AF334720

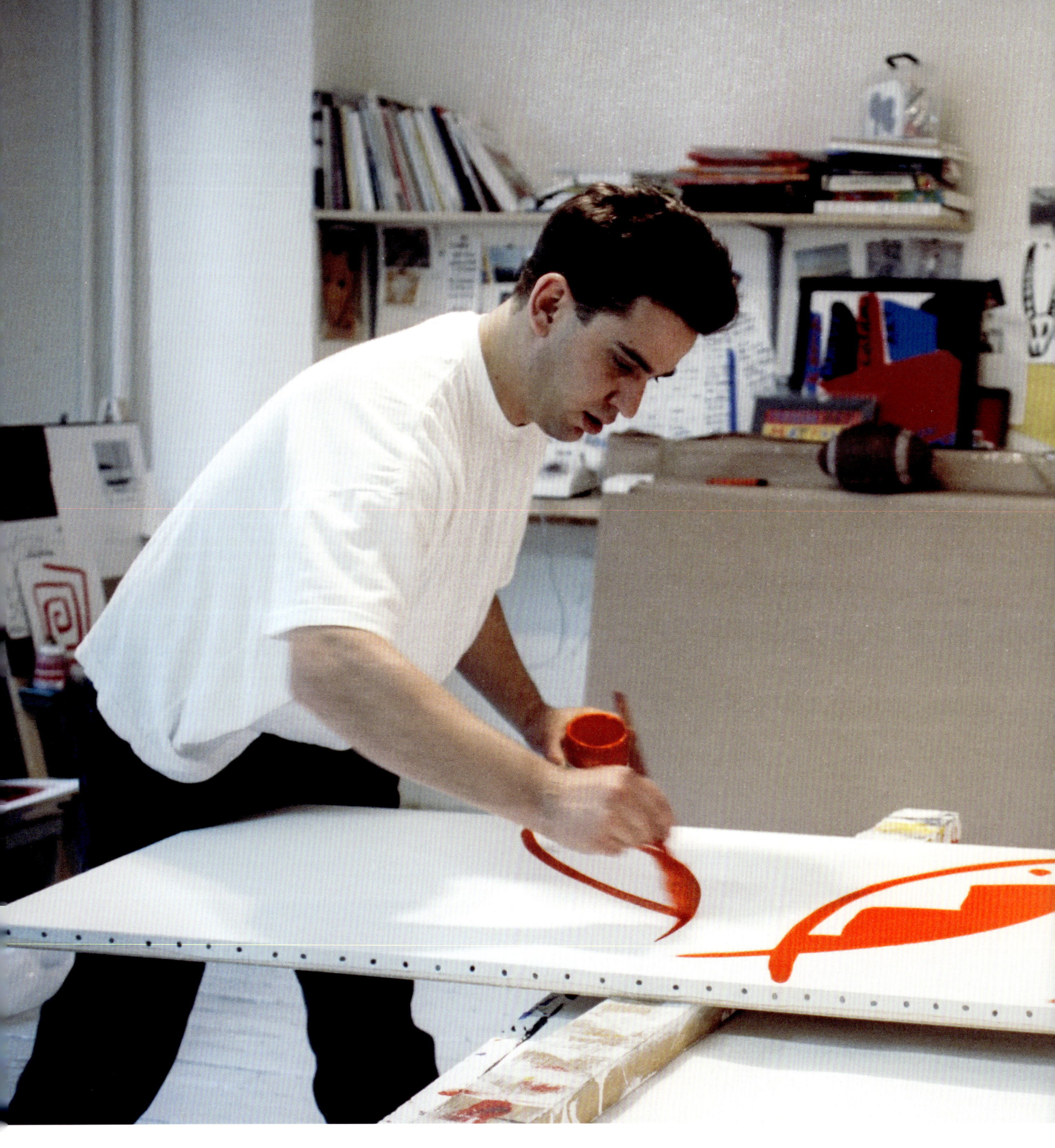

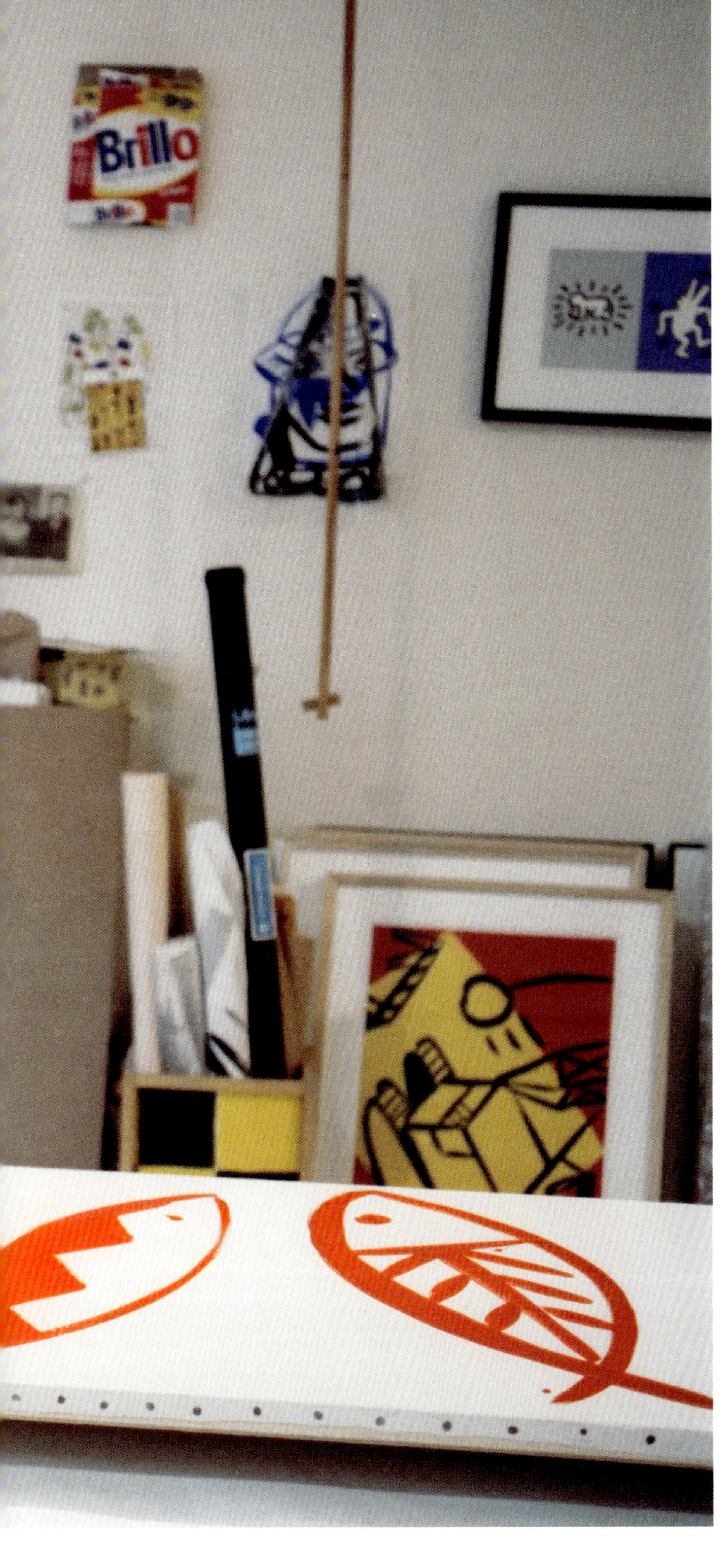

TOM SLAUGHTER

TOM SLAUGHTER

Essays and Contributions by

David Marshall Grant, George Negroponte,
Marthe Jocelyn, and Anne Pasternak

Foreword by
Glenn Lowry

The Artist Book Foundation
North Adams

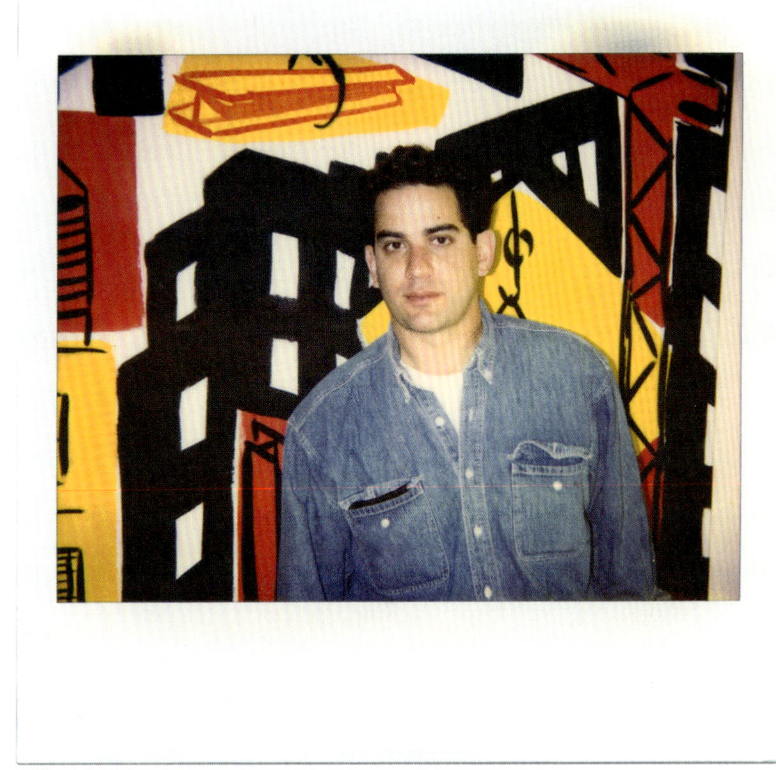

One of the thousands of Polaroids, dating from 1981 on,
that lined the hallway of Tom's studio.

FOREWORD 8
by Glenn Lowry

INTRODUCING TOM SLAUGHTER 12
by Hannah and Nell Jocelyn

THE NEGATIVE SPACE 18
by David Marshall Grant

1980–1990 24

THE OBJECT MAKER 68
by George Negroponte

1990–1998 74

EVERY SUMMER 128
by Marthe Jocelyn

1998–2006 138

OBJECTS 174

LOOK, AND REALLY SEE 186
by Anne Pasternak

2006–2014 192

UNMISTAKABLY HIS 242
Interview with Stephen Hannock,
Jean-Paul Russell, Robert Harms,
Ray Charles White, and Scott Kilgour

LIST OF PLATES 256

CHRONOLOGY 262

SELECTED PUBLICATIONS 264
Children's Books, Artists' Books,
Print Series, Catalogues,
Books and Magazines

SELECTED SOLO EXHIBITIONS 266

SELECTED GROUP EXHIBITIONS 267

SELECTED PUBLIC & PRIVATE COLLECTIONS 268

PHOTOGRAPHY CREDITS 269

ACKNOWLEDGMENTS 271

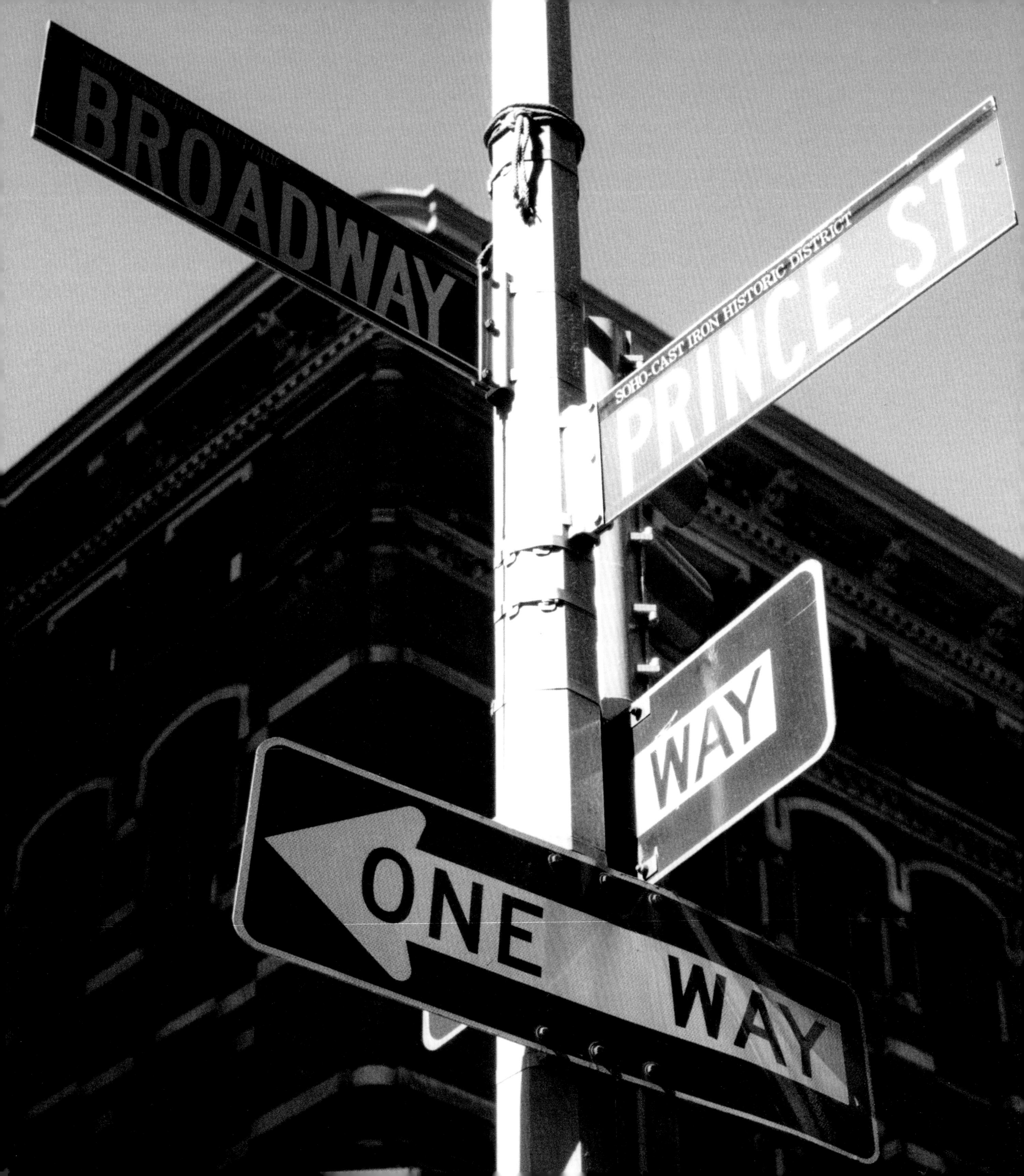

BROADWAY
SOHO-CAST IRON HISTORIC DISTRICT
PRINCE ST
WAY
ONE WAY

FOREWORD

Shortly before Tom died on October 24, 2014, he sent me a drawing of a
semi-naked woman unclipping her bra. It was typical Tom. Drawn over a letter
that I had sent him several months earlier acknowledging his support of the
Museum of Modern Art's exhibition of Henri Matisse's cutouts, the drawing was
a thank you for a thank you. Simultaneously cheeky and alluring, and realized in
Tom's fluid, almost effortless hand, the drawing turned my letter into a striptease.
He knew I would love it and I have kept it by my desk since the day it arrived—a
reminder of how much I loved Tom and how grateful I was to him for his
friendship and support.

I find myself still thinking about him. I see art that he was interested in and wish
he was here so we could talk about it together; I go to the beach and lie on
one of the towels he designed and remember how much fun it was to hang out
with him. From the moment I met him twelve years ago, I felt like I had not only
made a great new friend, but found the brother I never had. Tom, I think, felt
differently—he was not short of brothers—but we bonded quickly. He had an
easygoing quality to him that masked a more tightly coiled personality. He could
be funny and irreverent, and affected a laid-back attitude, but underneath that
casualness he was as determined and driven as anyone I have ever met.

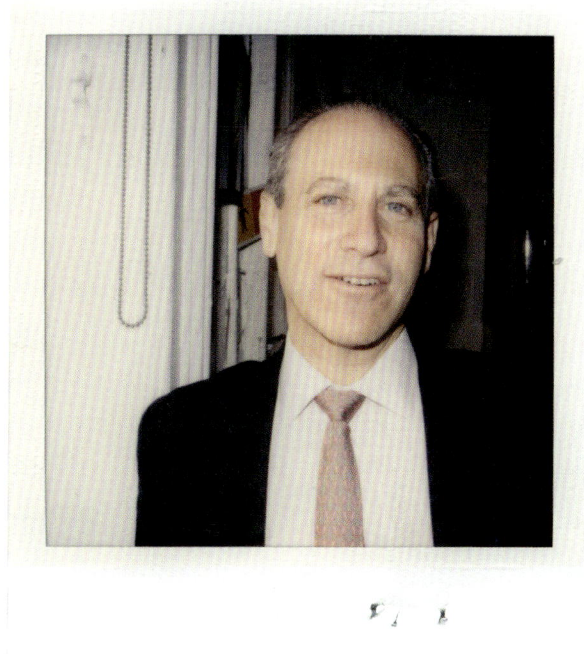

Tom loved his daughters, he loved making art, he loved elegant, sexy women, he
loved riding his crazy bike—I kept trying to convince him that the last thirty years
had seen many important innovations including gears and lighter frames, but he
would have none of it—he loved his family and his friends, and he loved a good
party, all pretty much in that order. In short, he loved life and lived it full throttle.

I got to know Tom well when he joined the board of PS1, shortly after it merged
with the Museum of Modern Art. He quickly became one of the most active
and vocal trustees. He immersed himself in the life of the institution and always
pushed for us to be better, and more daring. He was allergic to the status quo
and to the establishment. He bristled at the idea of convention. He was also a
closet engineer and architect, and never stopped opining about our various
architectural projects. Over the years, he emerged as perhaps PS1's most valued
and important trustee, joining the executive committee in 2008 and chairing the
nominating committee from 2008 until 2013.

His gift to PS1, and then as PS1 became MoMA PS1, was that he always spoke his
mind, he spoke the truth, he worked hard, and he was dedicated to making the
place better. His were always the sharpest comments at board meetings and he
caught every one of my mistakes. He was generous with his opinions—and they

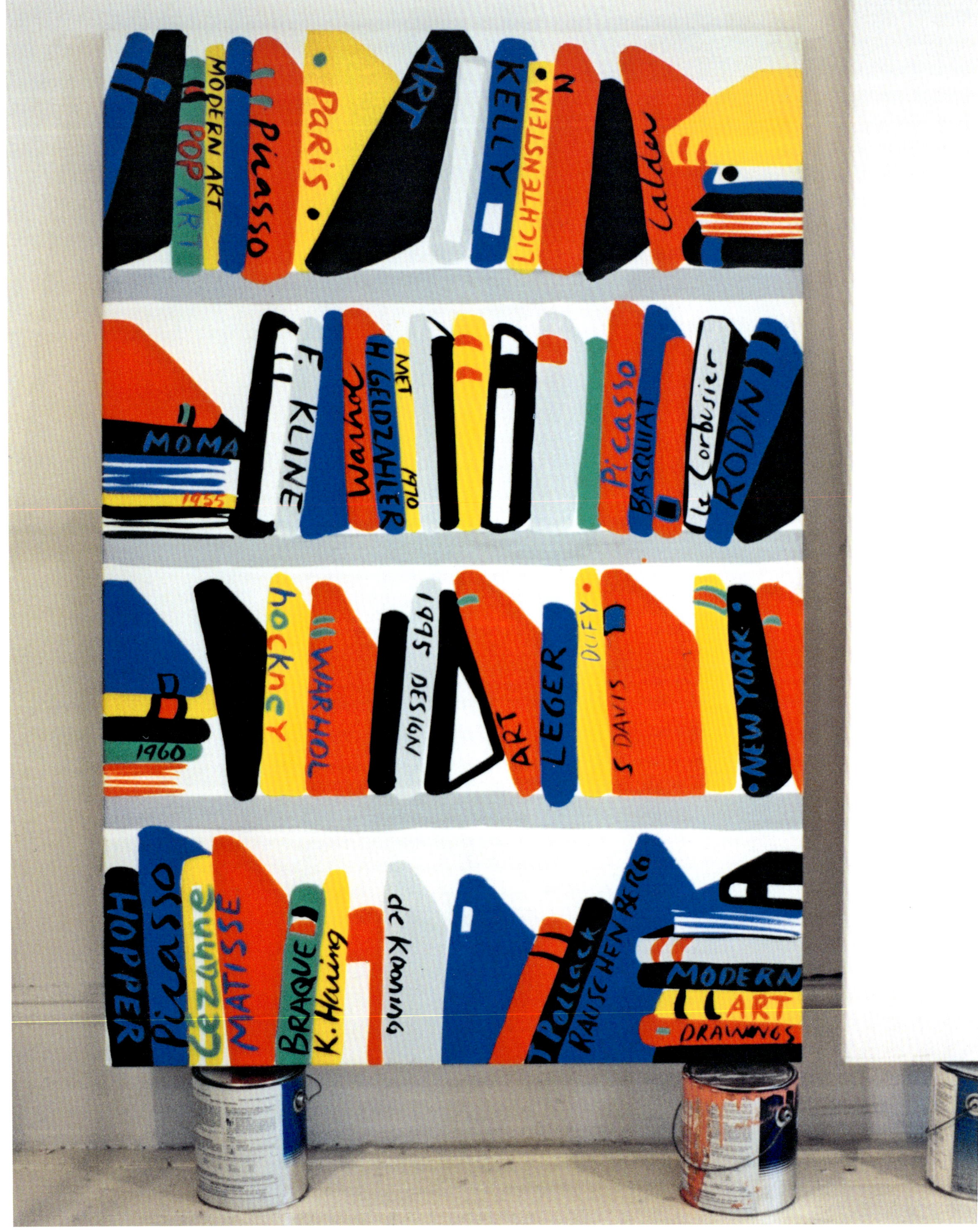

MODERN ART
POP ART
Picasso
Paris
ART
KELLY
LICHTENSTEIN
Calder
MOMA
F. KLINE
Warhol
H GELDZAHLER
MET
1970
PICASSO
BASQUIAT
Le Corbusier
RODIN
1455
hockney
WARHOL
1995 DESIGN
ART
LEGER
DUFY
S. DAVIS
NEW YORK
1960
HOPPER
Picasso
Cezanne
MATISSE
Braque
K. Haring
de Kooning
POLLACK
RAUSCHENBERG
MODERN
ART
DRAWINGS

were not in short supply—but he was equally generous in his openness to other people's ideas. He saved us on many occasions from ourselves, and he supported, unstintingly, the artistic and political causes he believed in. It would be easy to think of Tom as first and foremost a talented philanthropist given the range of institutions and projects he supported through the Horace W. Goldsmith Foundation.

But Tom was, above all, an artist. He thought like an artist and he acted like one. He had a gift for drawing and reducing a form to its essential shape. He loved to look at art, to turn it around and dissect it, and he was endlessly curious about how things were made—not just constructed but conceived. When I visited him not long before he died, as he was struggling and clearly exhausted, he was still drawing, forcing himself not to forget how to do what he loved. It was always exciting to talk to Tom about the art he was making or the artists that turned him on. We shared an admiration for Ellsworth Kelly and especially for Matisse, artists from whom he took a sense of line and color and rhythm. He was so excited that the Museum of Modern Art was going to present Matisse's cutouts in the fall of 2014; I only wish he had had the chance to see the show—I think he would have been enthralled.

Tom's art could be serious or jubilant, but it was always probing. He was so gifted that he could make anything look good. His designs found their way into books, onto posters, T-shirts, skateboard decks, and even towels. I think he enjoyed making illustrated children's books the most, because they let him share his own childlike enthusiasm with the world. He published ten and each is a gem.

As I think about Tom and how much I liked him, I realize that there are very few people with whom you can develop a deep personal affinity. Tom and I began our relationship on a professional level but it quickly became intensely personal. We shared being married to Canadian wives—with all that entailed, and believe me that was a lot—we shared the stories of our children, and we shared many common friends. I will never forget a dinner in Williamstown, Massachusetts, several years ago with Tom and my mother and sister, two intense women who can grill a stranger to the point of singing. I would have run screaming—in fact I usually did—but Tom charmed them both and my mother still wonders why I can't be more like him!

He made everyone he met part of his community and he made his community an indispensable part of his life. His art is joyous, even exuberant, and it brings pleasure to all who encounter it. No one can ask for a greater legacy.

Glenn Lowry

Director of the Museum of Modern Art

New York, NY

2016

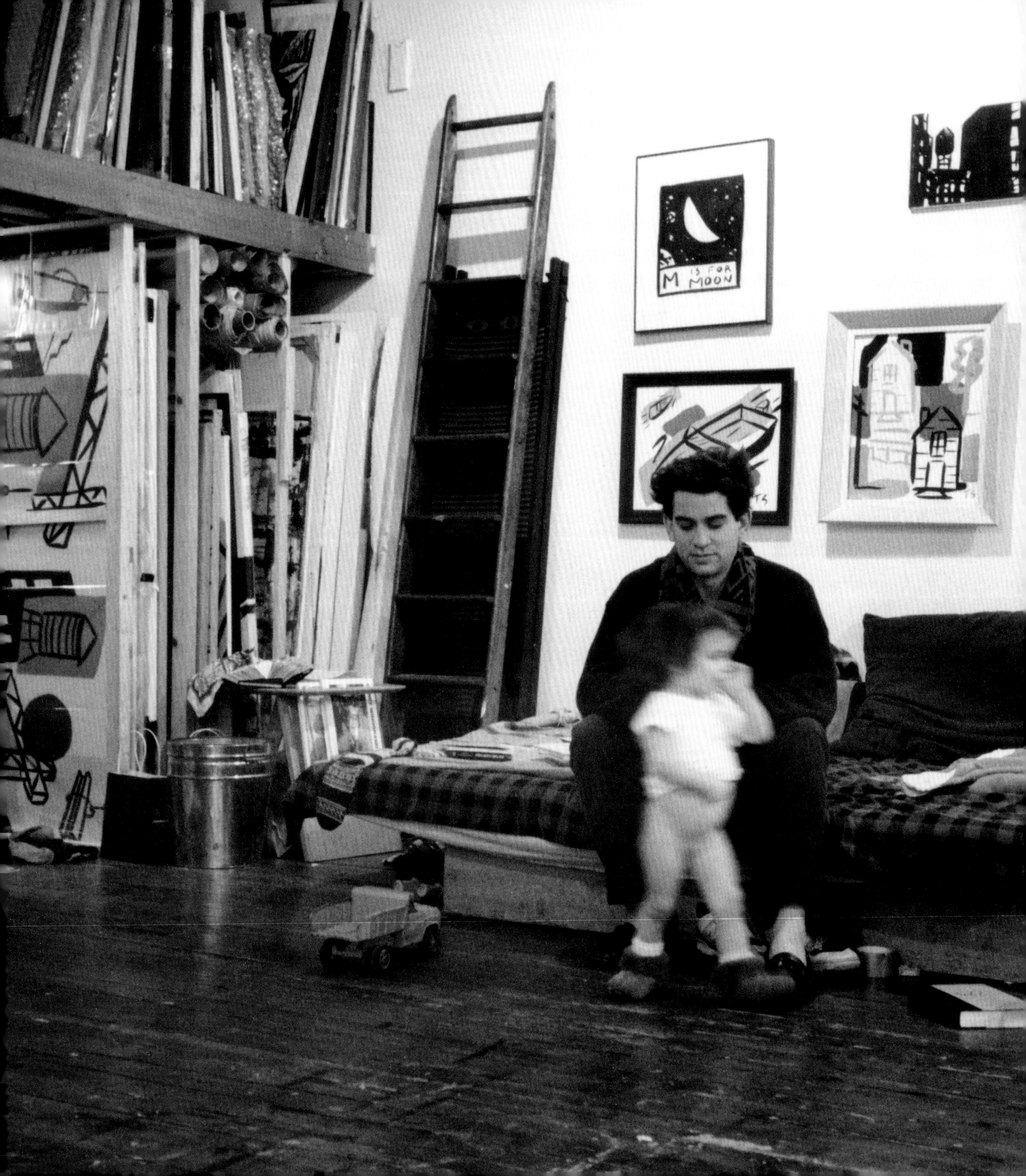

INTRODUCING
TOM SLAUGHTER

When our father did his first run of prints with Durham Press, in 1989, Henry Geldzahler, the curator of American Art for The Met, wrote an introduction to the series entitled "Introducing Tom Slaughter." In it he wrote:

> "The quality of freshness, the familiar world re-seen, from the water towers of New York City to the rural pleasures of boating, is the most immediately arresting aspect of Tom Slaughter's art. Strongly depicted large forms, most often in black over bold, bright colors, swiftly laid down, echo with resonances; Léger and Stuart Davis, Raoul Dufy and Roy Lichtenstein. All are artists who live their lives in the brilliant life of imagined skies where the time is always high noon or midnight. . . .One device developed by artists whose work is memorable is the creation over many years of an invented world, an identifiable *place*, that we need but glimpse to succumb to his spell. Tom's world is South-Eastern [*sic*] Canada, Ontario to be specific, on a hot summer day, and New York seen clearly, with the cunning of a New Yorker, from the vantage point of the rural, the Arcadian. The personality of his work is vigorous and bold, the alert attention of hard worker hard at rest, typically rowing his anonymous boat. . . . The strength, the gestural muscle of the drawing, telegraphs its information and its mood with equal clarity, reinforcing the quality of freshness with which we began this note."[1]

In his thank-you note to Henry, typed on lined paper with a typewriter and signed with his iconic hat, Tom wrote, "My 15 minutes may be over but I will always cherish your introduction to T. Slaughter cause you nailed it. A 16 penny nail one shot from a 28 oz hammer." Henry's description captured something so true about Tom's work and Tom's response captured something so true about Tom. In his metaphors as in his art and in his life, he was straightforward and vivid.

Tom was born in New York City in 1955. When he was eight, his family moved to Connecticut where he went to high school, and eventually to Connecticut College where he majored in art history. After graduating, he drove his pickup truck west, prospecting for tin in New Mexico and then working construction in Seattle. He met our mother, Marthe, during a visit home in January 1981 and decided it was time to come back to the city. Just a few months later, they moved in together—to the loft in SoHo, a retired garment factory that had a special dispensation from the city for artists. He lived there for the rest of his life. In the early eighties, his work started to appear in group shows; by the early nineties, he was established in the

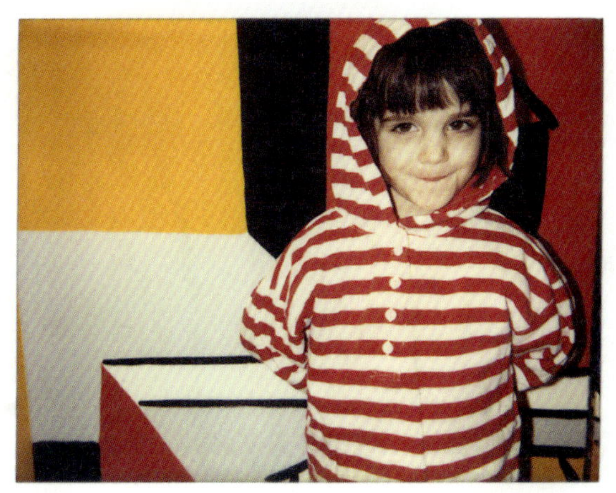

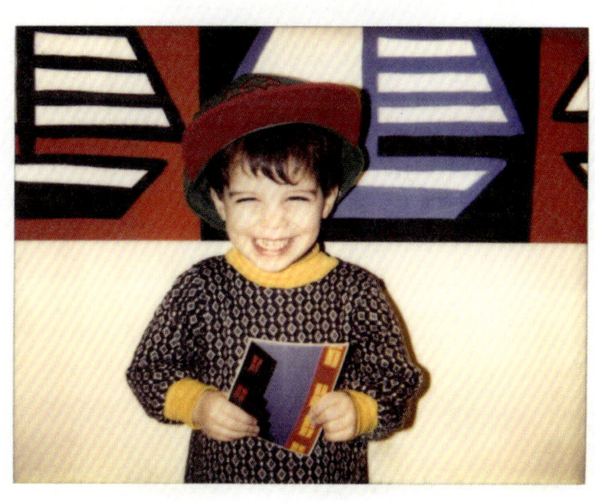

Hannah and Nell Jocelyn

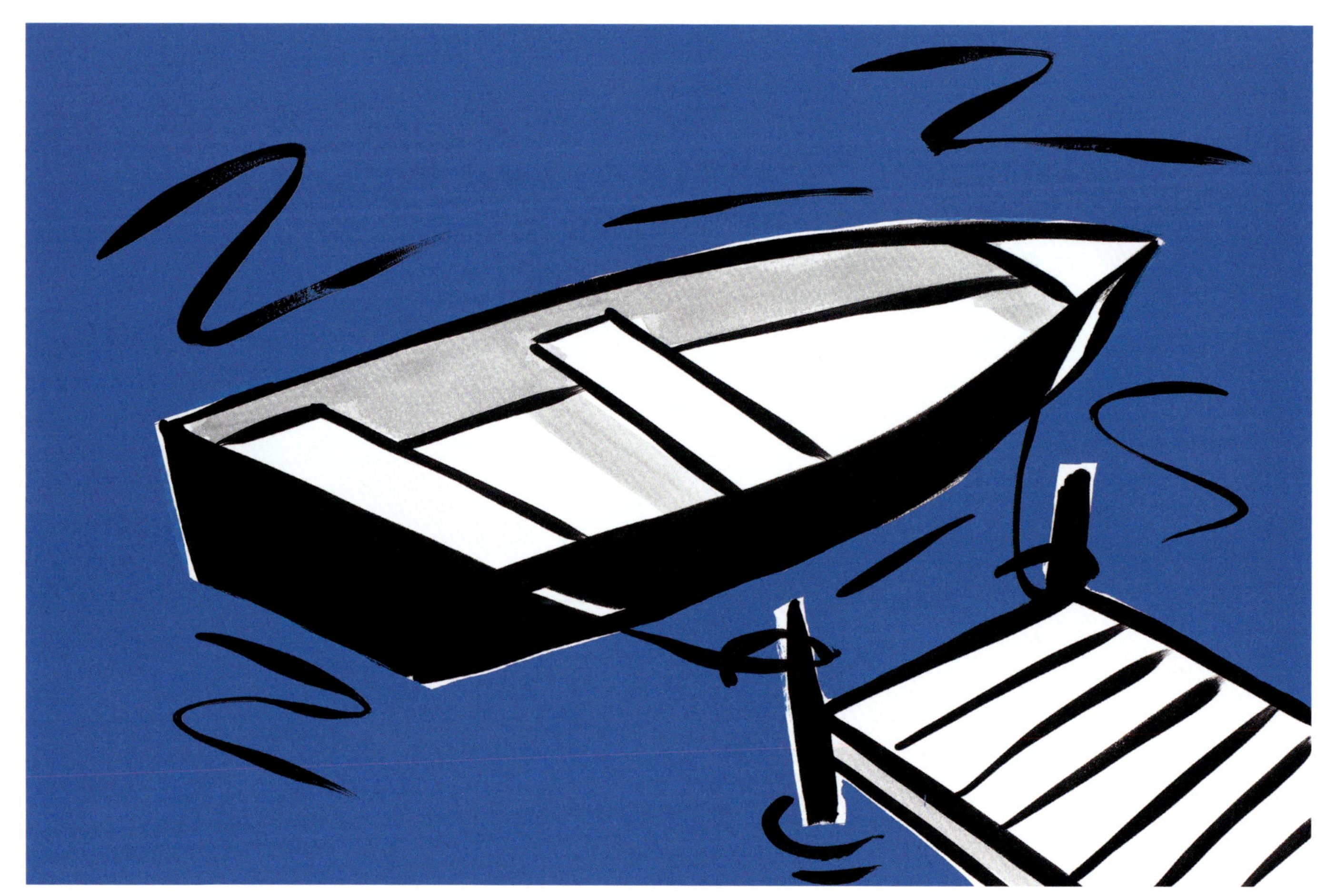

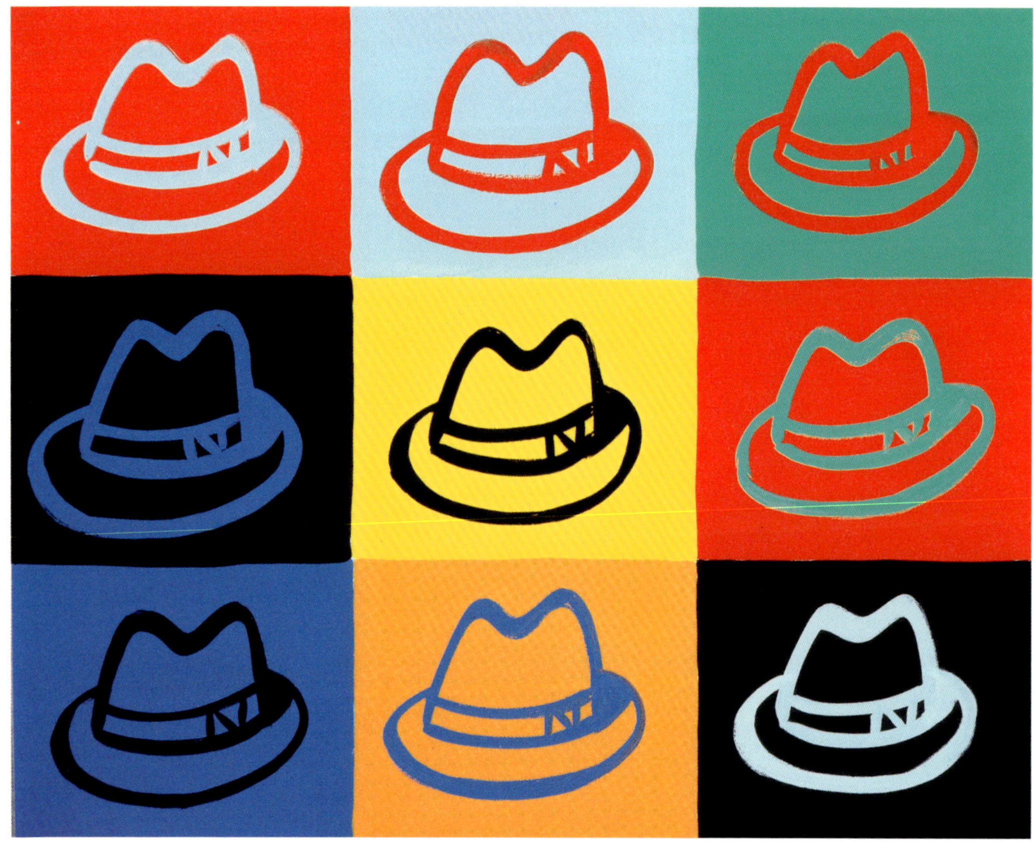

downtown New York art world and having solo shows around the world. His lines were loose, his scenes dynamic. He was making six-foot canvases, depicting the city in royal blues, vibrant reds and yellows, deep black—bright windows in a dark night, water-tower silhouettes, the chaos of construction.

To the world at large, Tom's work was an iconic representation of New York City. To us, it was just our life, rendered bright in primary colors. The walls (if you can call them that, at only six feet high) in our loft were collages themselves—covered in paintings, and photos, and photos of paintings; the flat surfaces were covered with matchbooks, Ray-Bans, Sclafani cans filled with brushes, and then sketches of those glasses, that can. For every object scattered around the house, a drawing could be found of the same, so that every scene we saw every day, we saw a hundred times more on paper. We played with carved and painted wood toys on wheels attached with wood glue; he illustrated our walks to school—the streetlights on the corner of Prince and Broadway, the neighborhood restaurant signage. We can remember chasing cousins through suited legs at gallery openings, sitting on the back of the bike as our dad rode slow circles around the studio waiting for inspiration, painting on our own miniature easels next to him working on his. He, along with our mother, filled our lives with things both beautiful and practical.

When we set out to create a monograph of our father's life and work, we were overwhelmed. Tom was prolific. If he painted one valentine, he painted twenty—then twenty more the next year. There was a repeating motion, almost a muscle memory, with which he created and refined his images. It was part of what made his work so recognizable, so unmistakable. We were stymied, too, by how to capture Tom's distinct sense of art direction. It was important to us that he be represented not just by his work, but by his style.

There are facts we could share—that his pieces appear in the permanent collections of MoMA, Cooper-Hewitt, and the Whitney; that he had an uncanny memory for art history, art works, and faces; that he liked the shade cast by the negative space in his paper-cuts when framed in a floating shadow box—but these facts don't communicate who he was as an artist and as a person: clear-eyed, sometimes blustery, full of humor. In his work, he valued simplicity without preciousness. It is stark and serene, graphic and handmade—riding the line between crisp and careless. In these pages, he is most often likened to Matisse (a comparison he would be honored by) we think because, like Matisse, he wasn't afraid of a crooked cut, or a color too rich, or an imperfect pattern. This lack of hesitation meant that in every piece, his hand is evident.

In the end, we, along with Jimmy Mezei, decided to try to make the book Tom would have made—designing and editing it in the loft, surrounded by his work, and trying to tell a simple story of a life in pictures. Over the years, Tom's style changed subtly, but his work always kept its immediacy and its vibrancy. He continued his practice of observation and distillation. As we grew up, he became more prominent as an artist, but he also began to illustrate children's books, for

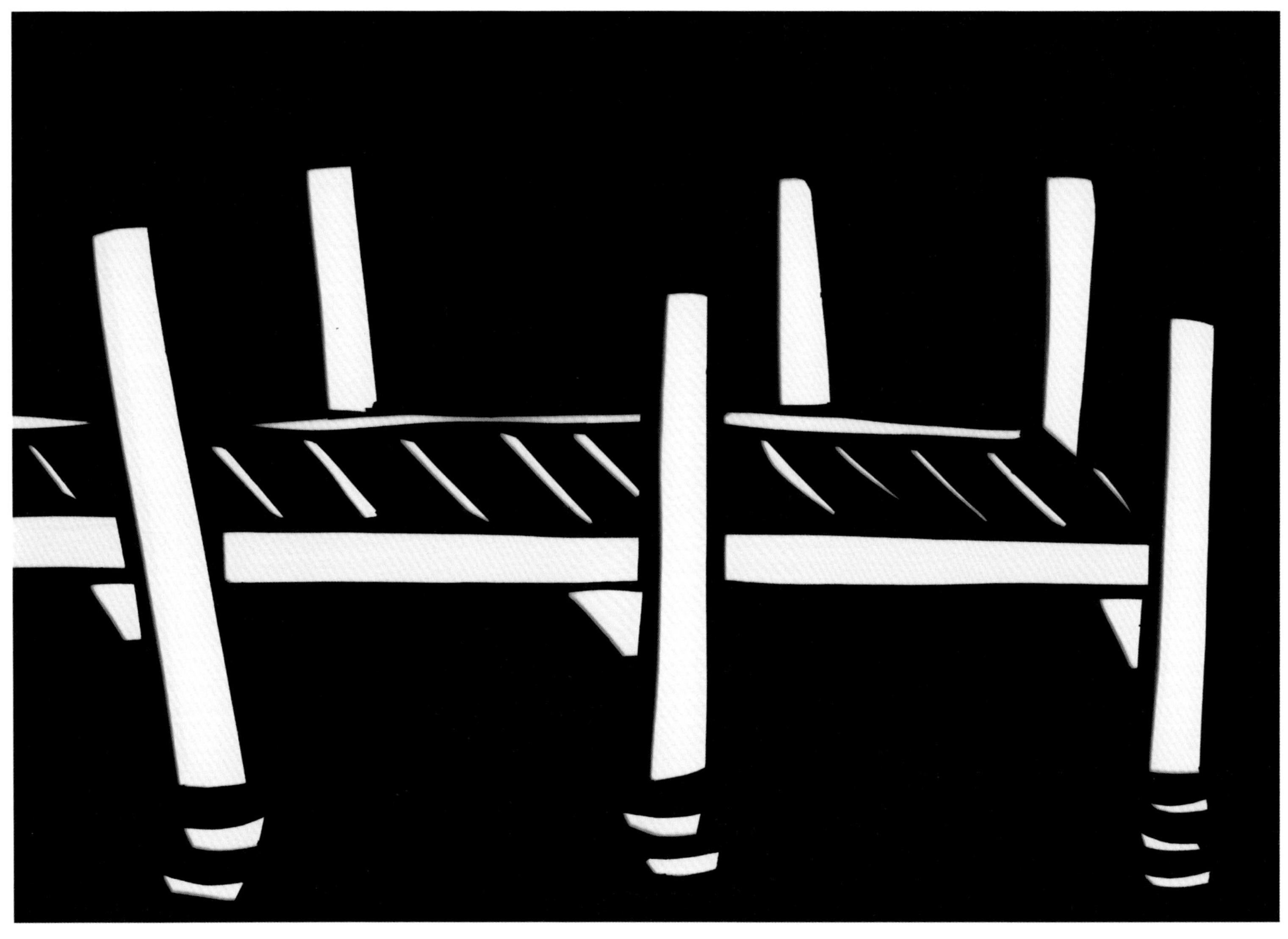

which his style was particularly well suited. He became a philanthropist, joining the board of the Horace W. Goldsmith Foundation in the nineties, but he was never entirely comfortable in his dual roles, never wanting his work making art to be influenced by his responsibility in supporting it. We saw fewer large-scale canvases and more notebooks, more watercolor, more brush pen. Less night, more day. More white space, more fluidity. Less southeastern Canada, more Suffolk County, Long Island. More design, more wallpaper, beach towels, and skateboard decks. He wasn't afraid to be commercial, knowing, as he had seen with his children's book illustrations, that his work was adaptable. Tom was a dweller in the day-to-day world, and so wanted his work to be accessible in any way possible, to as many people as possible. If someone was more likely to acquire a Tom Slaughter umbrella than a Tom Slaughter print or painting, that was fine with him. Like the subjects of the work itself, he did not want his images and art to feel exclusive. Throughout, always, and in whatever medium, he approached each piece with certainty. His lines and his cuts are bold, decisive. Whether he was branding BookExpo America, sketching the view from a sunny bench, painting a bike over blocks of color, illustrating a letter for a friend, cutting out the planks of a dock—he did so with strength.

Hannah and Nell Jocelyn

Tom Slaughter's daughters

New York, NY

2018

[1] Henry Geldzahler, "Introducing Tom Slaughter" in *Tom Slaughter: New York View, Construction Work, Hats and Boats,* exhibition catalogue (Amsterdam and New York: George Mulder Fine Arts, 1989).

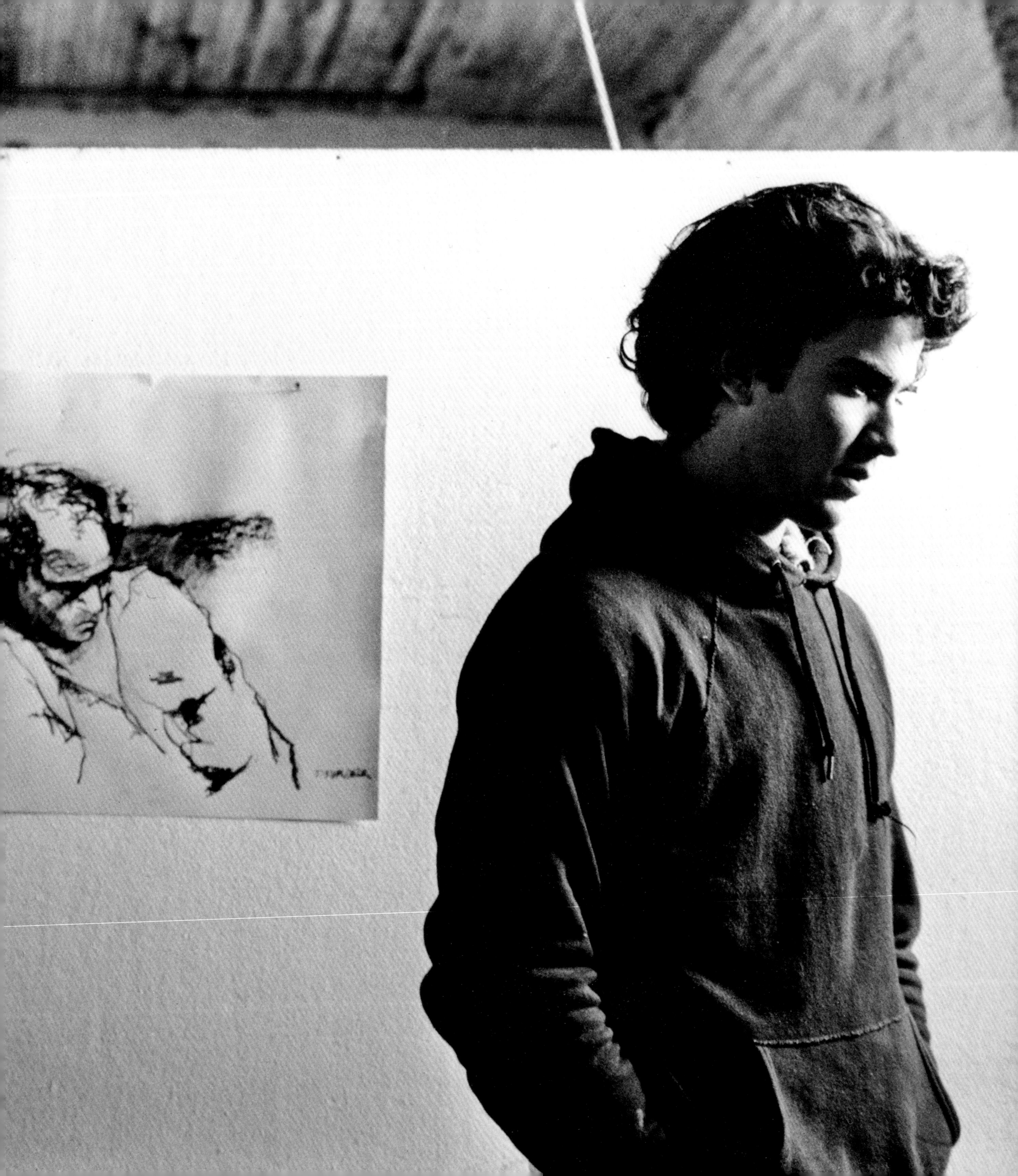

THE NEGATIVE SPACE

Tom Slaughter and I became friends when we were thirteen. I spent a lot of
time over at his family's home at 7 Bruce Lane in Westport, Connecticut. Before I
headed back to my house, we'd have a ritual cigarette leaning up against the cars
in the driveway. We talked about when we were going to lose our virginity,
Vietnam—you know, life's big questions. He wanted to be a great artist one day.

Tom found his calling in the Nine Building at Staples High School, which housed
the art classes. He started to learn how to draw by looking at Rodin sculptures
and Degas ballerinas. He had a great teacher, Jim Wheeler. One day he ran over
to find me. He was so excited to fill me in on a revelatory lesson, the most
profound lesson of all: shapes do not exist in a vacuum. There is something
called negative space, which exists in opposition to shapes, giving the drawing its
strength, its power, its beauty. One did not exist without the other. You didn't have
to draw perfect lines, you had to create negative space. I was a drama student
and was learning about a concept called subtext, reading Arthur Miller, Tennessee
Williams, and Eugene O'Neill. In our infinite wisdom we decided the two—subtext
and negative space—were the same thing.

We would take the train into the city and go to MoMA. He bought one ticket and
went in. I walked around to the north side of the building on 54th street and he
surreptitiously handed me the ticket through the metal fence of the sculpture
garden. After I entered using the same ticket, we met in the sculpture garden. He
was obsessed with Rodin and Henry Moore by then and we sat out there a long
time staring at the *Monument to Balzac*.

Once inside, his taste wasn't as much Monet as it was Matisse, Léger, Bonnard,
and Giacometti. When he discovered Edward Hopper, it was the start of his
greatest love affair with a painter. When we were at MoMA, we would play a
game. We would try to identify the artists without looking at the plaques. You
got no points for a Jackson Pollock. That was too easy. A Bonnard or a Vuillard?
That was a challenge.

After graduating from school, he bought a pickup truck and drove to New Mexico.
He craved adventure and the famous Western light he had read about. The big
sky. He found things to draw, first in charcoal, then in pastels or watercolors. It was
a long time before he started to use oils. He made his way as far as Seattle where
he lived in a loft under the shade of the King Dome. And he drew. He practiced.
He learned how to be an artist.

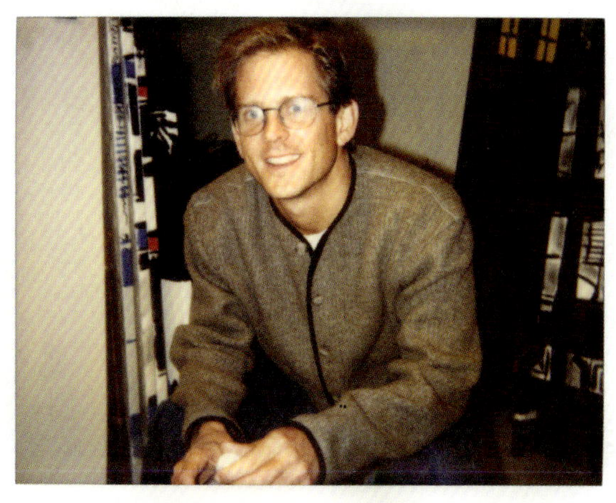

David Marshall Grant

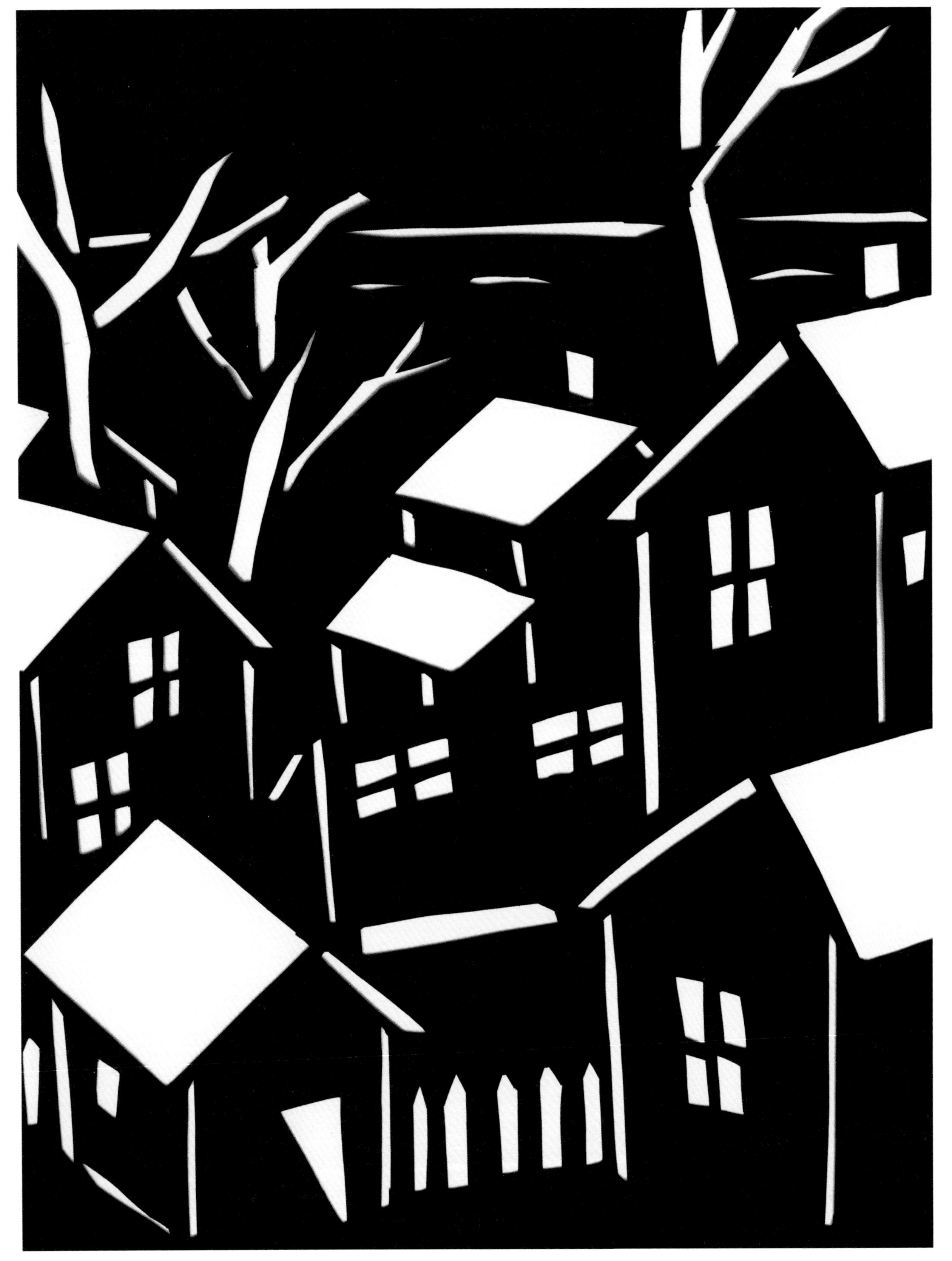

He came back to the city for a visit in 1981. We went to Cafe Central for dinner.
Bruce Willis was the bartender. I pointed out a waitress. He took her in.
"I'm going to marry her," he said. He left Marthe a pen and ink drawing that
night, went back to Seattle, packed up, and came back to move into the
loft on Broadway between Spring and Prince, which was his home and
studio for the rest of his life.

He became a New Yorker and found himself at the epicenter of an increasingly
vibrant art world. Keith Haring, Jean-Michel Basquiat—he saw every show, every
bit of graffiti. But he never lost his own vision. He got braver, bolder. His colors got
more vivid. He found the iconic images he would examine for his whole career—
boats, water towers, windows, hats.

I don't remember how it got there or exactly what it was, I think it was a
small red rowboat, but somehow it landed on Henry Geldzahler's desk. A few
months later, Tom got a call from Henry himself, saying he couldn't stop
looking at the painting. That began a great friendship and the recognition
Tom so greatly deserved. He had exhibitions in New York, L.A., Germany,
Japan—all over the world.

His art is full of cobalt-blue skies, flip flops, and jaunty sailboats. He saw
New York City much as E.B. White did—wandering around, re-examining this
spectacle, hoping to put it on paper. The boat pond in Central Park, the local
merchants, that perfect fall day. If it rained, he was more interested in the bright
yellow raincoat than in the dark sky. He was an optimist, a romantic. That's why so
much of his work is deceptively so simple; it's devoid of tricks.

But Tom always saw the negative space. In his art and his life, the edges and
corners were boundaries to a larger, more enigmatic vision. When you look
at his work, you are taken by its beauty, its almost childlike perfection, but also
how impossible that is to hold onto. It's as if as soon as you turn away, the
perfect blue sky will be gone forever.

David Marshall Grant

Actor, writer, and lifelong friend

Los Angeles, CA

2016

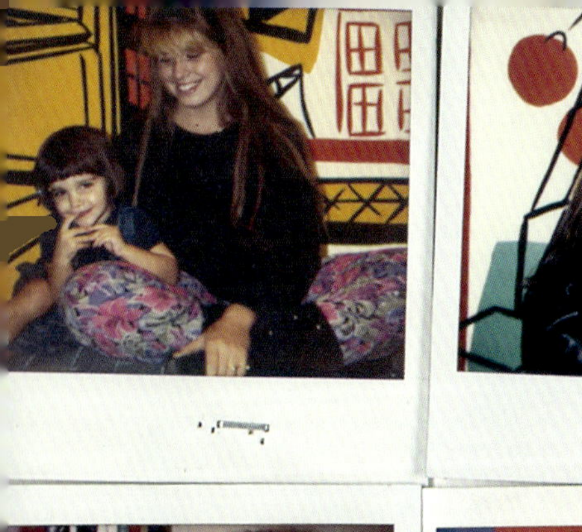
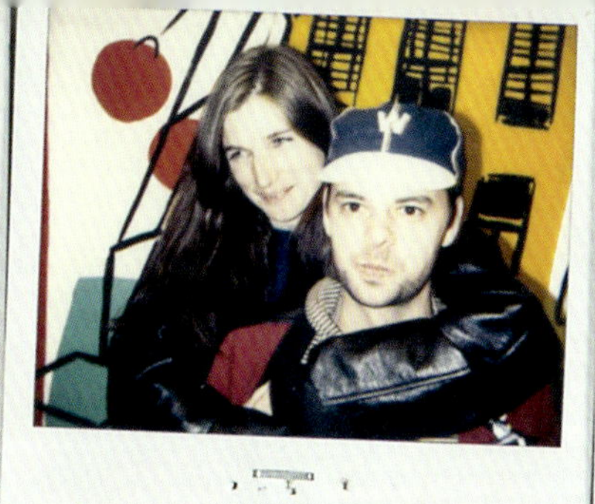
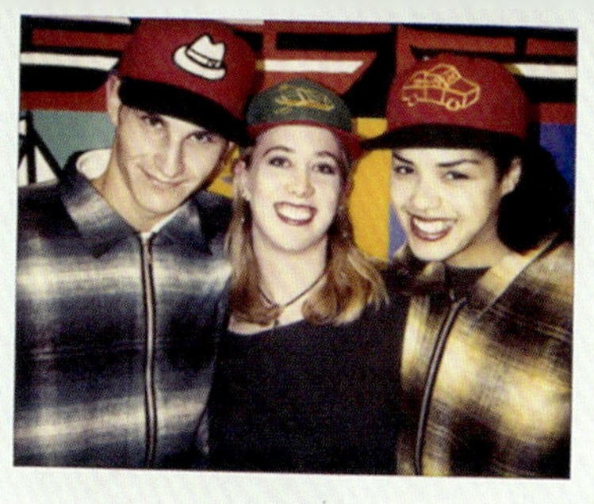
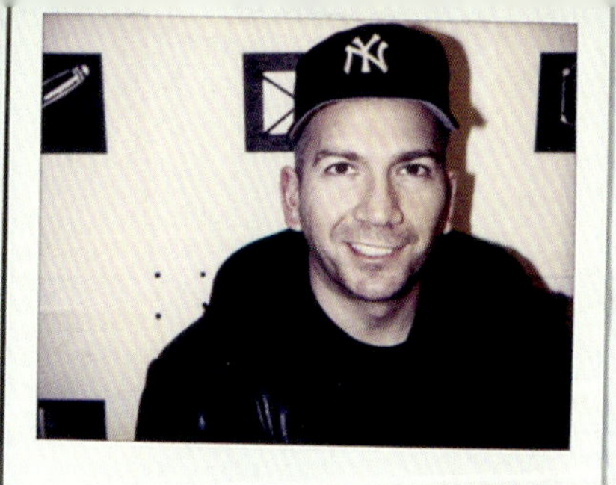
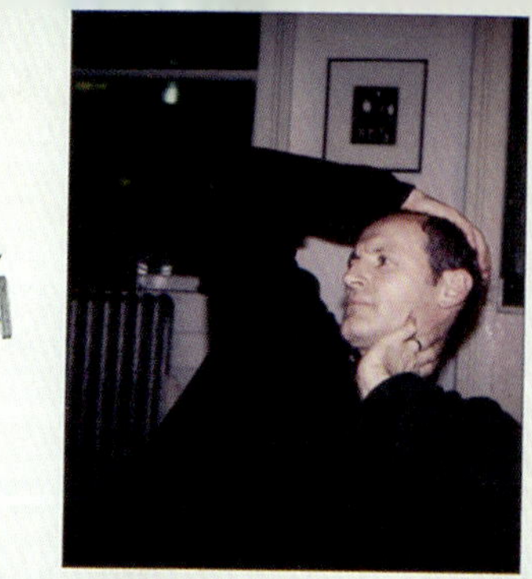
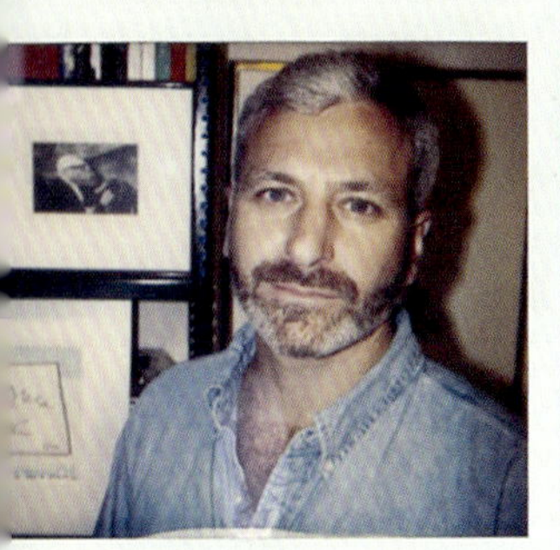
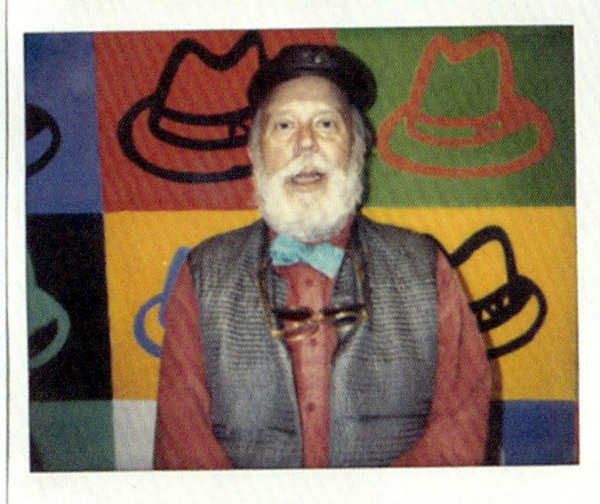
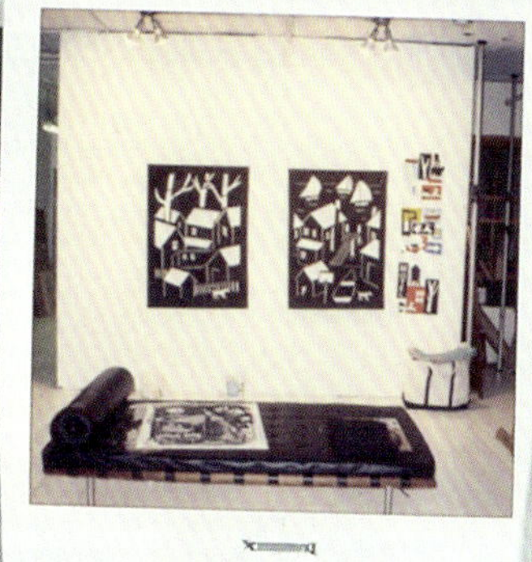
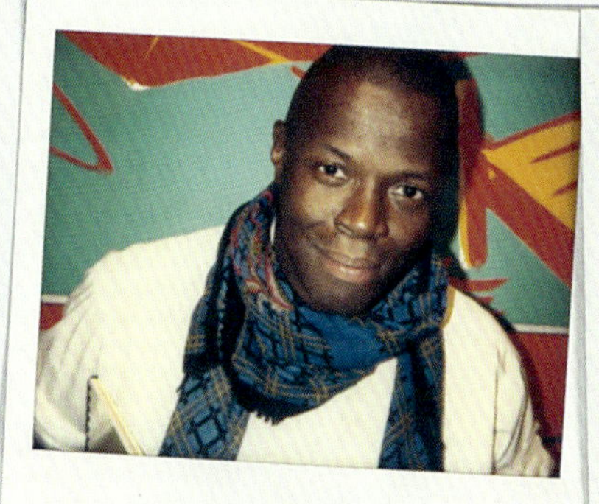
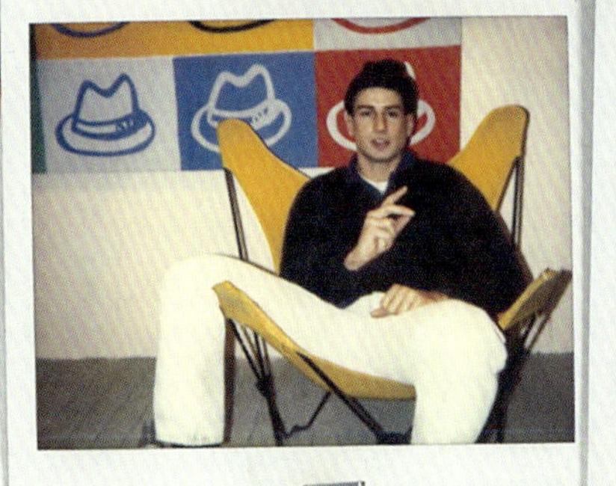
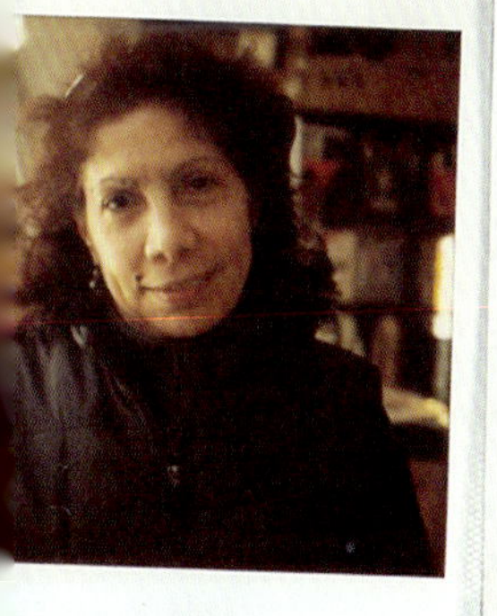
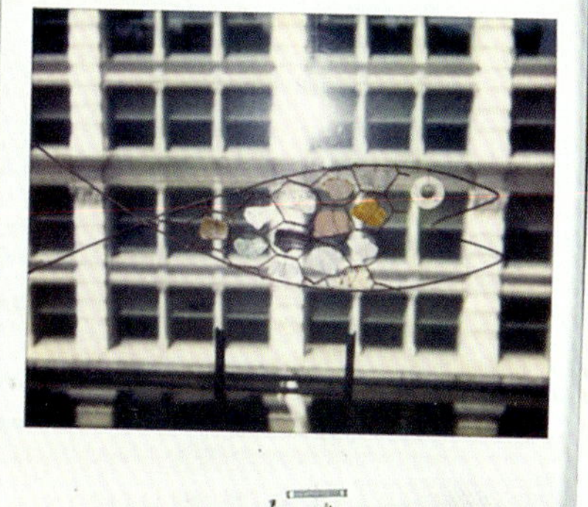
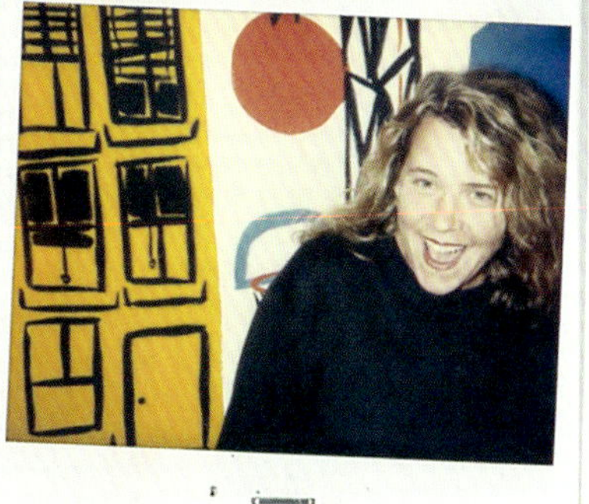
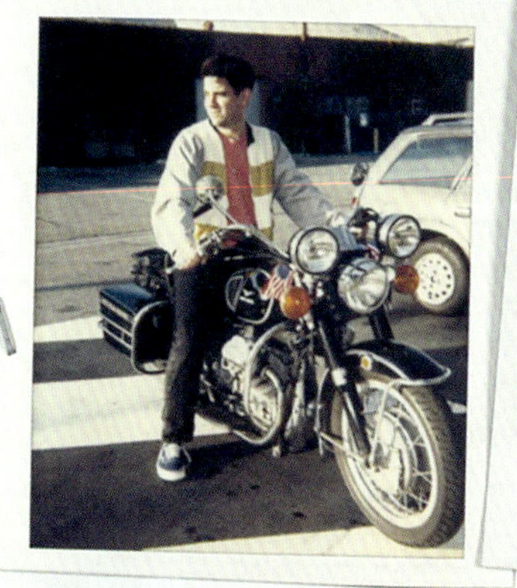
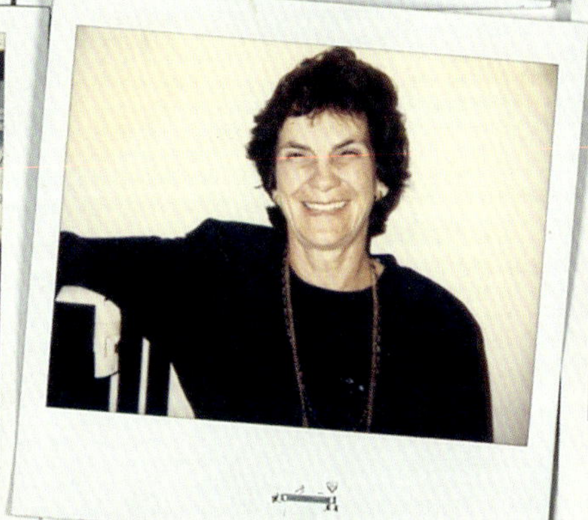
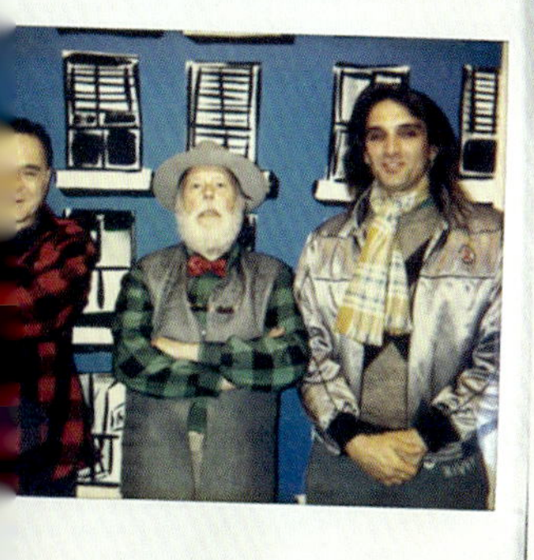
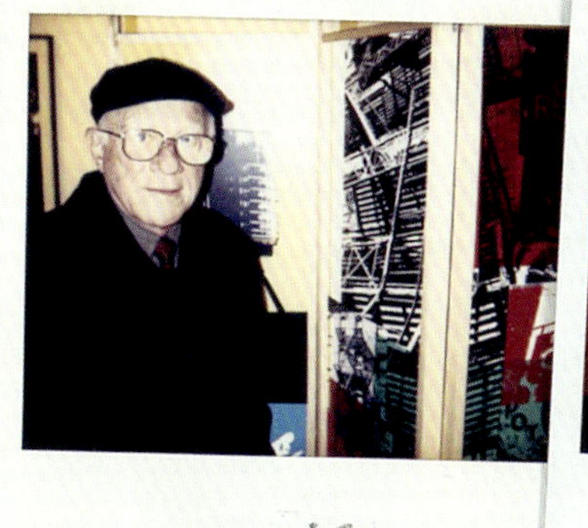
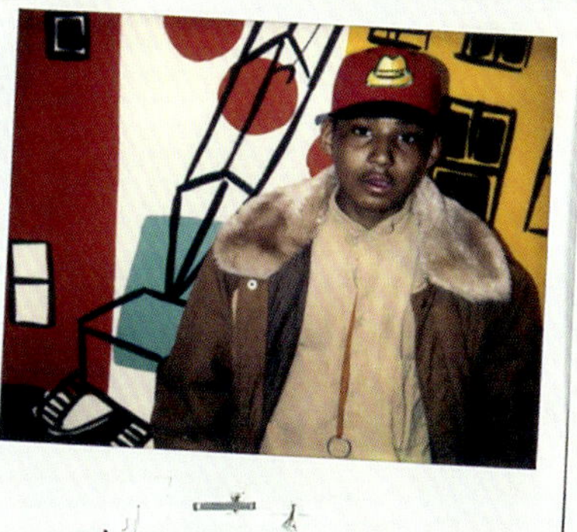
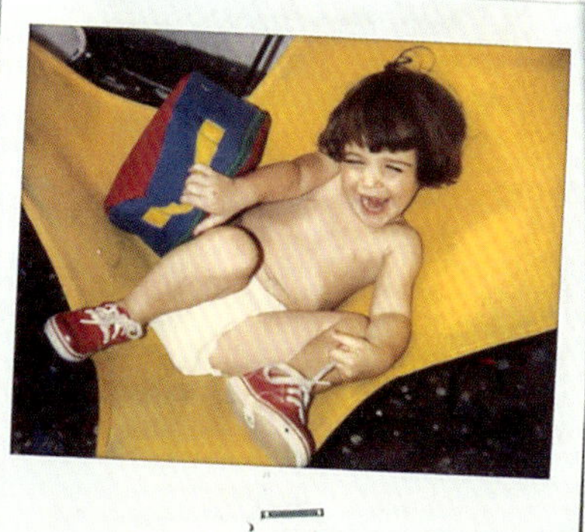
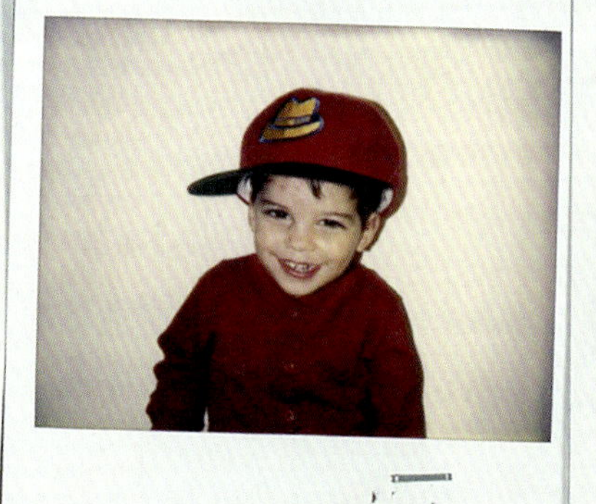
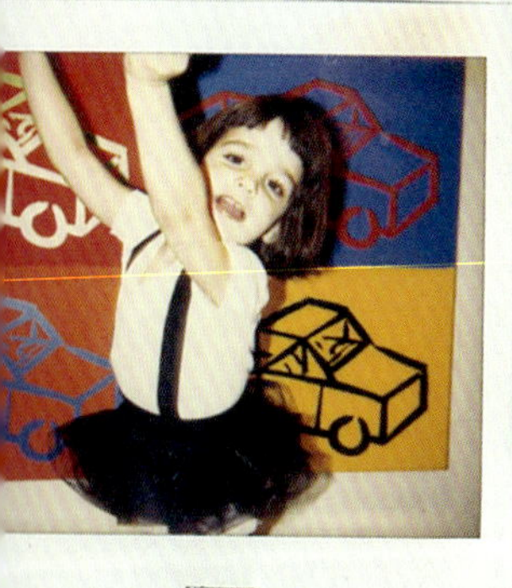
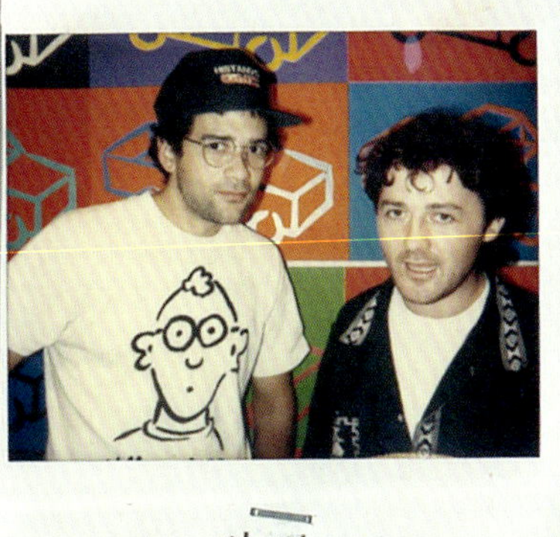
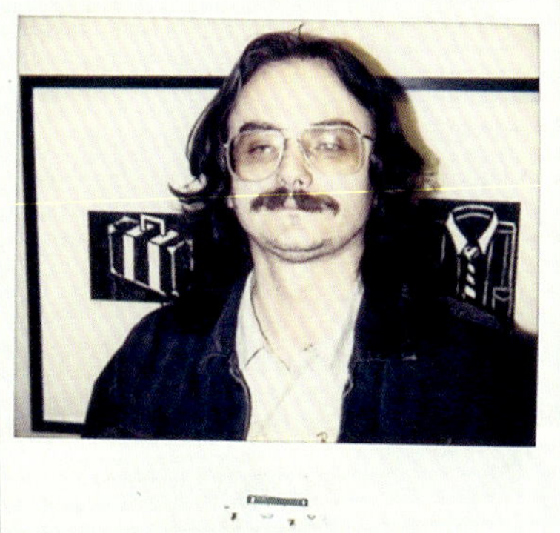
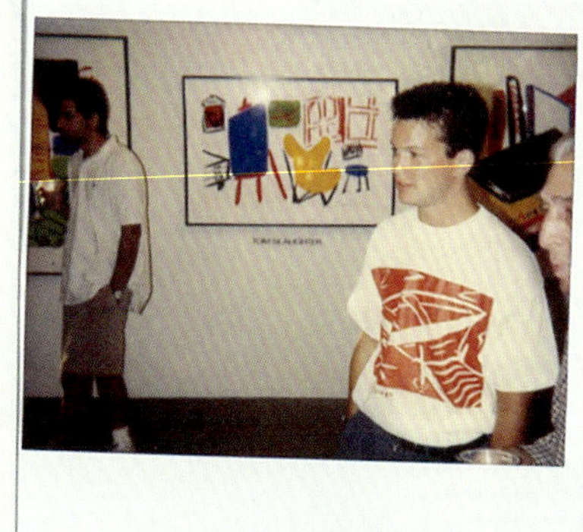
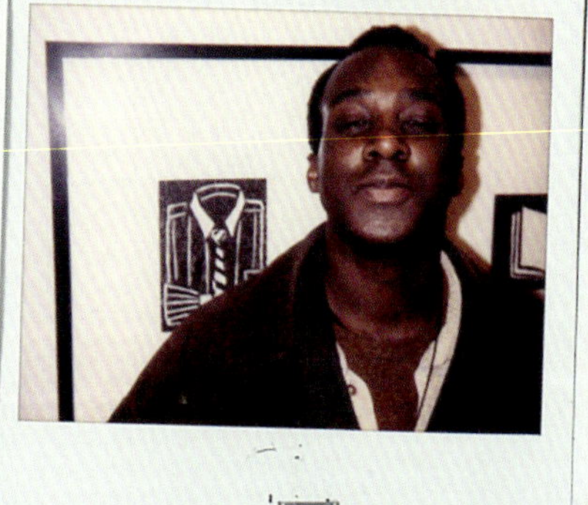
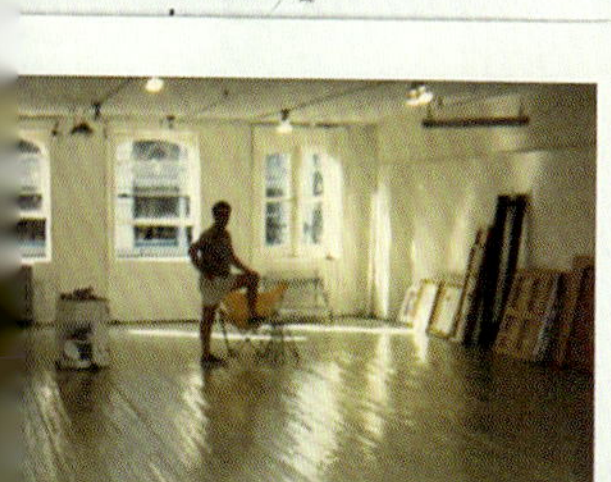
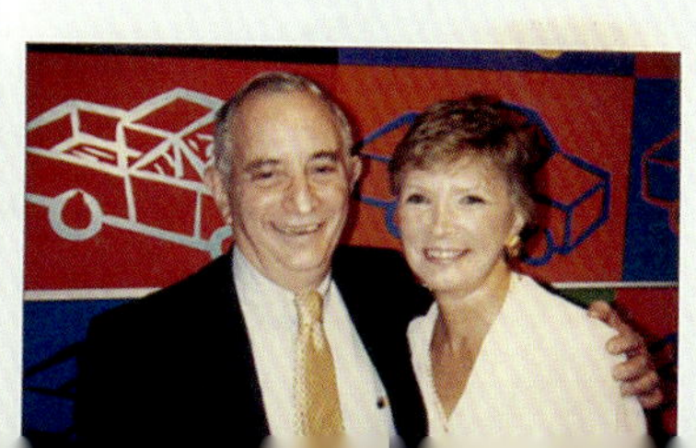
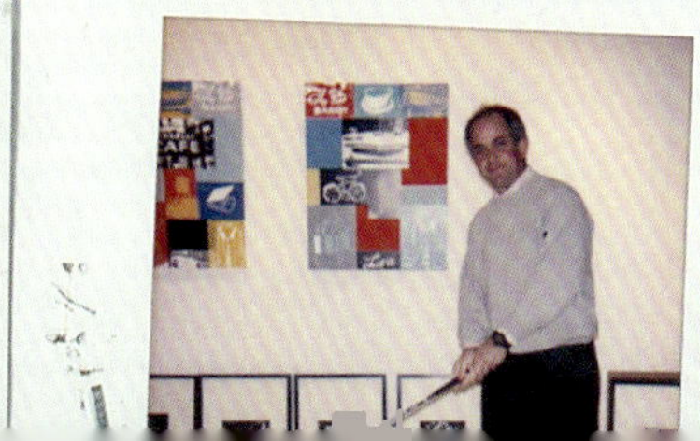
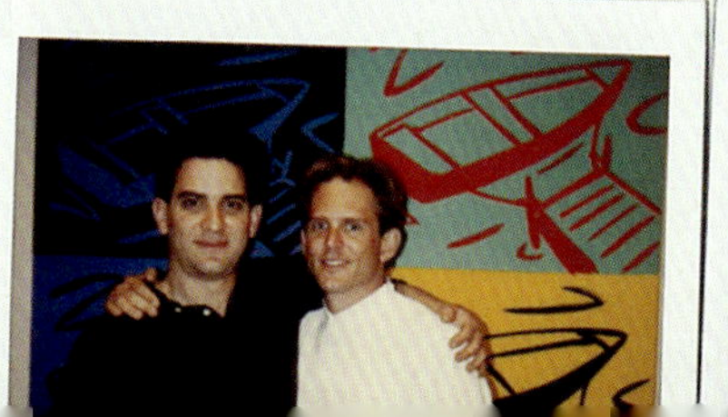
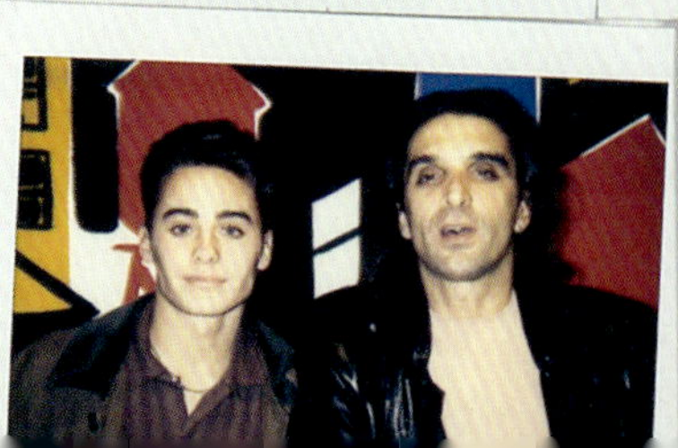

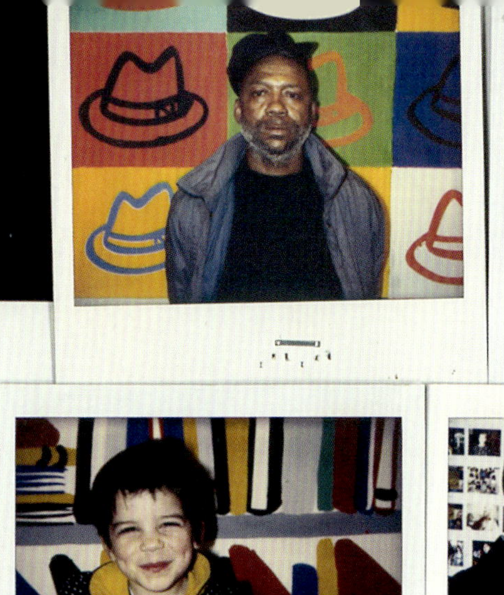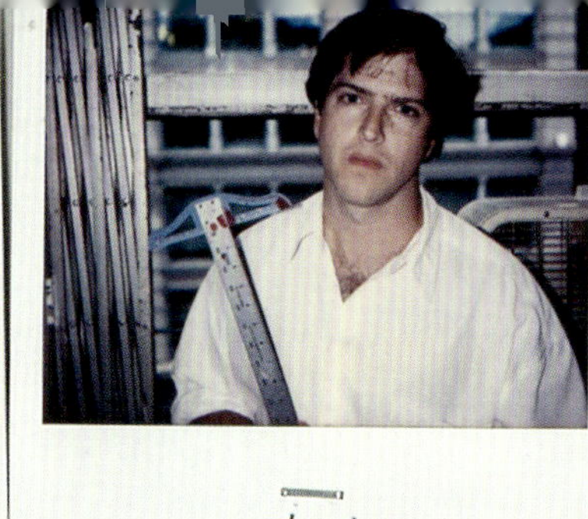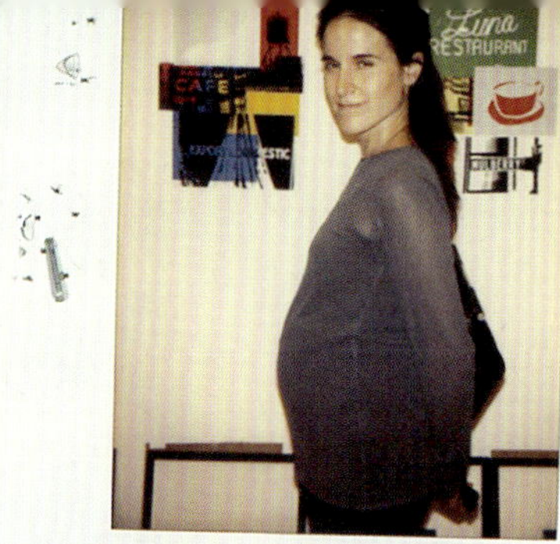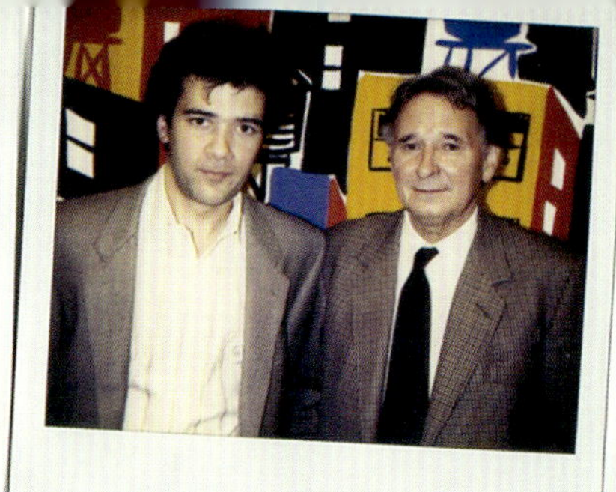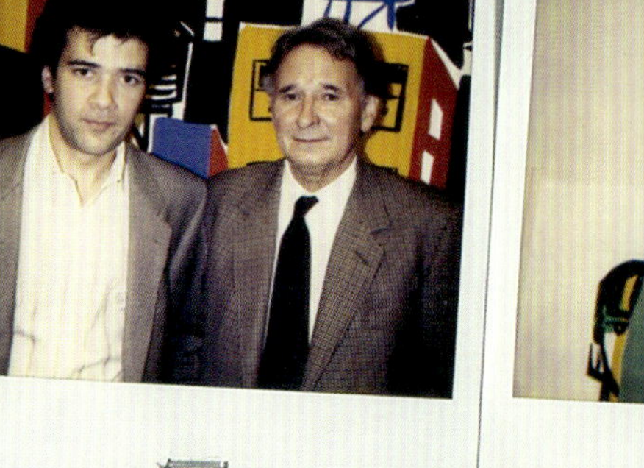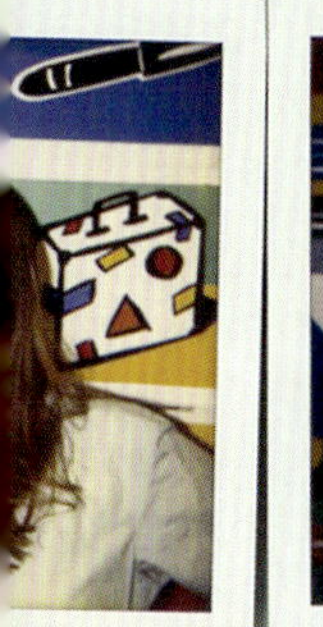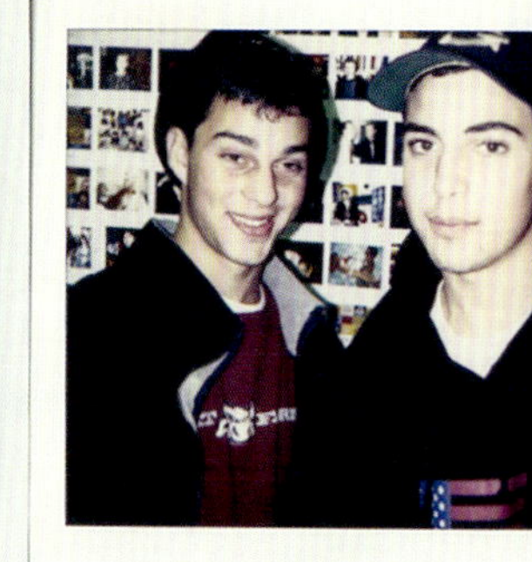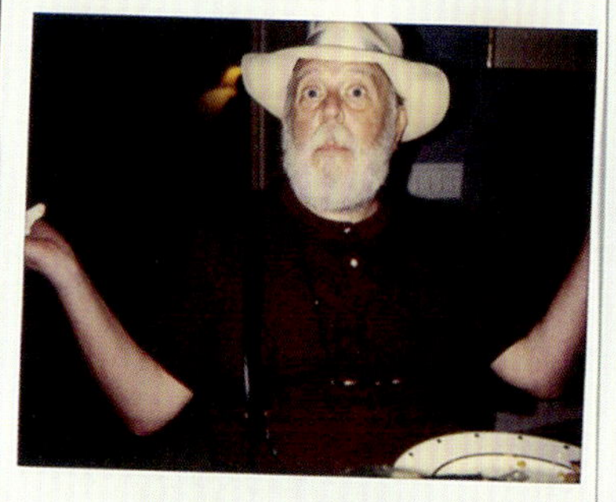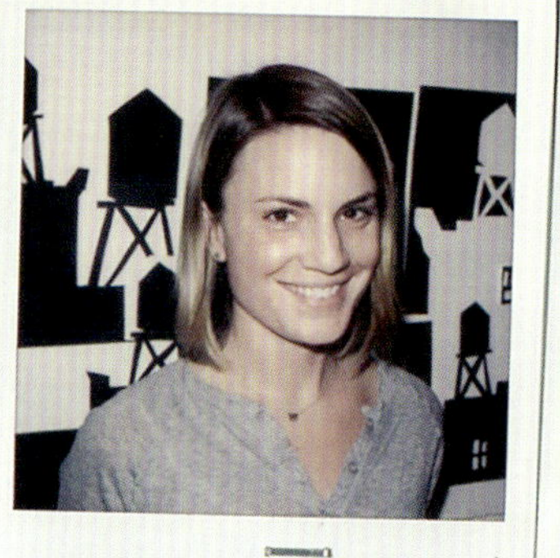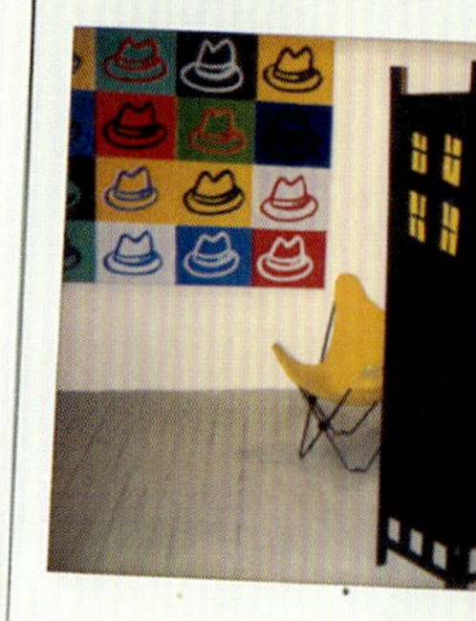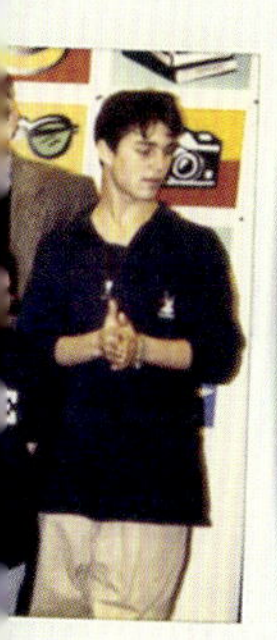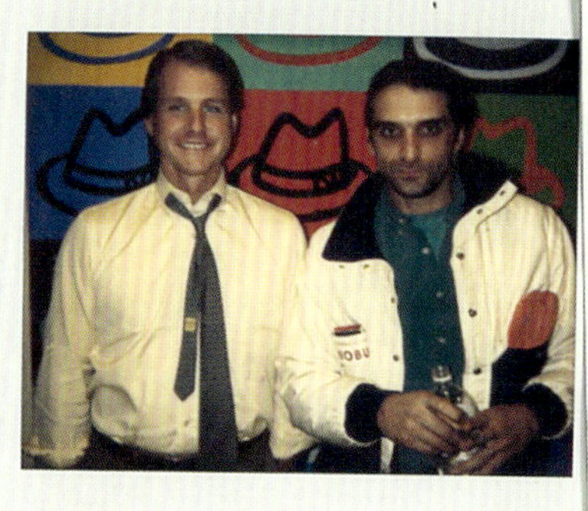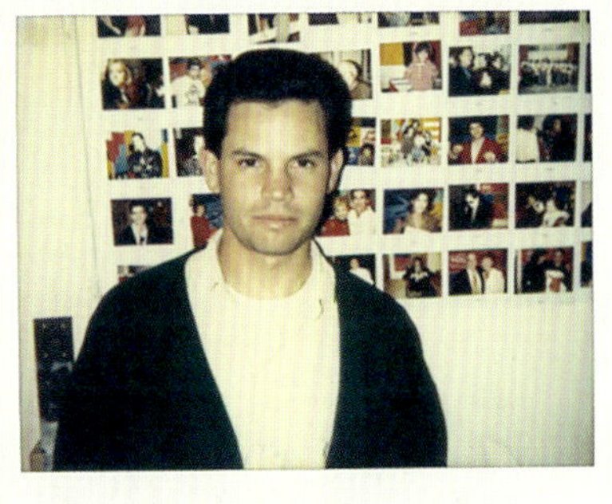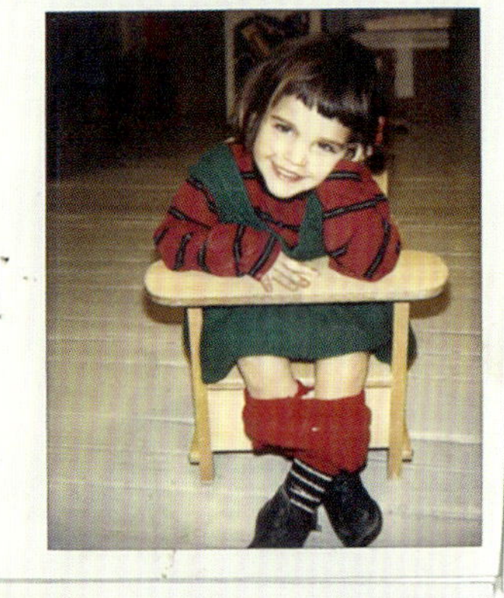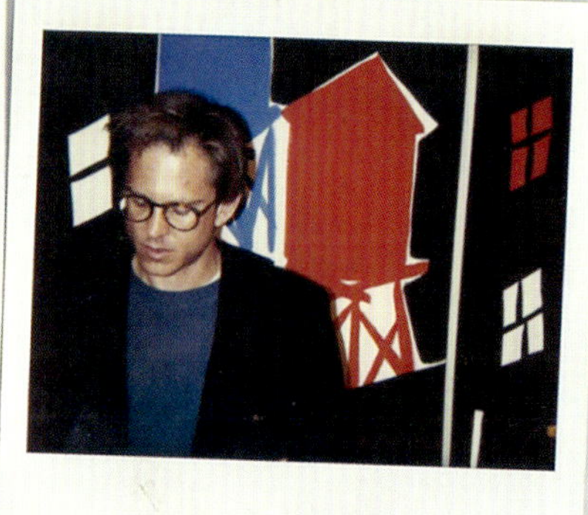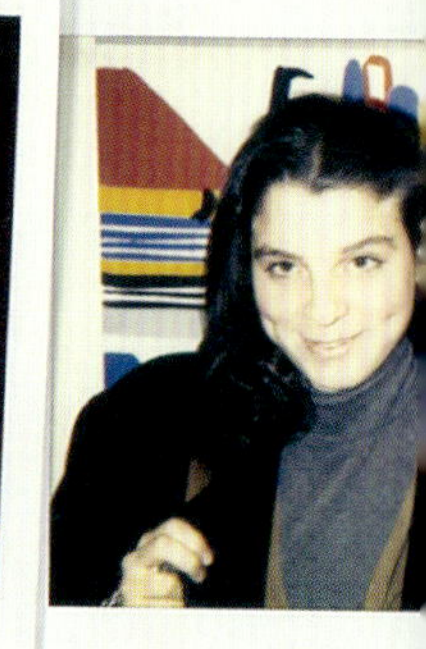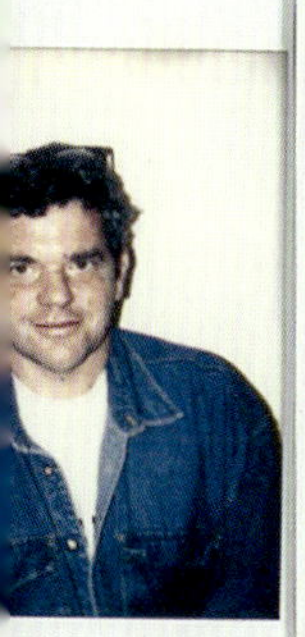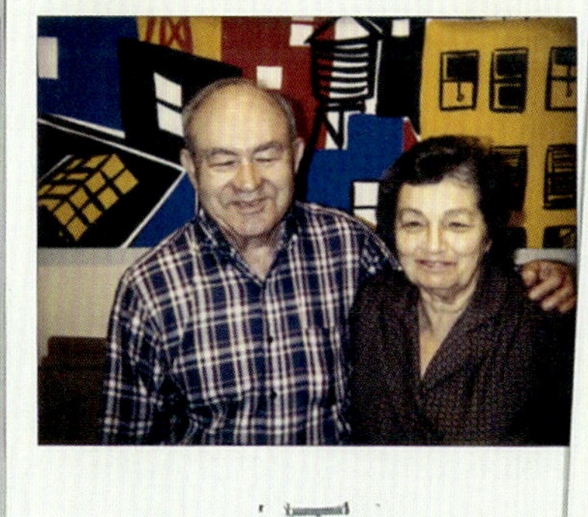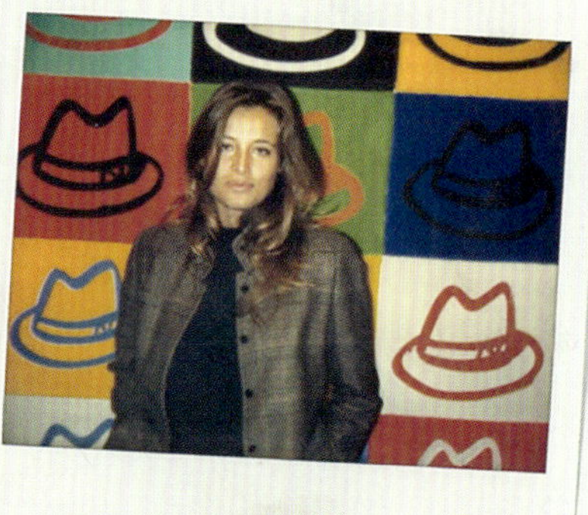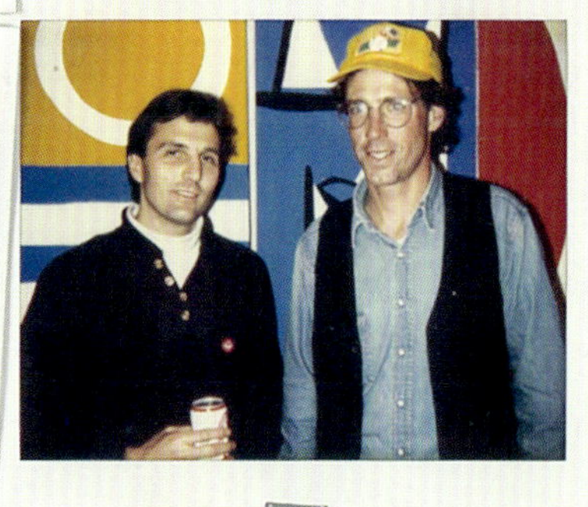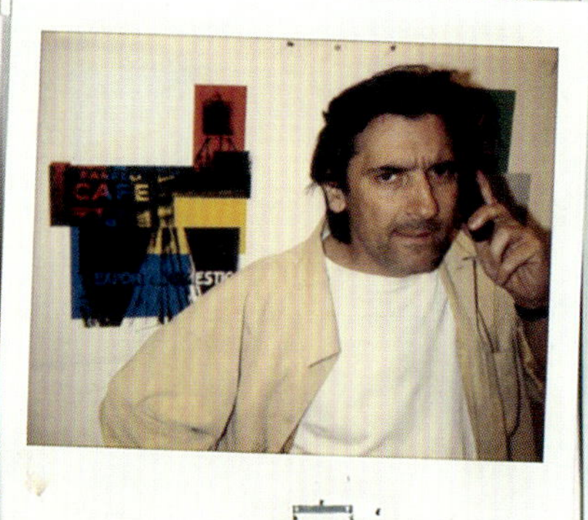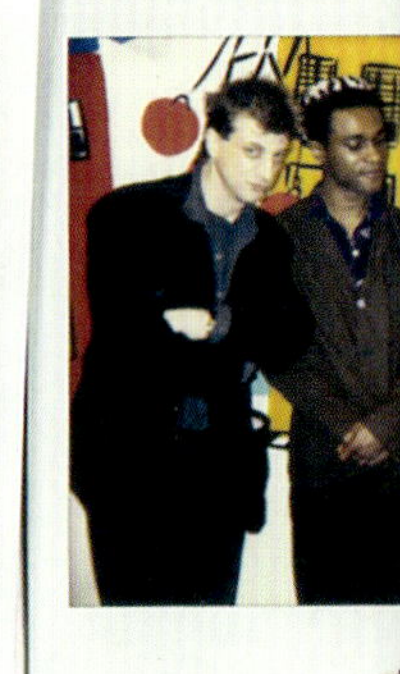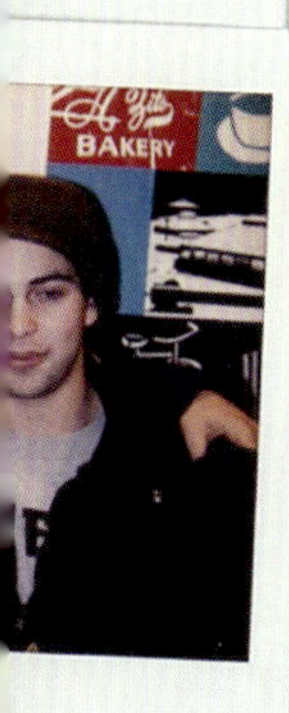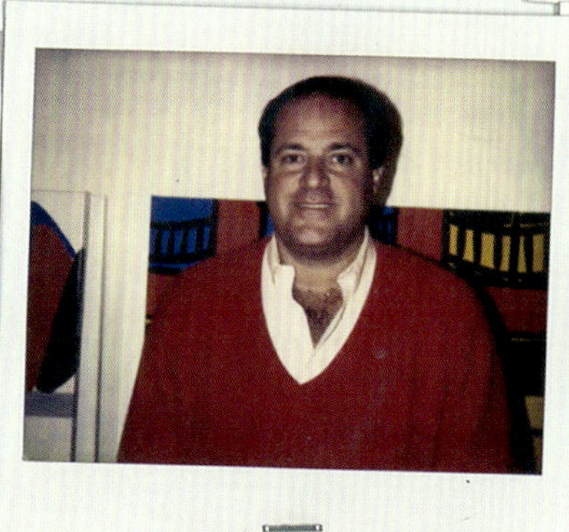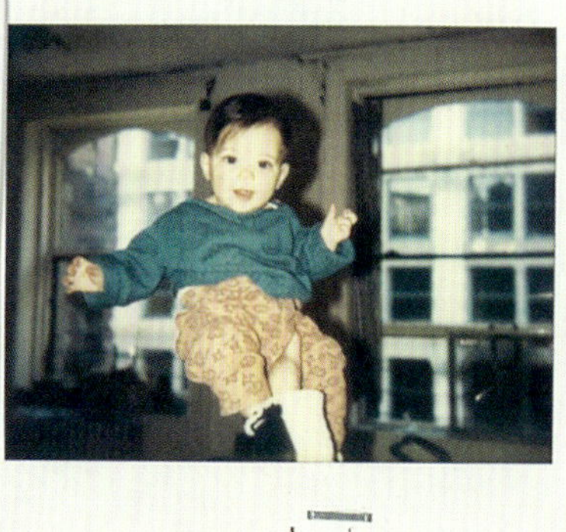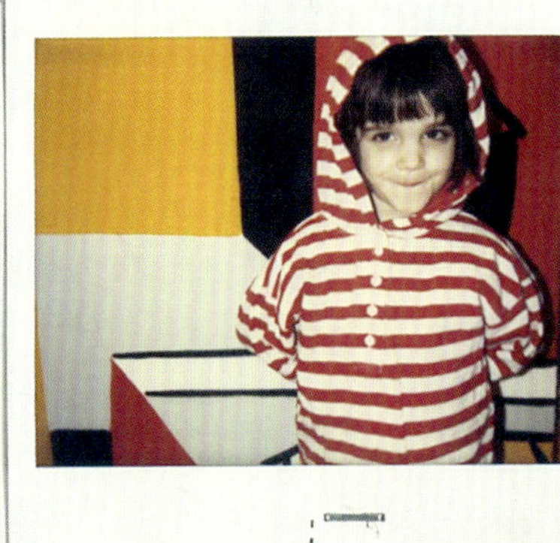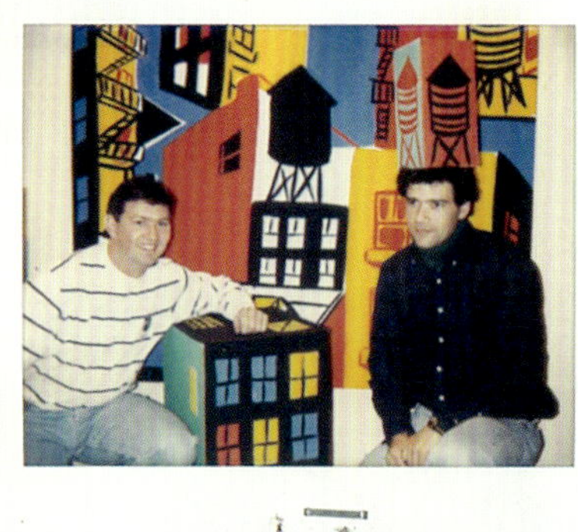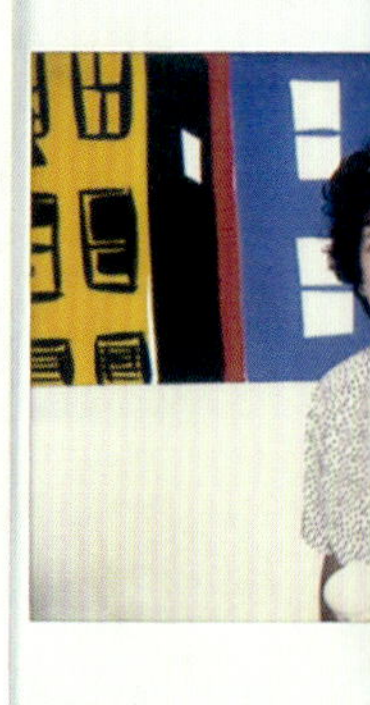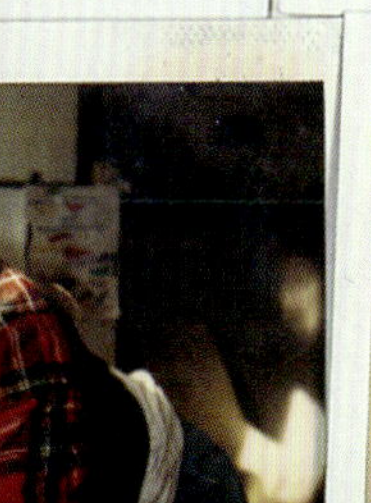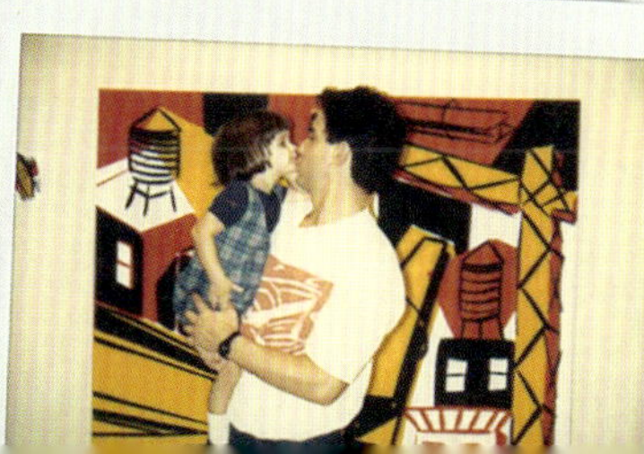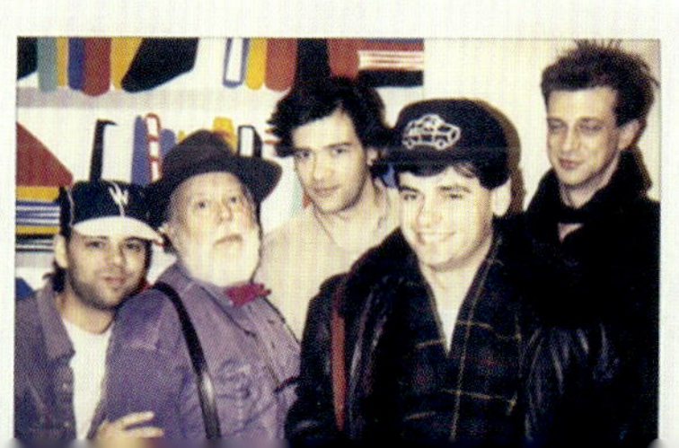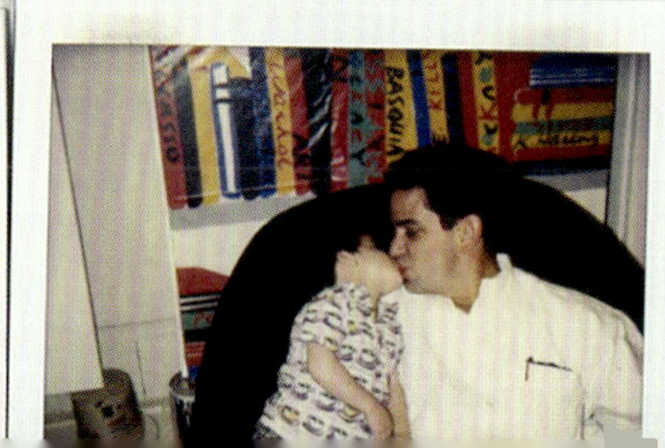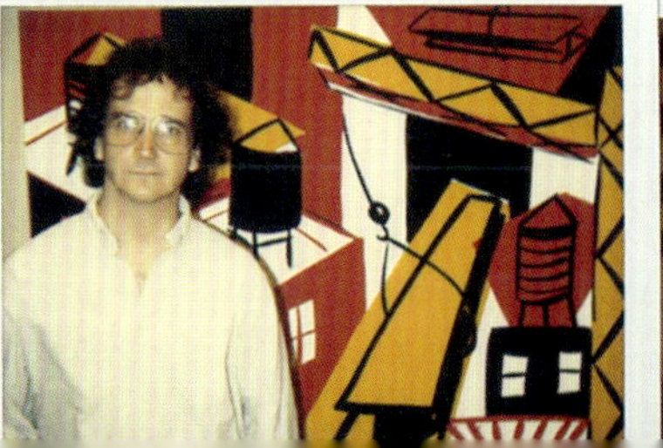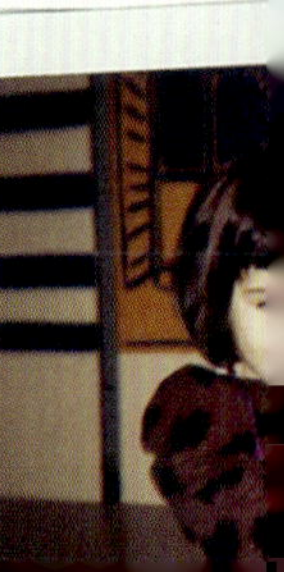

1980-1990

1980-1990

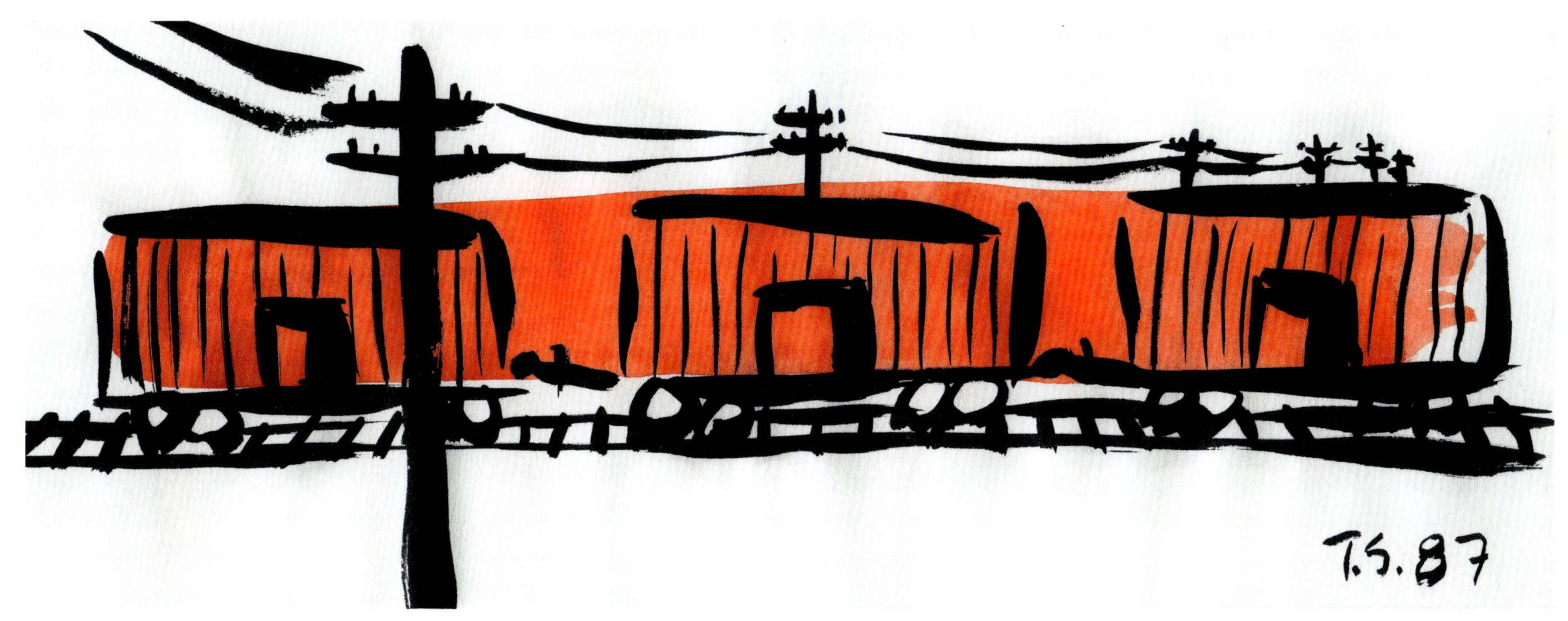

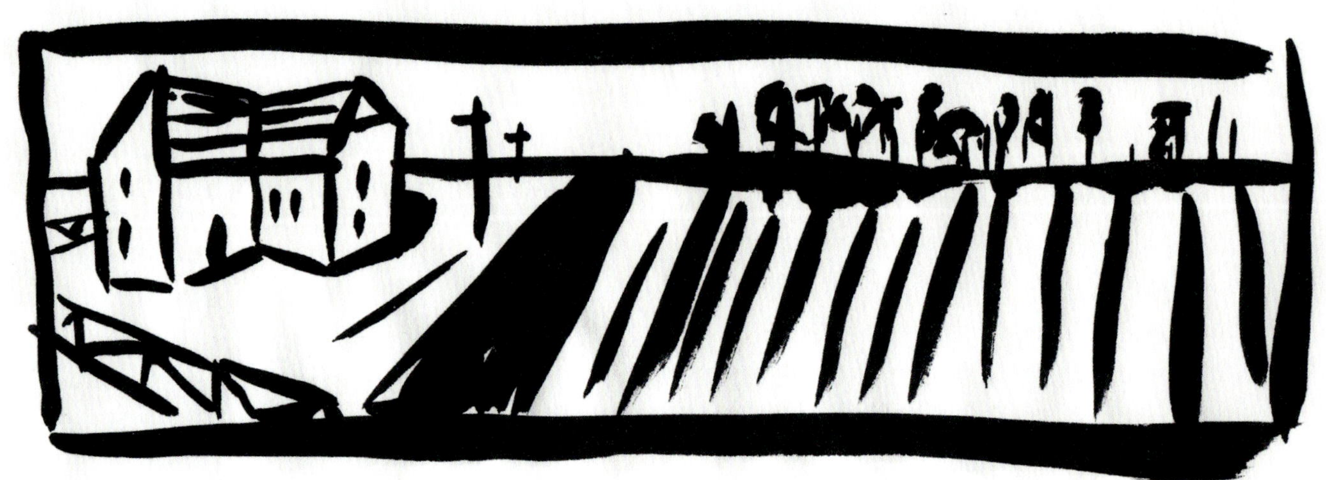

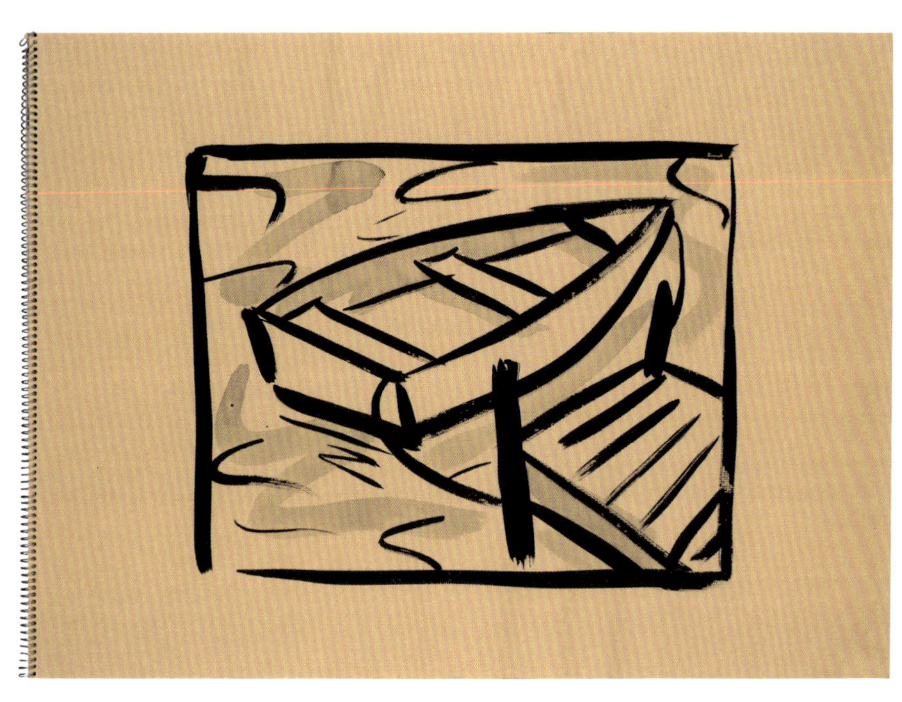

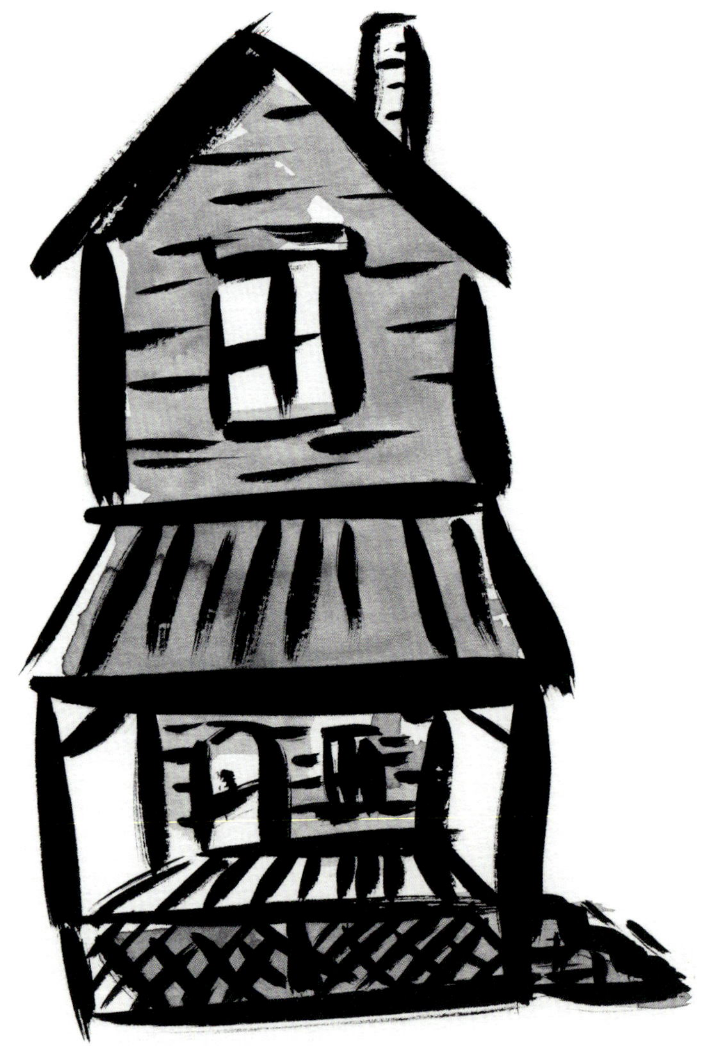

WHITE
PAINT

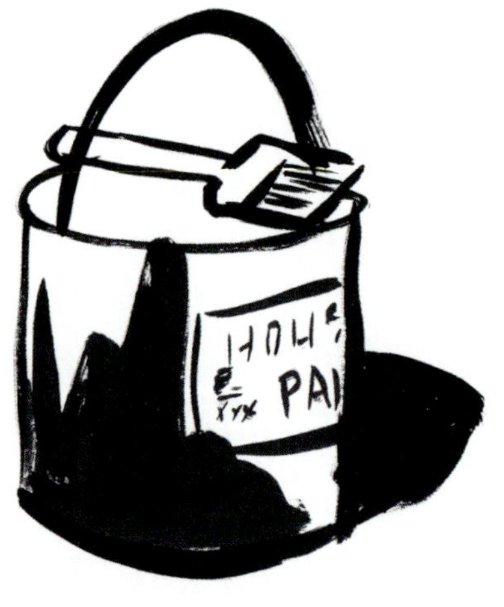
HOUSE
PAINT

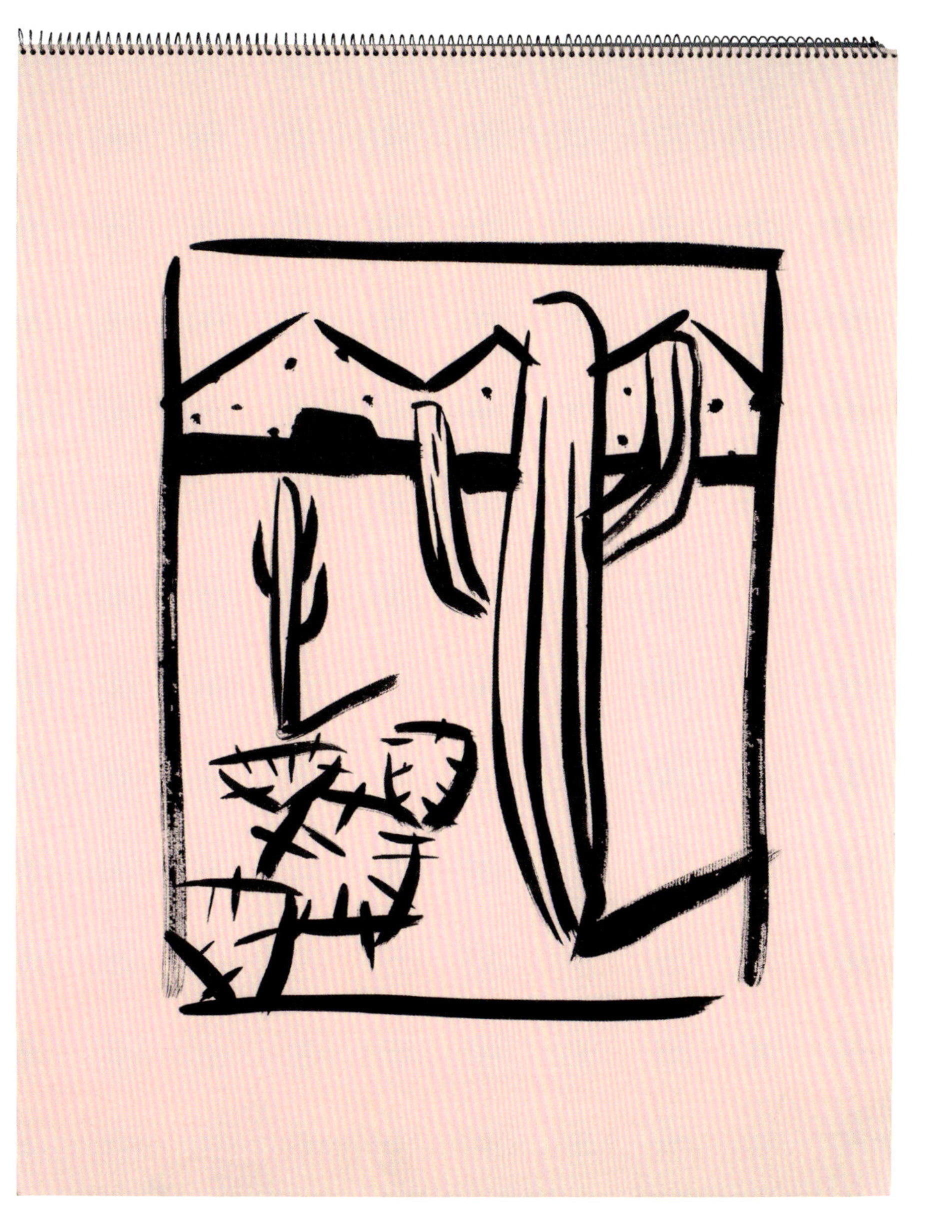

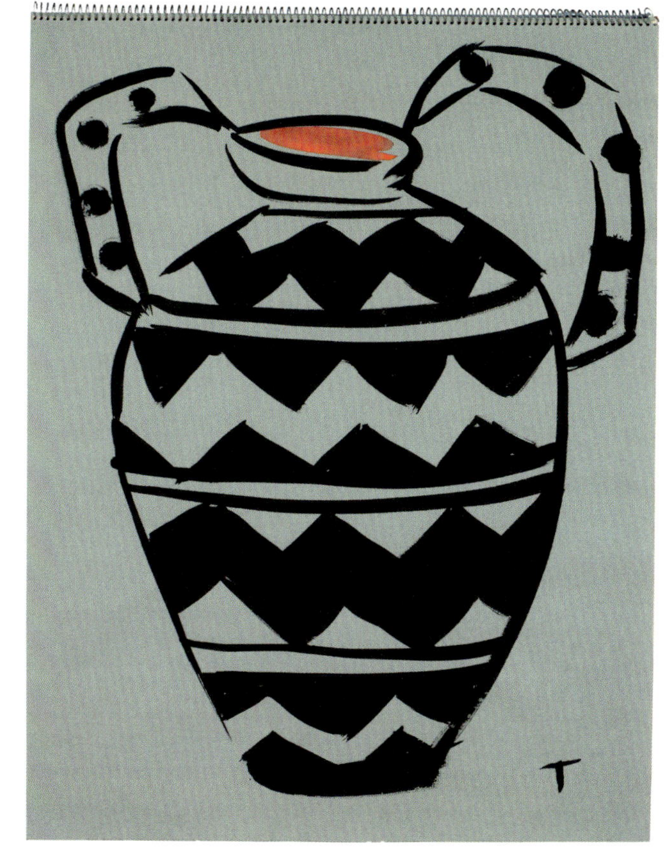

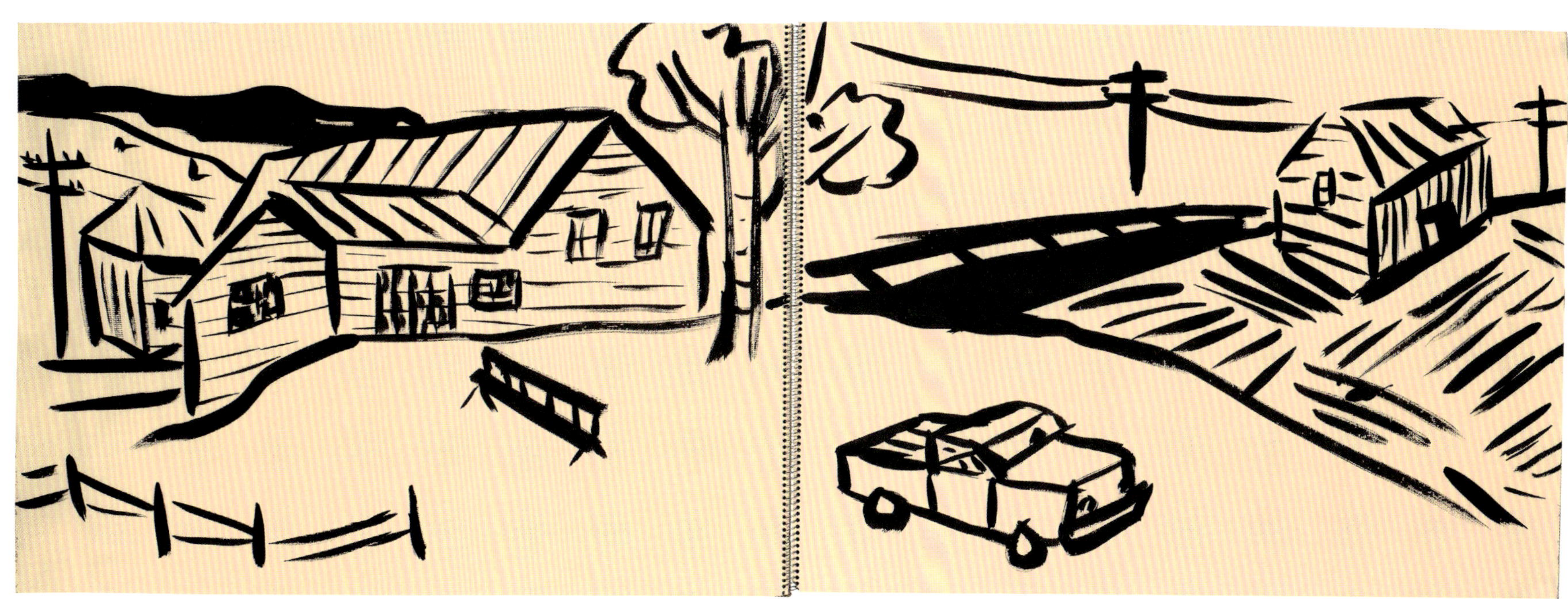

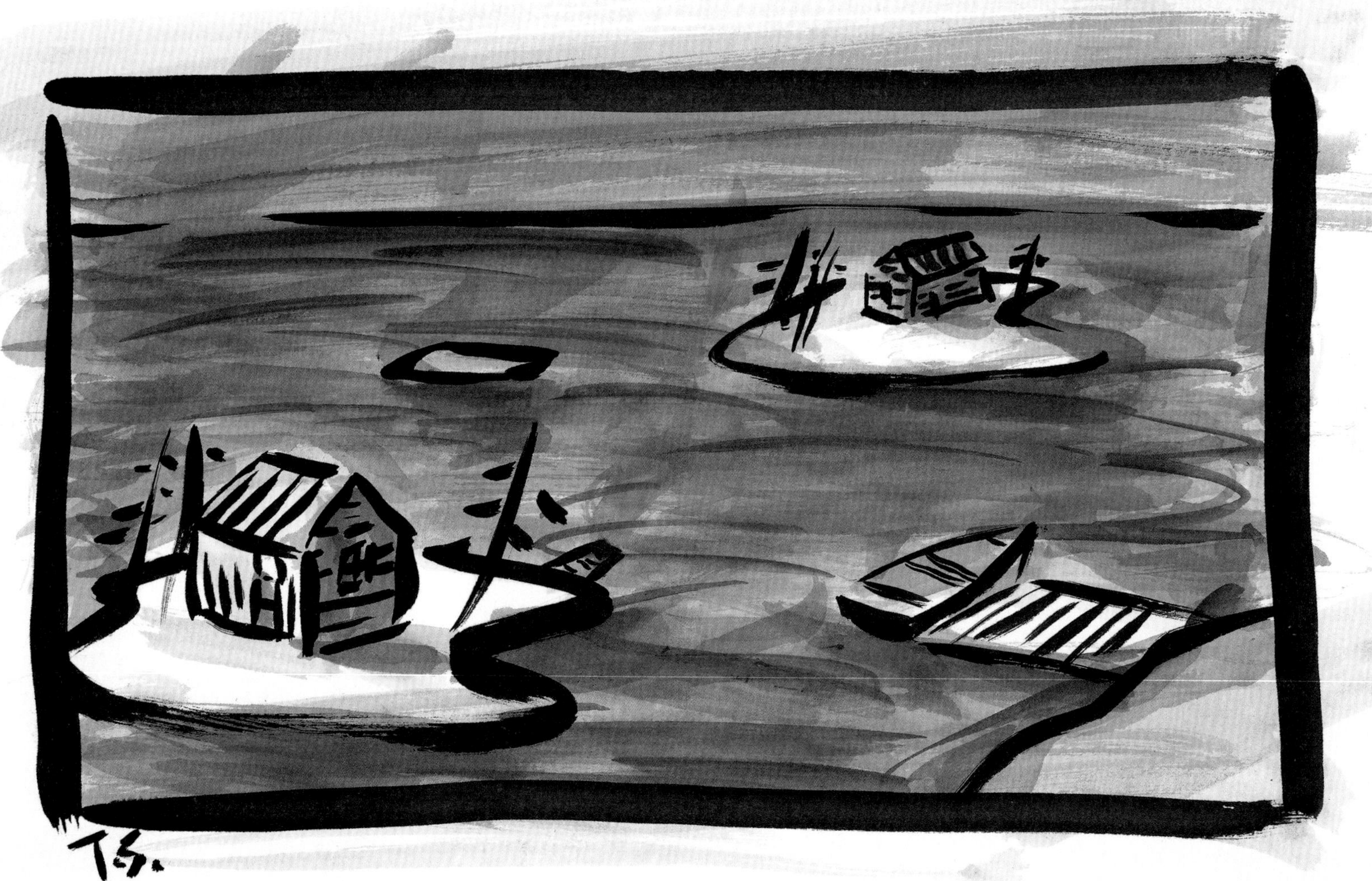

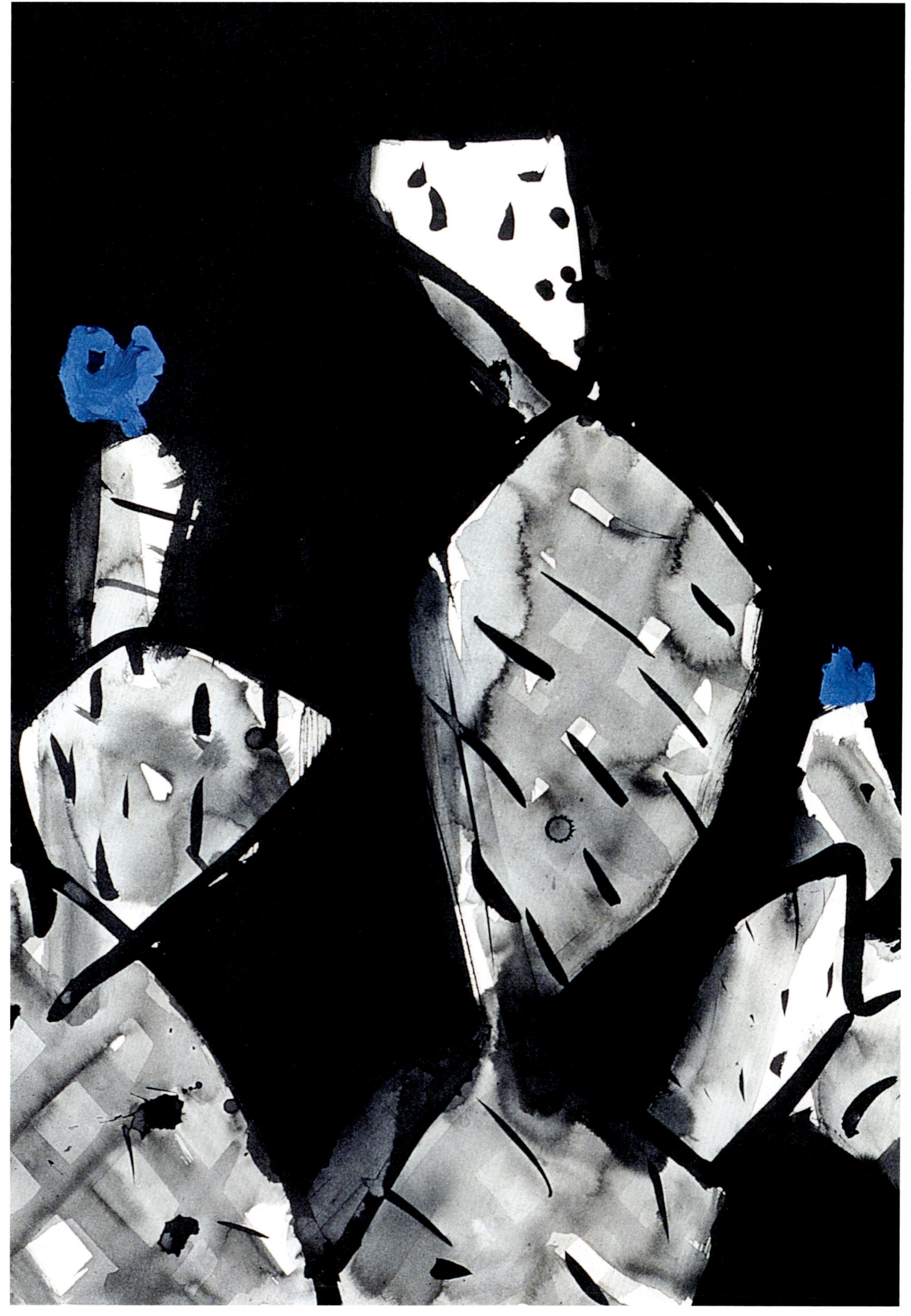

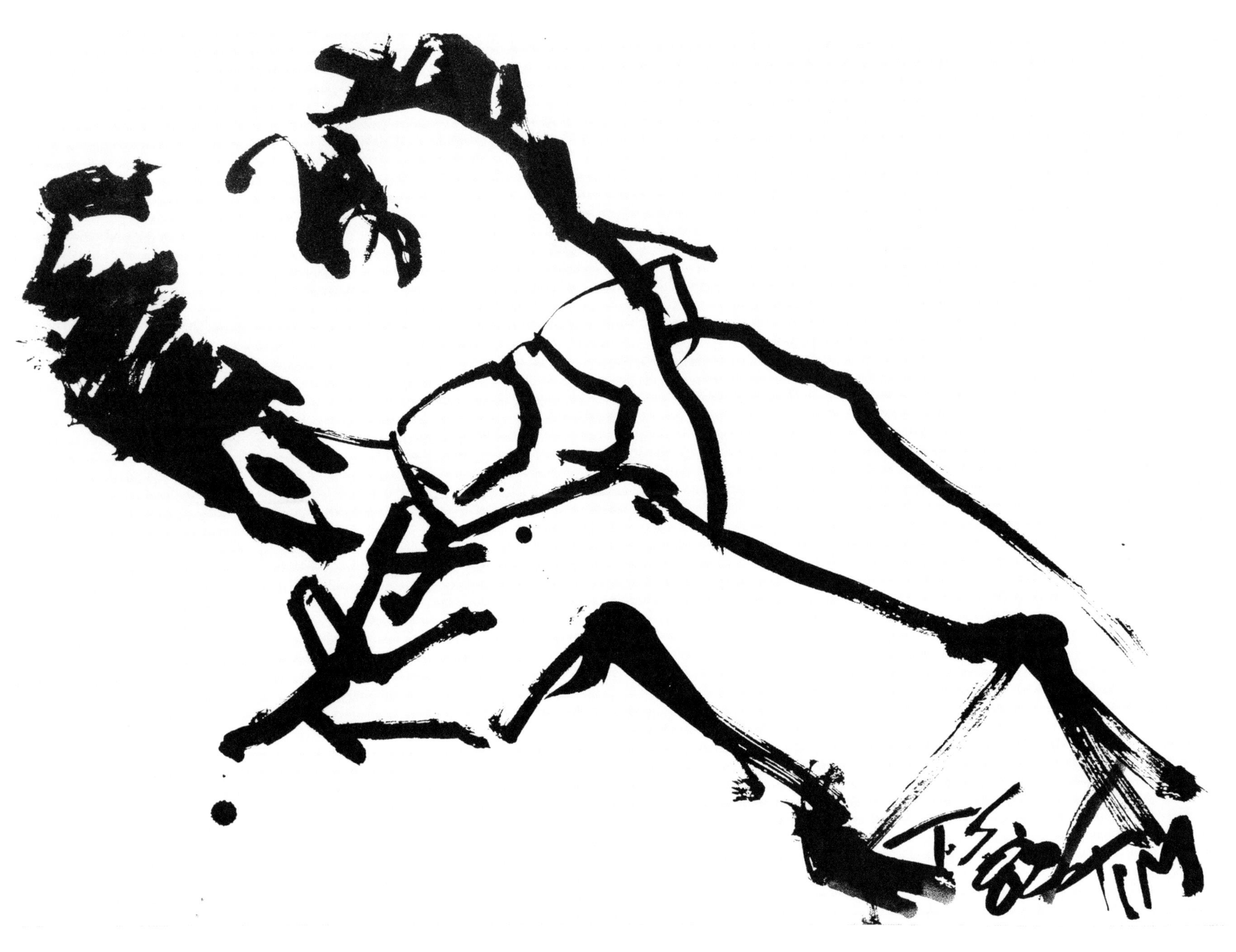

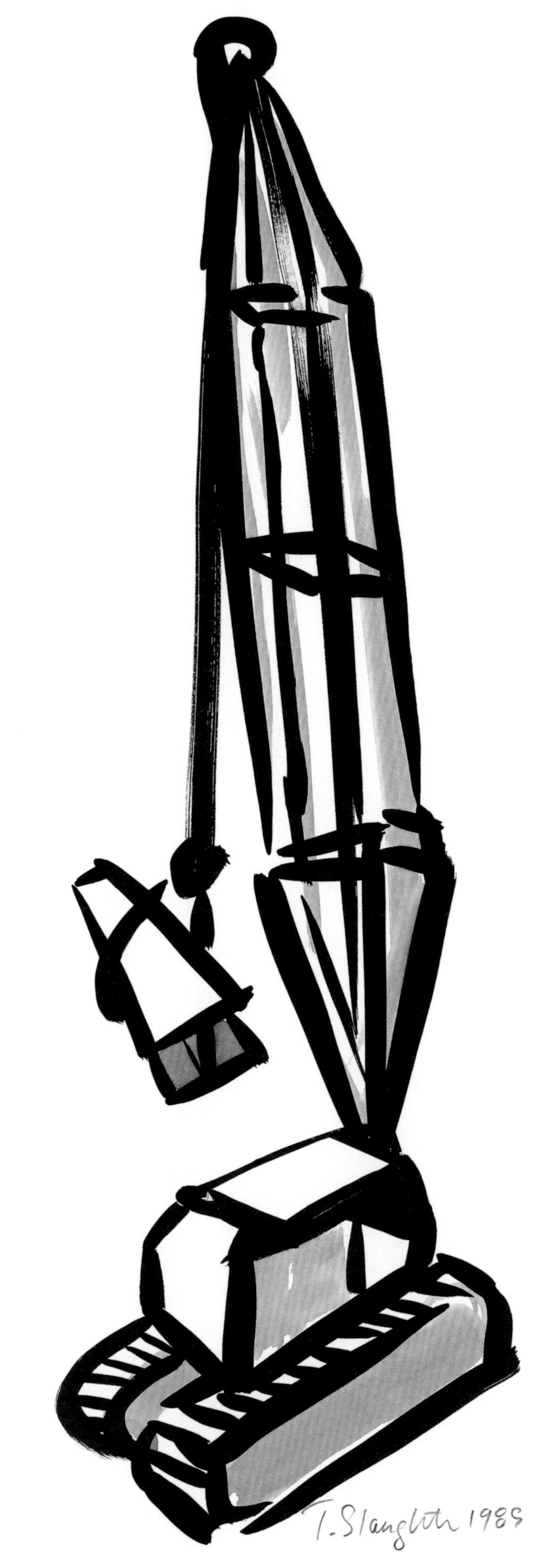
T. Slaughter 1988

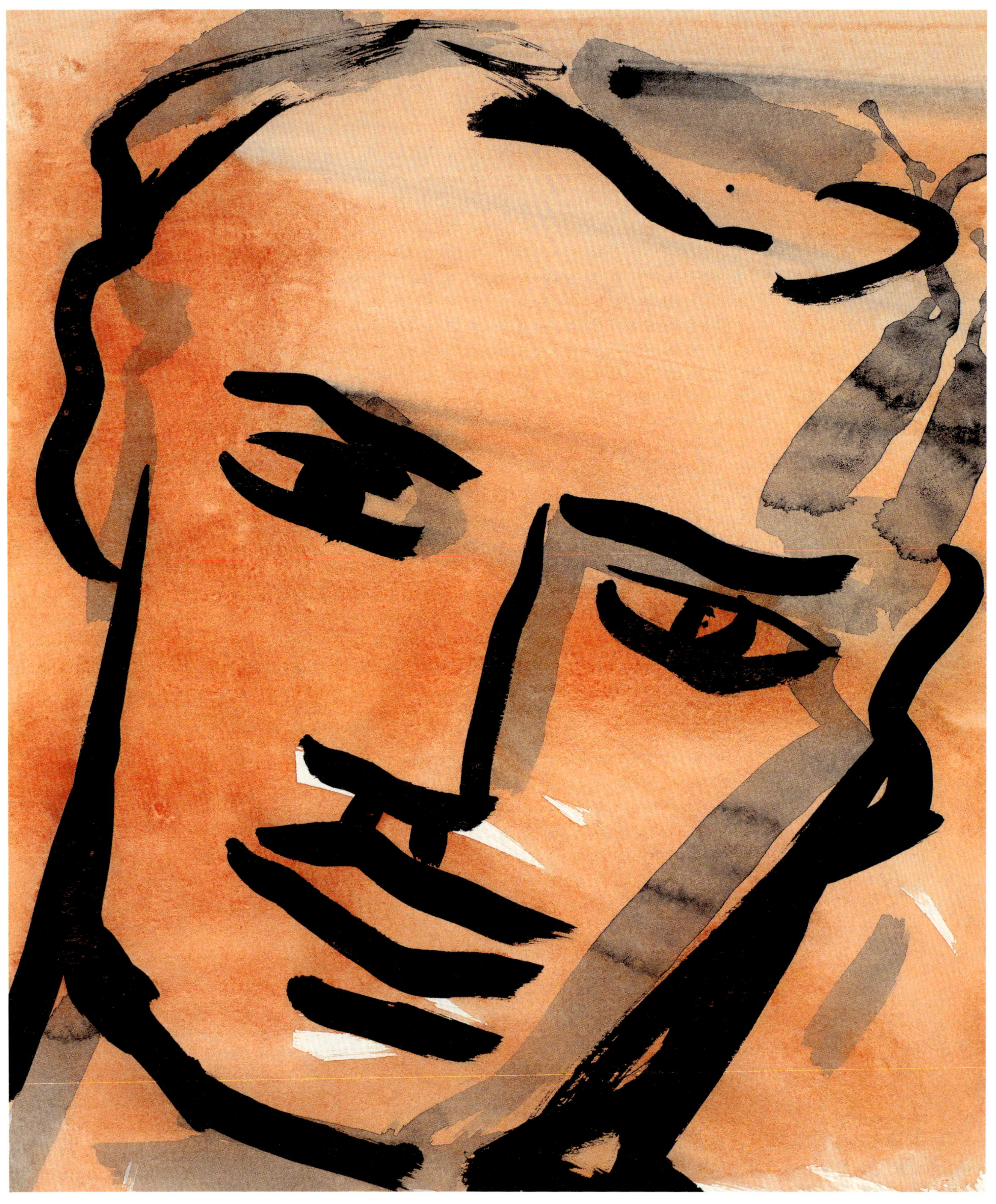

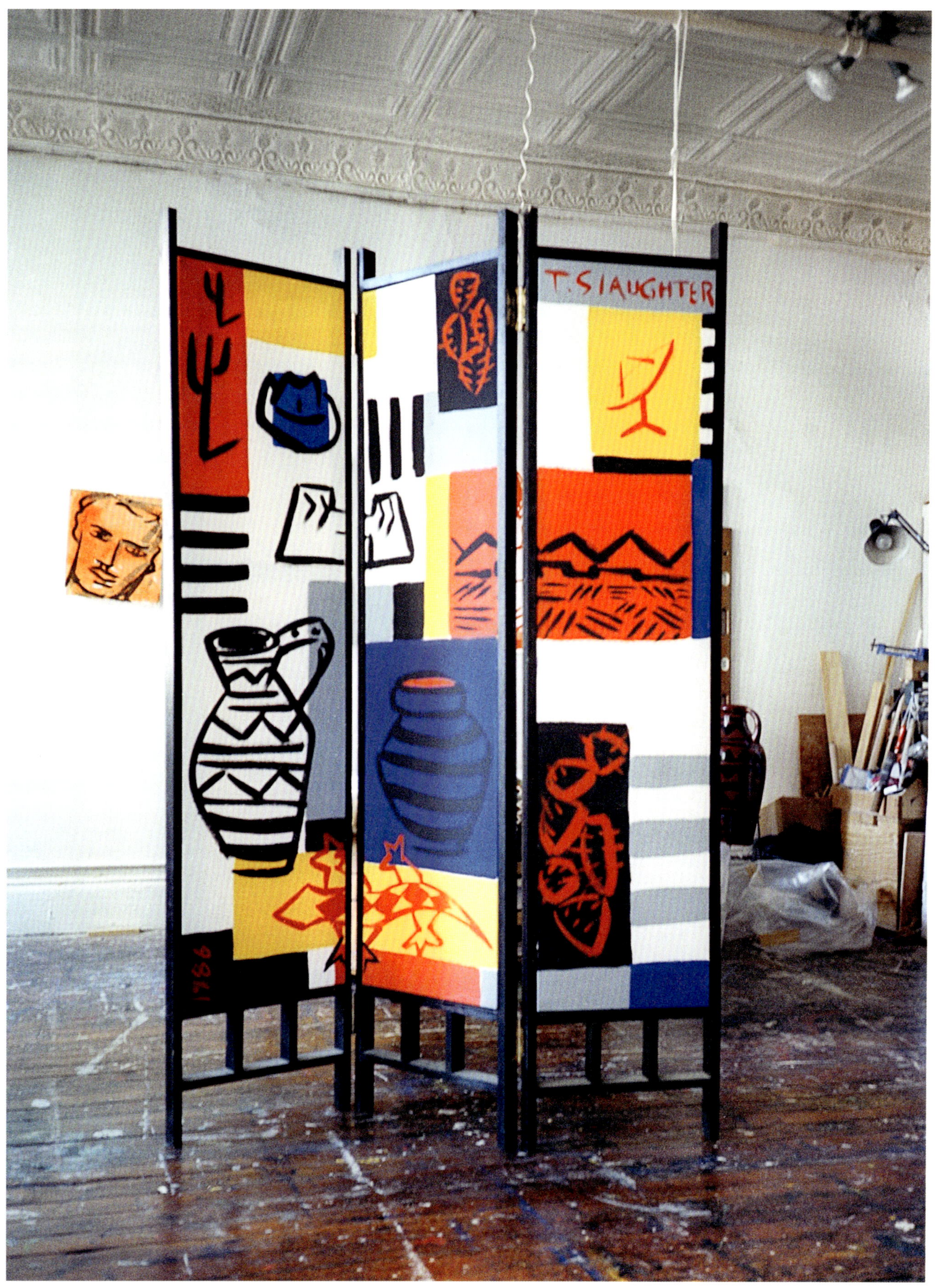

T. SLAUGHTER

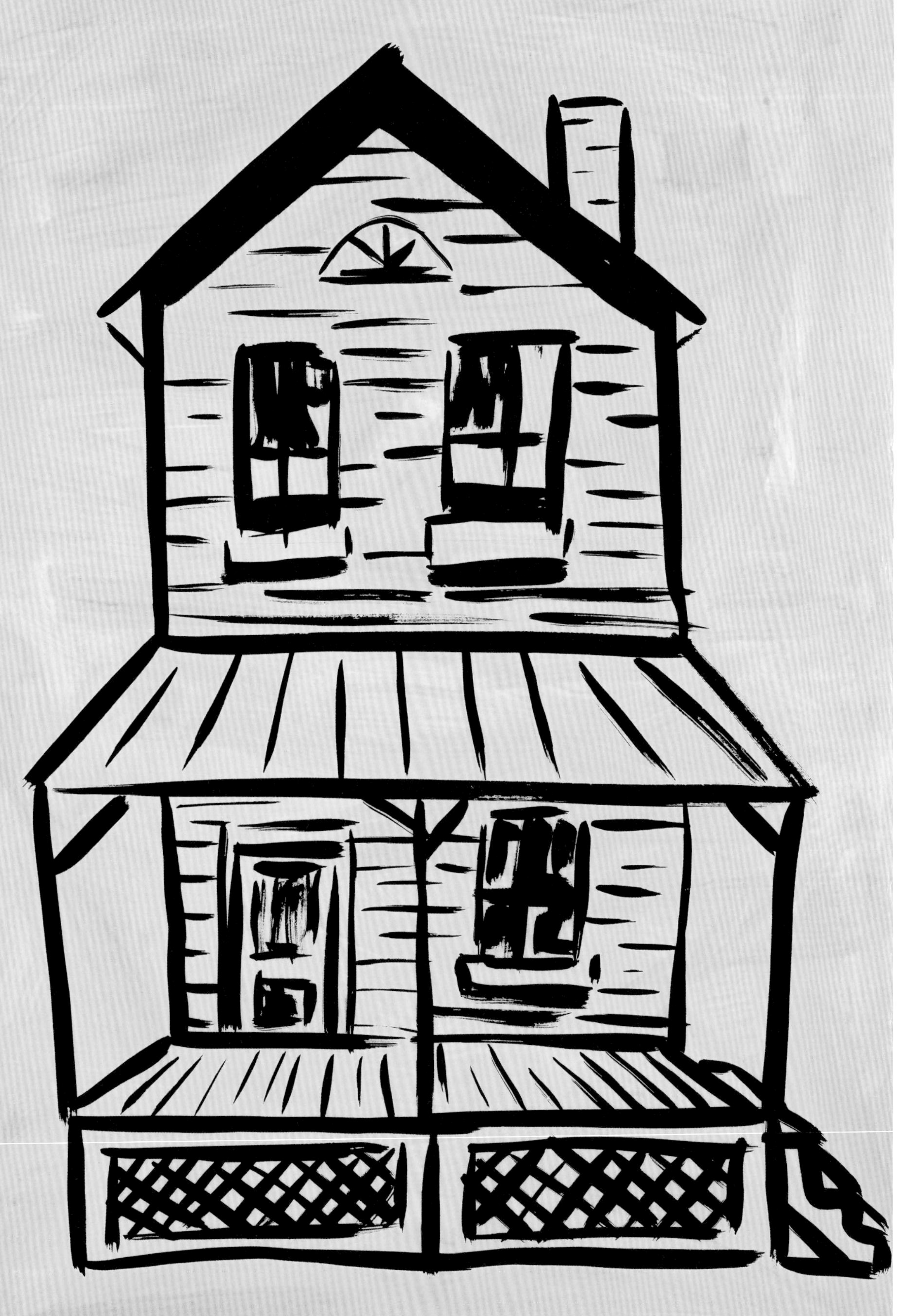

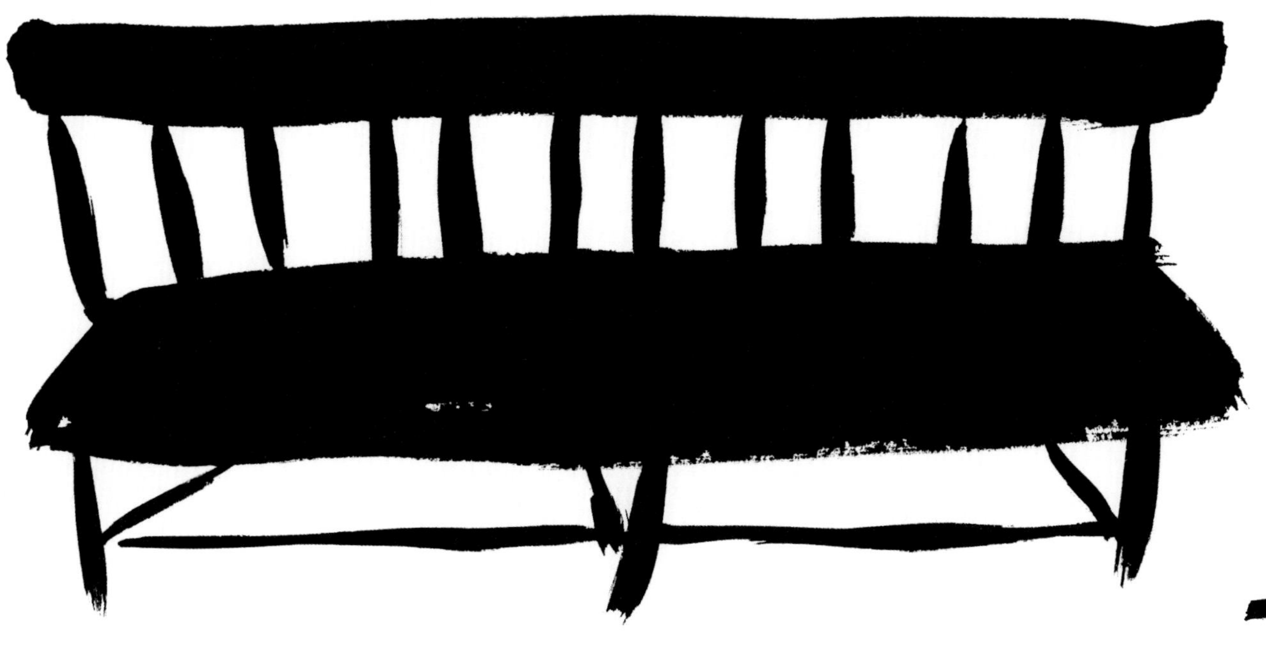

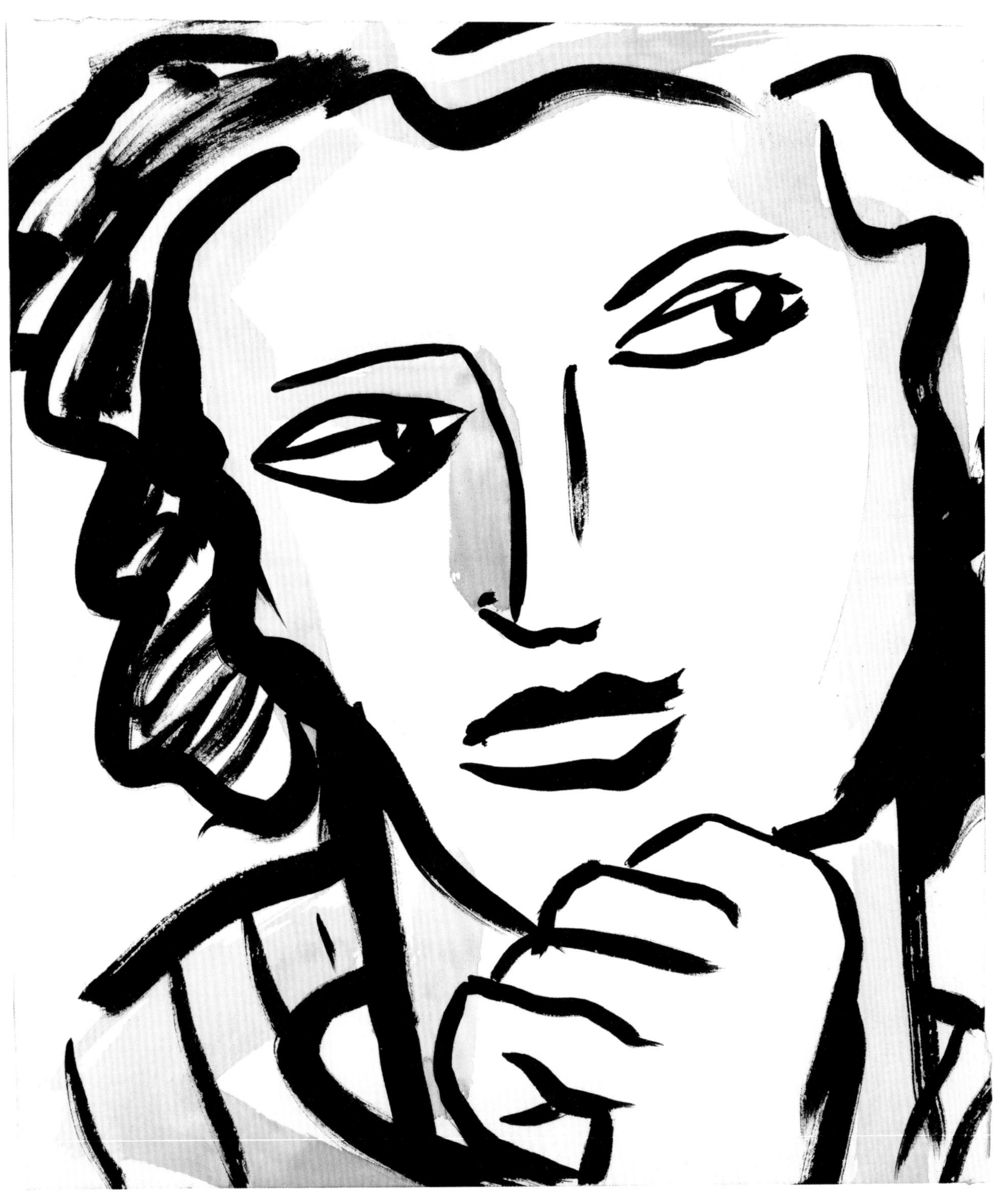

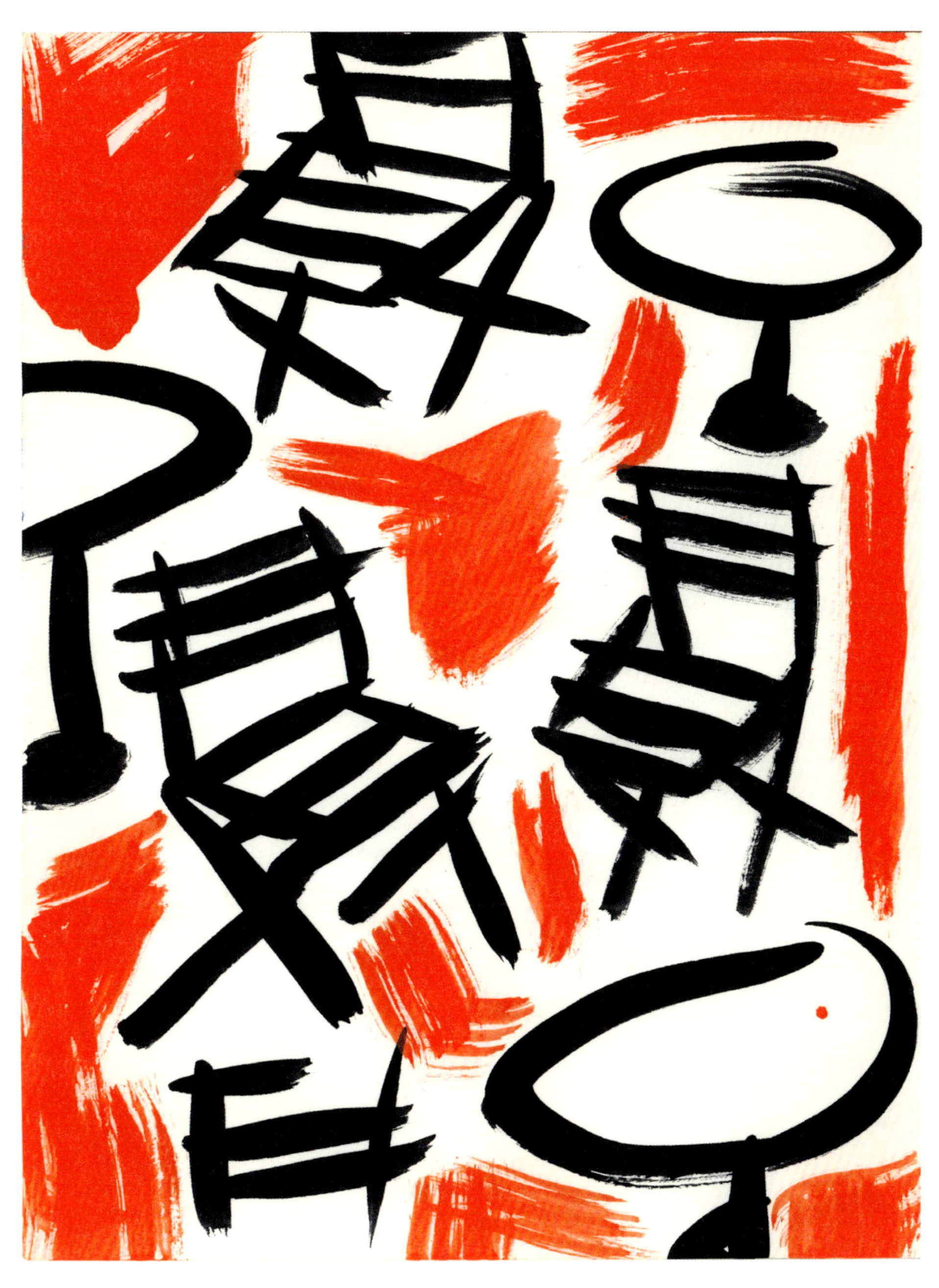

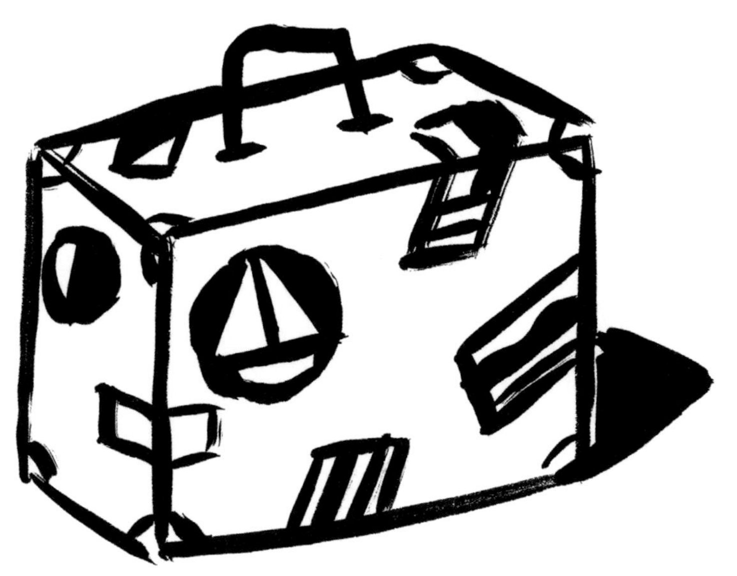

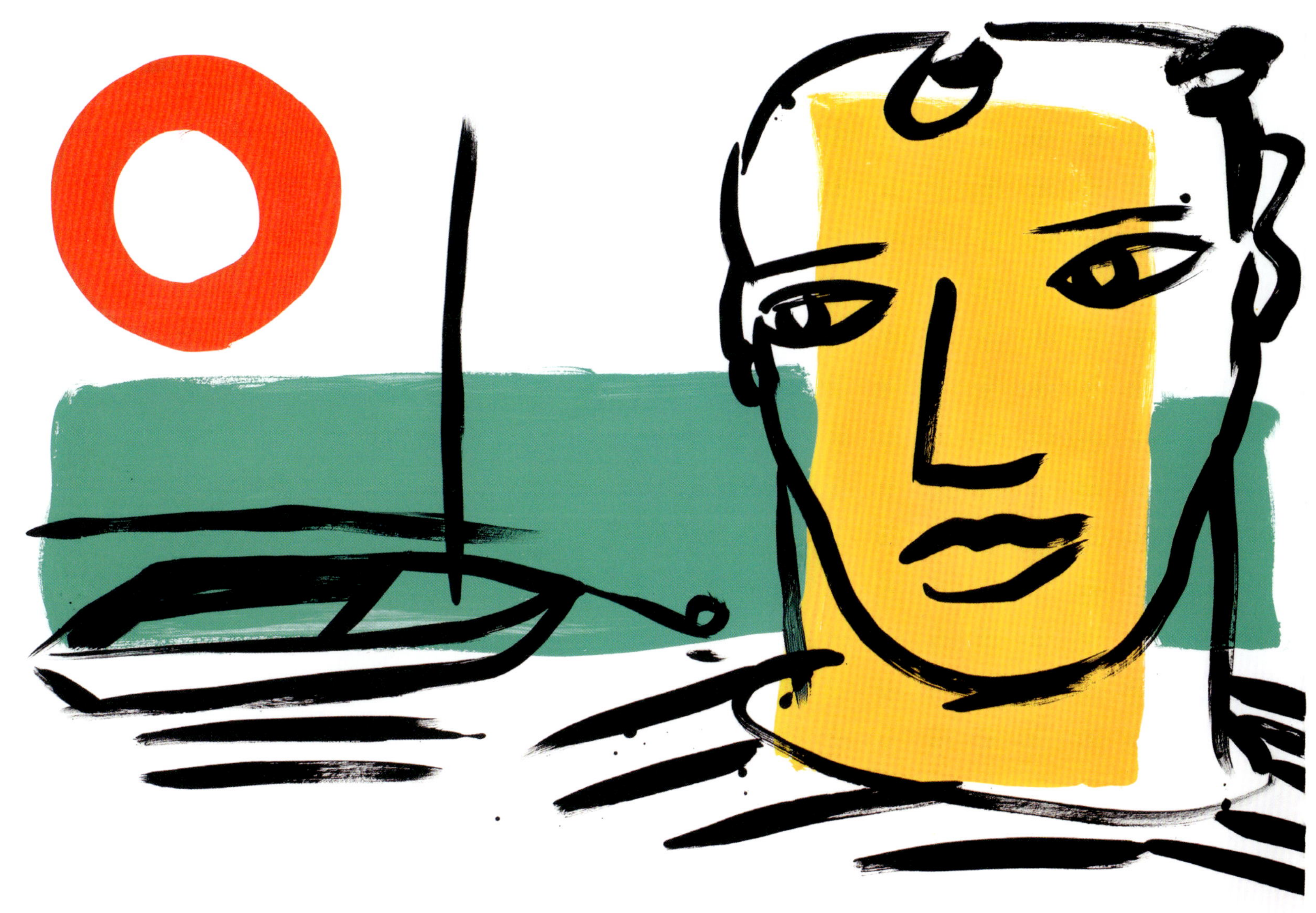

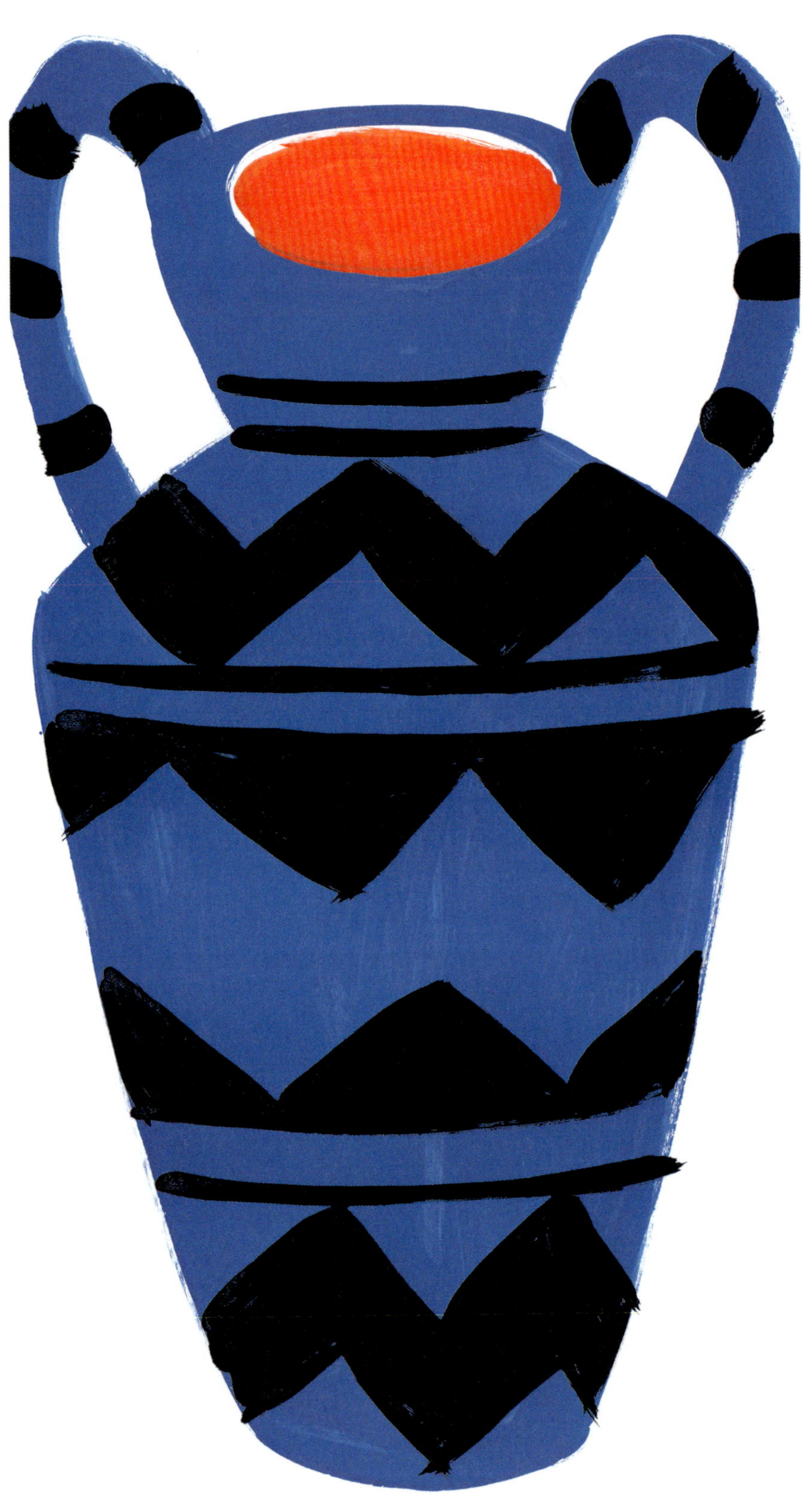

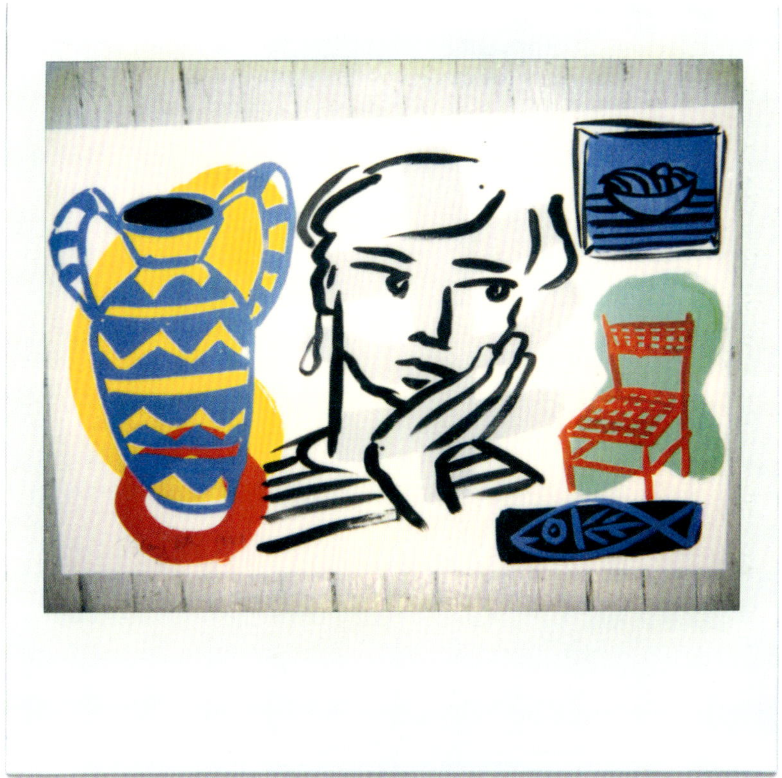

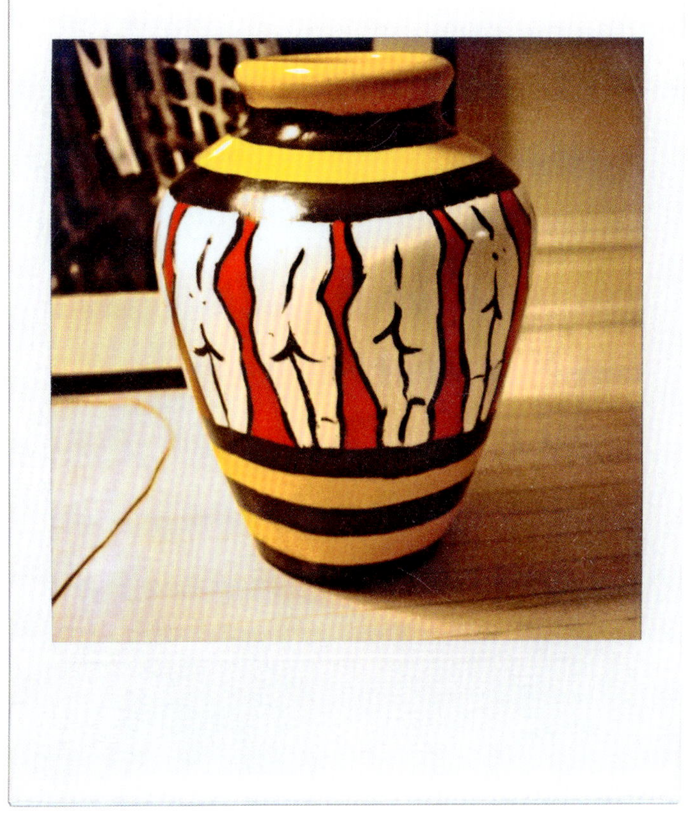

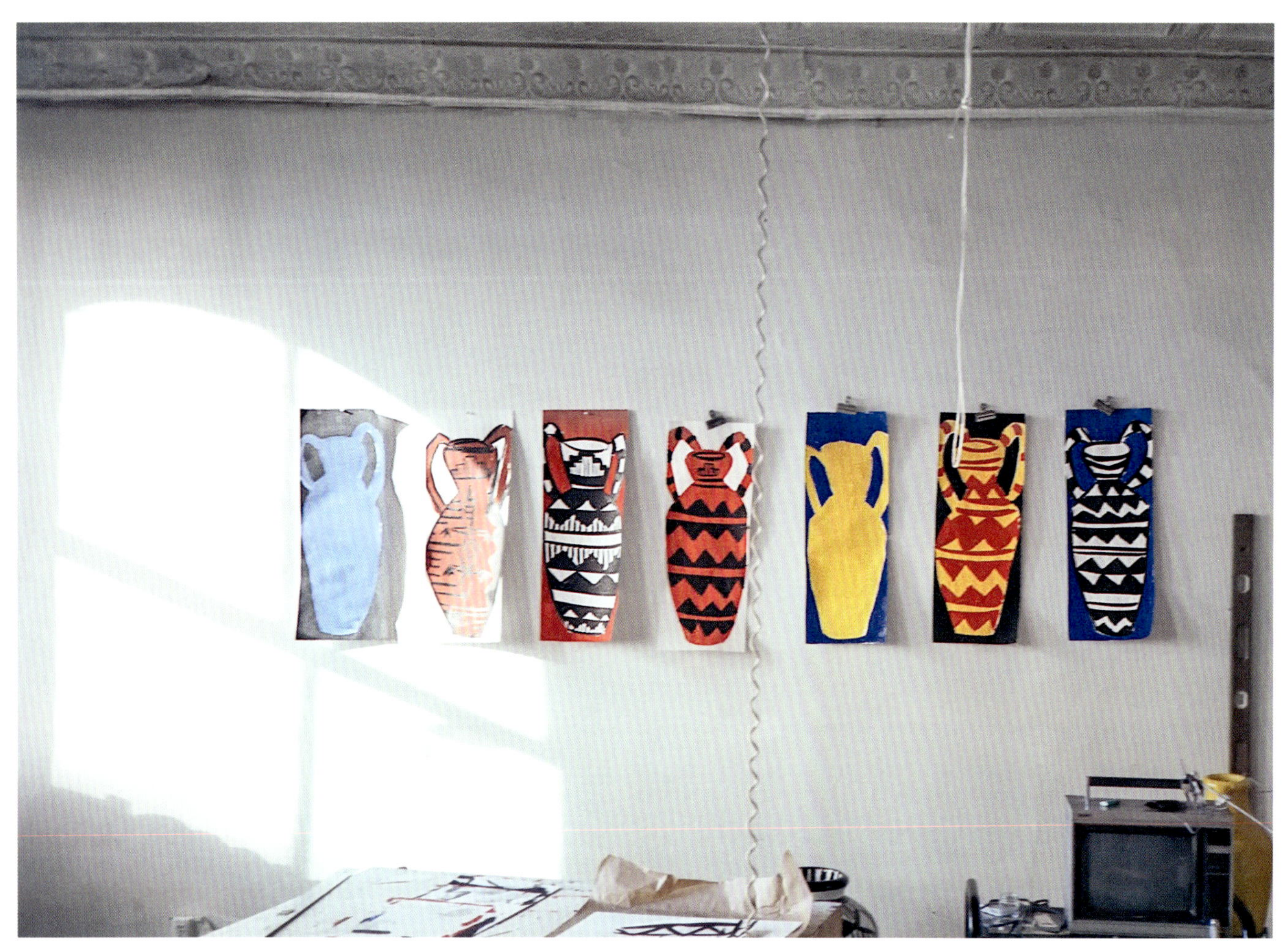

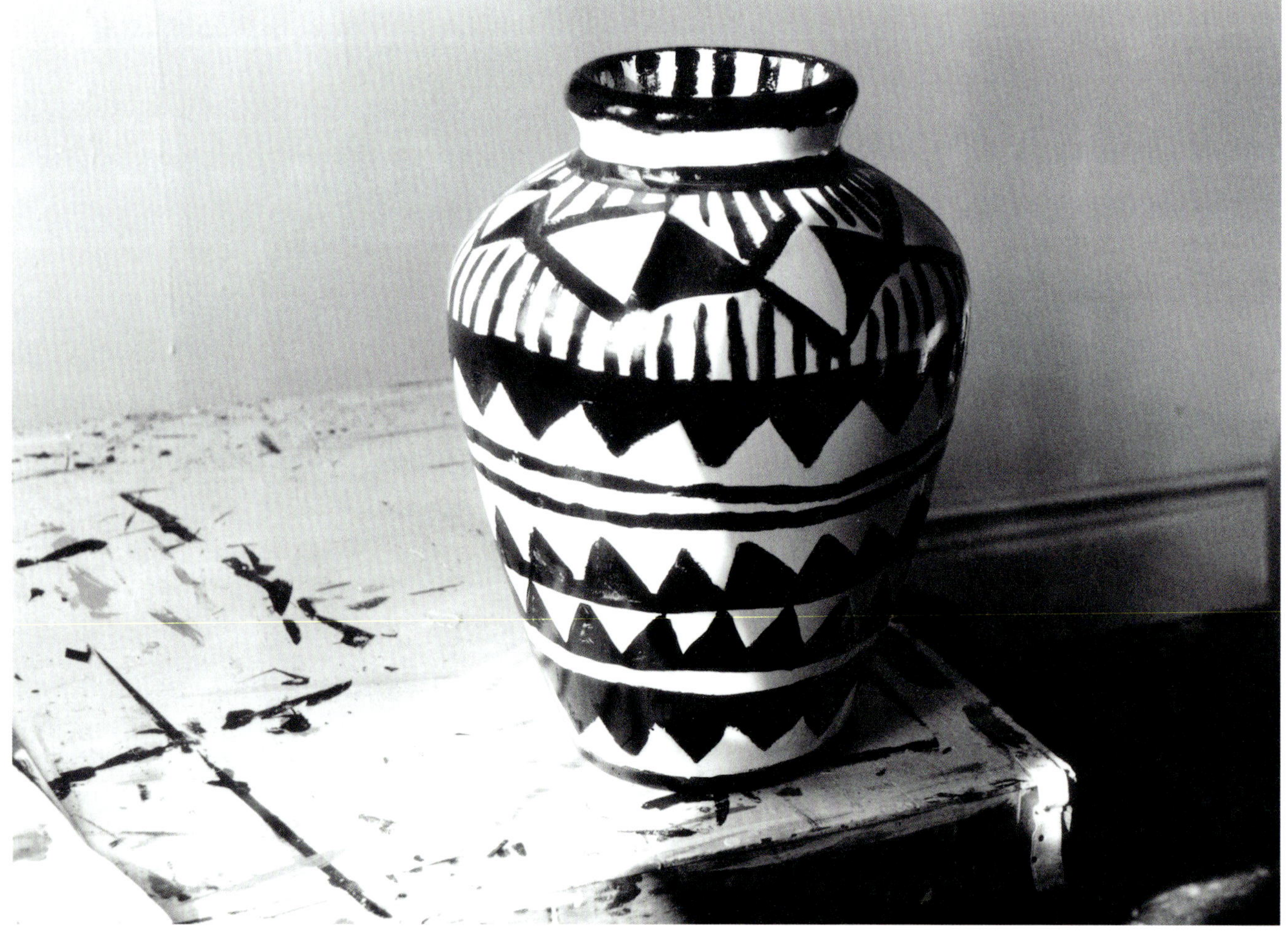

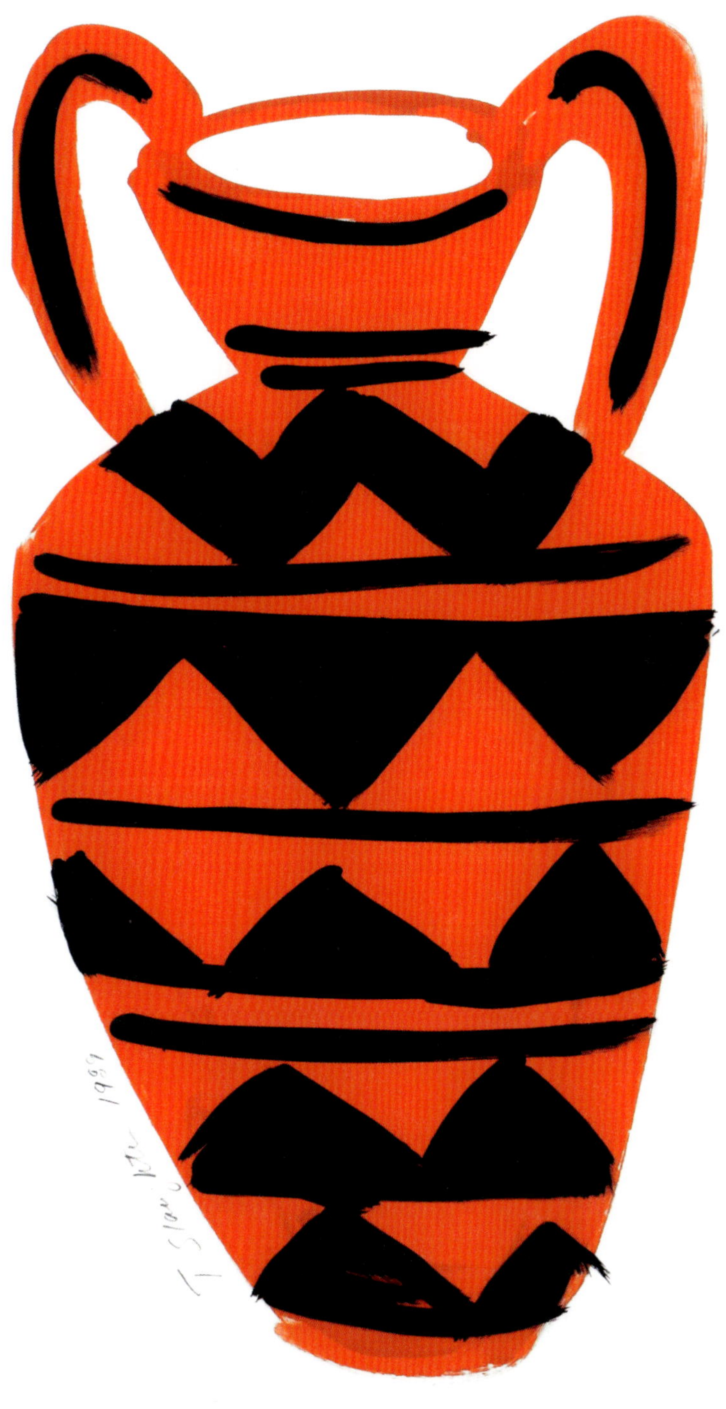
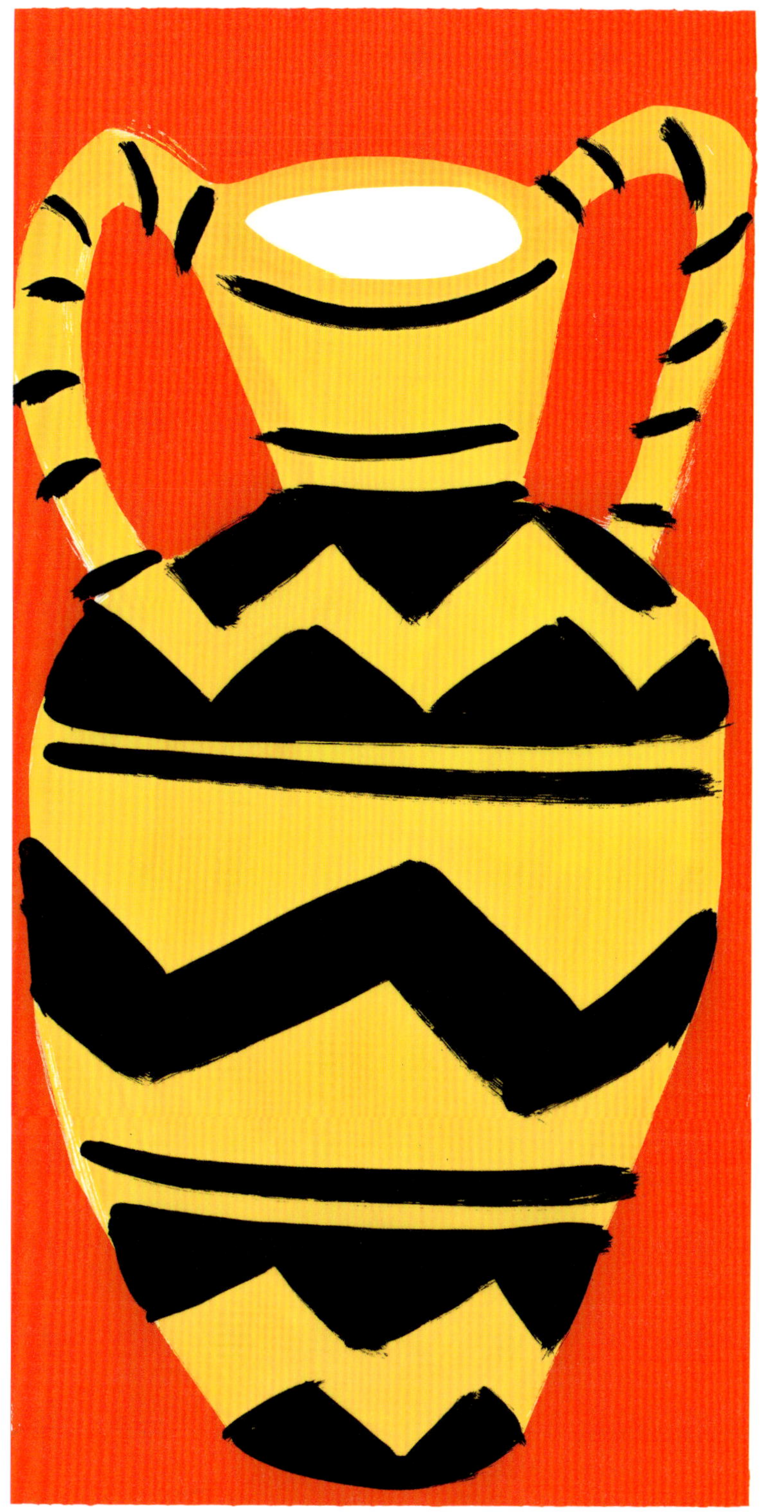

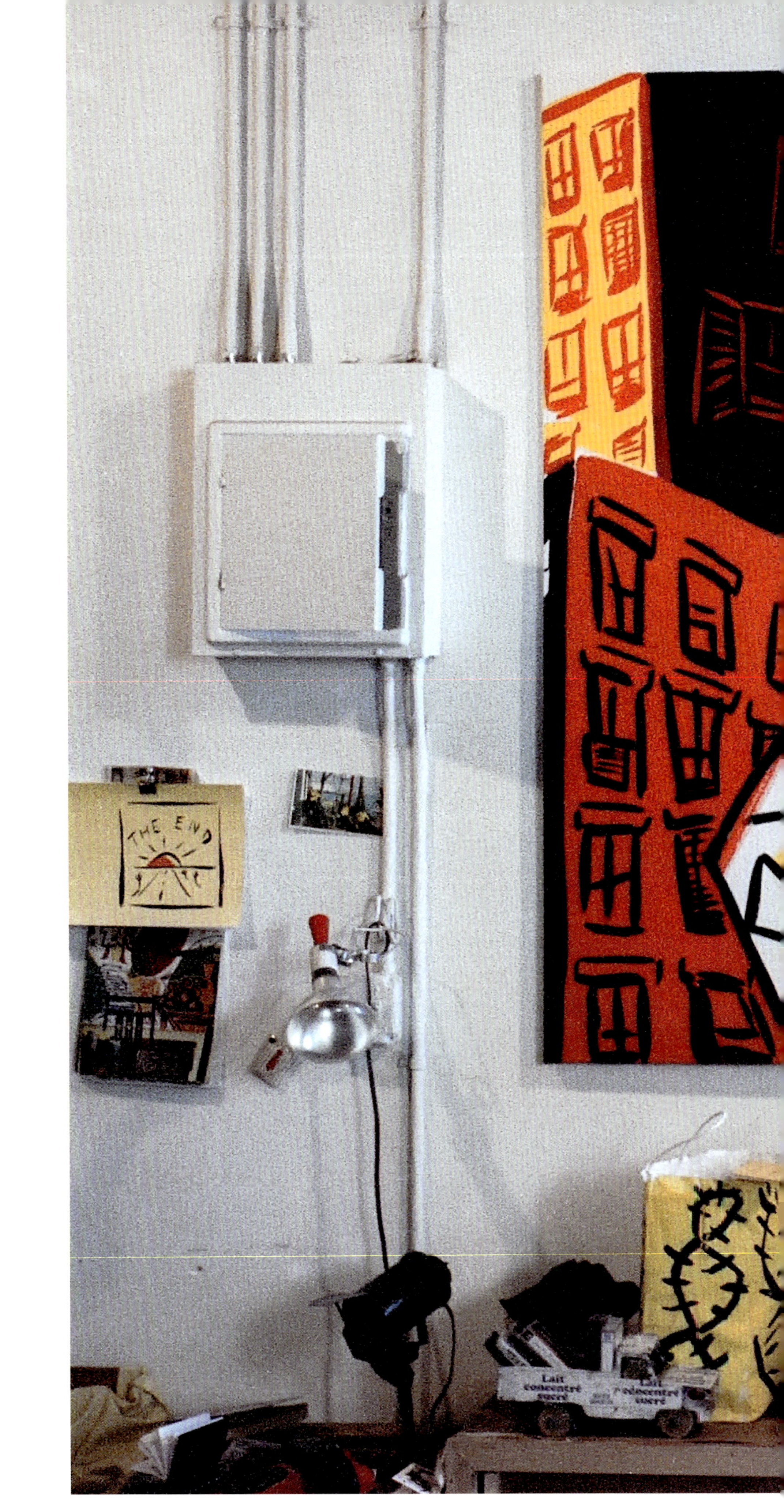
THE END
Lait concentré sucré
Lait concentré sucré

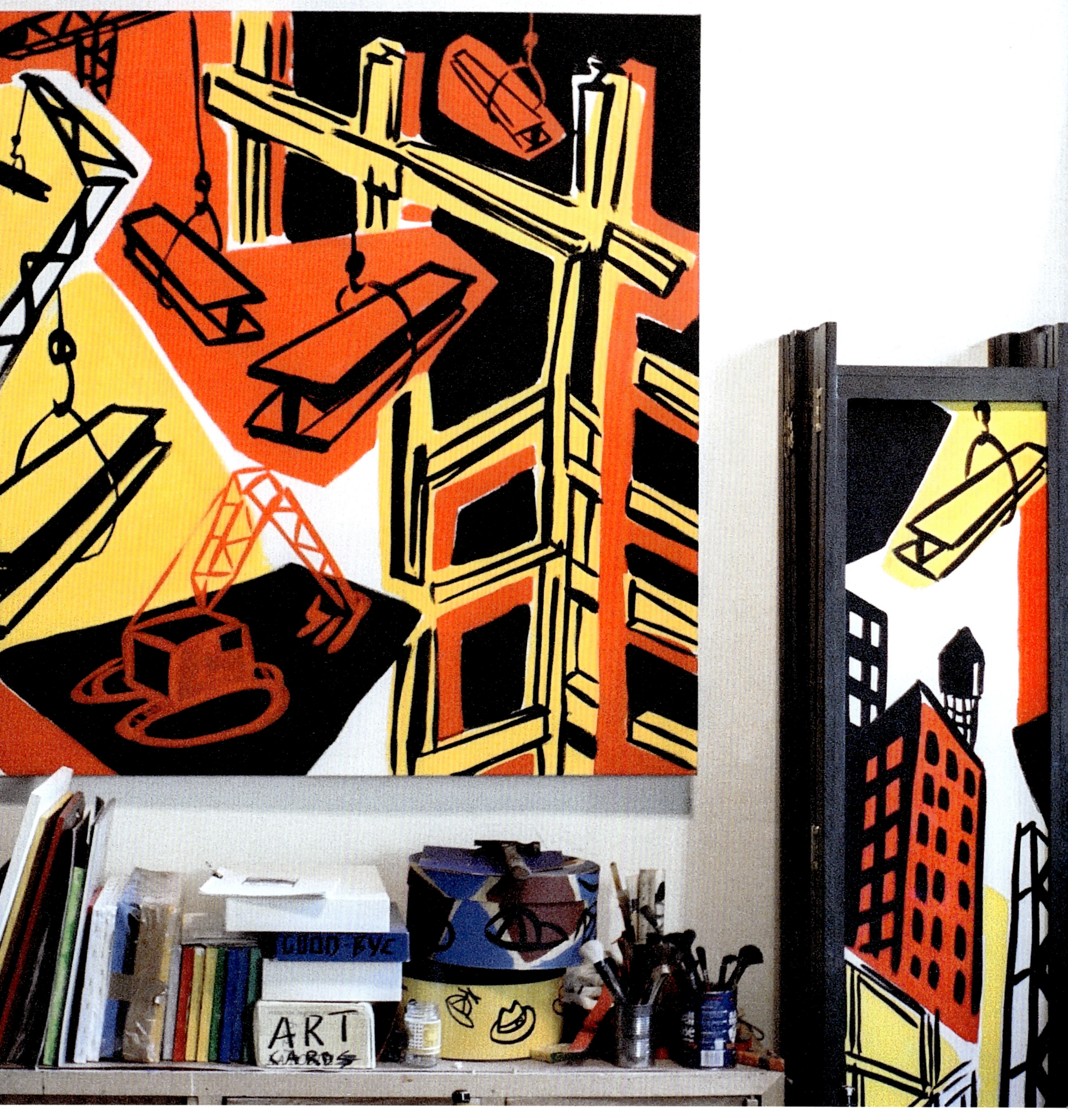

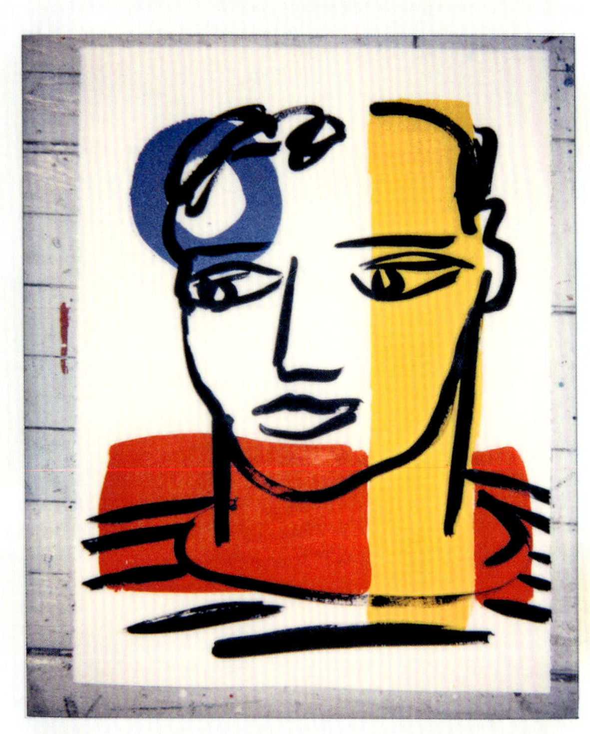

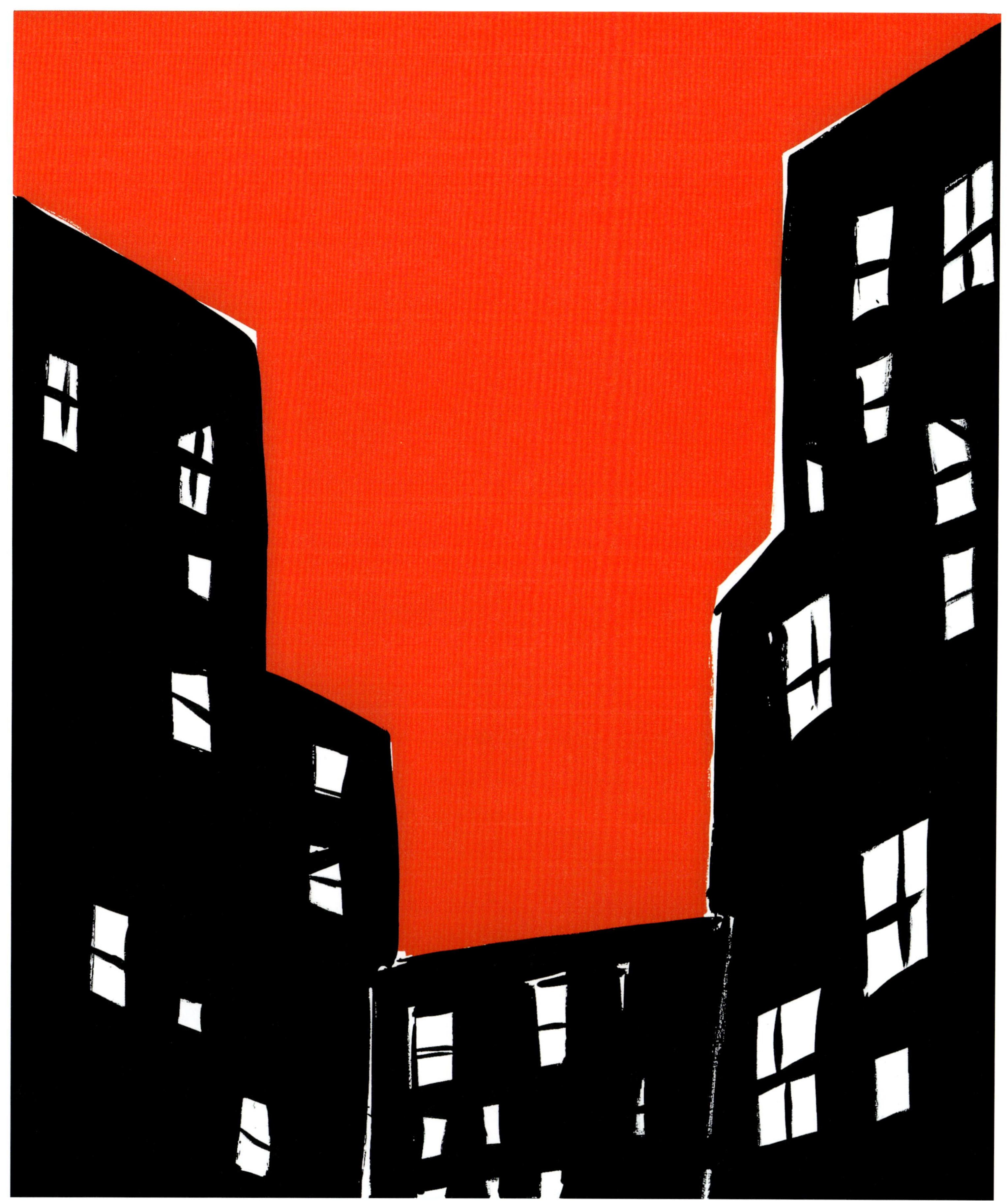

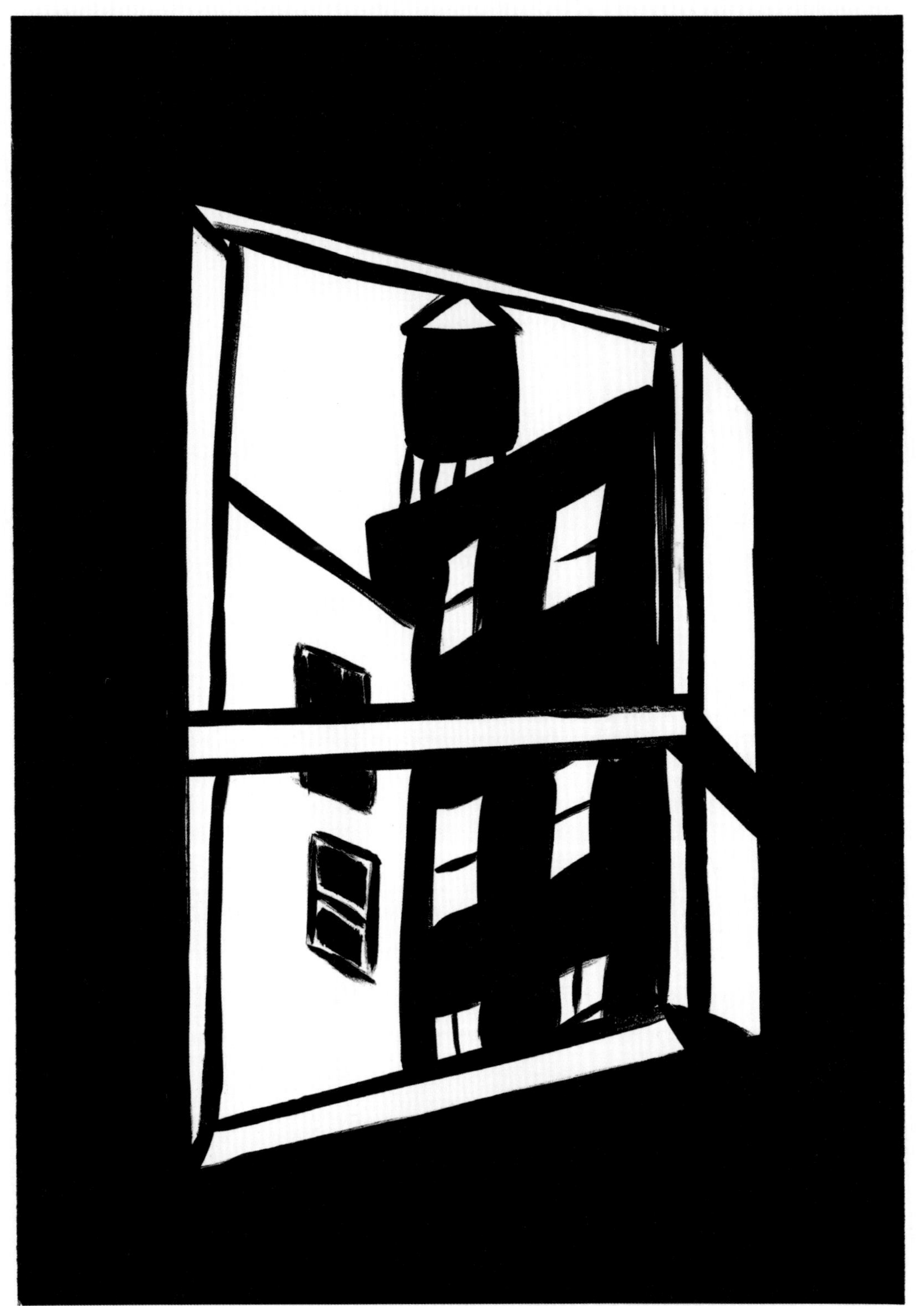

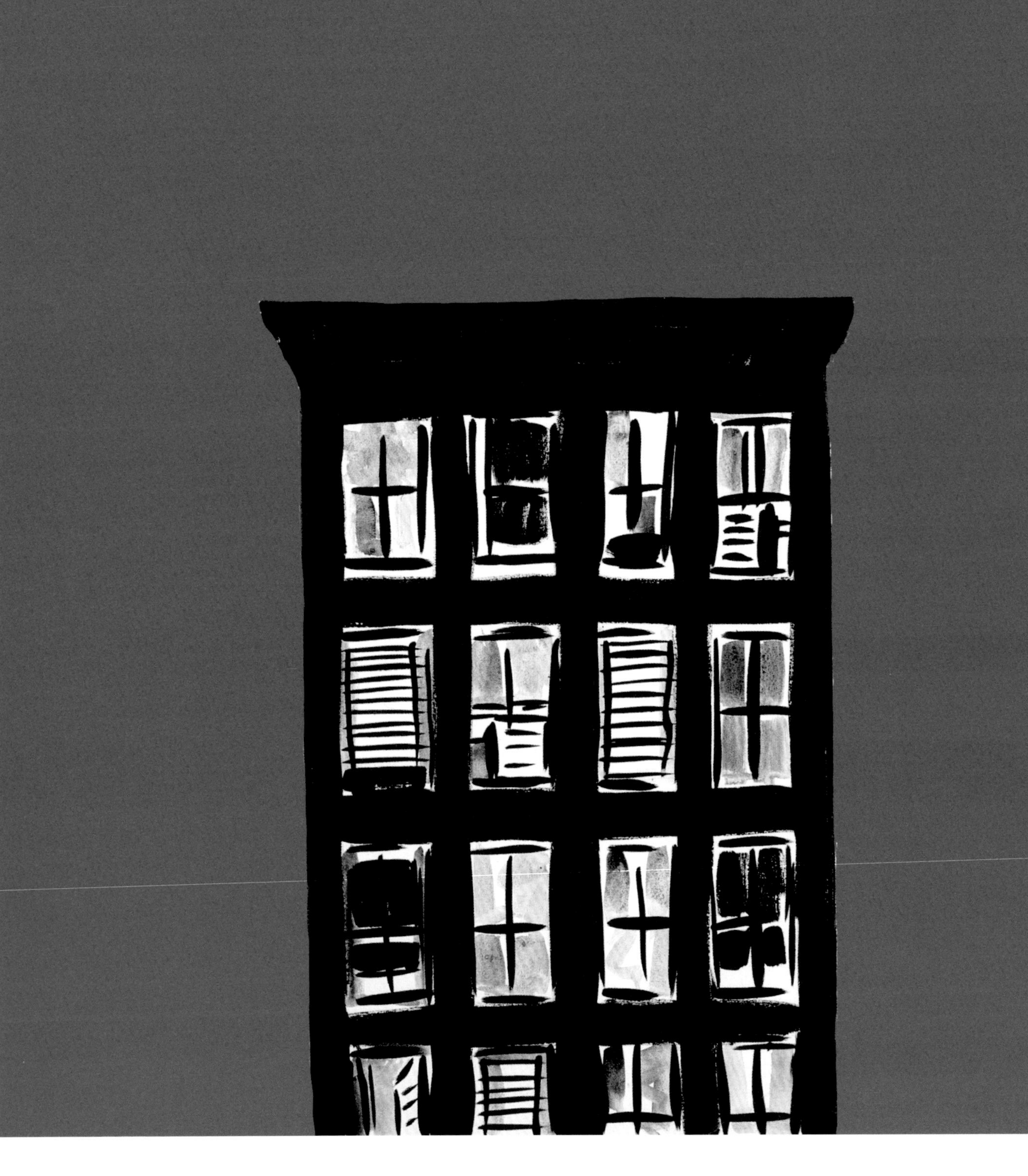

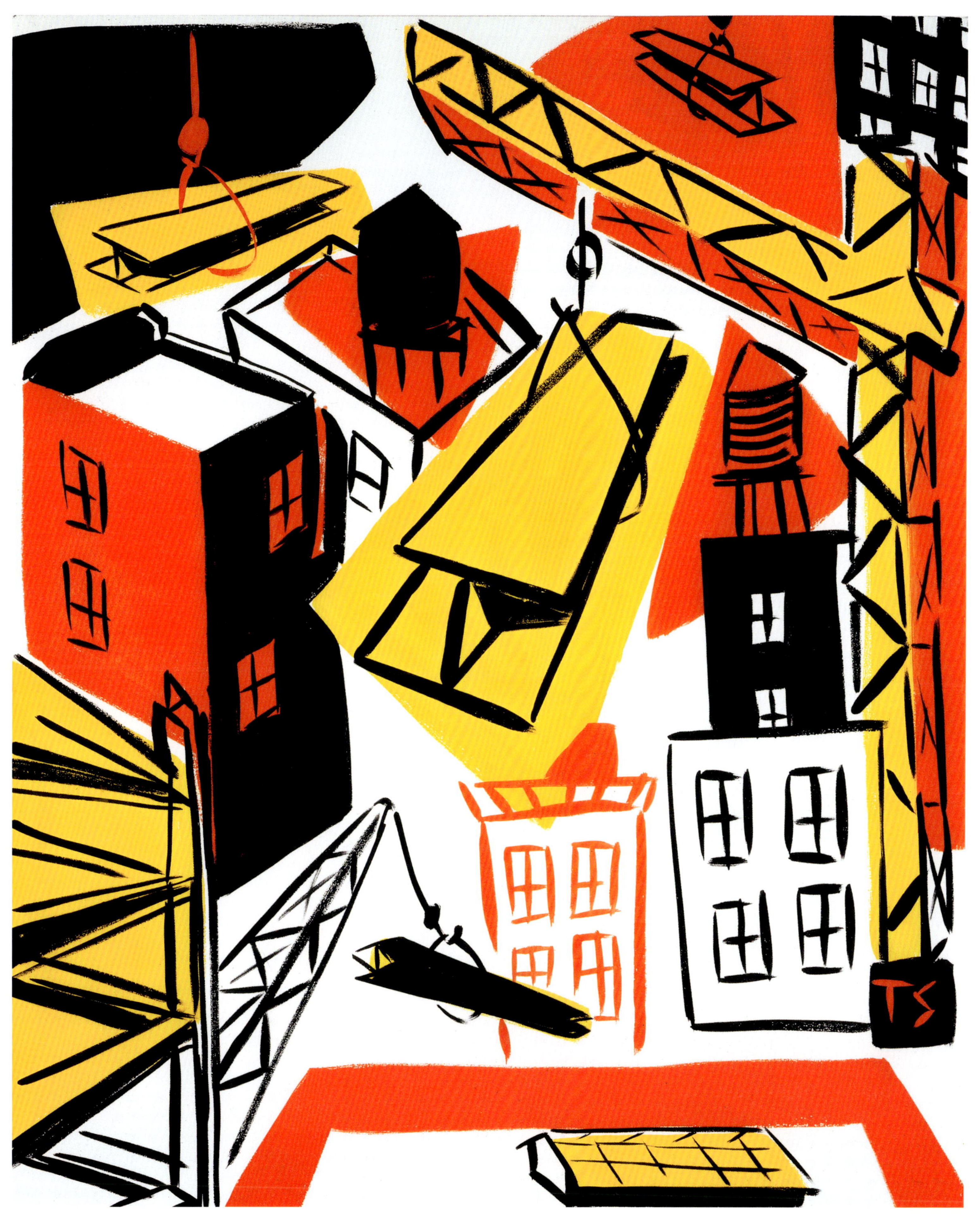

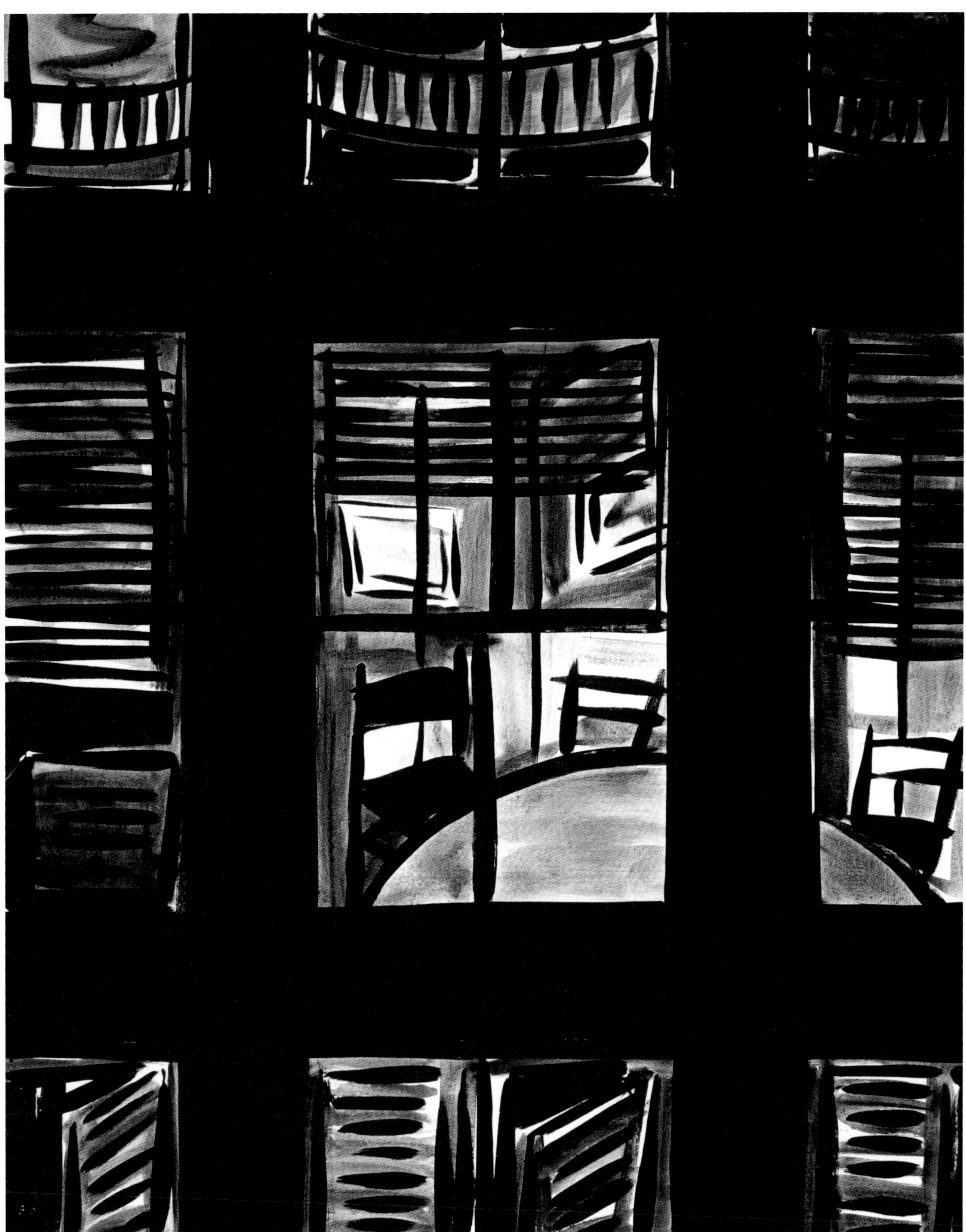

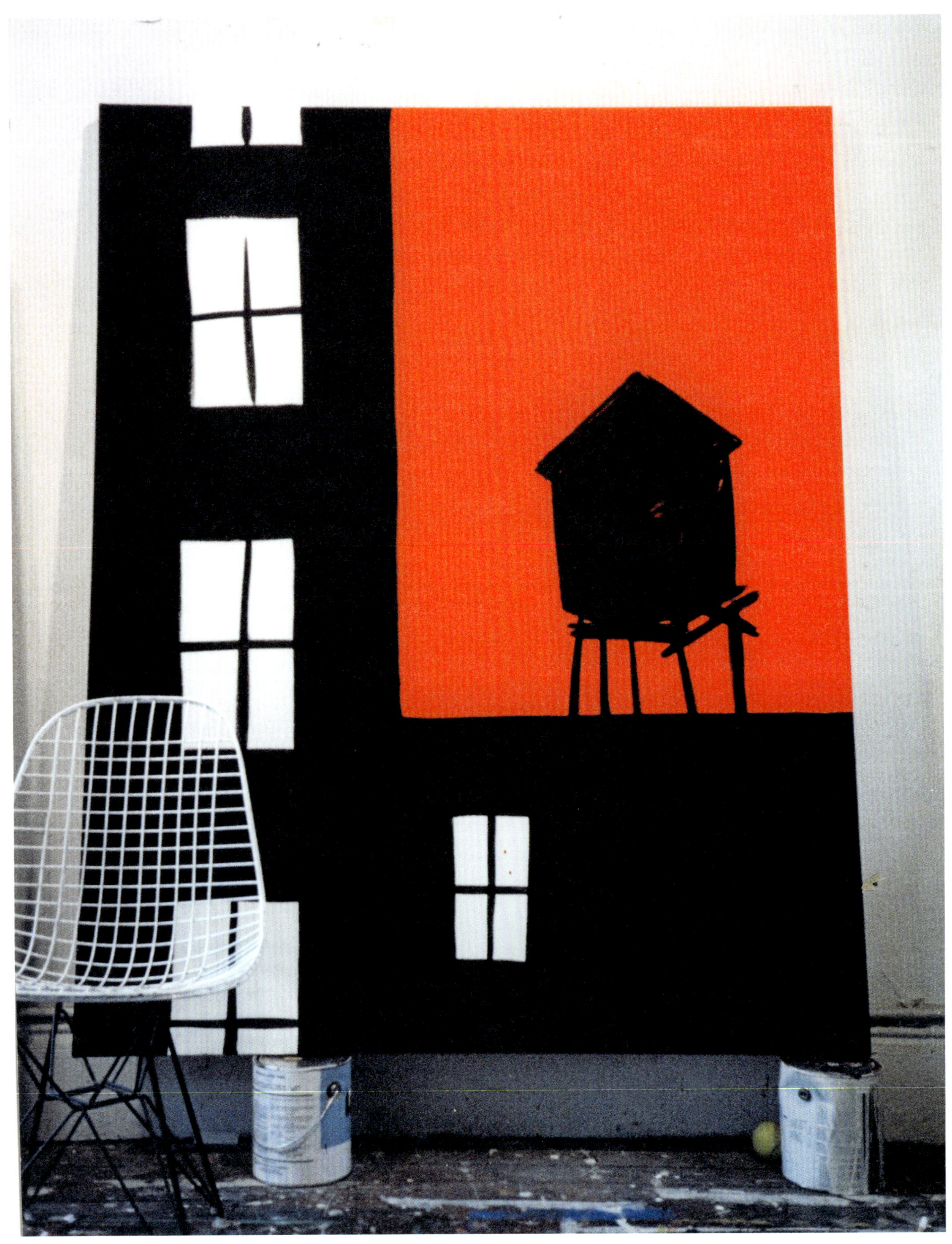

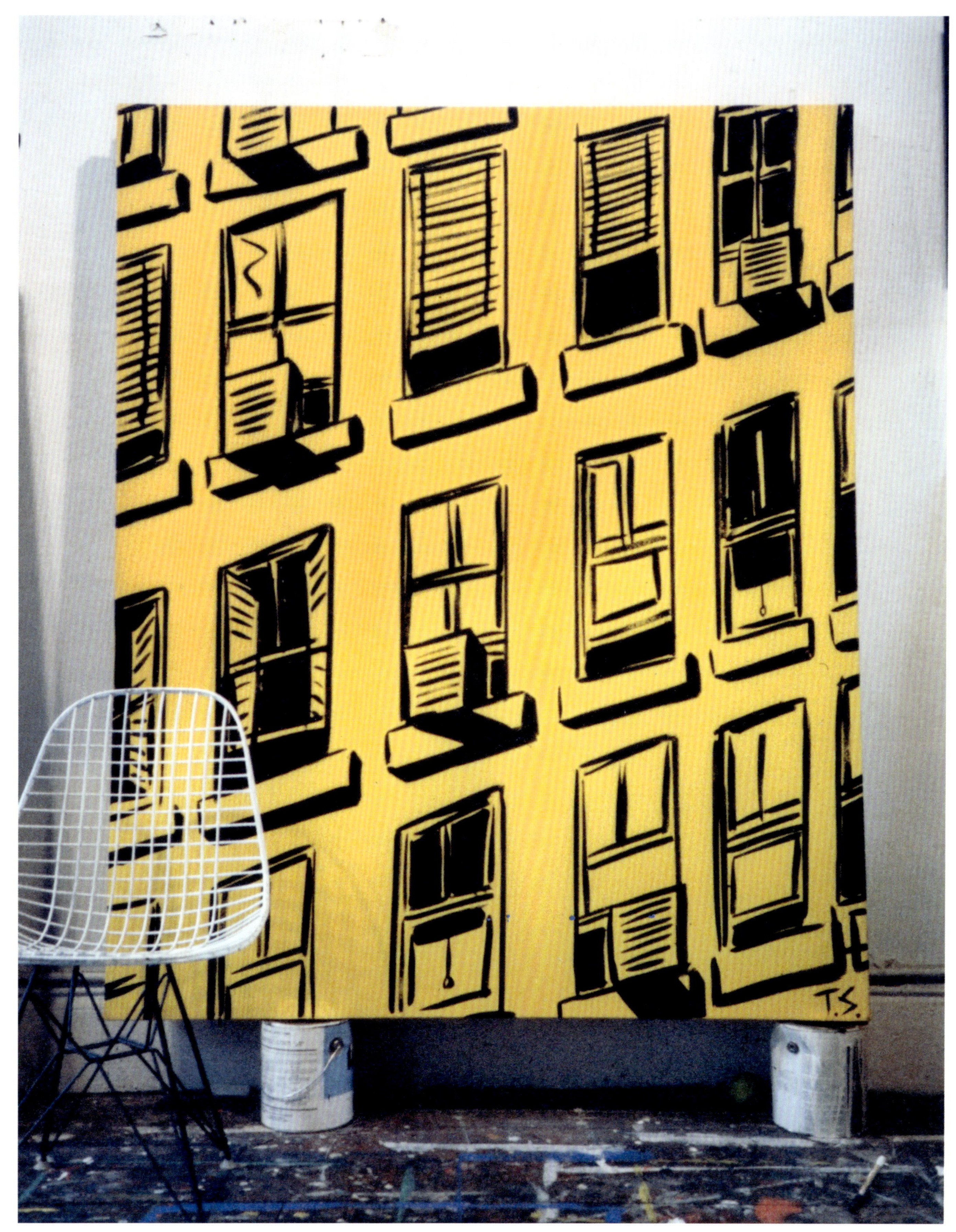

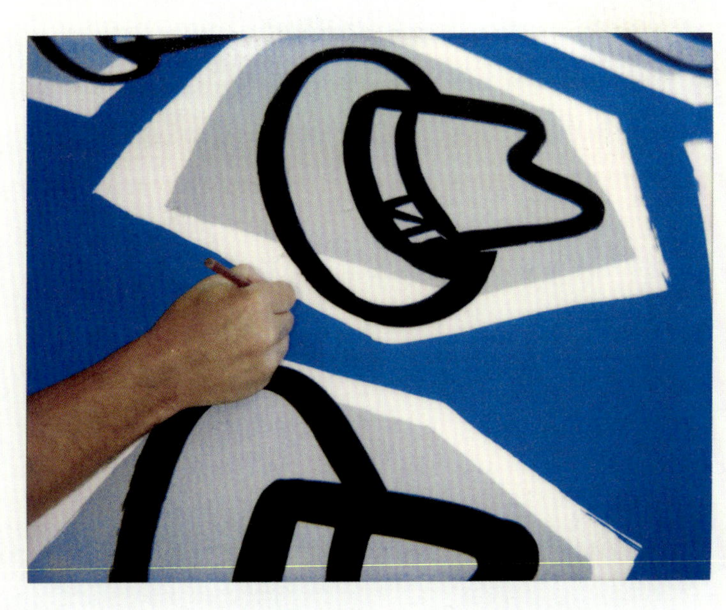

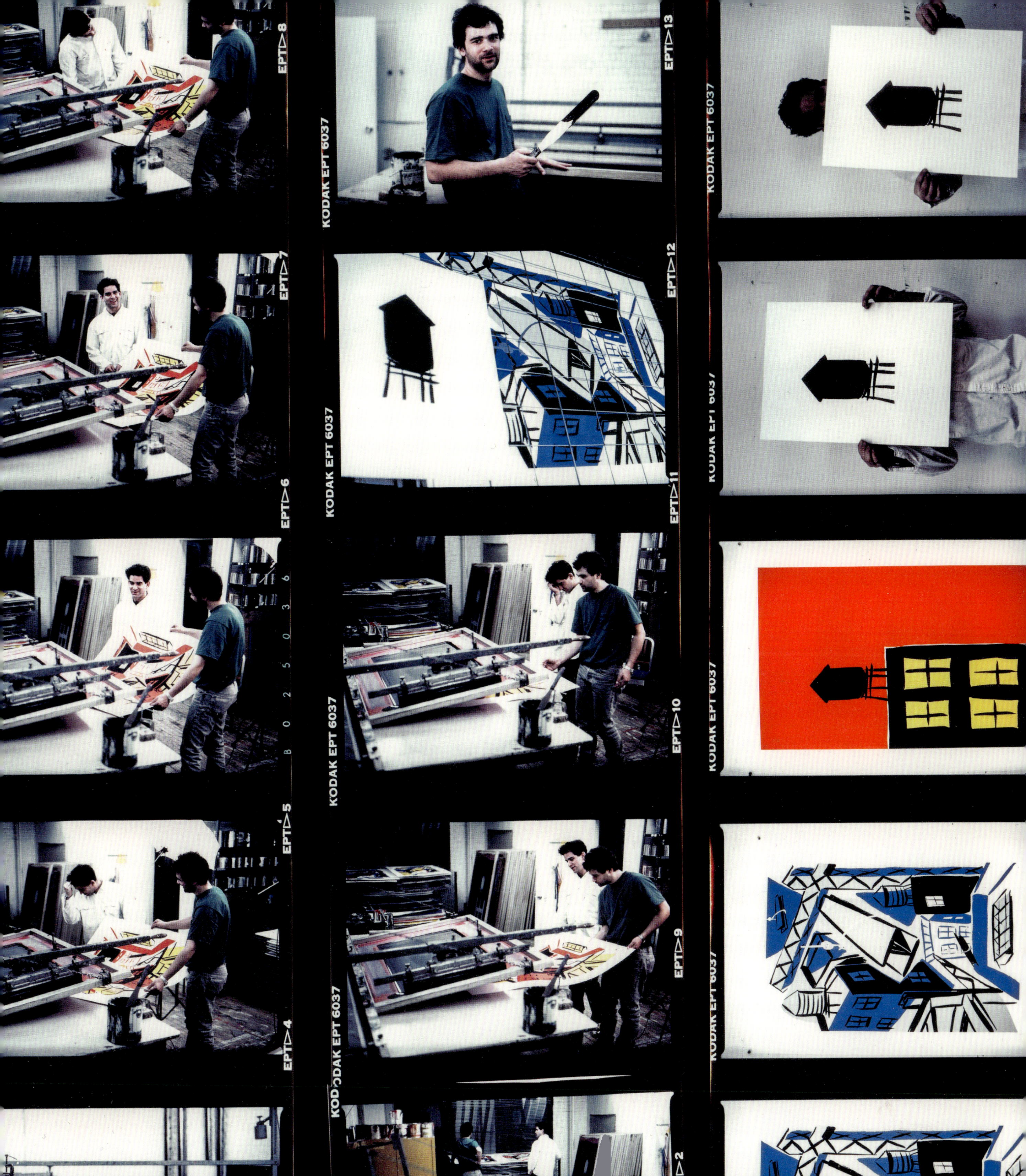

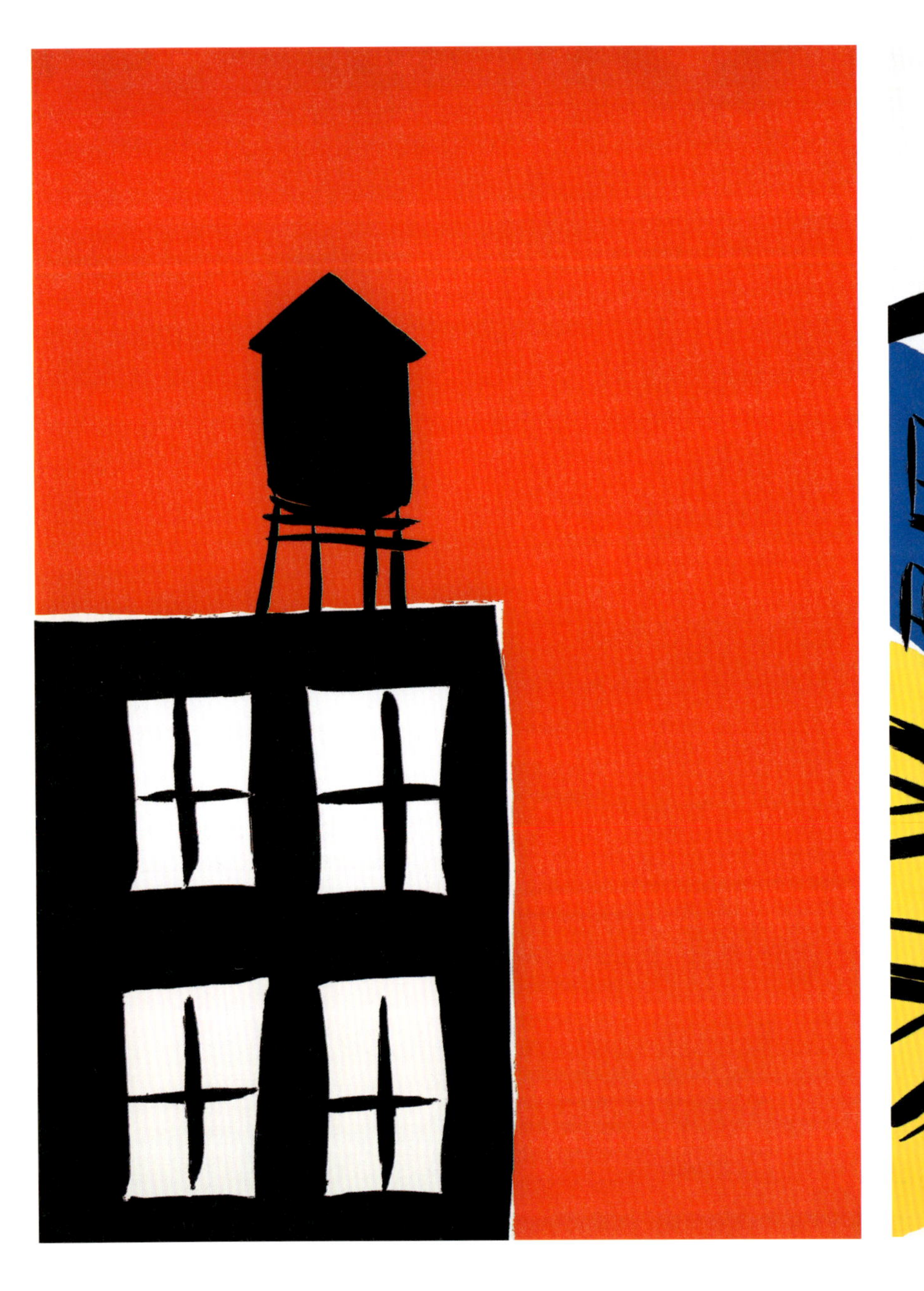
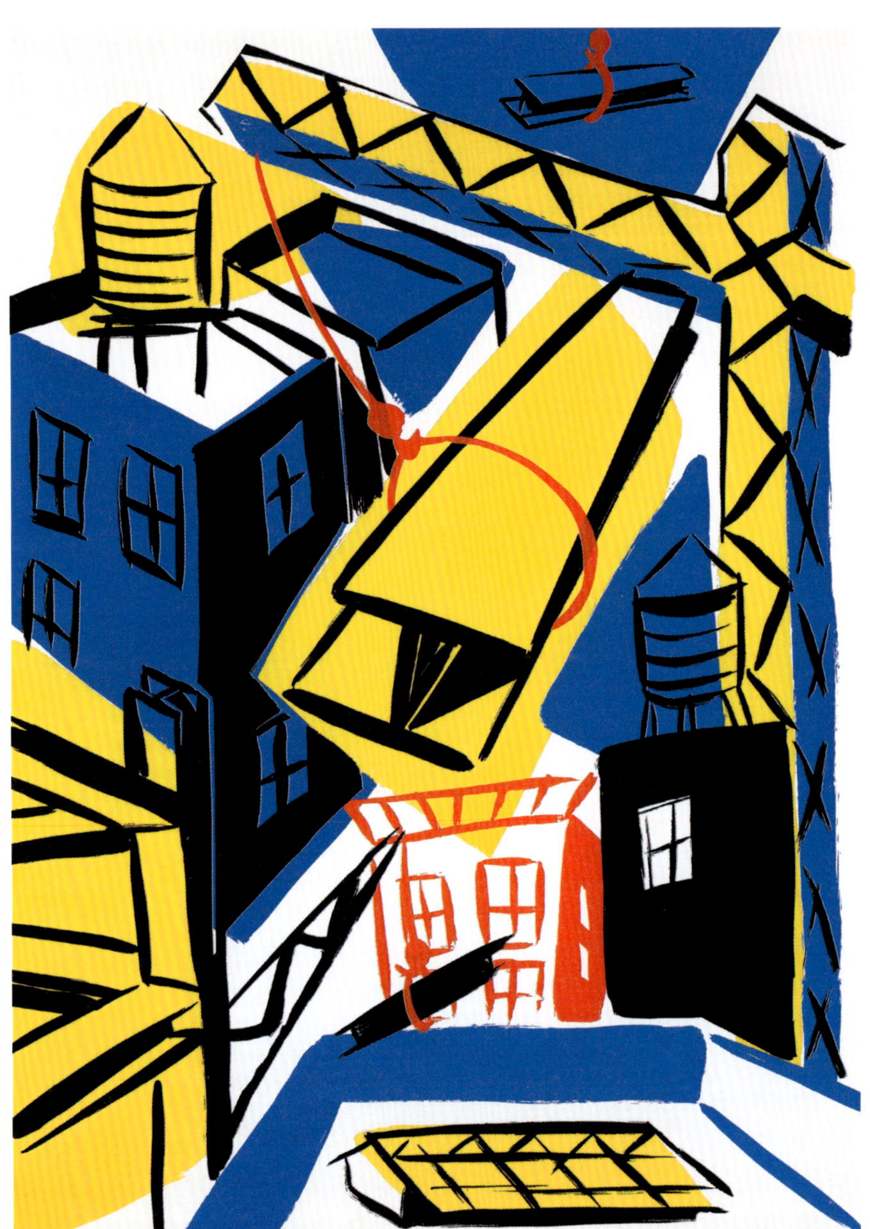

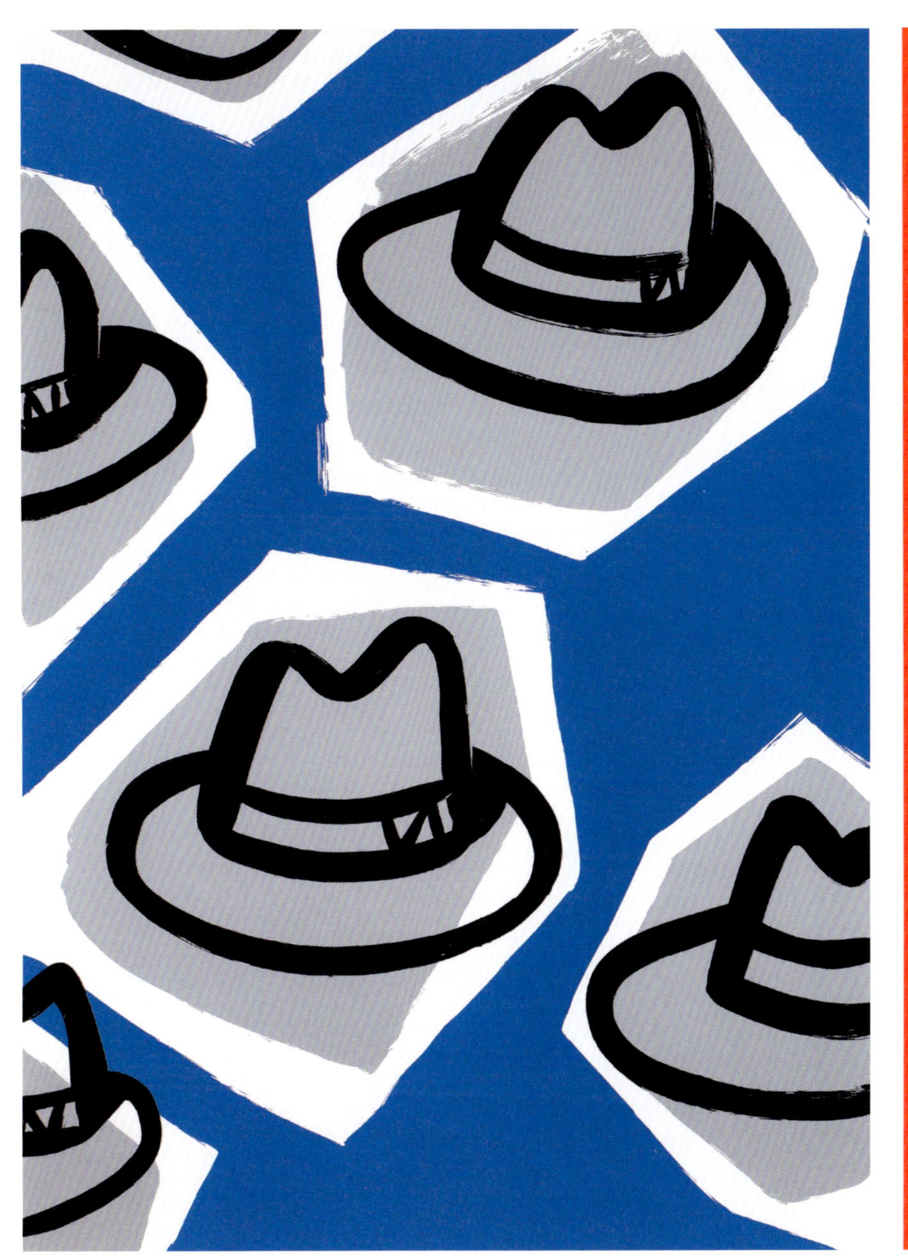
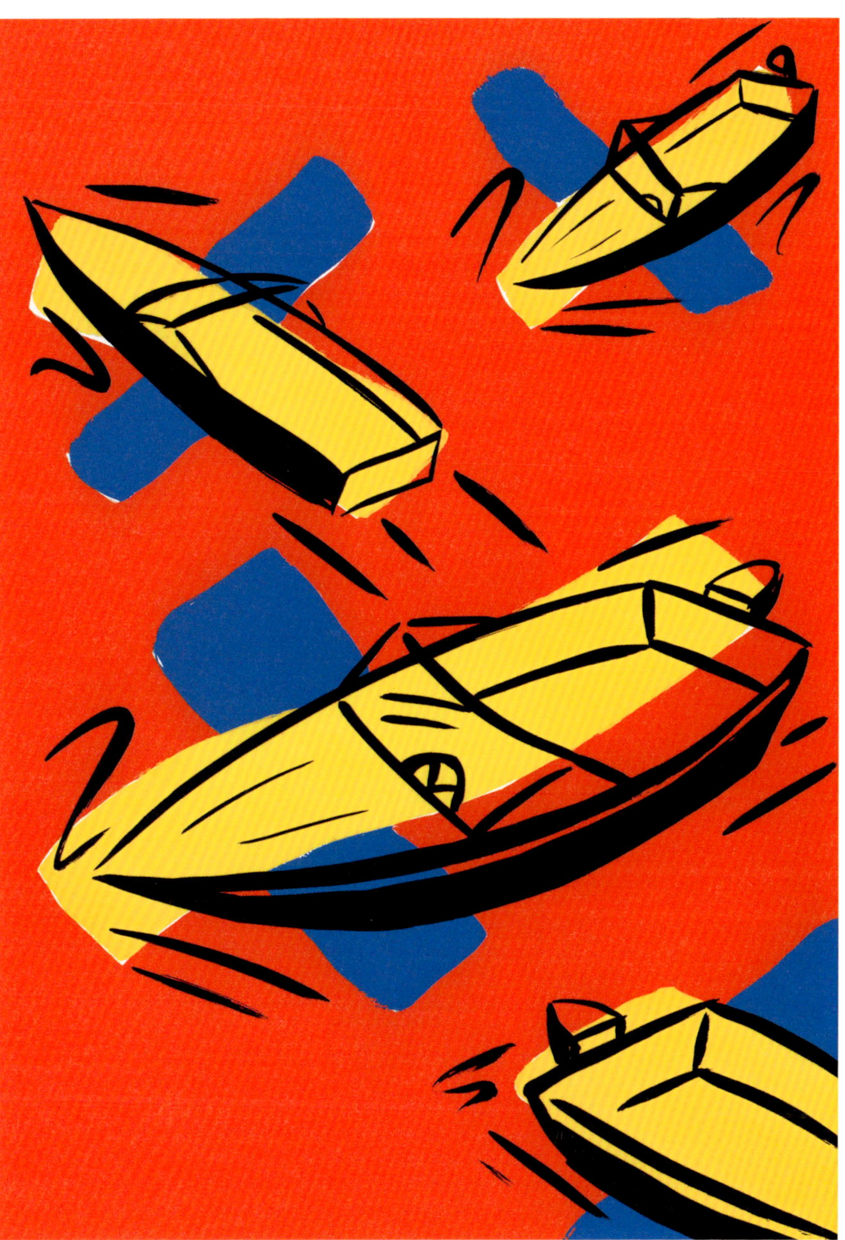

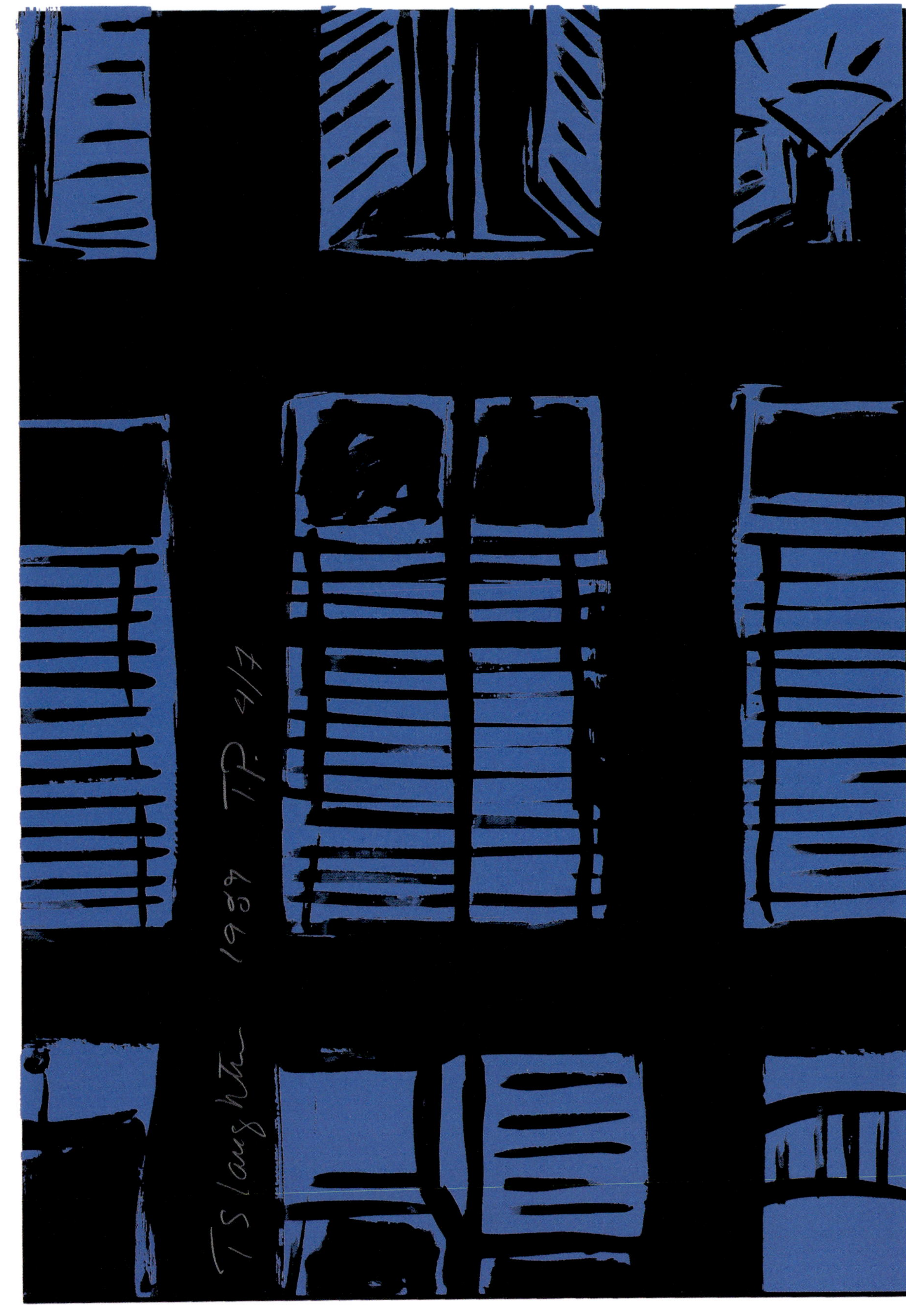

T Slaughter
1989 T.P. 4/7

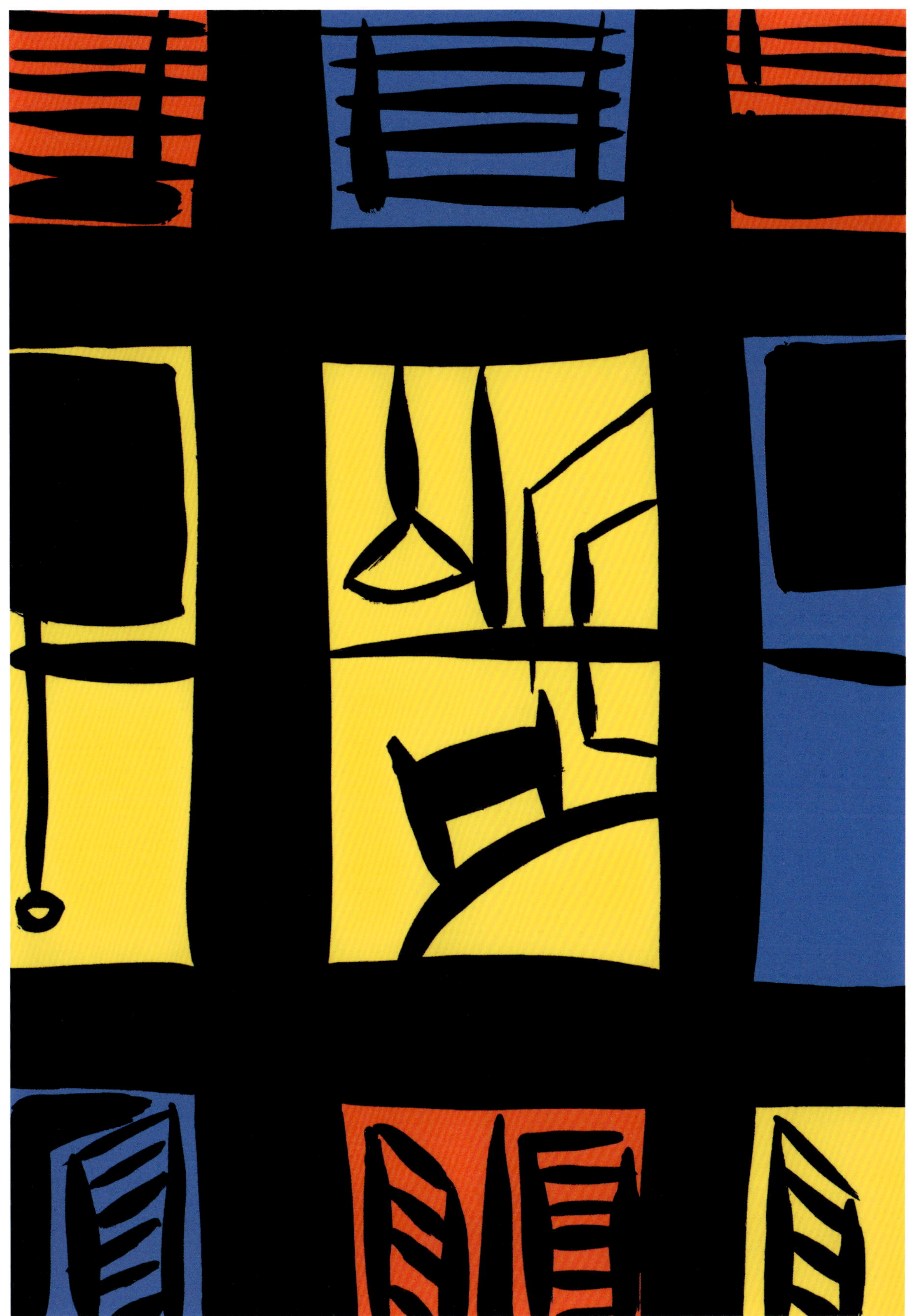

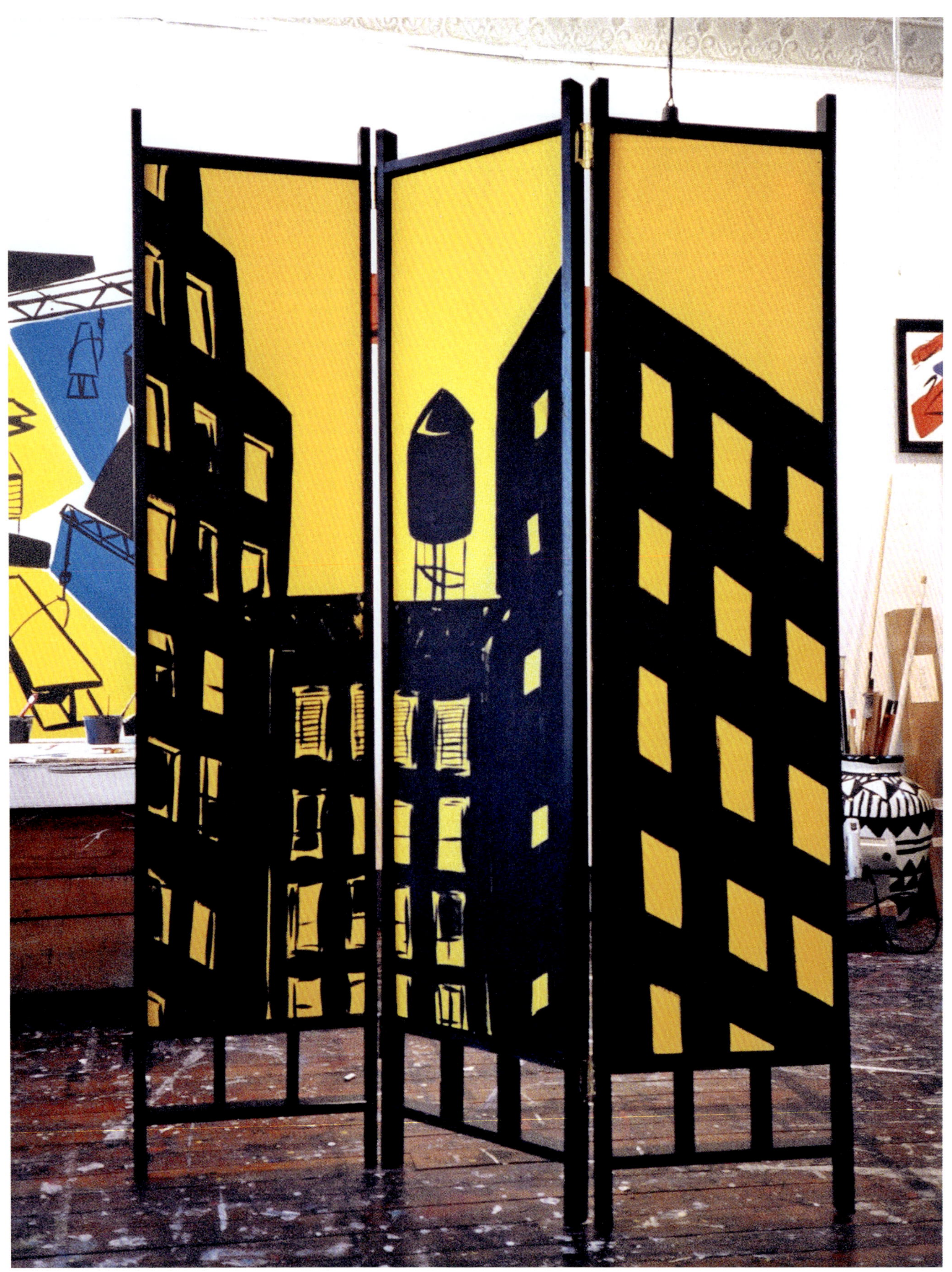

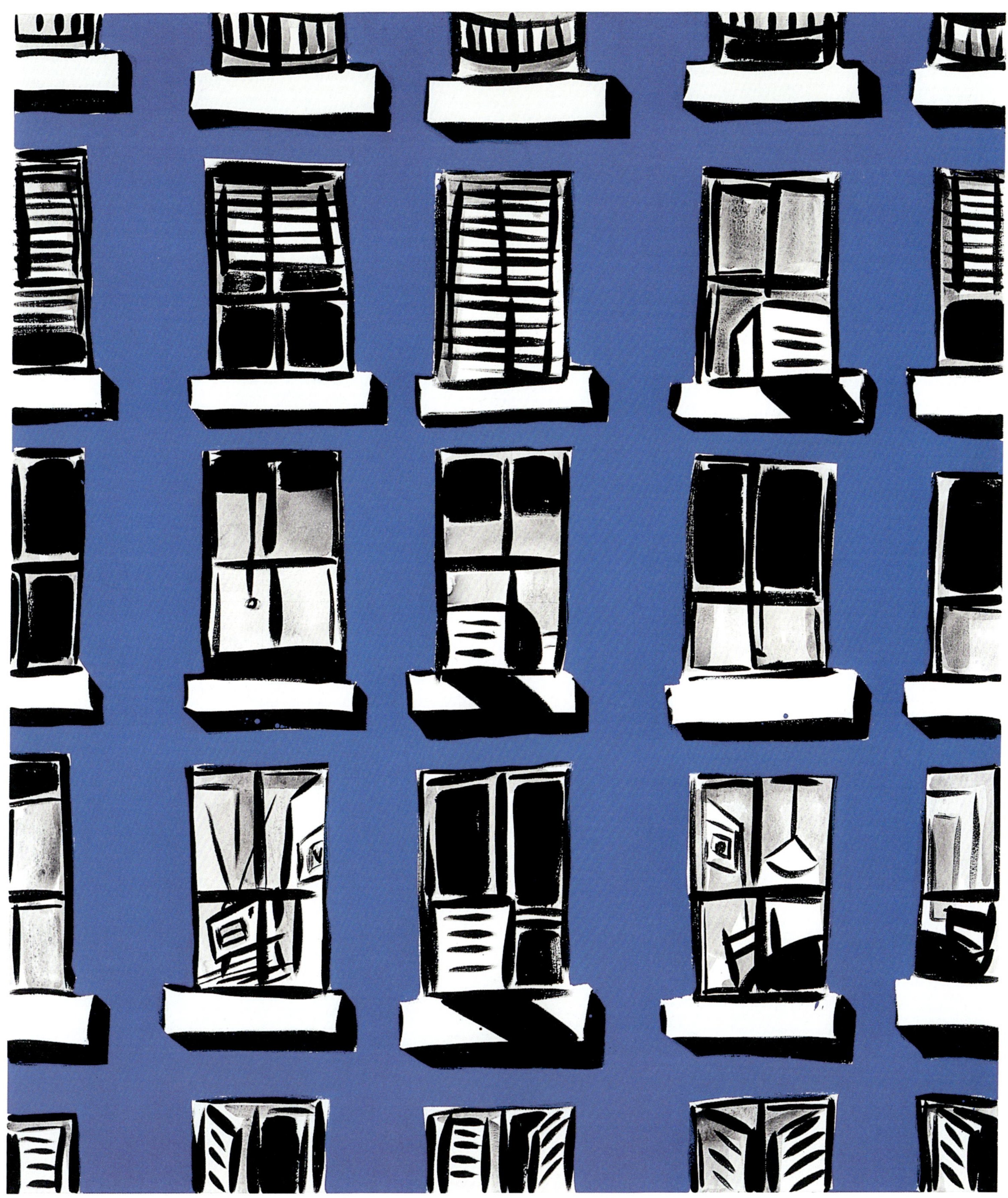

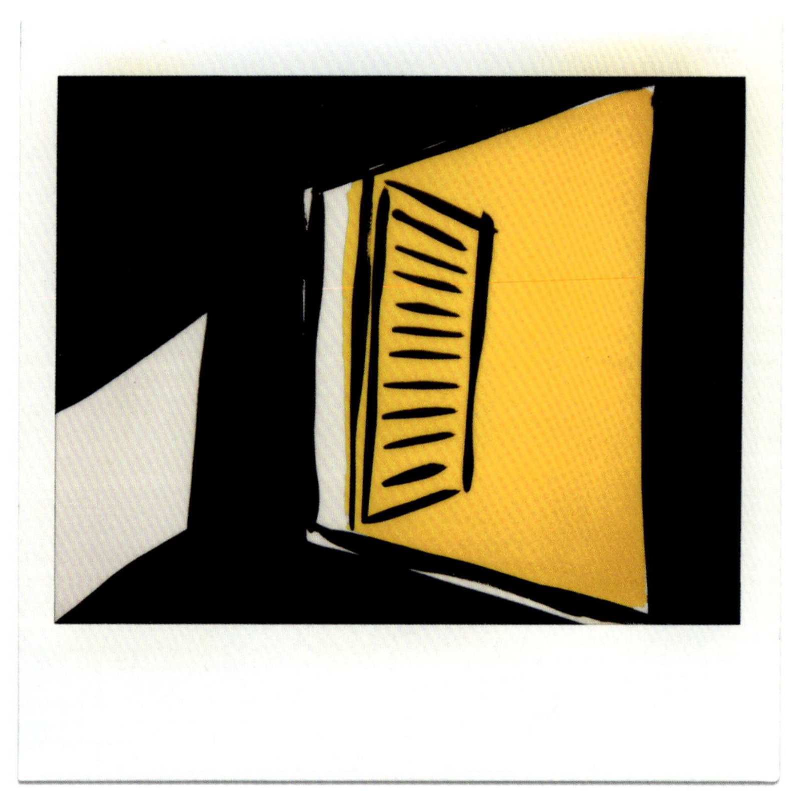

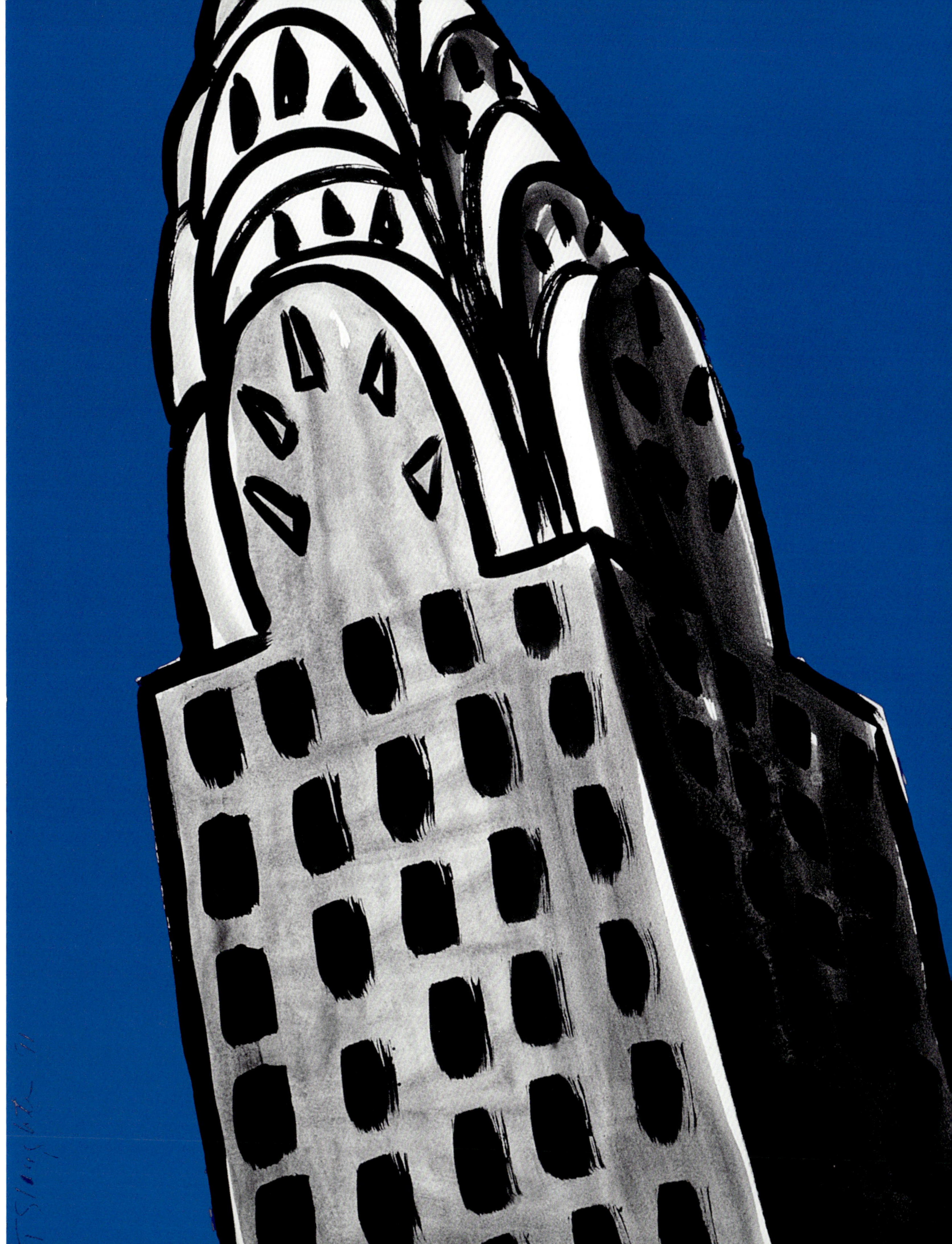

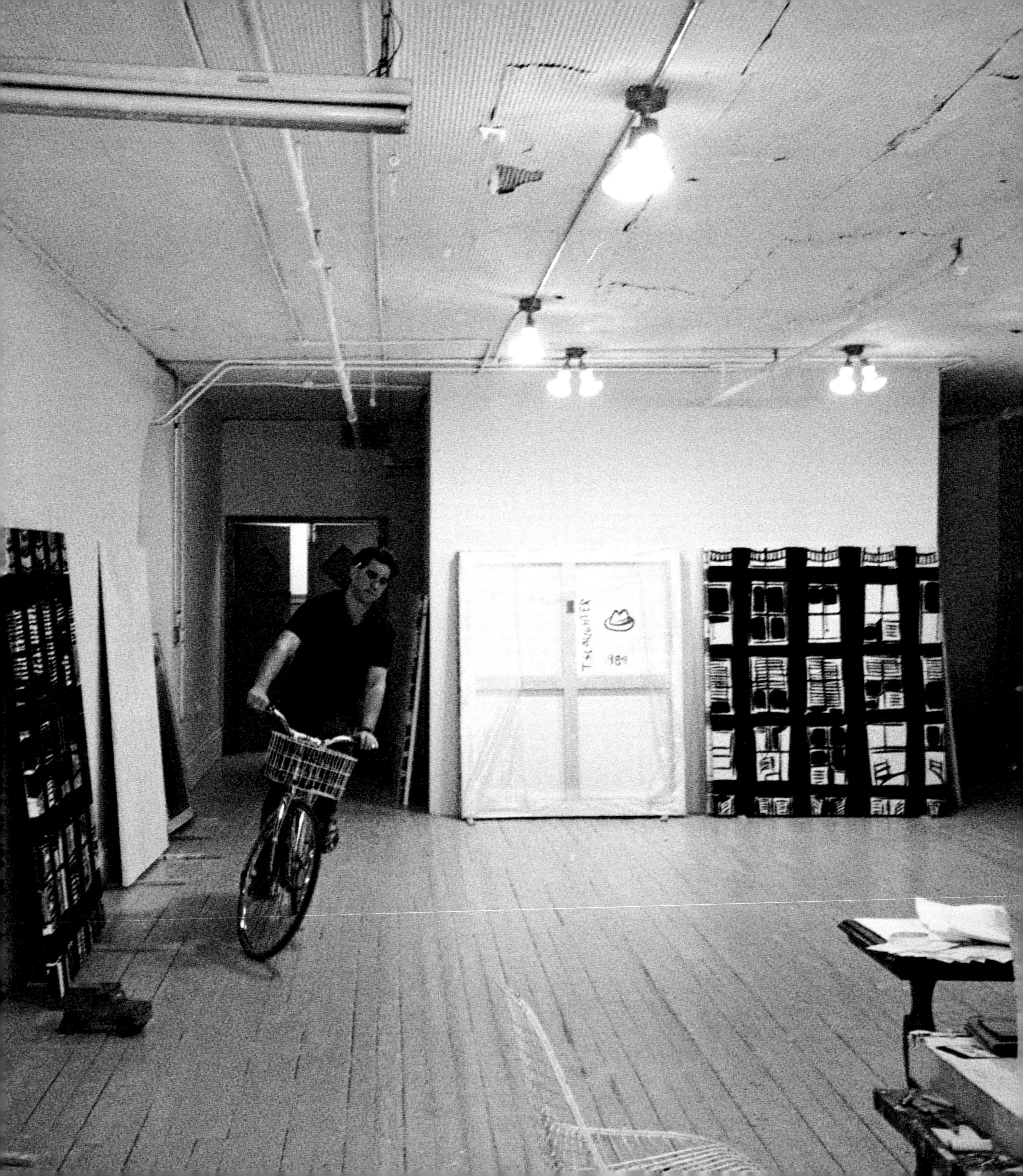
THE SLAUGHTER
1989

THE OBJECT MAKER

Tom built a civilization mostly from things he liked; he was the maker of objects and he owned them as if they had never existed before. Along the way he ignored most of the calamities in the world, choosing instead to paint whimsical images of rowboats, sailboats, anchors, lighthouses, binoculars, trucks, chairs, umbrellas, hats, Rosenwach Tanks, shirts and ties, and countless other things. He intrigued us with optimism, good faith, and sassiness. I never once detected any signs of psychic waste management in his delectable works of pure joy—no bitterness, no subversion. Tom did not participate in mockery or derision of any sort and always maintained a deeply felt sense of artistic dignity. His shorthanded notations were seamless ideograms: animated, real, and strictly grounded on their own terms.

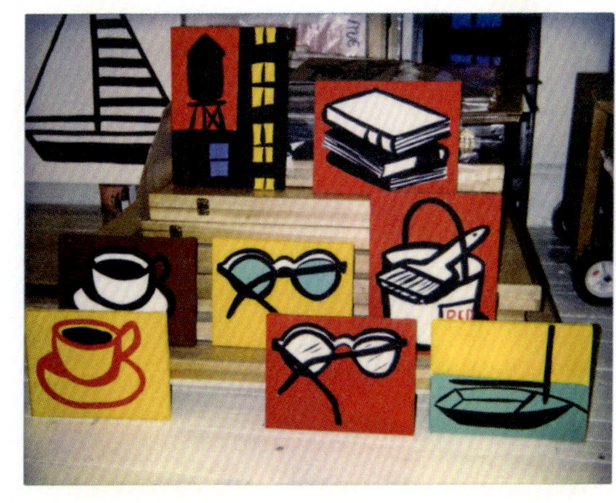

While Tom kept his unconscious at arm's length he always strove to link his images to an awareness of the life around him that unabashedly favored his daughters, Hannah and Nell; no doubt he dazzled them with his virtuosity and skill. Years earlier, Victor Hugo did exactly the same thing by leaving each of his five children a drawing he made that evening. Hugo's children found a small drawing tacked to their door in the morning: a devilish creature, a face with an enchanting grimace, or a clever visual pun. Like Hugo's world, Tom's was airtight—sealed and fortified. His entire body of work moved forward like an army advancing toward victory one step at a time. His images impersonated material that could be found almost anywhere, but my sense is that there was a deeply personal code at work. Behind the scenes a battle had been waged to find the visual essence of each image, lines denoting volume and density.

Tom worked like a human switchboard: clued-in and alert. He achieved a rare mixture of everyday images, partially abstracted, yet conveying the spirit of popular culture. He outsmarted most pictorial conventions by veiling his images in the colloquial, tipping his hat to Keith Haring, and absorbing popular culture of the seventies. Tom detected a form of salvation in Haring and liked that halo of attention. Like Haring, Tom wanted to circulate his images in a worldwide fashion for all to behold: his signature became ubiquitous. For so many young artists at that moment, inspiration could be found in the aisles of a supermarket, on the sidewalk, on restless walls, beach blankets, and almost everywhere. The populist ambience of the early seventies and eighties was contagious; the notion of the masterpiece was struck from language and replaced by tags on walls. Artists rejoiced in the remedial, perfunctory, and democratic. Equally true, Tom could be the young prosecutor: often denouncing formalism, abstraction, and everything I loved.

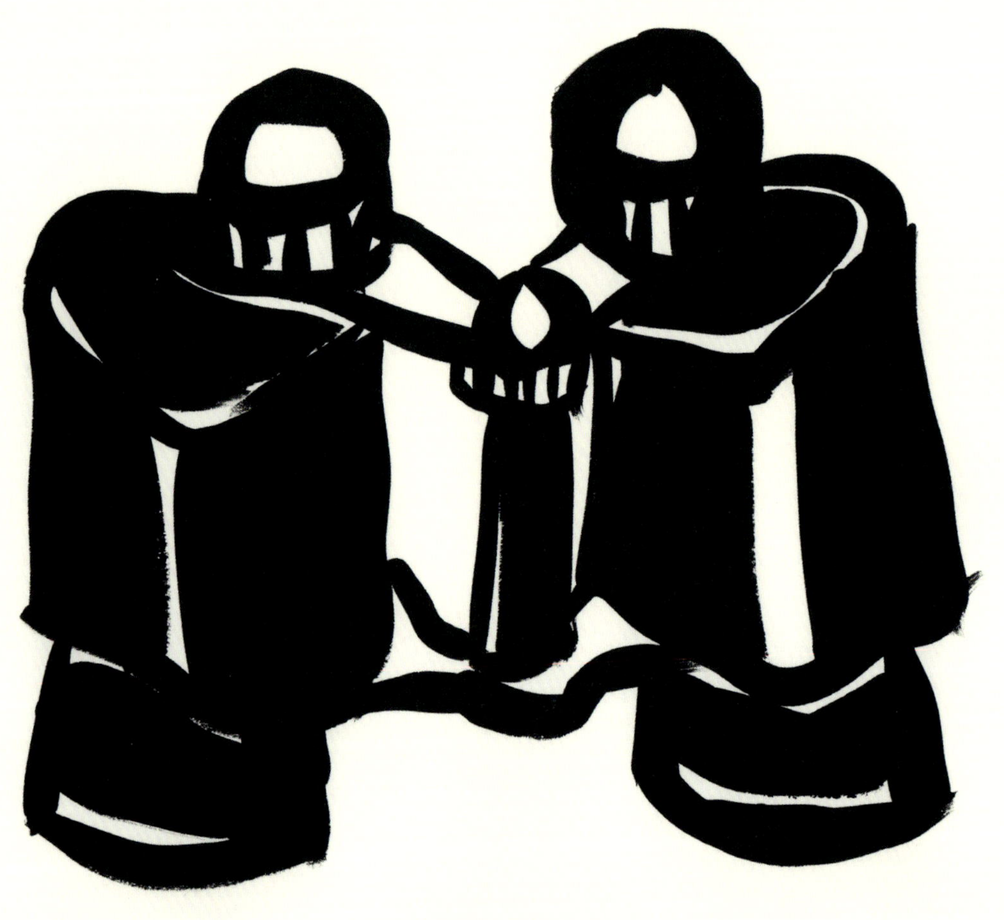

I am quite sure Tom always counted on his own stubborn logic because
all along the way he made magic. His industriousness was delivered
with machine-like precision and his mark was bold, thick, hardheaded, and
evenly weighted. His aesthetic roots appear connected to a form of early
twentieth-century proto-Cubism that was often typified by a baseline of radical
and simple geometry. At that time, Braque and Picasso also severely limited their
palettes and introduced us to a new formula for reduction. Tom added more to
his own stew through the lens of Warhol: mass media, a touch of gossip visible
in his own Polaroids, and a pinch of conspicuousness sprinkled freely. Tom
was a visual conductor of the brashest kind: if Warhol wanted to be a machine,
Tom was a camera. Was his manifesto sanitized or too idealized? He always
kept me guessing.

Tom lived in his utopia because the paradise-garden stabilized him; it was his
indispensable inner sanctum. He could also be urgent and insistent, and his
work conjured up the sheer necessities of beauty and decency, like the work
of Ellsworth Kelly. This was the "French" side of things and it meant an awful
lot to Tom. It was his idea of modern, of daring, and in New York City, very much
a gamble. Tom was deeply sensitive to all visual language even if it wasn't
necessarily his. He was more open and generous than he let on. Tom's touch
could compress images but without doing harm to them—a remarkable feat.
His sensibility elbowed forward but retained an elegant and tough-minded
robustness that always tested his own hard-won glimpse of reality.

Bravura took Tom places; he defied the provincial by storm. He disparaged
elitism but so often wore a fading Chemise Lacoste shirt, with alligator. Go figure.
Tom never curbed his delight as he raced from desire to consummation; he made
countless images of which he was the titleholder. His pursuit was dogged,
relentless, and strong-willed like that of a discoverer. Never nebulous or unsure,
he kept pace with himself at all times. Toward the end of his life Tom started
to resemble the great master Henri Matisse. As always, a notebook was ever
present and the stride of his hand increased. A simple sketch of a chair
was broken down into rudimentary lines and shapes; gravity dissipated and
lines reformed on the surface of the page. His imagination permitted a new,
idiosyncratic absence without familiar reasons. A different sense of self seeped in.
Tom was making abstraction.

George Negroponte

Artist

New York, NY

2017

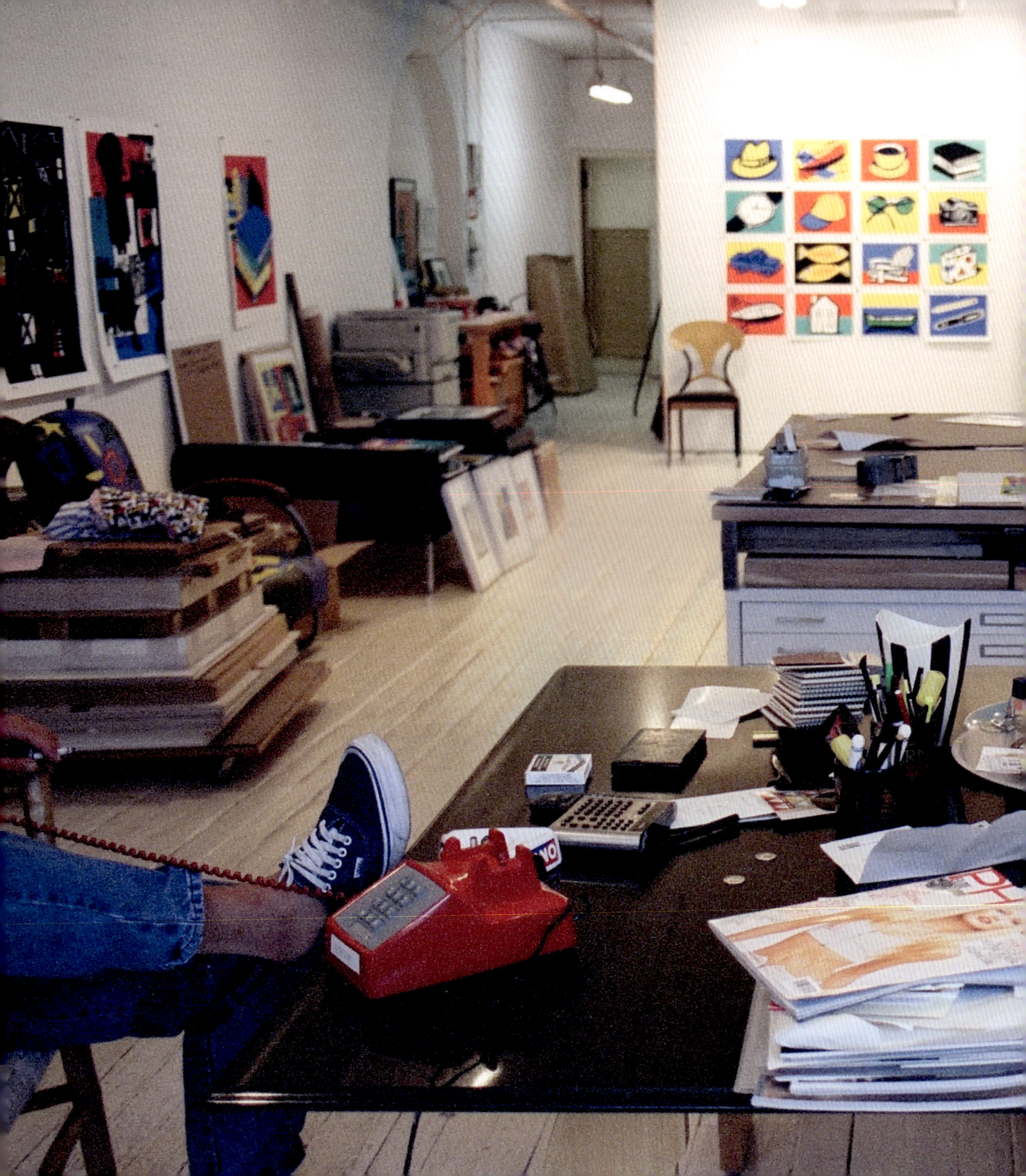

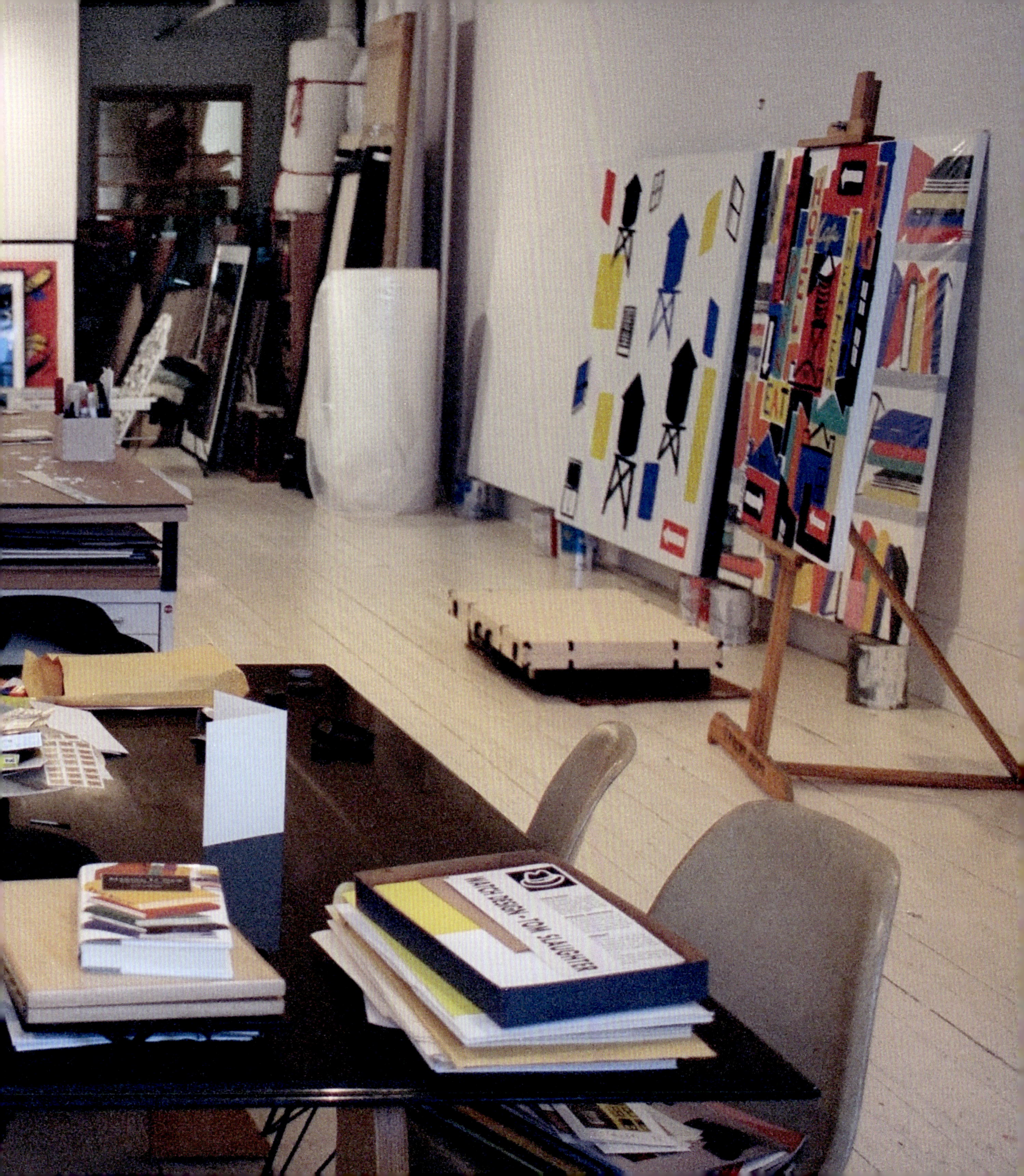

1990–1998

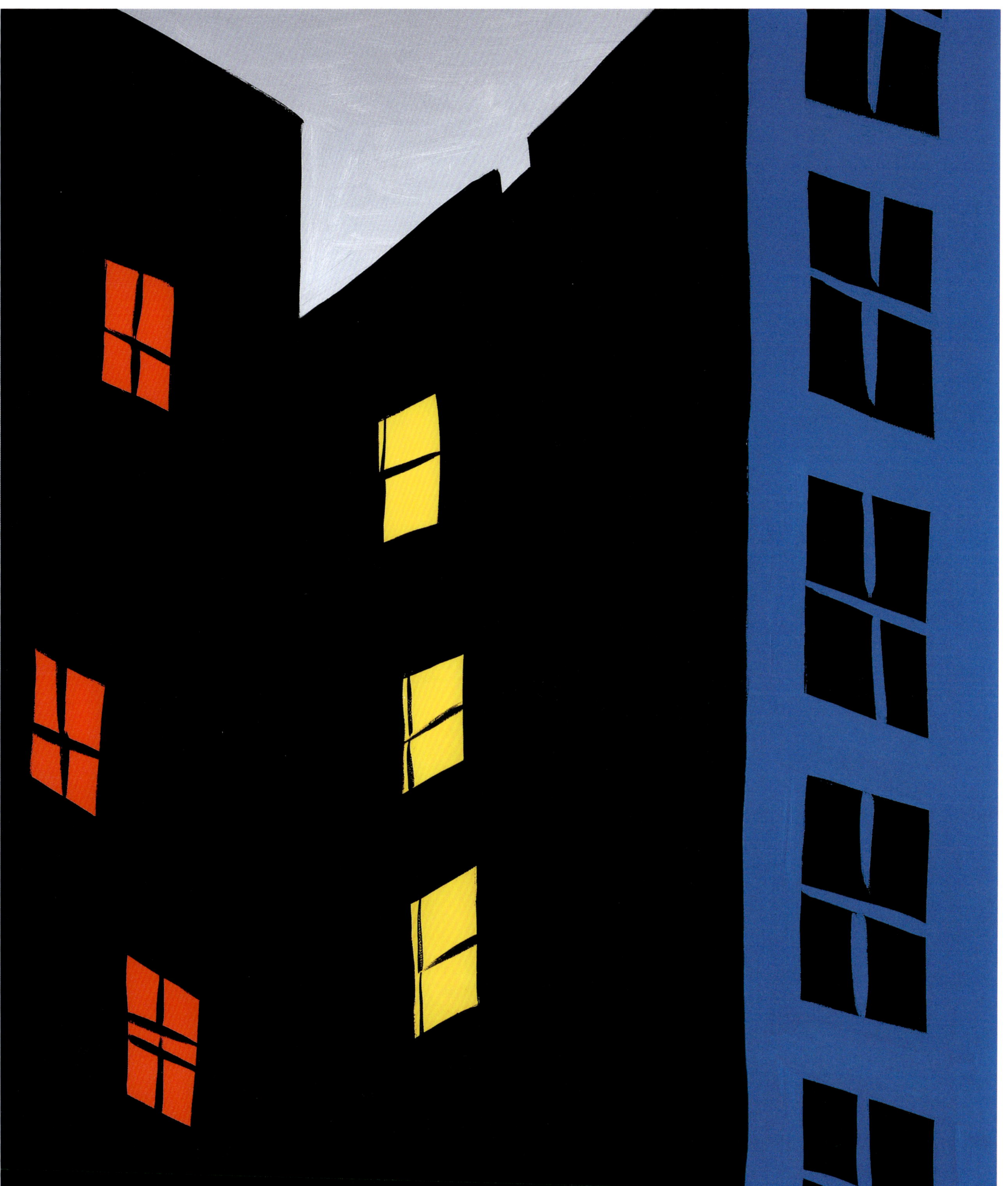

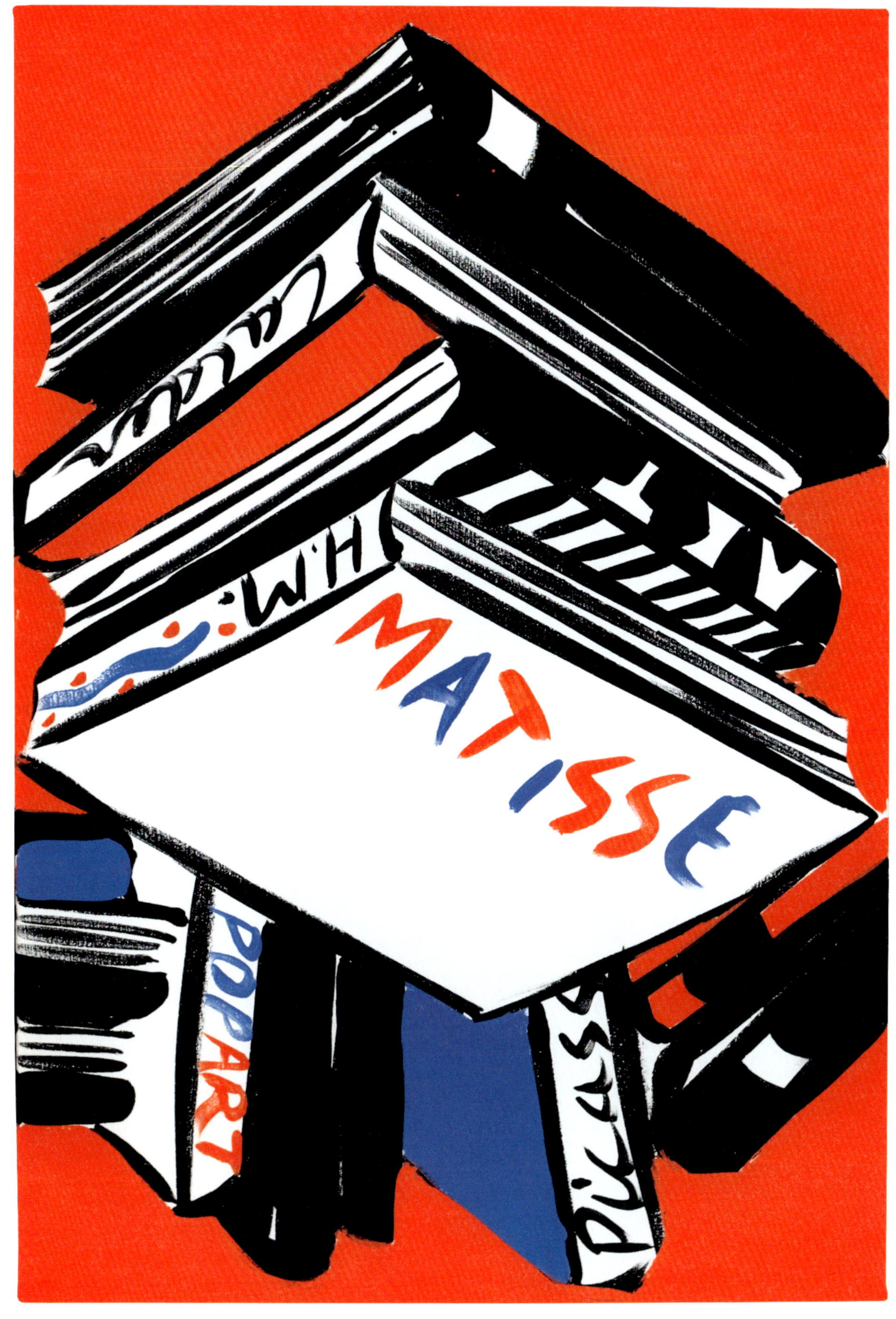

MATISSE
H.M.
POP ART
Picasso
ART
Calder

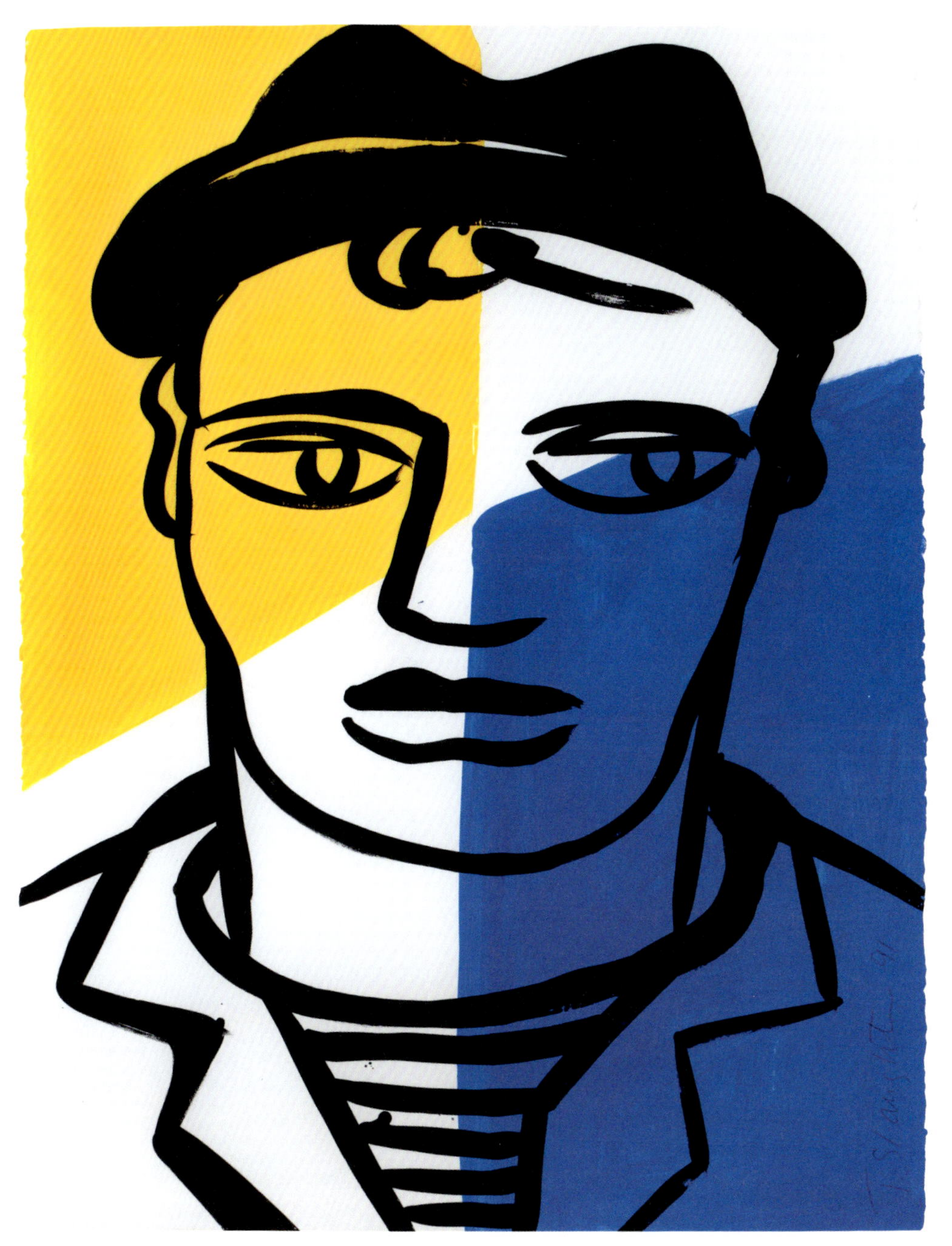

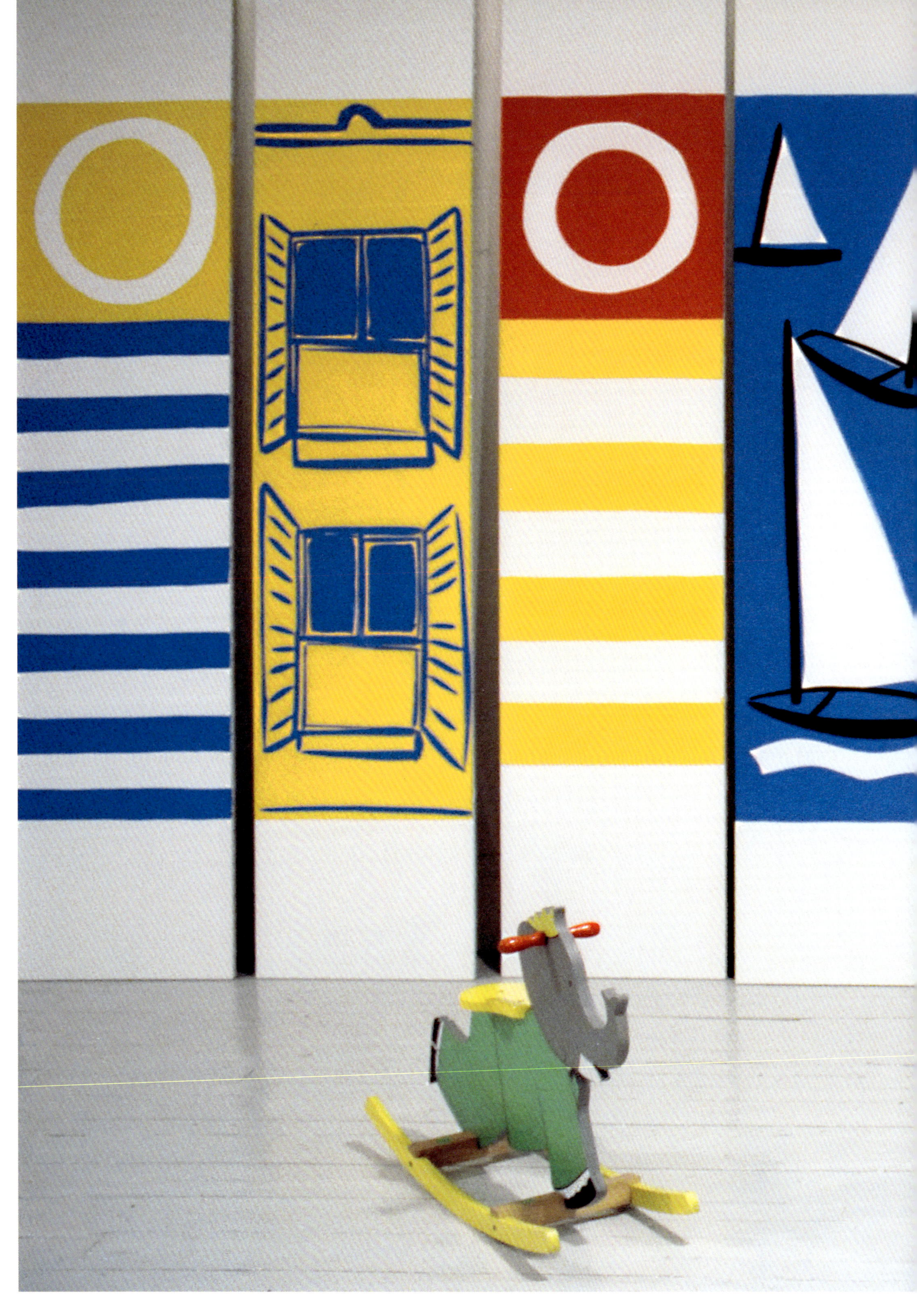

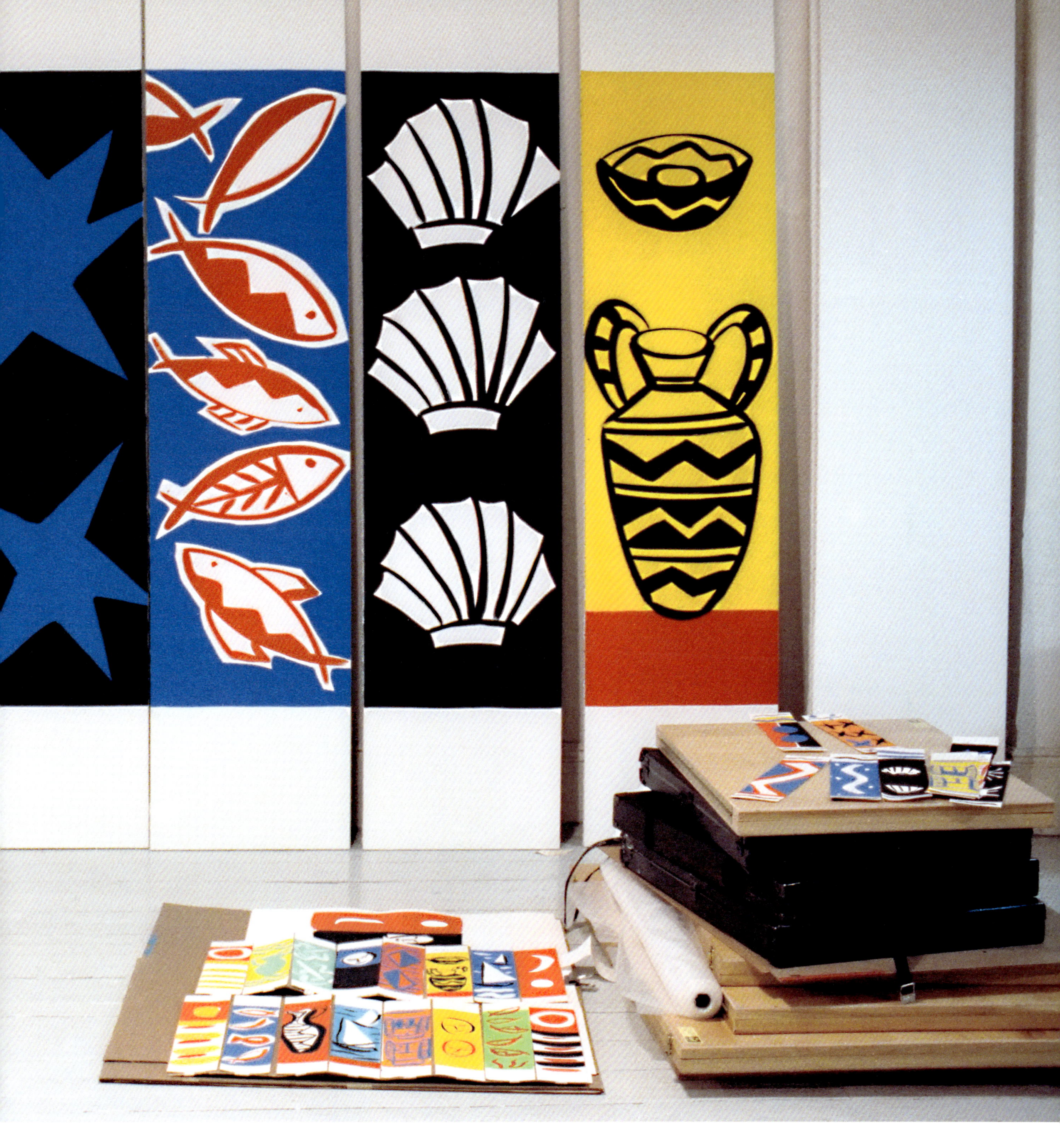

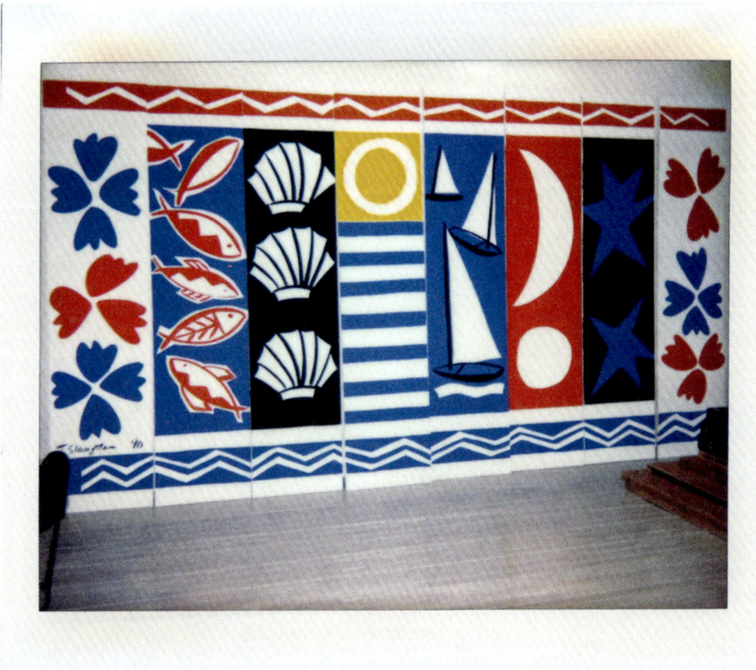

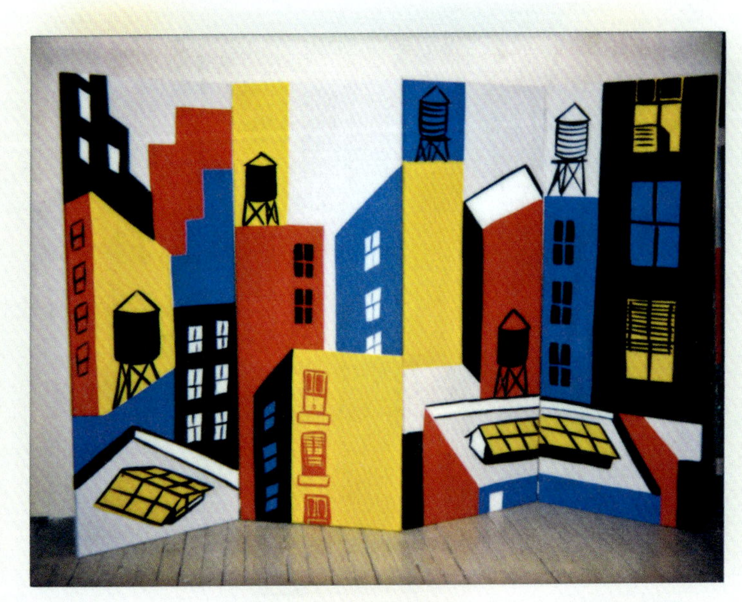

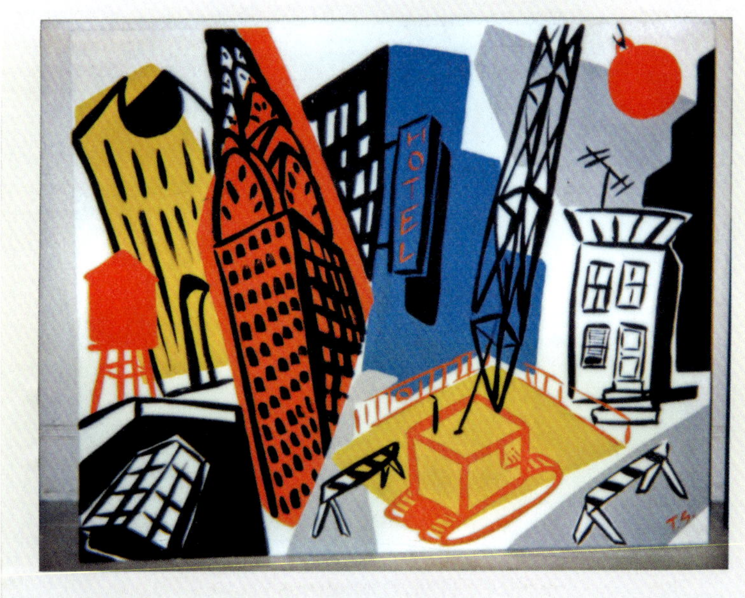

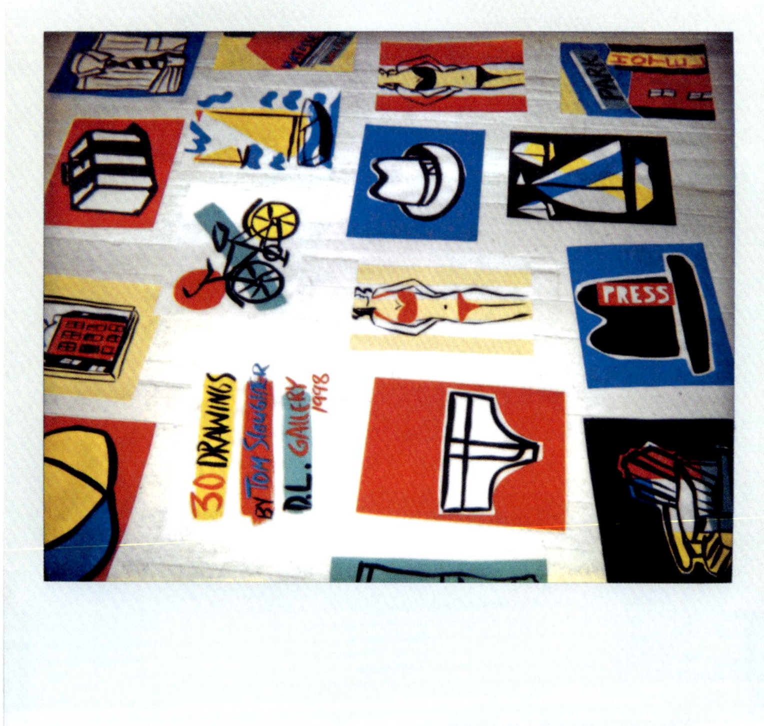

30 DRAWINGS
BY Tom Slaughter
D.L. GALLERY 1998
PRESS
HOTEL

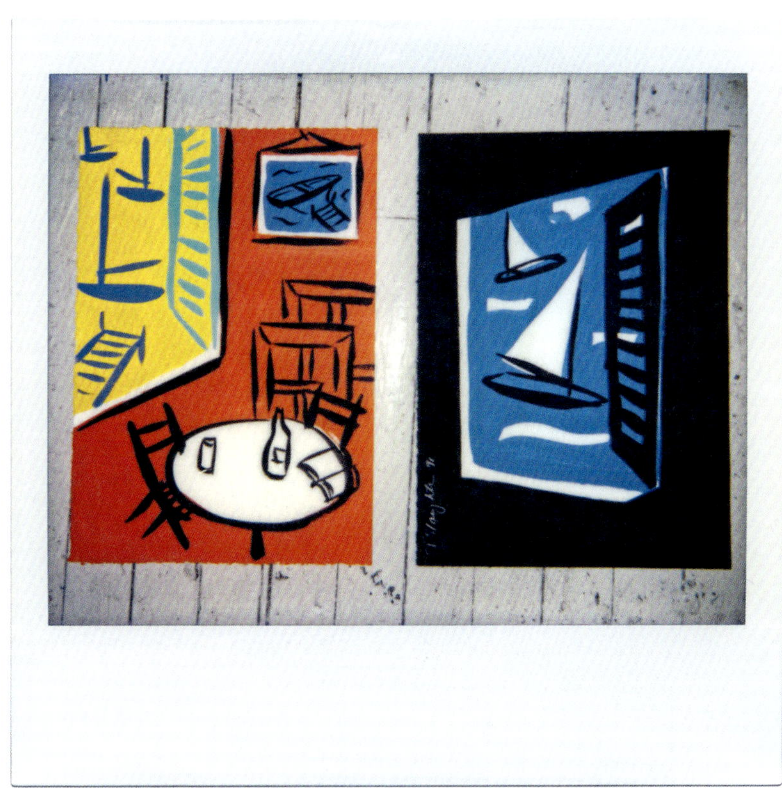

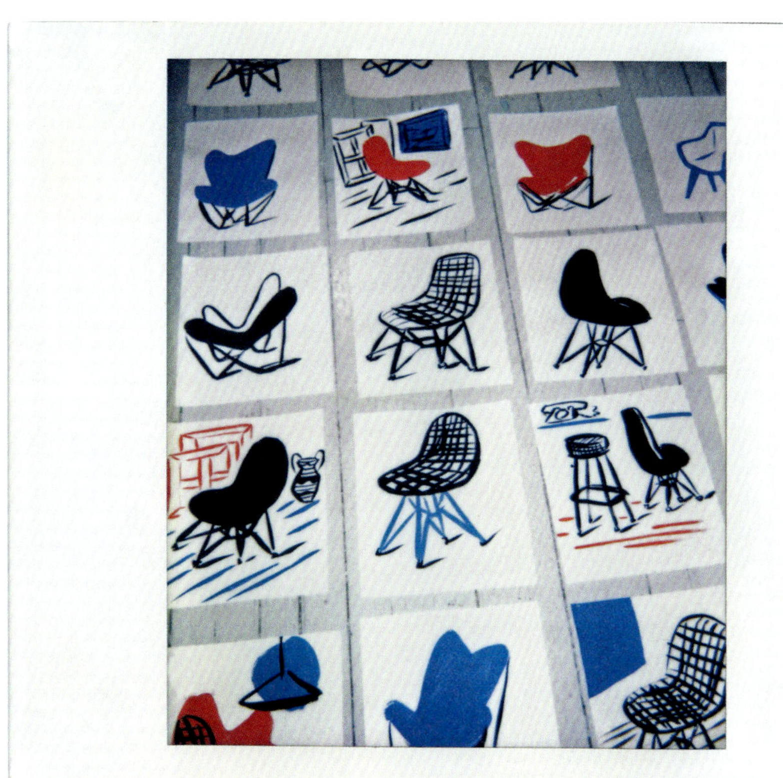

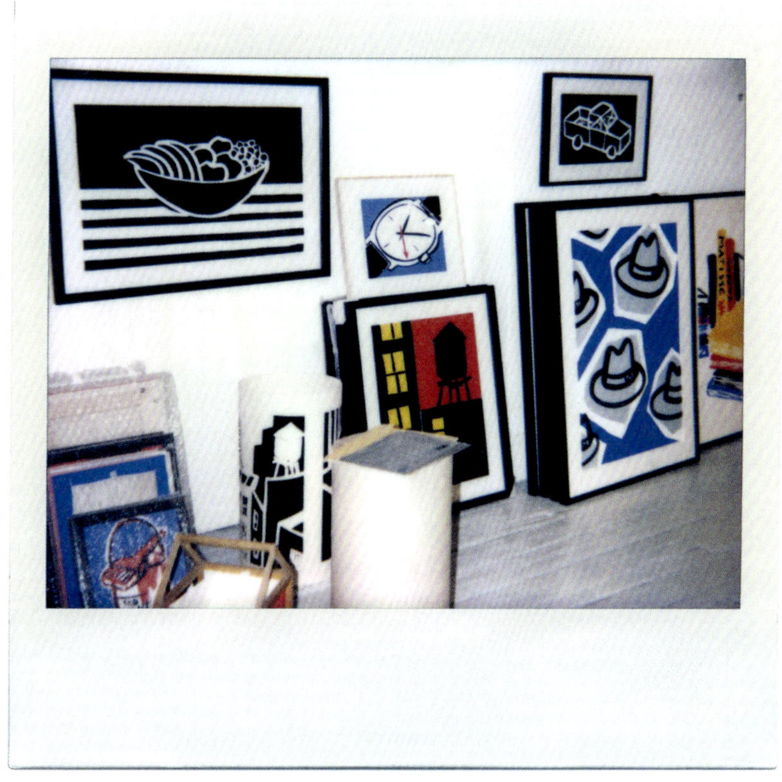

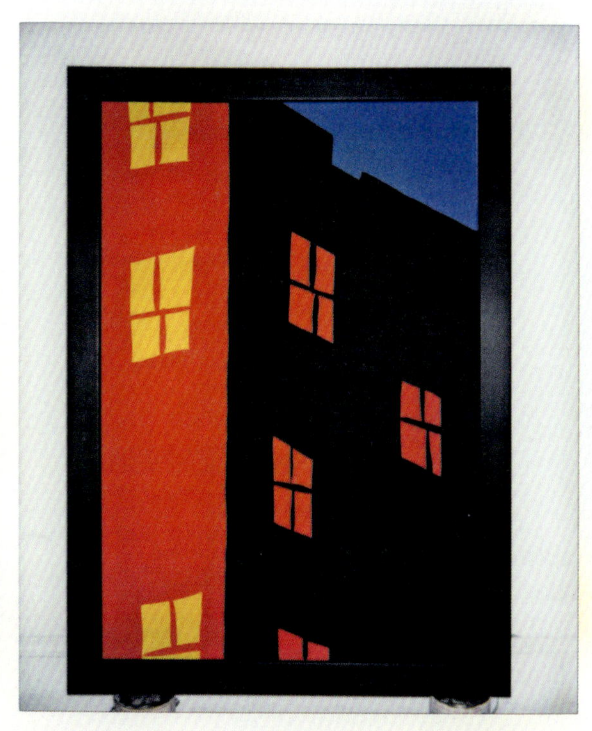

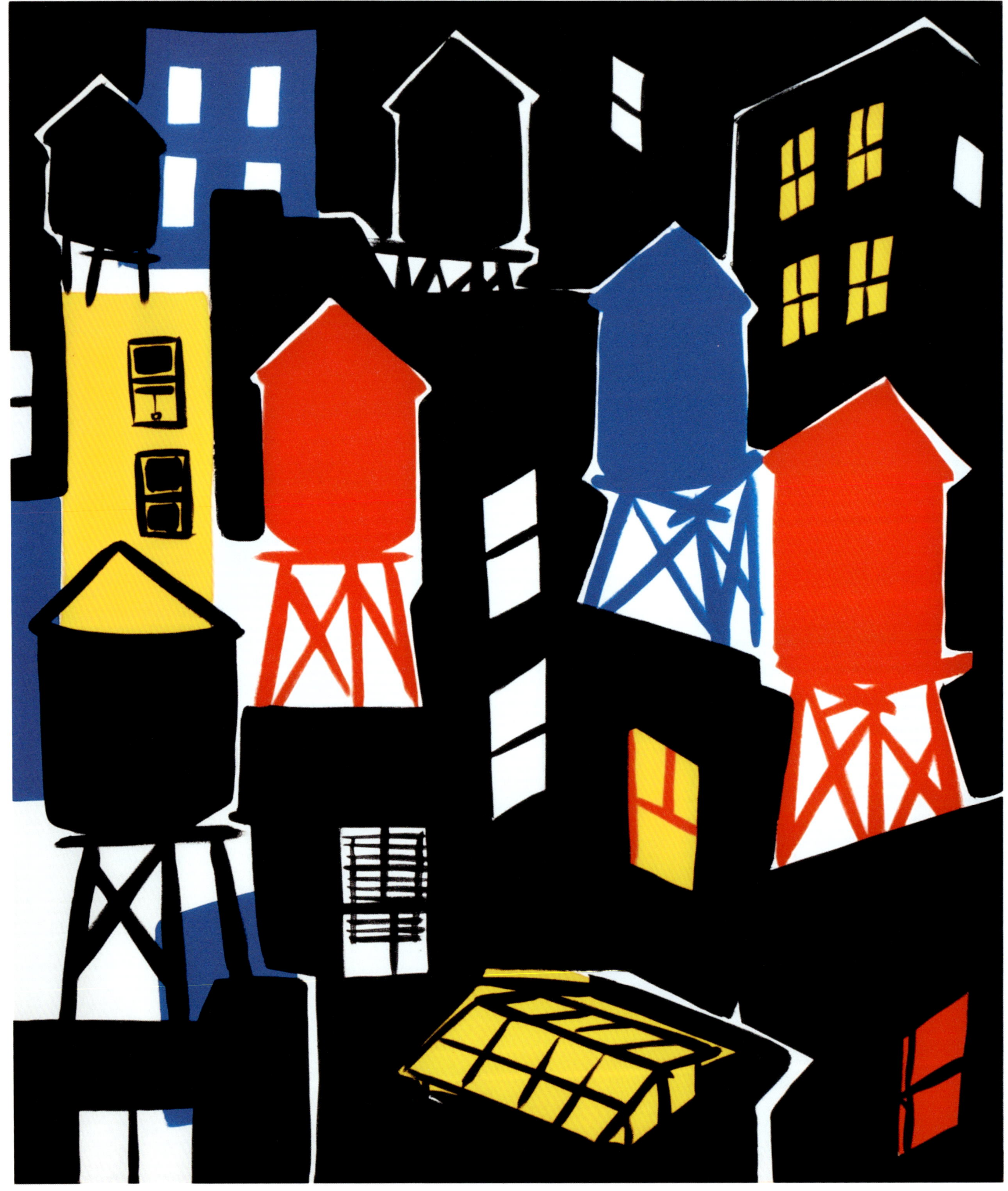

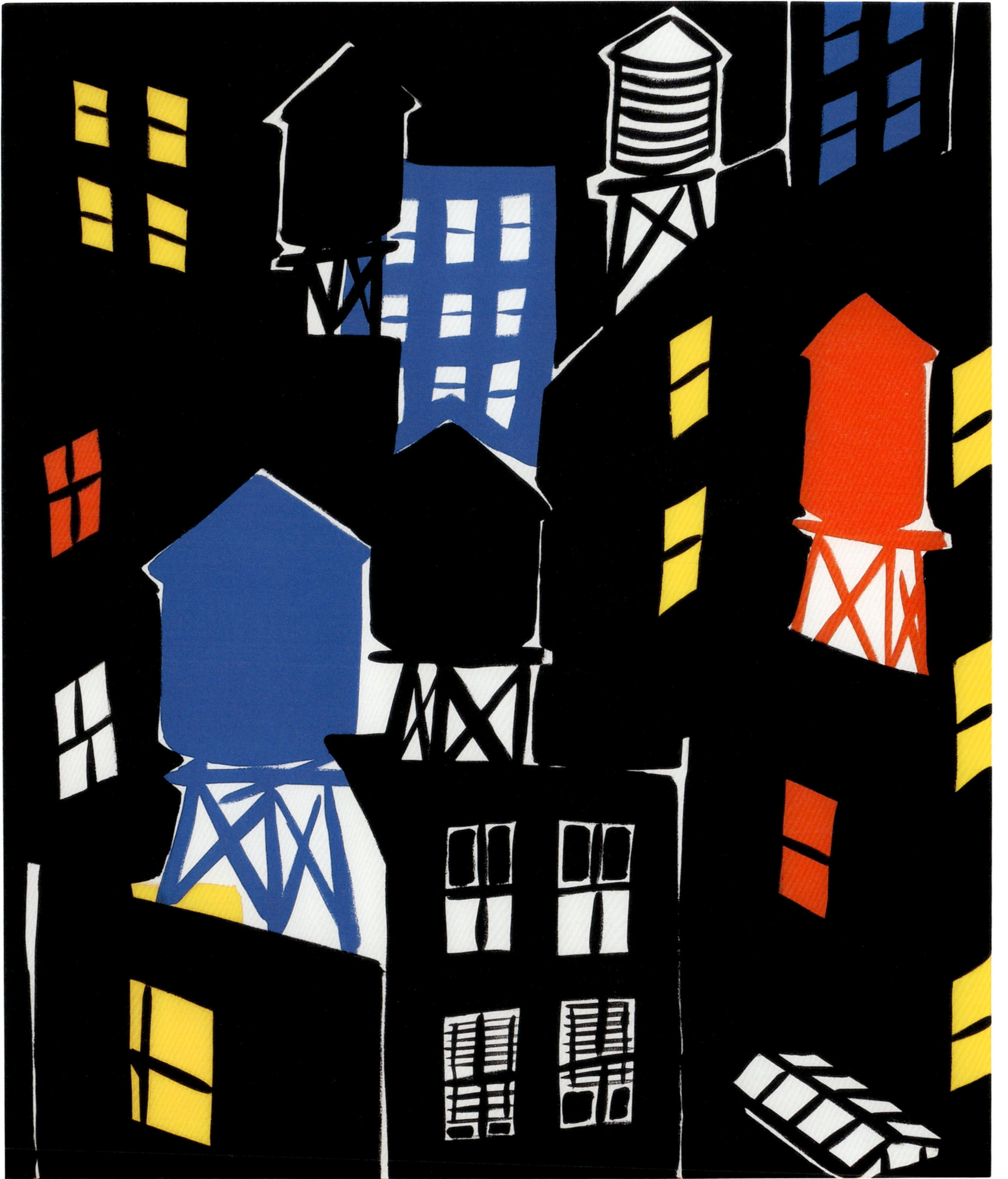

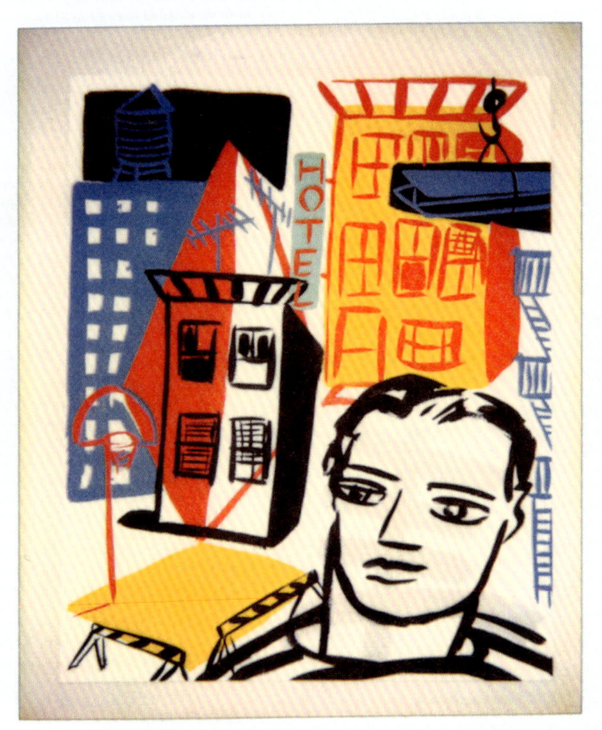
HOTEL

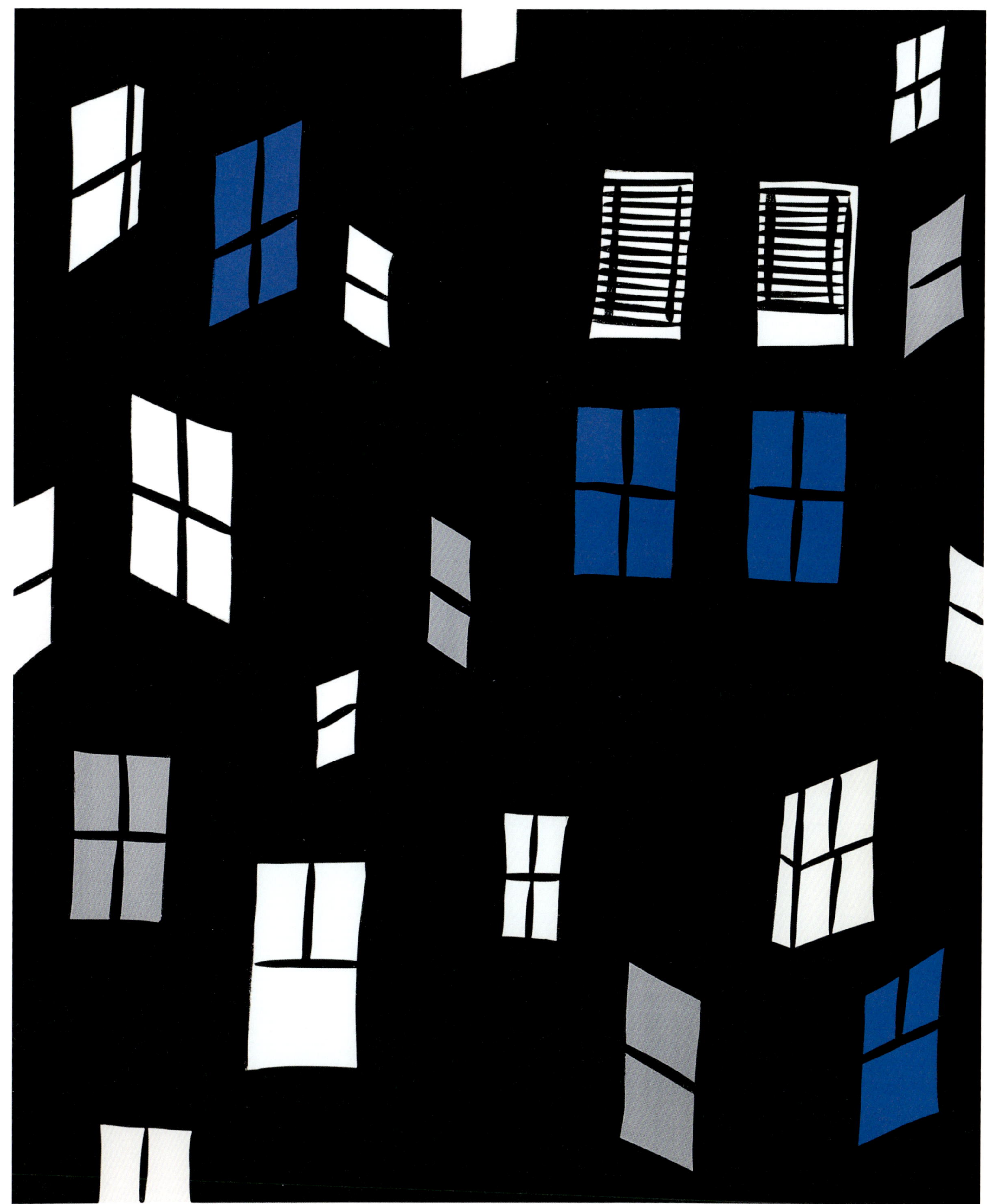

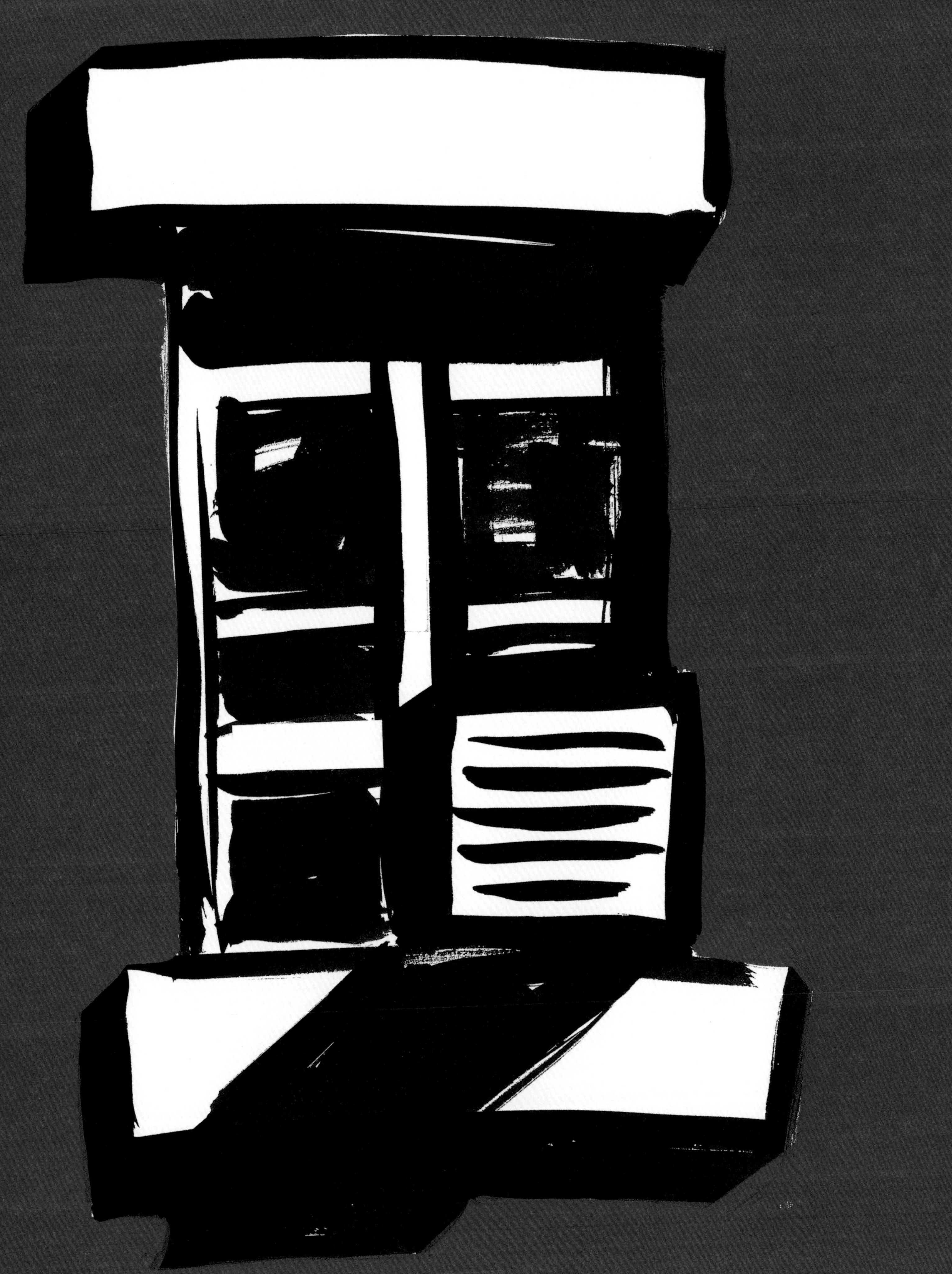

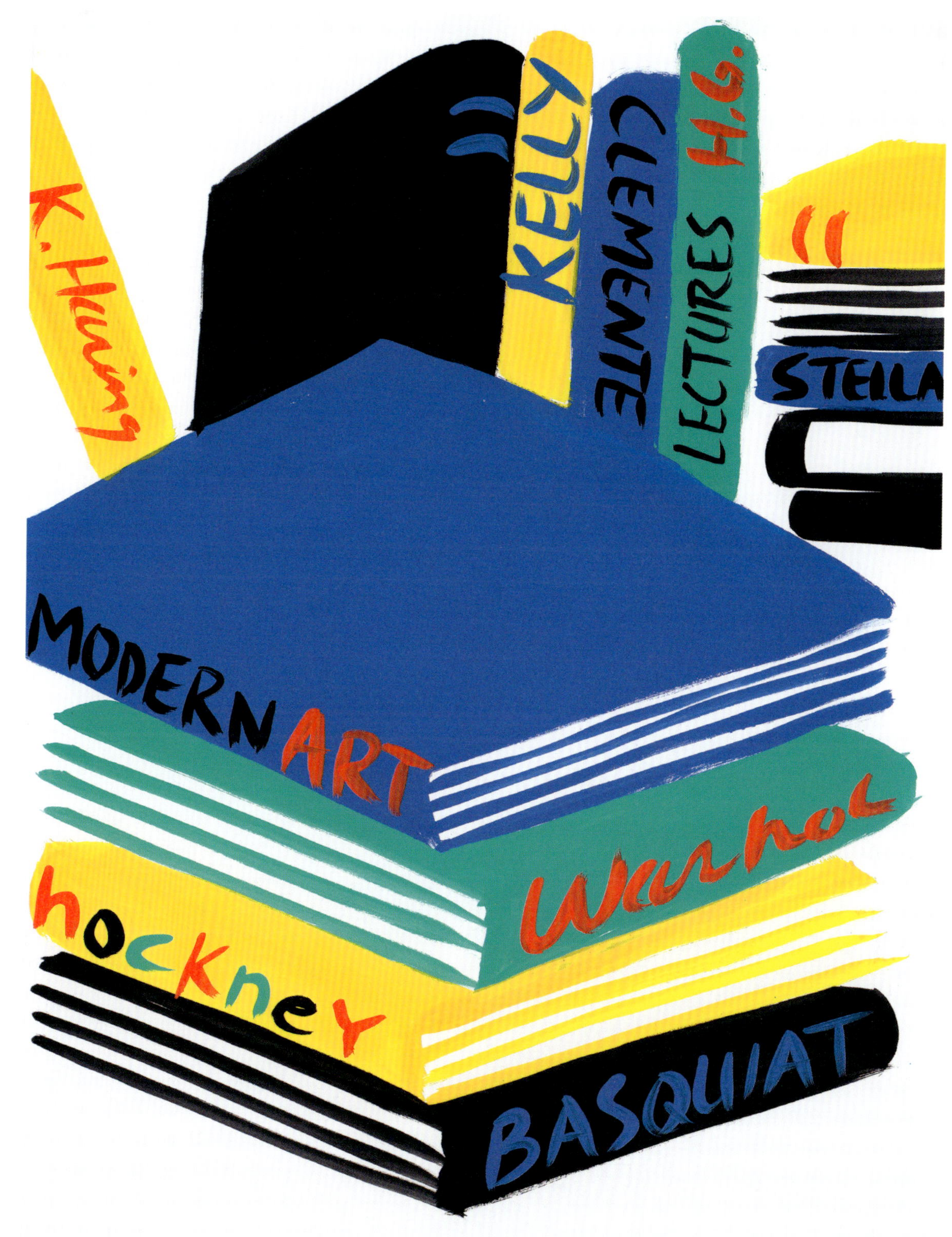

K. Haring
KELLY
CLEMENTE
LECTURES
H.G.
STELLA
MODERN ART
Warhol
Hockney
BASQUIAT

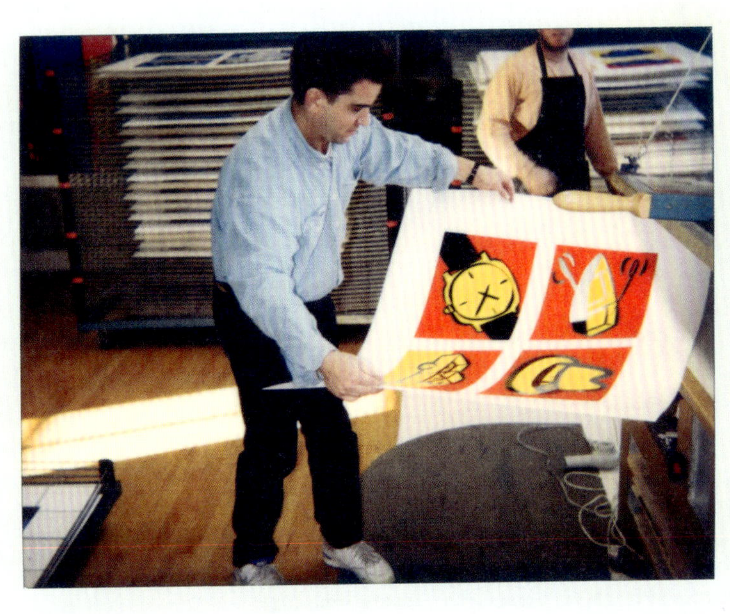

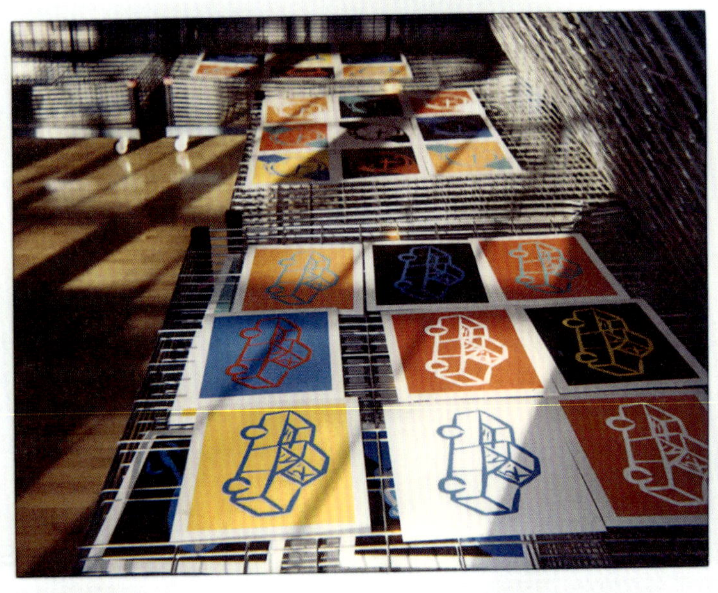

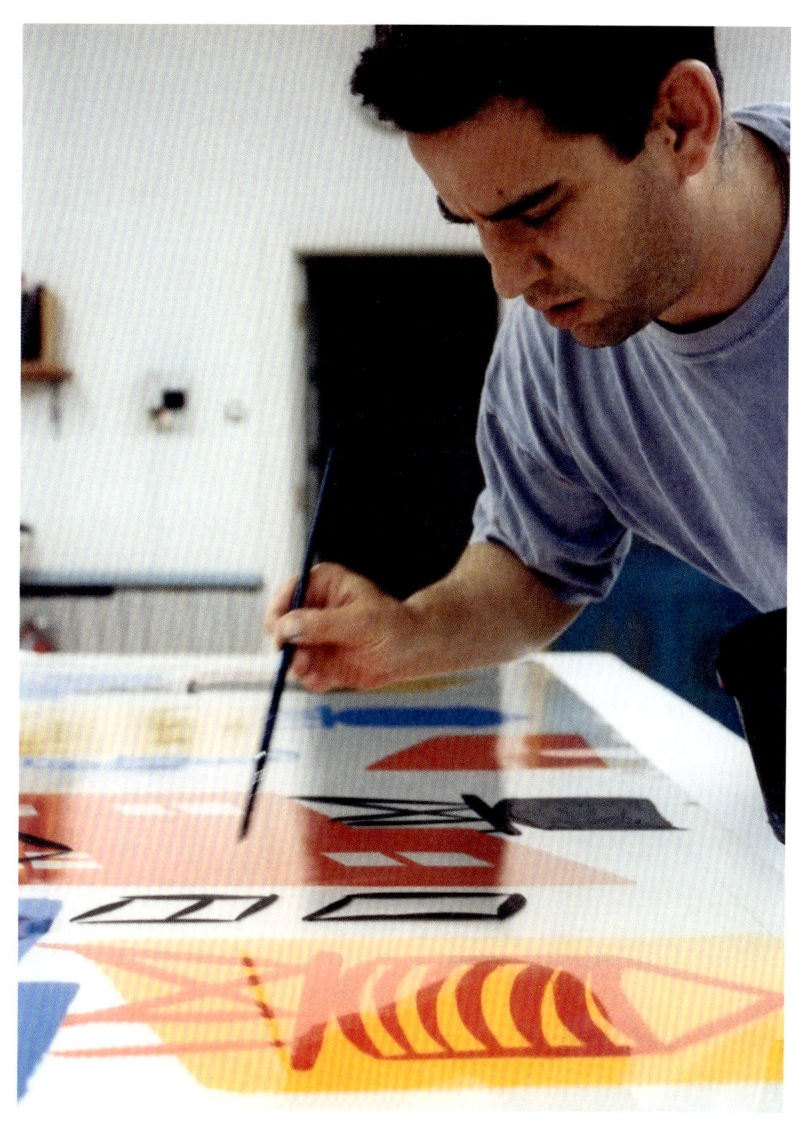

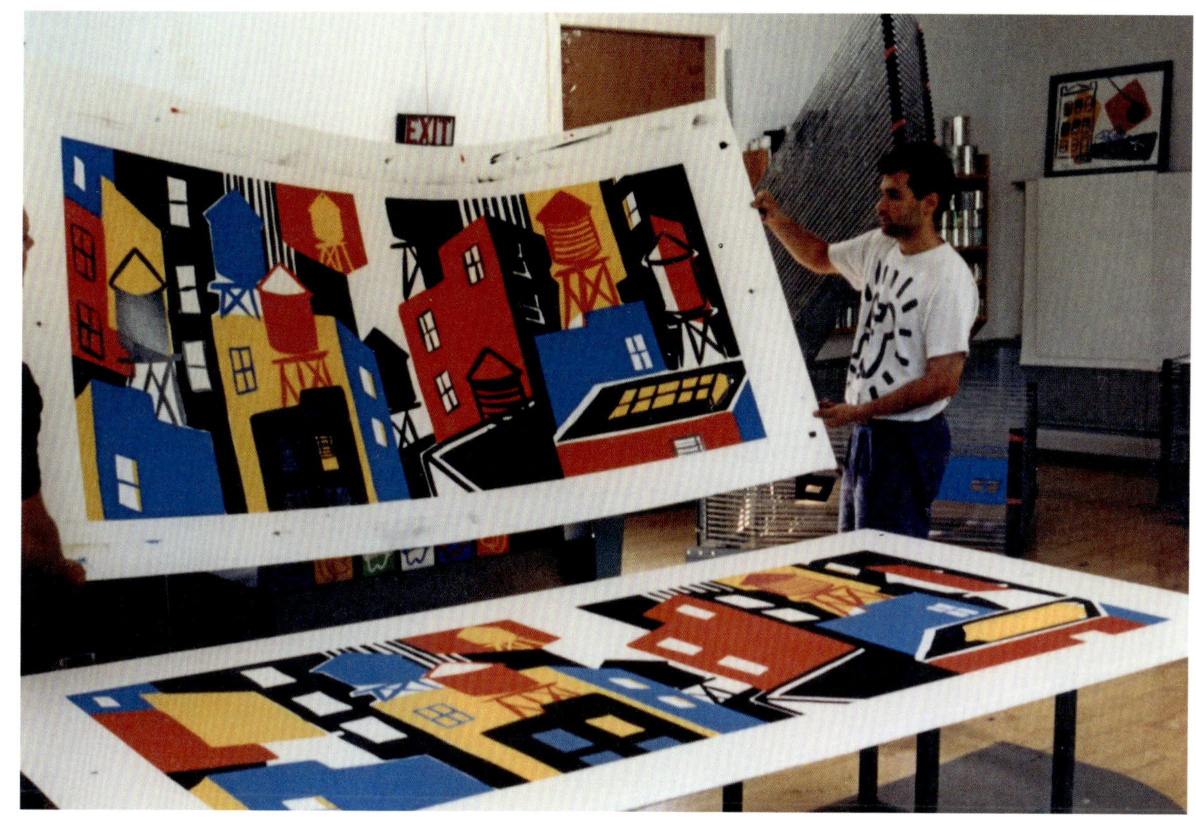

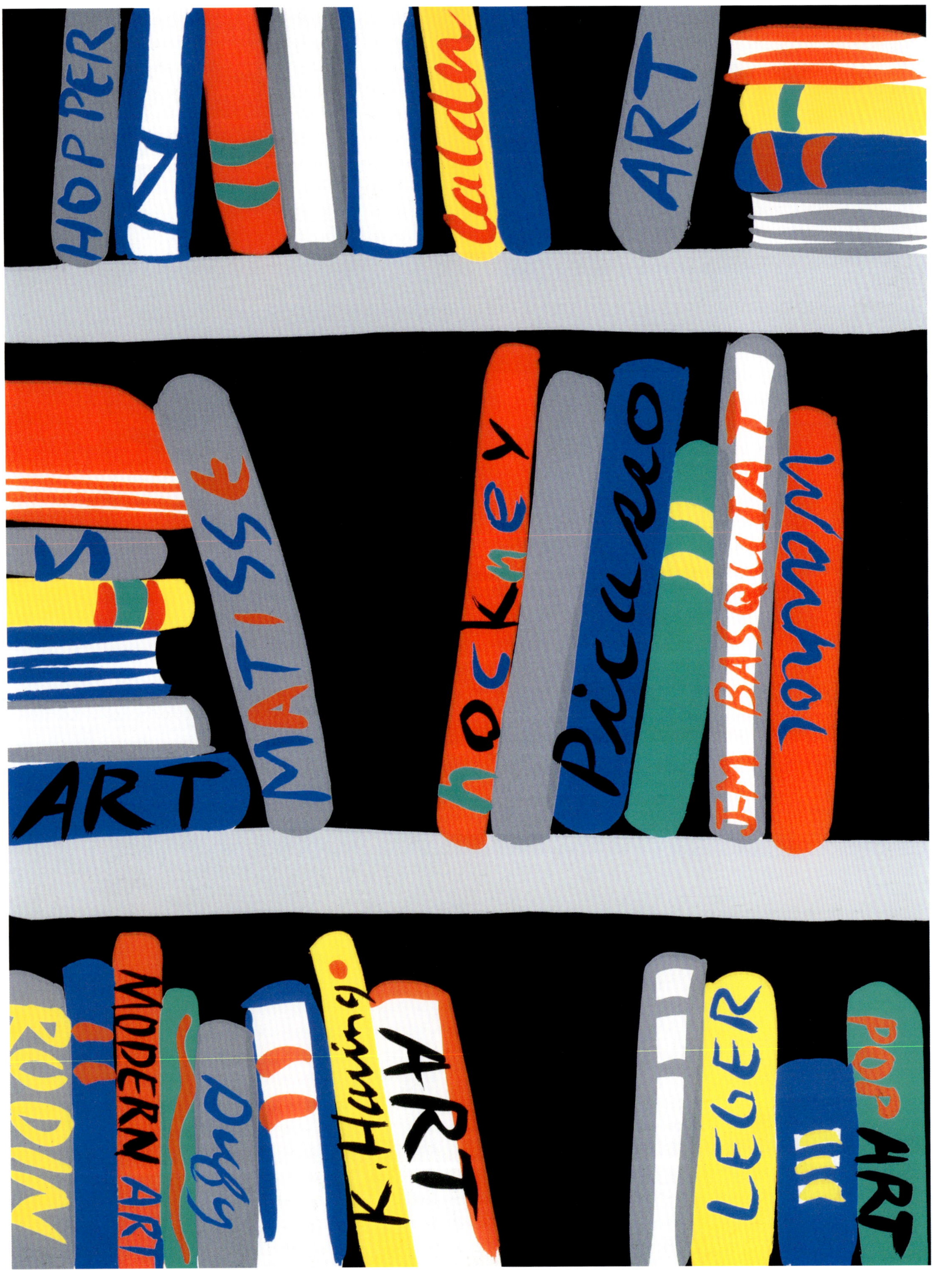

HOPPER
Caldn
ART
MATISSE
ART
hockney
Picasso
Picasso
JM BASQUIAT
Warhol
RODIN
MODERN ART
Dubg
K.Haring
ART
LEGER
POP ART

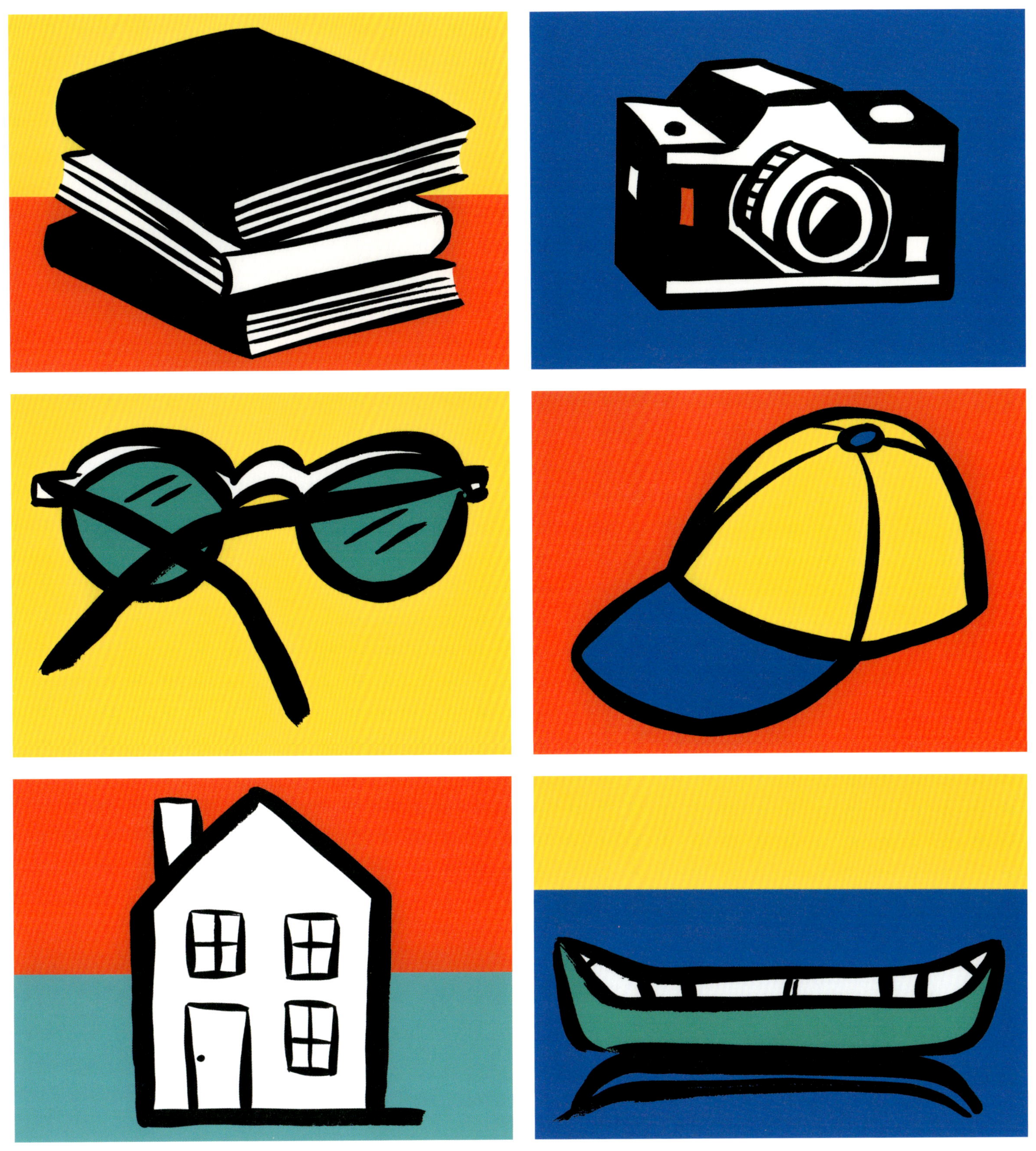

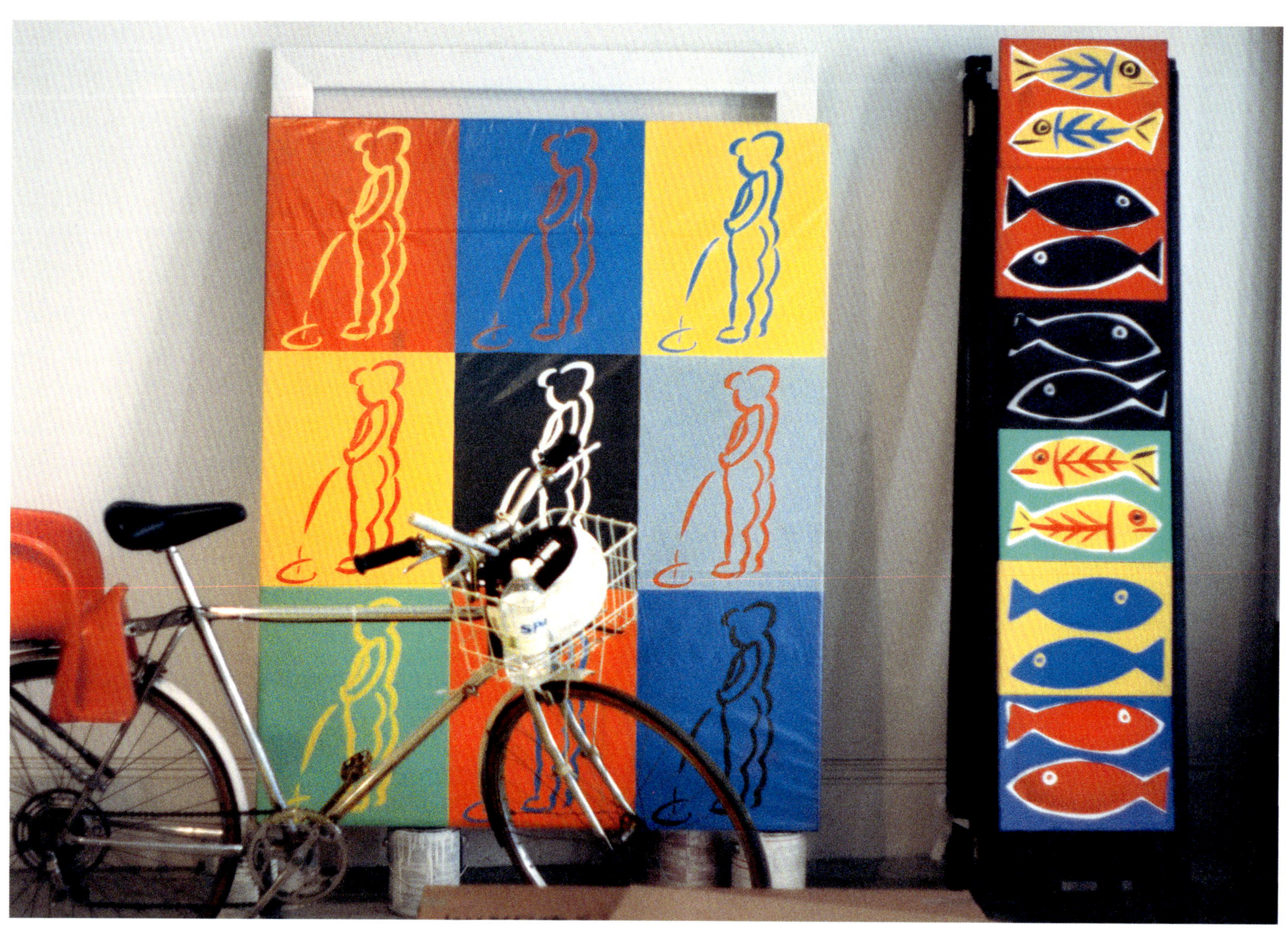

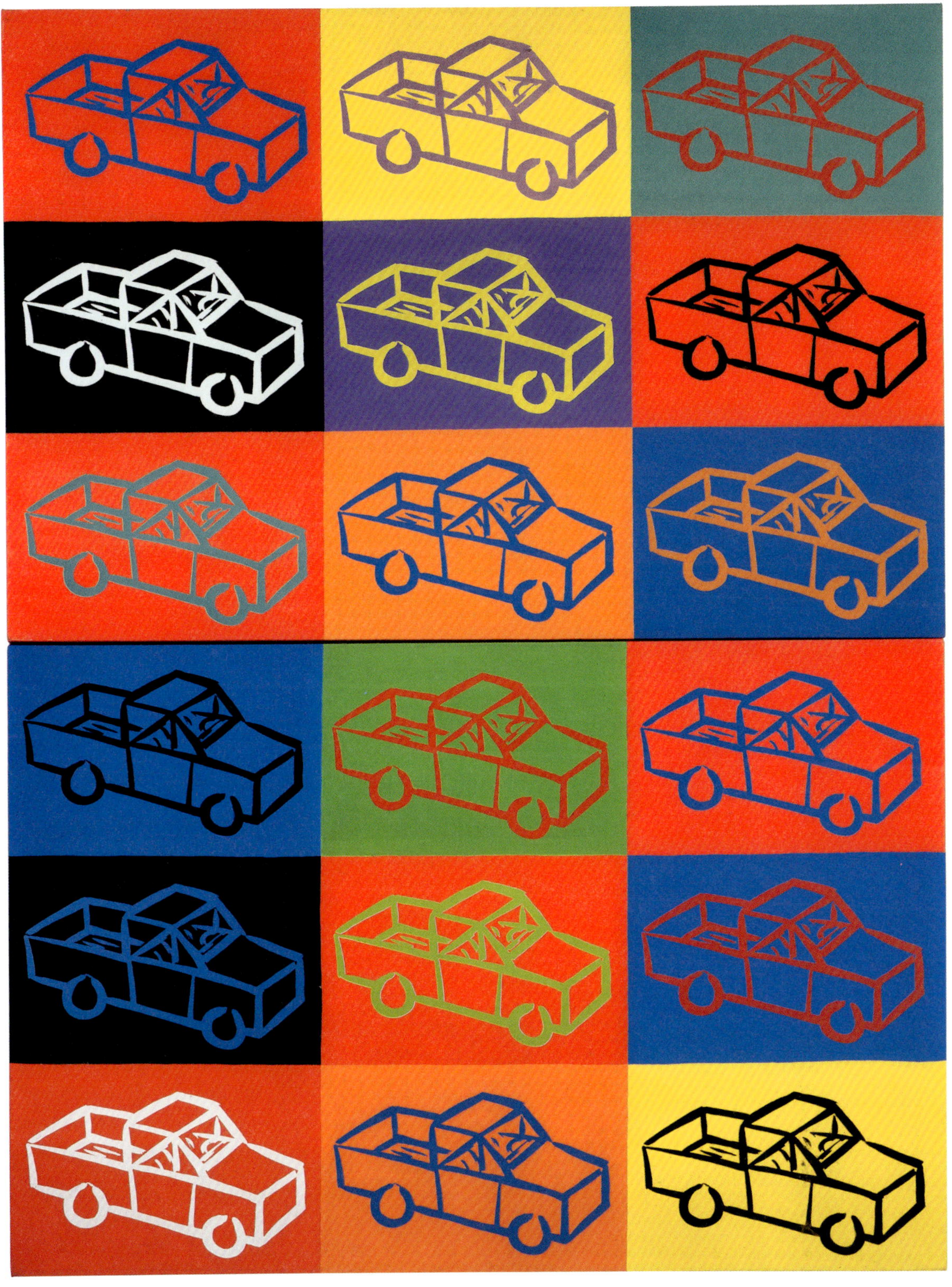

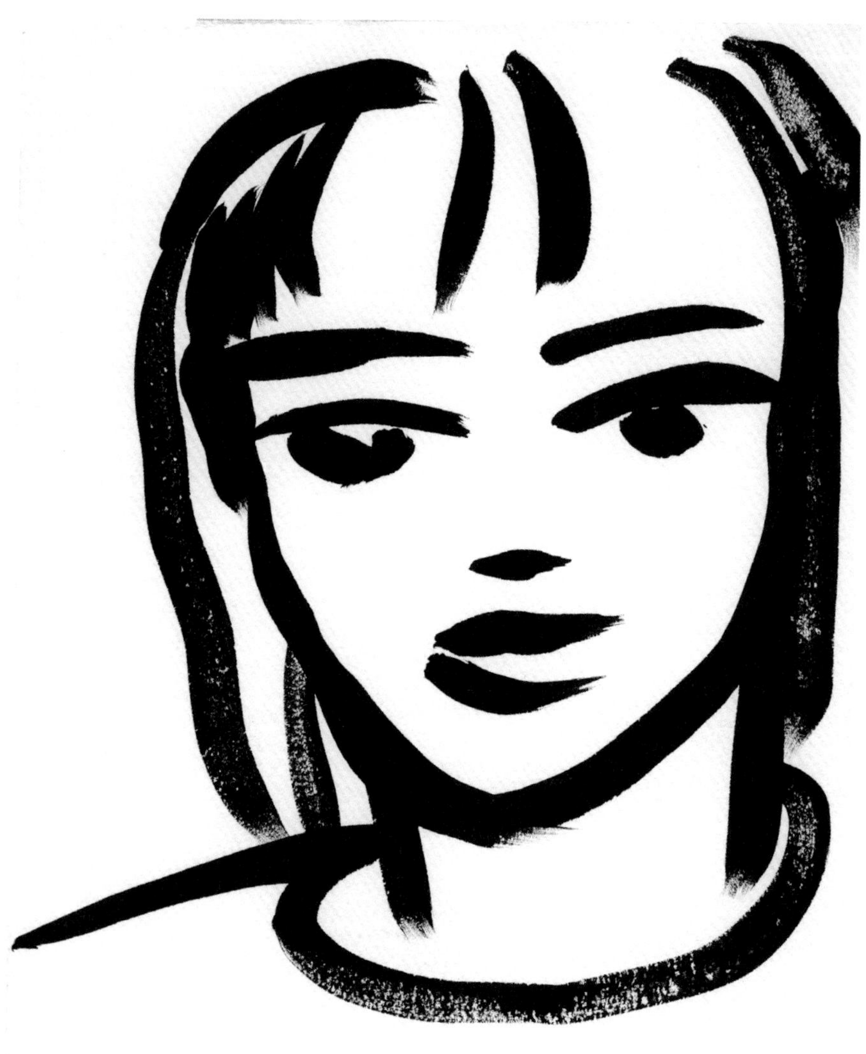

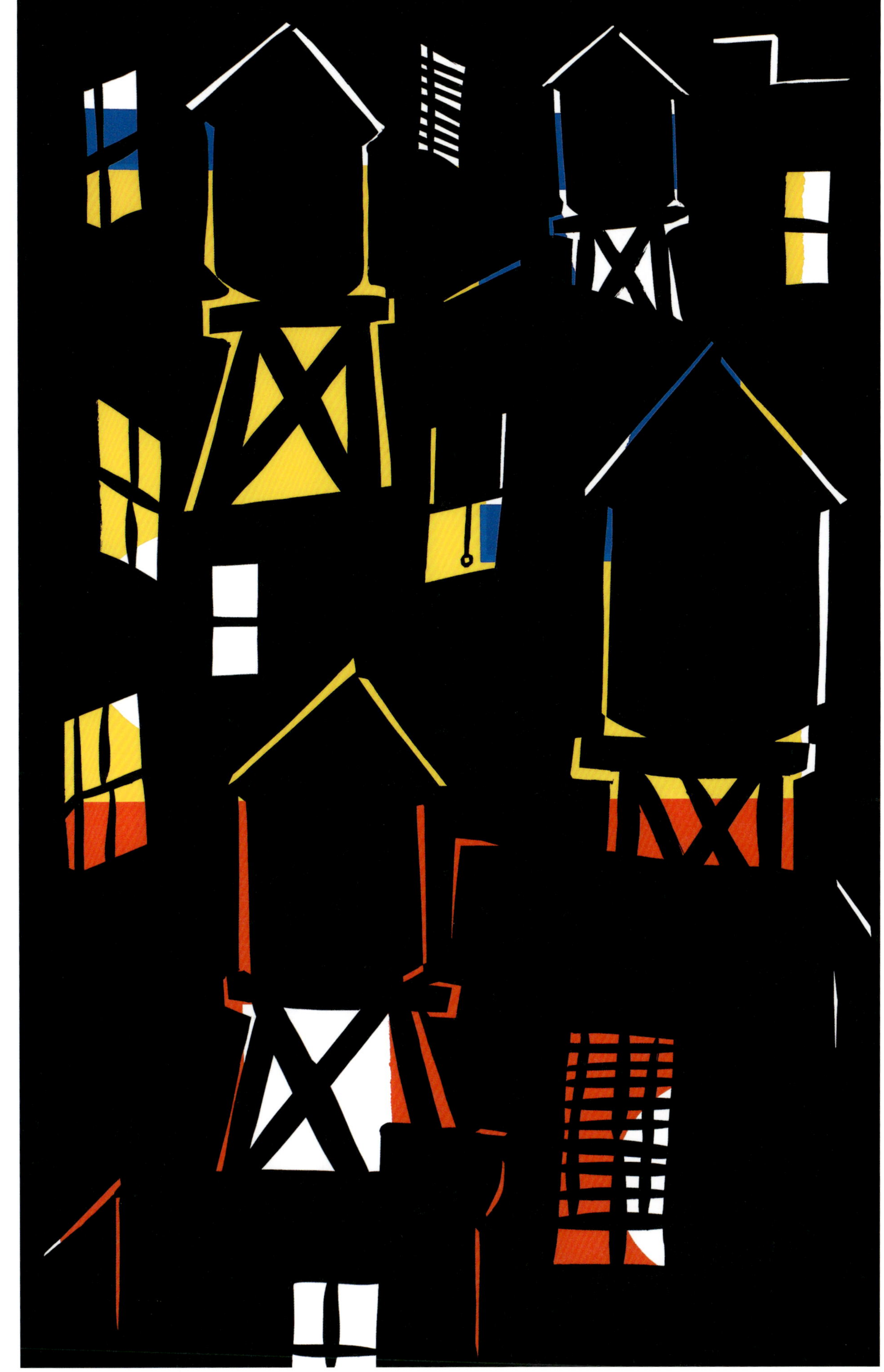

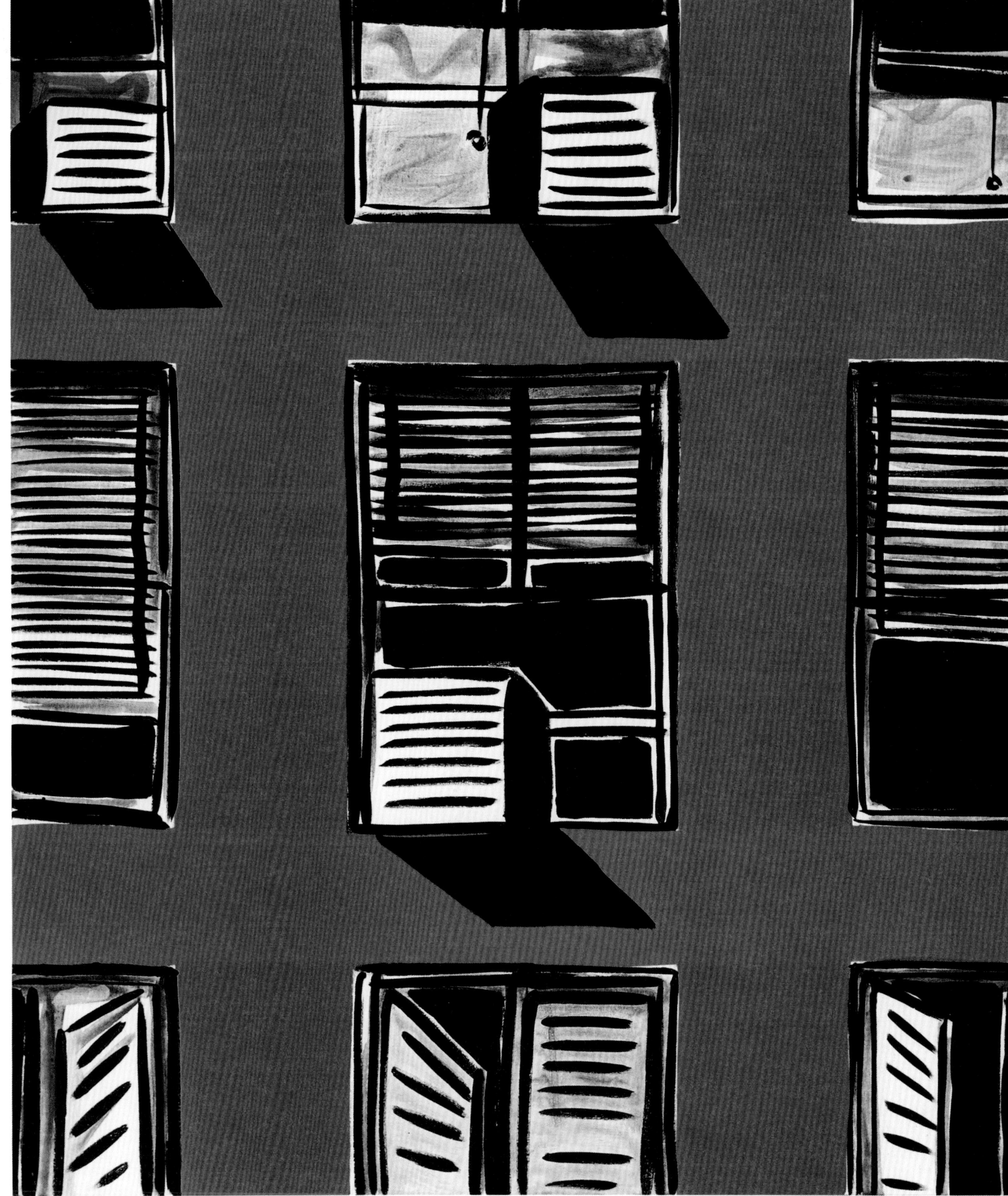

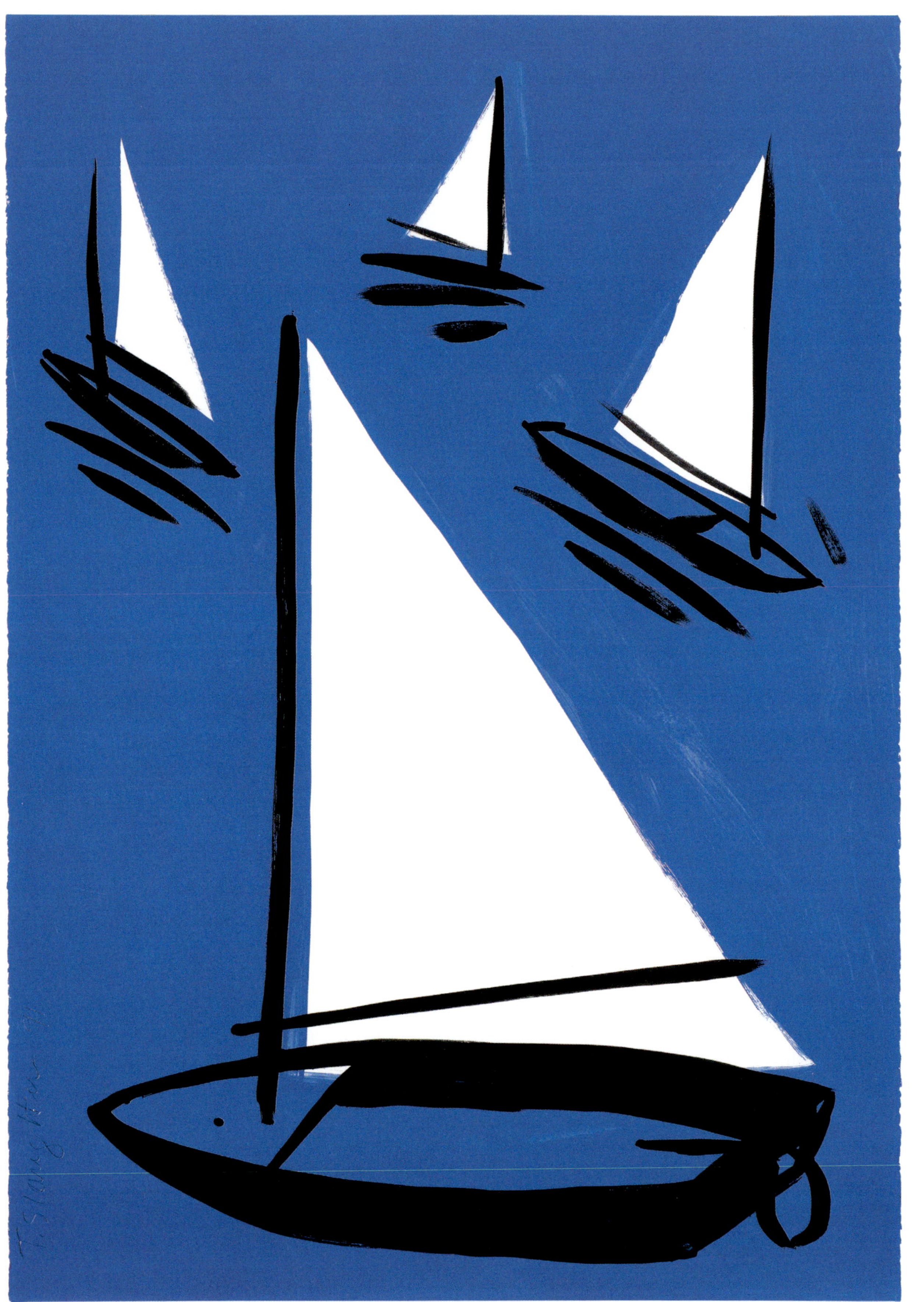

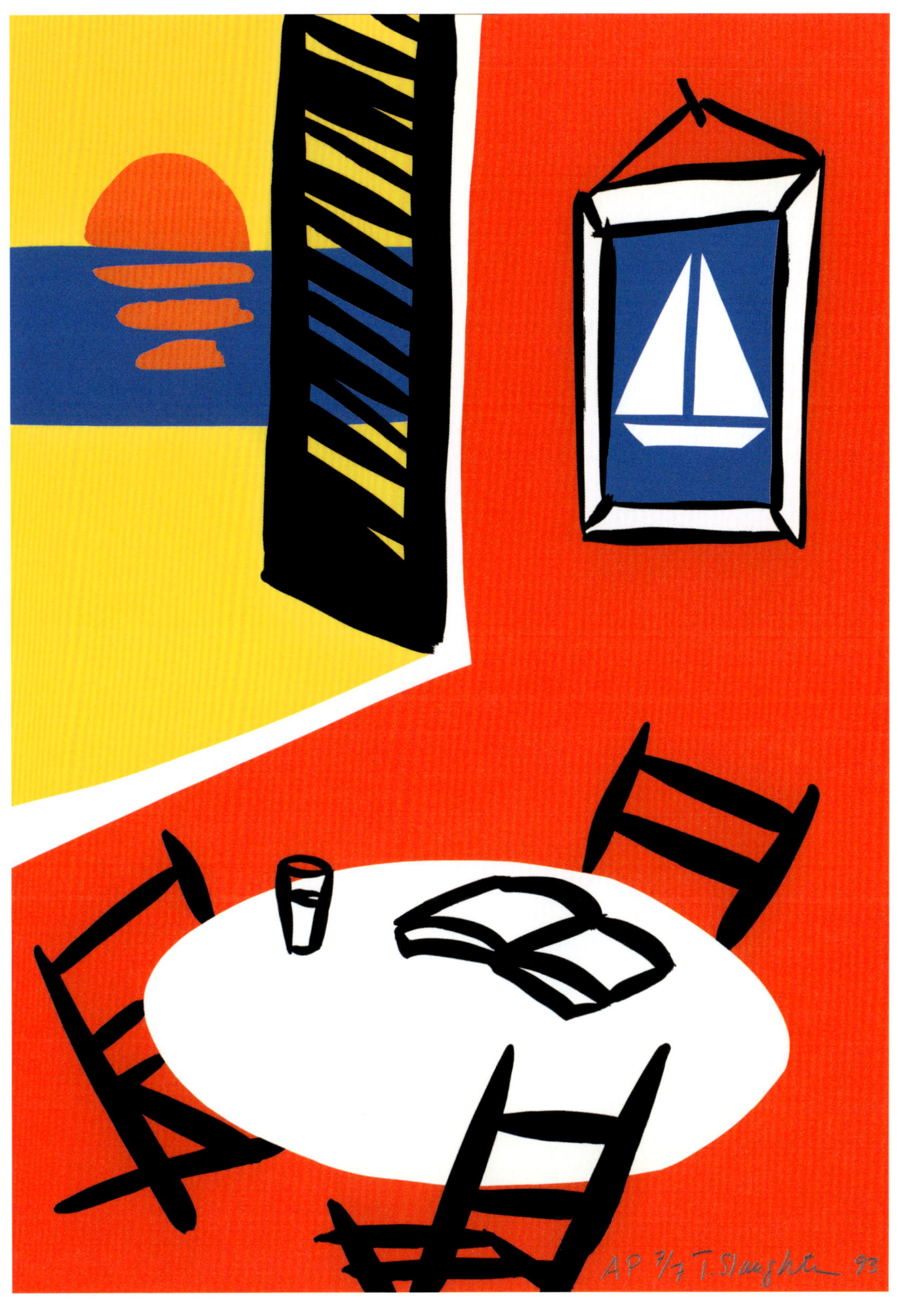

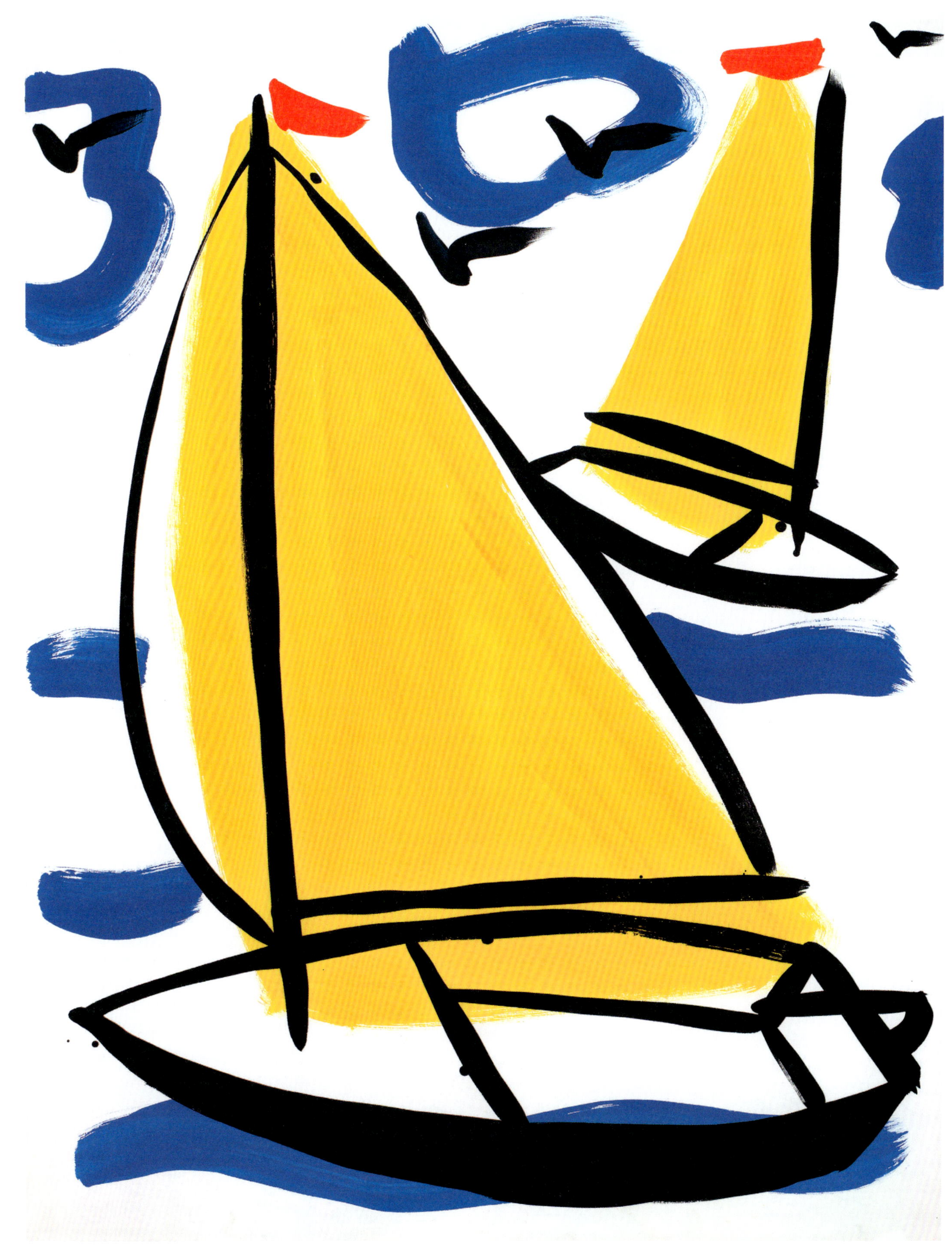

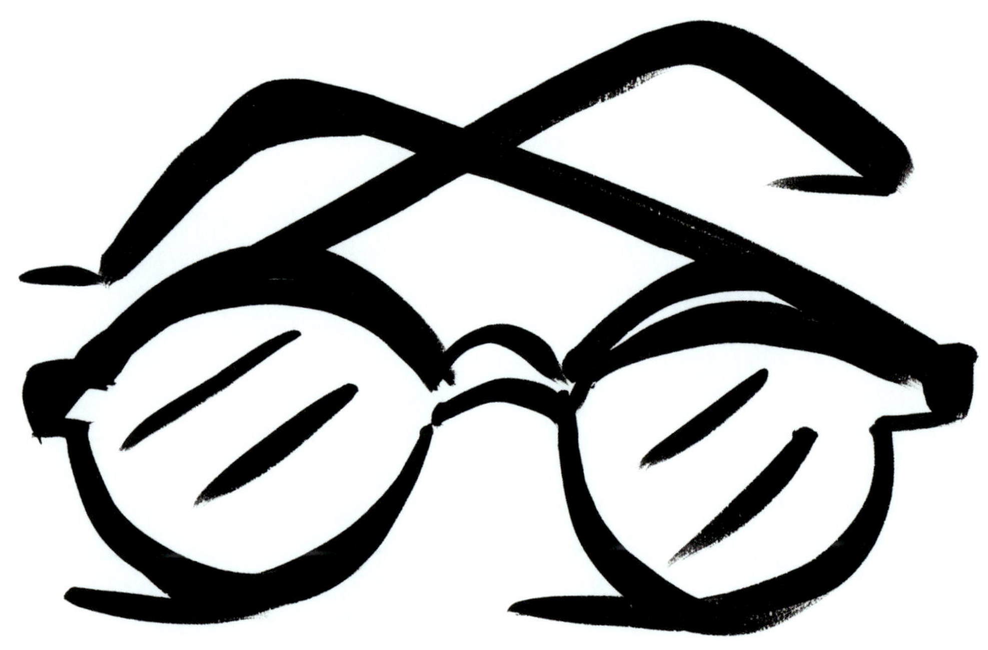

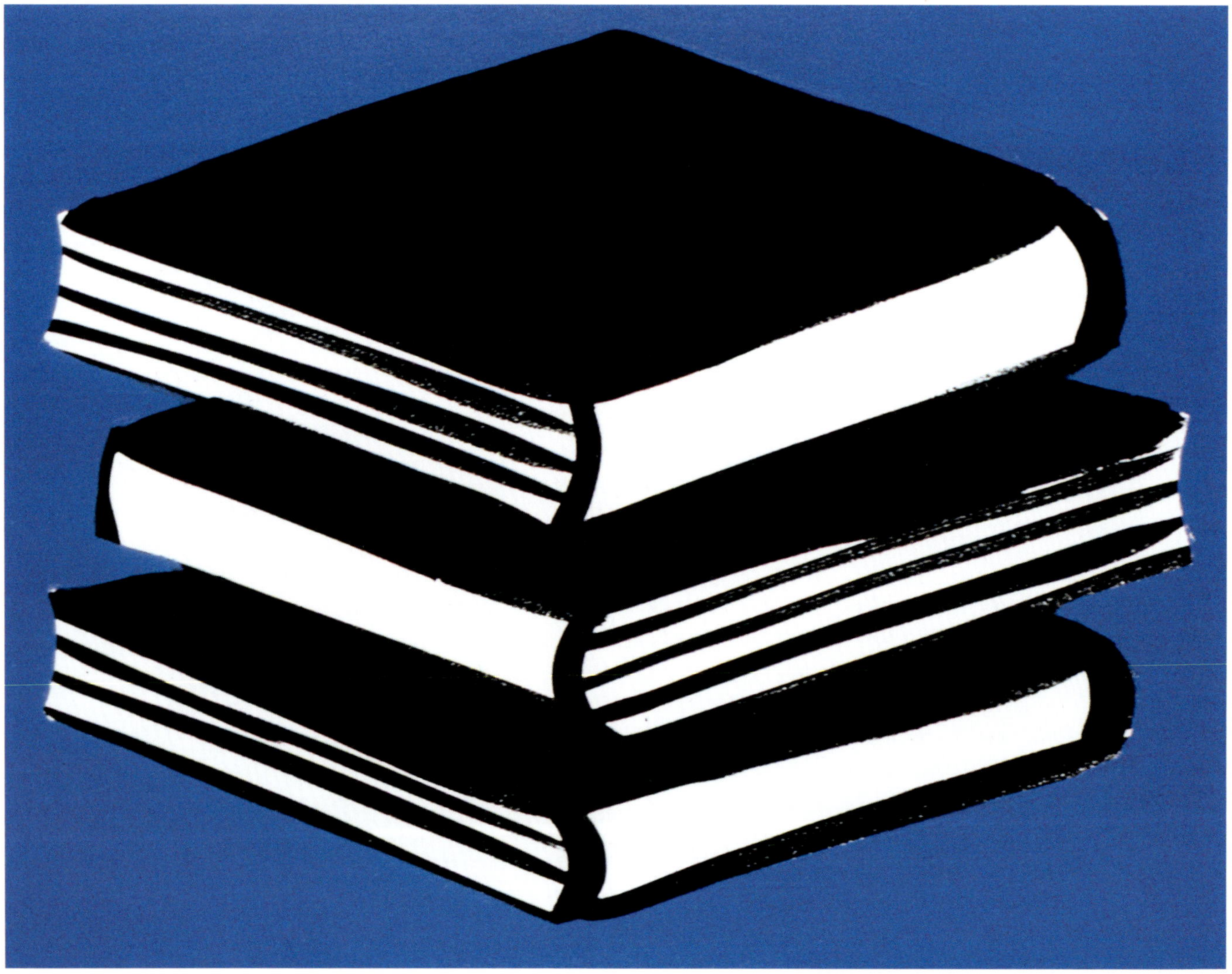

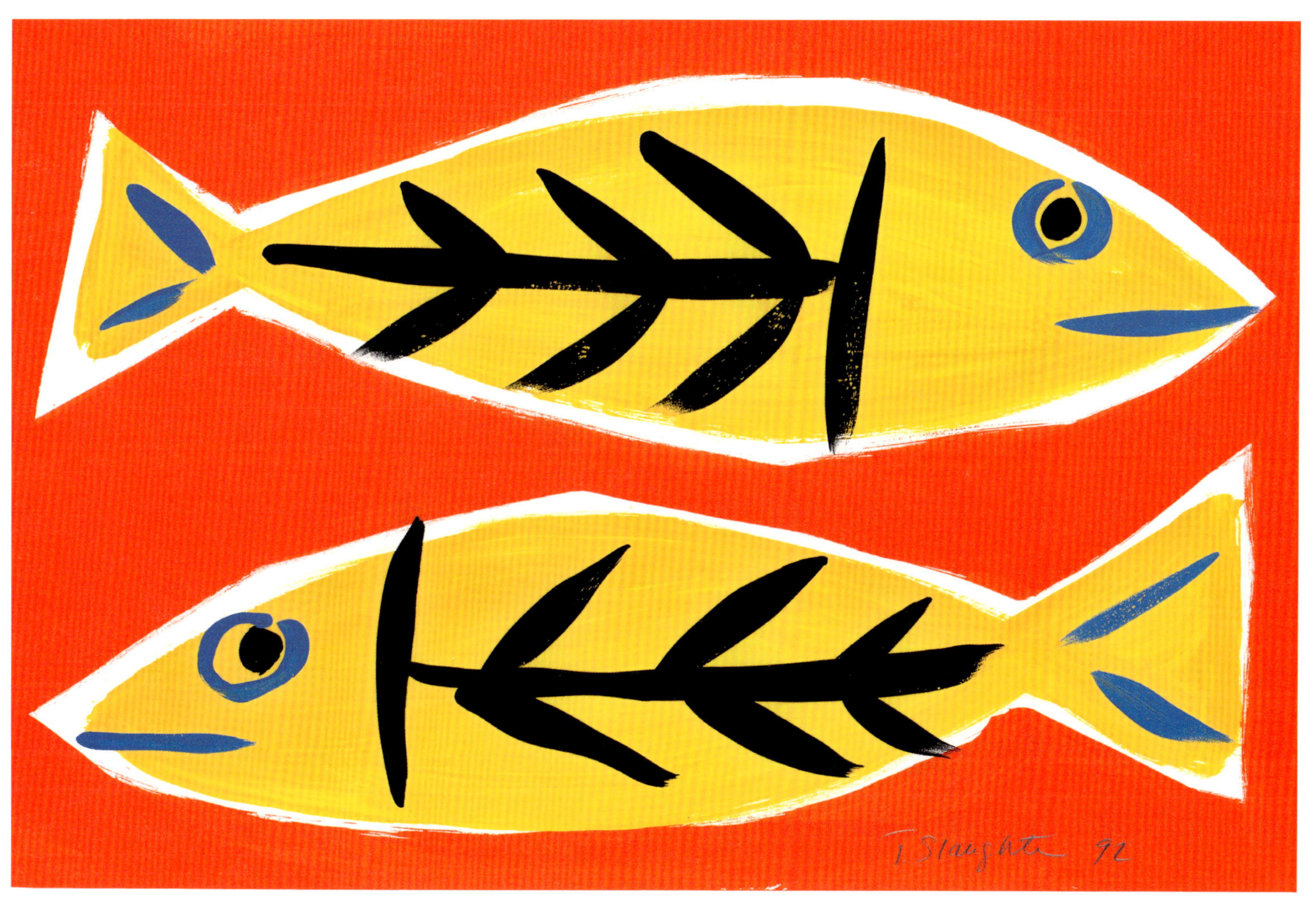

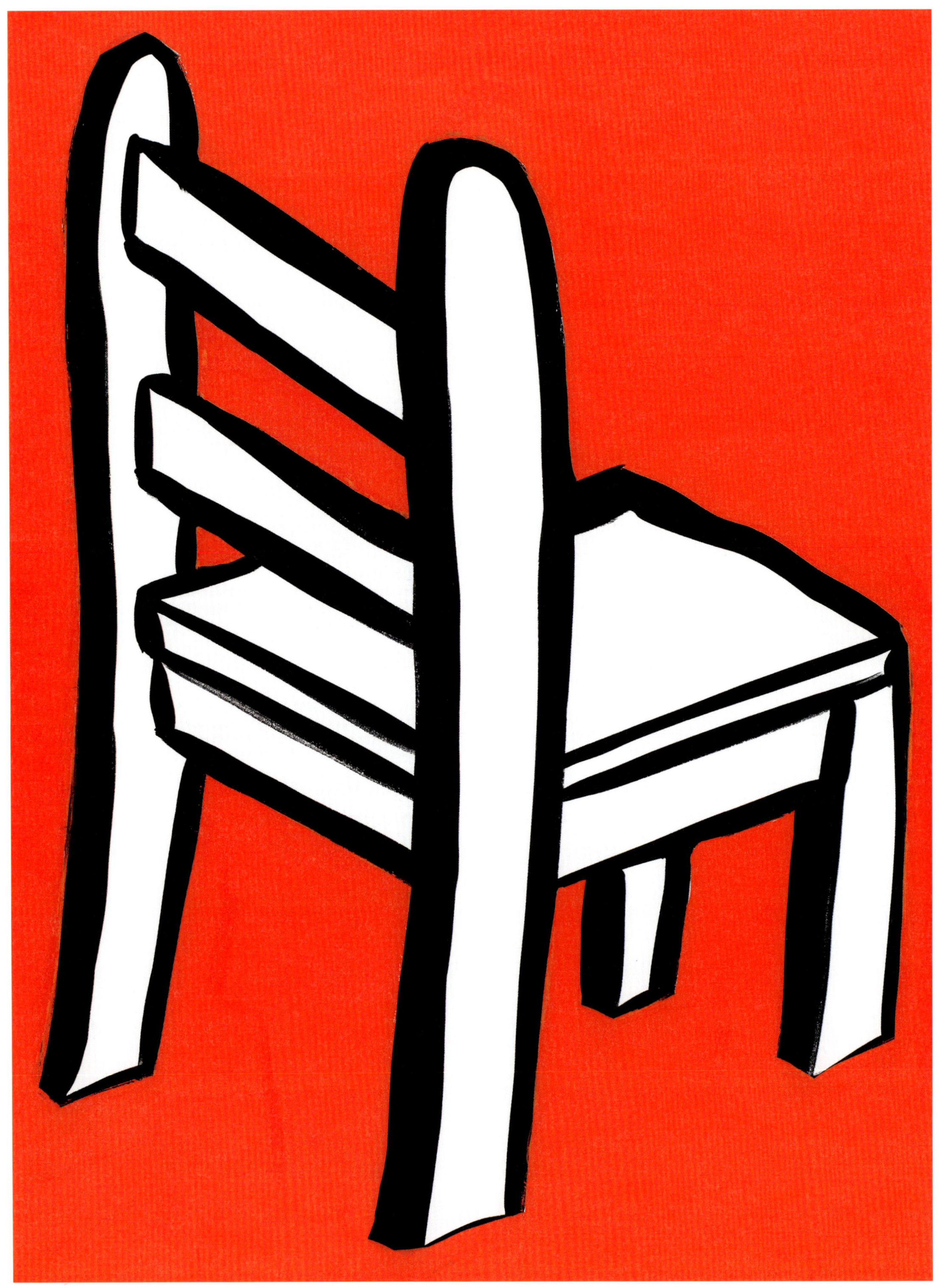

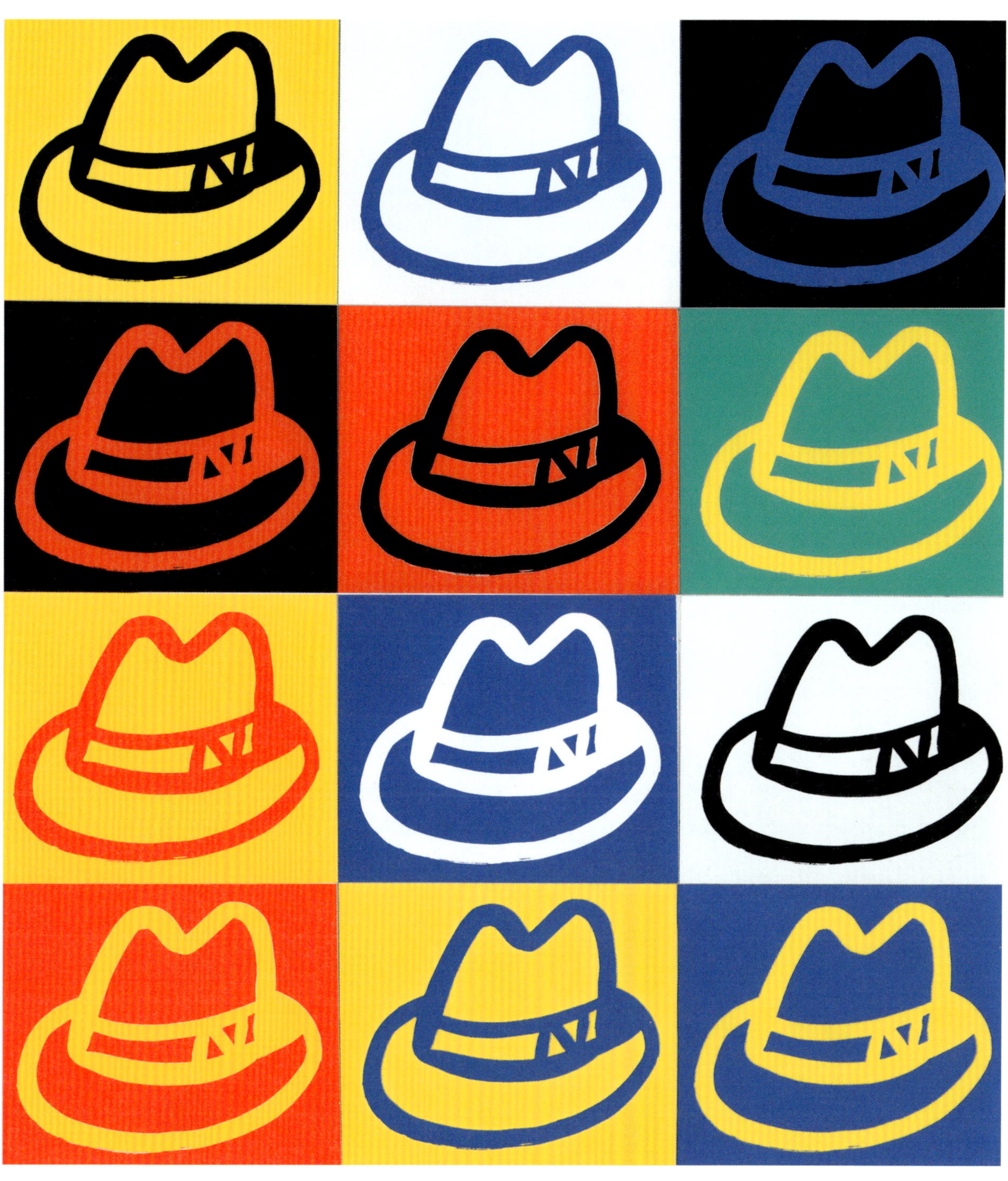

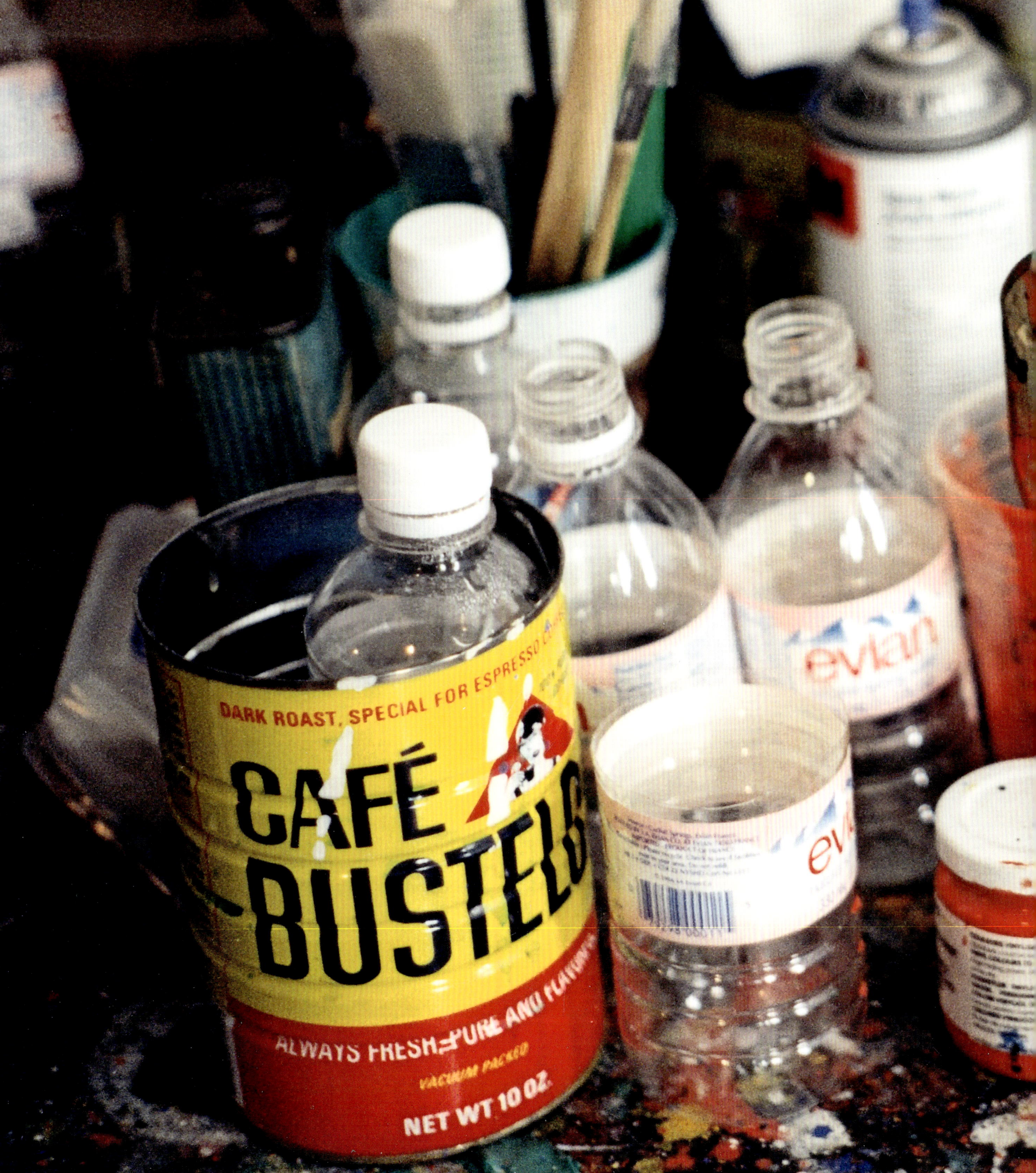

DARK ROAST, SPECIAL FOR ESPRESSO
CAFÉ
BUSTELO
ALWAYS FRESH—PURE AND FLAVORFUL
VACUUM PACKED
NET WT 10 OZ.
evian
evian

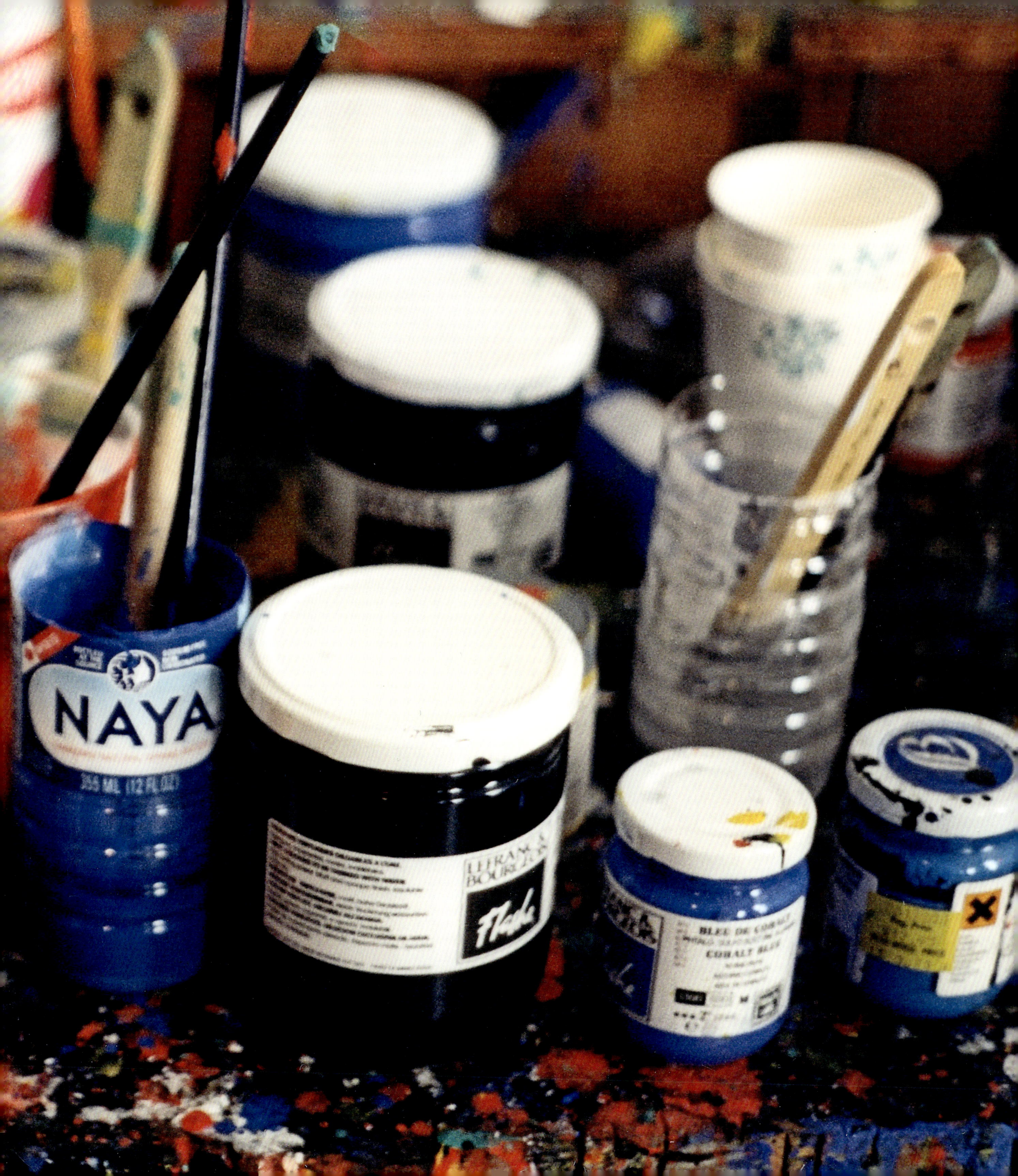

NAYA
355 ML (12 FL OZ)
LEFRANC &
BOURGEOIS
Flash
BLEU DE COBALT
COBALT BLUE

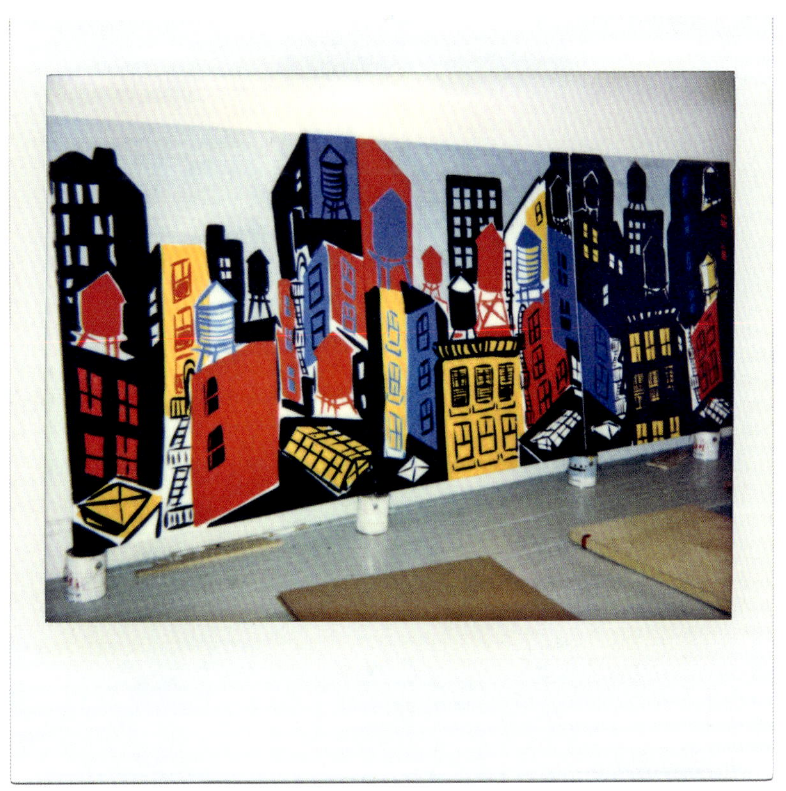

Tom Slaughter's paintings have a very specific effect. Like Brazilian music, as in Jobim, or Caetano Veloso, they are instantly pleasing. Two cases: First, there is the water tower. As painted over and over by Slaughter, most often as a bold silhouette, it is at once totemic and comforting in its familiarity. Those structures that are to New York what rooftop gardens are to Rome, atelier walls of glass to the Latin Quarter in Paris, palm trees to L.A., have resonances that, like so many of Slaughter's other paintings, hint at his desire to be nowhere in place, but somewhere else in time. Say 1948. Say John O'Hara's New York. When men still routinely wore good felt hats, usually of a gray or putty color, smoked cigarettes, drank martinis and loved little props such as ashtrays and pencils. Like so many of Slaughter's images, there's a kind of true sweetness at play, underscored by an insistence that the visual world of small domesticities is almost compulsively scrutinized. Second, there is the hat itself. The hat became, for many years, the logo of a restaurant on 42nd Street, the West Bank Café, which was and is a gathering place for show people, a hub for long talks after performances at Playwrights Horizons right across the street as well as the colony of little theaters farther west. The West Bank matchbook featured that hat in black against a yellow background. I still have books of them from the mid-'80s. They are a small treasure, little celebrations of what Slaughter is jazzed by. . . .

Slaughter is curious about the tools we use. Such as books. He adores the way they look and the way they feel; he paints their heft and mass and shape much in the way that Giorgio Morandi painted bottles. They're more. . . .

Slaughter's cabinet of wonders is like a Joseph Cornell box, thrown together in the hopes that the contents amount to something mysterious and larger. There's also some unpretentious formalism at work: you can feel the affection for Mondrian in Manhattan, for Stuart Davis anywhere, for Braque's little tableaus, for Matisse both in Morocco and in Nice. Slaughter evokes something sweet, and something gone. The pictures can be considered wistful celebrations of what Robert Hughes, in *The Shock of the New*, exquisitely calls "the landscape of pleasure."

Jon Robin Baitz

Writer and producer

New York, NY

2003

Jon Robin Baitz, "Tom Slaughter," *BOMB* magazine 84 (July 2003).

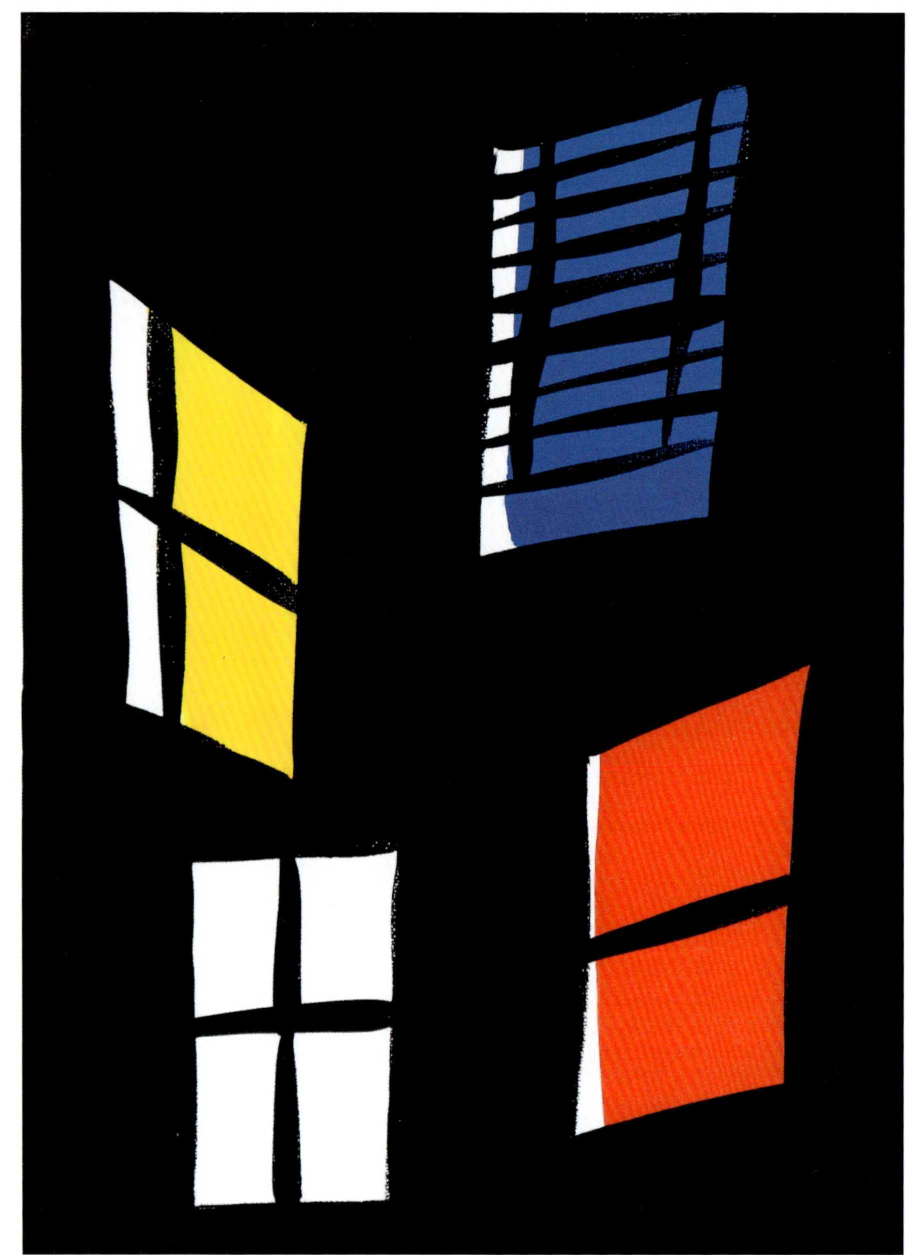

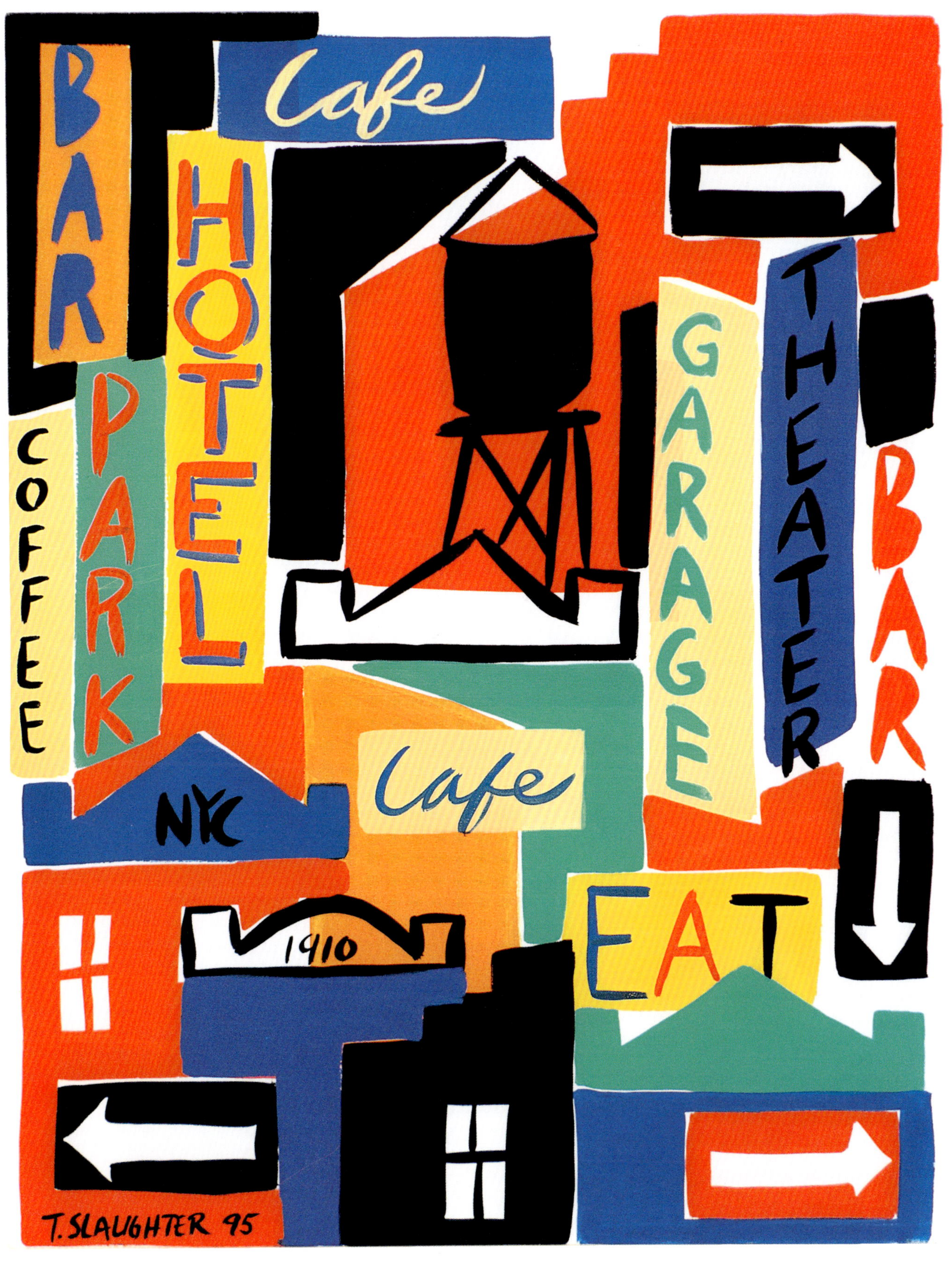

BAR
Cafe
HOTEL
COFFEE
PARK
GARAGE
THEATER
BARR
NYC
Cafe
1910
EAT
T. SLAUGHTER 95

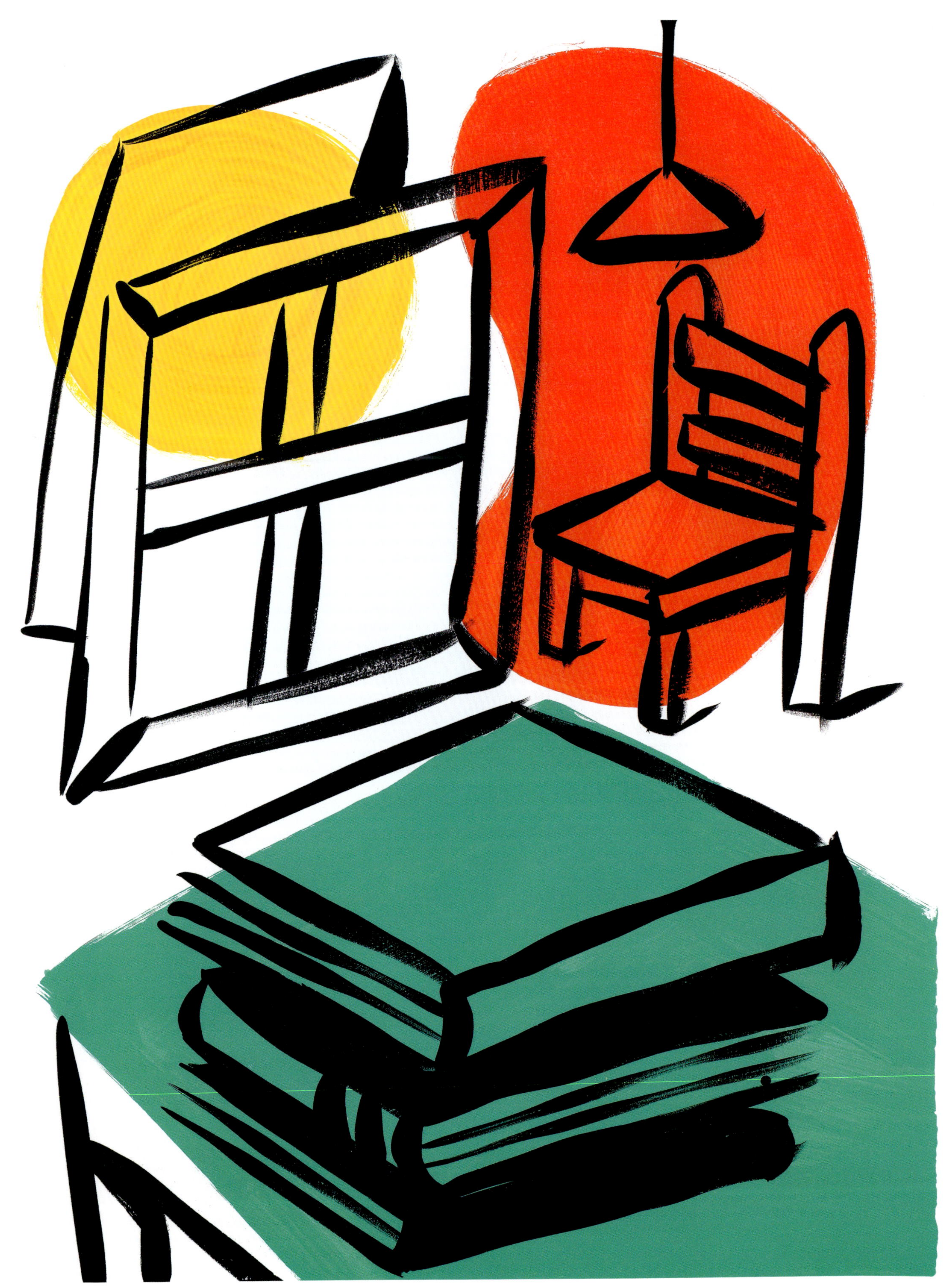

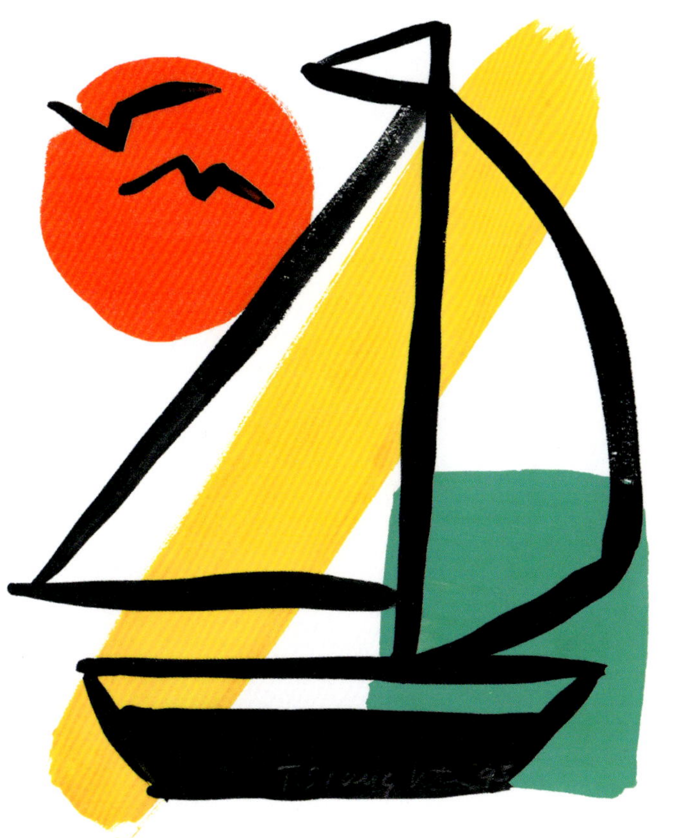

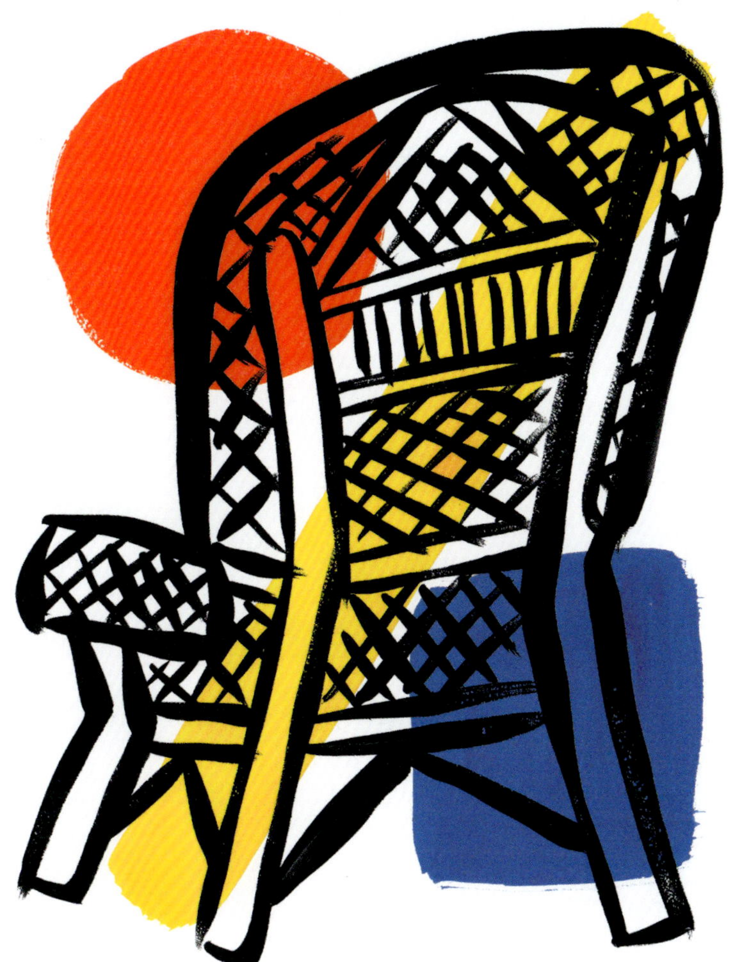

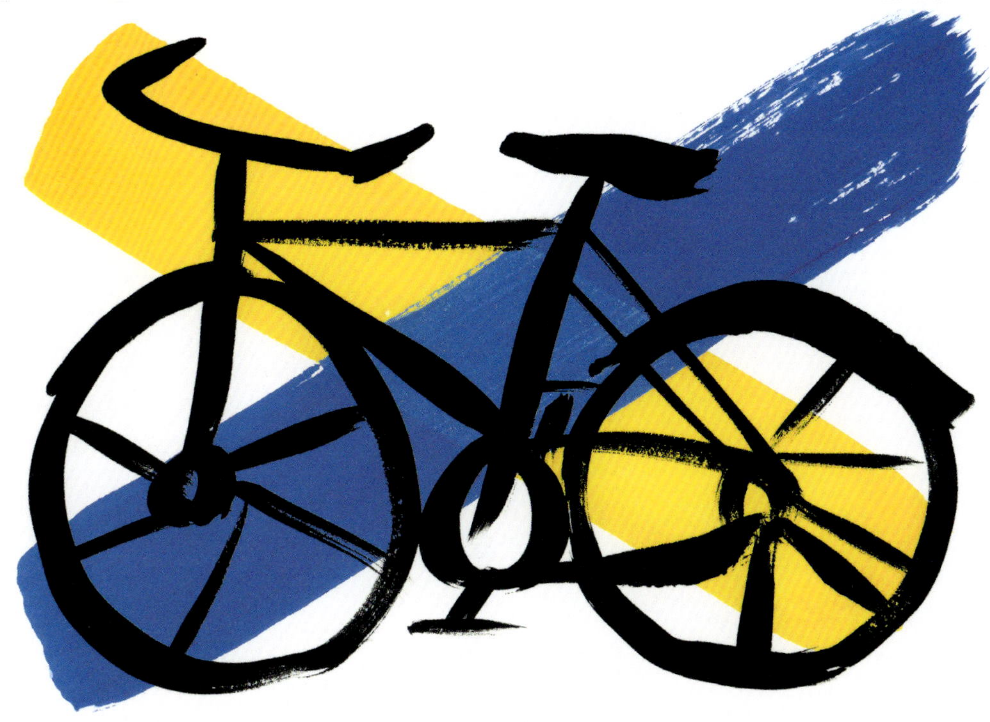

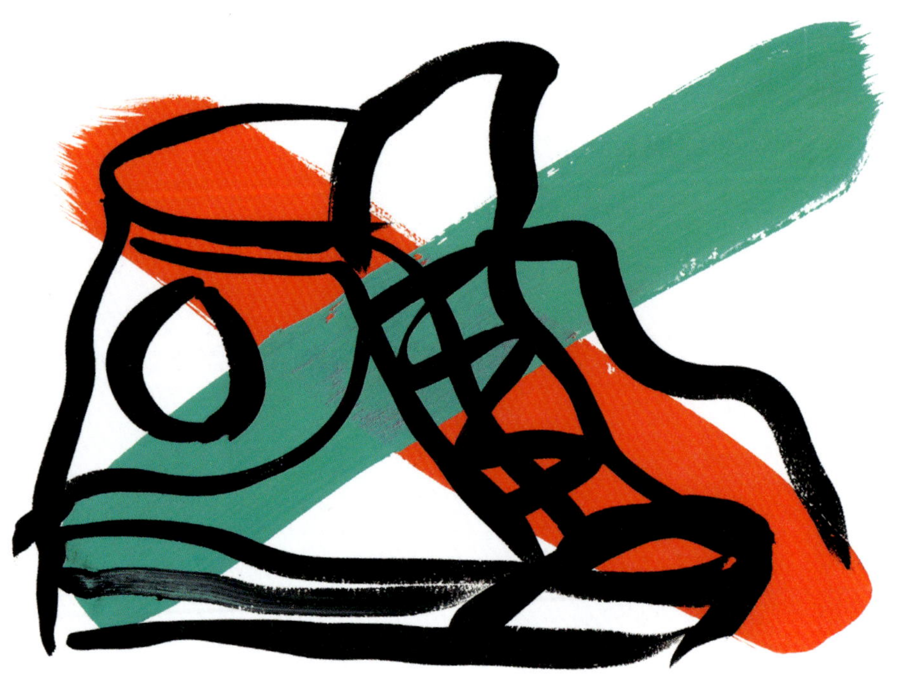

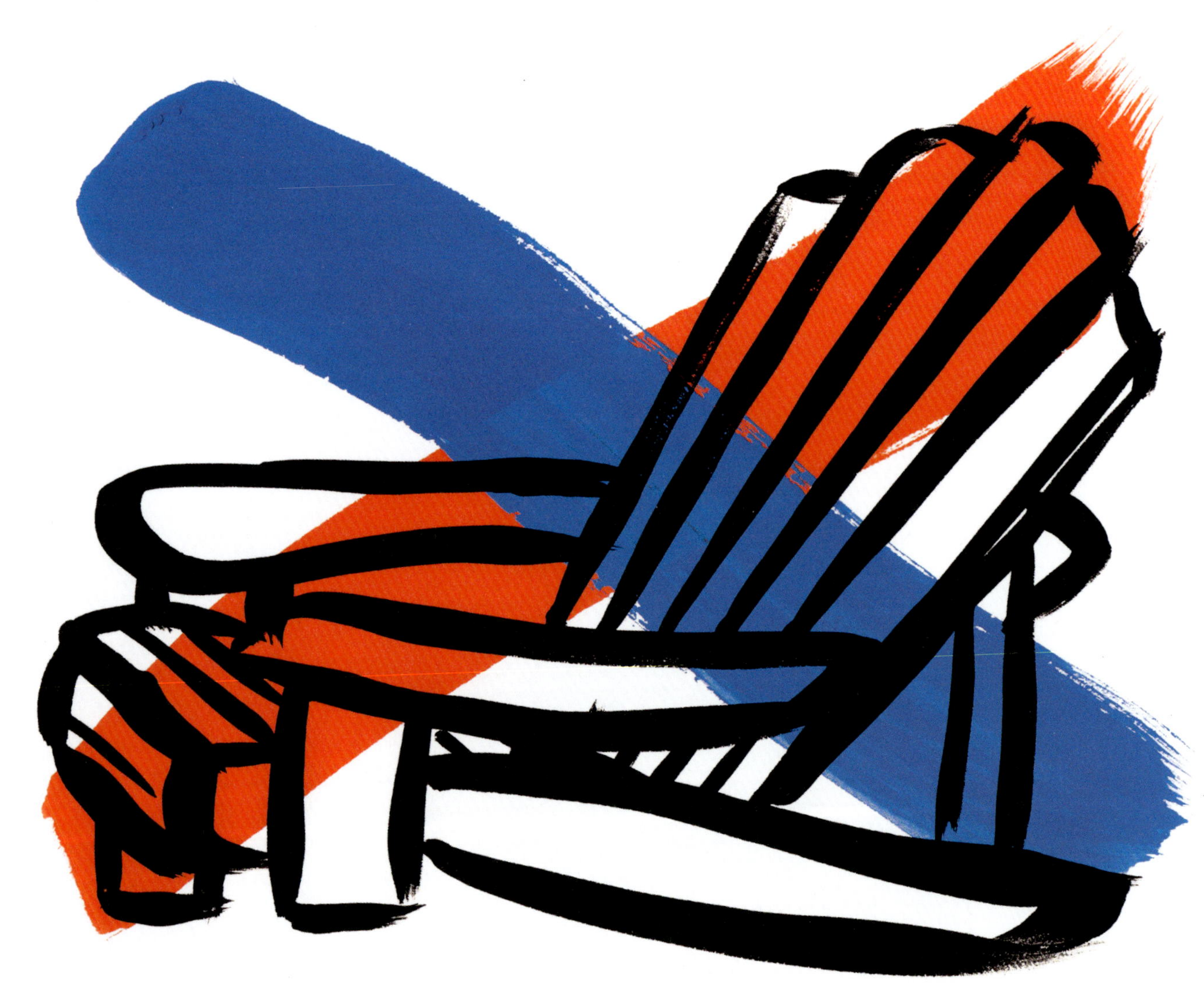

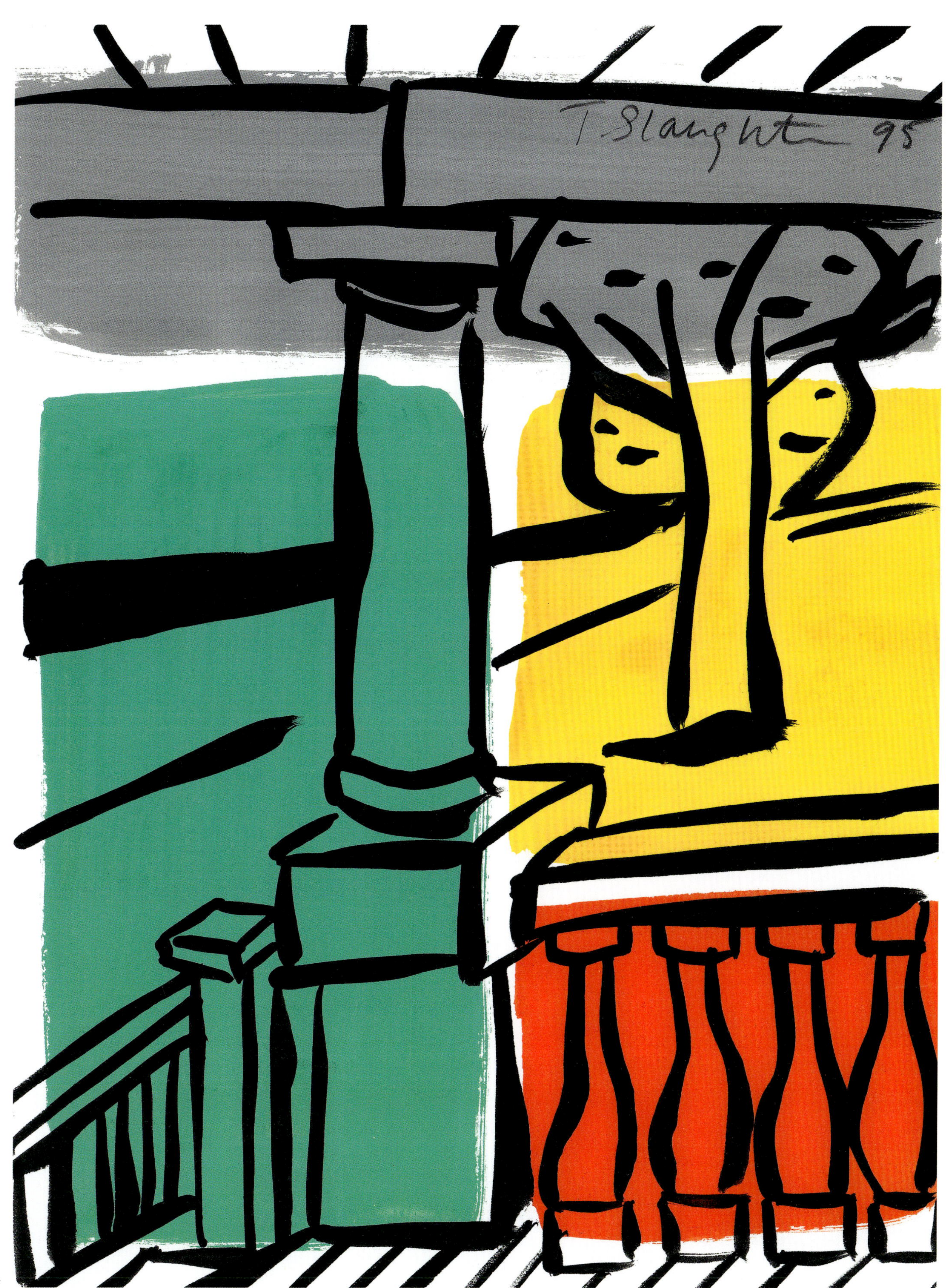

T Slaughter 95

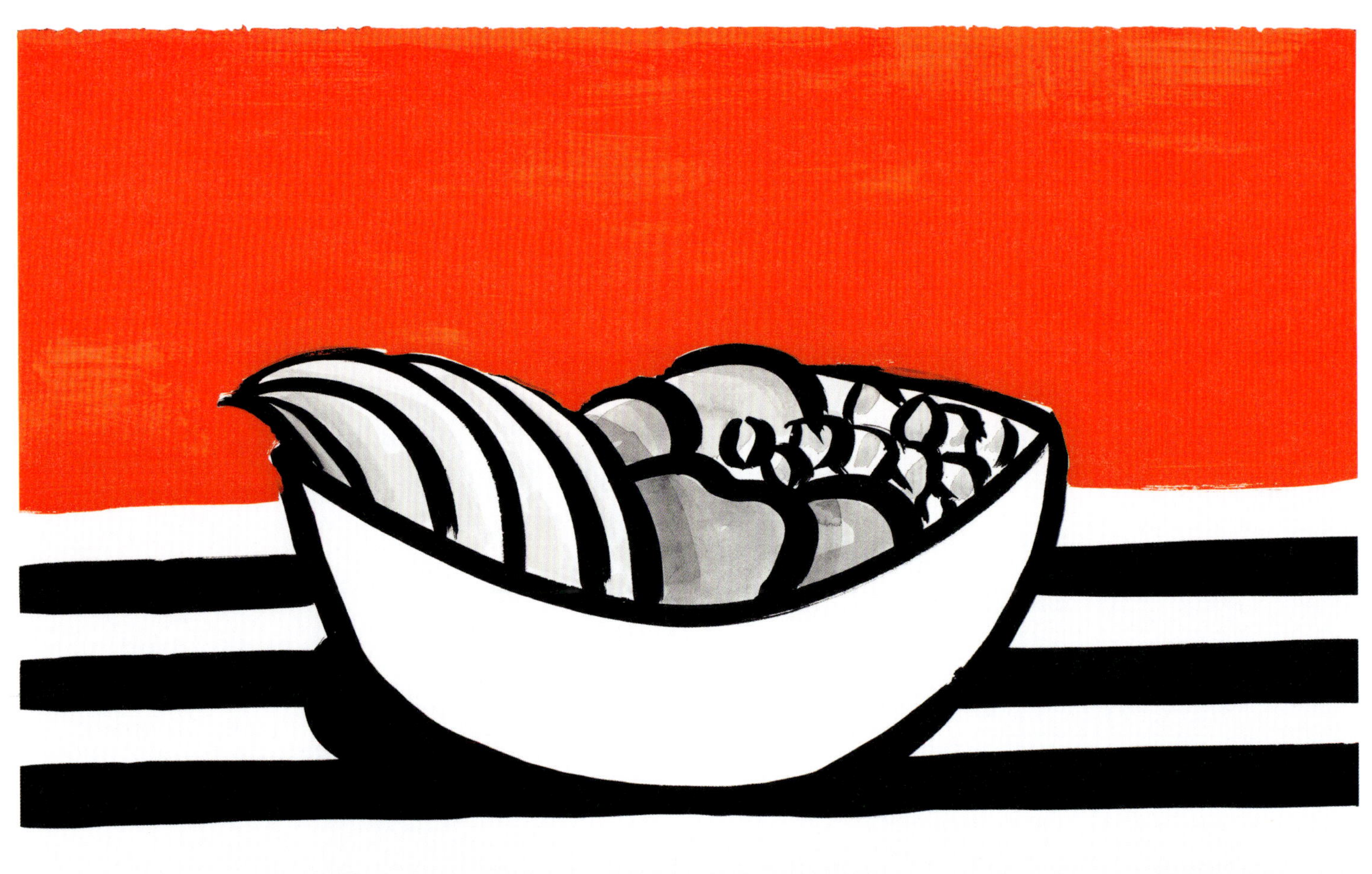

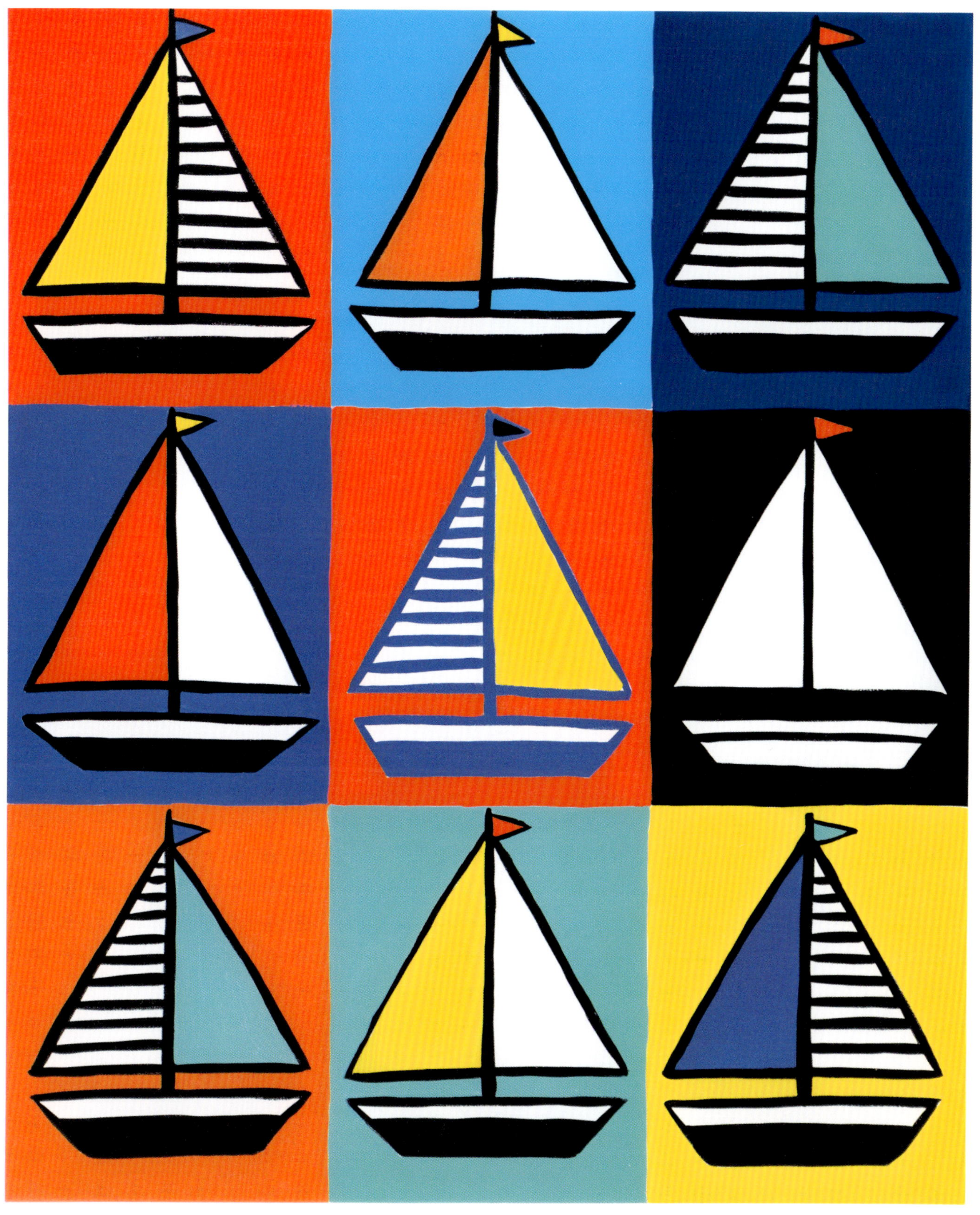

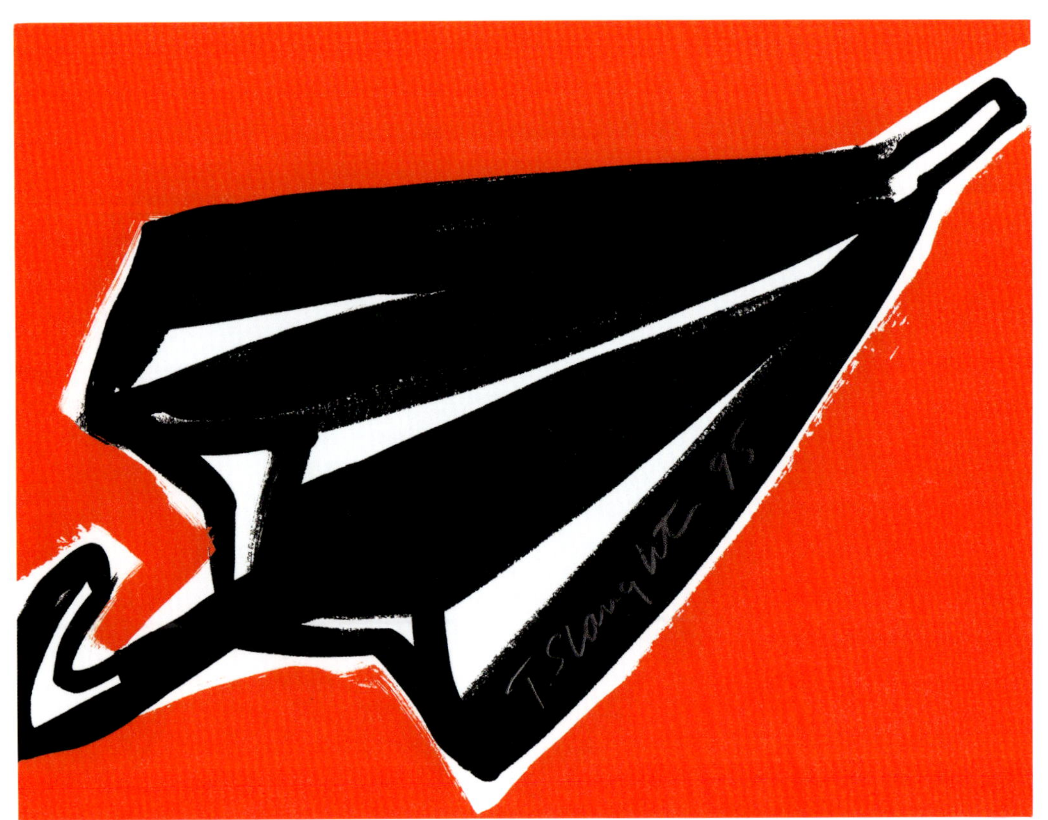
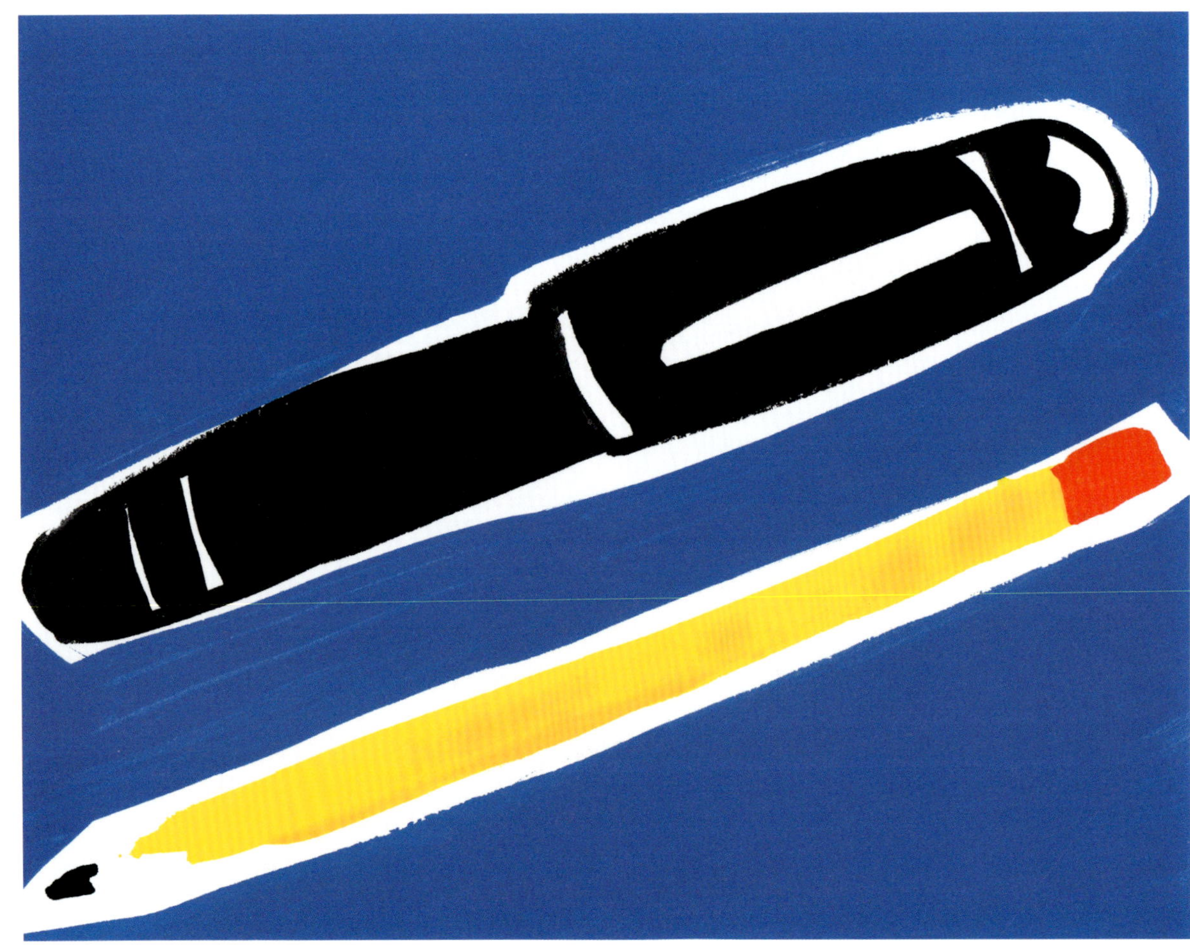

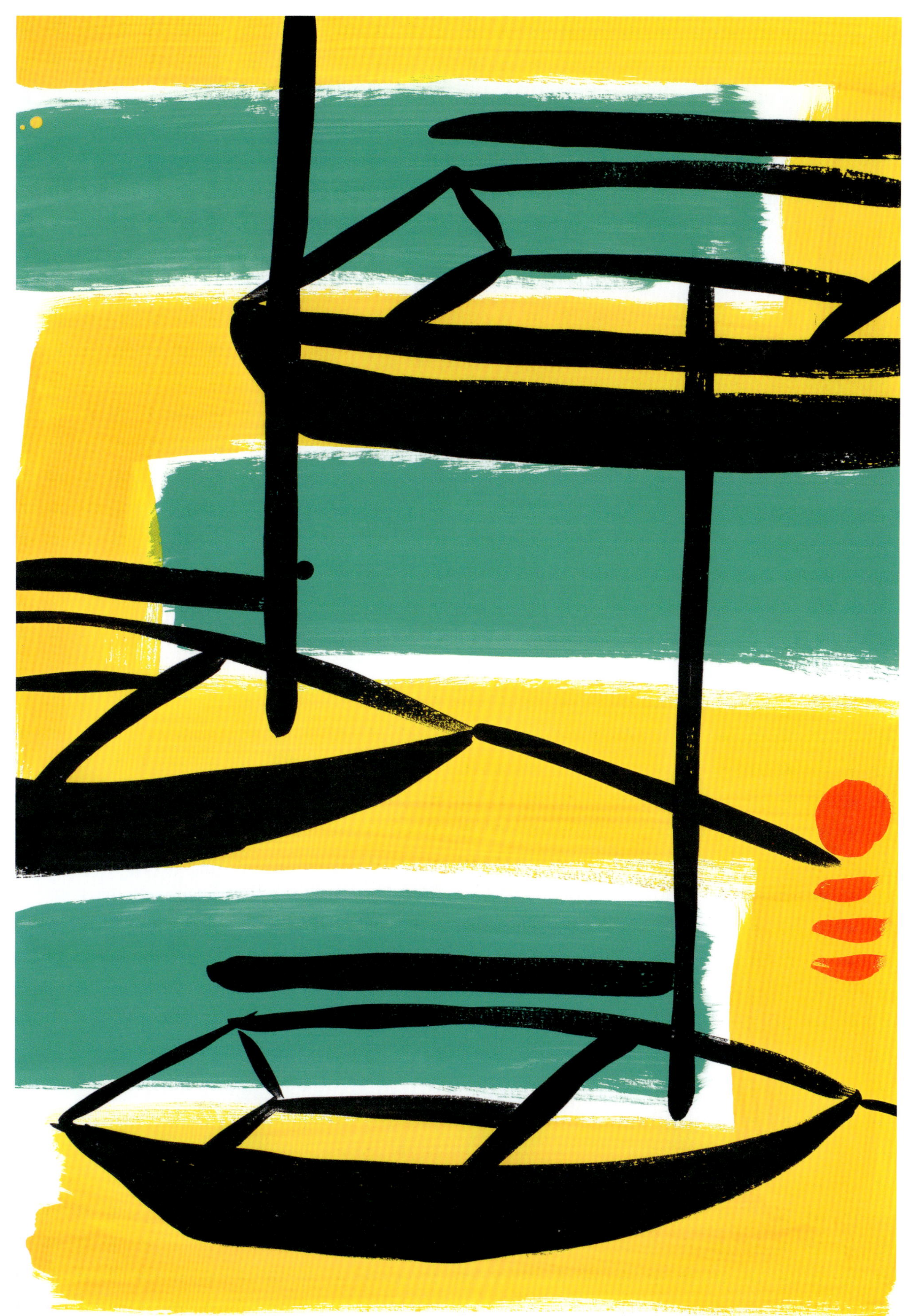

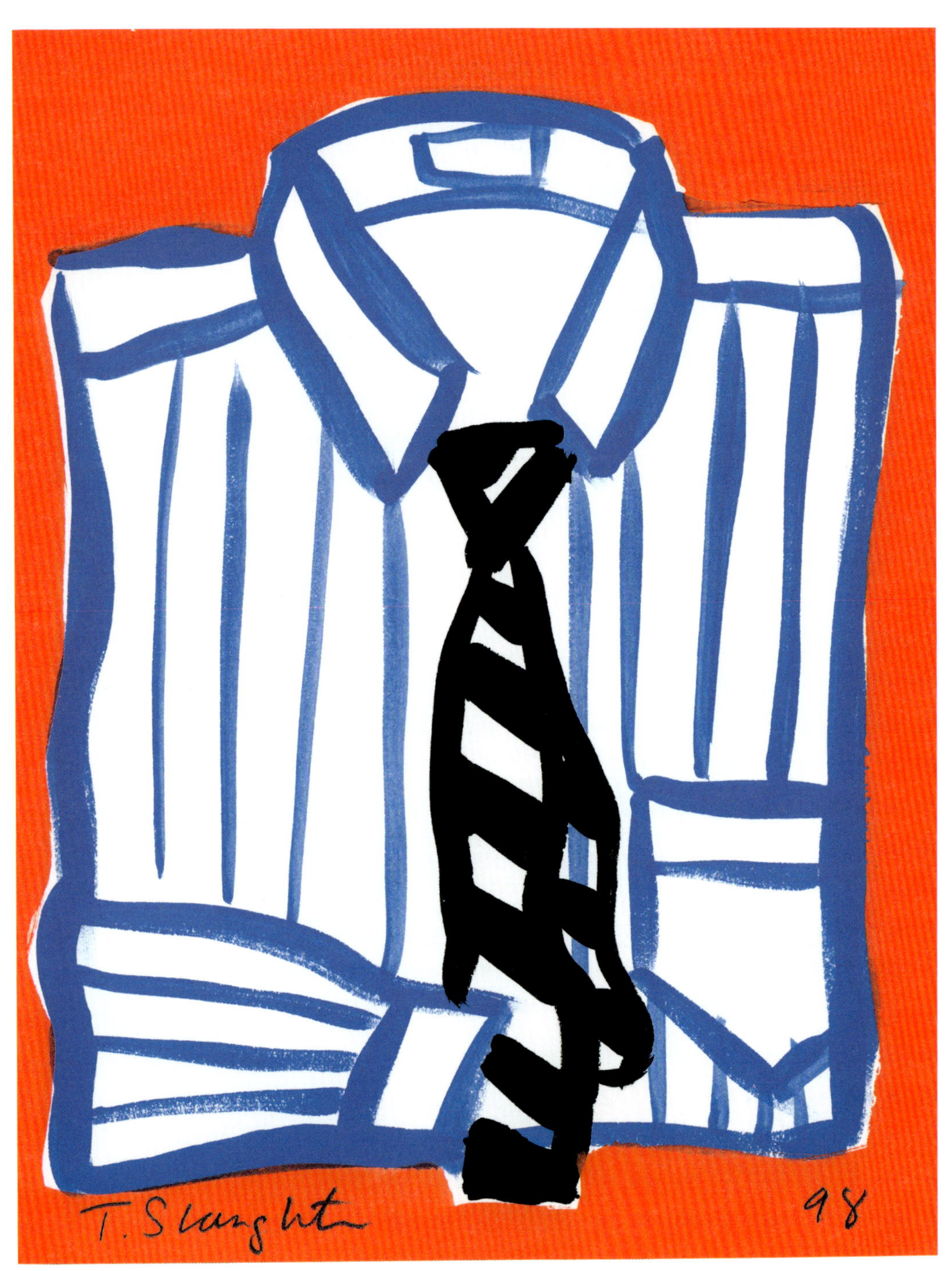
T. Slaughter
98

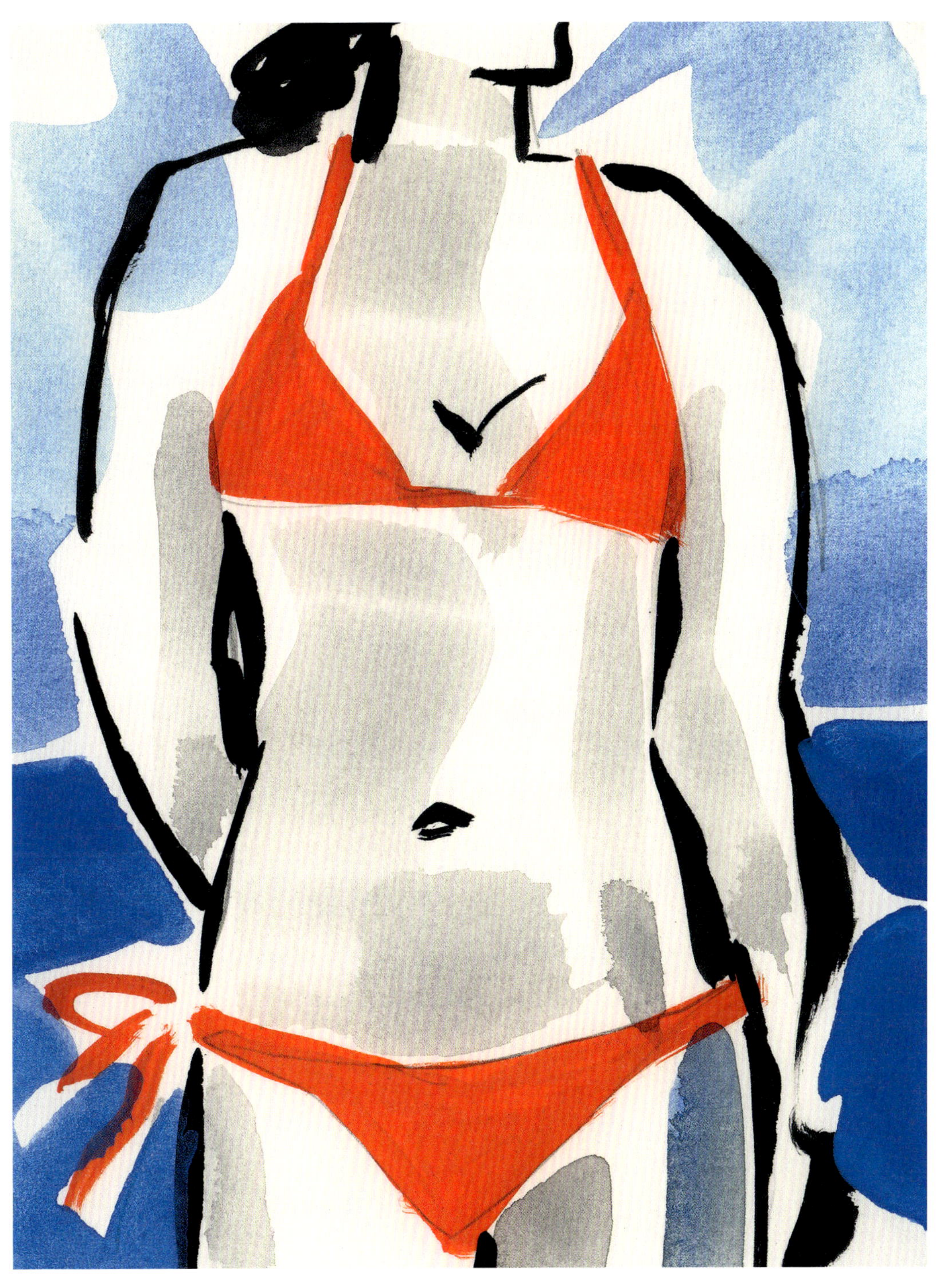

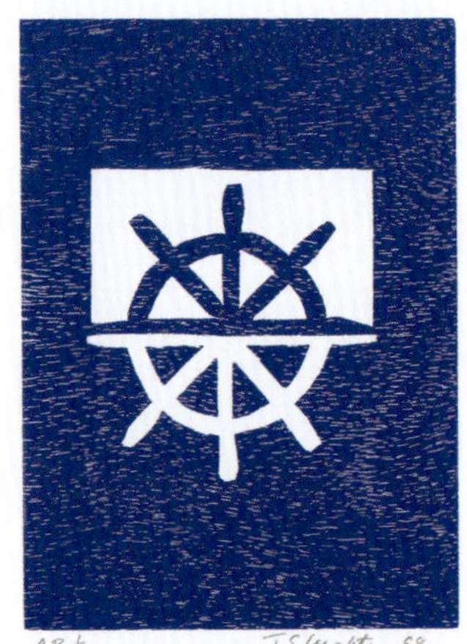

AP 4/7   T. Slaughter 98

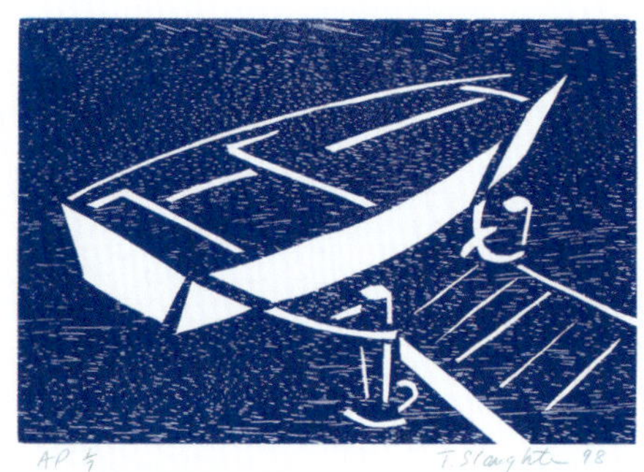

AP 4/7   T. Slaughter 98

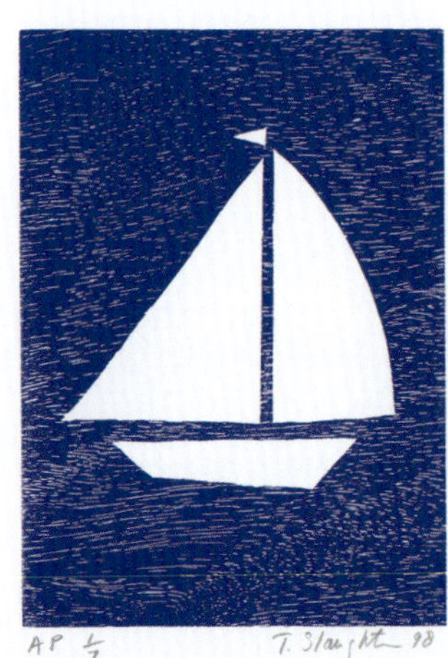

AP 4/7   T. Slaughter 98

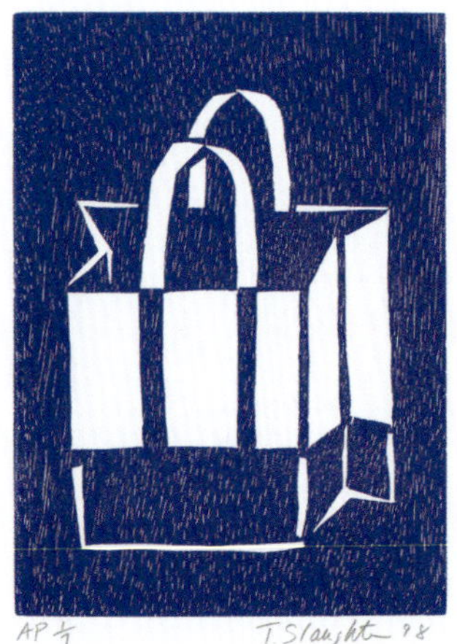

AP 4/7   T. Slaughter 98

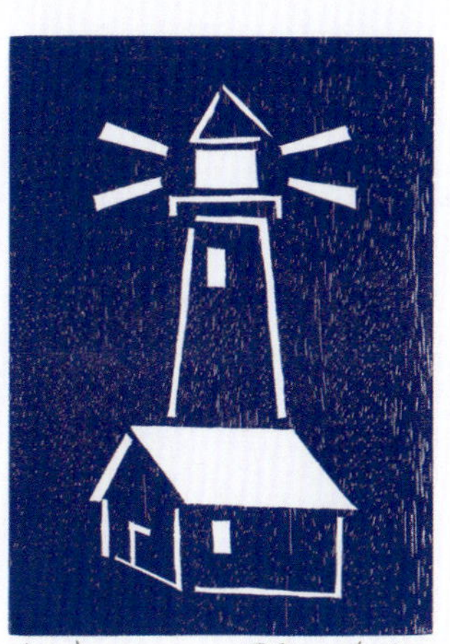

AP 1/7
T. Slaughter 98

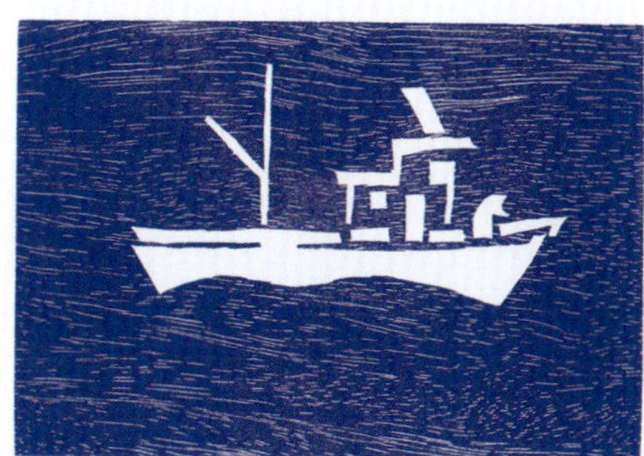

AP 1/7
T. Slaughter 98

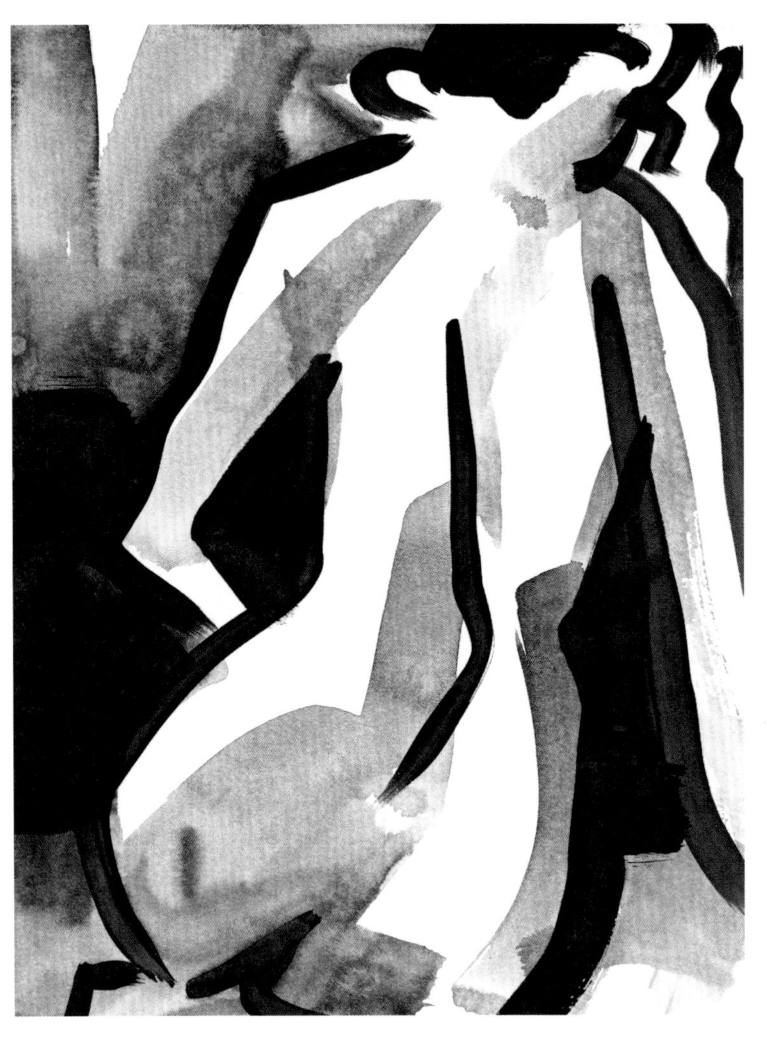

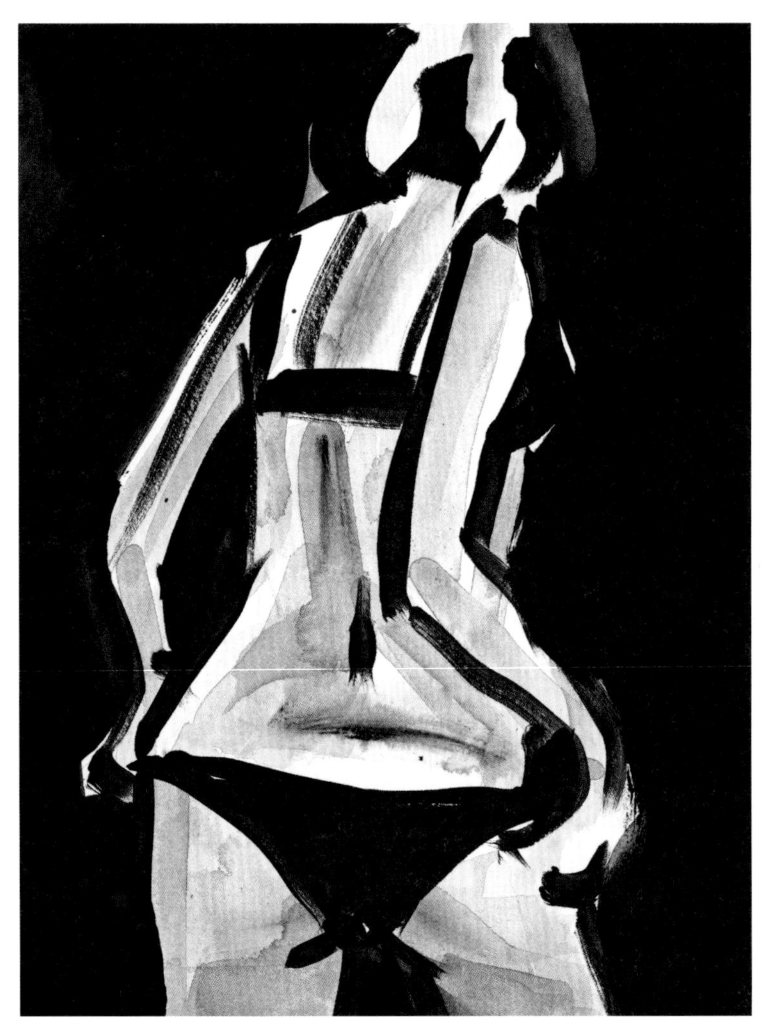

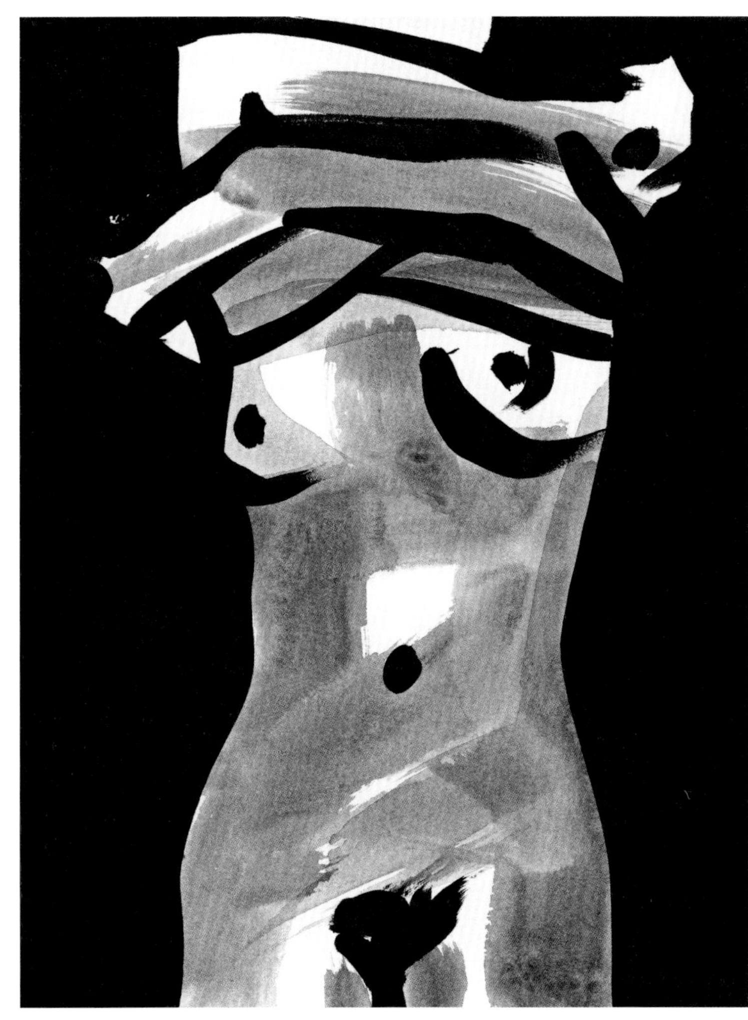

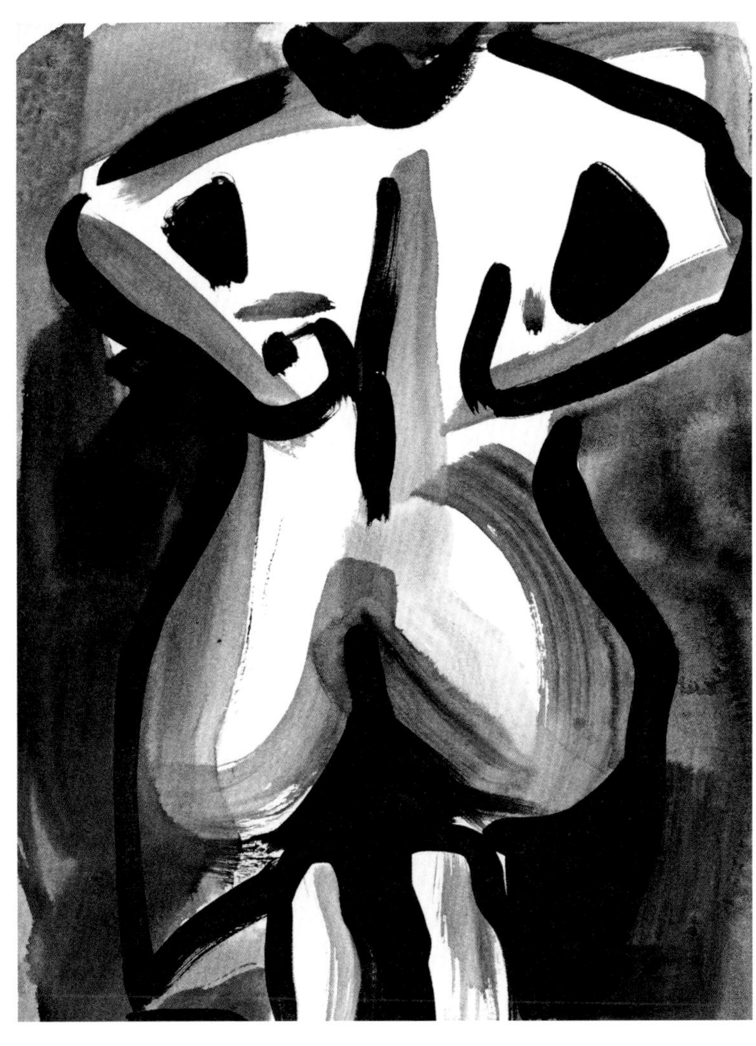

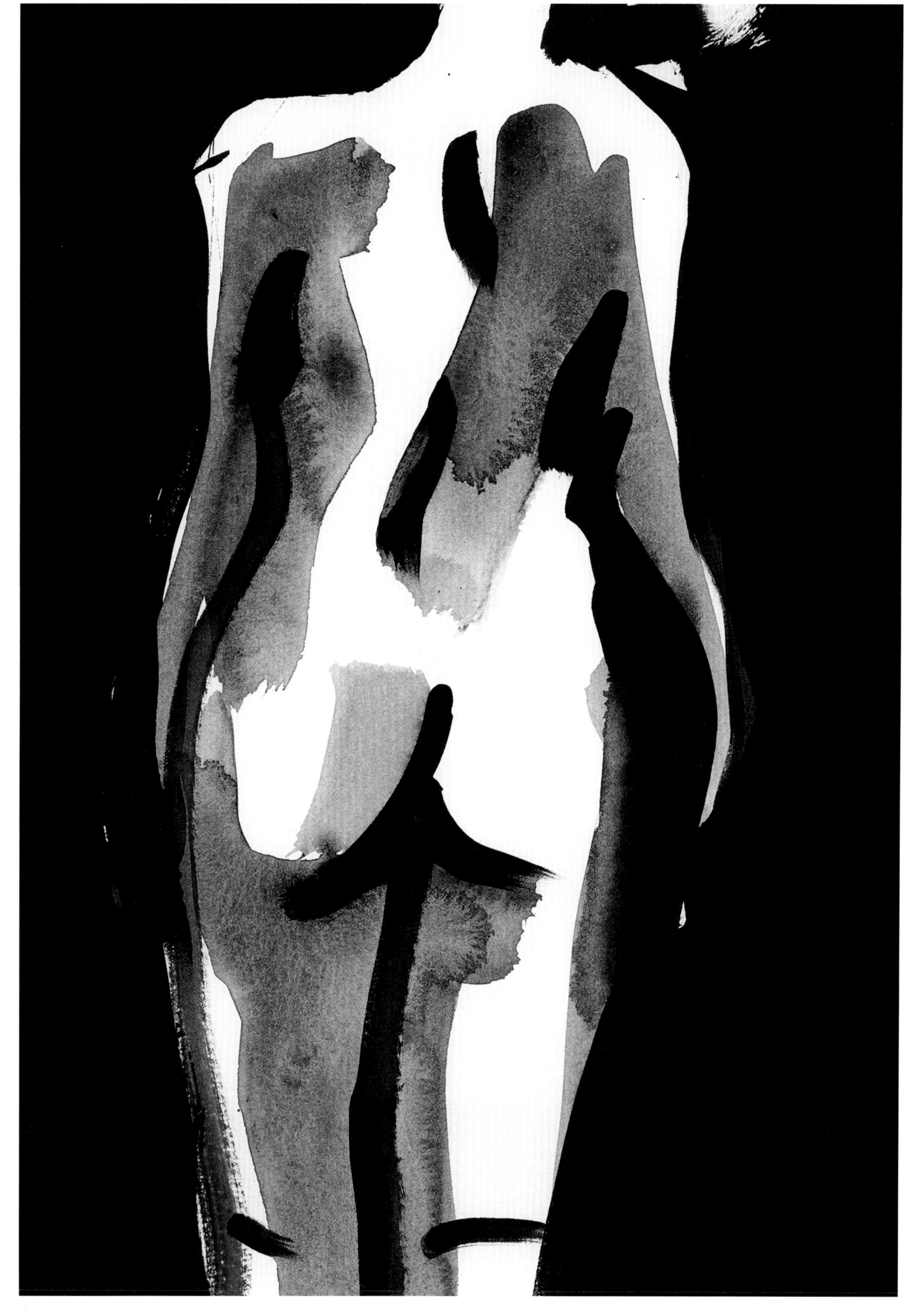

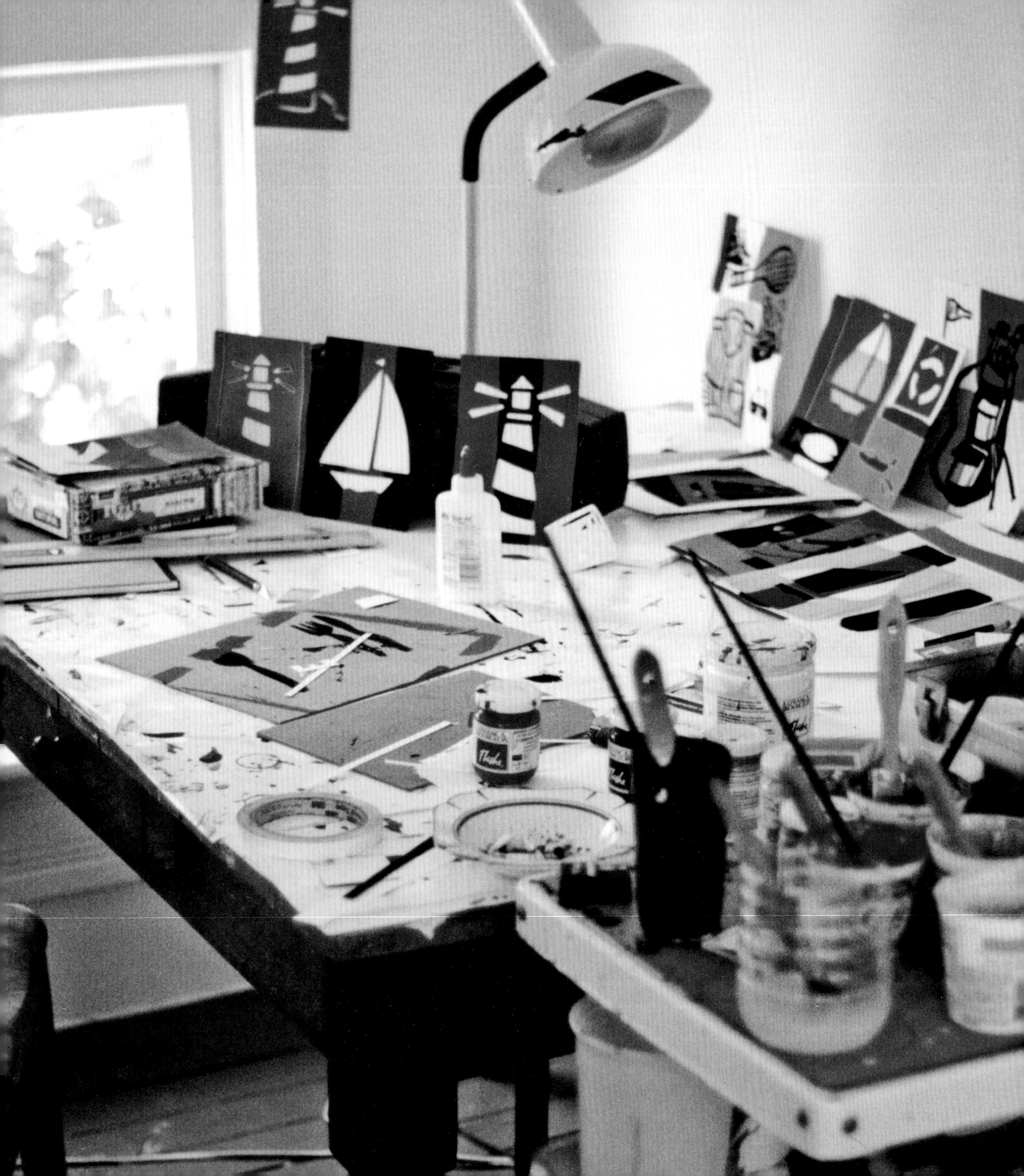

EVERY SUMMER

Looking at Tom's ten picture books all together, a reader sees exactly what Tom set out to create—a gorgeous body of work that is smart, playful, and instantly recognizable as being his.

Our loft on Broadway was twenty blocks from the World Trade Center with an unimpeded view from the fire escape. We watched together on September 11th, 2001, as the towers fell. Weirdly enough, this led fairly directly to Tom making his first picture book. In an attempt to see the world from a different vantage point, we spent the following year in Stratford, Ontario, where both girls had been born and where we visited every summer.

Far from New York City, Tom needed diversion. He threw himself into making a counting book. He had an old table in the attic beside north-facing windows. His method was simple, Matissean. He painted paper in solid colors of gouache. He cut the paper into shapes, usually with an X-Acto blade instead of scissors. After many variations, he glued the cut pieces down. Some of the images for *123* were already part of Tom's iconography. For others, like the beach balls, he drew inspiration from beloved illustrator heroes like Dick Bruna. My only contribution was to recognize Tom's unconscious numeric layers in the early pages and urge him to continue with that. One apple missing one bite. Two pairs of glasses, each with two lenses. Three sailboats sporting three sails, and so on.

Tom liked the idea of creating "legacy" images, to be taken from one book and re-used in the next, creating a brand for himself as an illustrator, and exciting familiarity in the child reader. He had a line rattling around in his head: "One, some, many. Hardly any." On a park bench one afternoon before a matinee, I started with those words and wrote the rest of our first collaboration. "Two, a few, a few is more than two. . . ." Almost simultaneously, we made the next book, about opposites. Echoing *One Some Many*, the opening lines of *Over Under* are "Big. Small. Not at all." Alongside the reliable balls and sailboats, he made seals, an owl, and a rooster for the first time.

Meanwhile, Tom had created a complicated silk-screened alphabet print and was keen to recycle some of that work. We came up with a clever spin, choosing objects that began with the same letter in English, French, and Spanish! "A" was easy: airplane, avion, aeroplan. "B" was done; we already had balls. We inched our way through to the hard ones: J, K, Q, X, and Y. He found an etching of a kiwi in an old nature book and purloined the silhouette. But quetzal? "What the hell is a quetzal?" The only "Q" noun to appear in all three languages. *ABC x 3* includes a quetzal.

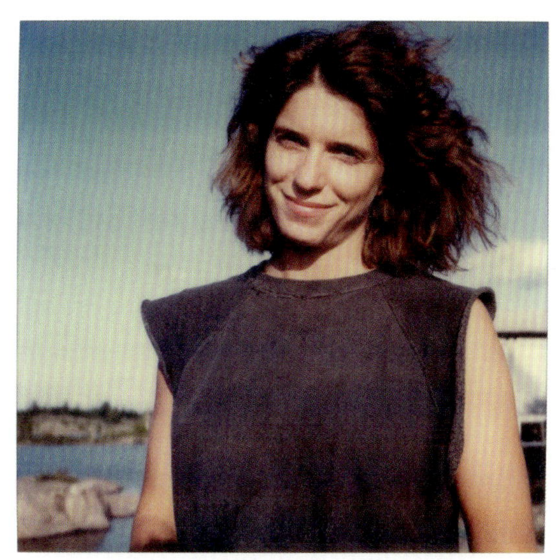

Marthe Jocelyn

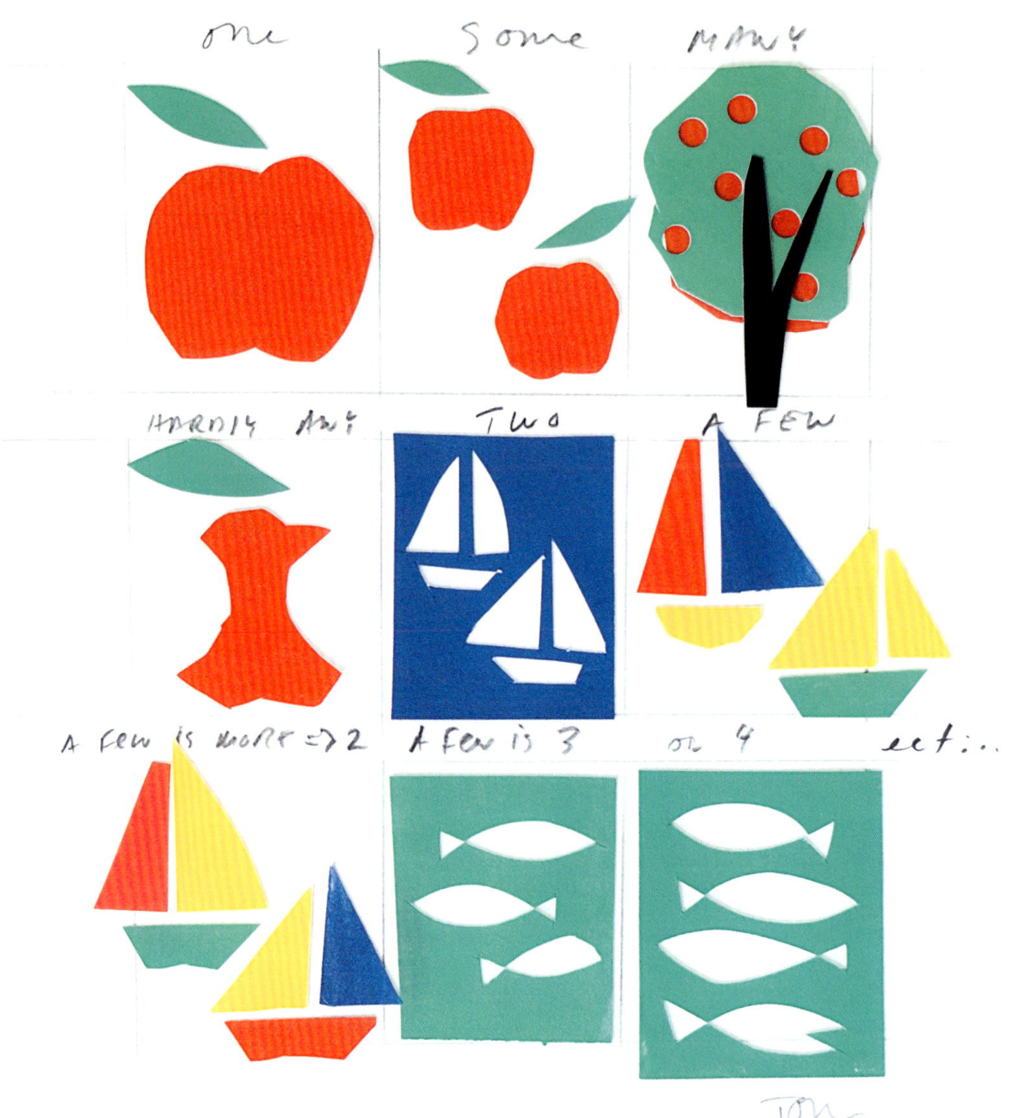

one
Some
MANY
HARDLY ANY
TWO
A FEW
A few is more =>2
A few is 3
or 4
ect...
Ton

EATS was conceived to showcase the growing gallery of animals, and where
Tom introduced a subtle visual narrative; a delicate screen of bamboo for
the panda, a parade of tiny ants about to be devoured by the anteater.
In the opening sequence, a worm eats an apple, and then a bird eats a worm.
We stopped before bumping into the problem of showing a cat eating a bird
and perhaps a pit bull eating a cat. But we liked the idea of something on one
spread being redefined after the page turn. *Same Same* inspires a child's early
understanding of classification, and is my favorite of the books that Tom and I
made together. The publicity tagline was, "A first concept book. A first art book."
The illustrations in a picture book are a child's first exposure to art, and Tom's
work is particularly accessible.

Our final collaboration happened during and after the end of our marriage.
Which Way? asks questions about where to go and how to get there, perhaps
symbolic of decisions we were making after so many years together. Tom, for the
first time, created actual scenery, as well as a compass, lots of traffic signs, and
one of his earliest maps—soon to be a favorite motif in his bigger collages.

Moving to Blue Apple Books, Tom was assigned a debut text by author
Susan A. Shea called *Do You Know Which Ones Will Grow?* This gorgeous
lift-the-flap book required precision, inventiveness, and even a recurring human
character—something he'd previously avoided. The cover announces "paintings
by Tom Slaughter," celebrating his visible brushwork and mastery of the page.

Boat Works is Tom's second solo picture book, a culmination of his love for
nautical images and happily including versions of knots made from thick rope,
like the bracelets he'd worn all his life.

Tom's final picture book is *What Is Part This, Part That?* by Harriet Zeifert.
The illustrations blend relaxed and playful new imagery with his traditional
bold style, reflecting highlights from his early career. The bowl of fruit,
for instance, is a nostalgic echo of Tom's very first still-life paintings—inspired
by Roy Lichtenstein—and nearly identical in composition to the originals. The
taxi, the teapot, the anchor, the fish, the boats—all are familiar, yet refreshed
icons in the Slaughter vocabulary.

Tom was the ideal artist to illustrate for children. Vibrant color, simple shapes,
noisy, irregular, and charming. I am so lucky to have been part of the process.
We are all so lucky to have his books.

Marthe Jocelyn

Author and illustrator

Stratford, ON

2018

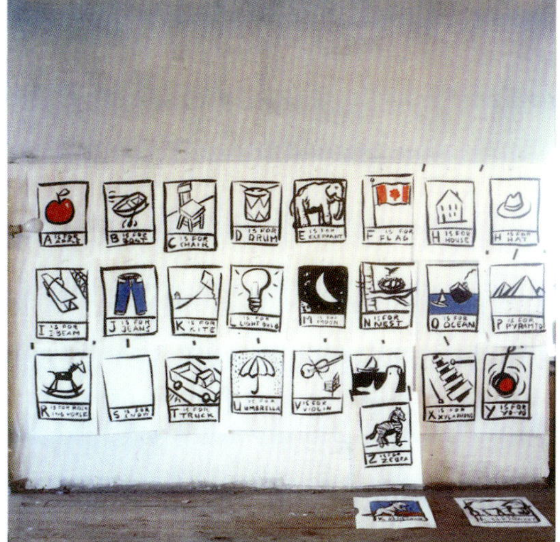

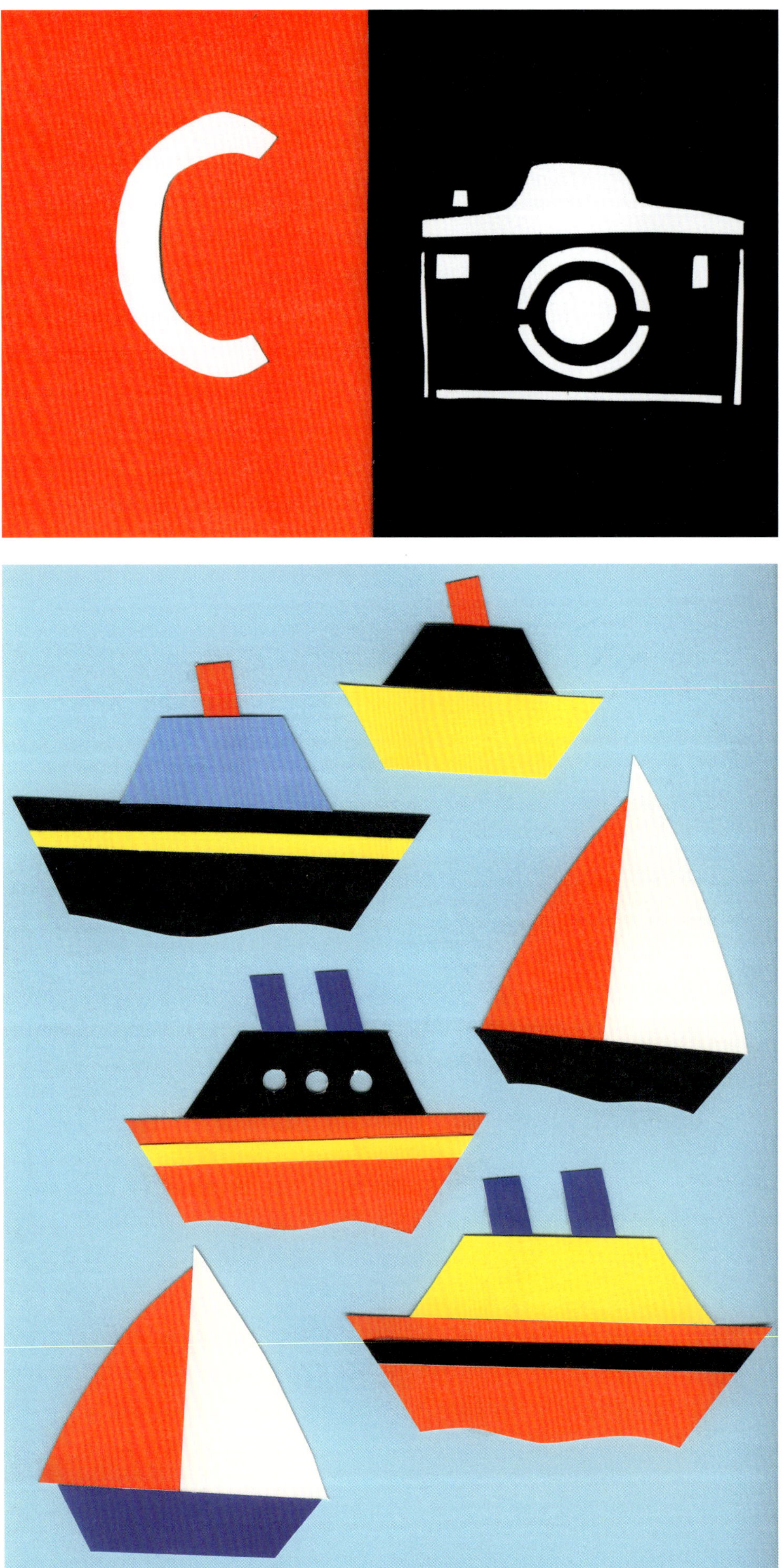

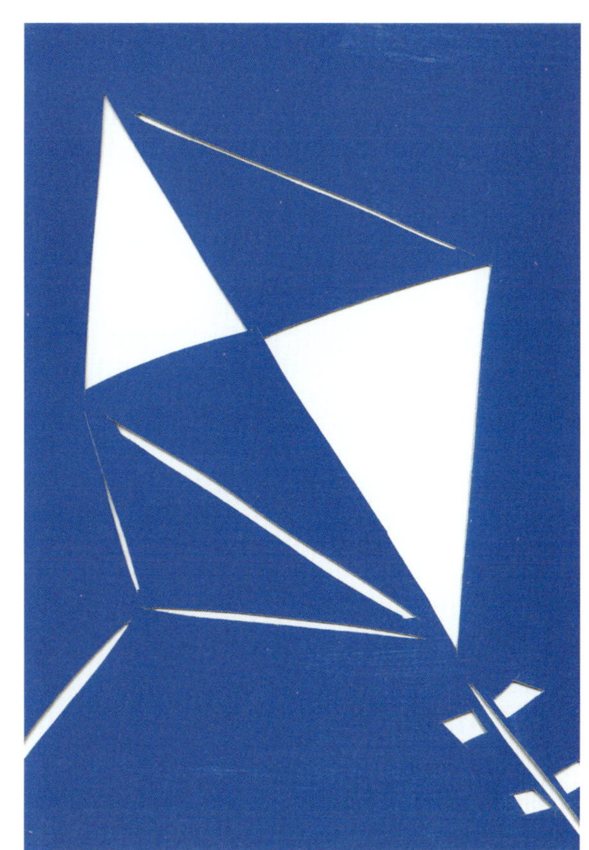

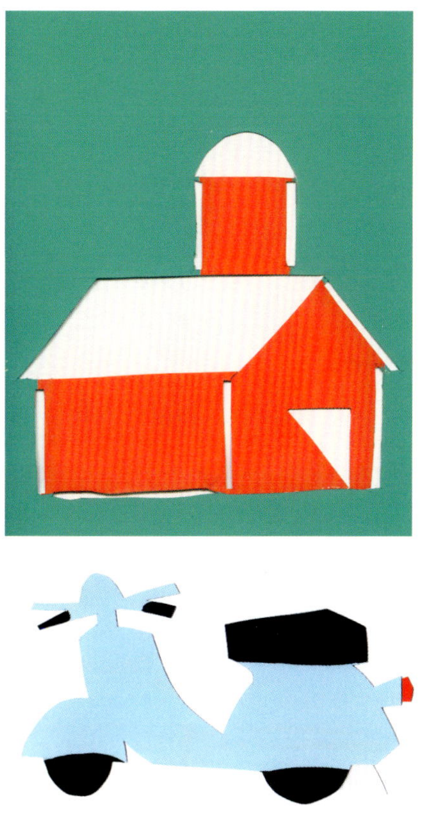

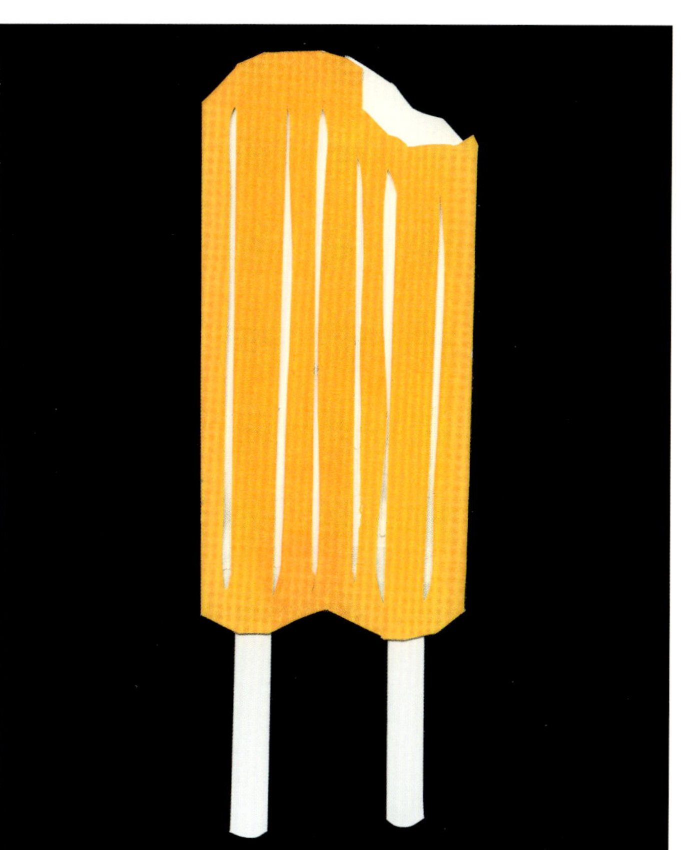

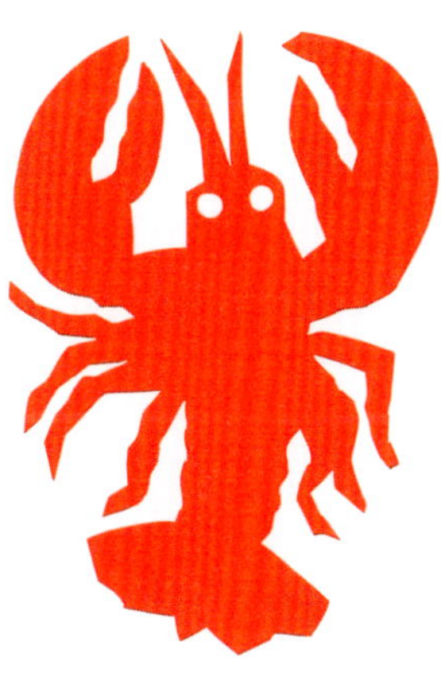

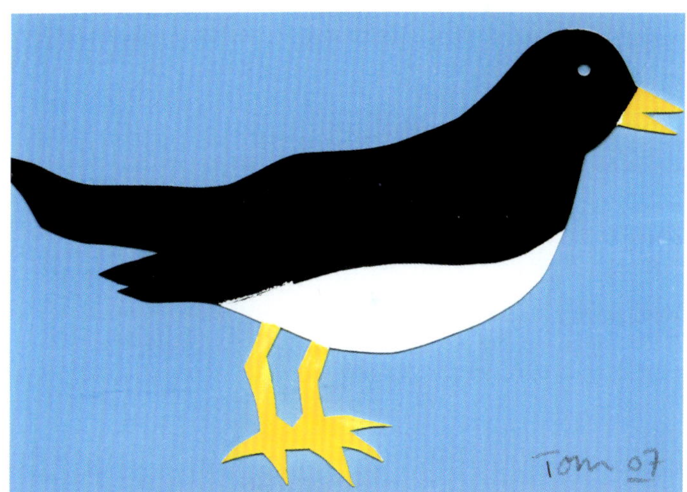
Tom 07

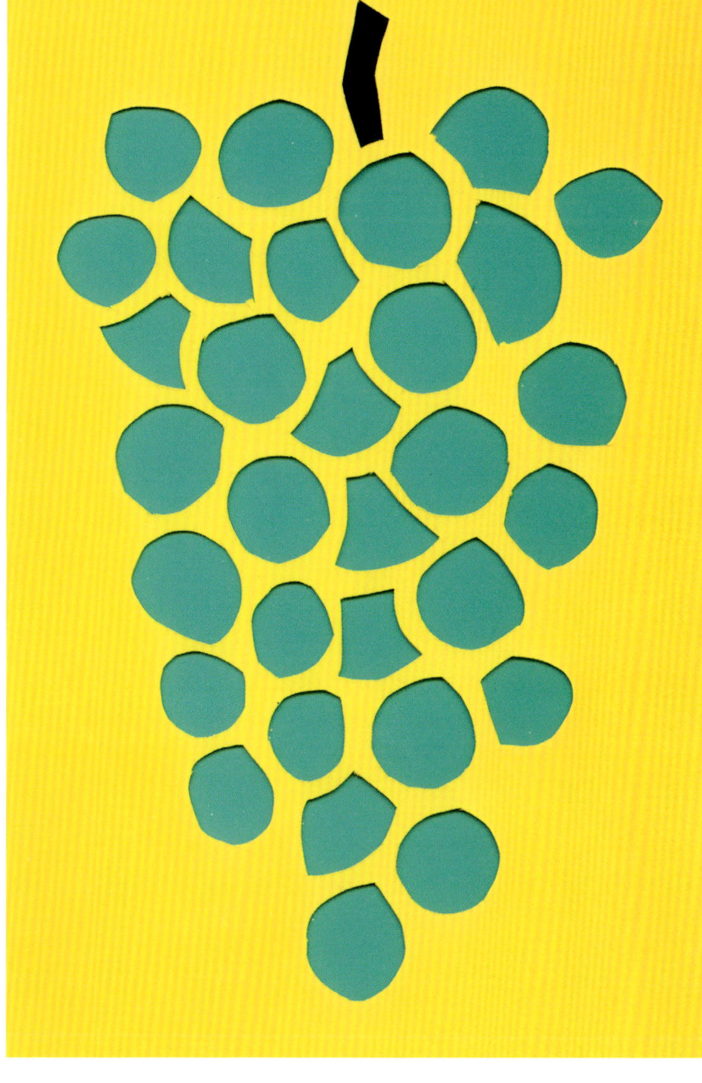

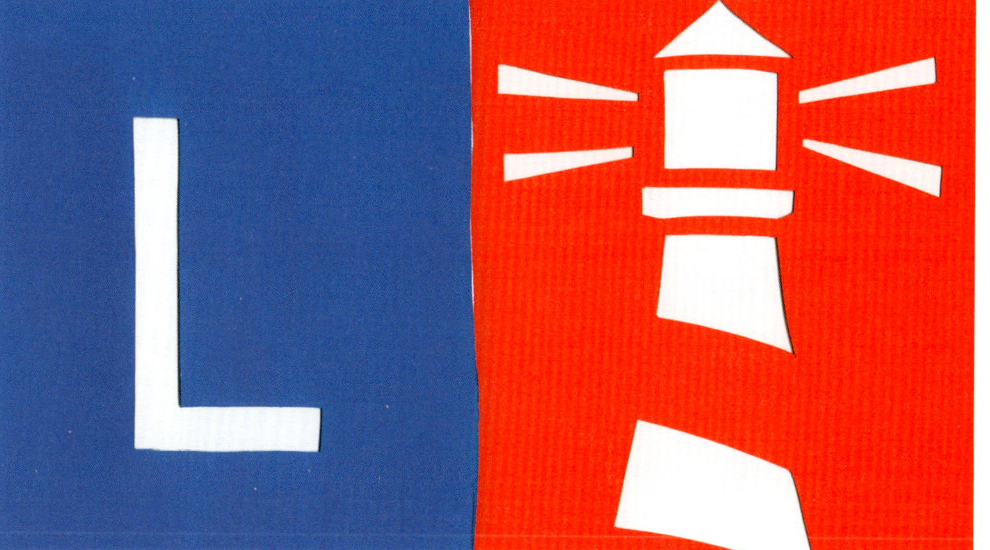
L

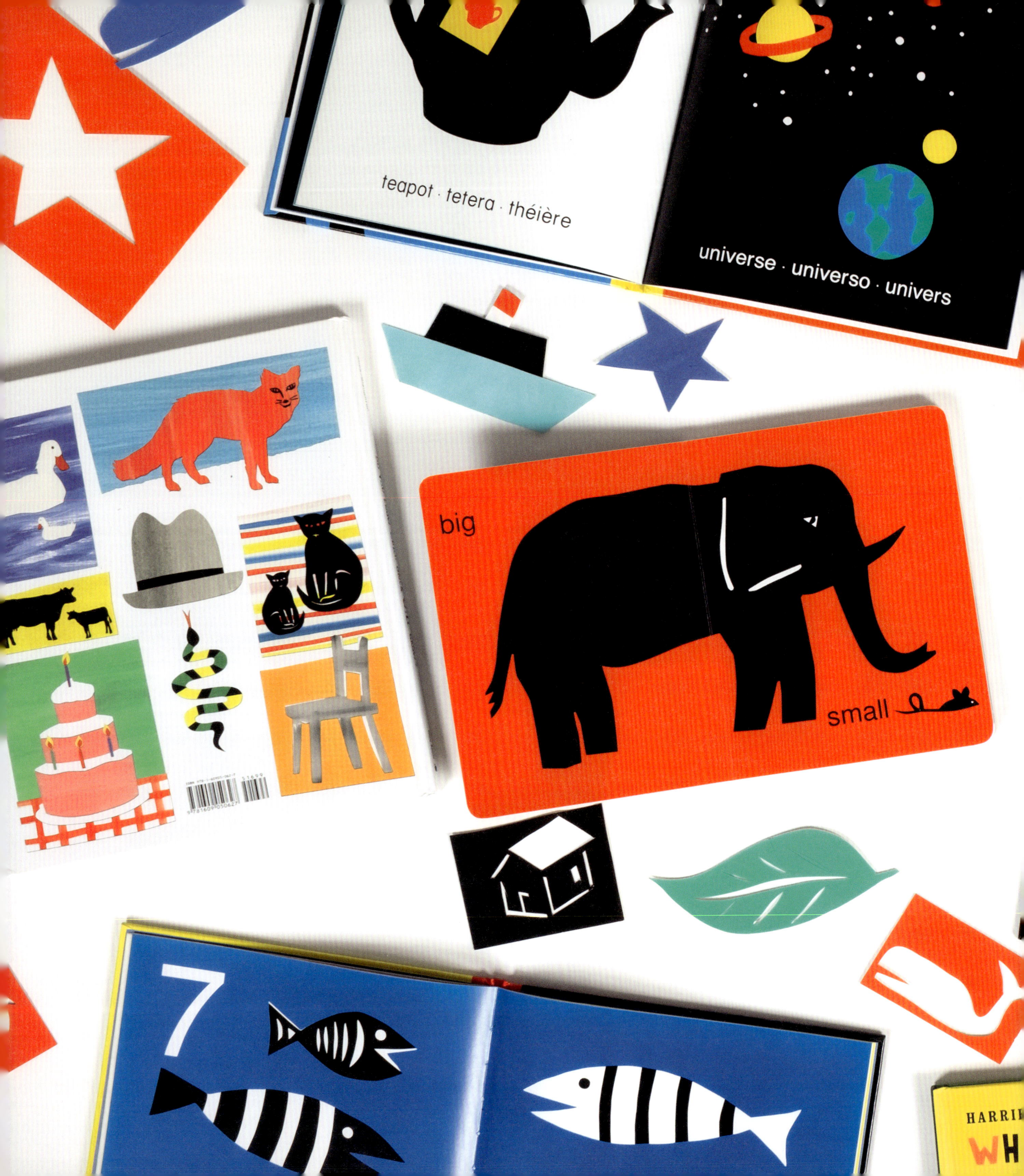

teapot · tetera · théière
universe · universo · univers
big
small
7
HARRI
WH

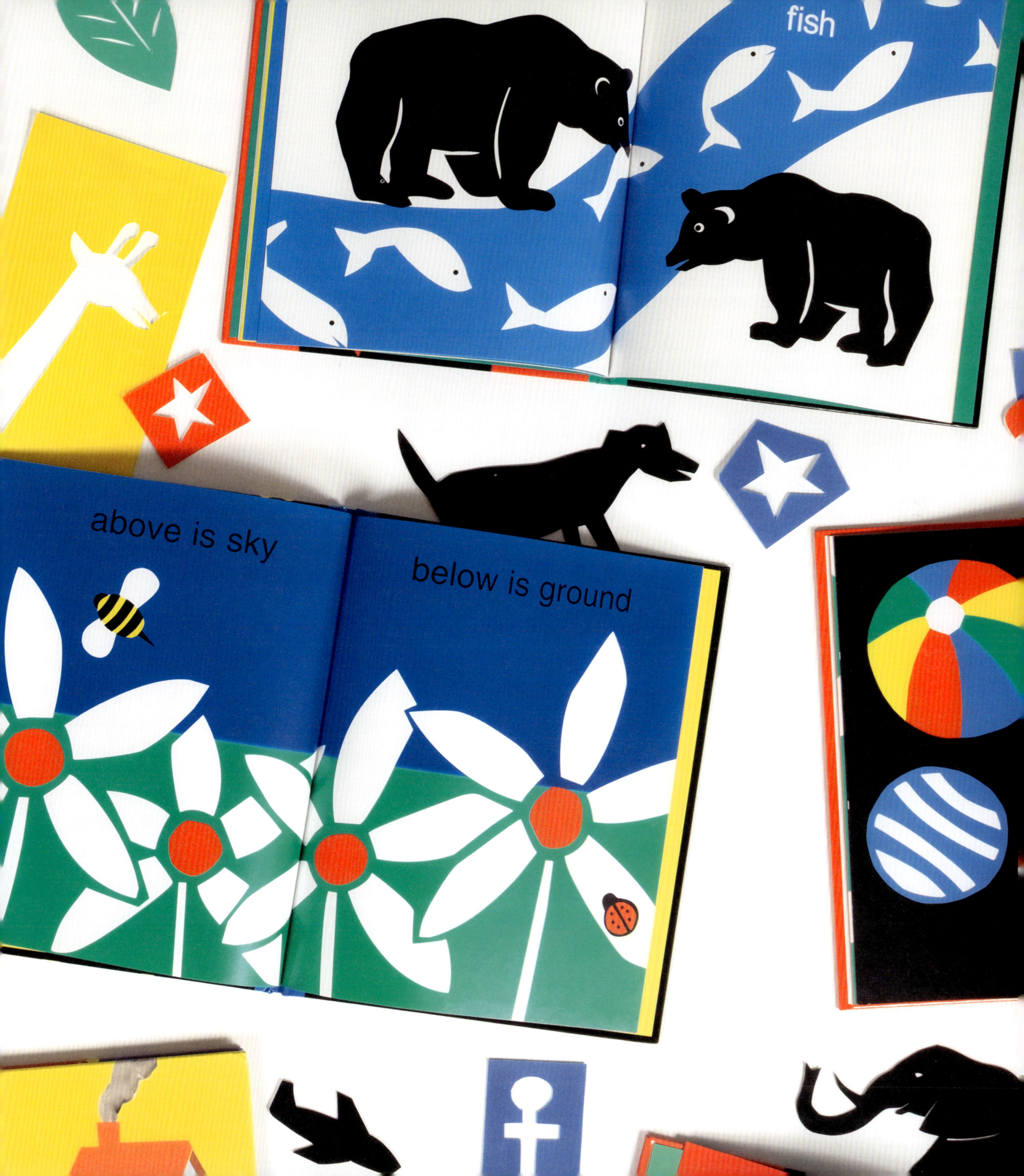

fish
above is sky
below is ground

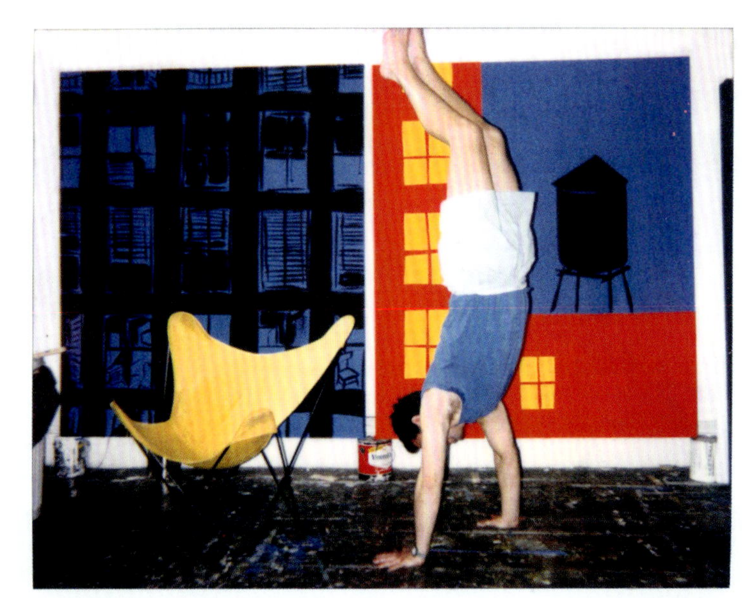

Tom could charm men, women, and children as easily as he could paint a sailboat or a pair of flip-flops or a New York skyline. The charm was innate, as was his artistic talent. Picasso said it took him four years to paint like Raphael but a lifetime to paint like a child. Luckily for us, Tom never lost that childlike innocence.

Jim Kempner

Gallery owner and art dealer

New York, NY

2017

1998—2006

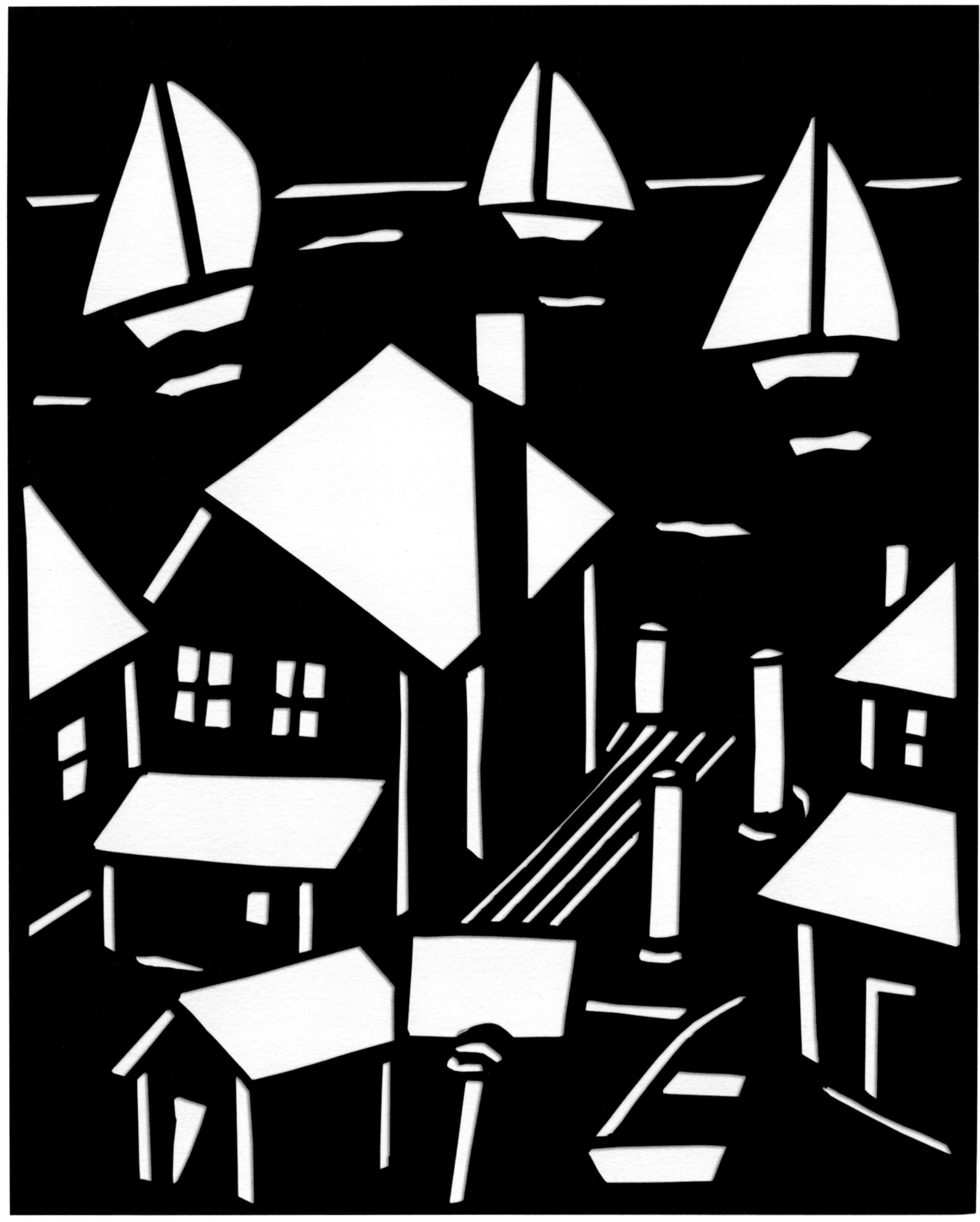

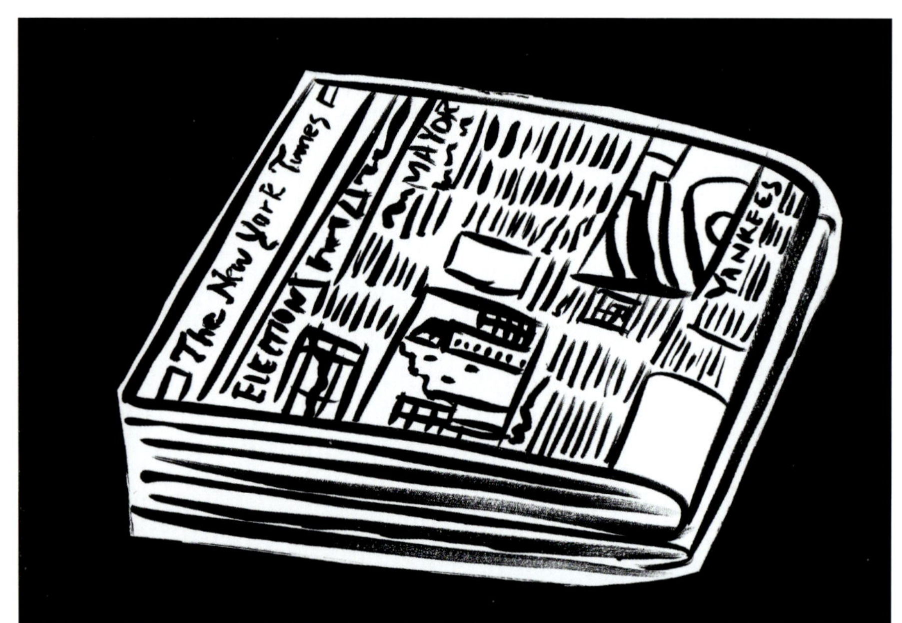

The New York Times
ELECTION
MAYOR
YANKEES

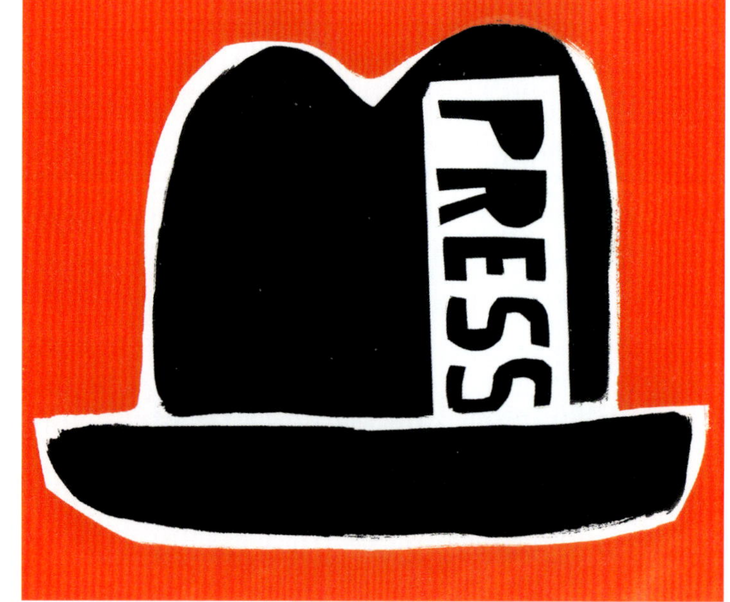

PRESS

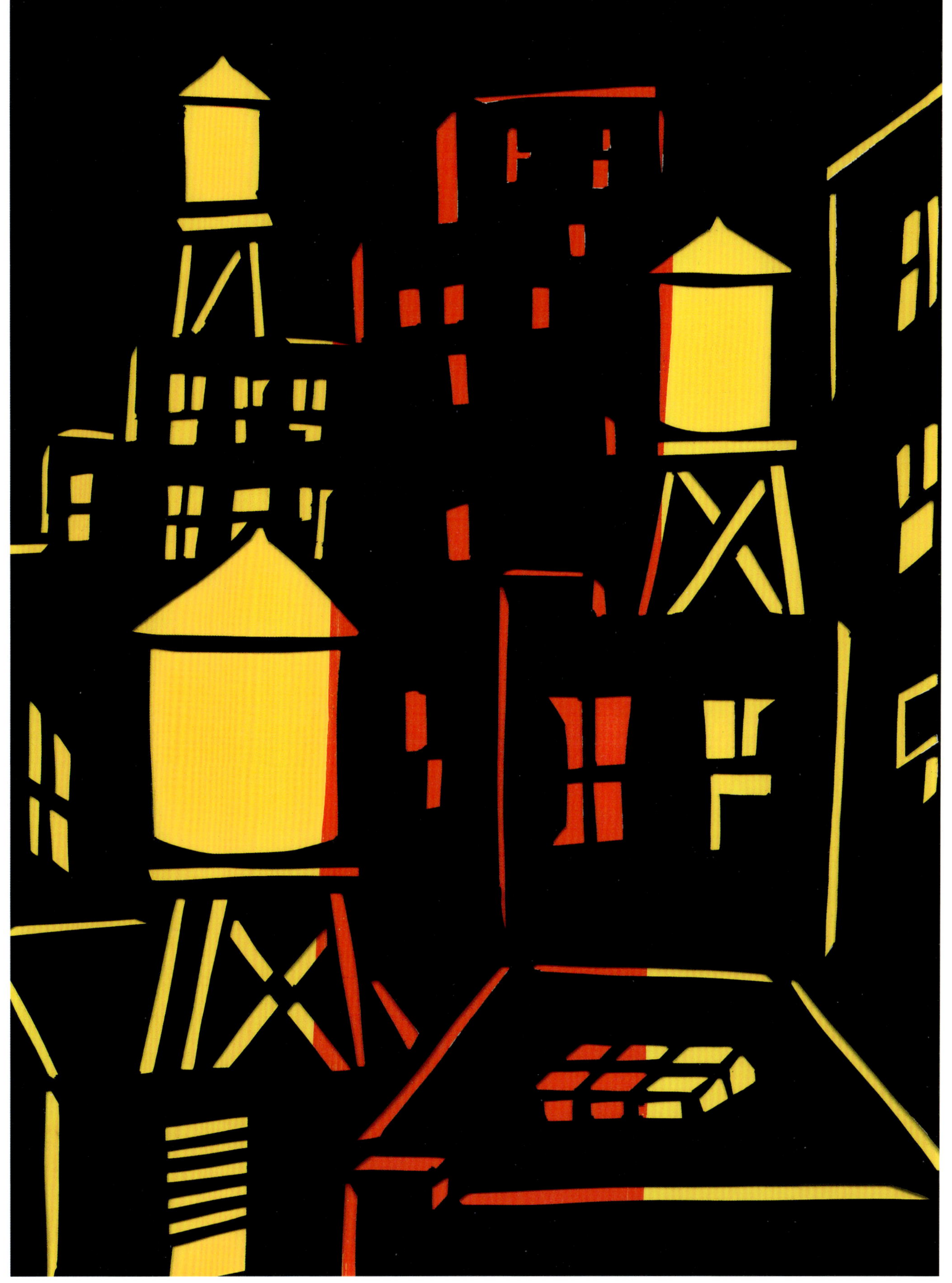

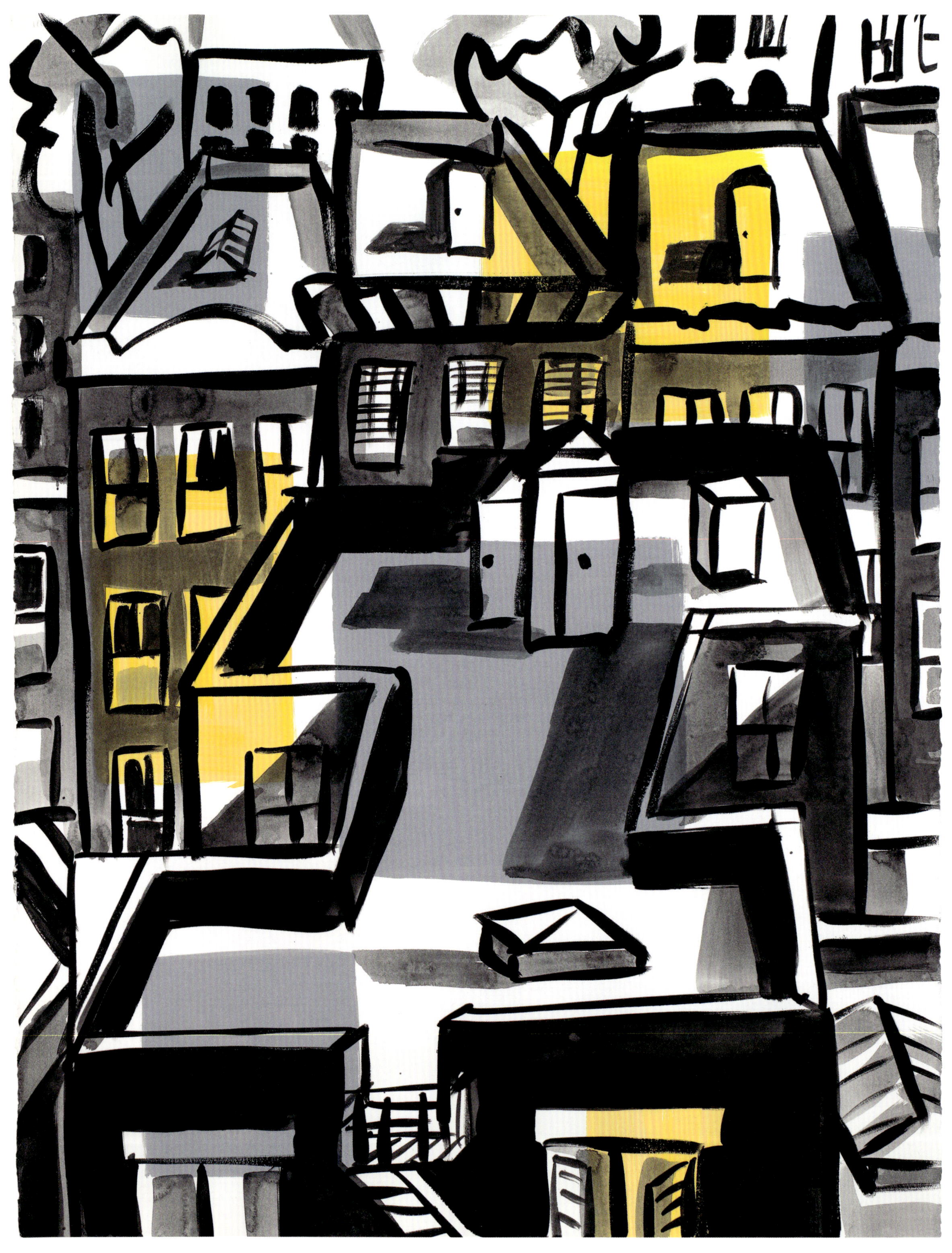

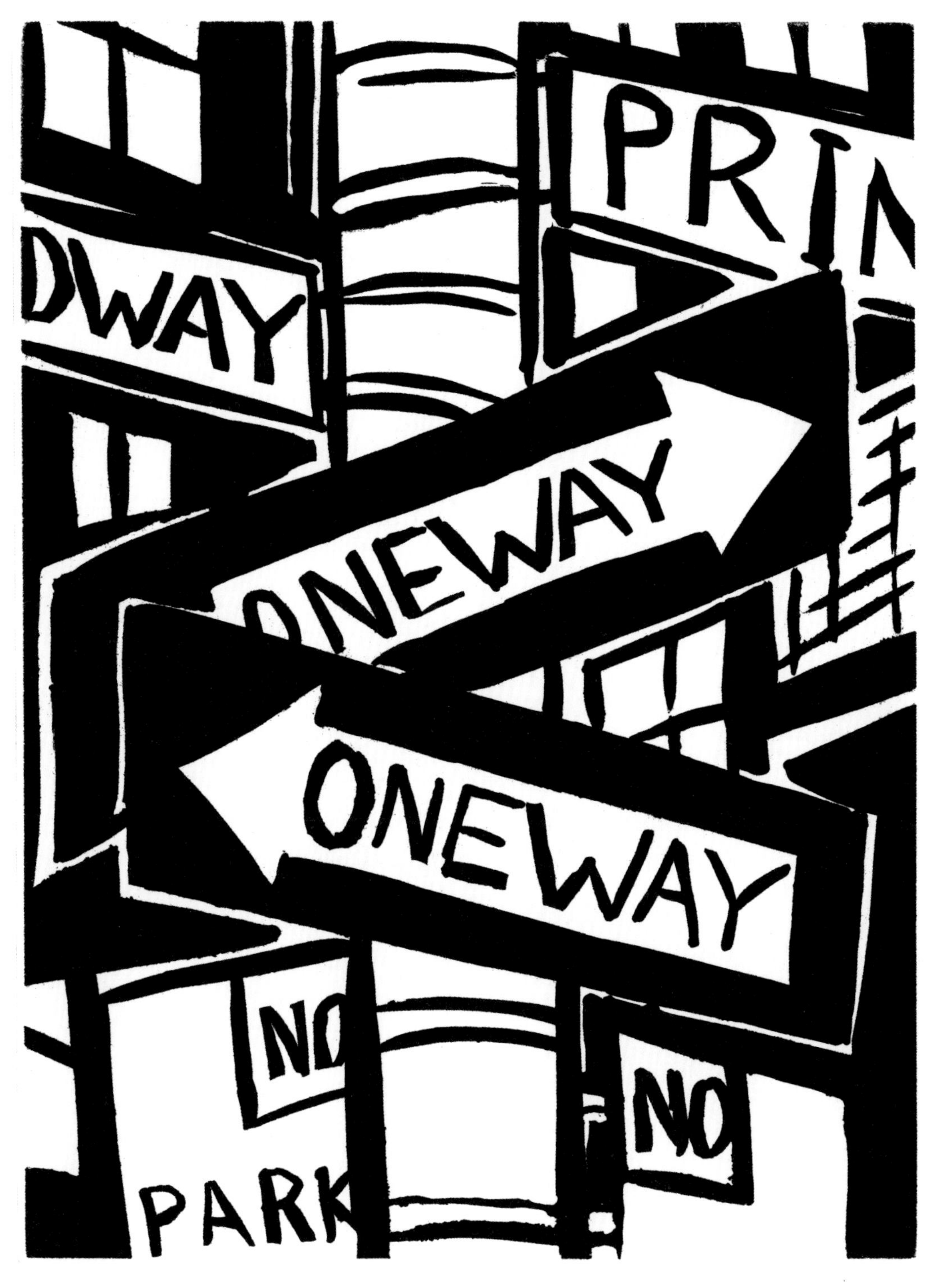

DWAY
PRIN
ONEWAY
ONEWAY
NO
NO
PARK

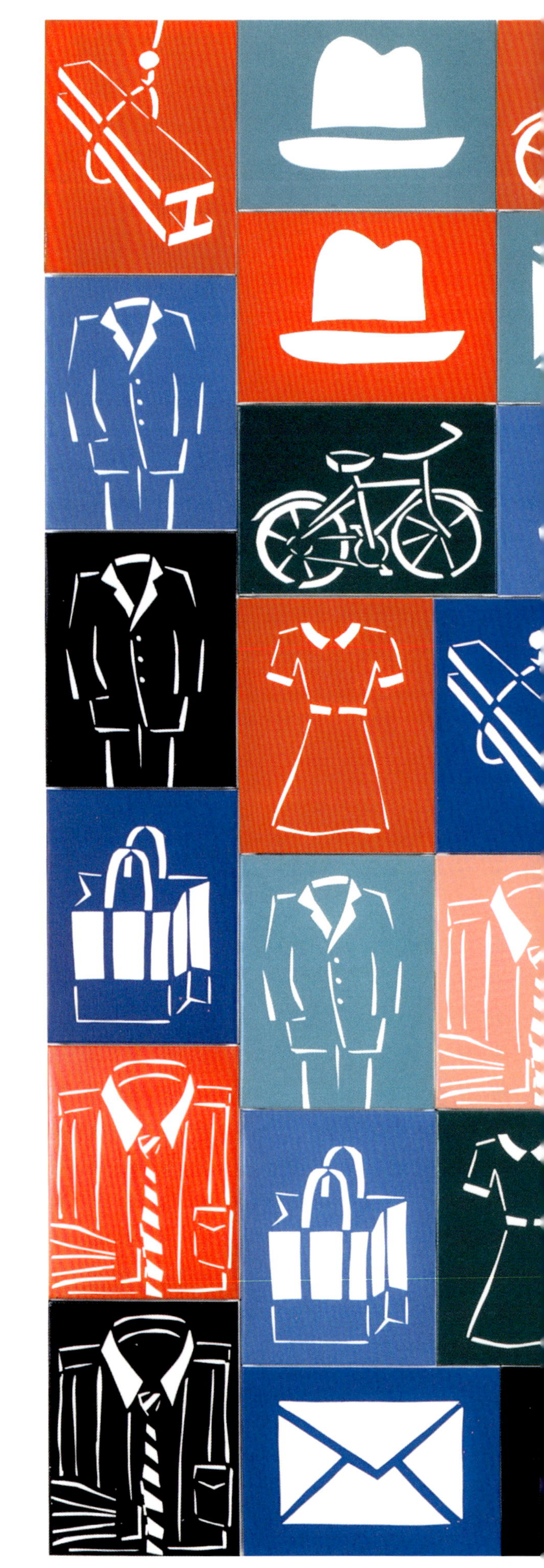

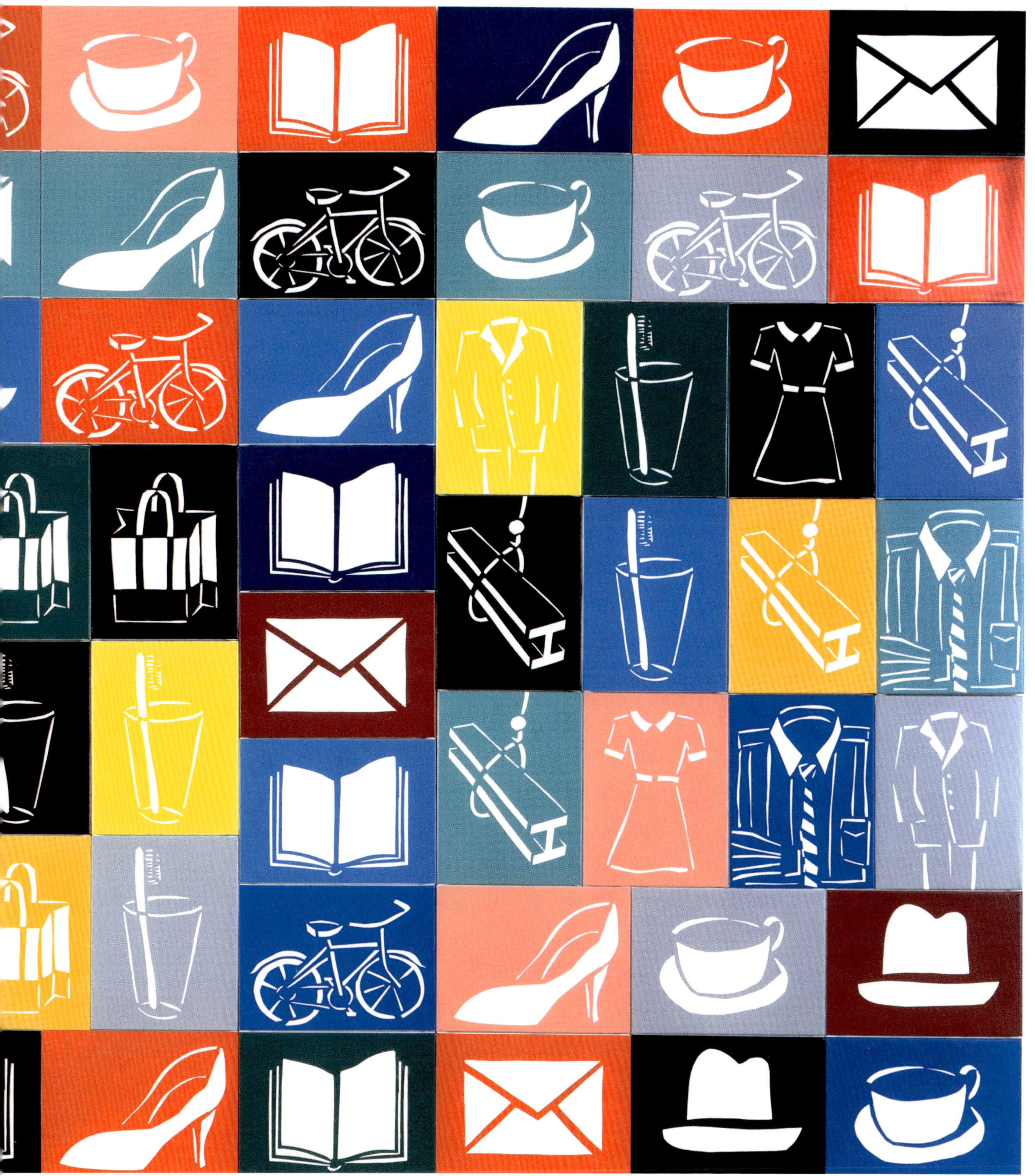

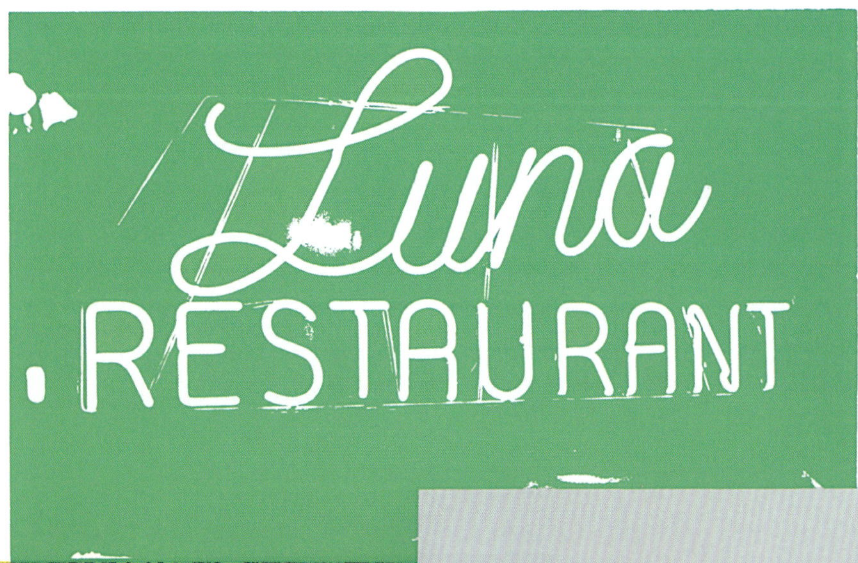

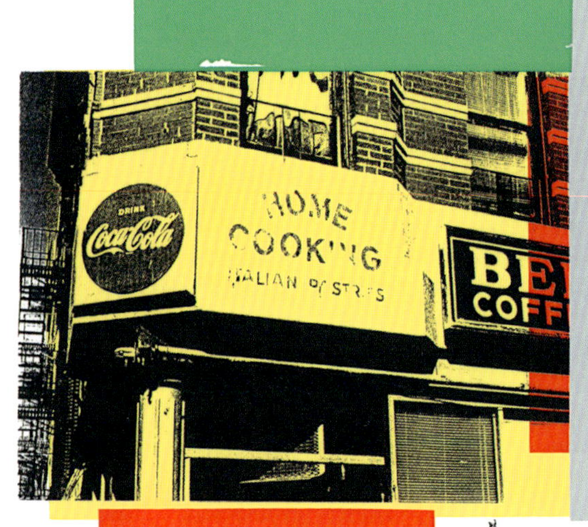

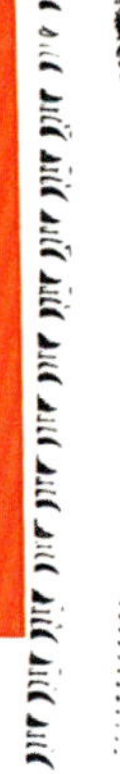

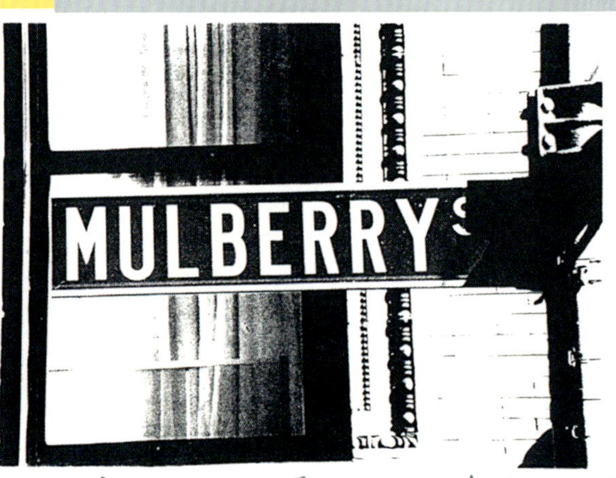

A.P.   T. Slaughter 01

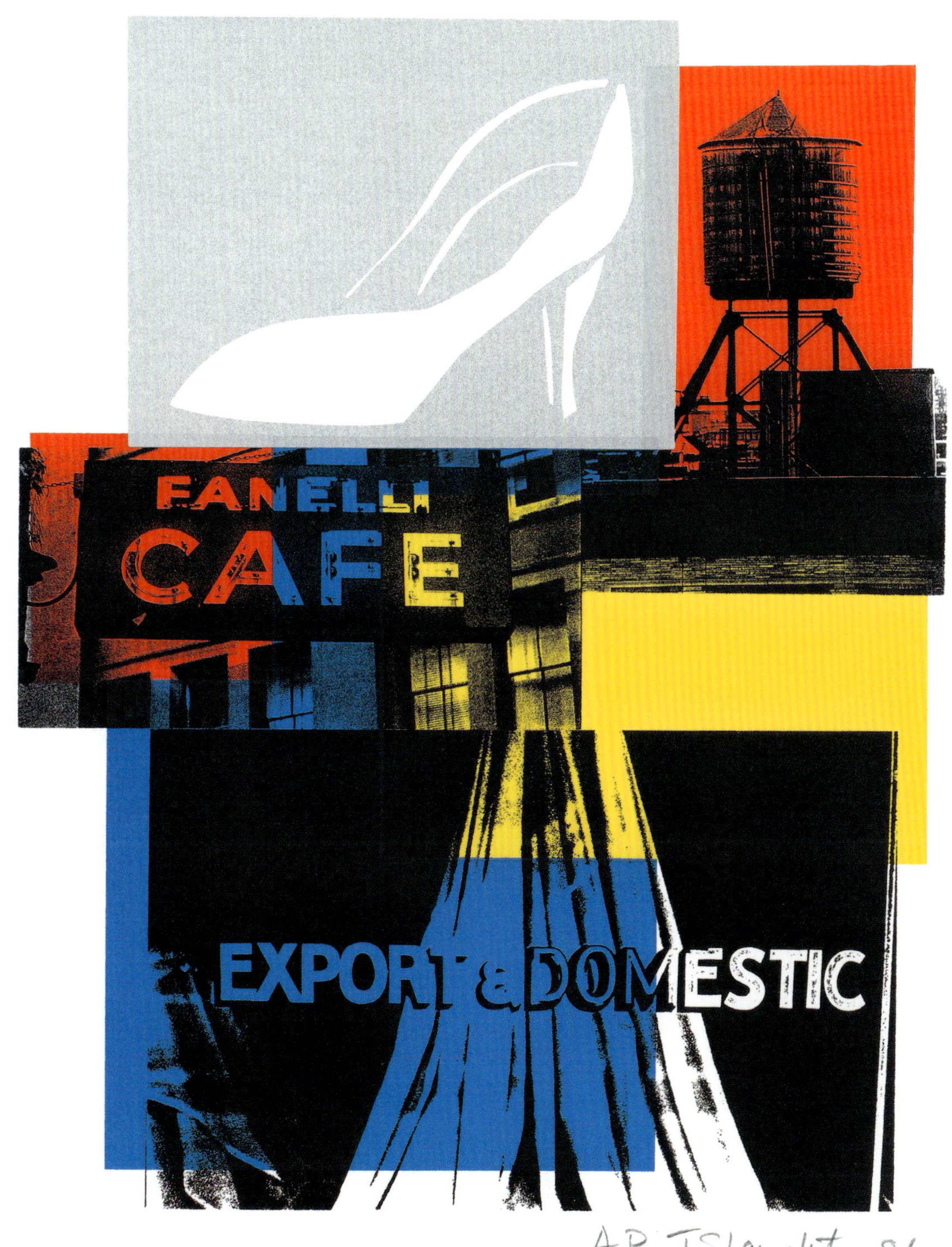

FANELLI
CAFE
EXPORT & DOMESTIC

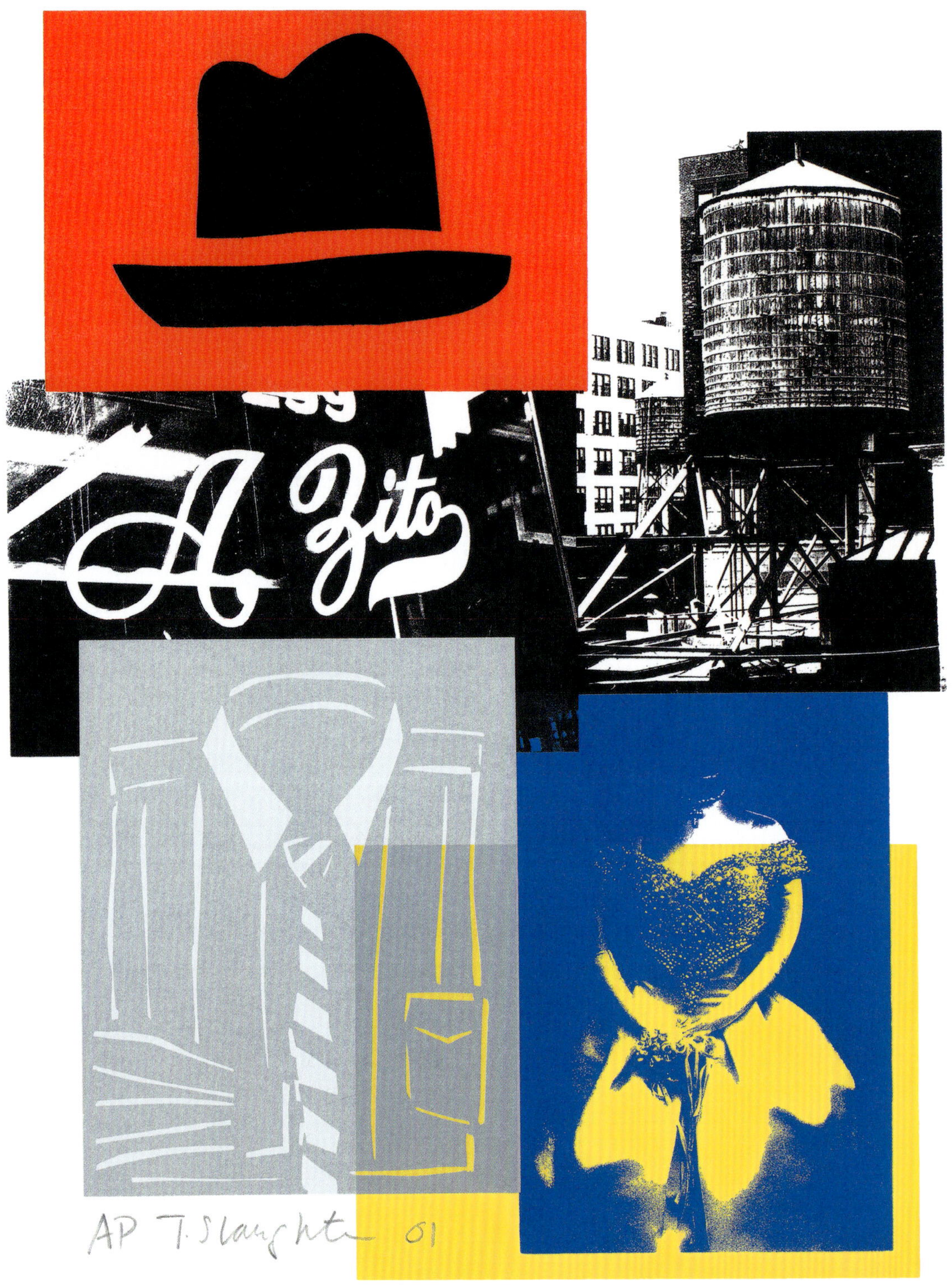

A Zito
AP T. Slaughter   01

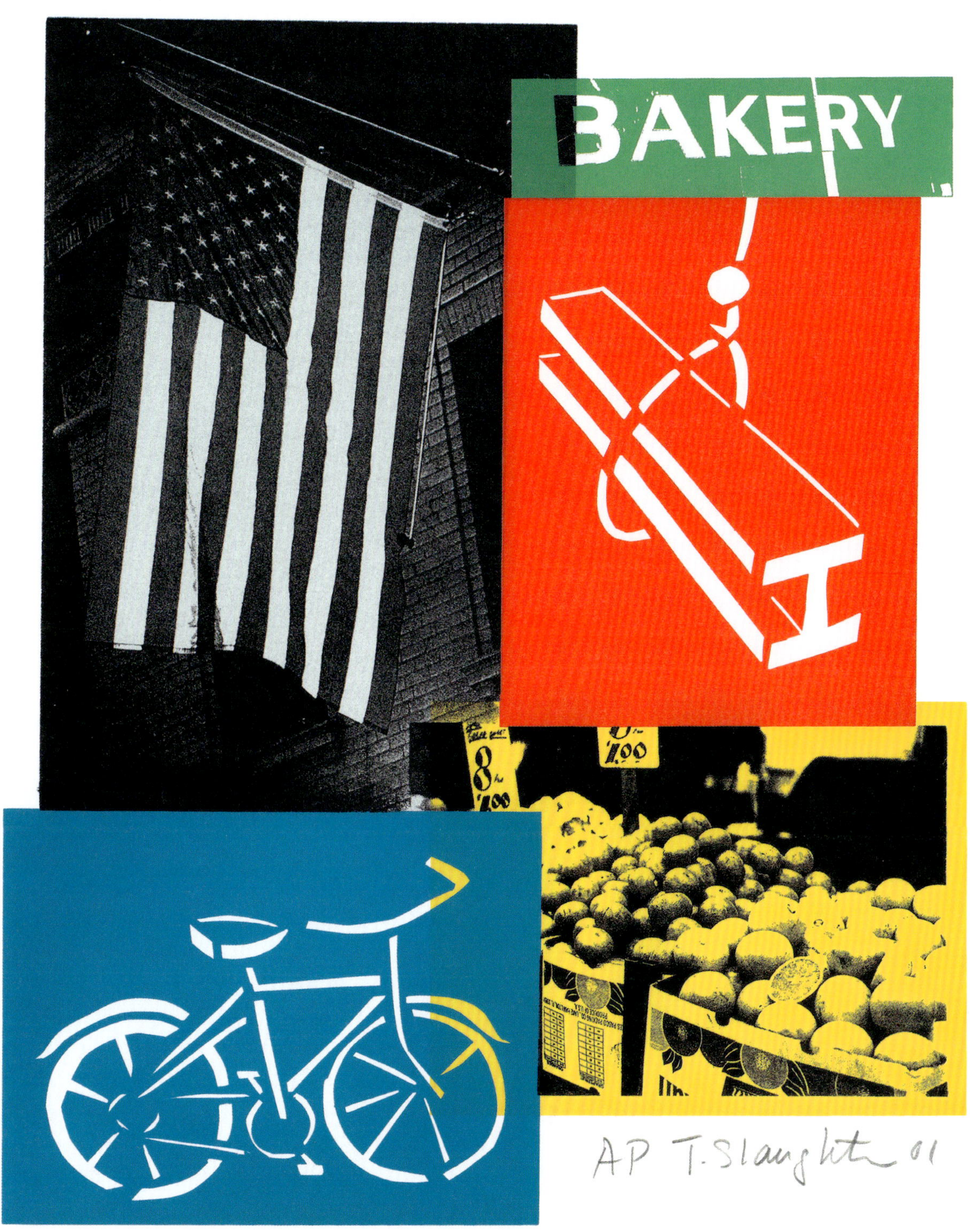

AP T.Slaughter 01

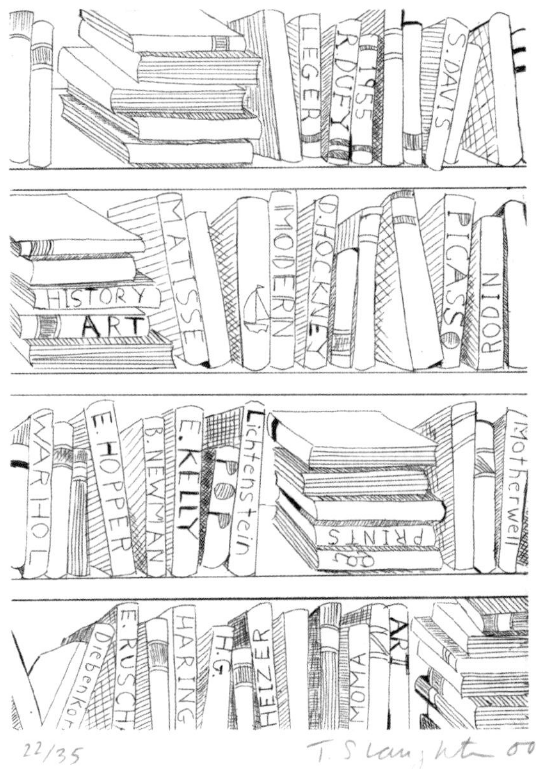

22/35   T. Slaughter 00

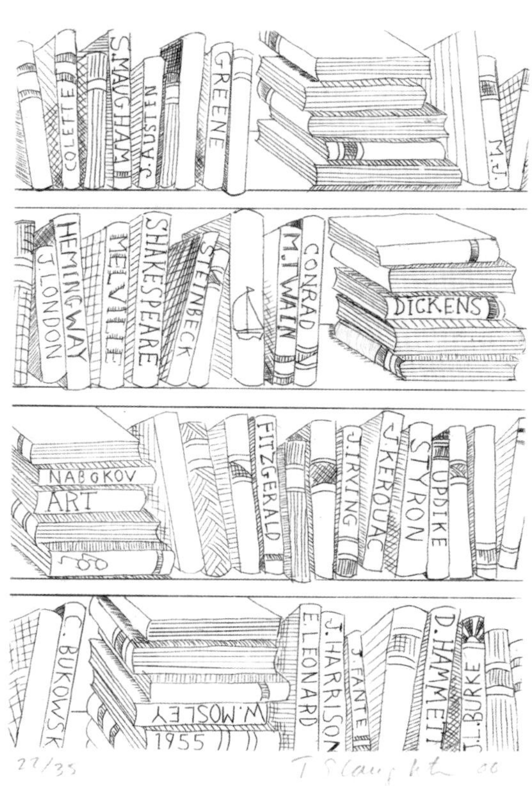

COLETTE
S.MAUGHAM
J.JOYCE
GREENE
M.P.
HEMINGWAY
J LONDON
MELVILLE
SHAKESPEARE
STEINBECK
M.TWAIN
CONRAD
DICKENS
NABOKOV
ART
FITZGERALD
J.IRVING
J.KEROUAC
STYRON
UPDIKE
C.BUKOWSKI
W.MOSLEY
1955
J.HARRISON
E.LEONARD
TANTE
D.HAMMETT
J.L.BURKE
27/35
T.Slaughter 00

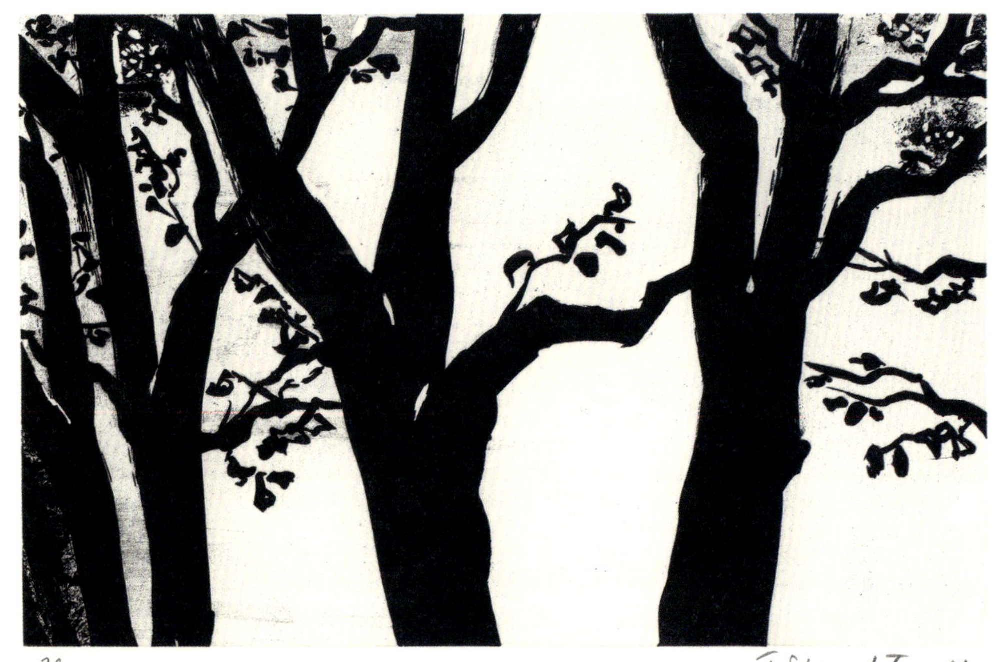

20/30
T Slaughter 01

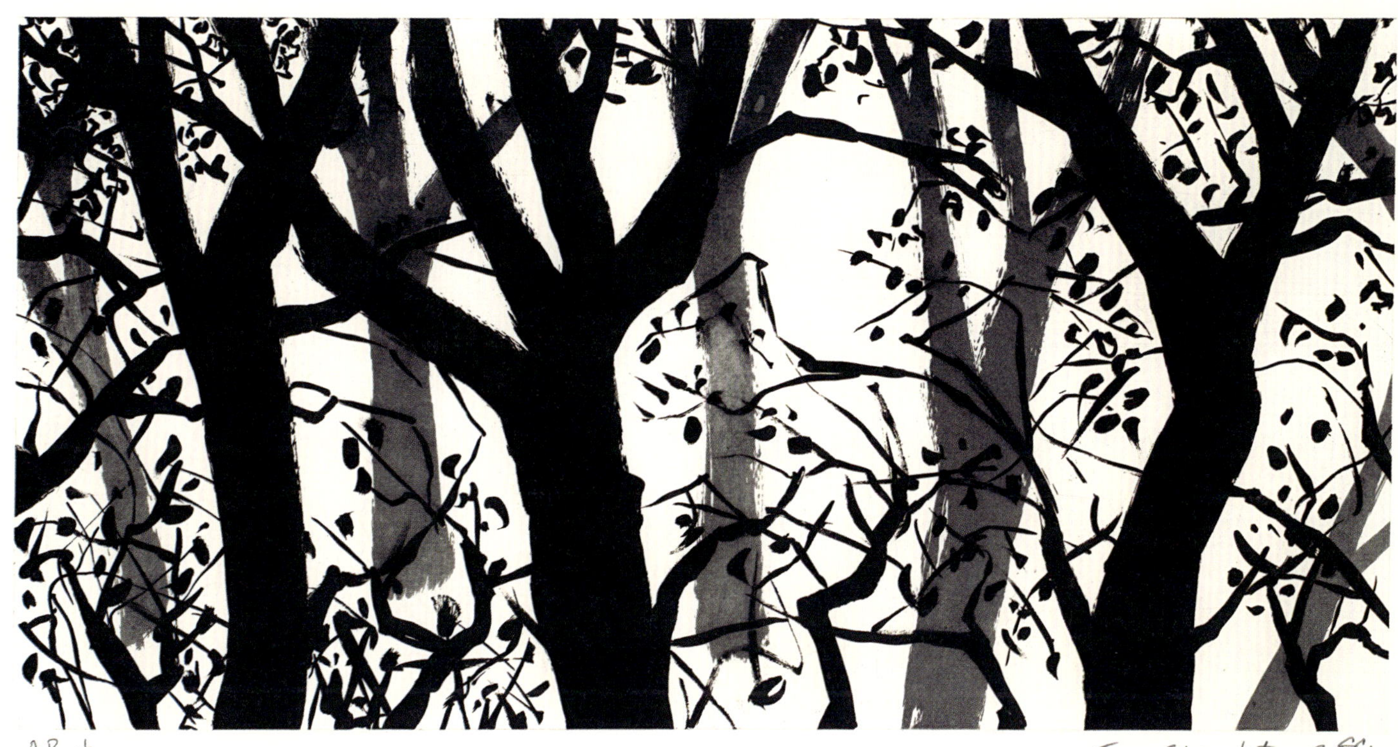

A.P. ½
Tom Slaught 2001

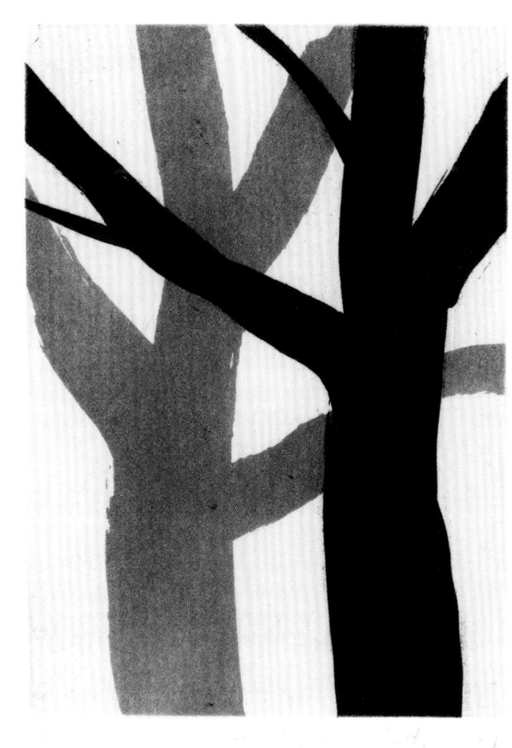

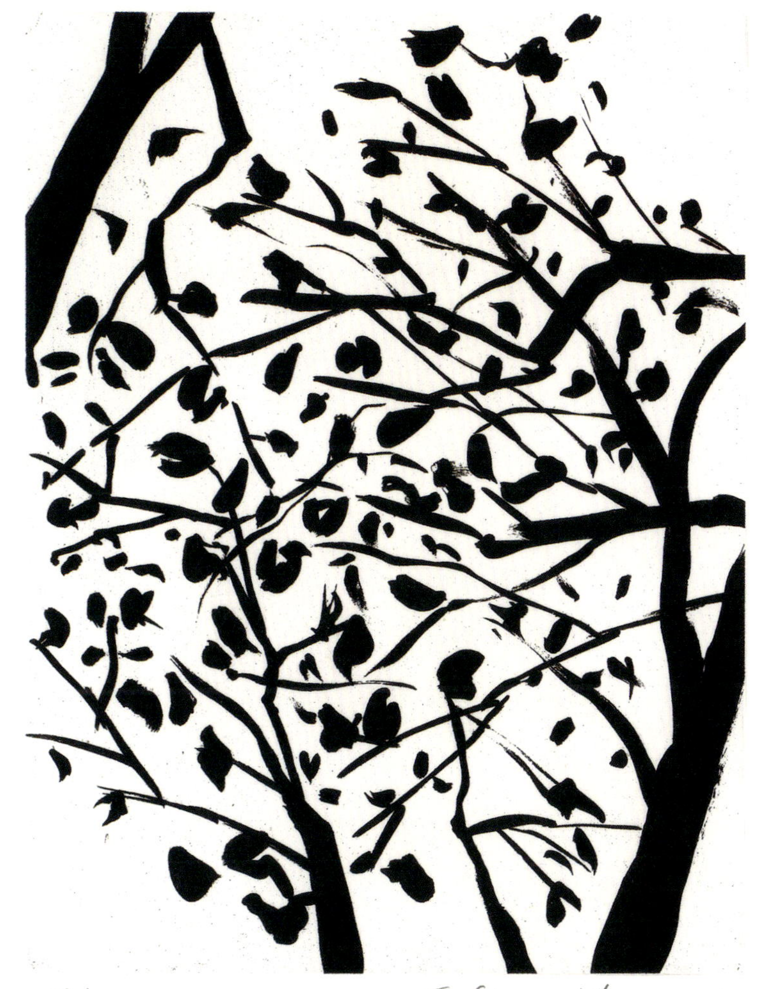
19/40
T. Slaughter 01

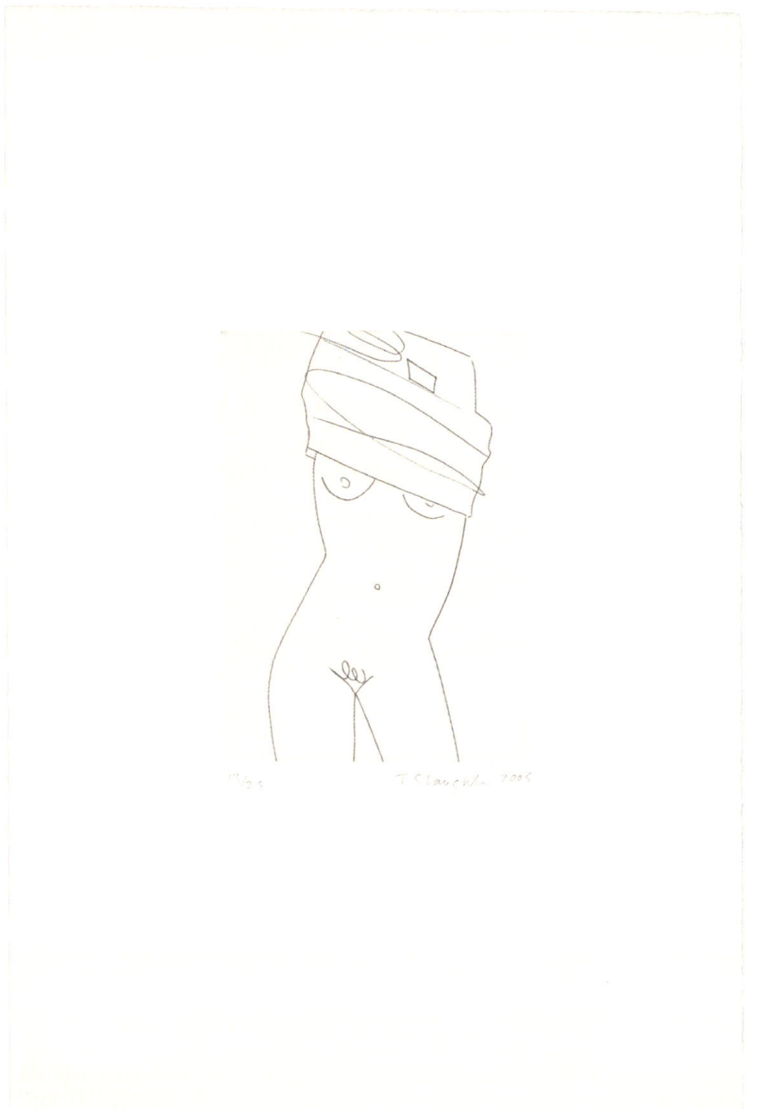

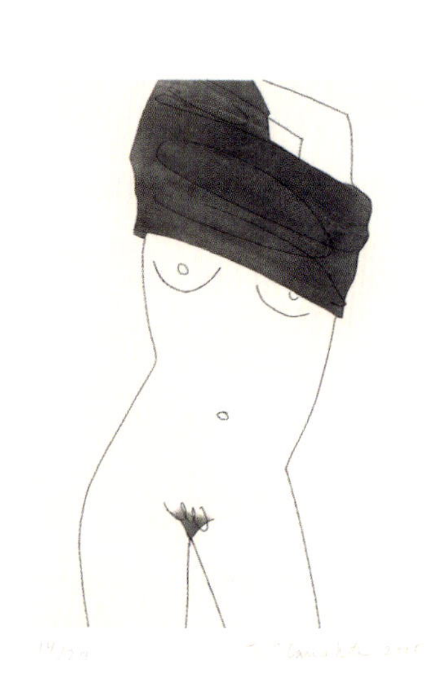

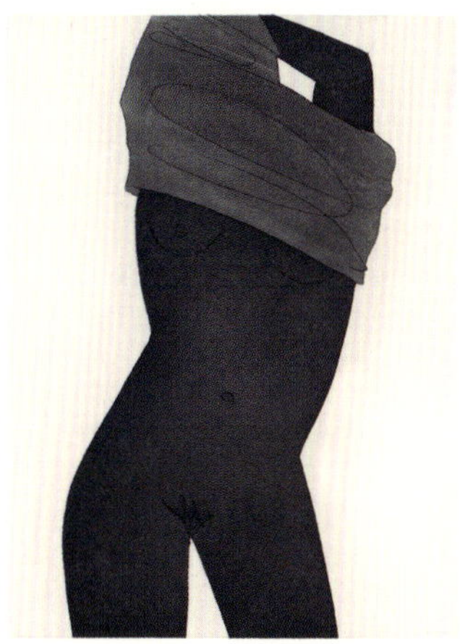

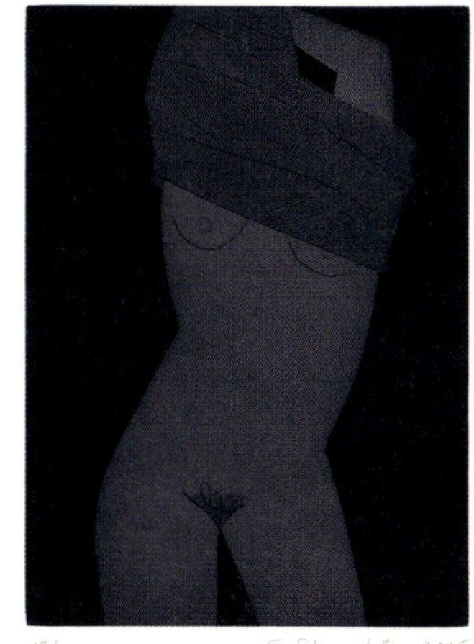

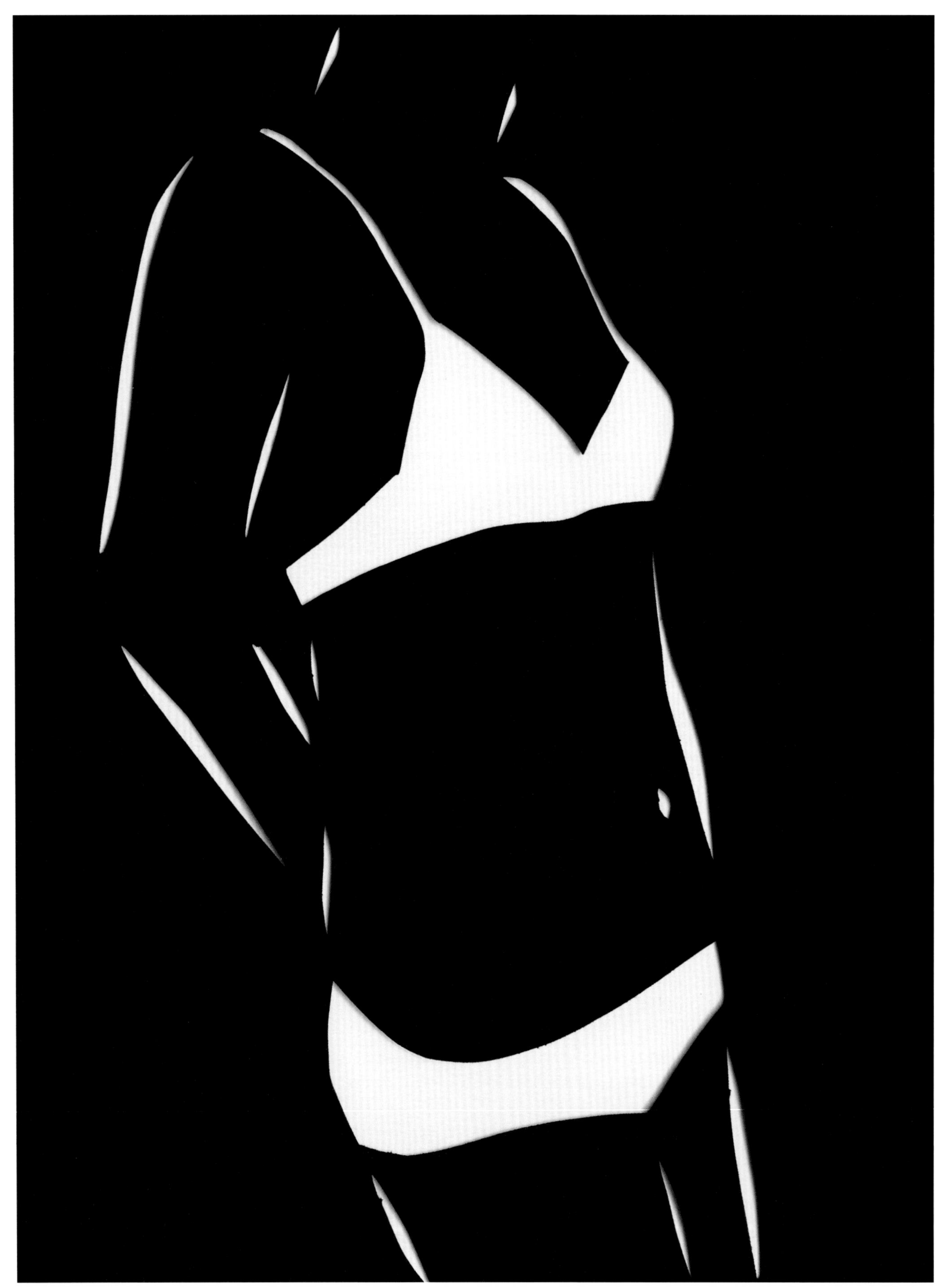

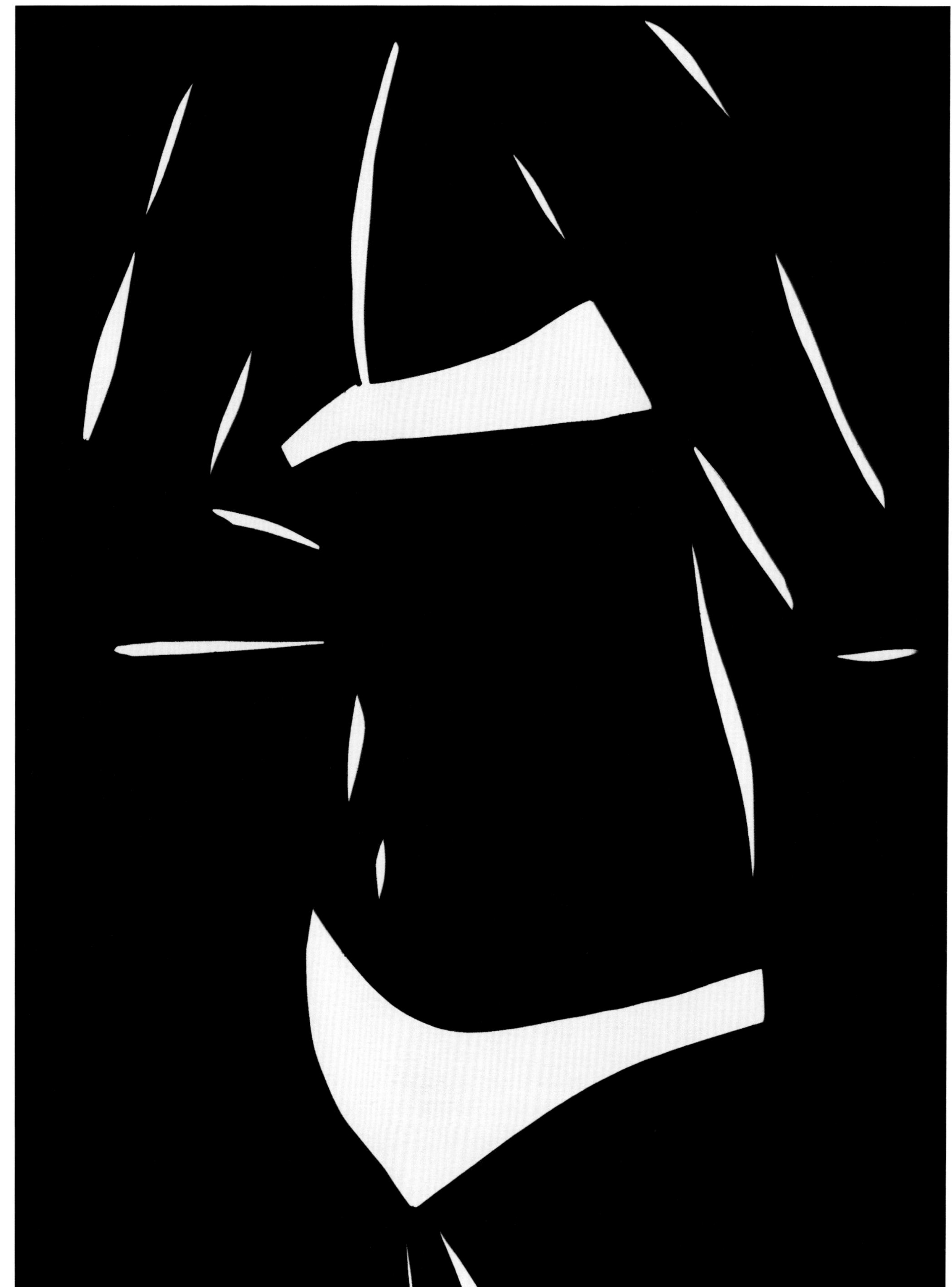

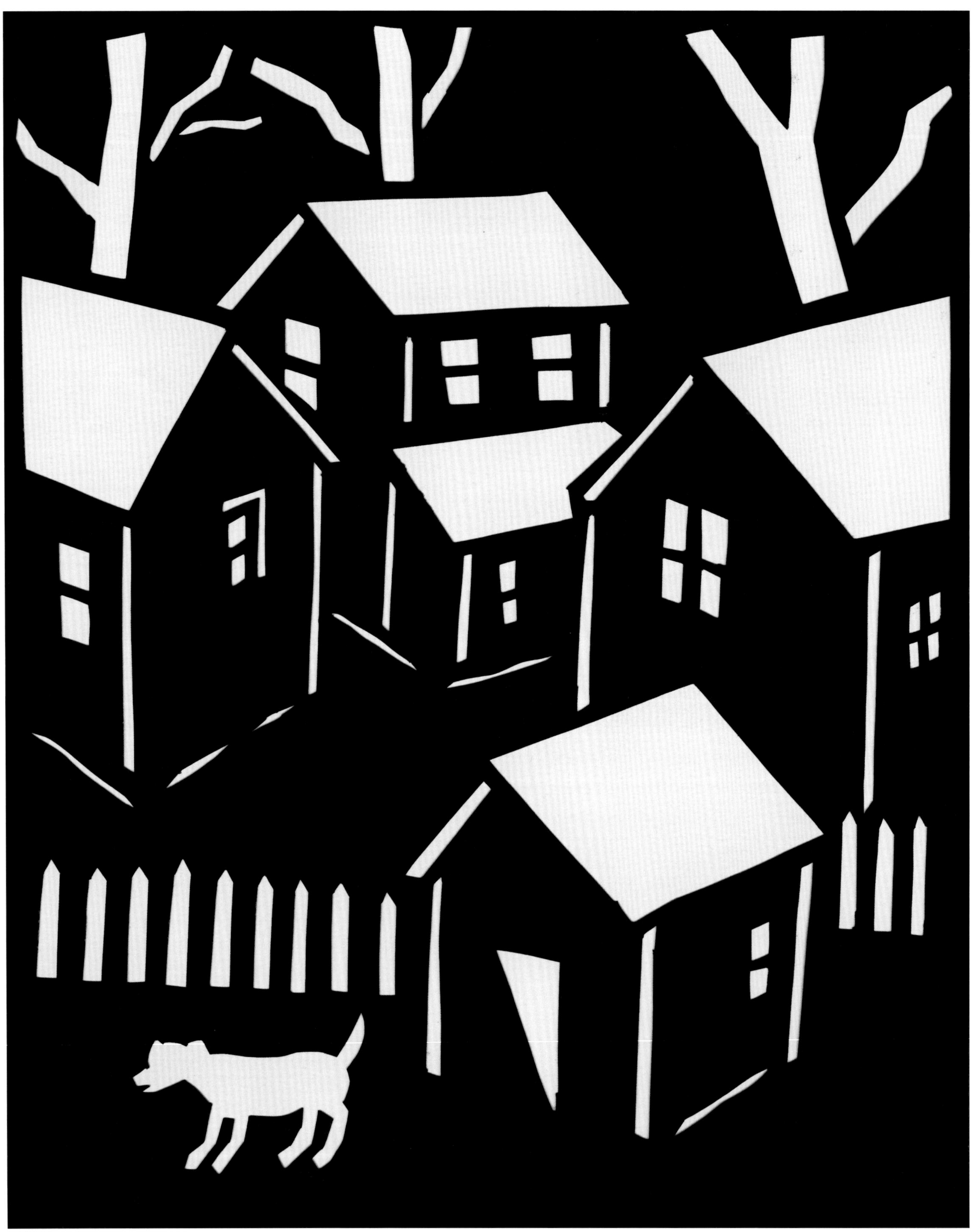

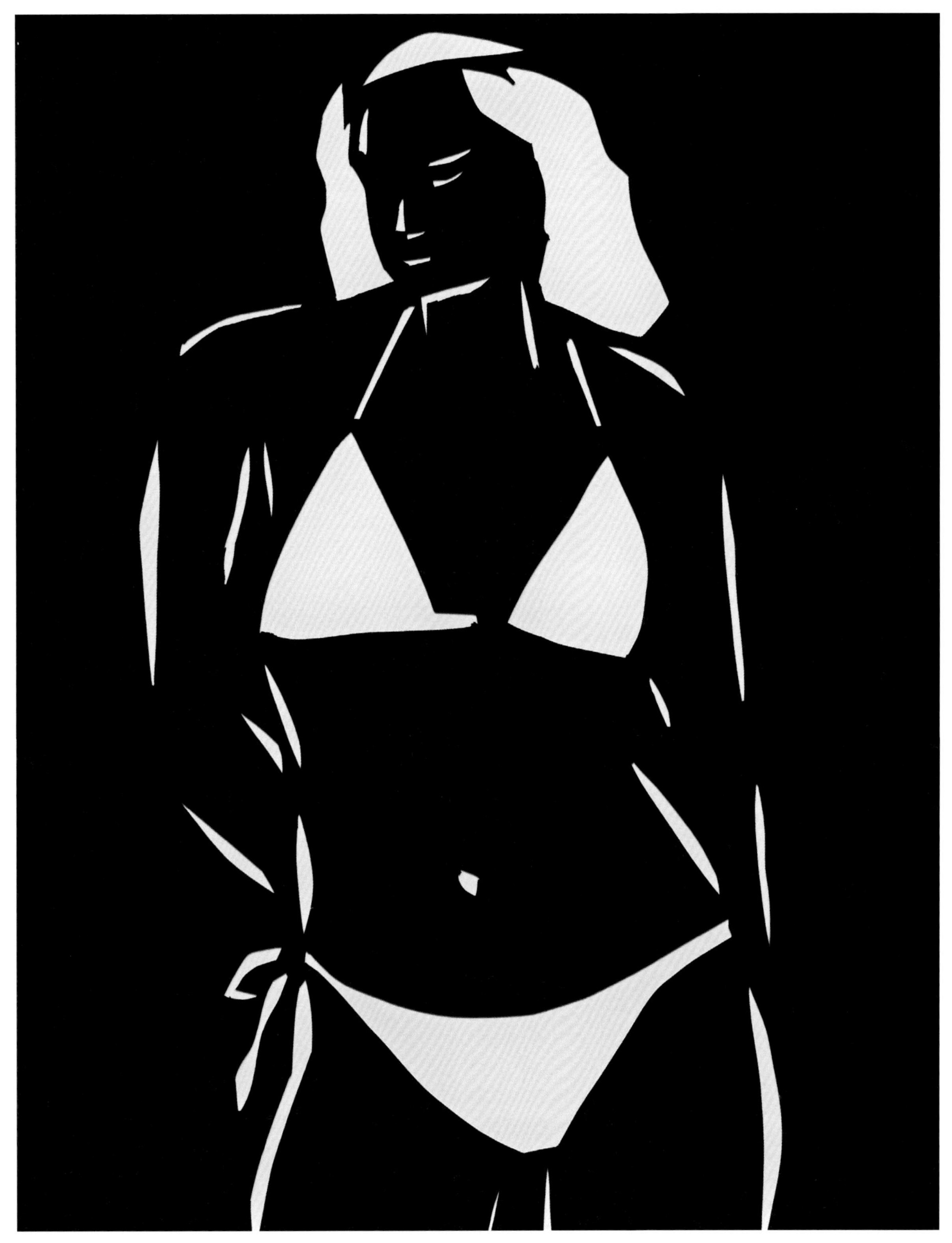

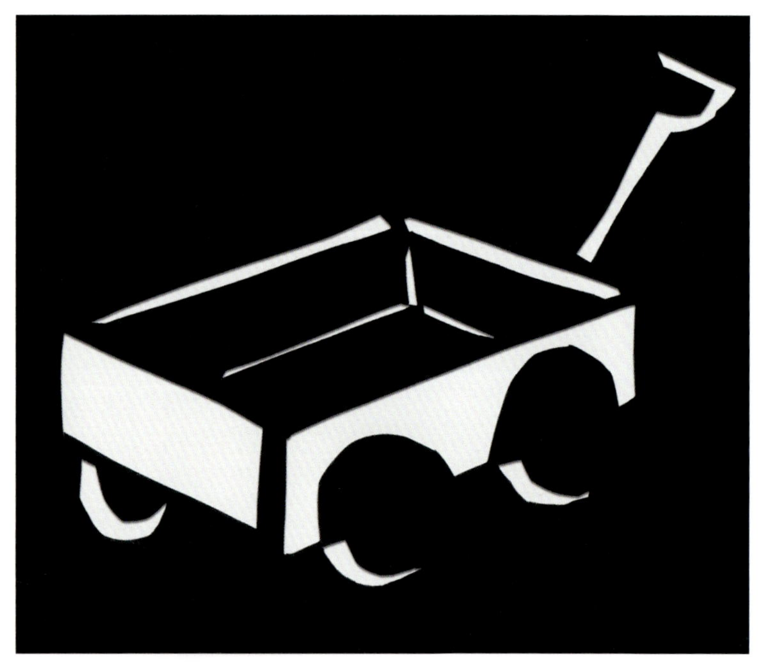

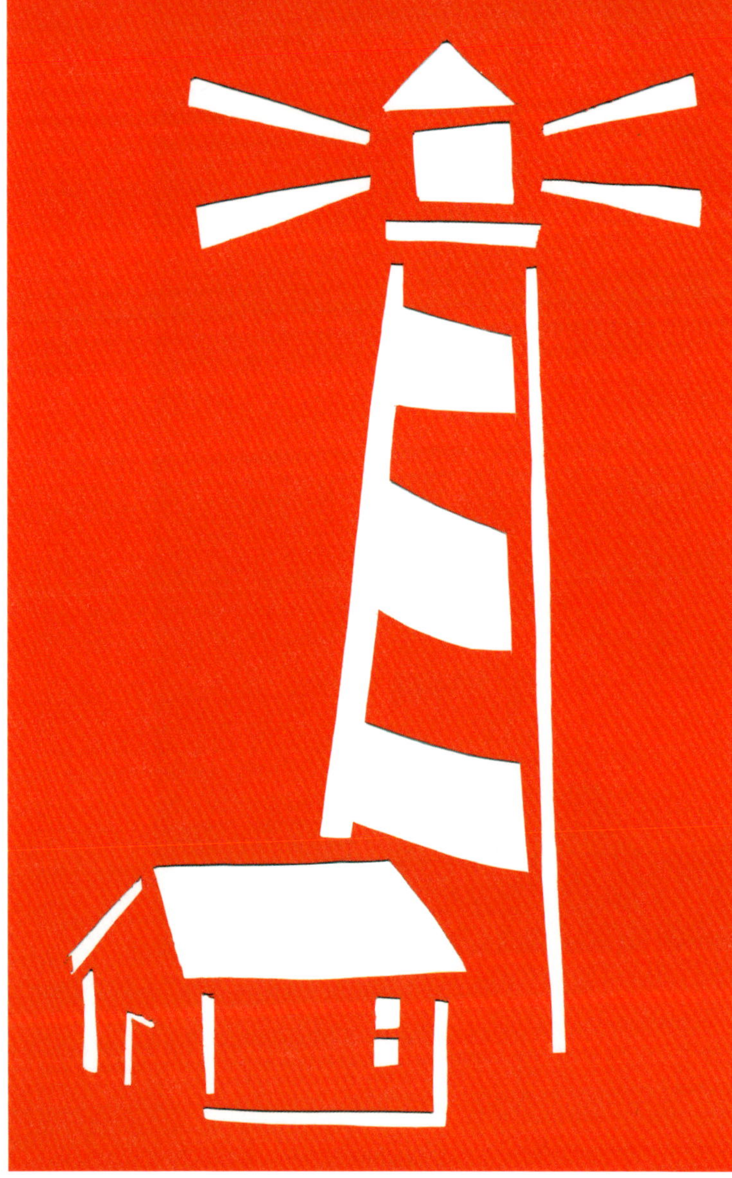

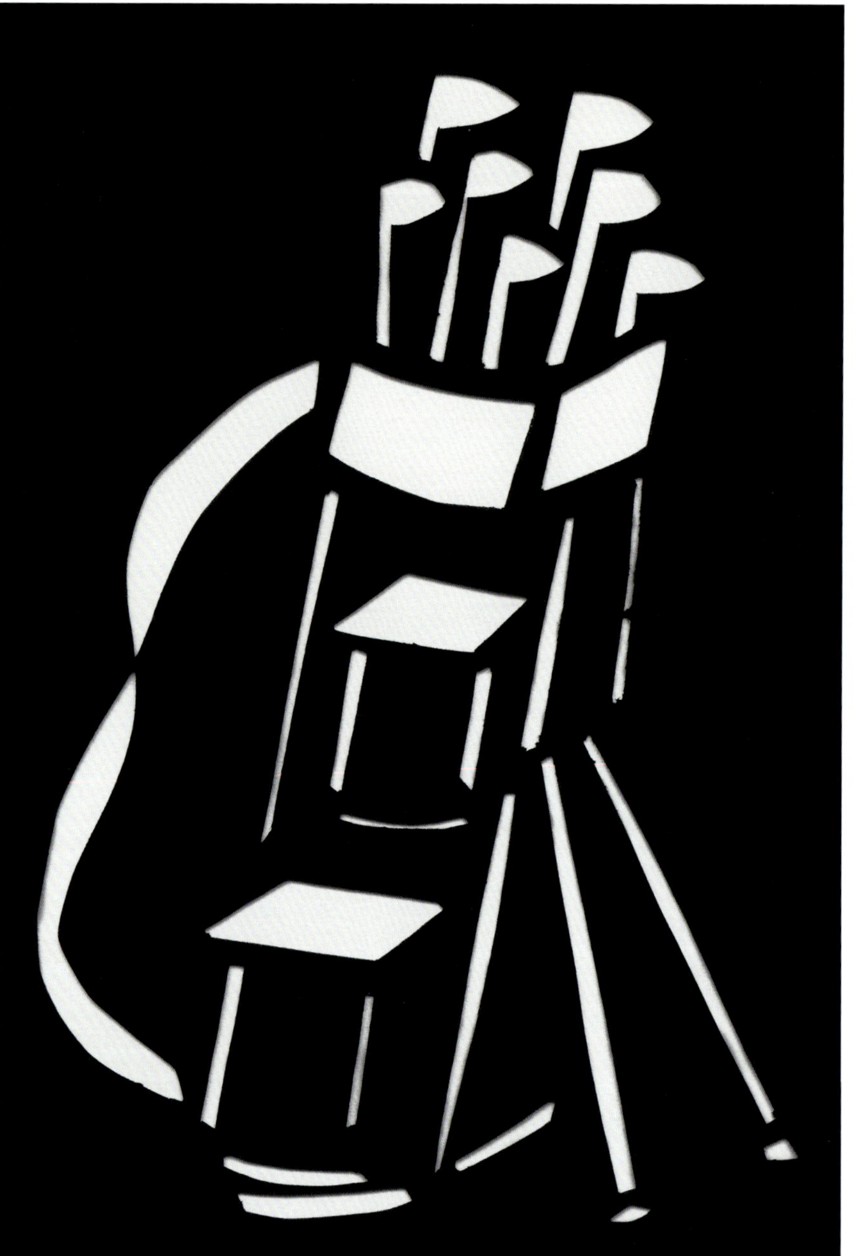

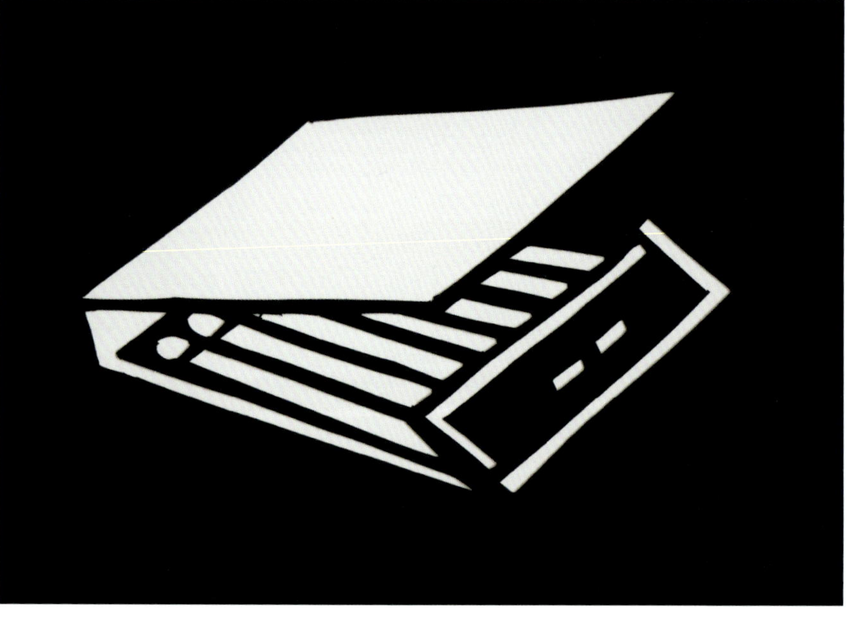

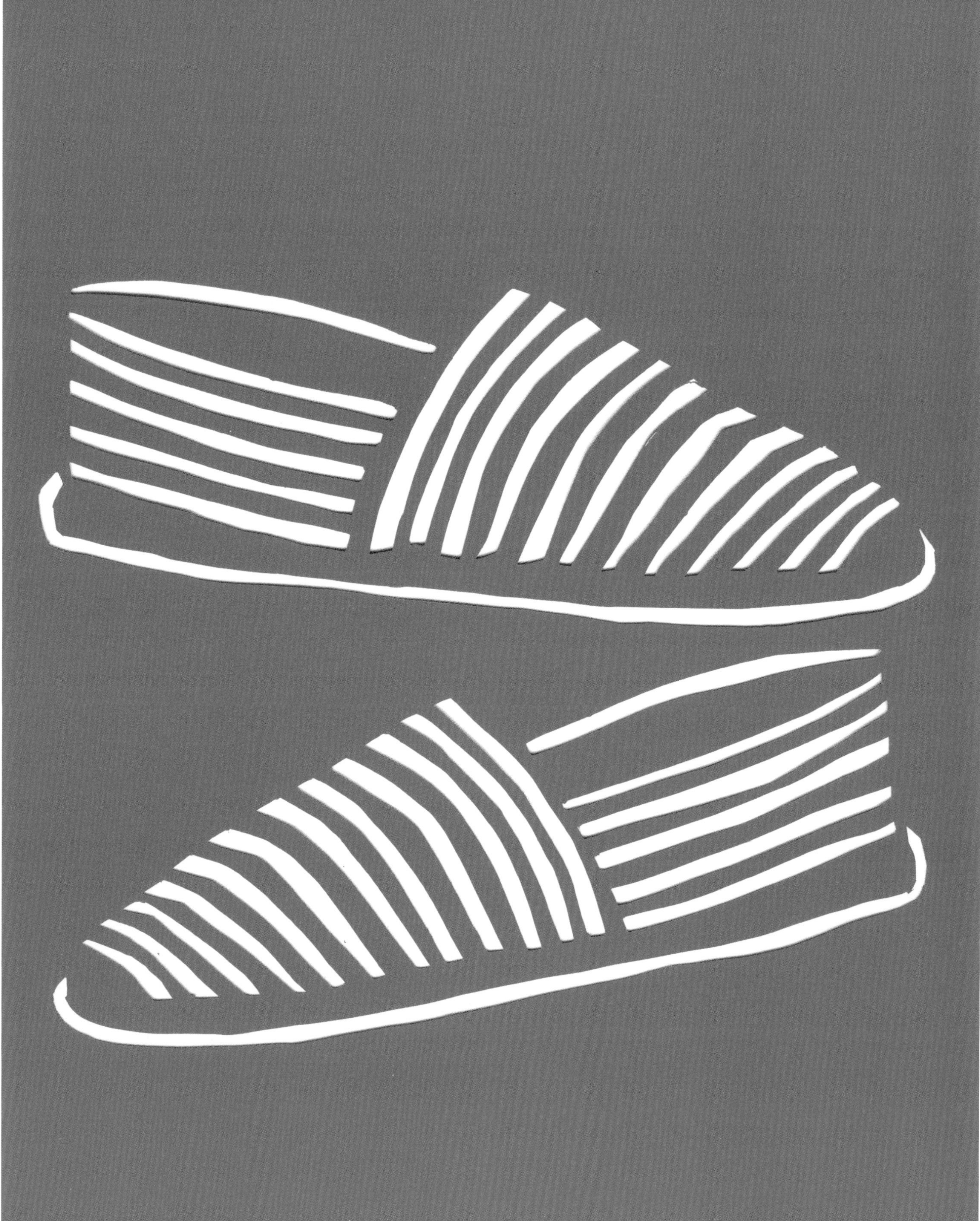

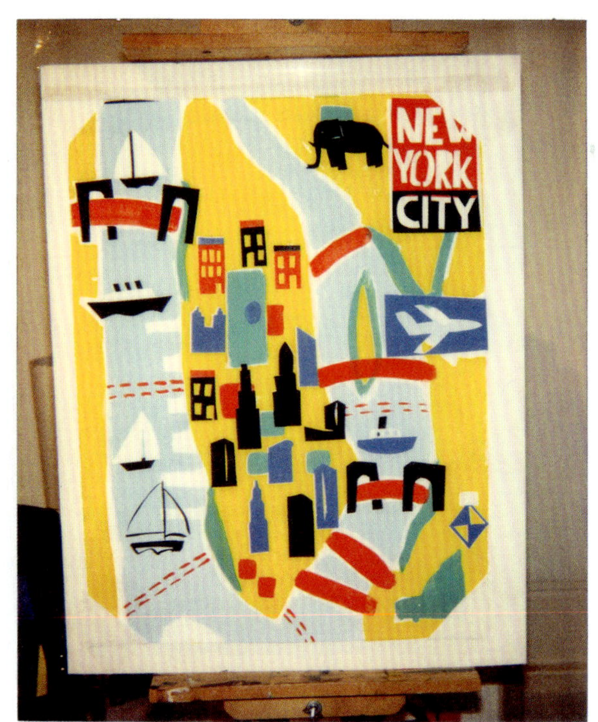
NEW
YORK
CITY

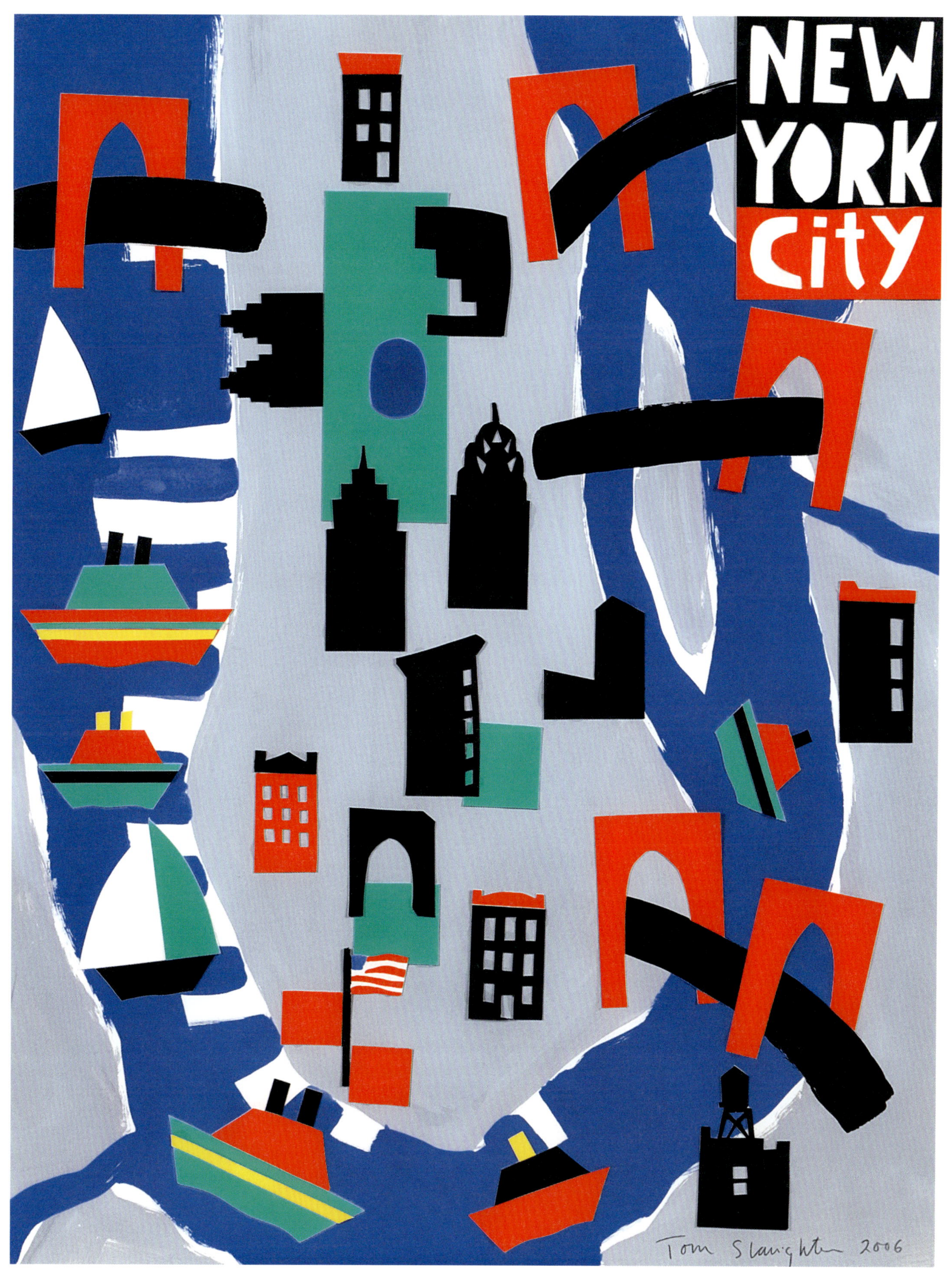

NEW YORK
CITY
Tom Slaughter 2006

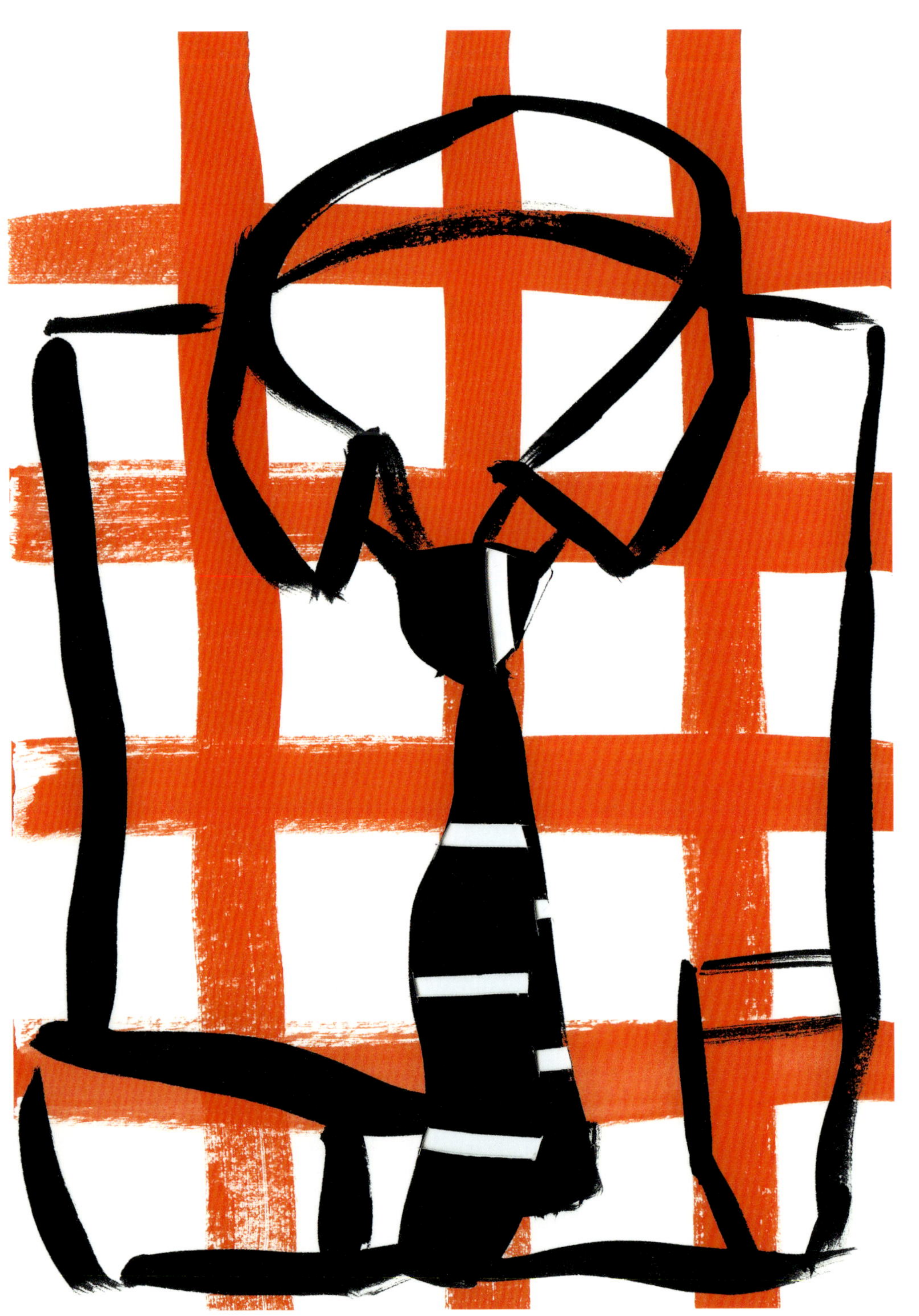

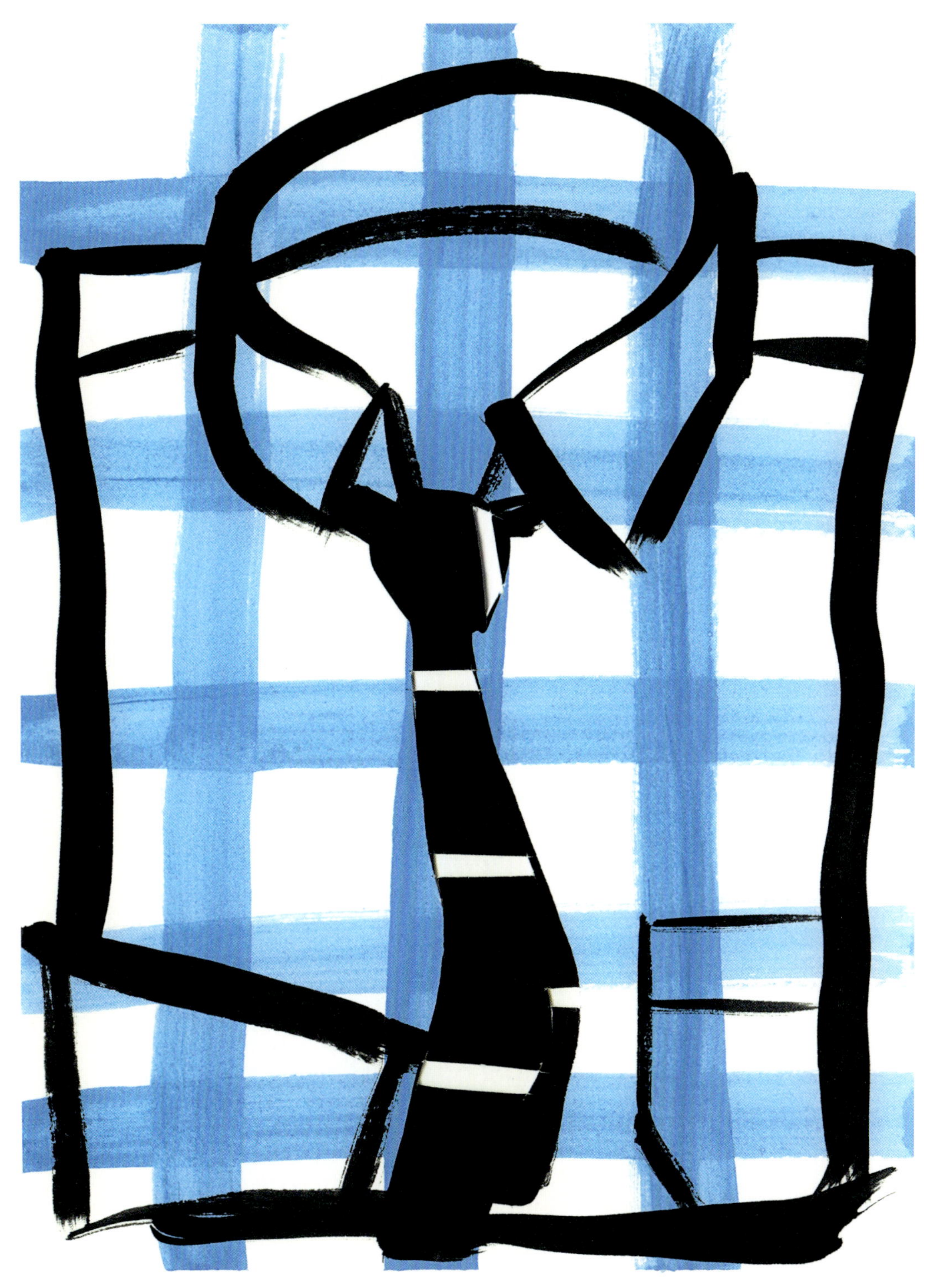

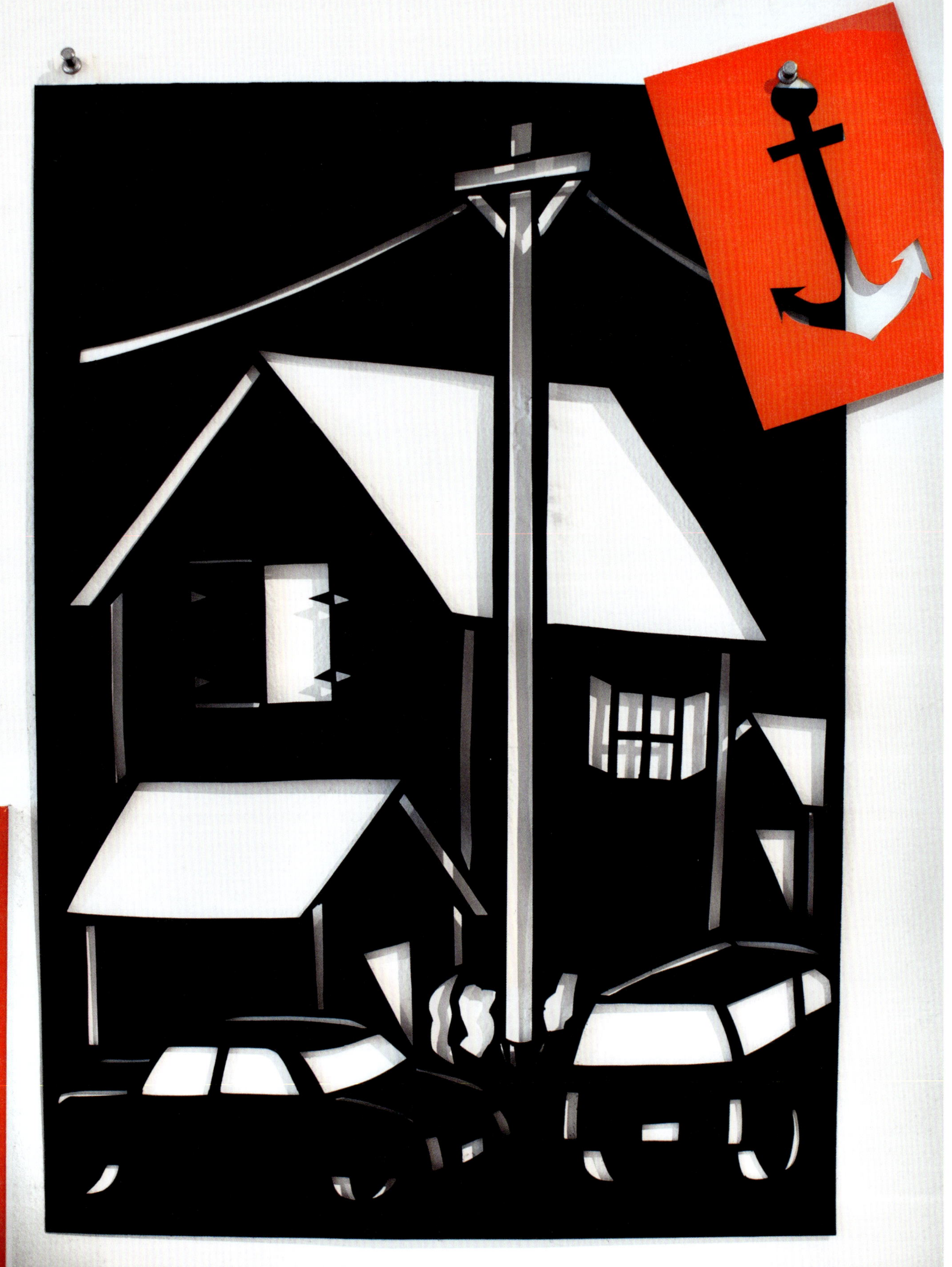

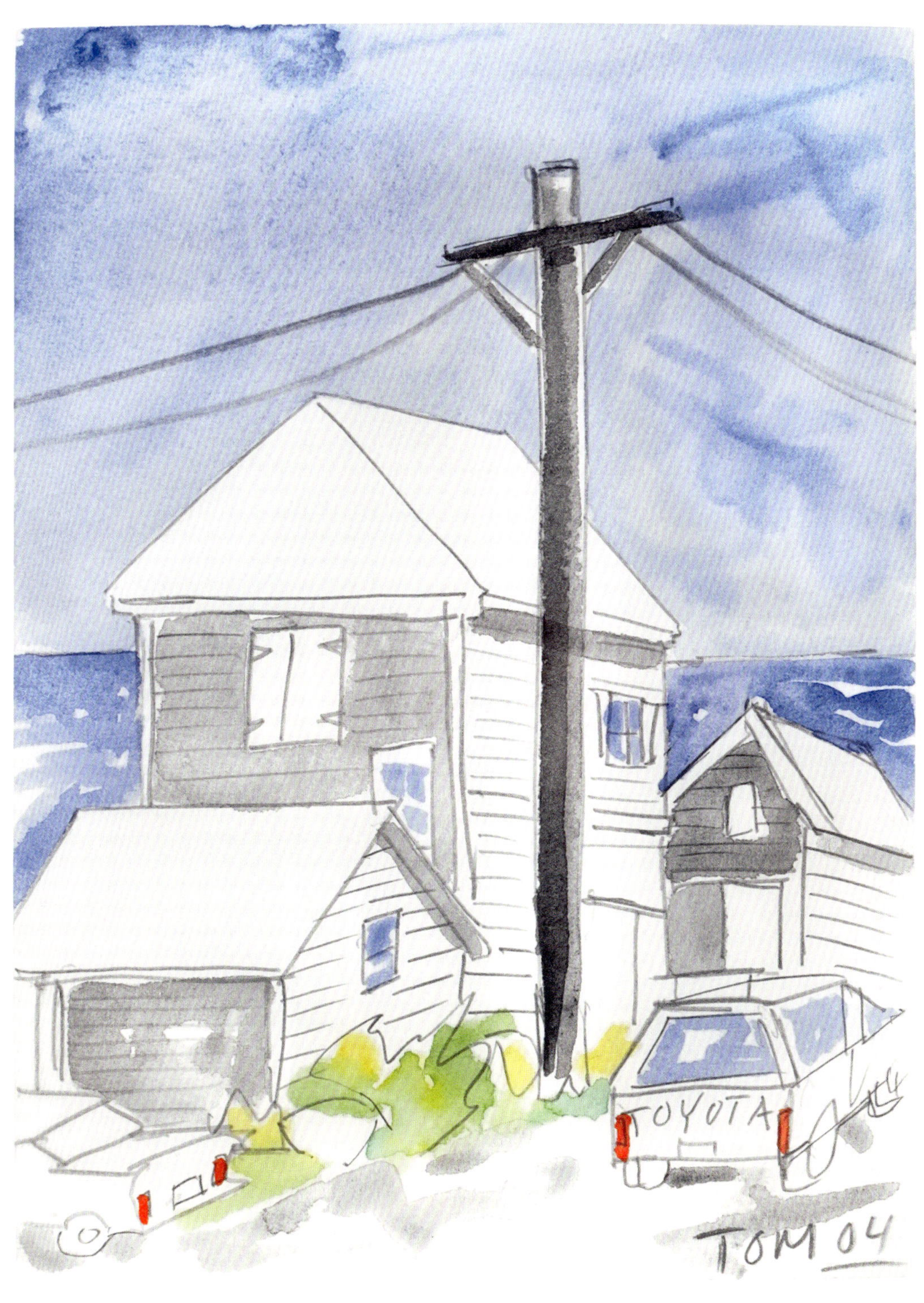
TOYOTA
TOM 04

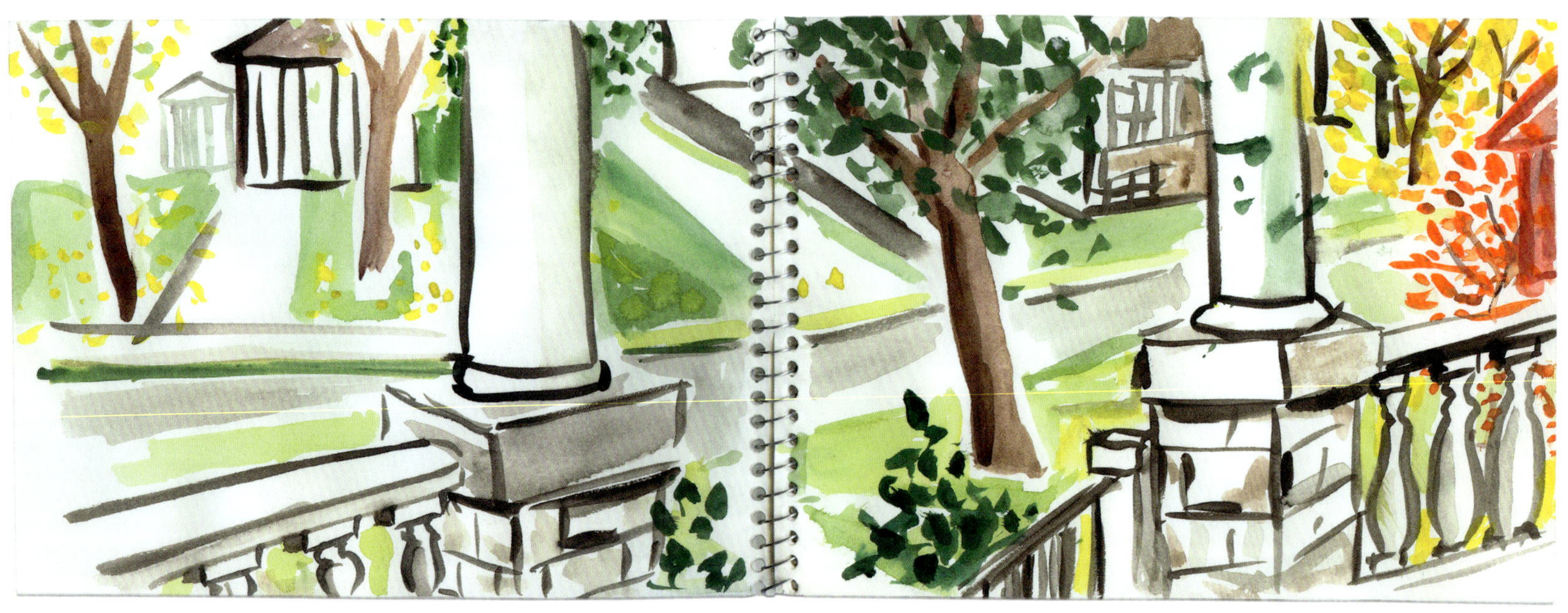

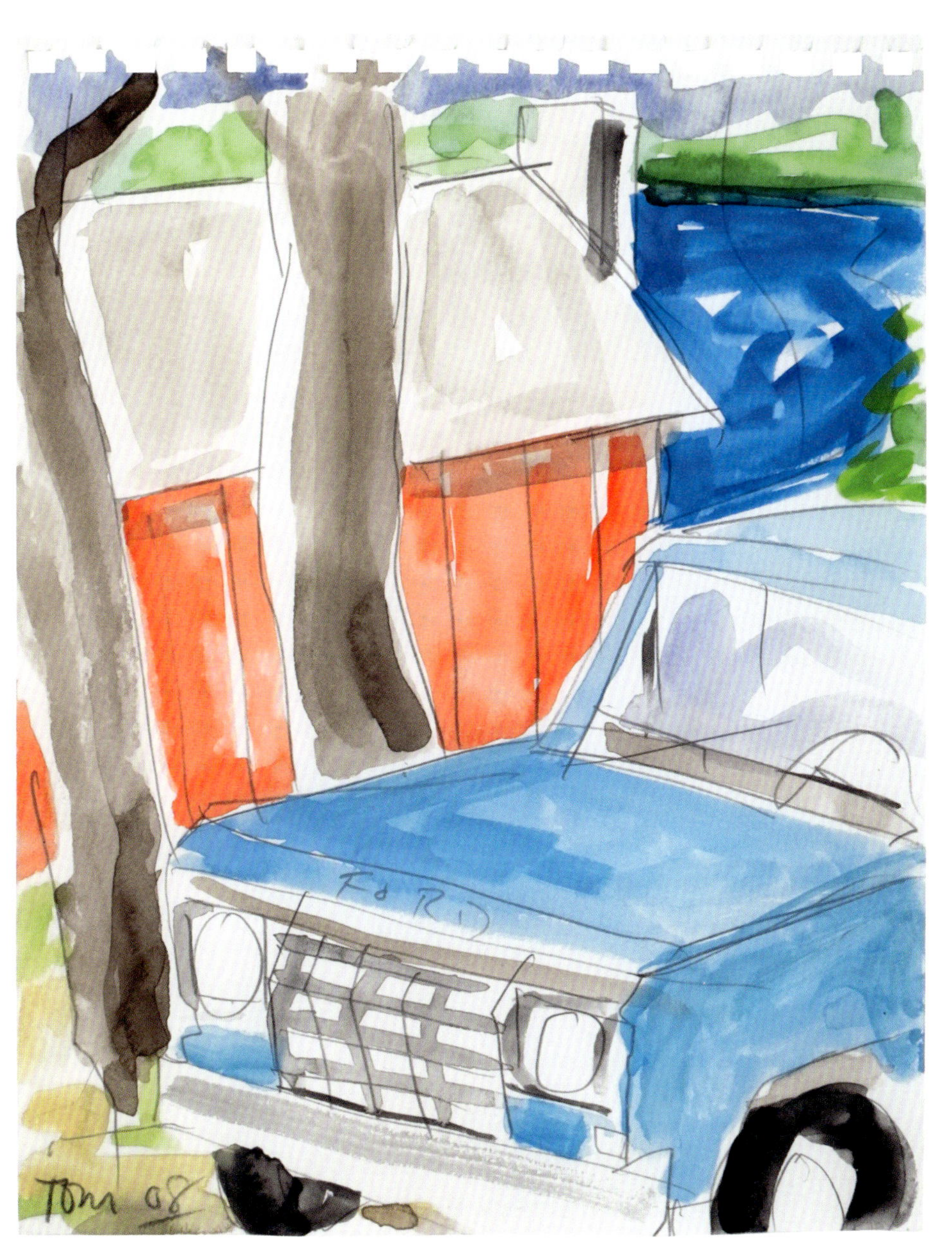
FoRD
Tom 08

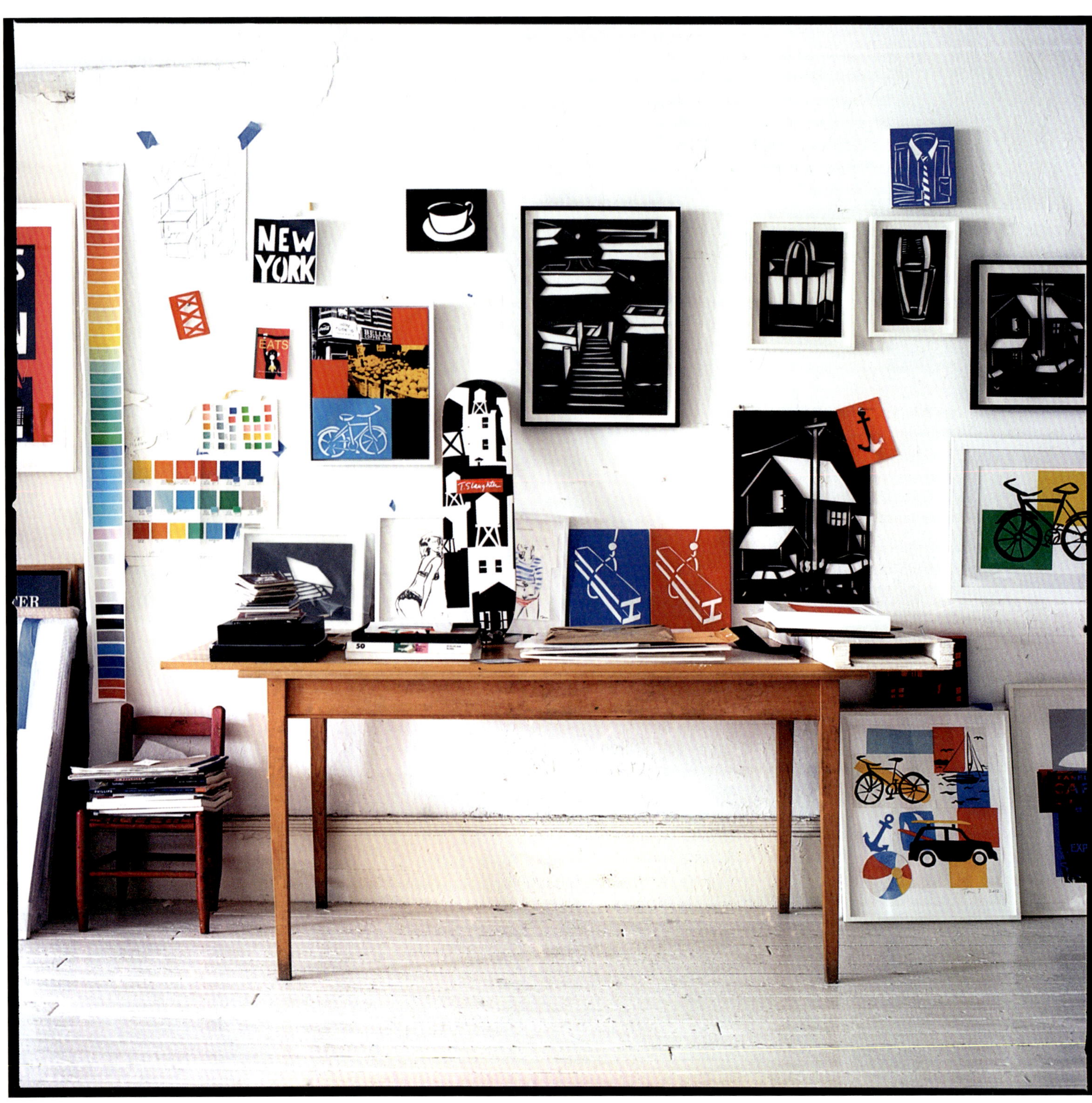

Tom Slaughter's art is about pleasure, and more specifically the pleasure of everyday objects. Yes, he did make forays into portraiture and the figure but those series are islands in a vast sea of images of objects. I used the marine metaphor deliberately, because so many of the images were nautical, but there were also urban images, vehicular images, and domestic images. Apparel also frequently appeared in his work—perhaps because he had an eye for simple, elegant design.

This repetitive drawing of a small array of objects was very much a part of Tom's process, notably, his endless attempt to achieve a distilled perfection through replication. The paradox of this emphasis on iteration is that it alludes to two things that seem to be the opposite in our understanding of the world: the meditative effect of repetition that is achieved in the distilled brushwork of Zen masters like Shunso Joshu versus the distancing effect achieved by art using mechanical reproduction that was perfected in the twentieth century—perhaps most explicit in Andy Warhol's silkscreened works.

Returning to the notion of pleasure, there are no wars, natural disasters, or economic crises in the art of Henri Matisse, Raoul Dufy, or Stuart Davis—artists who I know from many chats with Tom were crucial influences on his work. He took a similar celebratory approach to art-making, delivering sensual visual pleasure to his viewers even during turbulent times. From the rounds that Tom and I made through the galleries of New York and Toronto, I know that he also appreciated issue-oriented work by Leon Golub, Nancy Spero, and Jean-Michel Basquiat. However, he knew full well the source of his creative spark and, accordingly, delivered insights to his viewers into the enjoyment of objects.

Andy Fabo

Artist

Toronto, ON

2017

OBJECTS

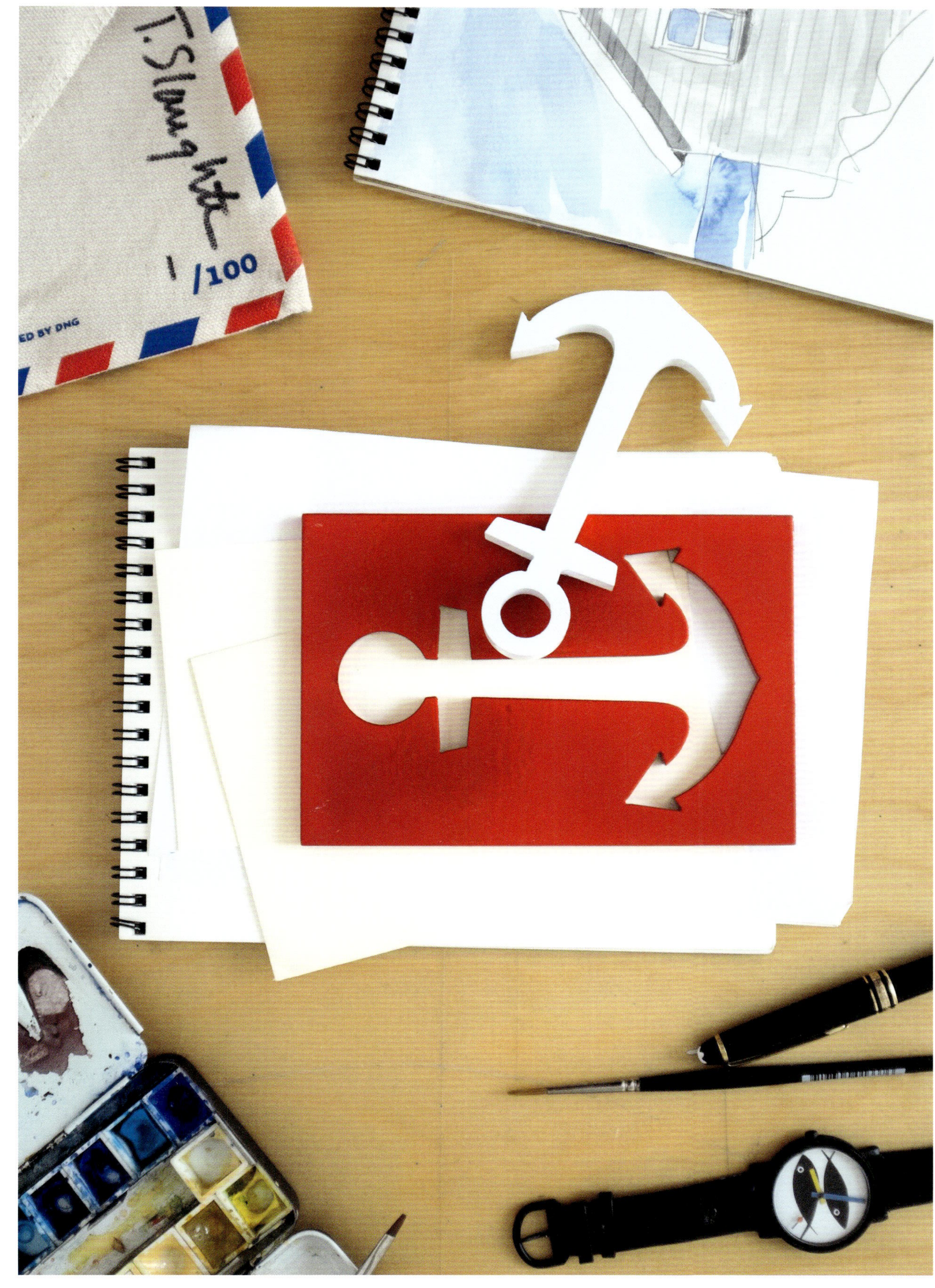
T.Slaughter
— /100
ED BY DNG

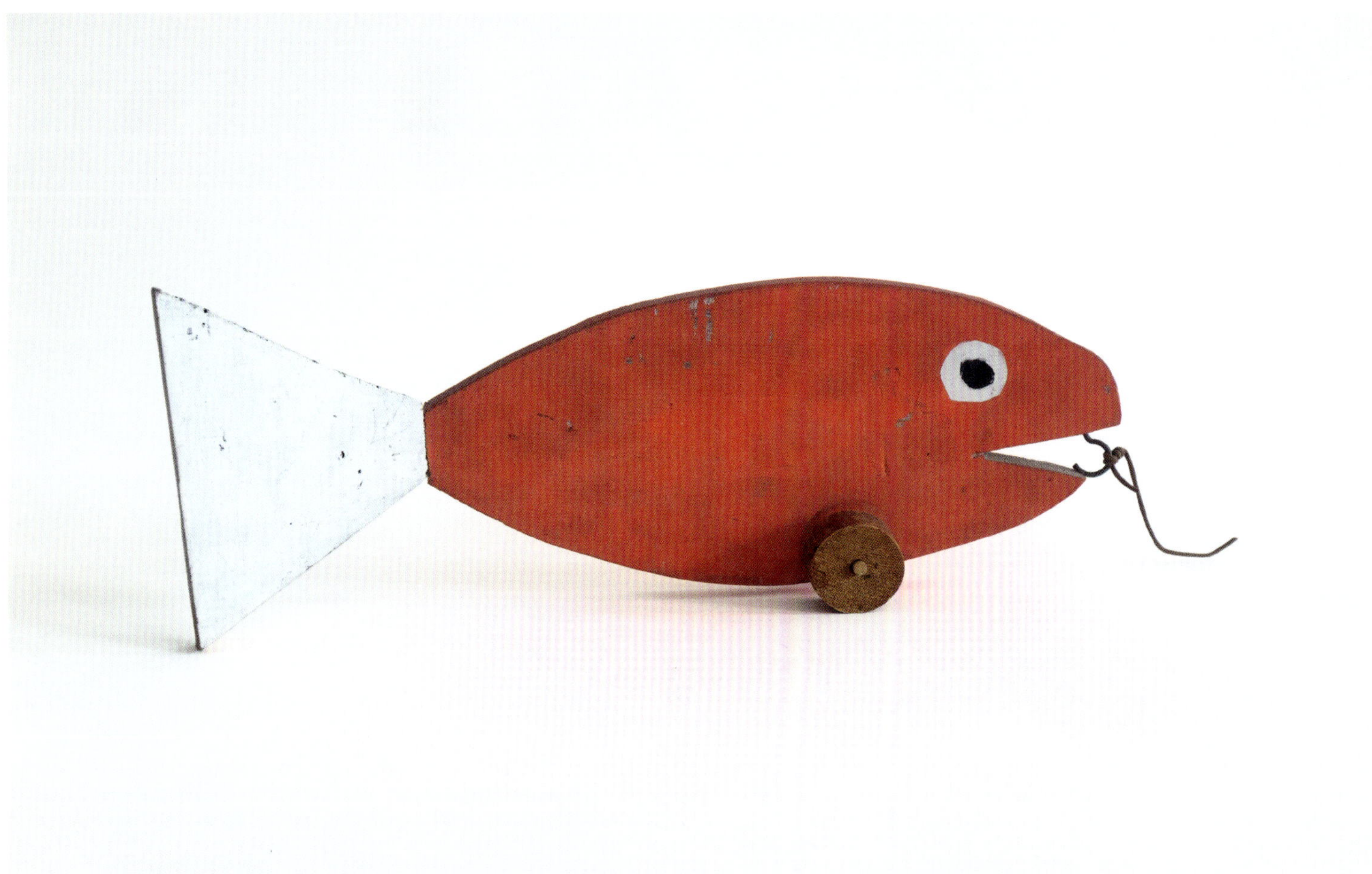

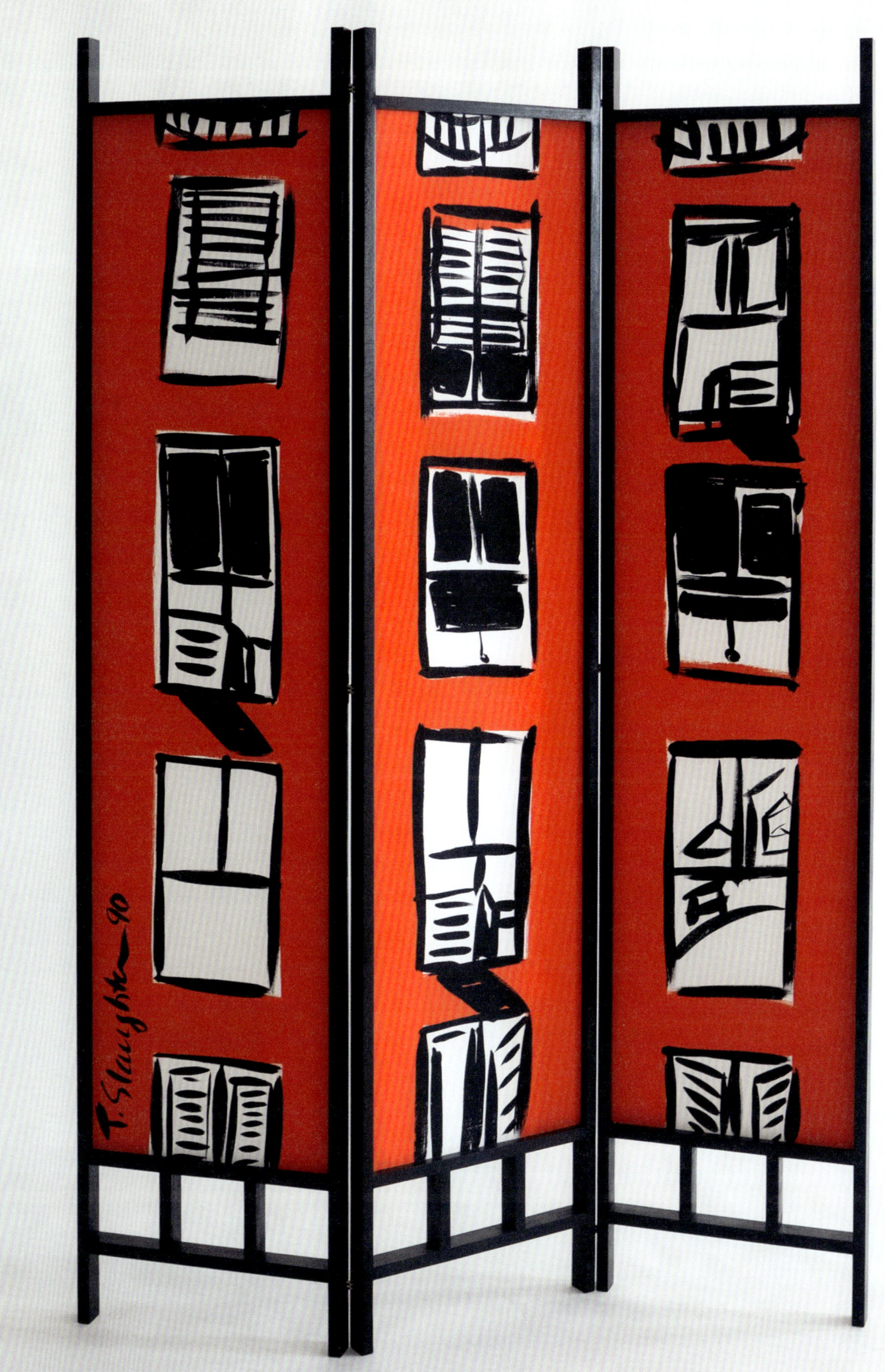

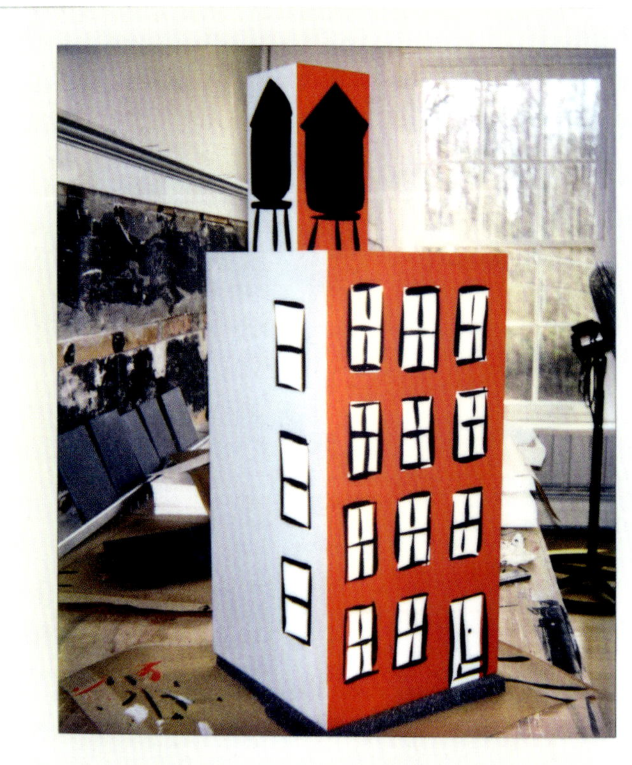

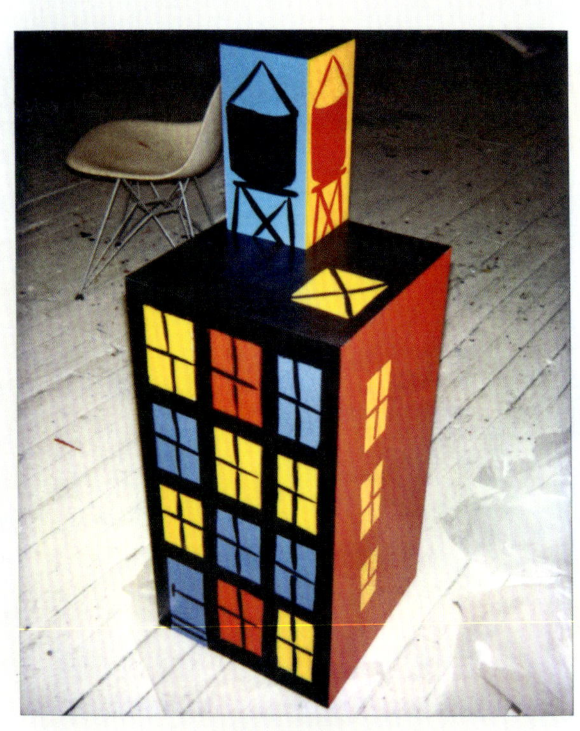

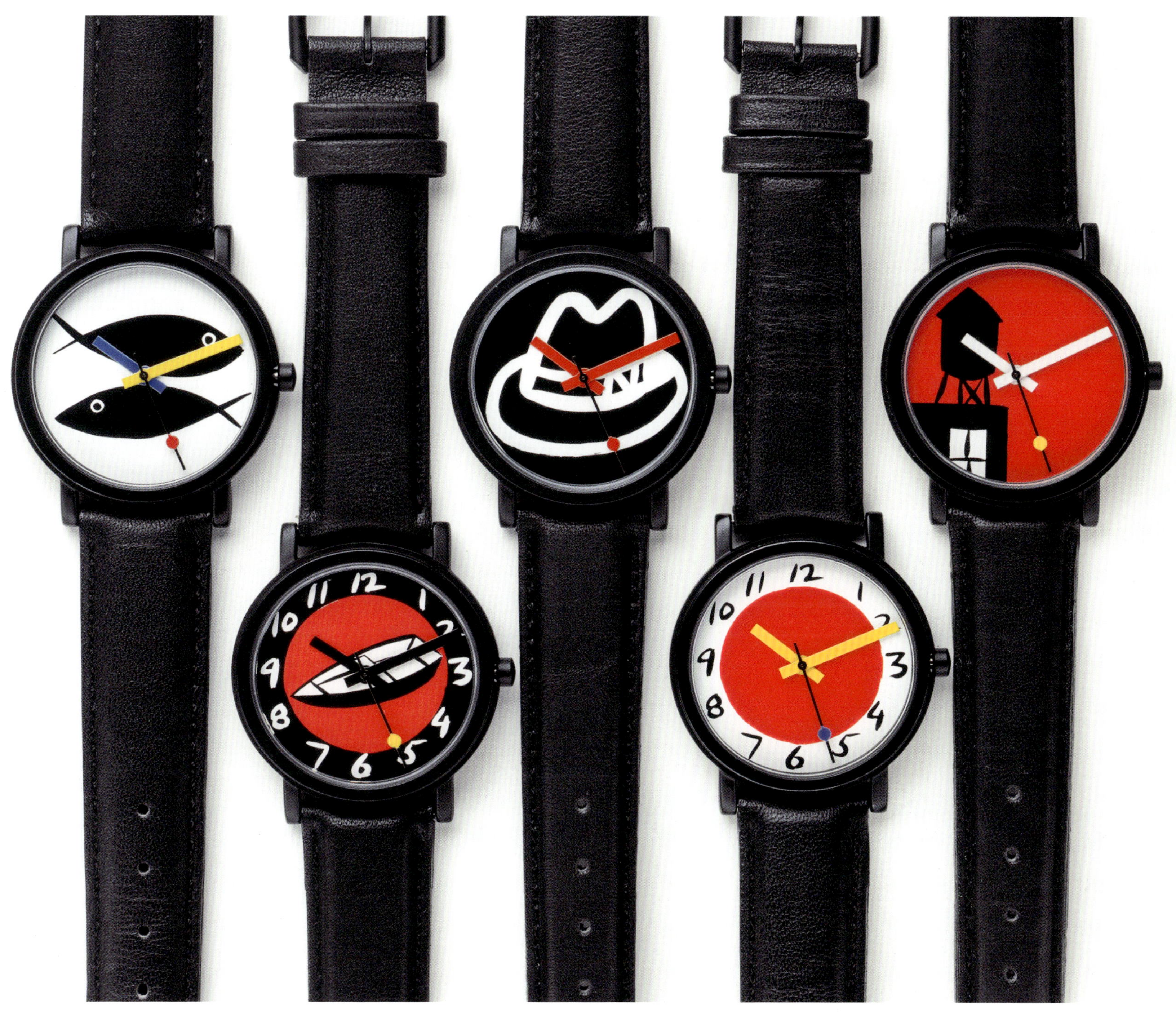

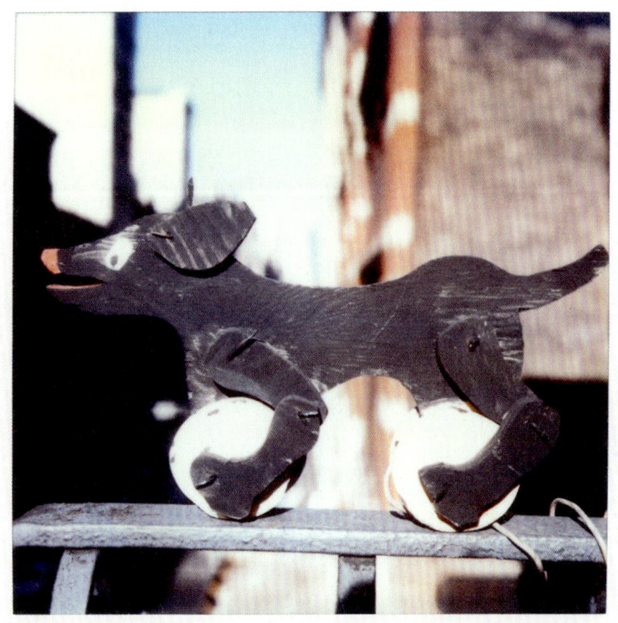
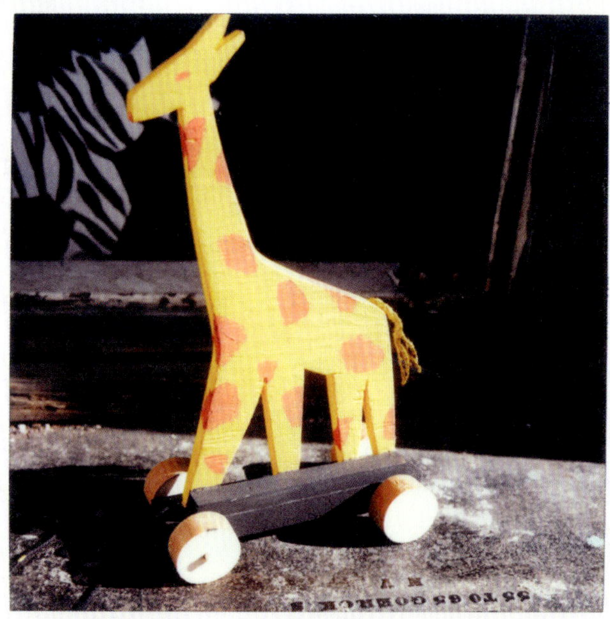
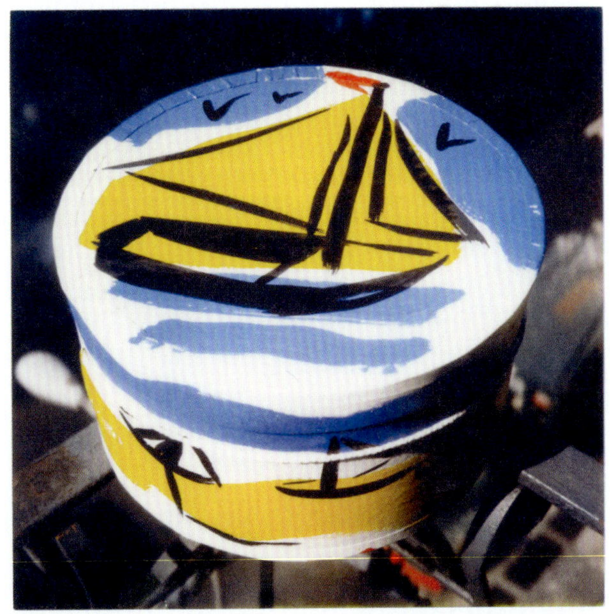
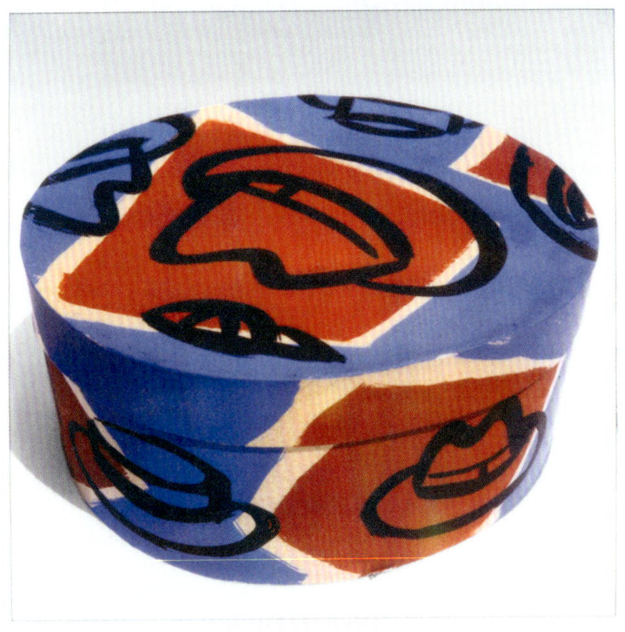

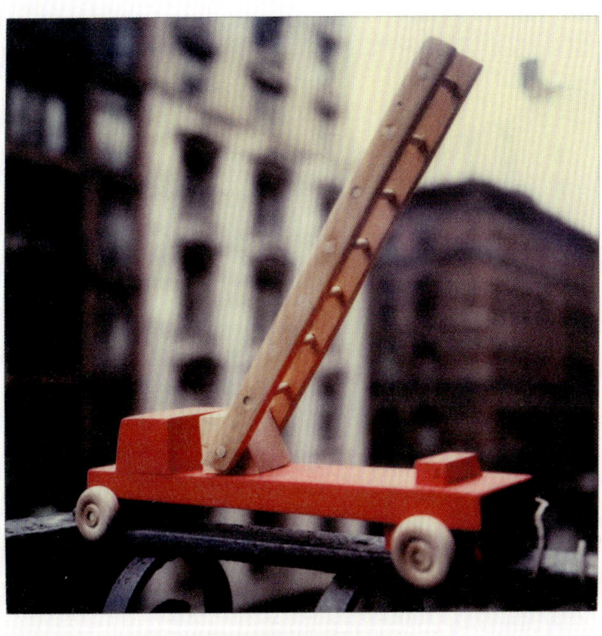

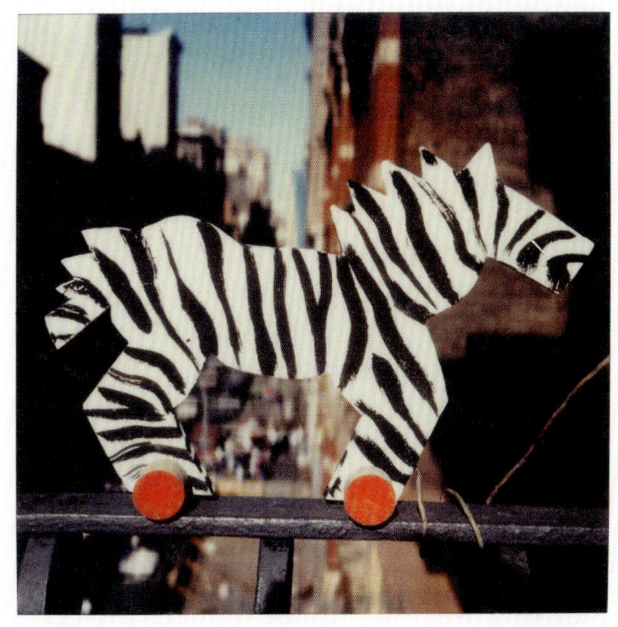

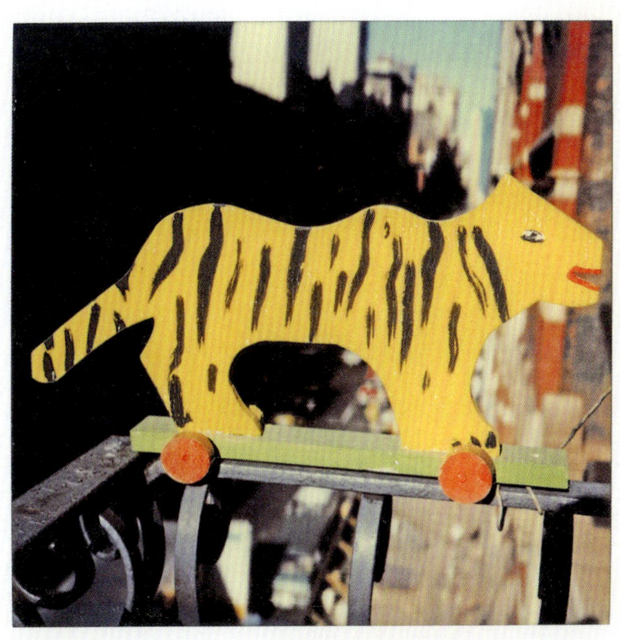

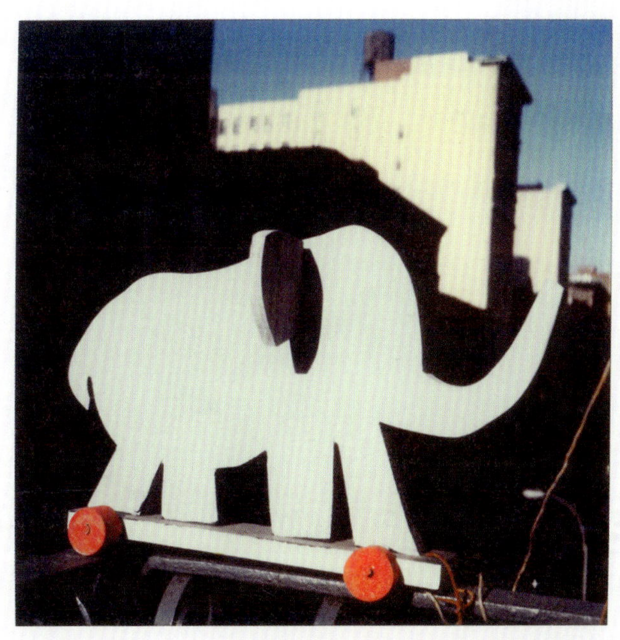

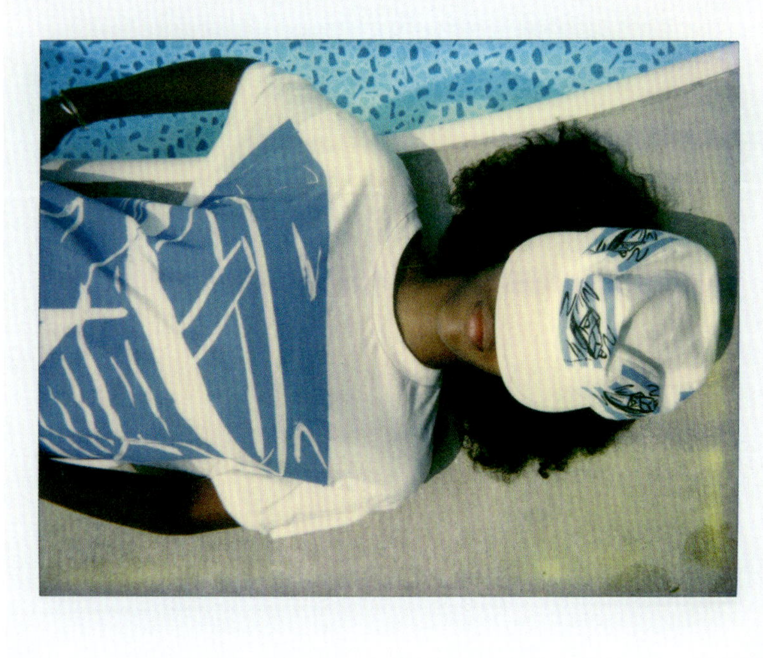

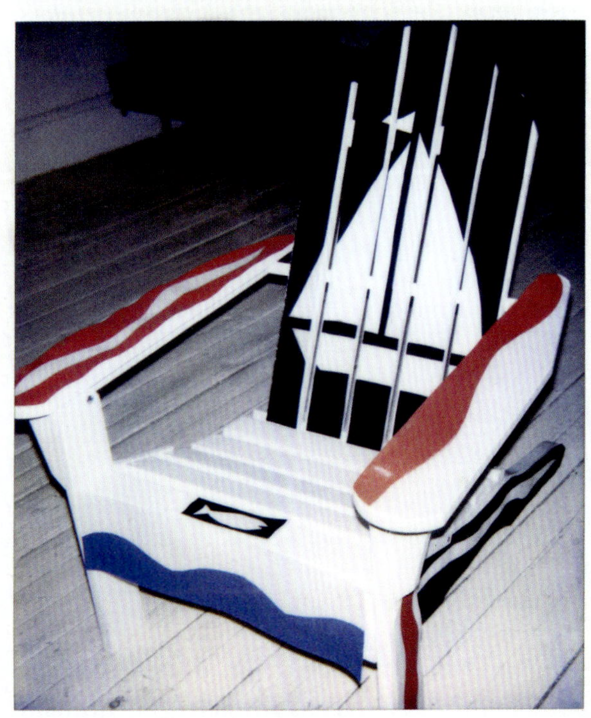

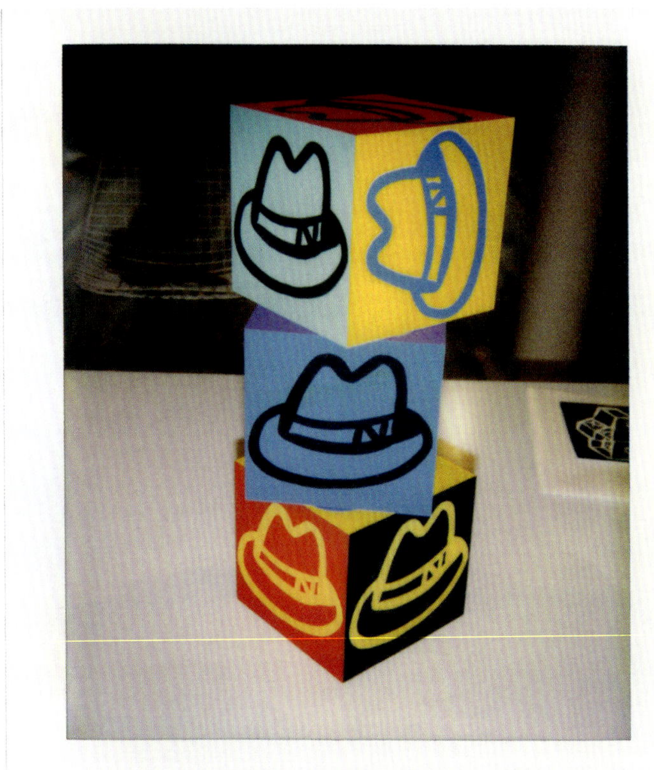

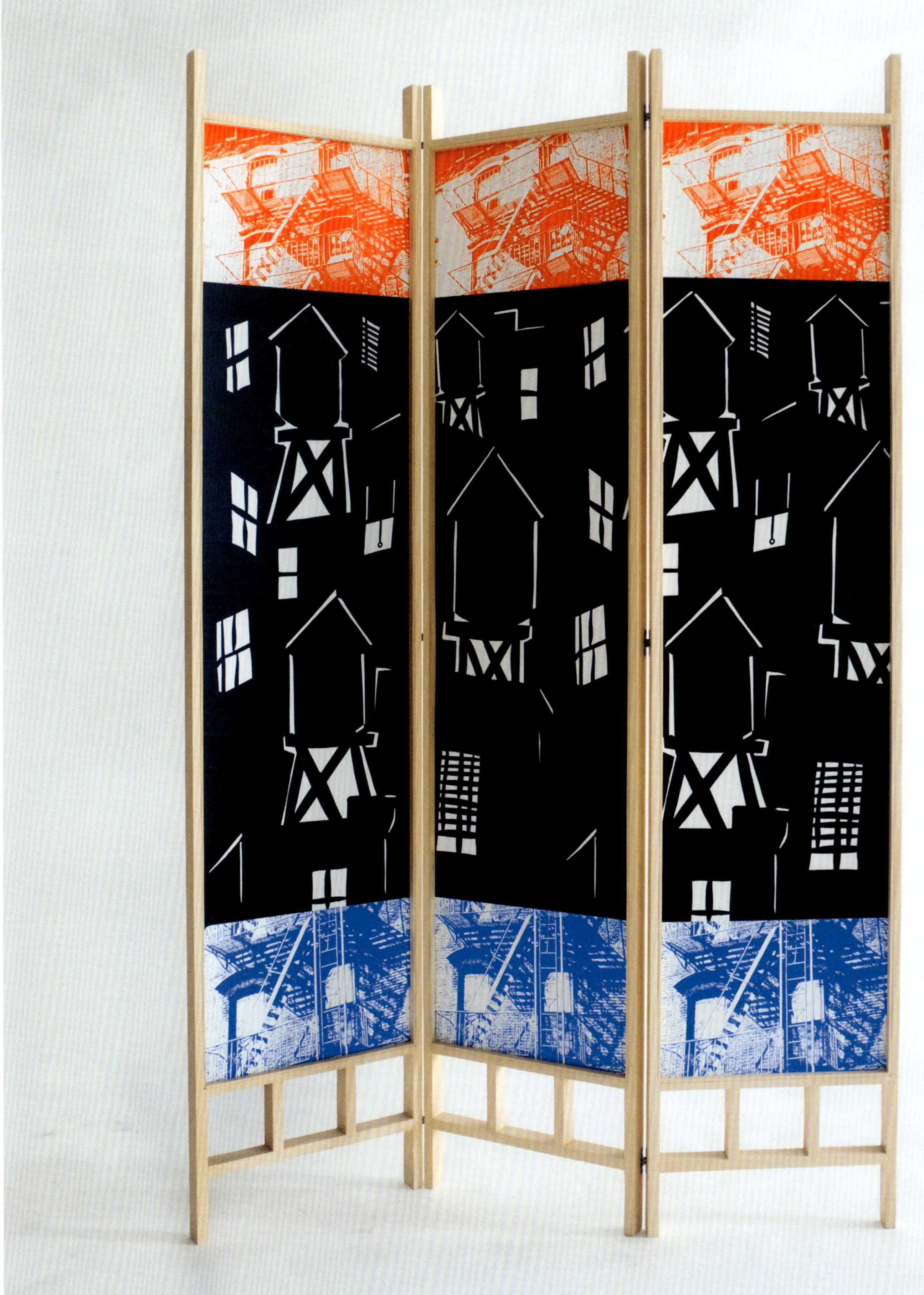

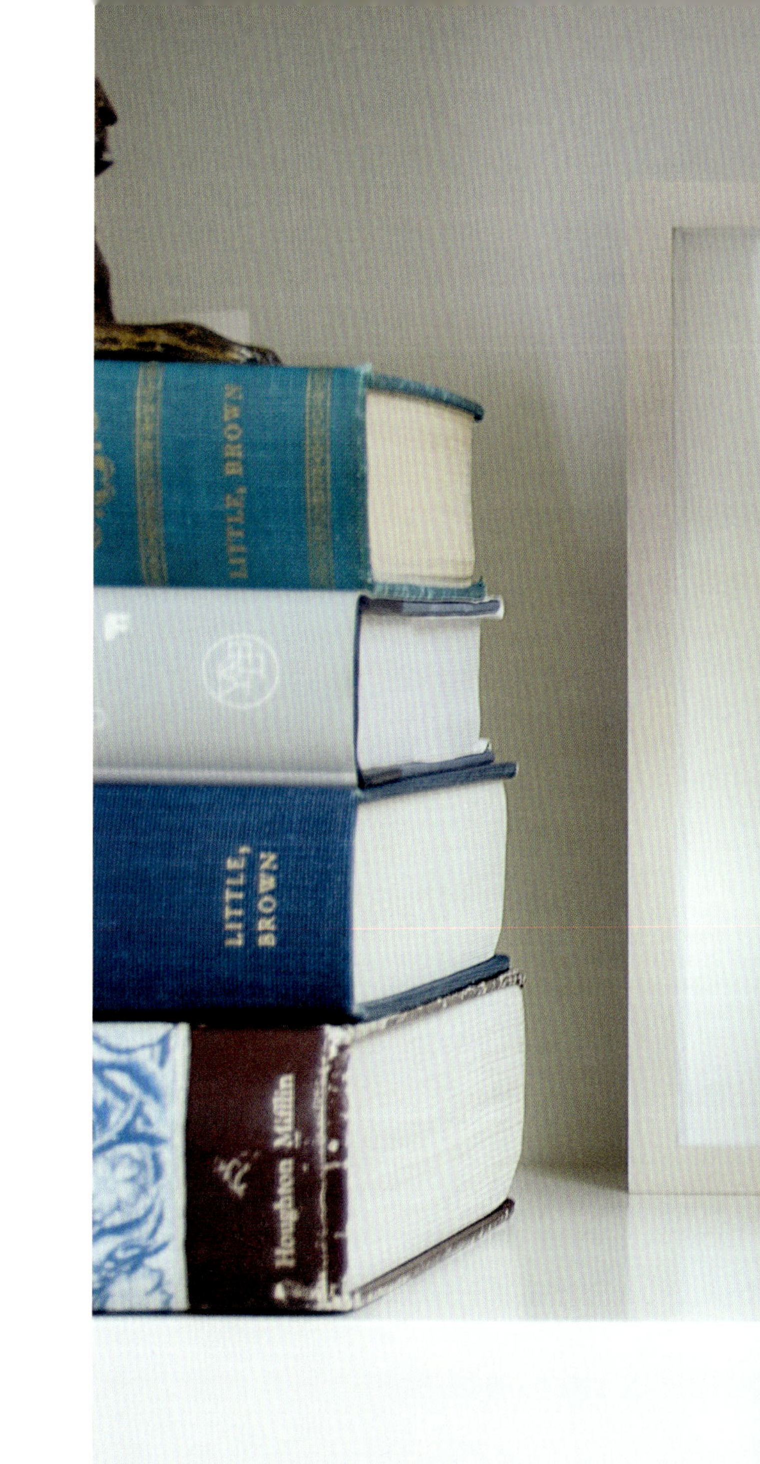

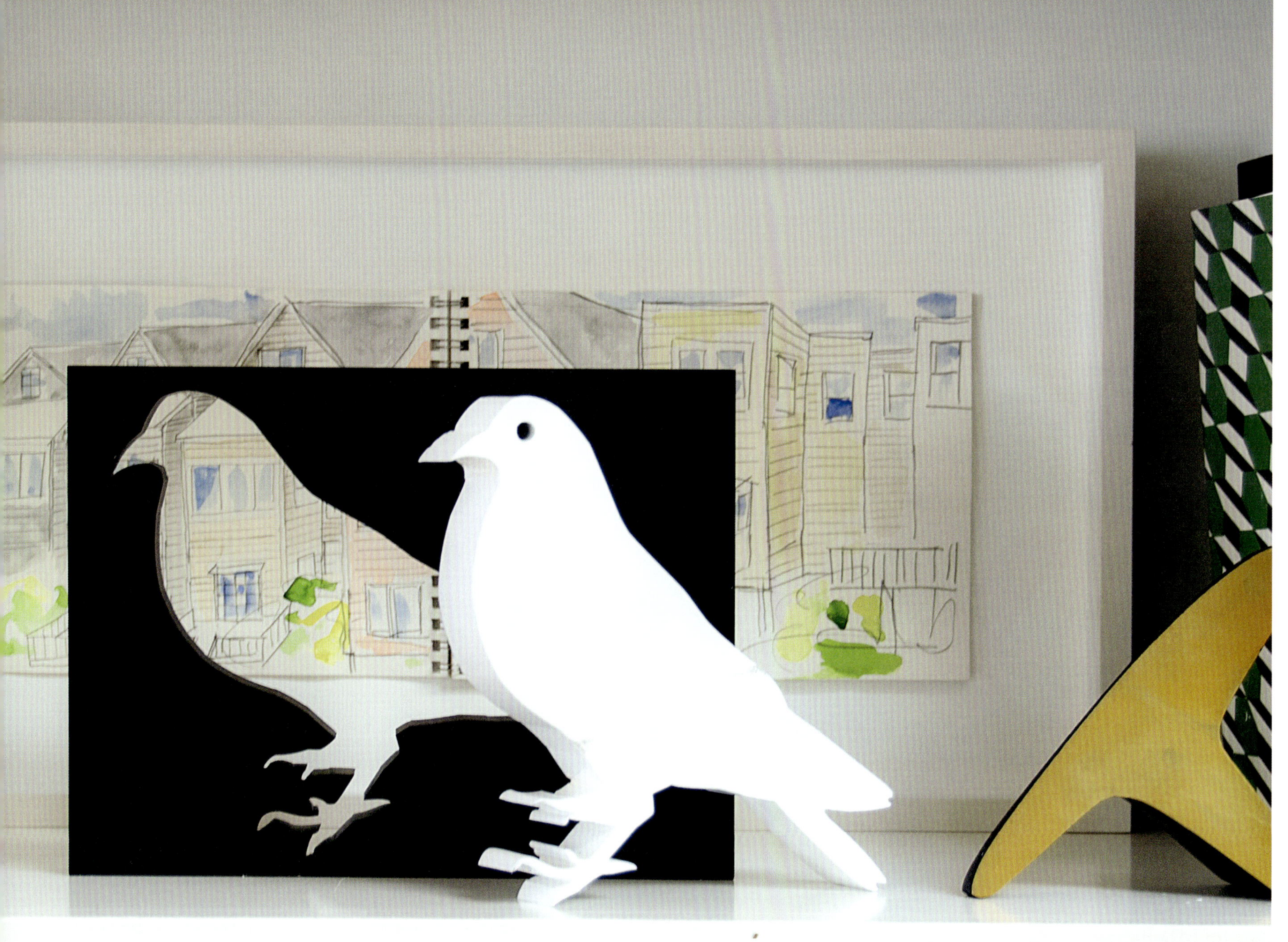

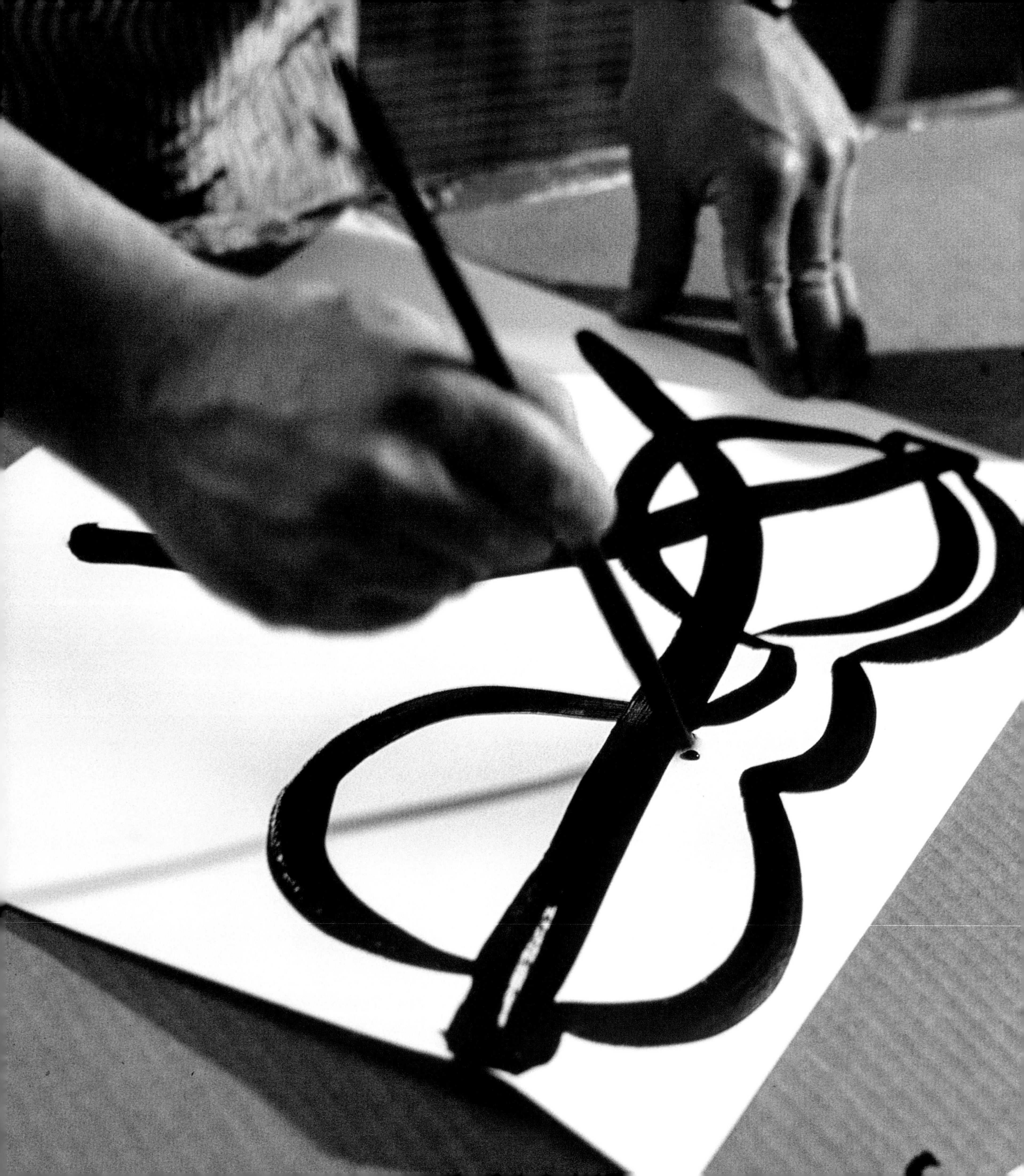

LOOK, AND REALLY SEE

It's best to see art with artists. My favorite artist to see exhibitions with
was Tom Slaughter.

I first met Tom through our mutual friend Jerry Joseph, the owner of Jerry's
restaurant, a popular SoHo hangout for artists and art lovers from the late eighties
until it closed in 2008. Jerry was a board member of Creative Time, the ambitious
public arts organization I then directed, and he knew we needed money. Tom
was a board member of the Horace W. Goldsmith Foundation, and Jerry hoped
Tom would invite us to apply for a grant. I'm sure it was out of affection for Jerry
that Tom took the meeting; knowing him as I do now, I know he would have rather
been in the studio painting or out seeing a new exhibition. But he would also hate
to disappoint another nonprofit arts leader with her hand out.

Tom was handsome, with a head of wavy black hair, piercing brown eyes, thick
eyebrows that arched toward his temple, and full lips, yet I was most struck by
his demeanor. He was intense, irreverent, opinionated, and whip smart. When we
met, his emotional armor was on, and I confess it took a while to make a dent.
But as we discussed art, his manner changed. His eyes brightened, his mind
opened, and so too did his heart. It wasn't long before Tom made the first of his
grants to Creative Time—grants that were critical, and even transformative, to the
organization's work. Grants that helped us realize now legendary projects such
as Paul Chan's *Waiting for Godot* in the Lower 9th Ward of New Orleans, Kara
Walker's *A Subtlety* at the Domino Sugar Factory on Brooklyn's waterfront, Nick
Cave's *Heard NY* in Grand Central, Paul Ramirez Jonas's *Key to the City* in all five
boroughs of New York, and Trevor Paglin's *The Last Pictures*, a time capsule that
continues to make the rounds of the geosynchronous orbit.

It wasn't long before Tom and I became fast friends. From the get-go, it
was obvious he was a man of many passions. He was passionate about good
philanthropy—the kind that forges a real partnership of commitment and
trust between donor and beneficiary. He was a passionate board member for
the organizations he served, including PS1 and the Public Theater. He was
passionate about good, simple food. (I recall, for example, his lecture on the best
apples as we headed to the Union Square farmers' market one fall morning after
a long stint in isolation at the hospital after his stem-cell transplant.) Tom was
particularly passionate about women. He made them feel beautiful. Most of all,
he loved his daughters. For this passion, I have no words to do his love justice.

Tom also really loved art. He loved making art. He made big paintings of brightly
colored everyday things, such as bookshelves, glasses of water, airplanes, boats,

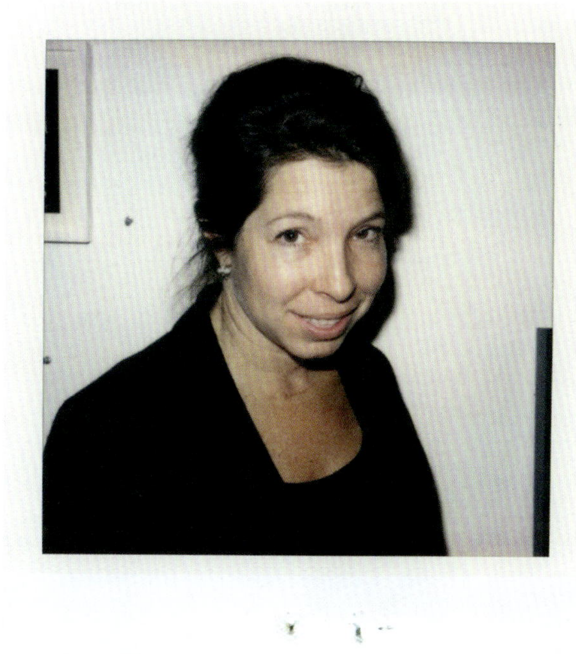

Anne Pasternak

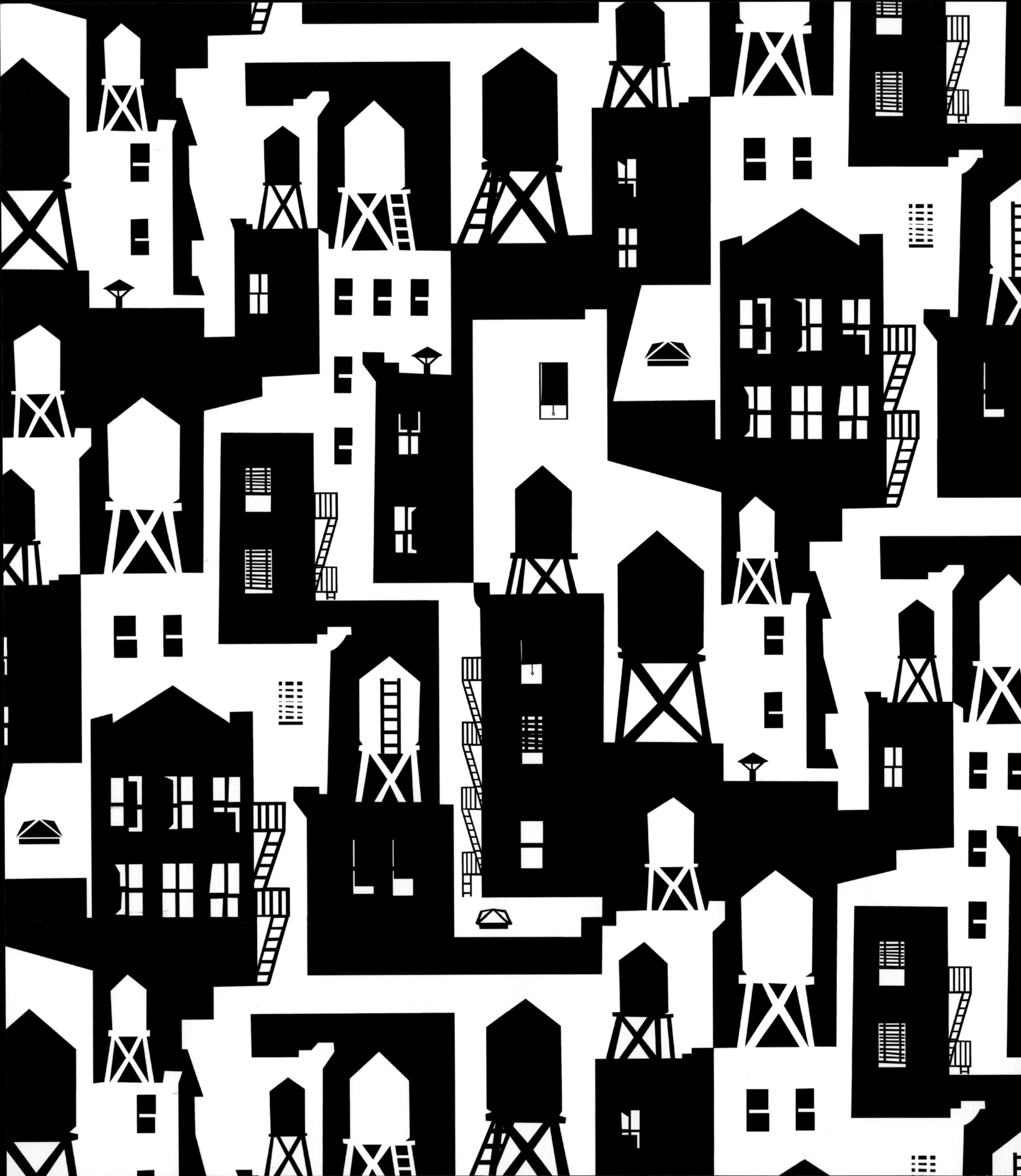

cars, and New York City water towers. He made art accessible for everyone,
no matter how young or of what income. He made Mattisean cut-out collages
of animals and objects, and they became delightful books for kids. He loved
designing posters for his favorite theater company, The New Victory, on 42nd
Street, because its programs catered to children. He made wallpaper of his
bookshelf and water-tower images. (When I put up his water-tower wallpaper
in my bathroom, he insisted on overseeing the installation. He could not have
been more thrilled.) He made inexpensive print editions of ice-cream sandwiches,
surfboards, and sneakers. He even made images for pillows and iPhone cases.
Tom was always making things.

Our friendship took us to many places, especially places filled with art.
Before he got sick, hardly a day went by without Tom seeing an exhibition. He
was always happy for other artists when they did well. I marveled that he never
seemed jealous of anyone's success. He loved all sorts of art: high and low, bright
and dark, accessible and difficult. He took me to galleries I had never heard of.
He spoke with great knowledge about each show. I loved how he delighted in
a simple line, a stroke of the paintbrush, a drip of color.

When I became the director of the Brooklyn Museum, I took reminders of Tom
with me. His anchor paperweight sits next to my keyboard. A drawing hangs
on the wall by my phone. Our gift shop is now stocked with his books, which
I continue to gift to the newborns in my life. (He'd be happy that children still
delight over his pages.) Most of all, I carry Tom's memory with me as I walk
through the galleries at night, imagining what his reaction might have been
to a painting by Marsden Hartley or Stuart Davis, an African beaded mask, or
an ancient Egyptian figure. I can't ever know the conversations that might have
ensued, but I can imagine how his bright brown eyes would have lit up, how
he would release his deep, generous laugh, and how his curious mind and
keen eye would inspire me to look, and really see, through a lens of
goodness and beauty.

Anne Pasternak

Director of the Brooklyn Museum

New York, NY

2017

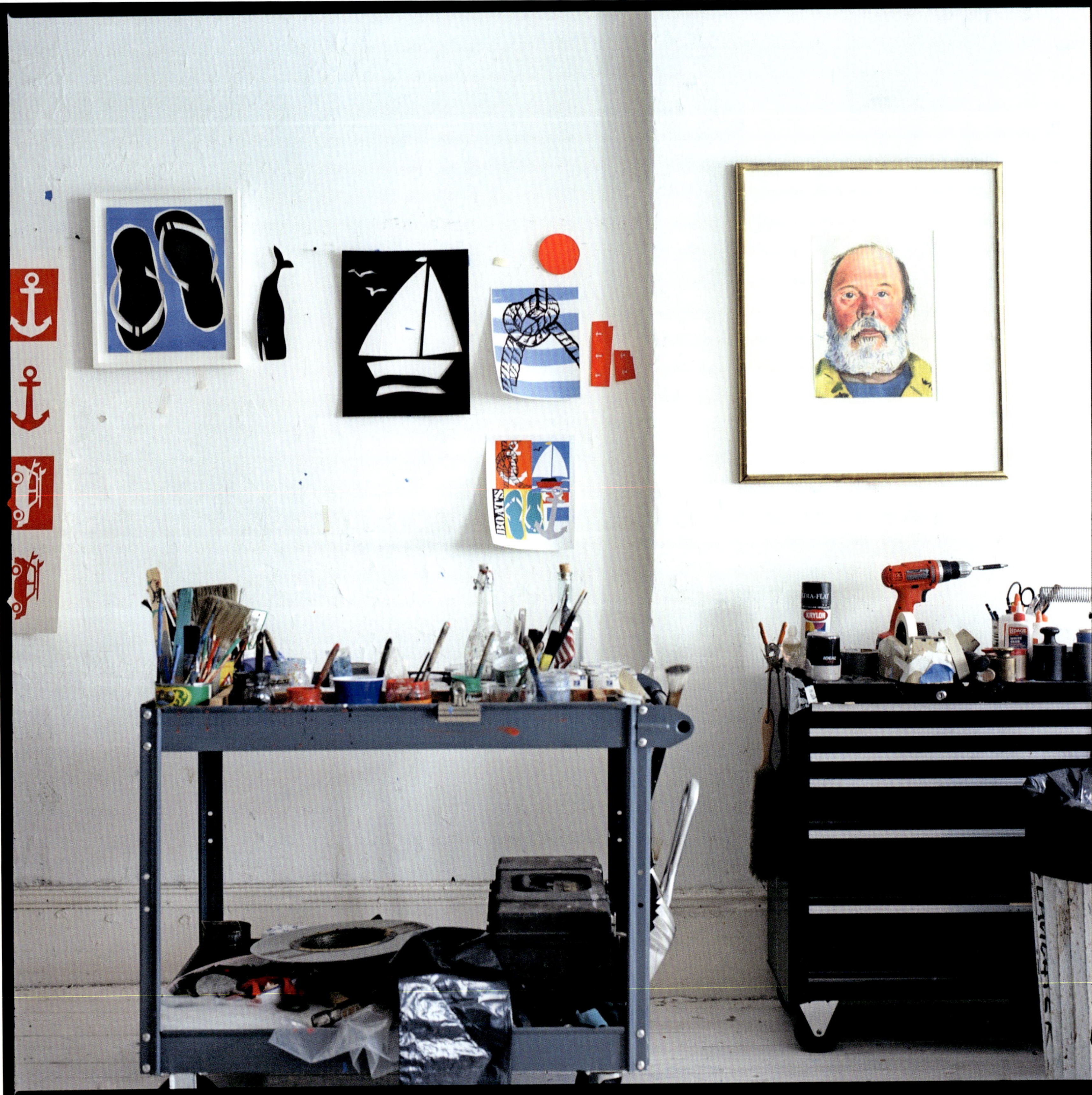

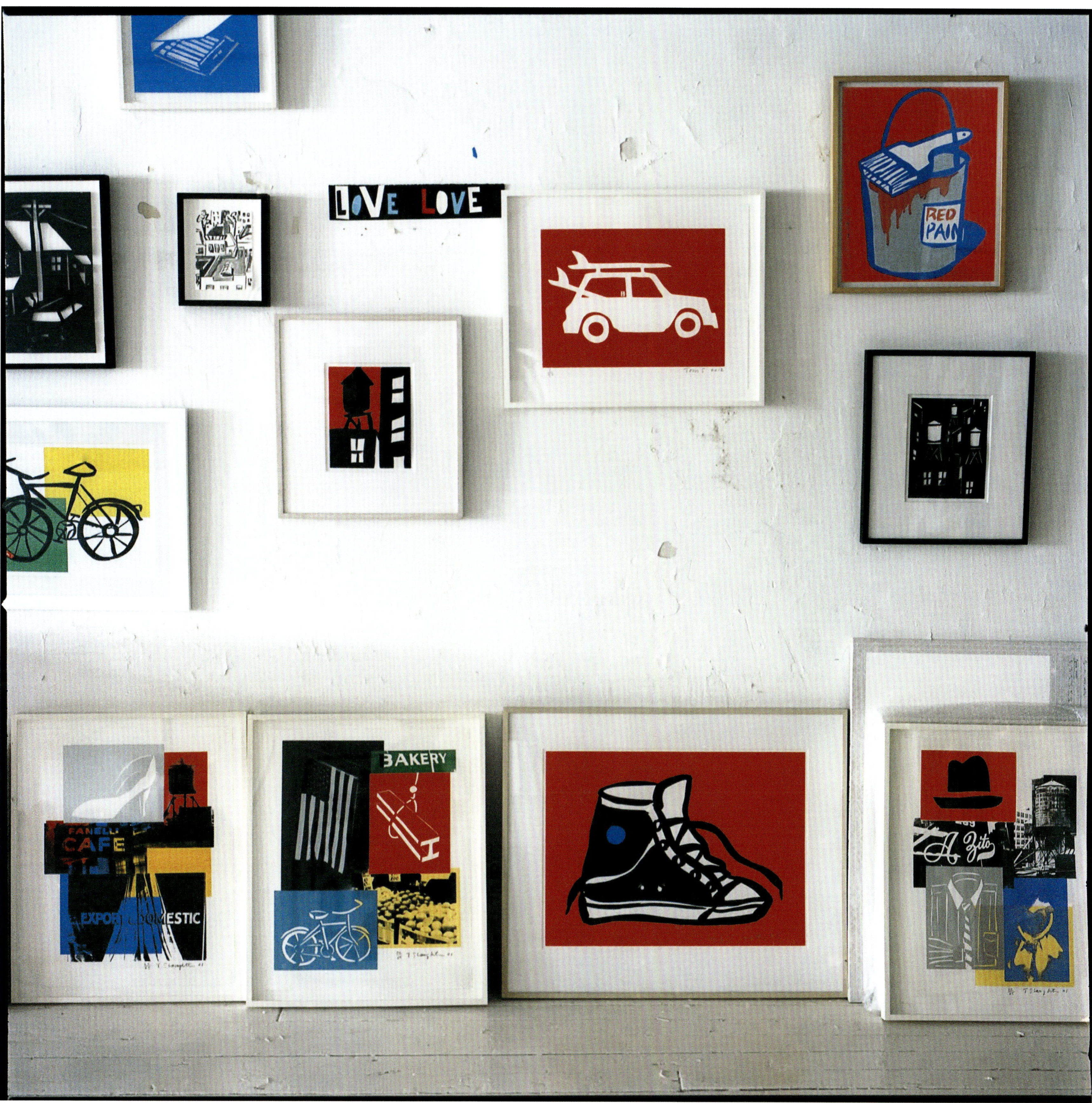

2006—2014

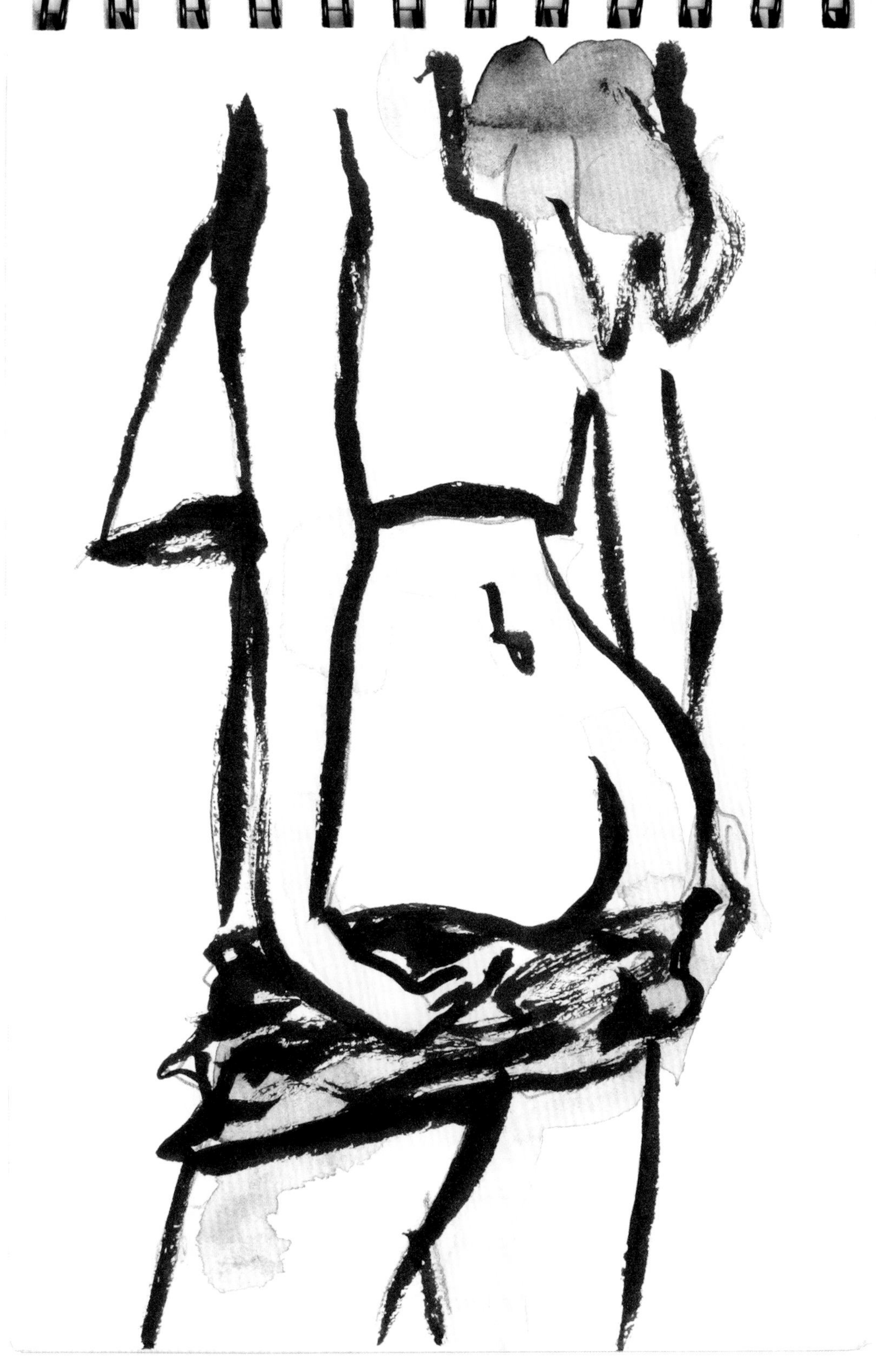

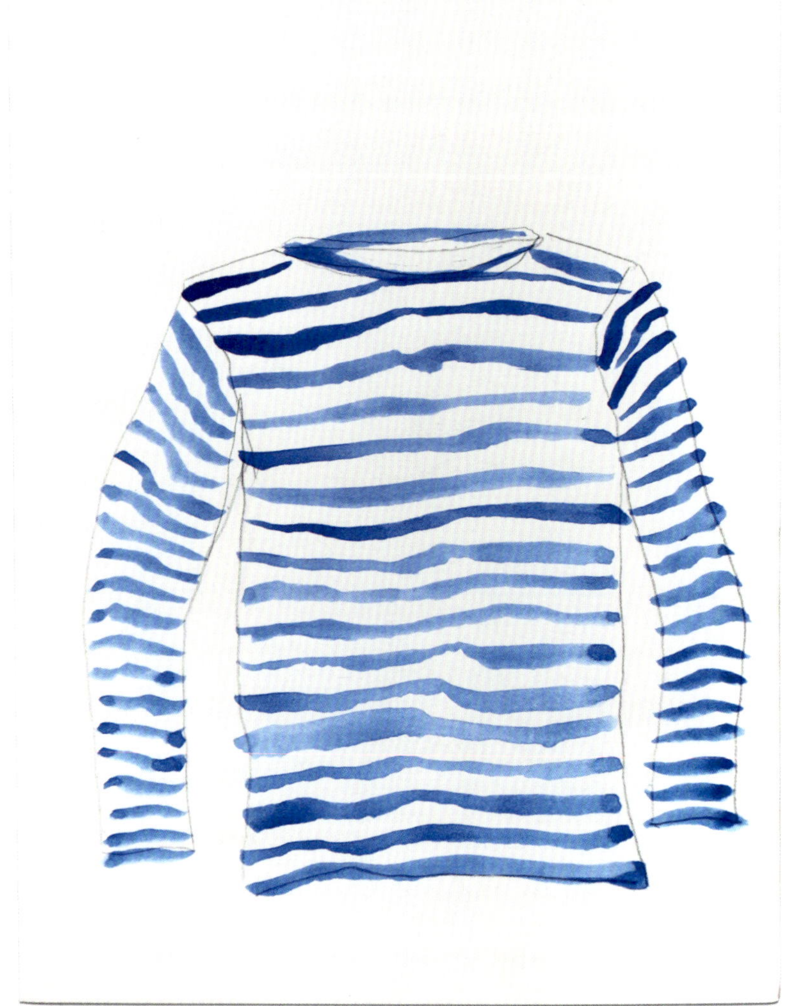

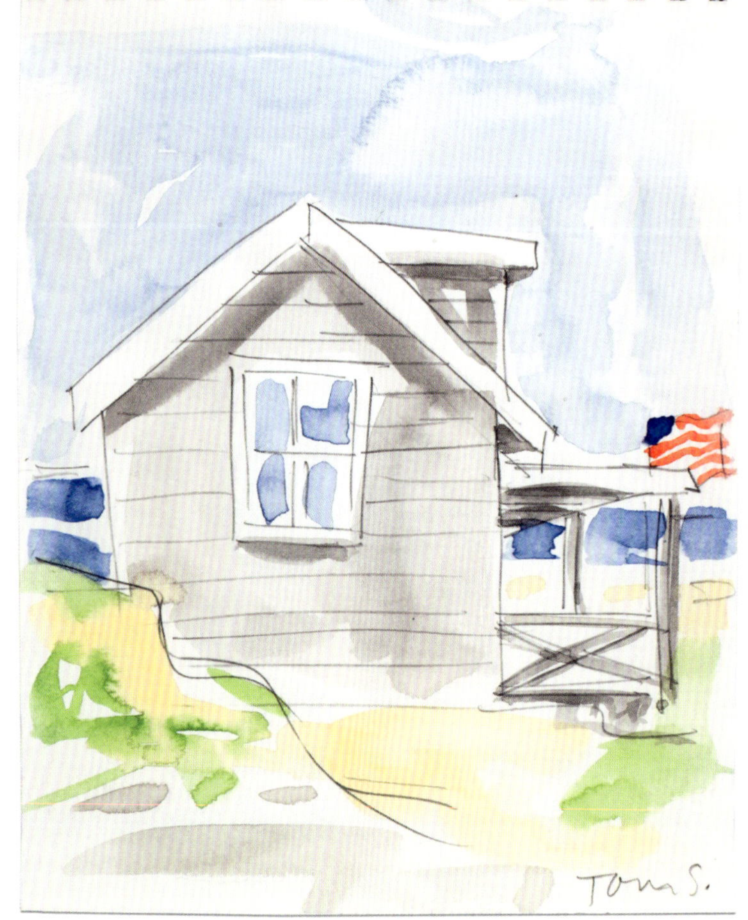

Tom S.

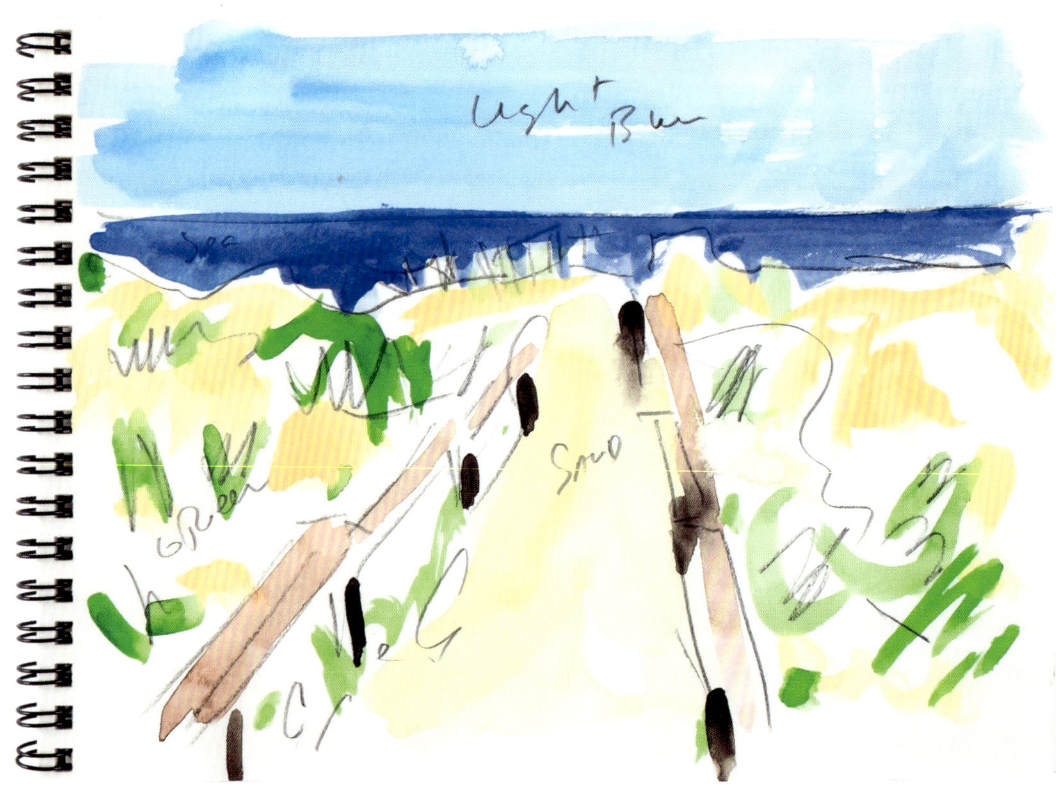

Light Blue
Sea
Green
Sand

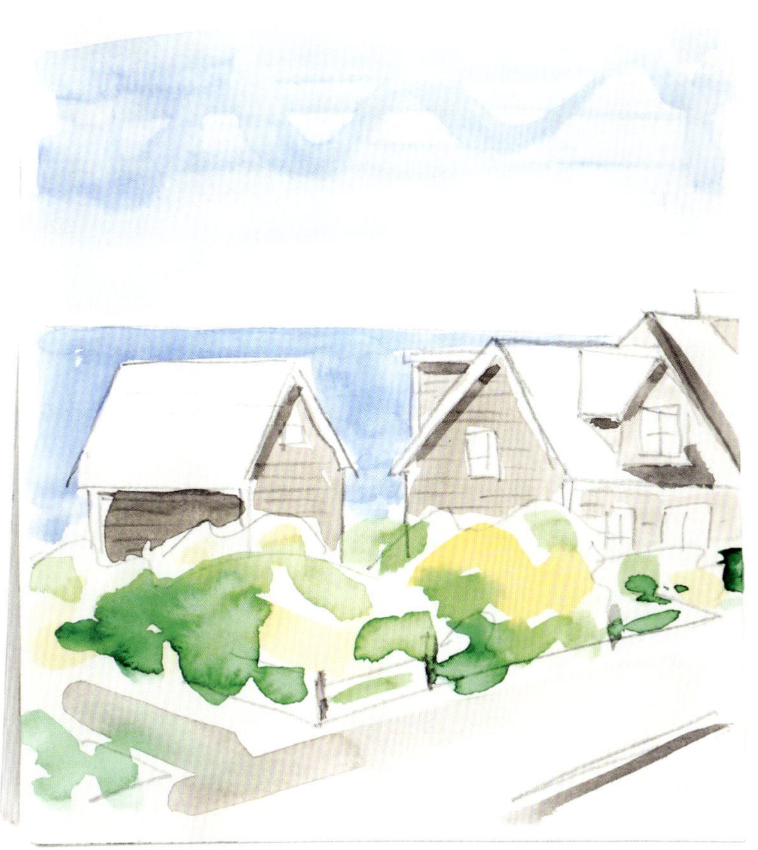

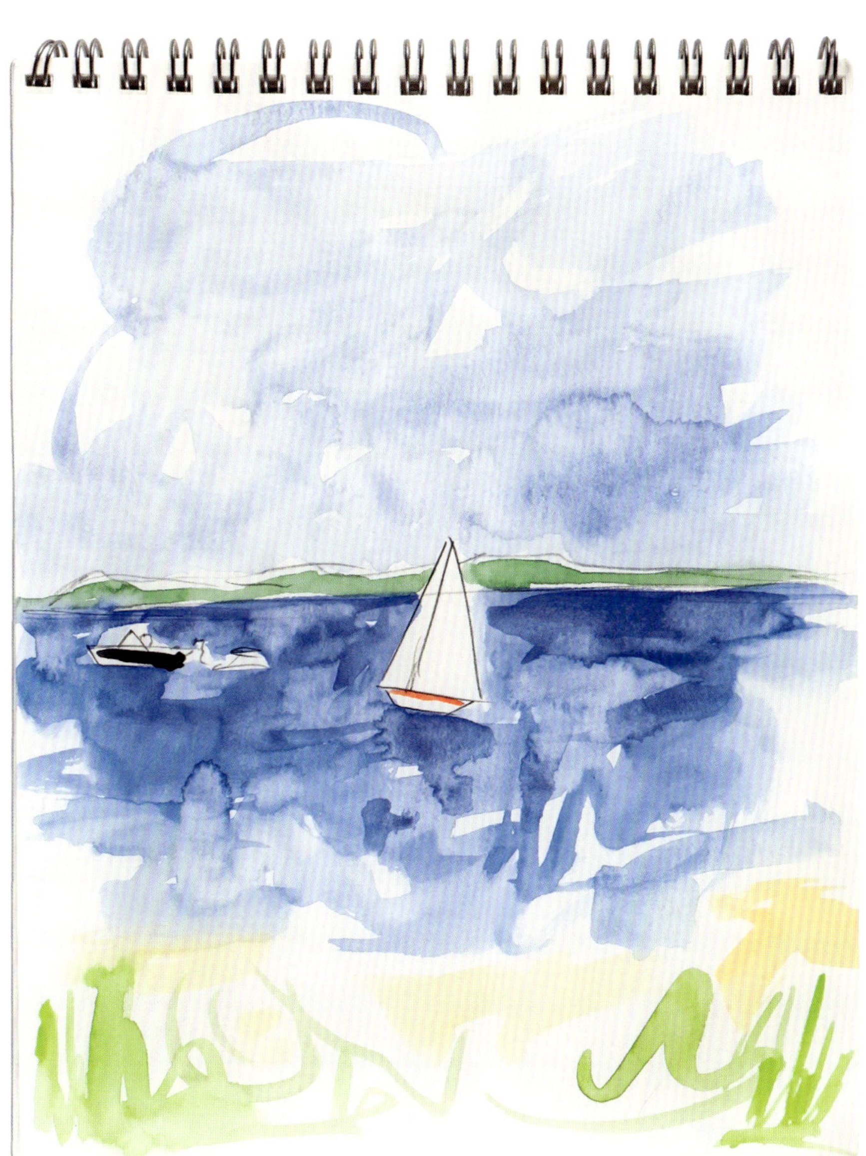

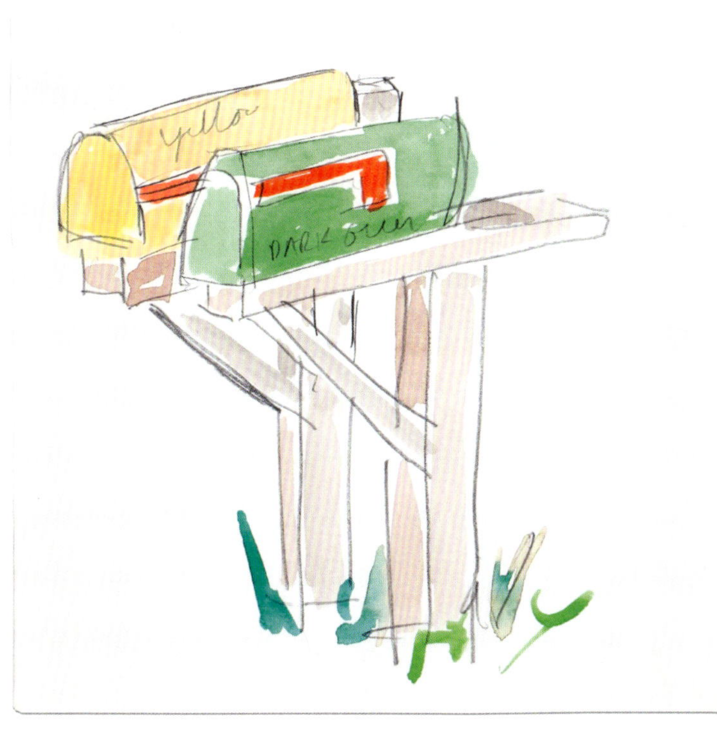
Yellow
DARK green

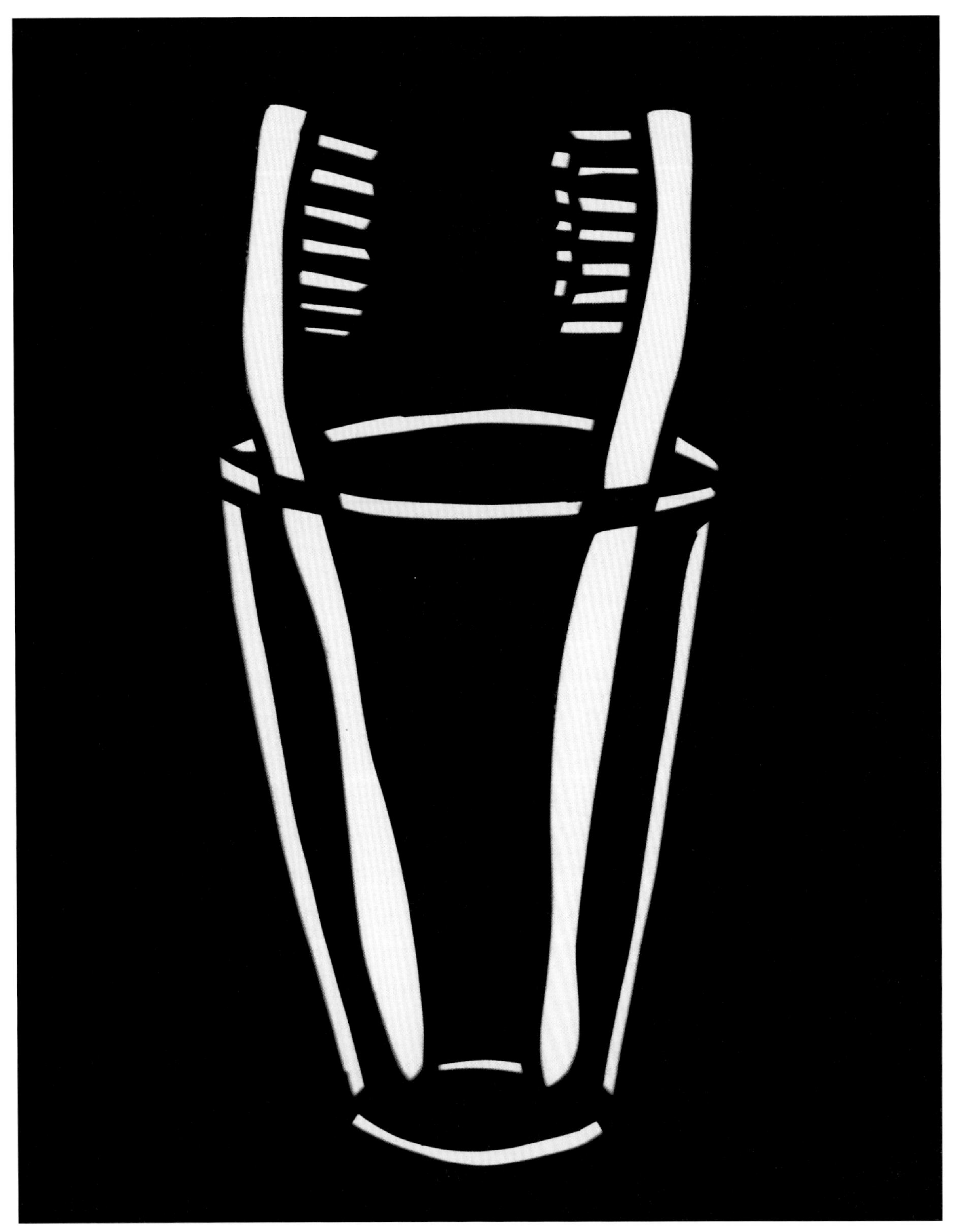

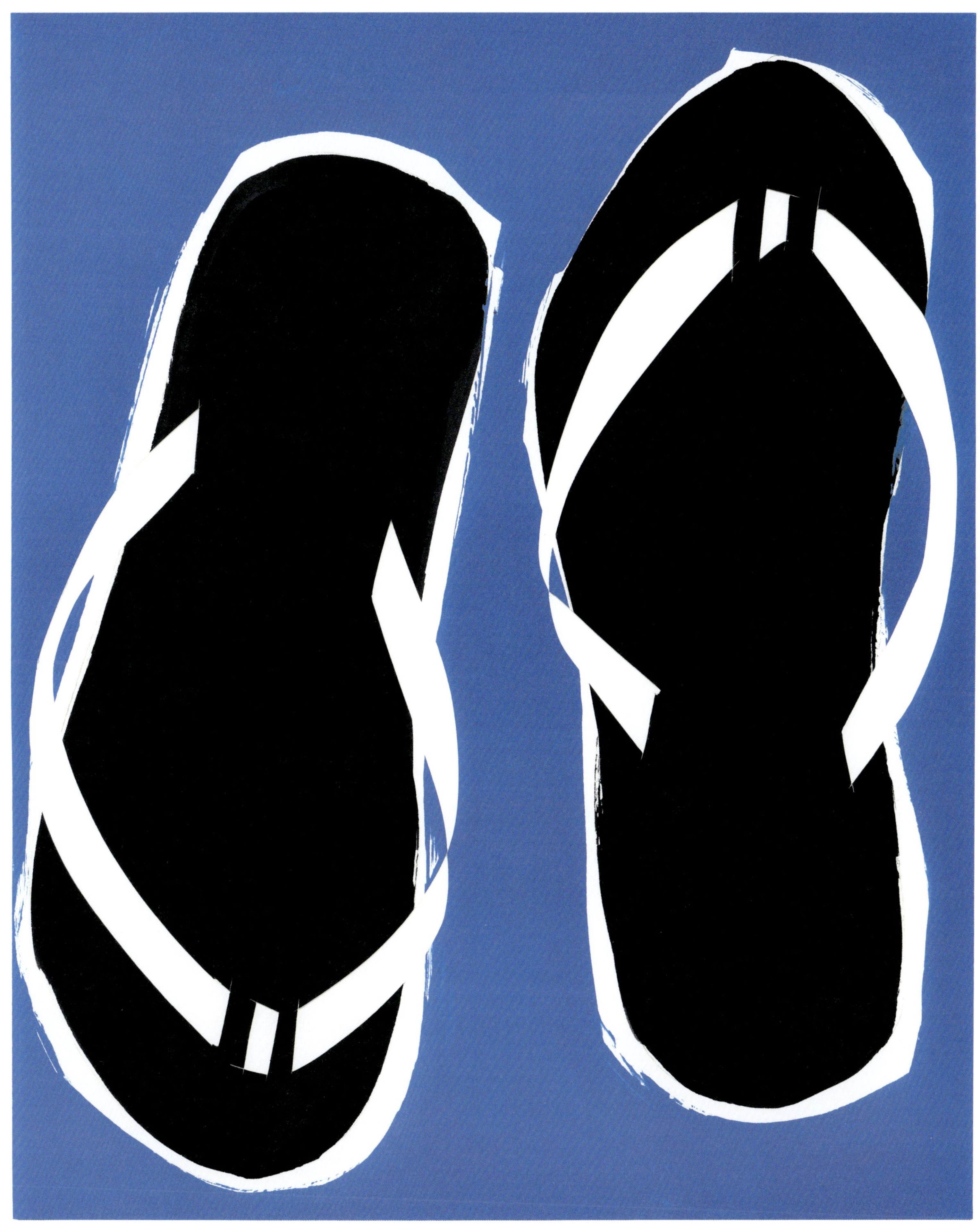

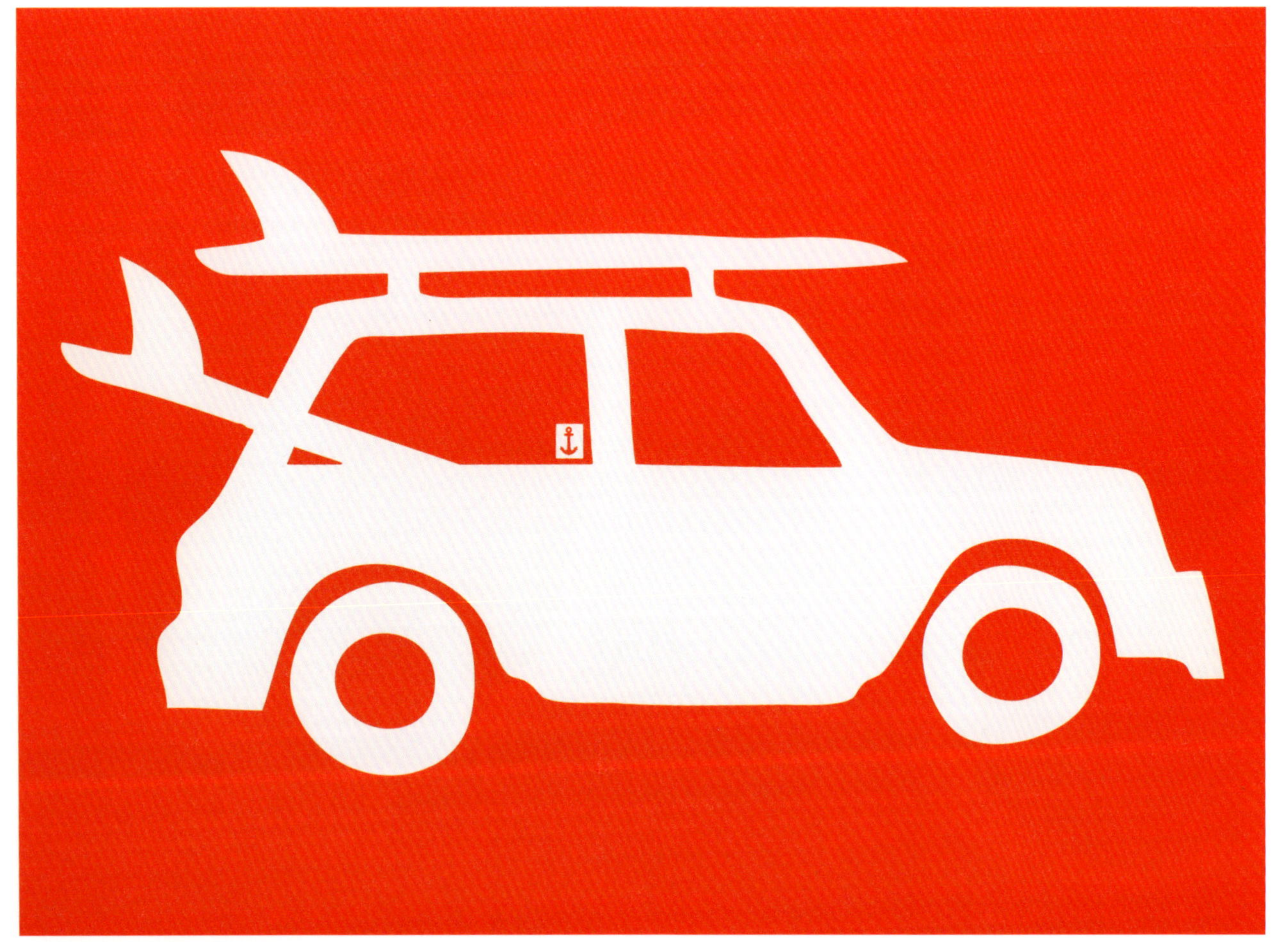

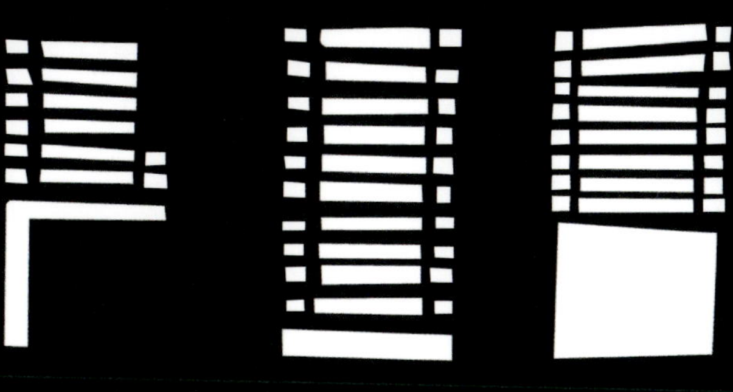
YES
WE
CAN

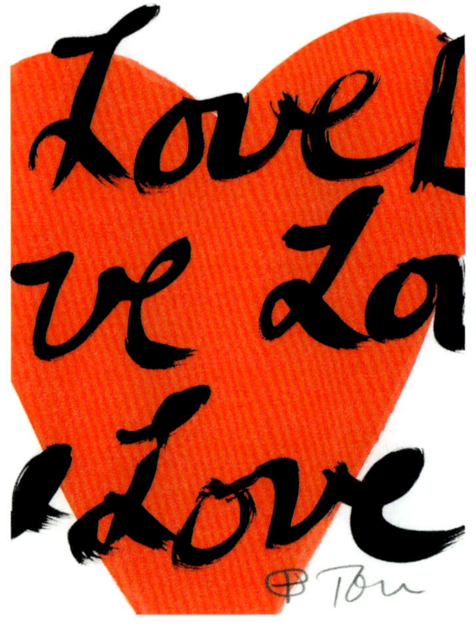
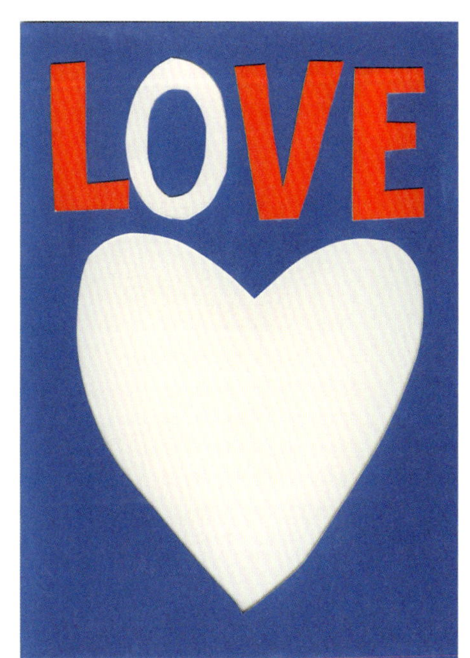
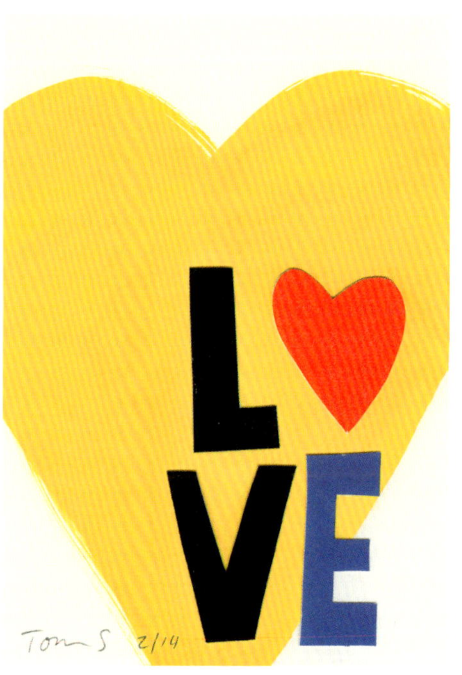
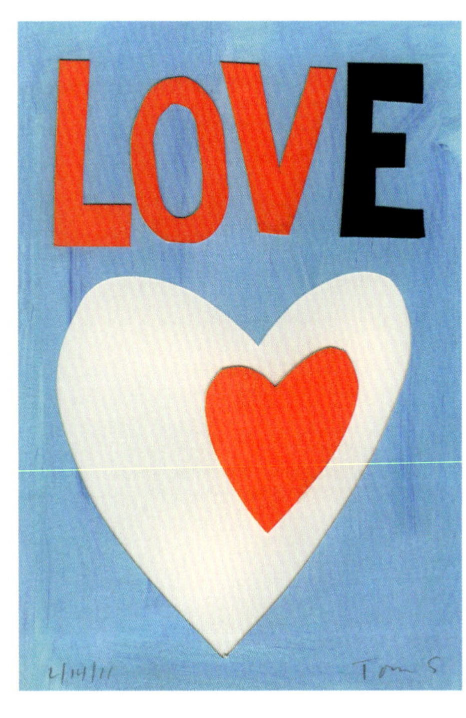
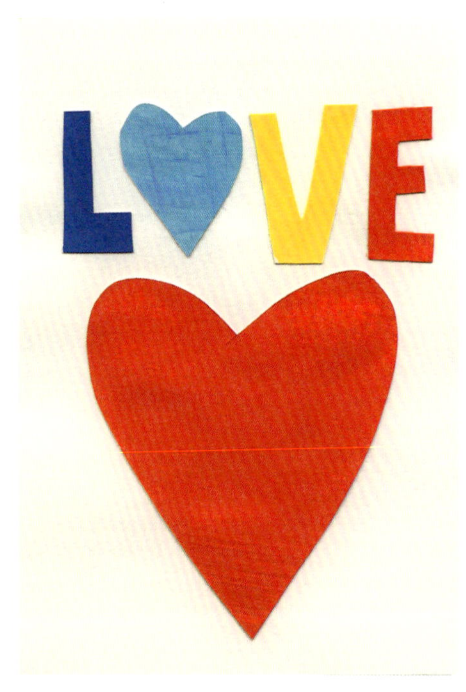
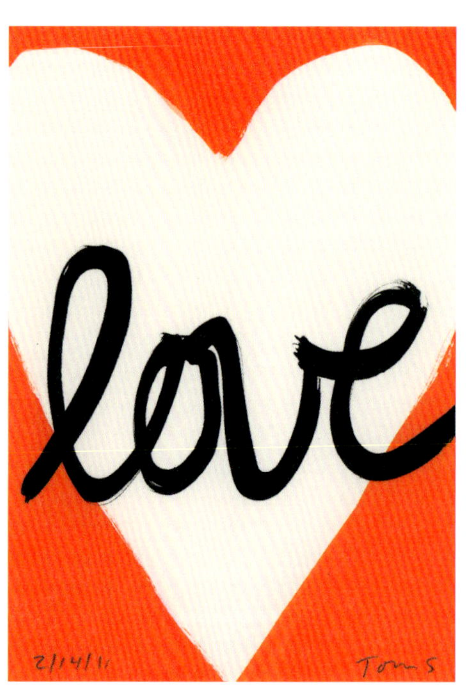

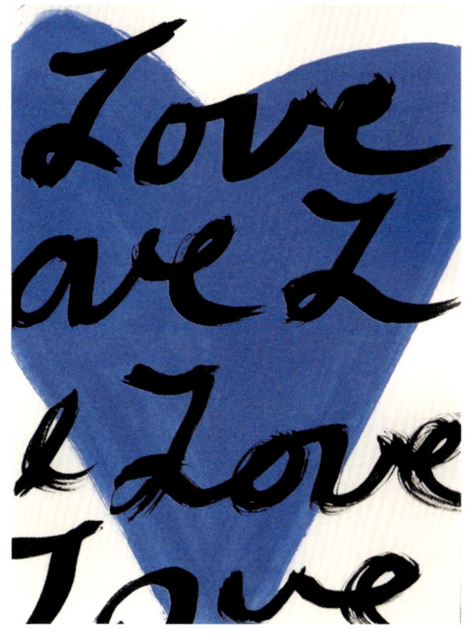
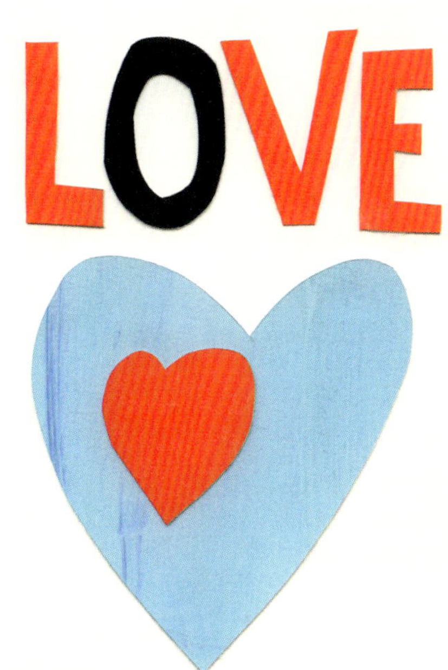
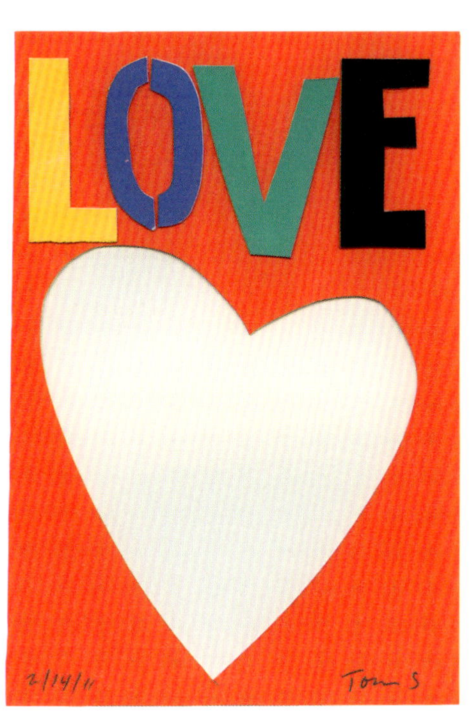
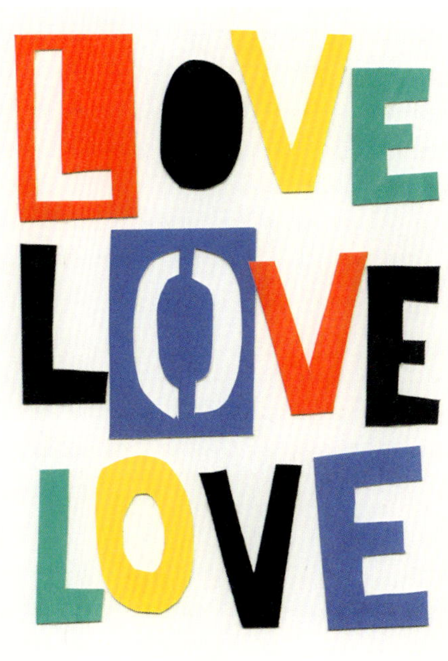
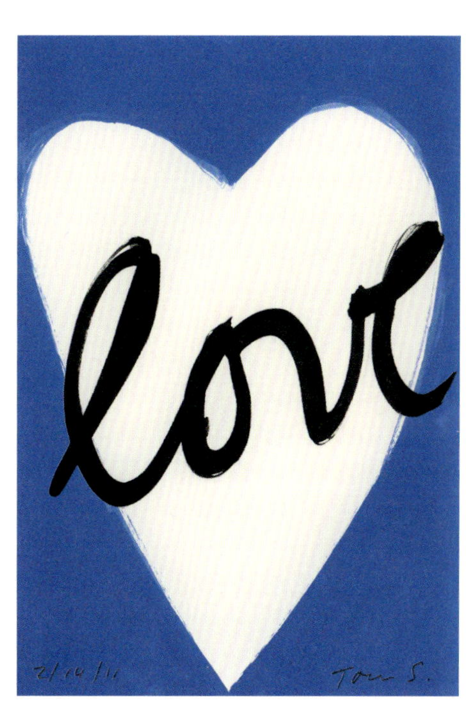
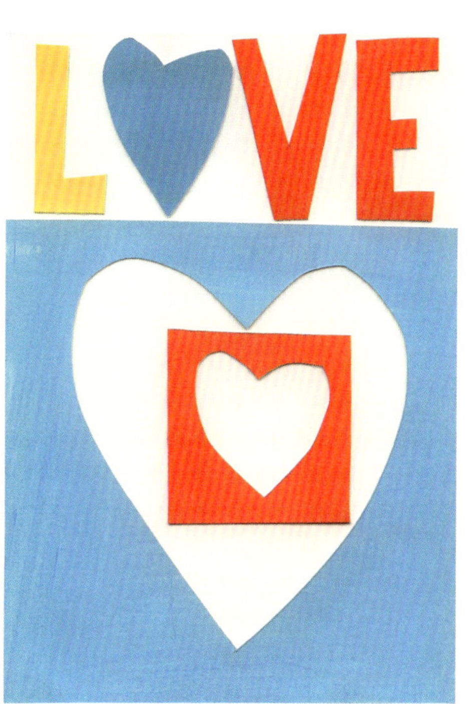

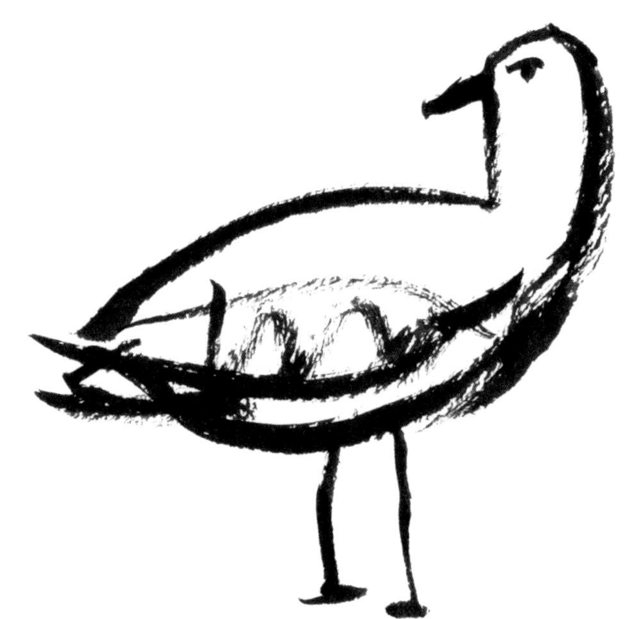

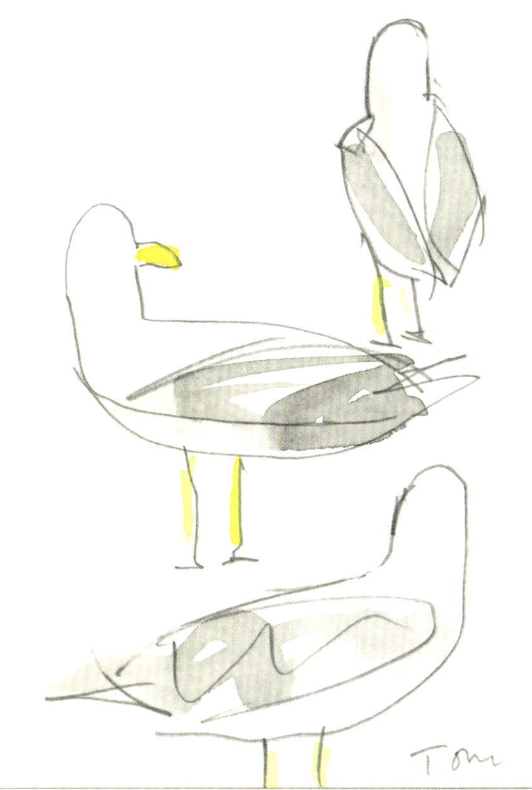
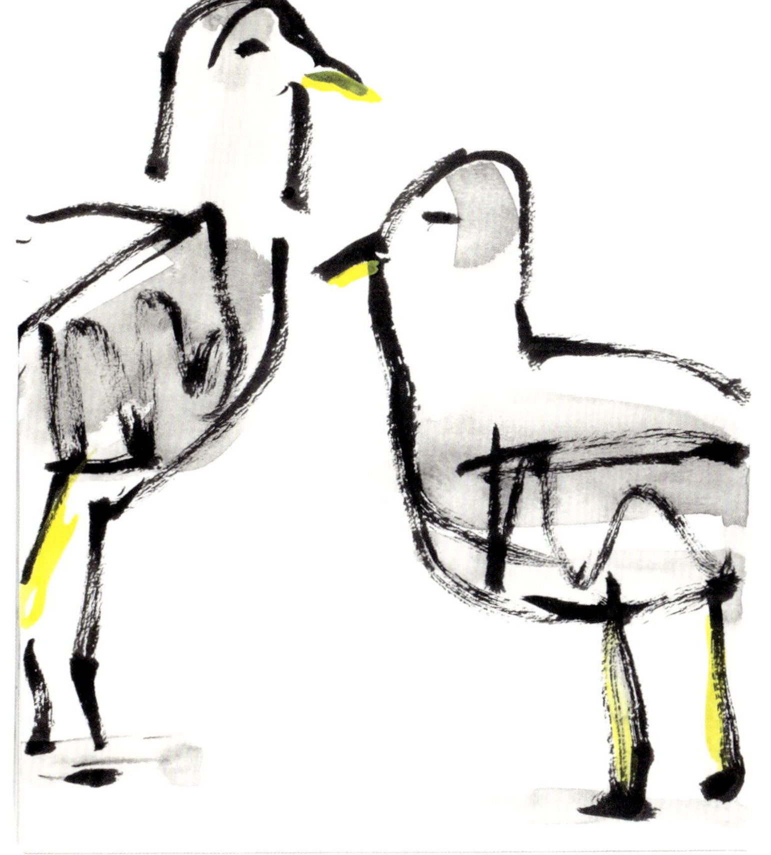
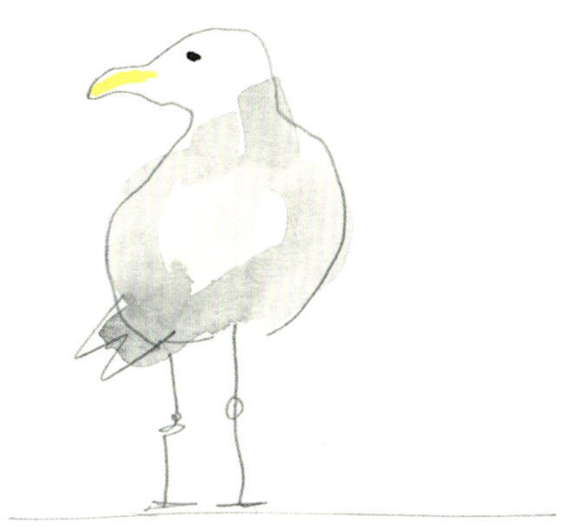

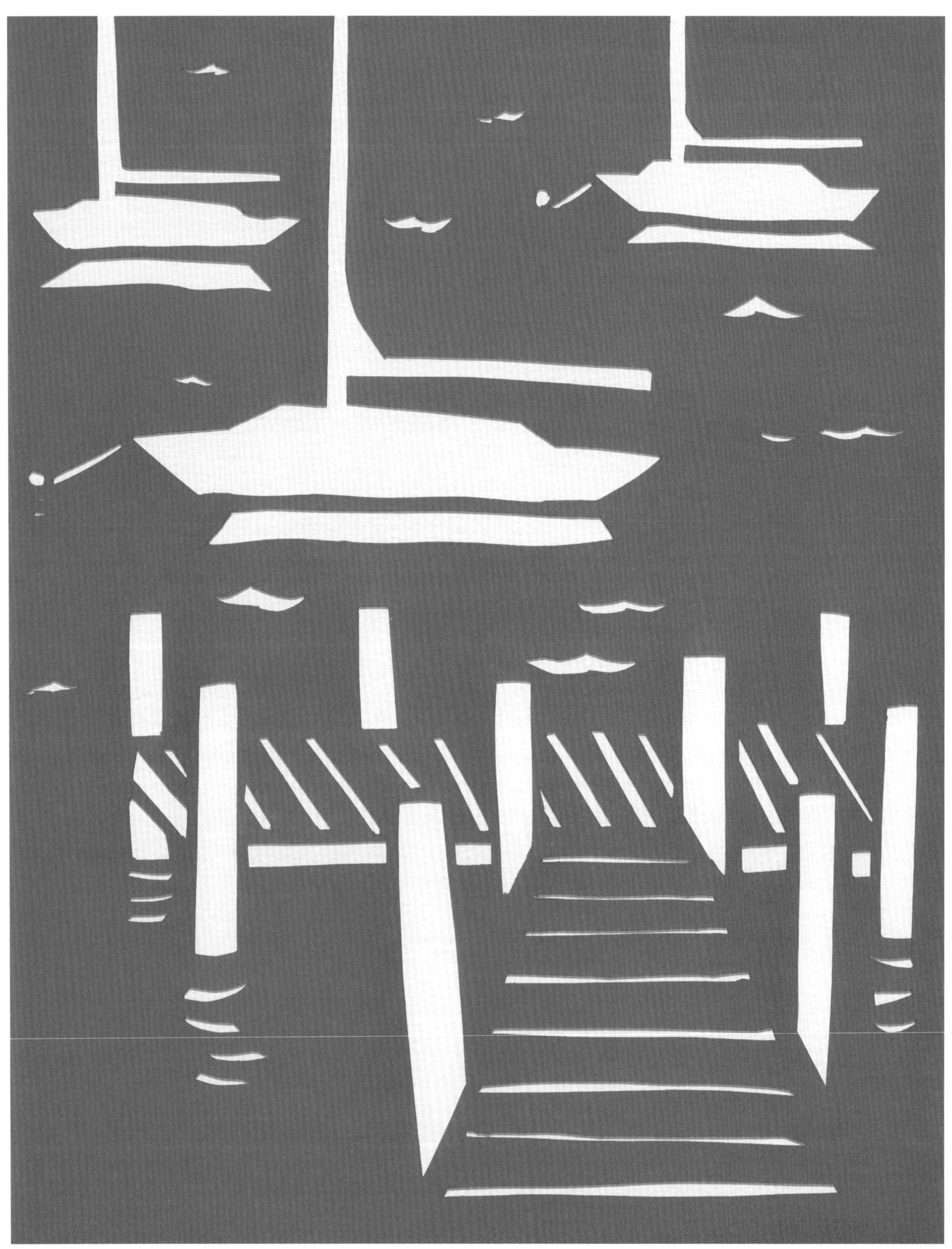

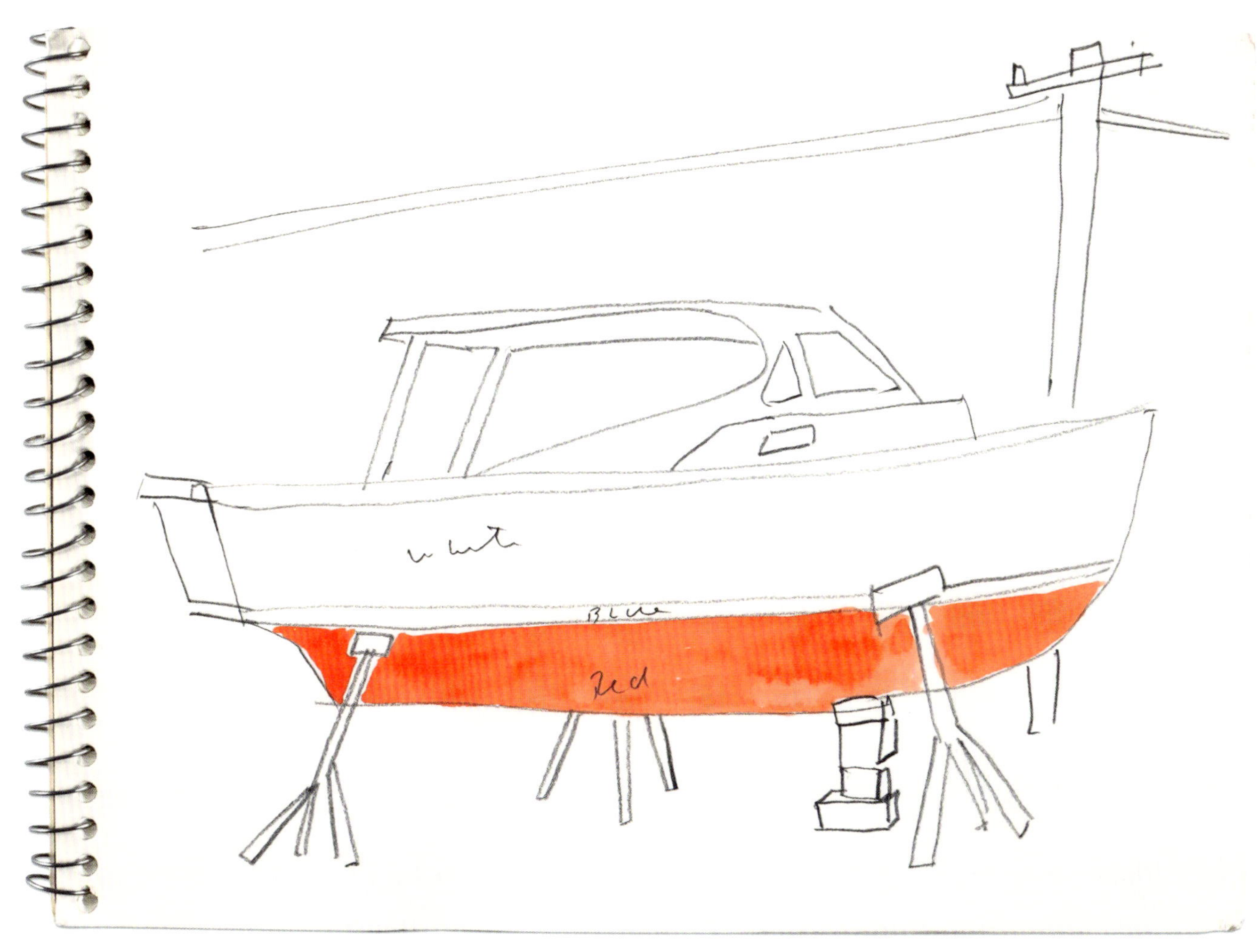

white
Blue
Red

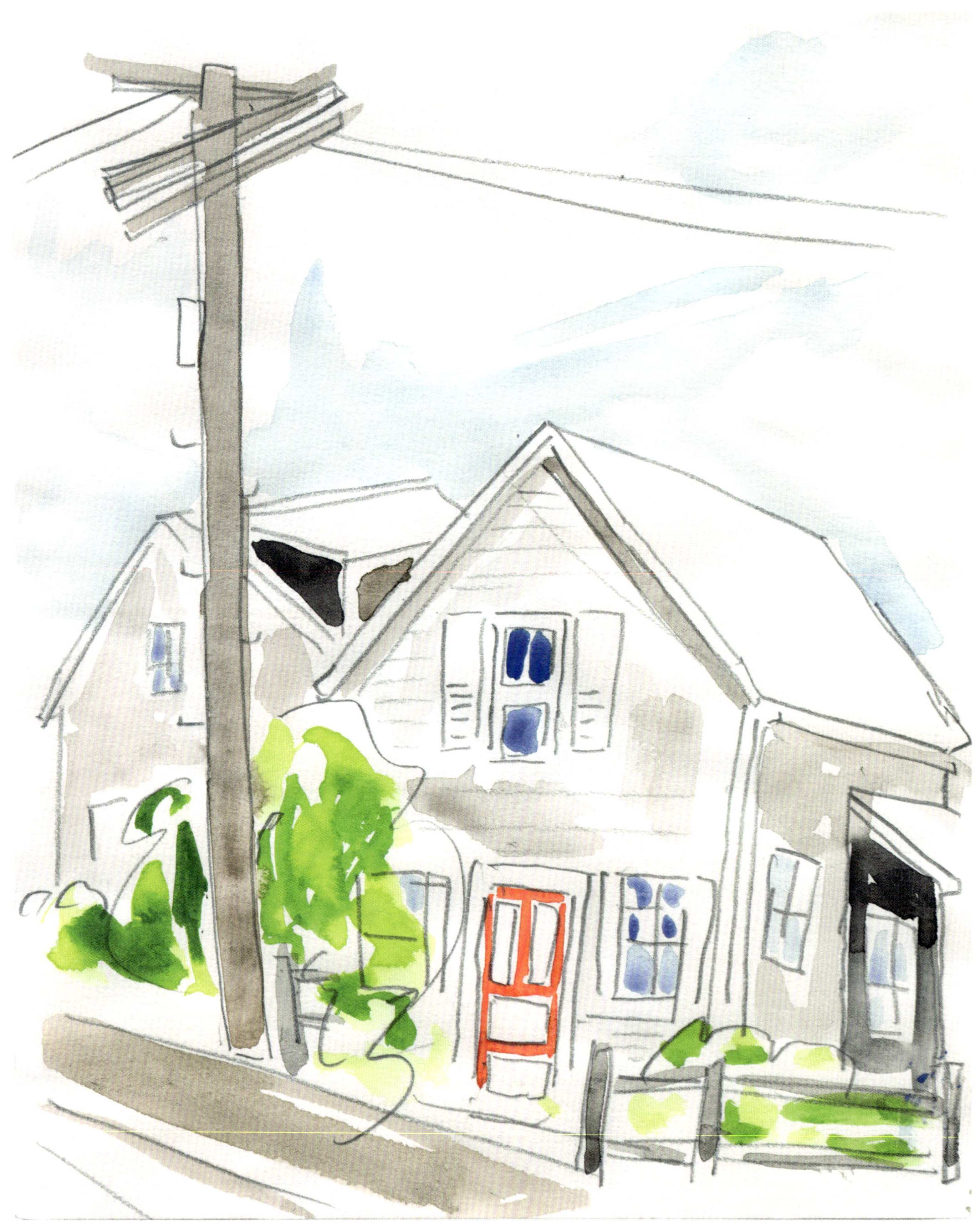

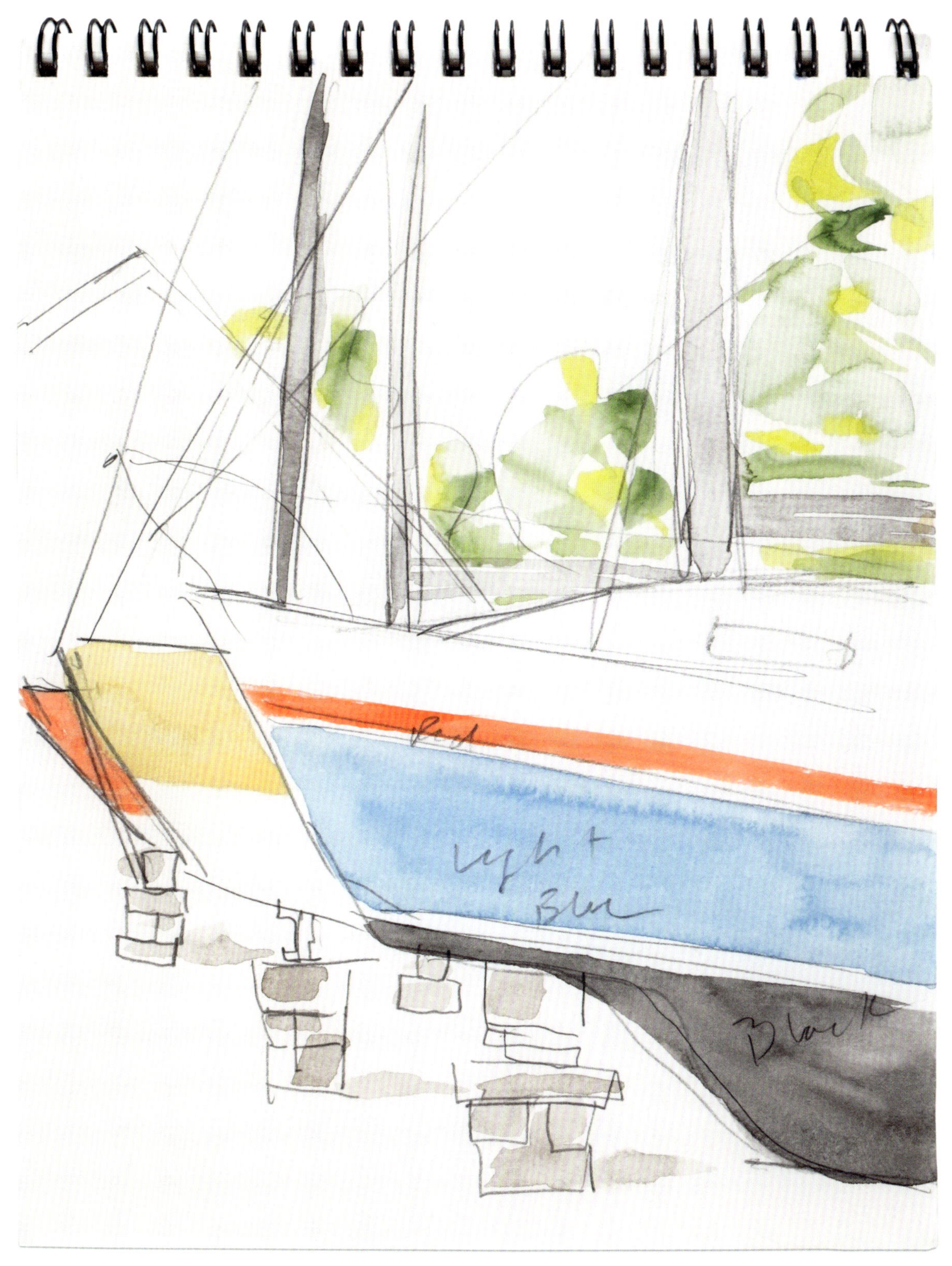
Red
light
Blue
Black

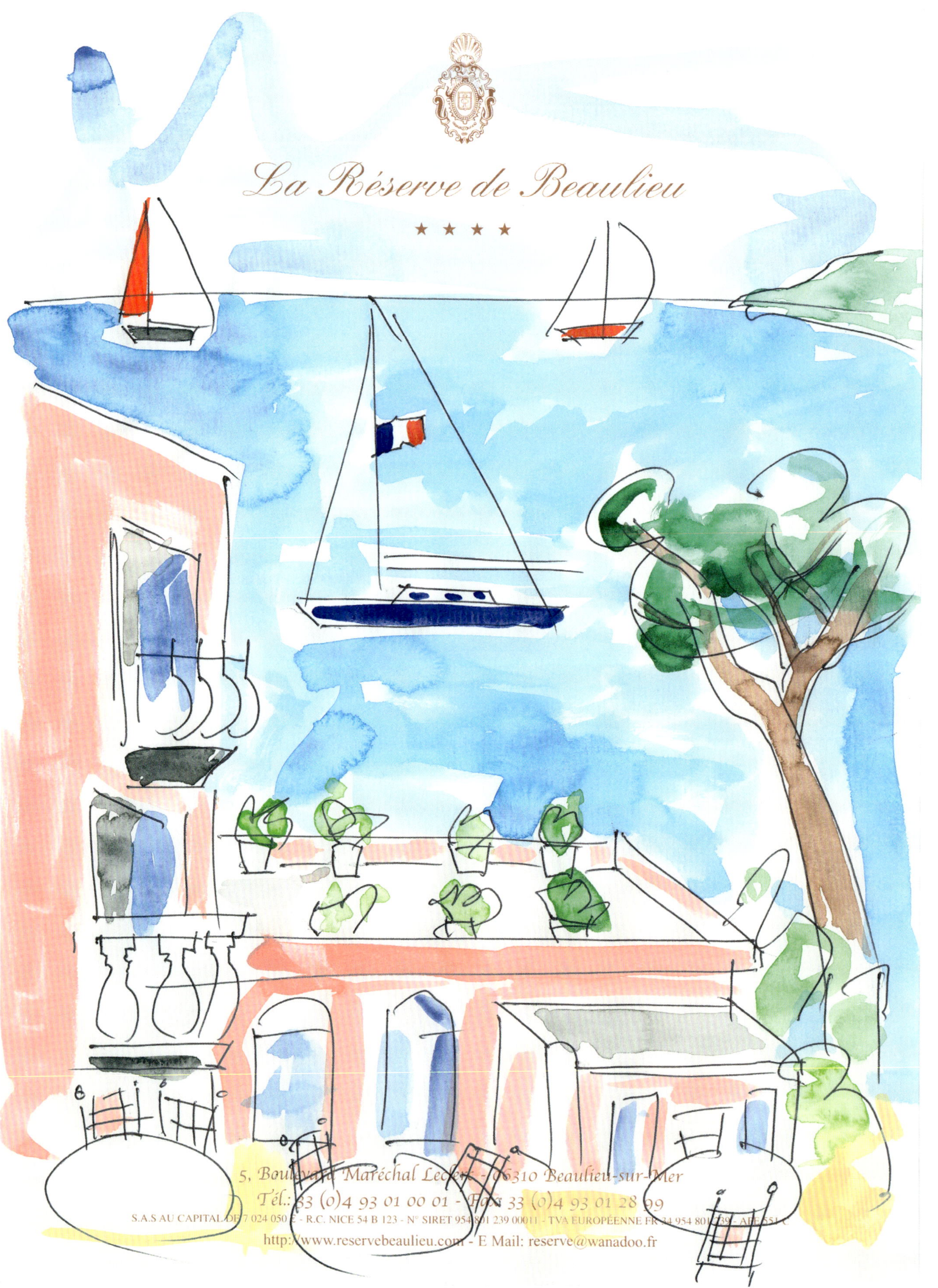

La Réserve de Beaulieu
★ ★ ★ ★
5, Boulevard Maréchal Leclerc - 06310 Beaulieu-sur-Mer
Tél. : 33 (0)4 93 01 00 01 - Fax : 33 (0)4 93 01 28 99
S.A.S AU CAPITAL DE 7 024 050 E - R.C. NICE 54 B 123 - N° SIRET 954 801 239 00011 - TVA EUROPÉENNE FR 34 954 801 239 - APE 551 A
http://www.reservebeaulieu.com - E Mail : reserve@wanadoo.fr

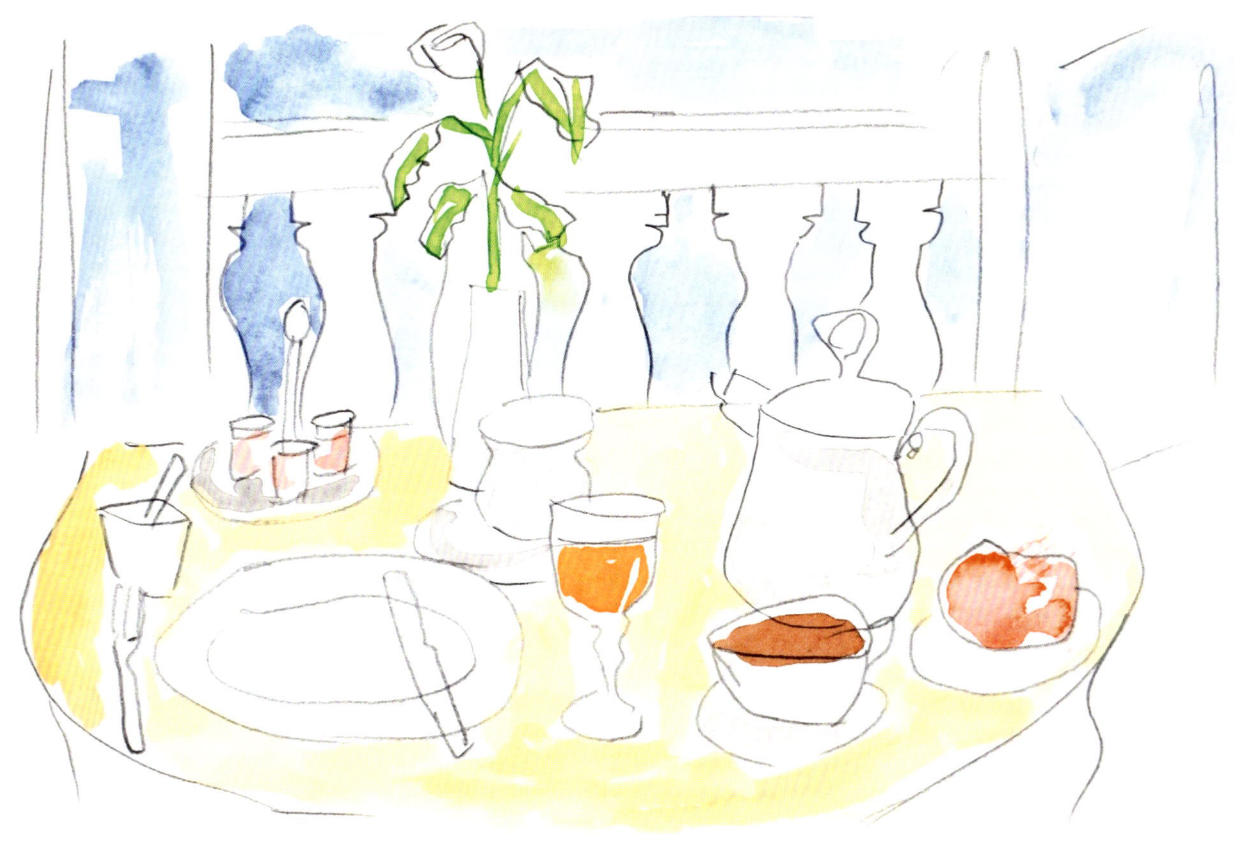

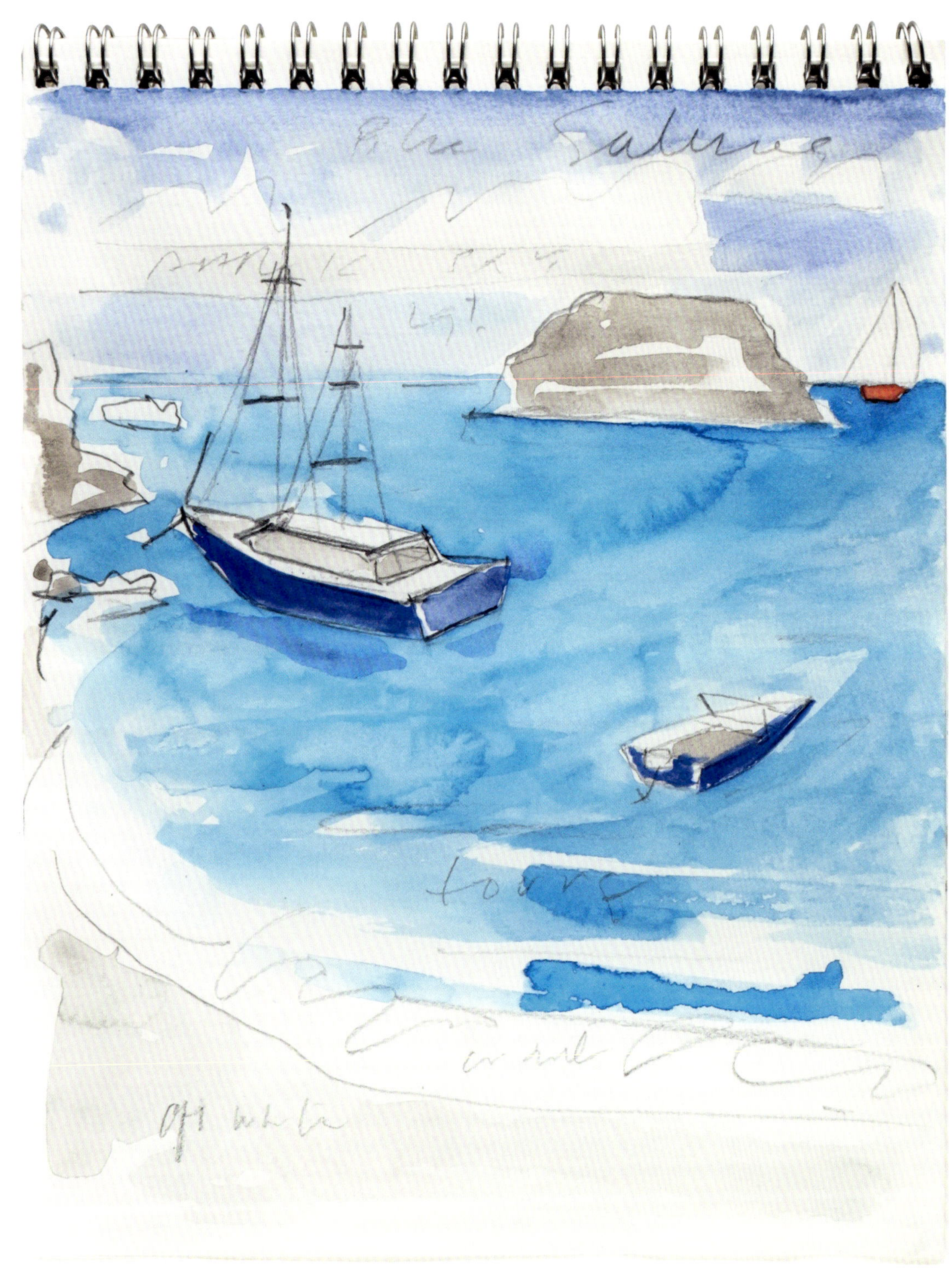
Blue Salines
off white

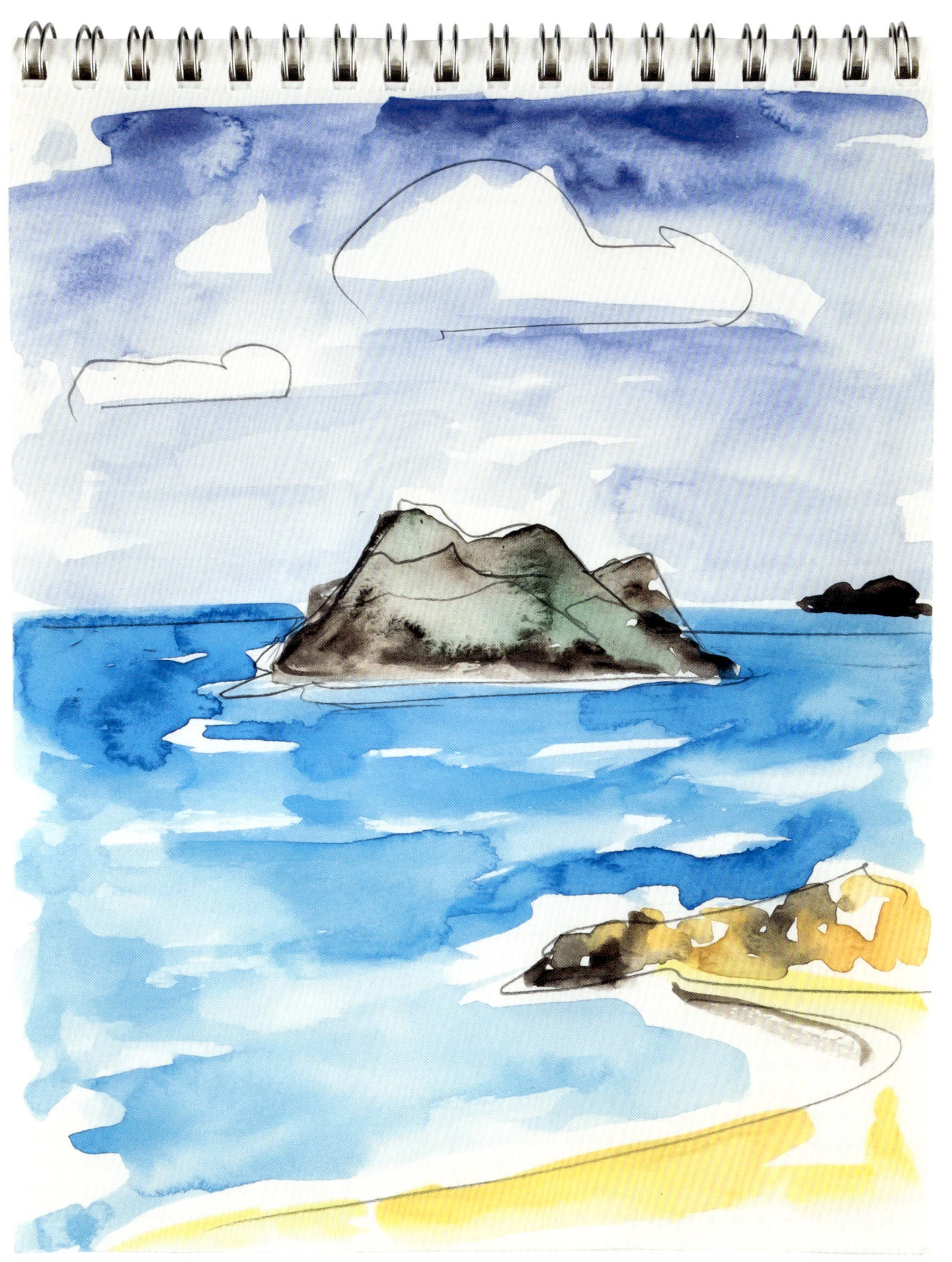

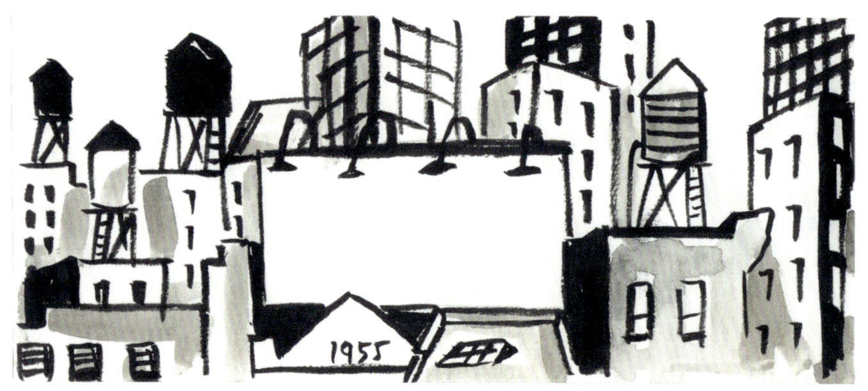

1955

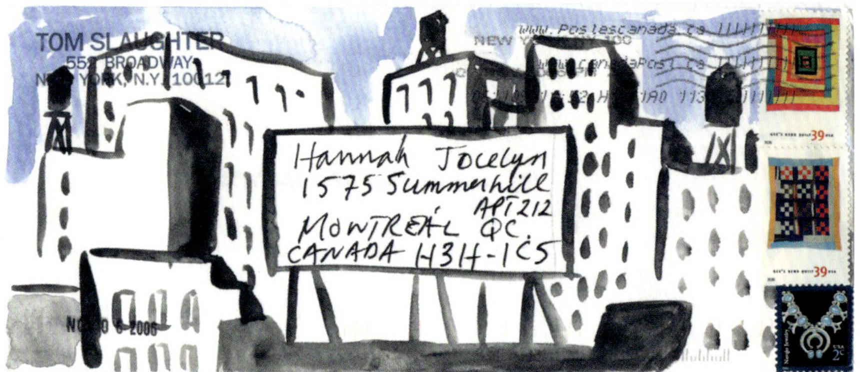

TOM SLAUGHTER
555 BROADWAY
NEW YORK, N.Y. 10012
Hannah Jocelyn
1575 Summerhill
APT 212
MONTREAL QC.
CANADA H3H-1C5

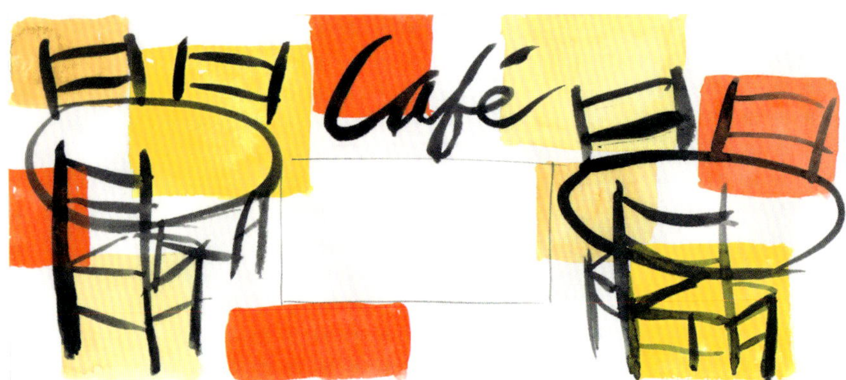

Café

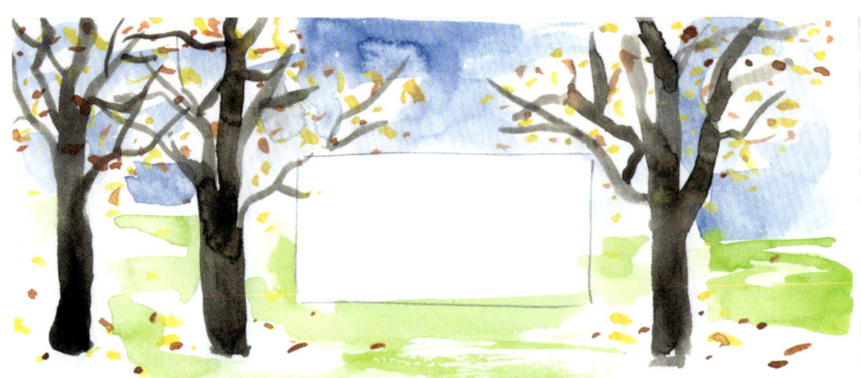

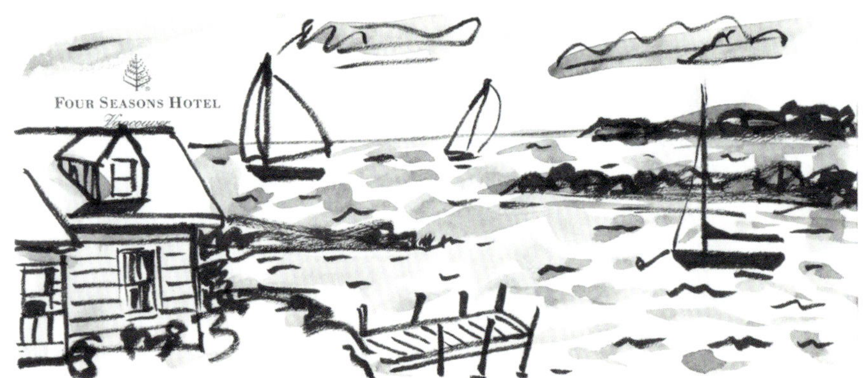

FOUR SEASONS HOTEL

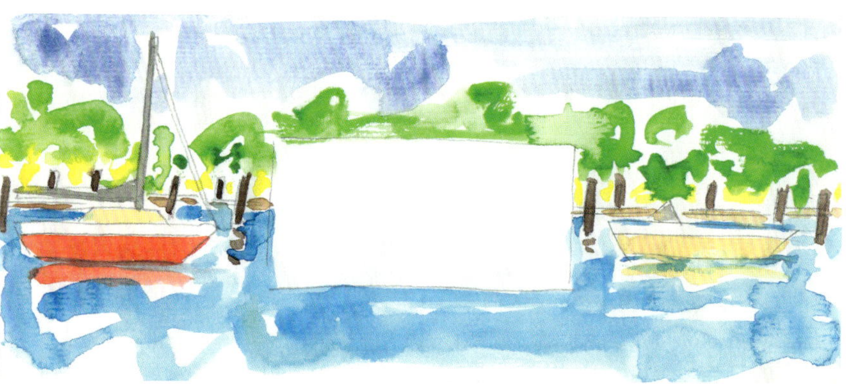

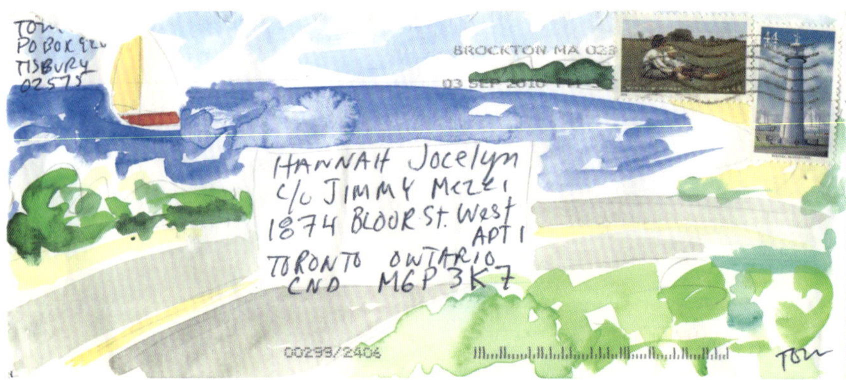

TOM.
PO BOX 820
TISBURY
02575
BROCKTON MA 023
HANNAH Jocelyn
c/o JIMMY McZEi
1874 BLOOR St. West
APT 1
TORONTO ONTARIO
CND M6P 3K7
00293/2406

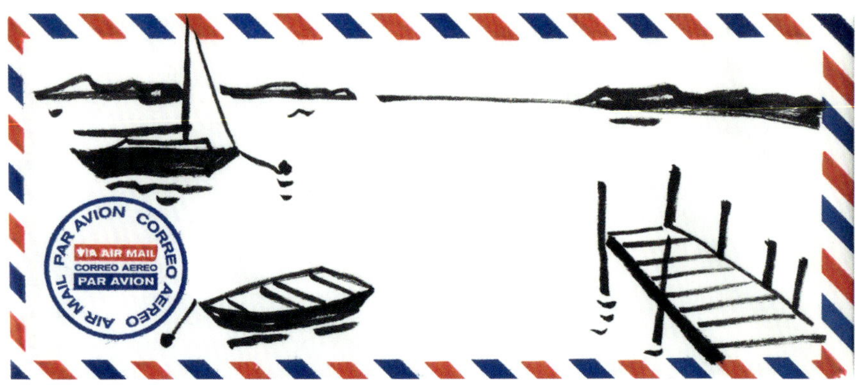

PAR AVION CORREO
VIA AIR MAIL
CORREO AEREO
PAR AVION
AIR MAIL

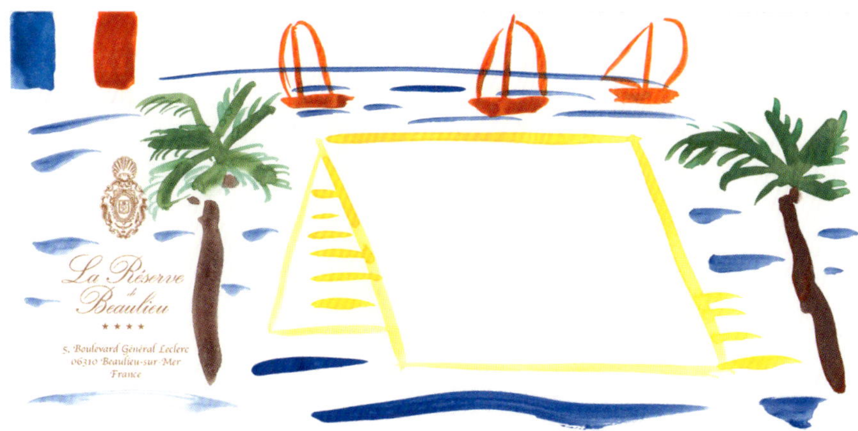

La Réserve
de
Beaulieu
★ ★ ★ ★
5, Boulevard Général Leclerc
06310 Beaulieu-sur-Mer
France

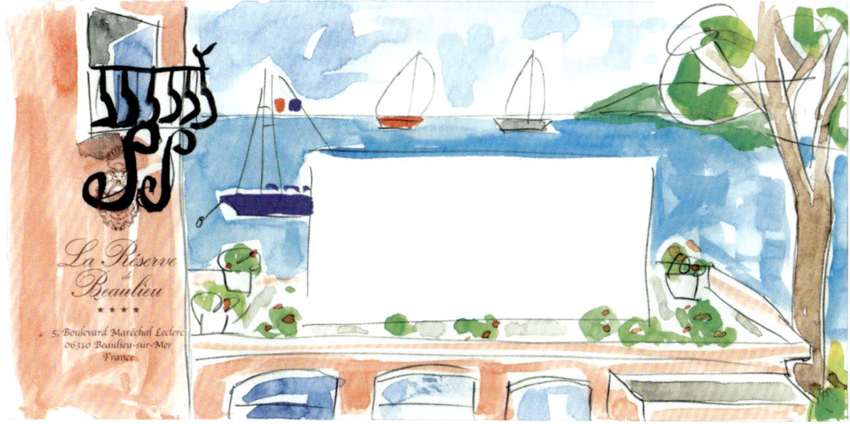

La Réserve
de
Beaulieu
★ ★ ★ ★
5, Boulevard Maréchal Leclerc
06310 Beaulieu-sur-Mer
France

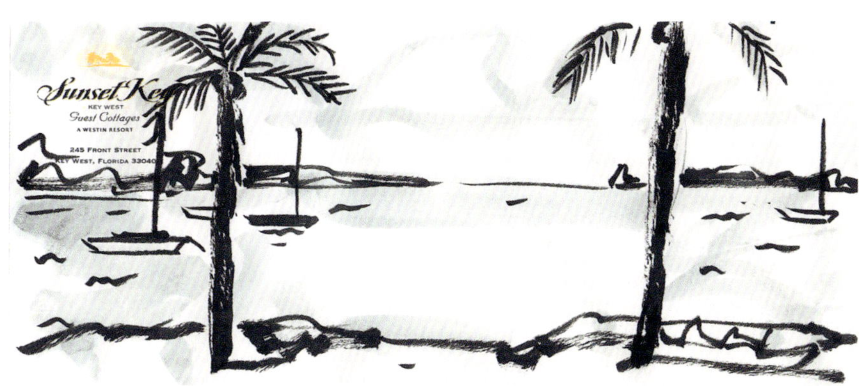

Sunset Key
KEY WEST
Guest Cottages
A WESTIN RESORT
245 FRONT STREET
KEY WEST, FLORIDA 33040

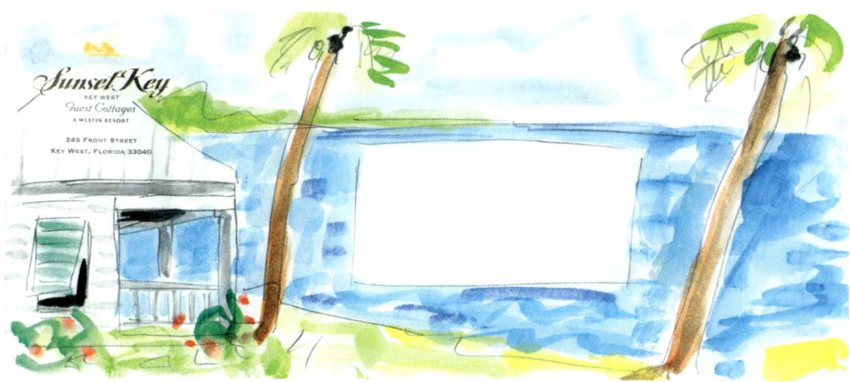

Sunset Key
KEY WEST
Guest Cottages
A WESTIN RESORT
245 FRONT STREET
KEY WEST, FLORIDA 33040

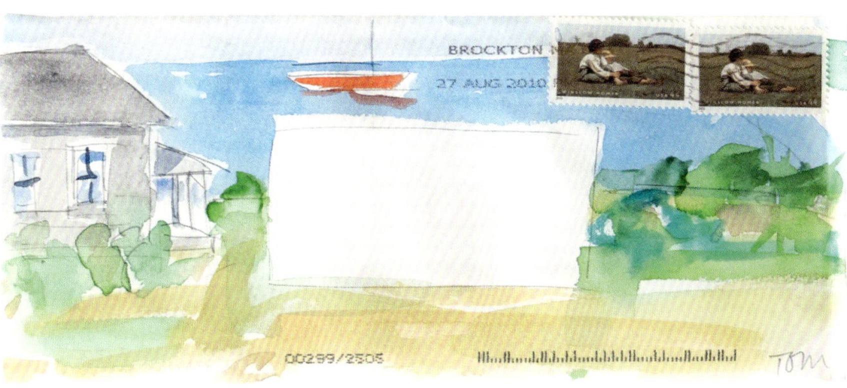

BROCKTON M
27 AUG 2010
00299/2505
TOM

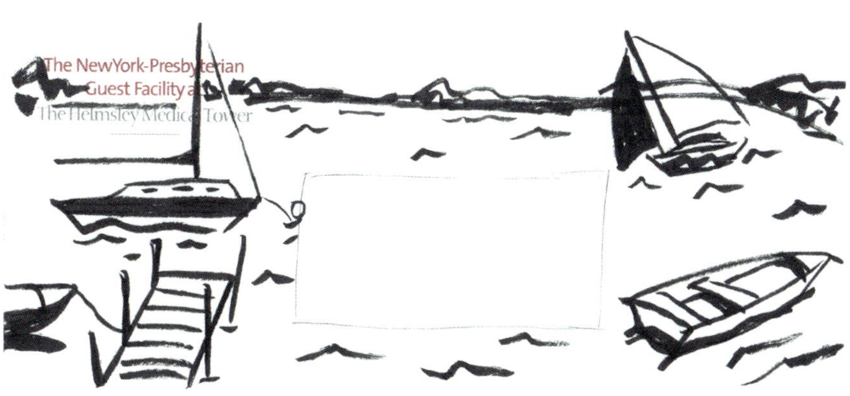

The NewYork-Presbyterian
Guest Facility at
The Helmsley Medical Tower

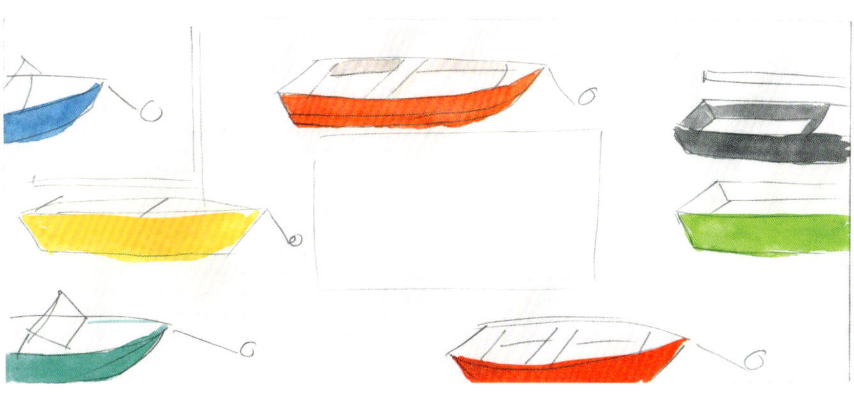

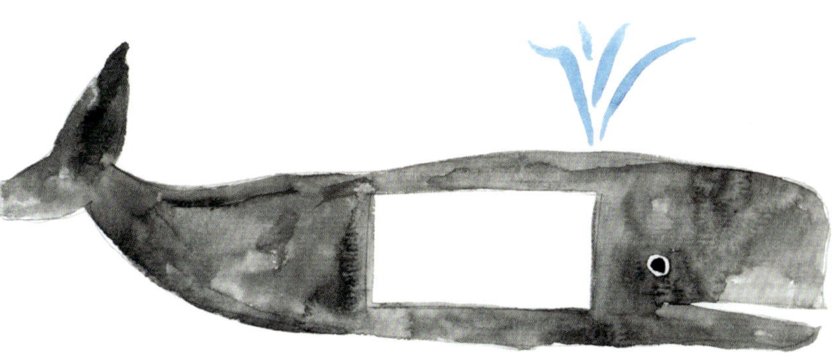

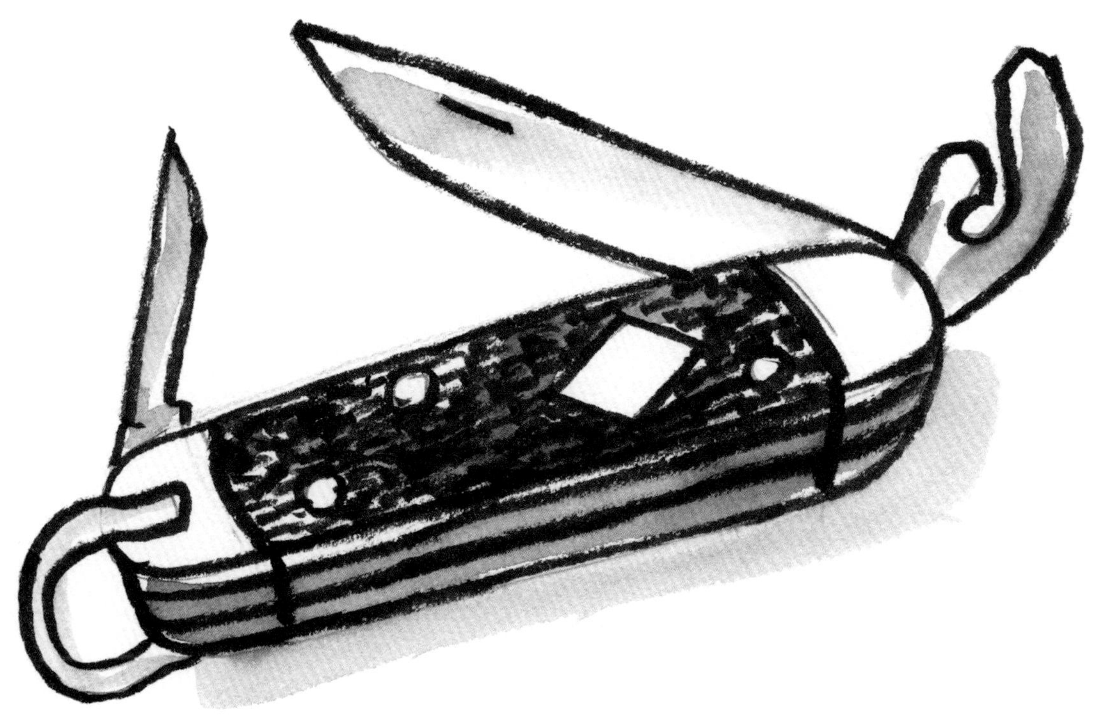

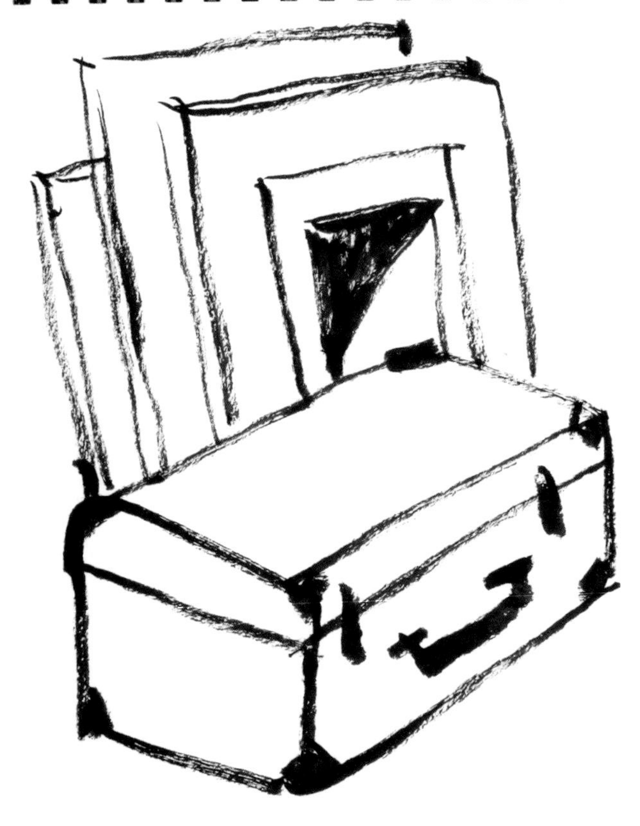

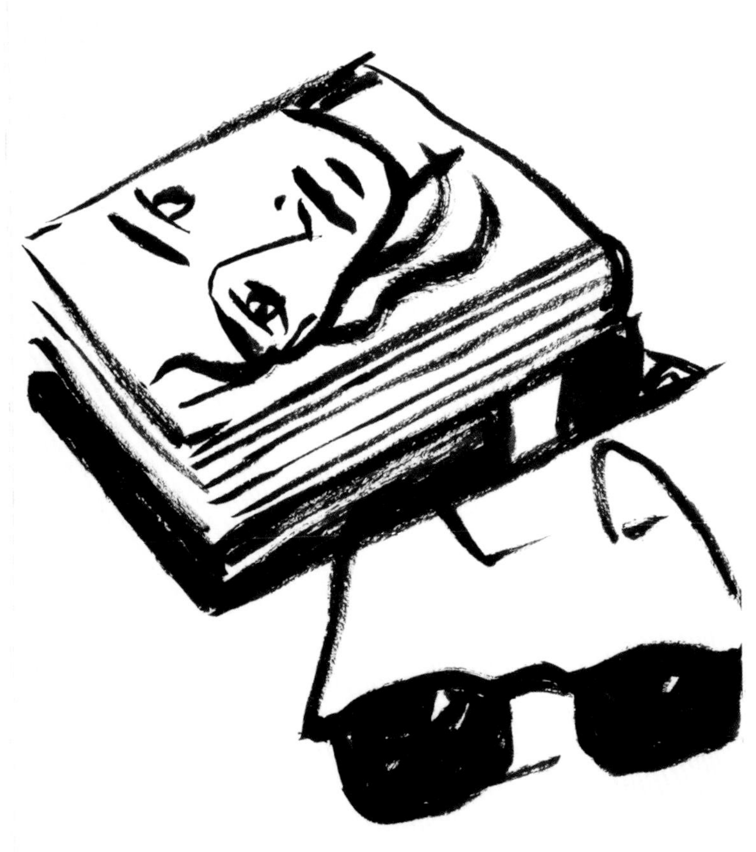

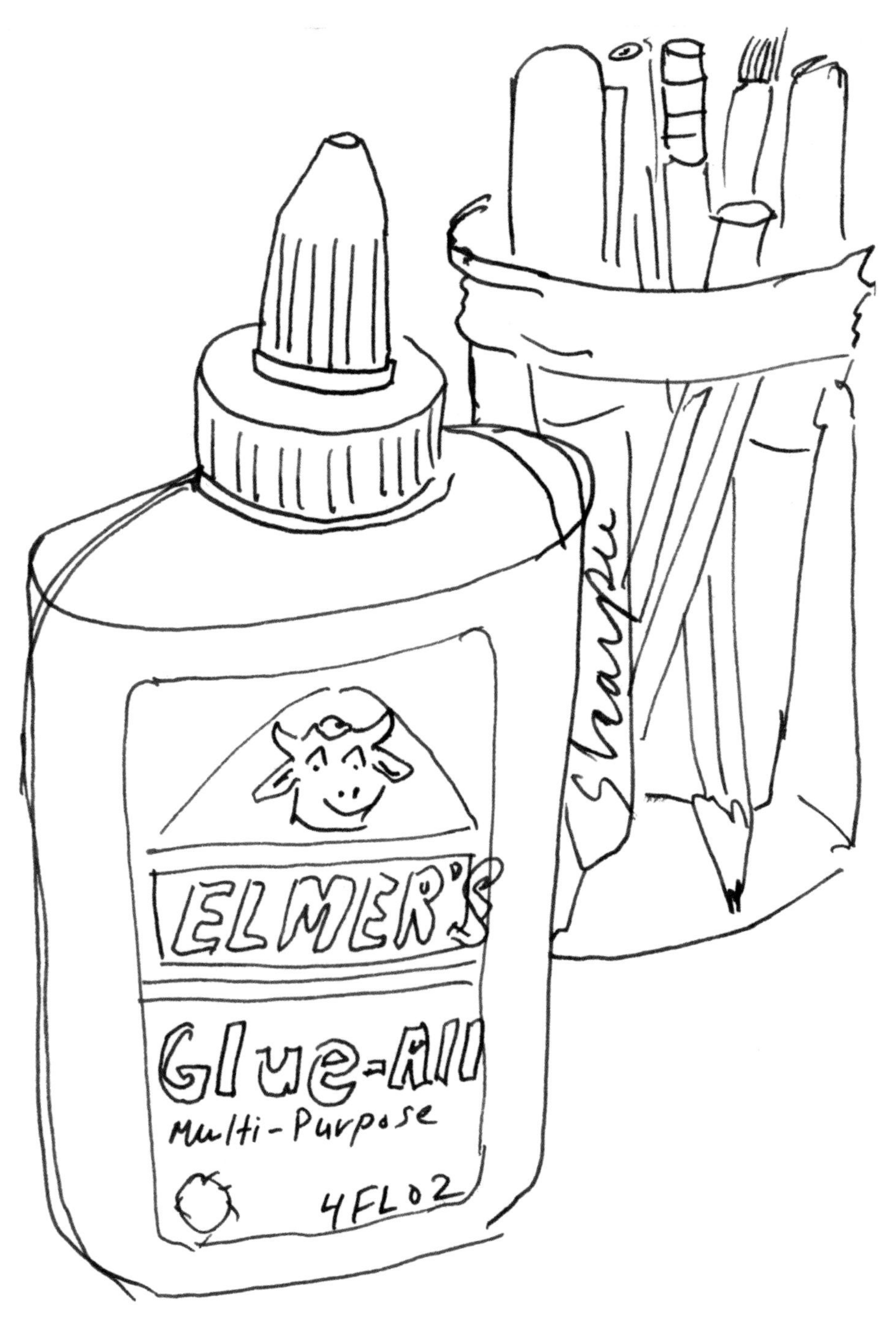
ELMER'S
Glue-All
Multi-Purpose
4FL OZ
Sharpie

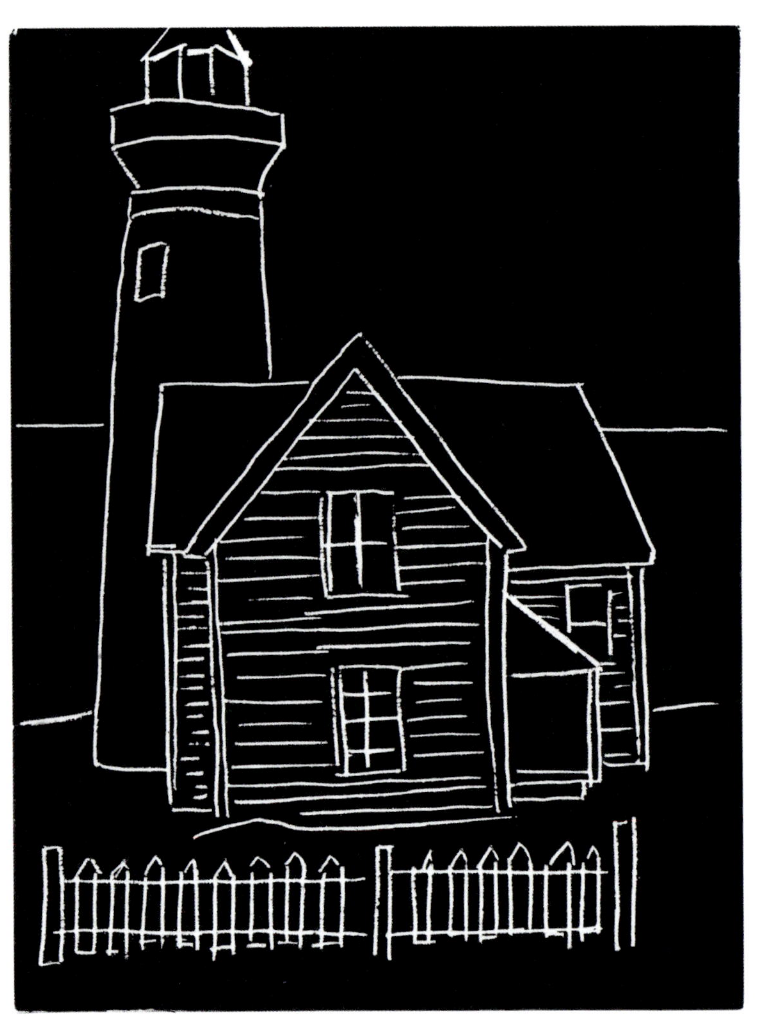

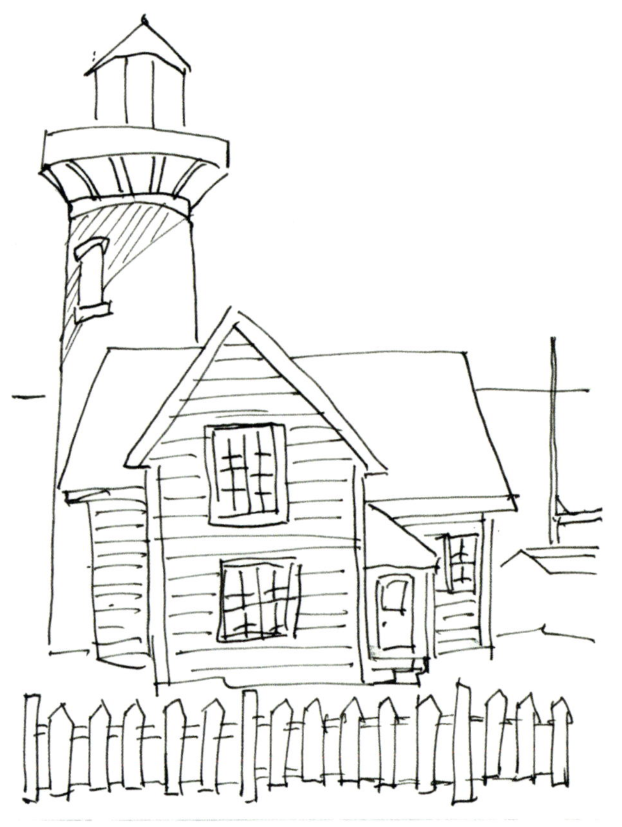

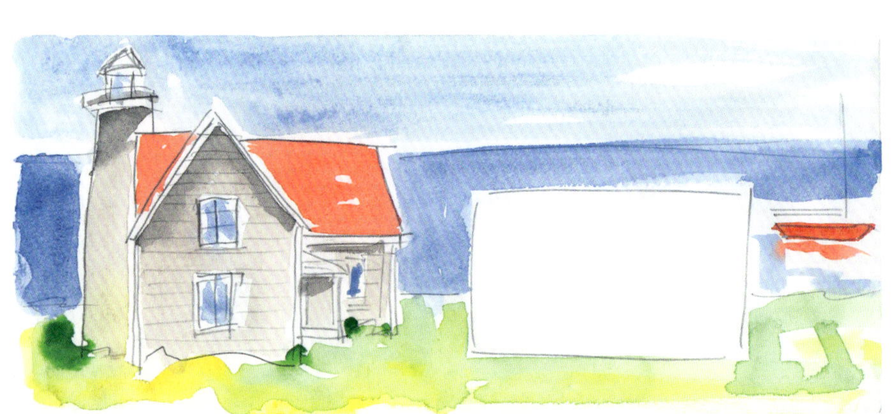

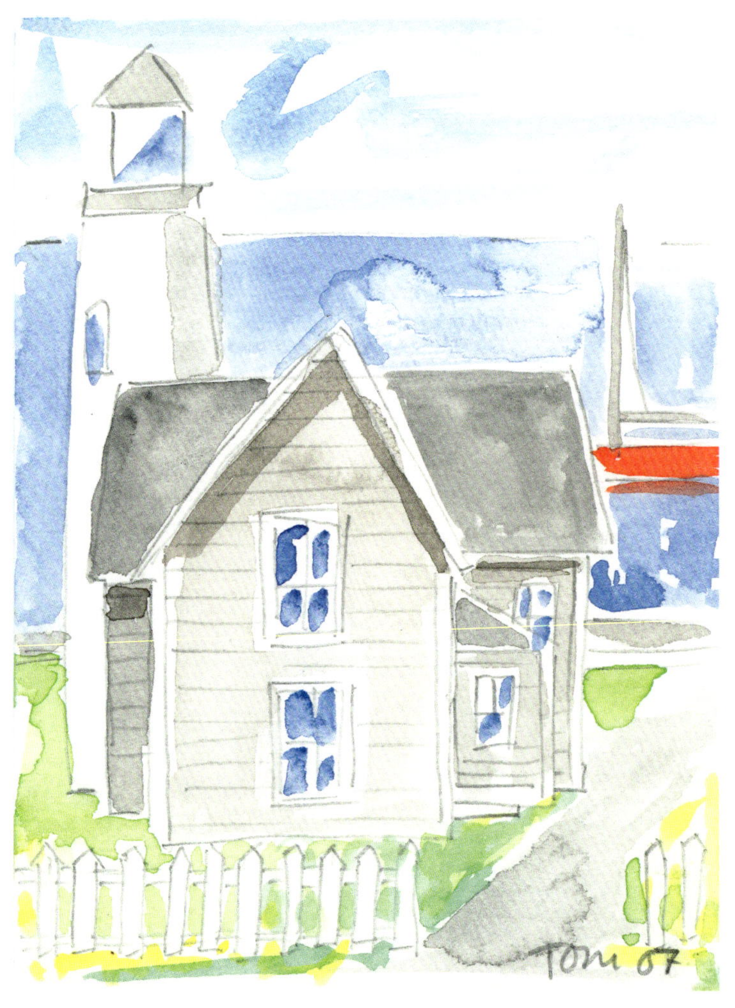

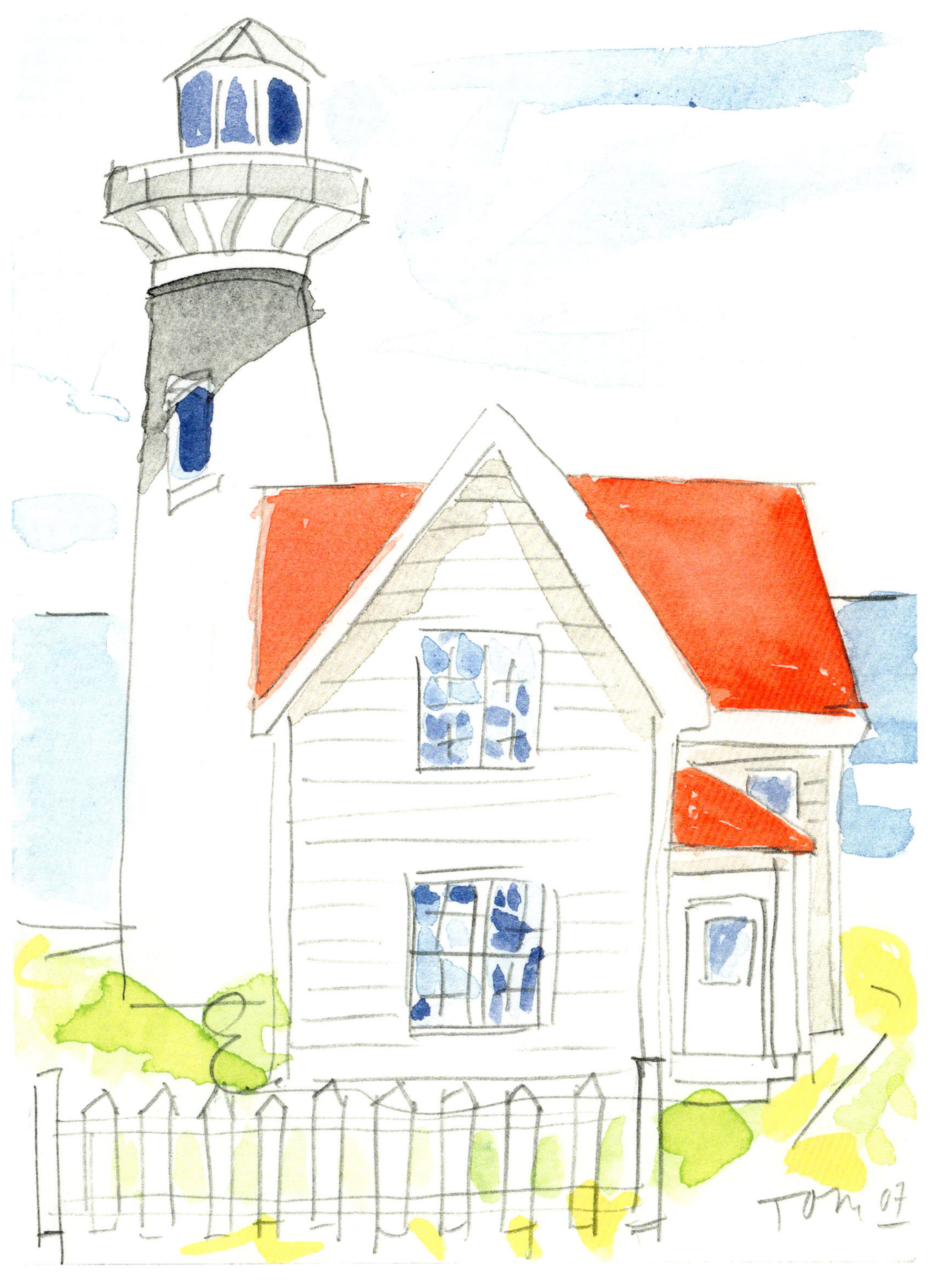

Tom 07

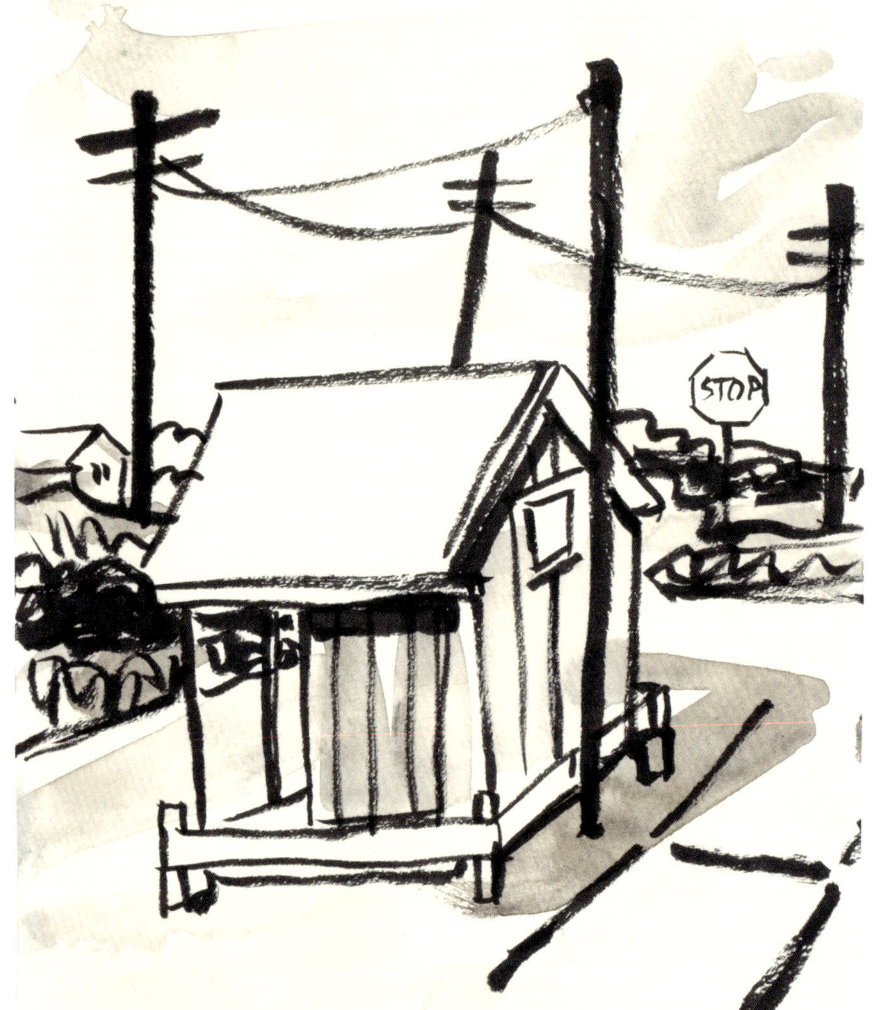

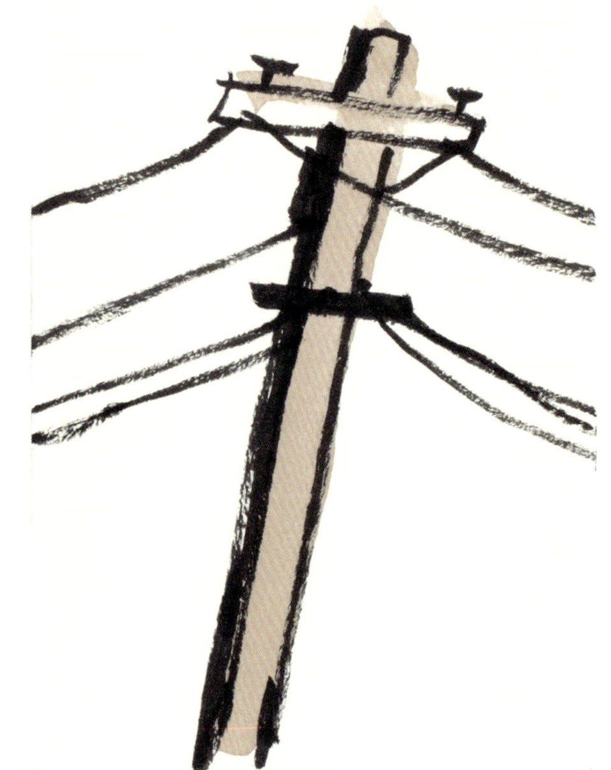

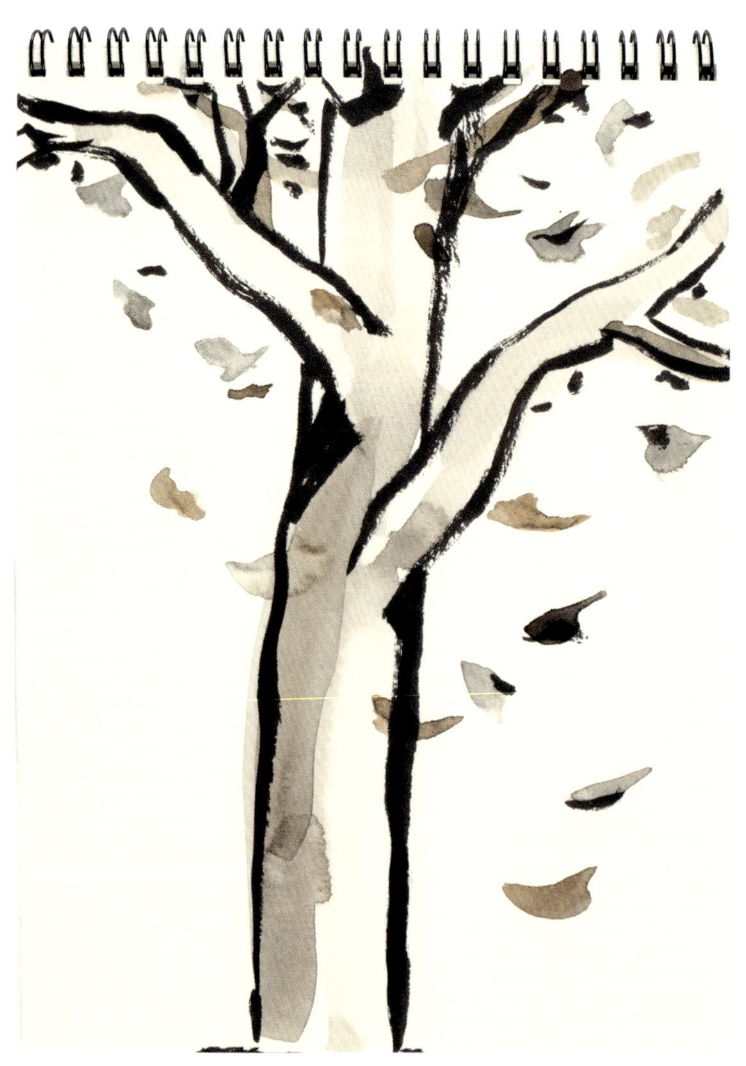

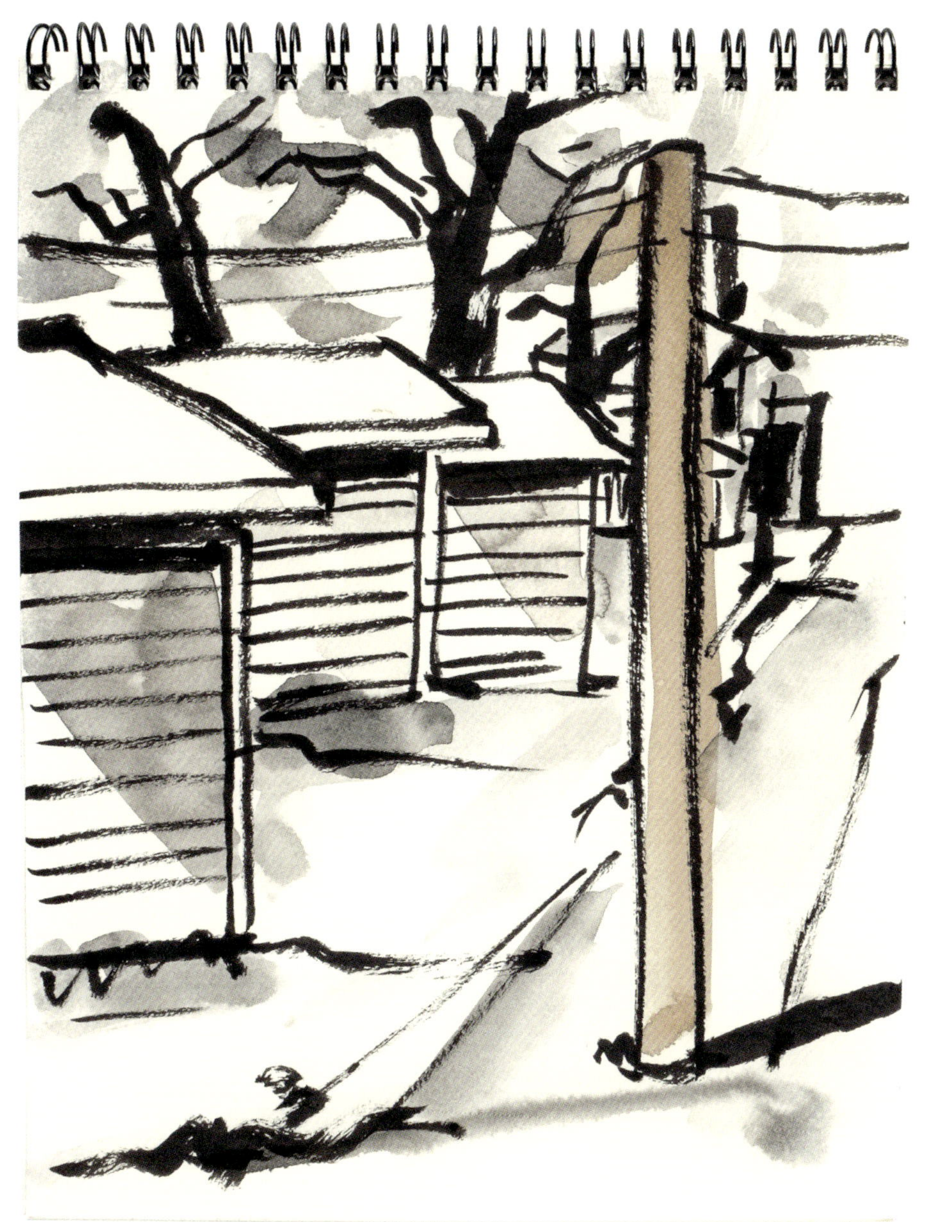

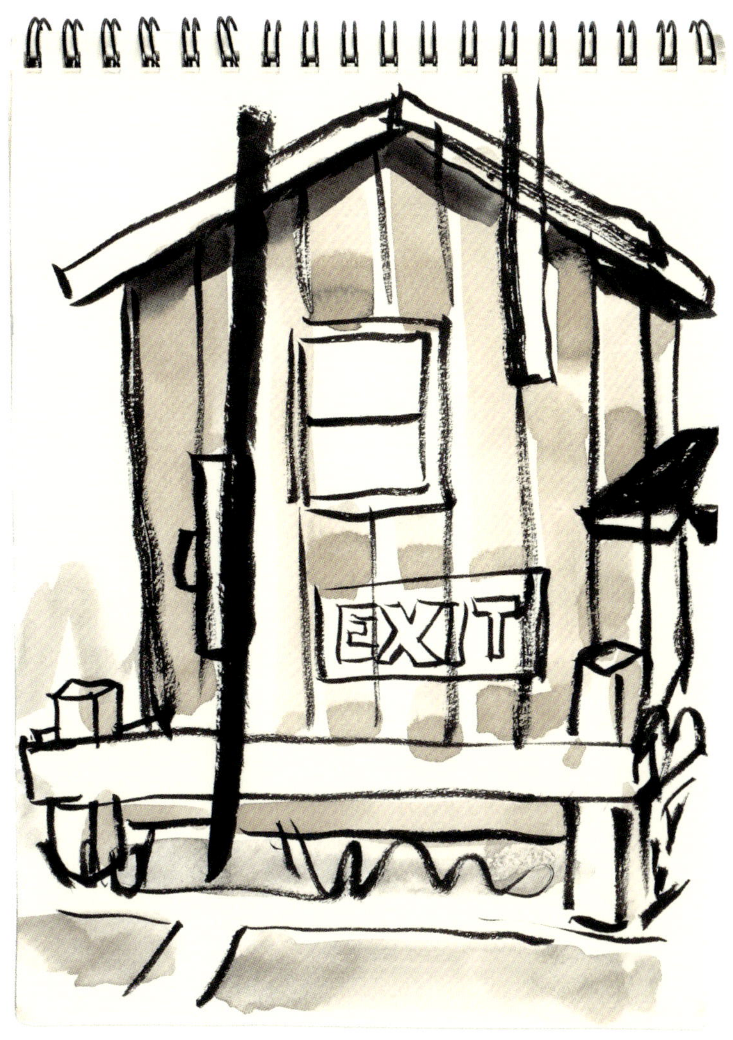
EXIT

WATCH YOUR TONGUE.

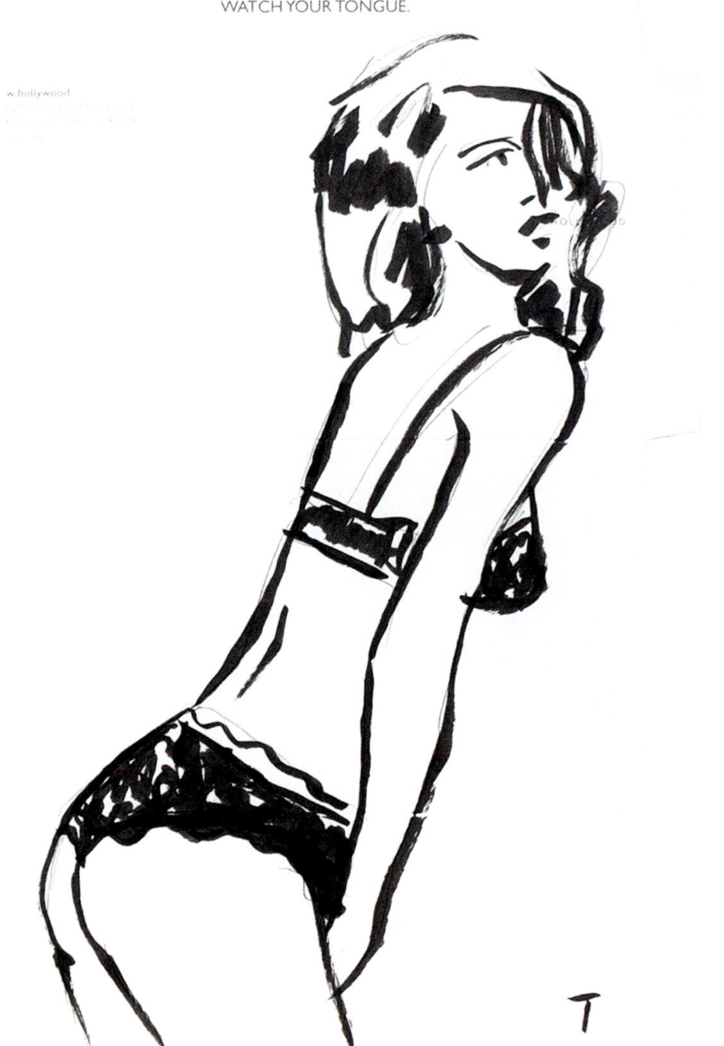
w hollywood

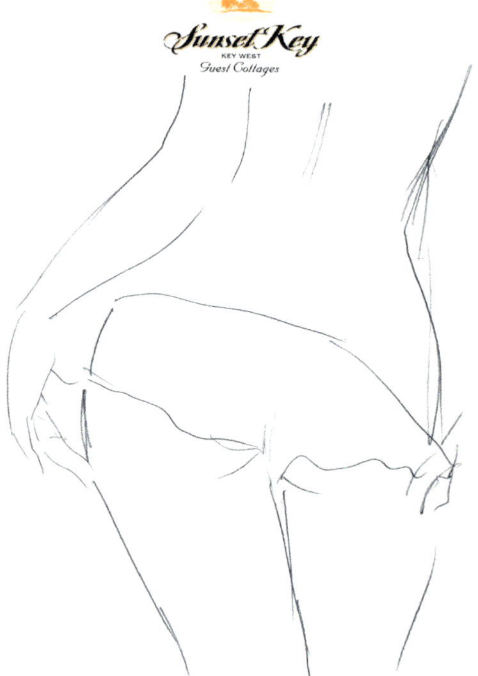
Sunset Key
KEY WEST
Guest Cottages
245 Front Street Key West, FL 33040 (305) 292-5300 1-888-477-7sun Fax: (305) 292-5395
WWW.SUNSETKEYISLAND.COM

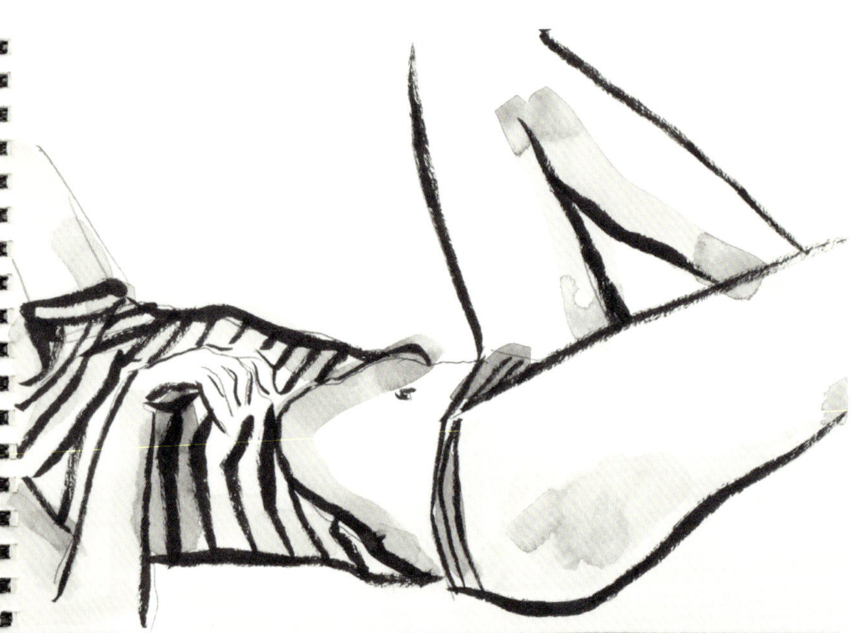

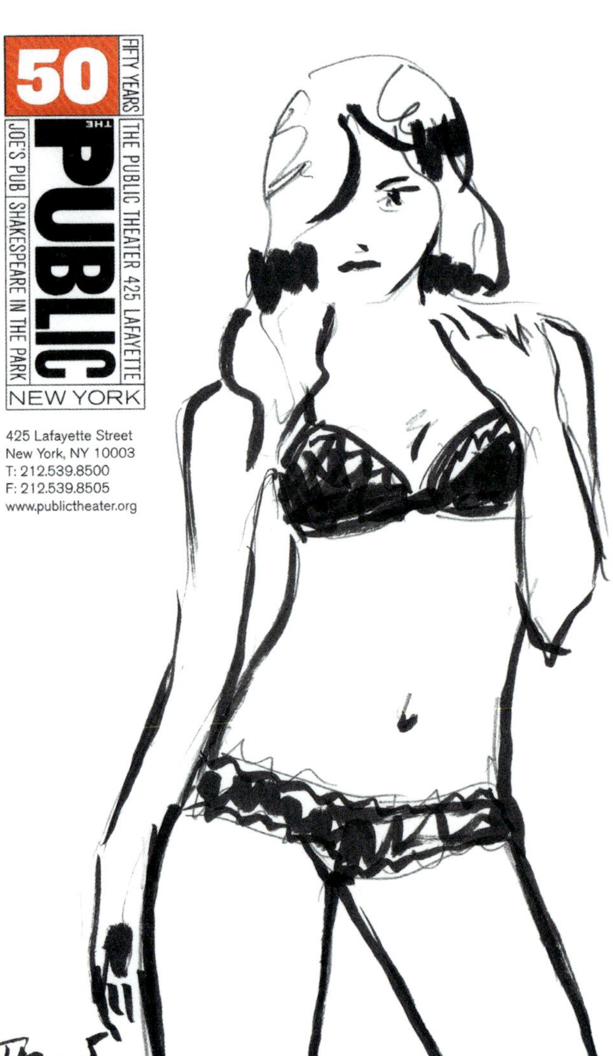
50
FIFTY YEARS
THE PUBLIC THEATER 425 LAFAYETTE
THE
PUBLIC
JOE'S PUB SHAKESPEARE IN THE PARK
NEW YORK
425 Lafayette Street
New York, NY 10003
T: 212.539.8500
F: 212.539.8505
www.publictheater.org

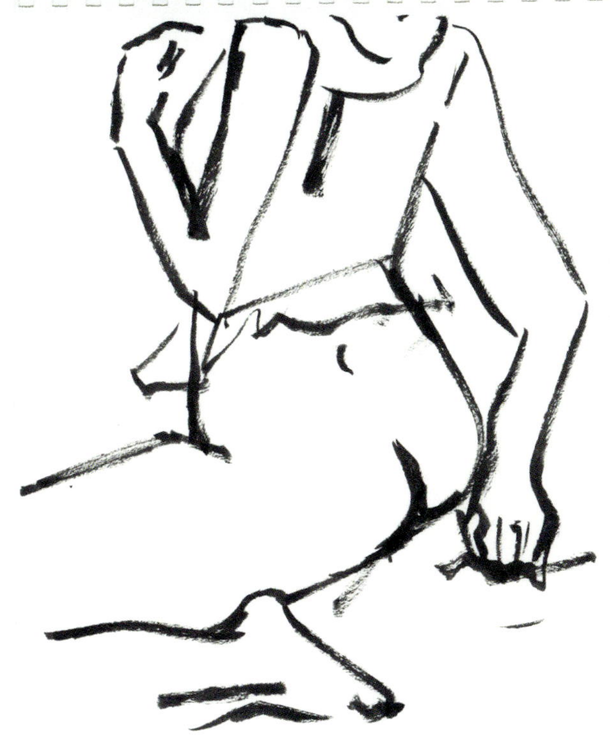

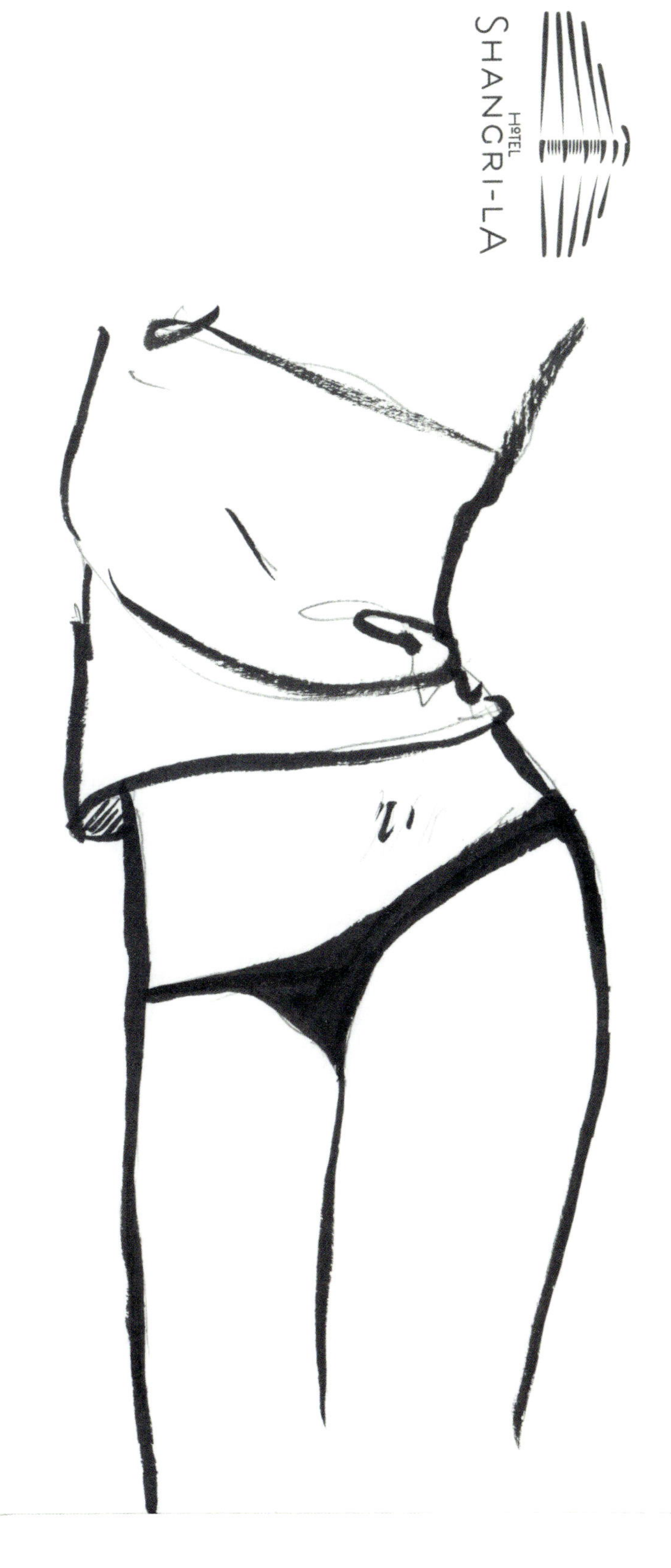

THE SHORE CLUB

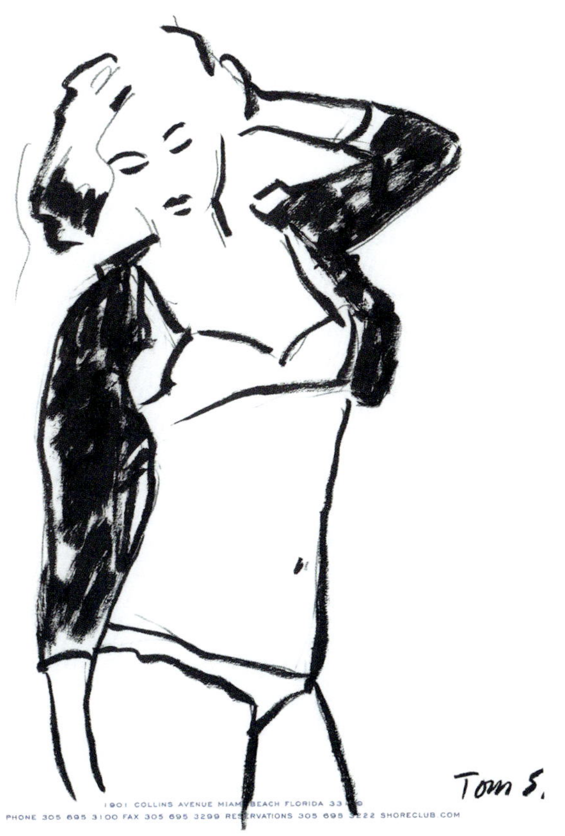

1901 COLLINS AVENUE MIAMI BEACH FLORIDA 33139
PHONE 305 695 3100 FAX 305 695 3299 RESERVATIONS 305 695 3422 SHORECLUB.COM

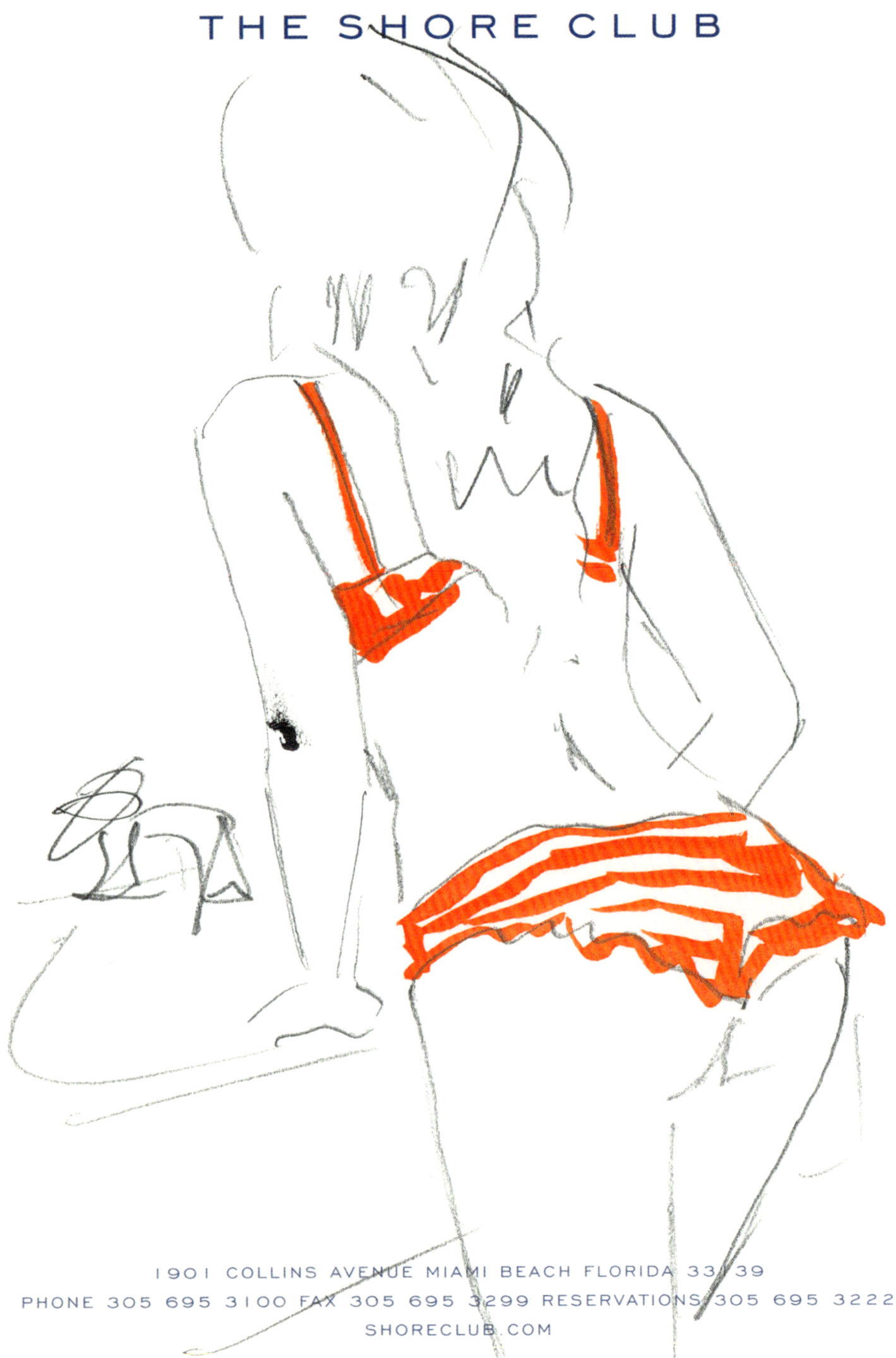

1901 COLLINS AVENUE MIAMI BEACH FLORIDA 33139
PHONE 305 695 3100 FAX 305 695 3299 RESERVATIONS 305 695 3222
SHORECLUB.COM

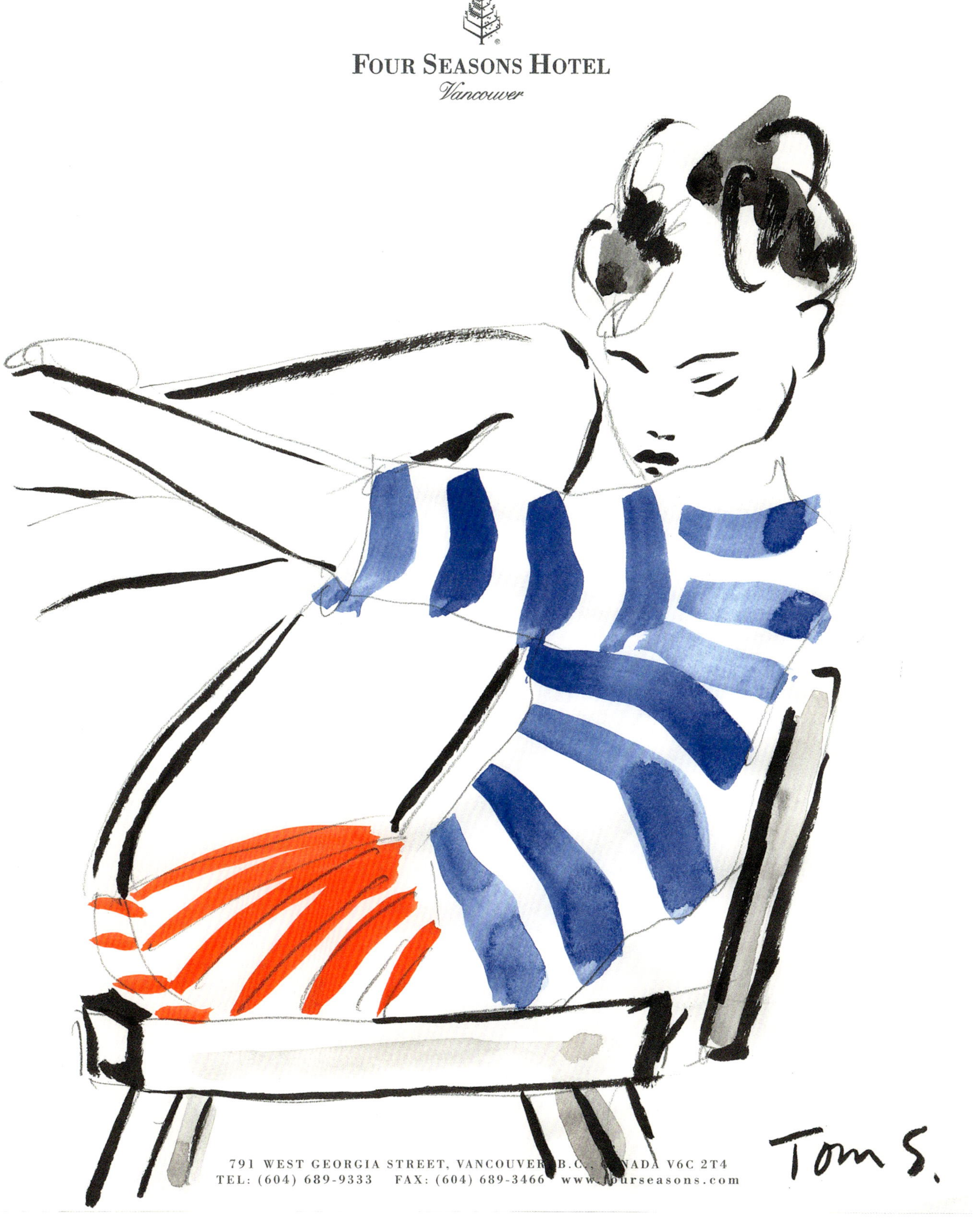

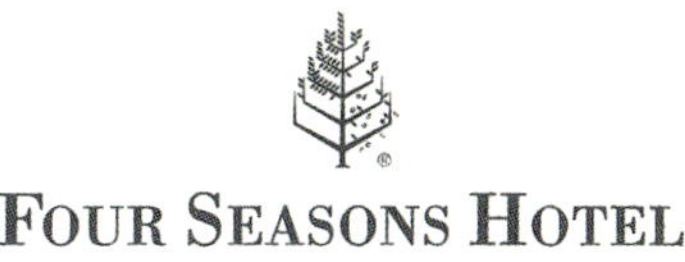

FOUR SEASONS HOTEL
Vancouver

791 WEST GEORGIA STREET, VANCOUVER, B.C., CANADA V6C 2T4
TEL: (604) 689-9333   FAX: (604) 689-3466   www.fourseasons.com

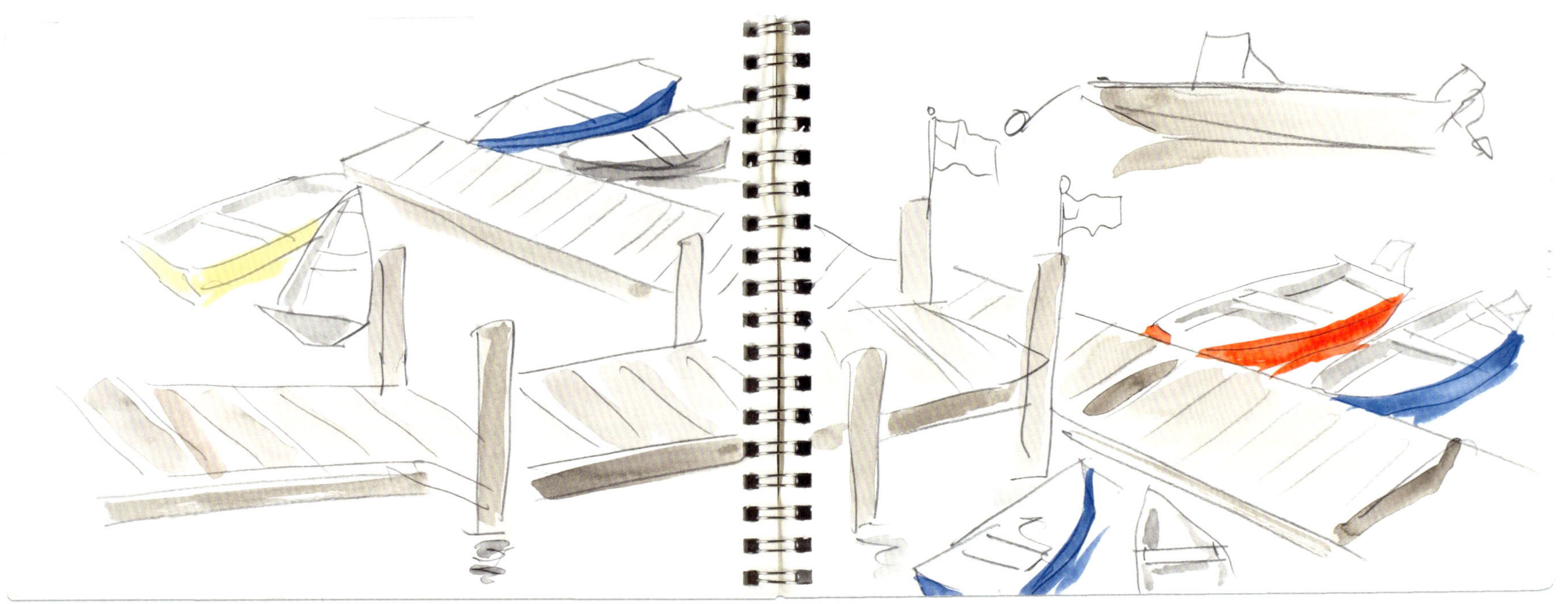

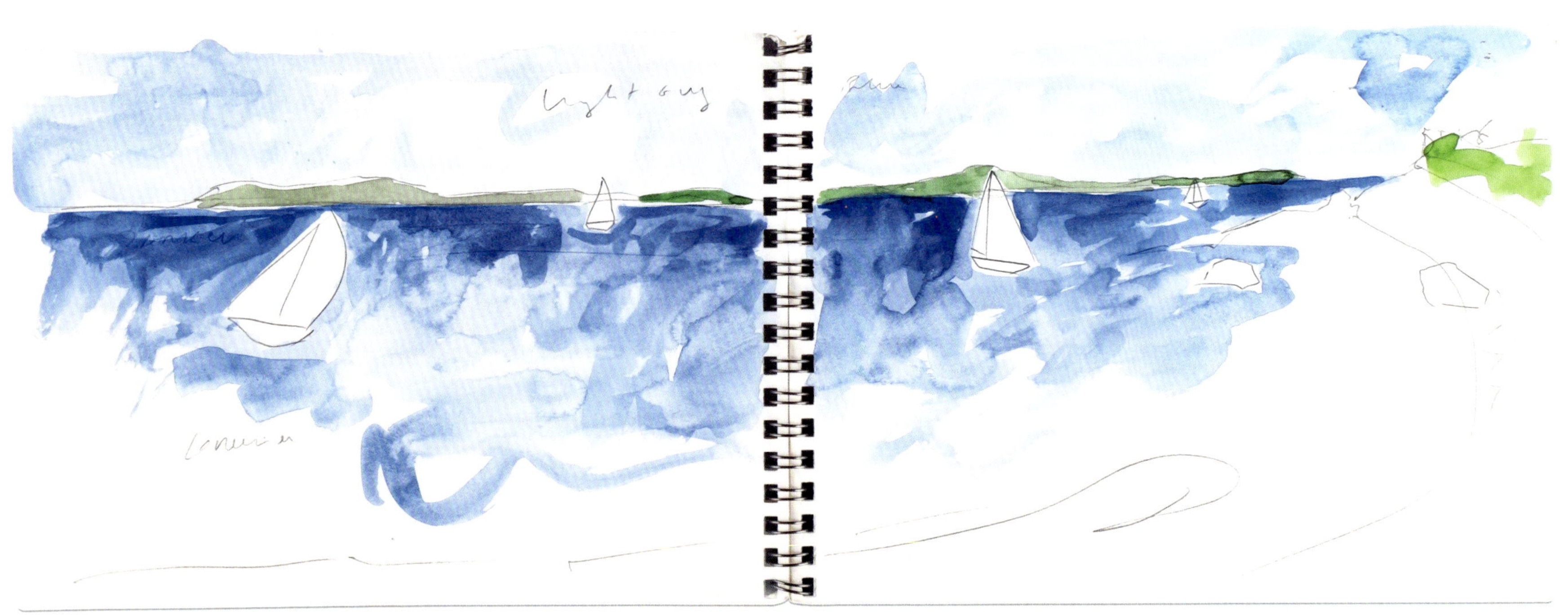
light grey
blue

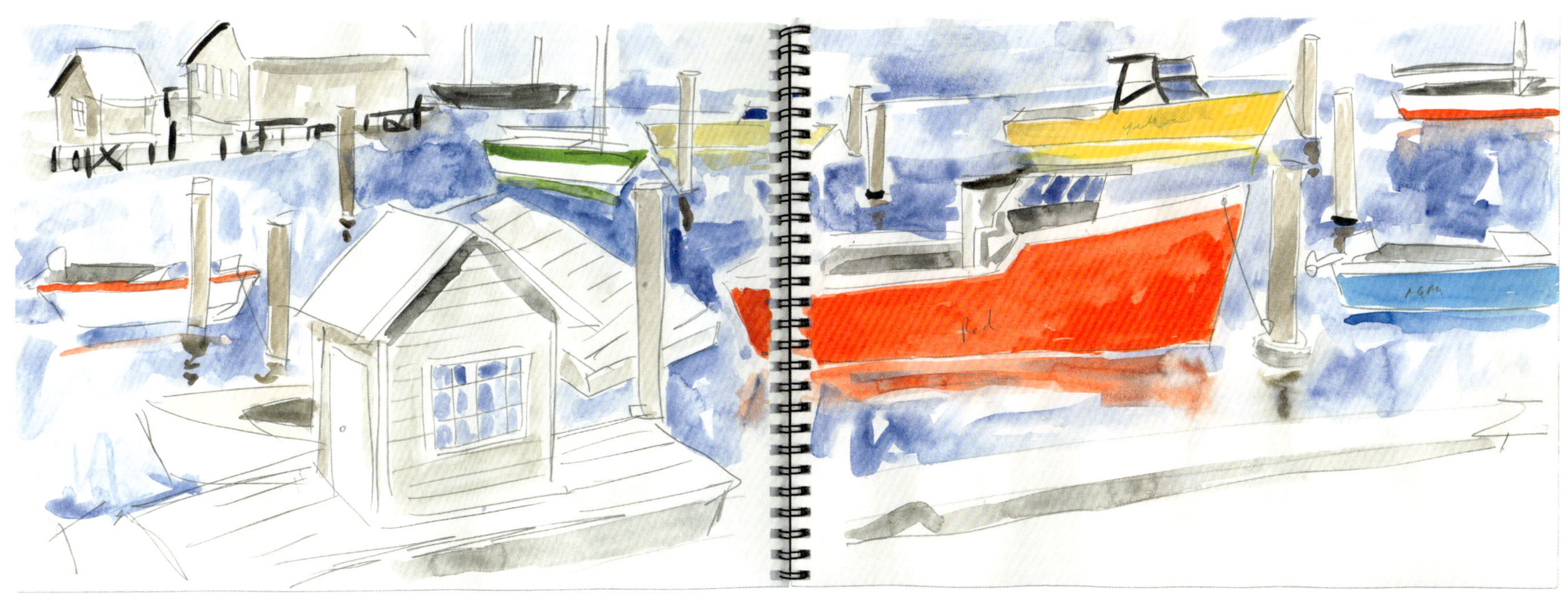

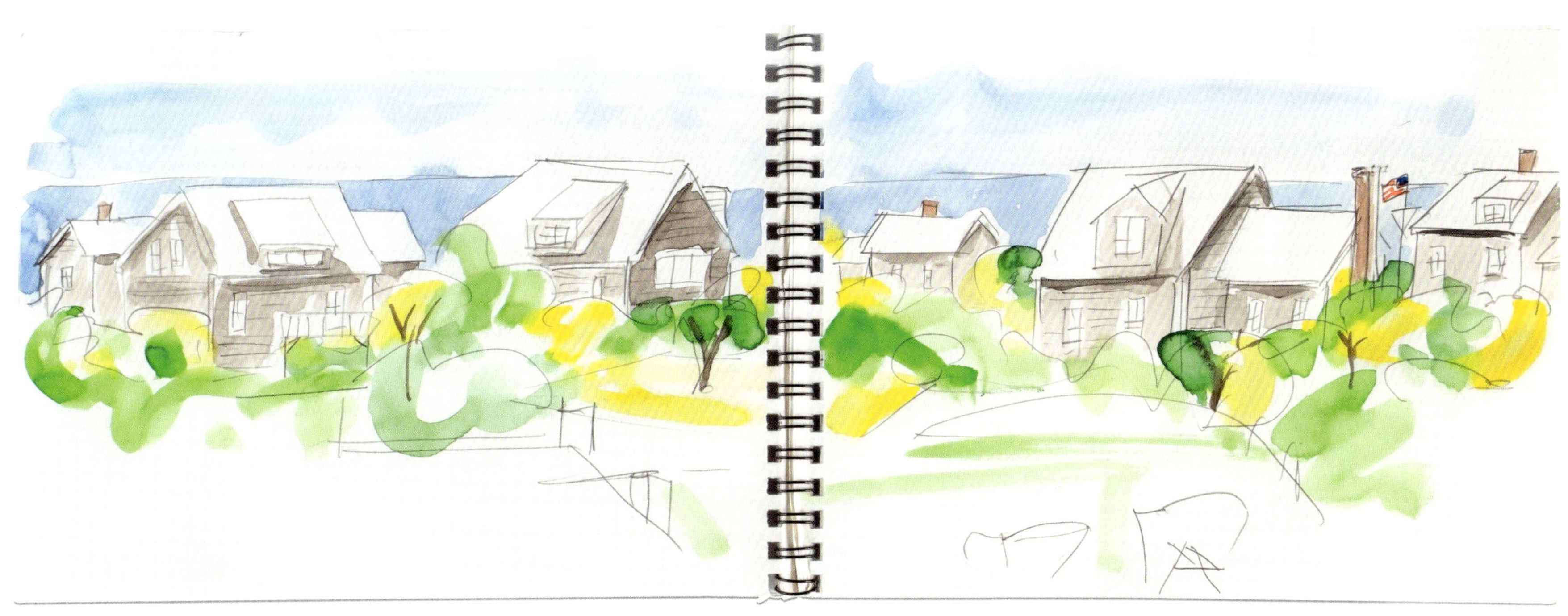

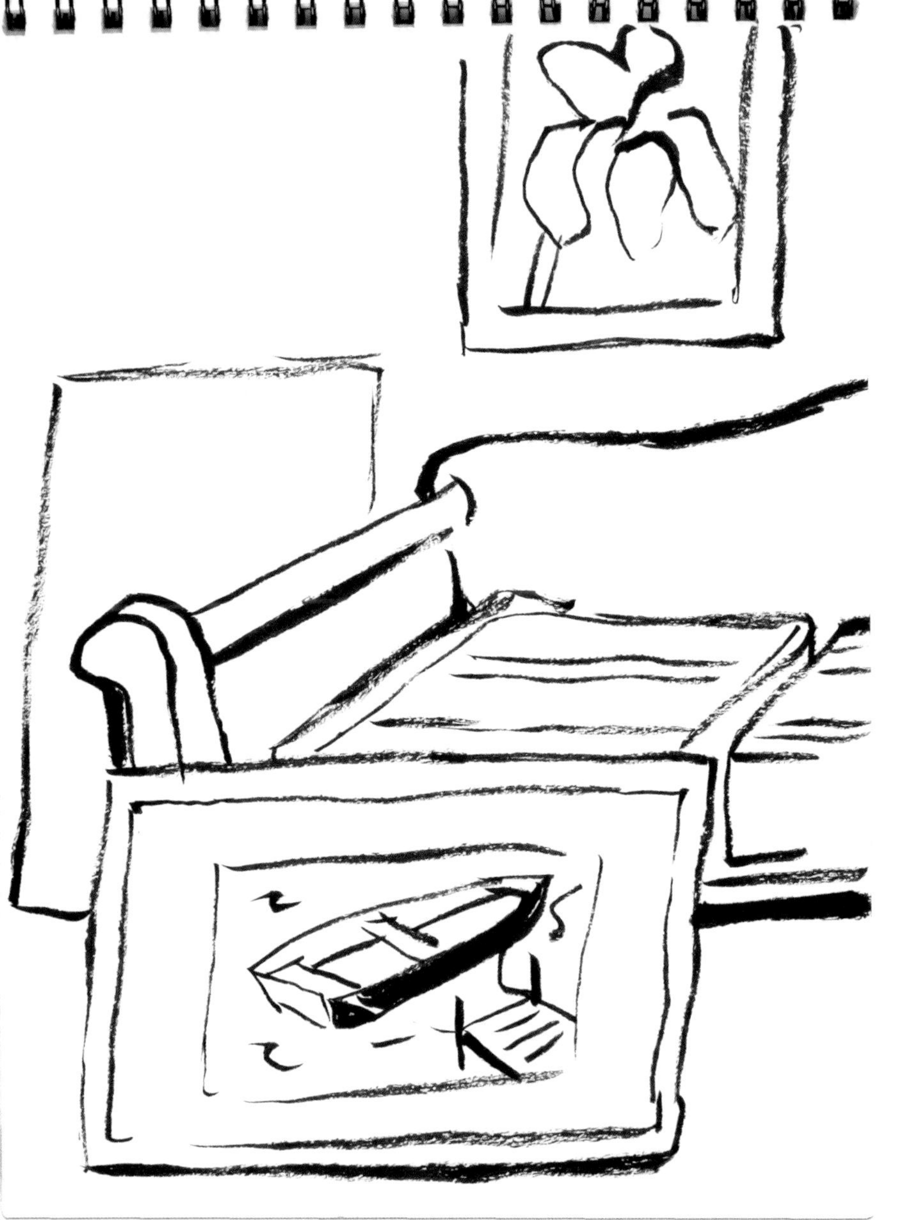

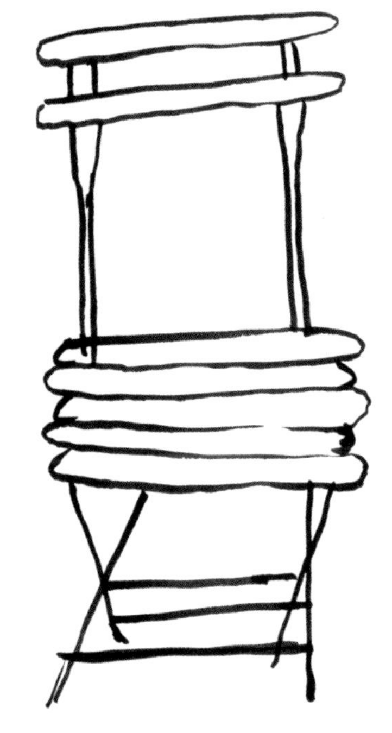

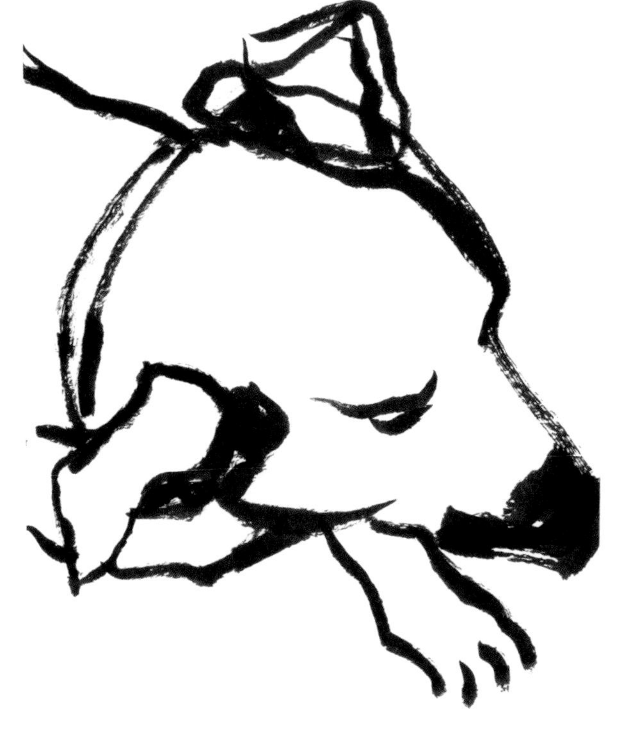

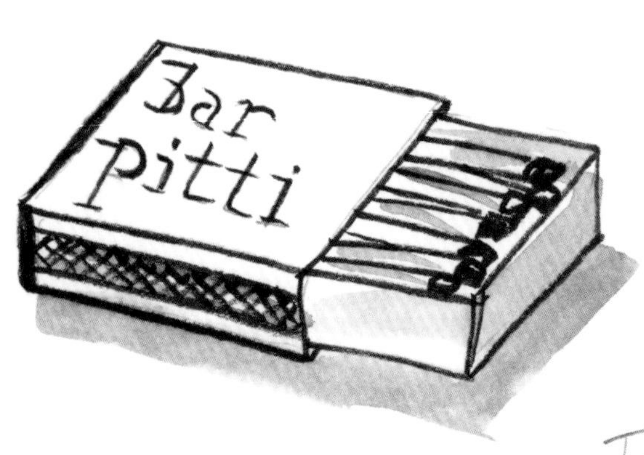

TomS

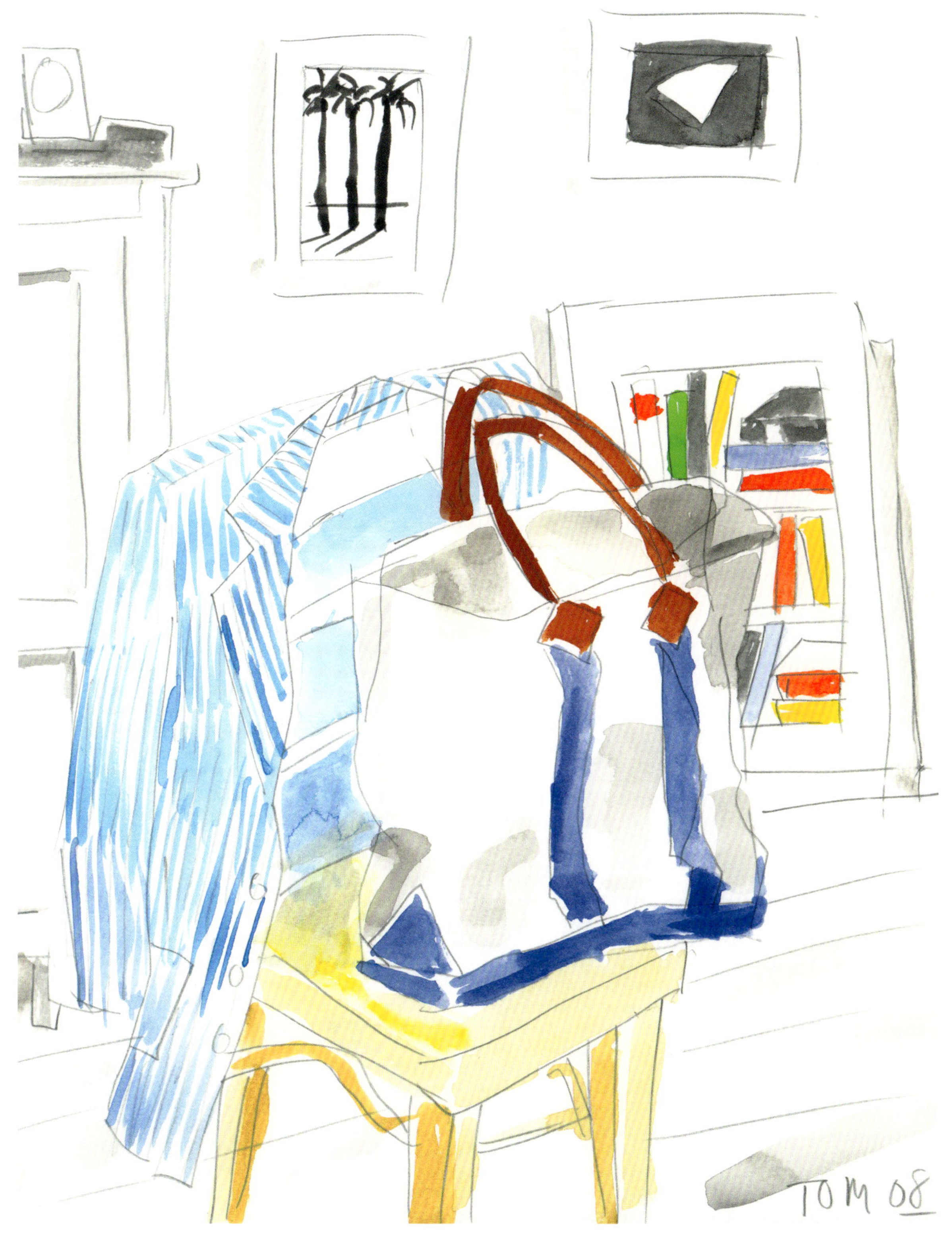

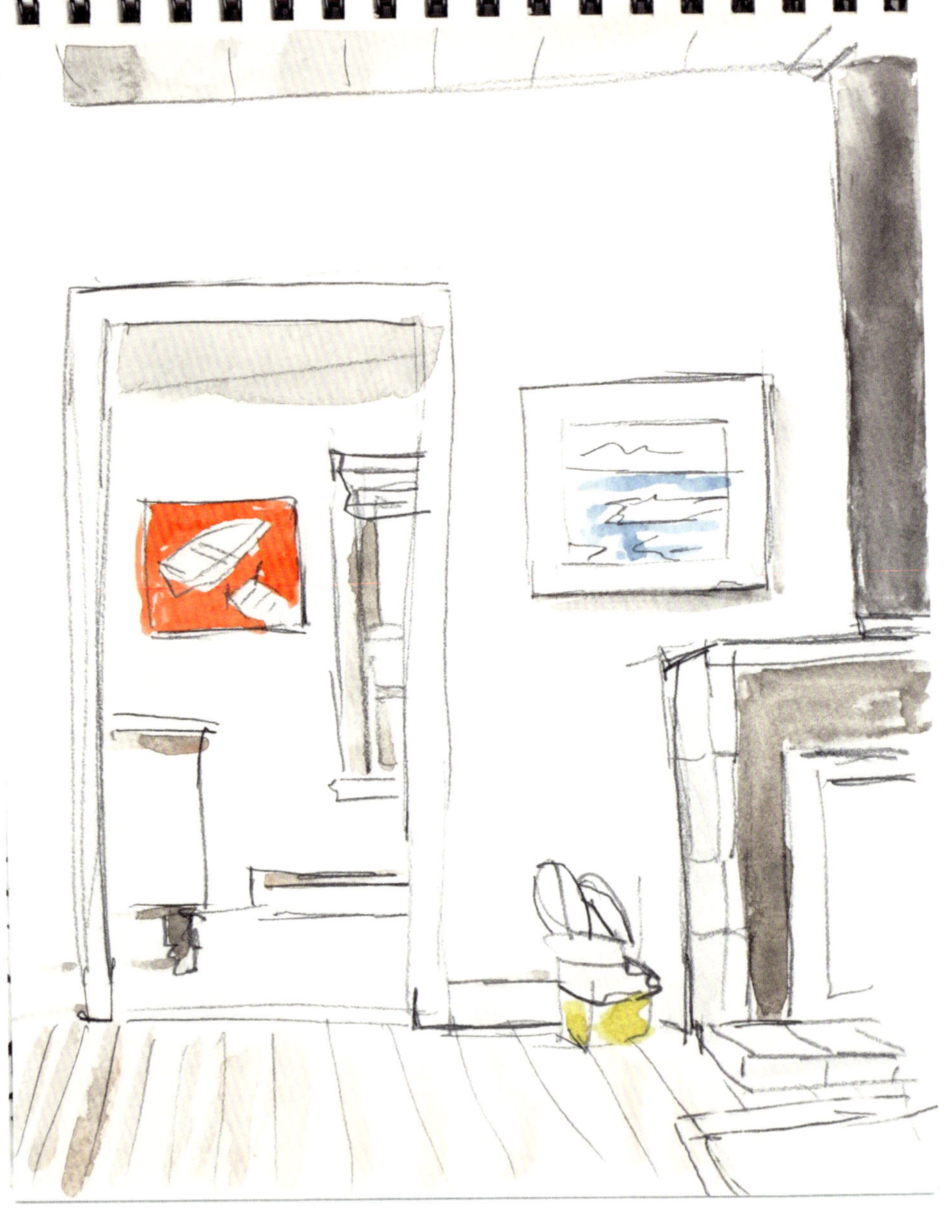

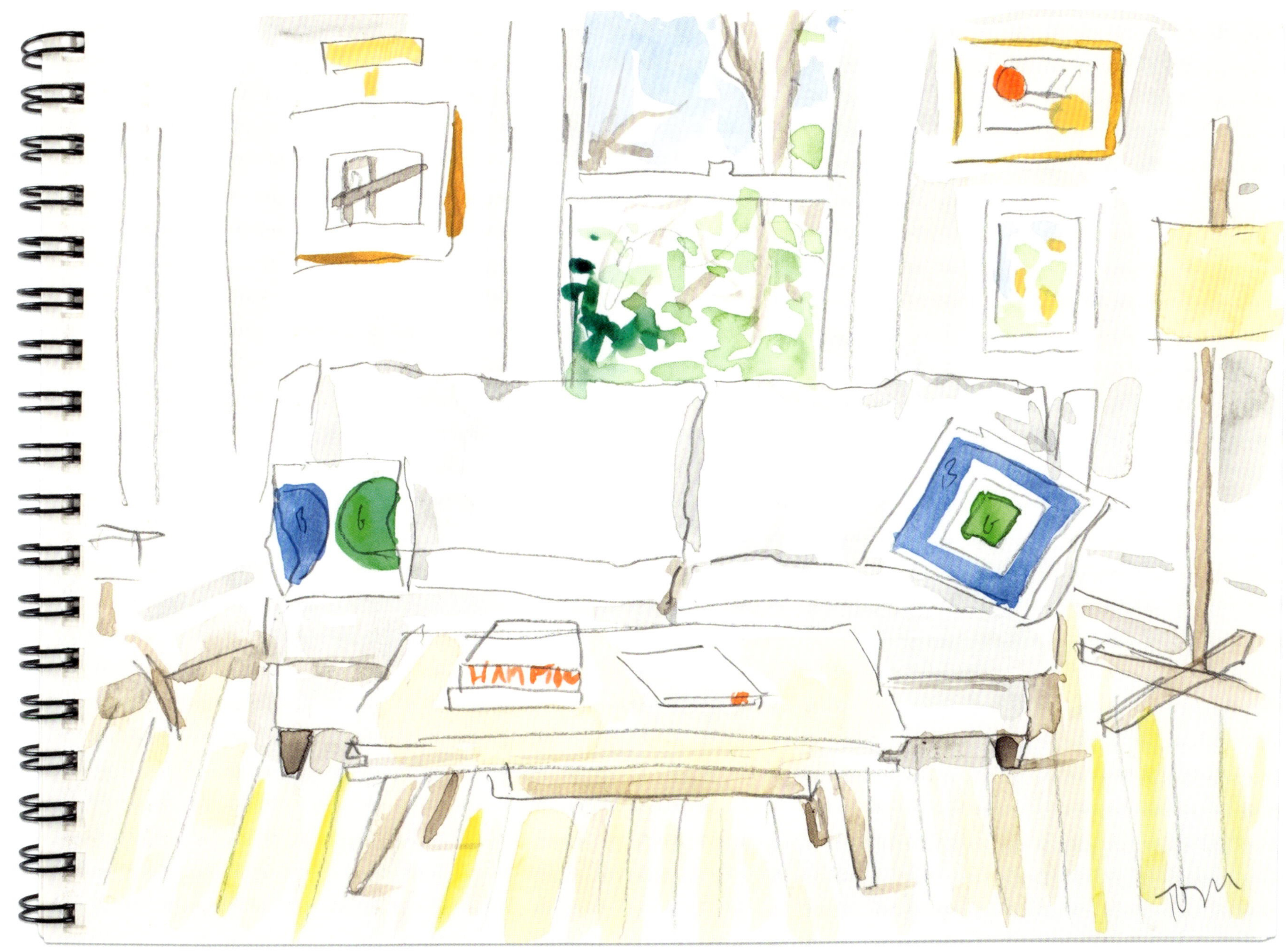

HAMPTO
B
G
B
G

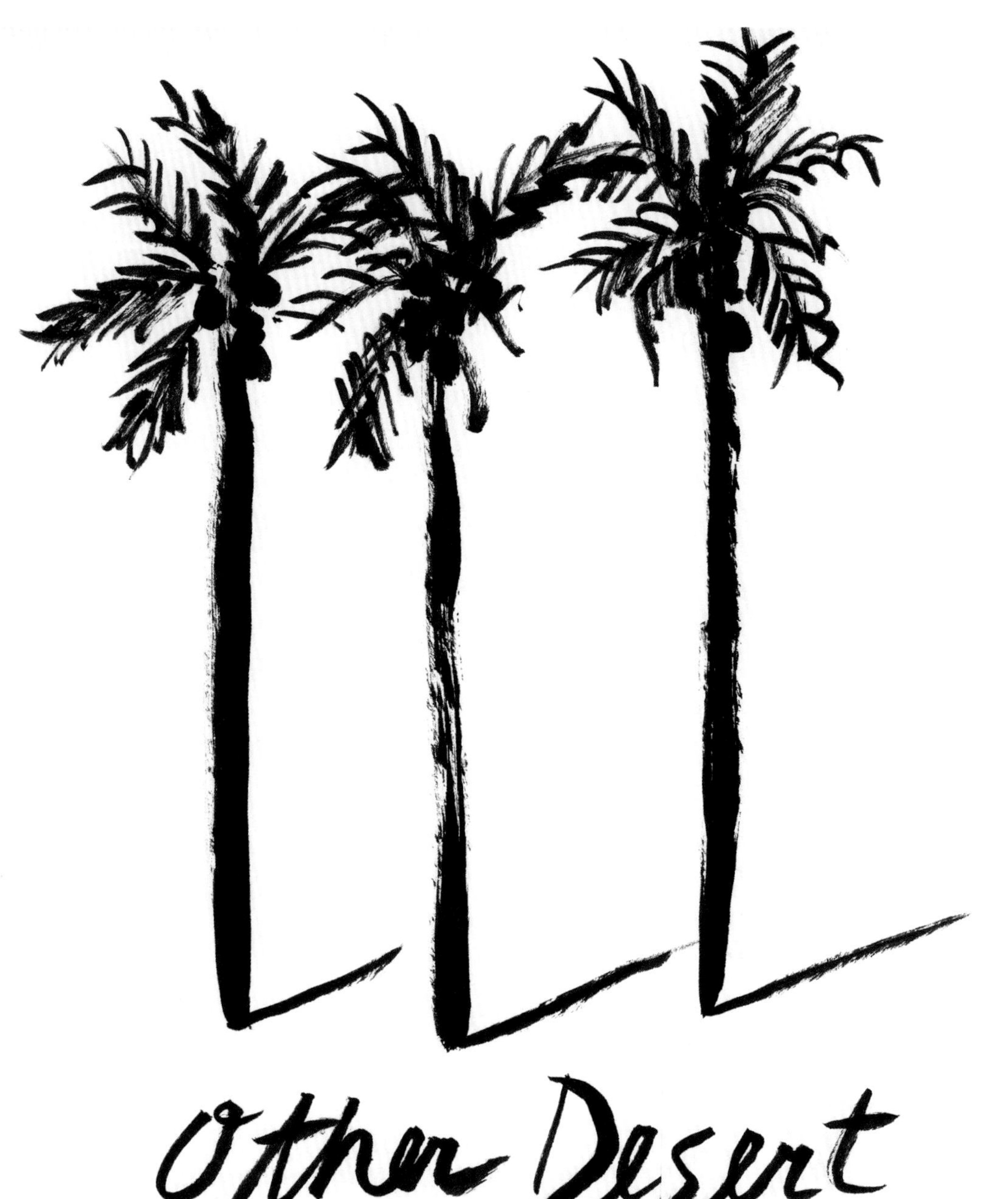

Other Desert Cities

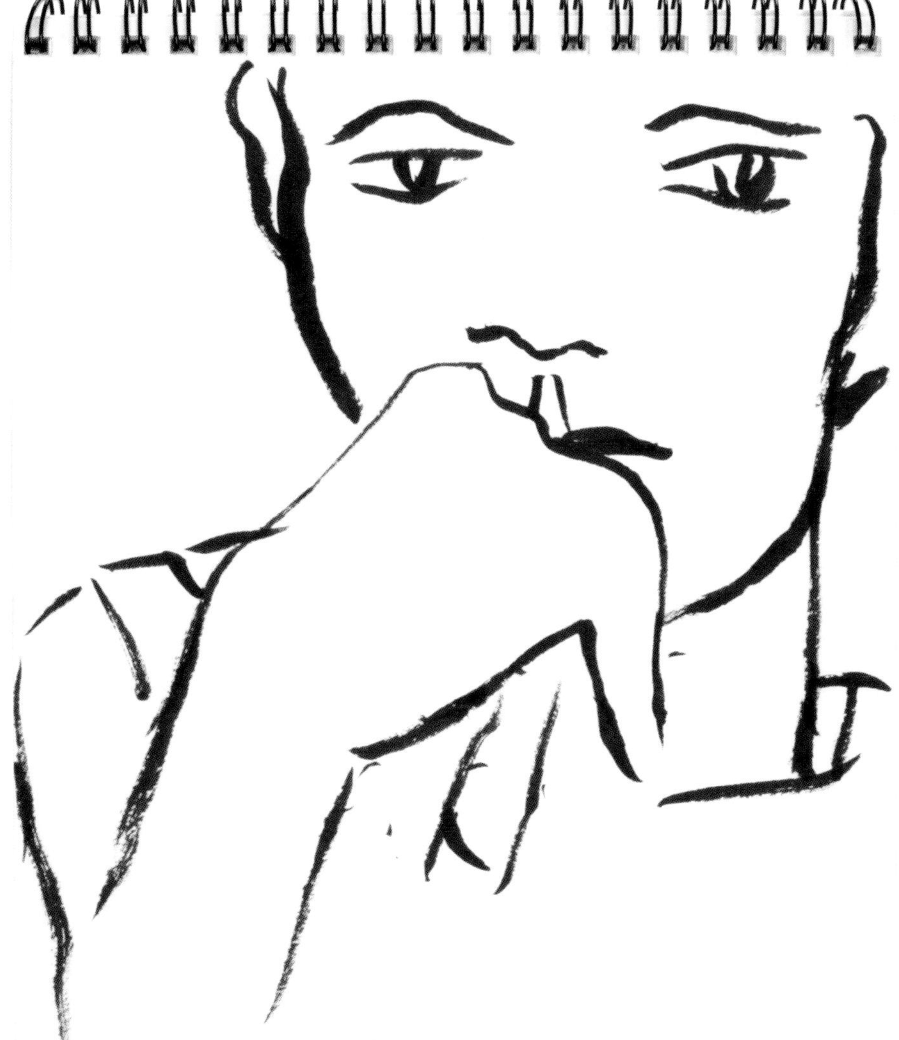

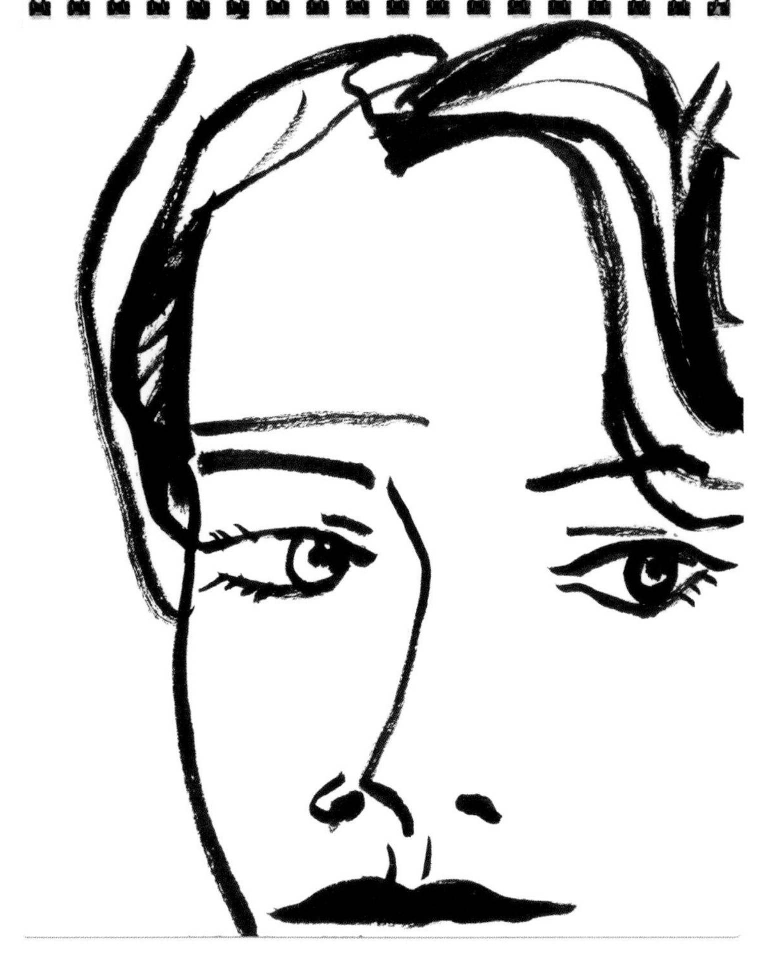

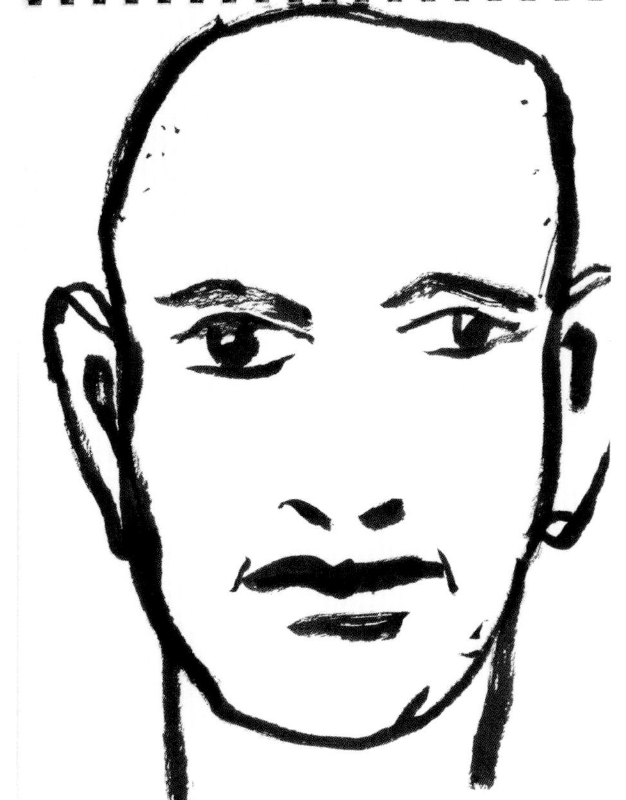

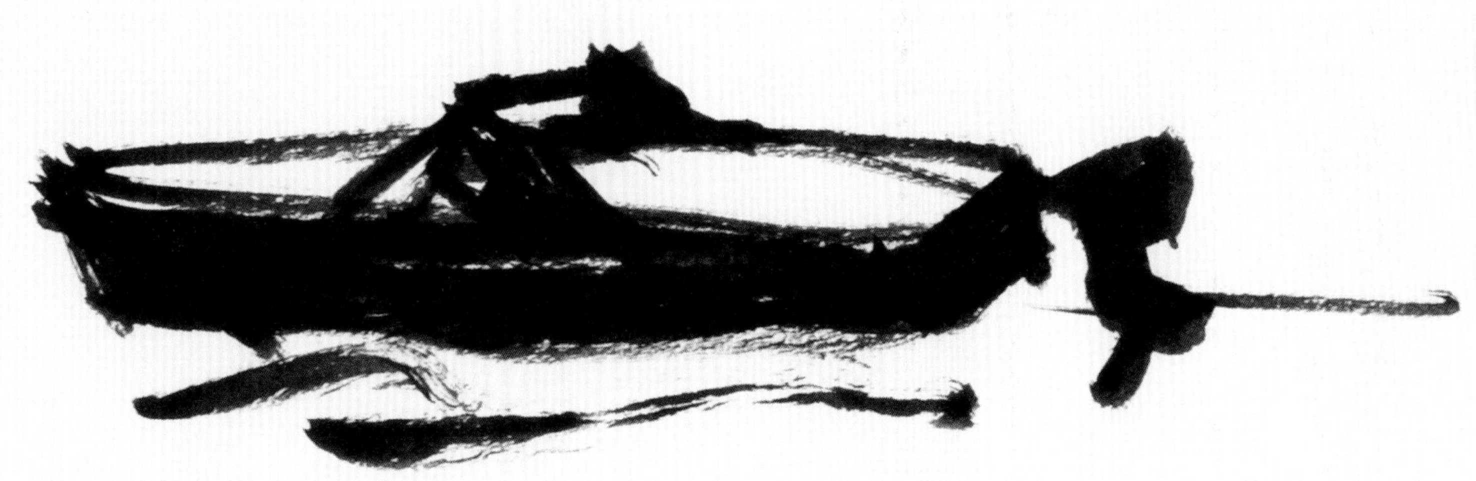

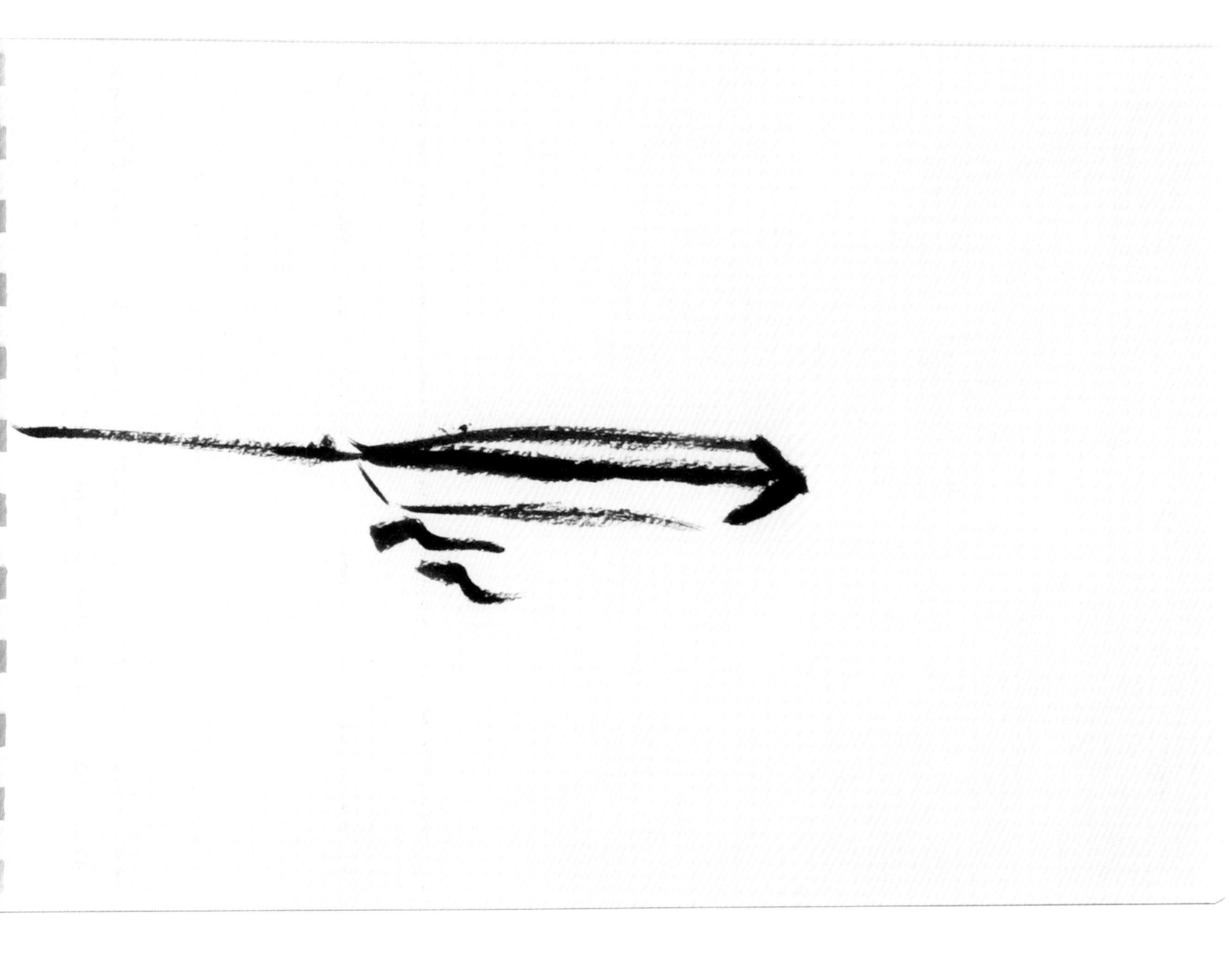

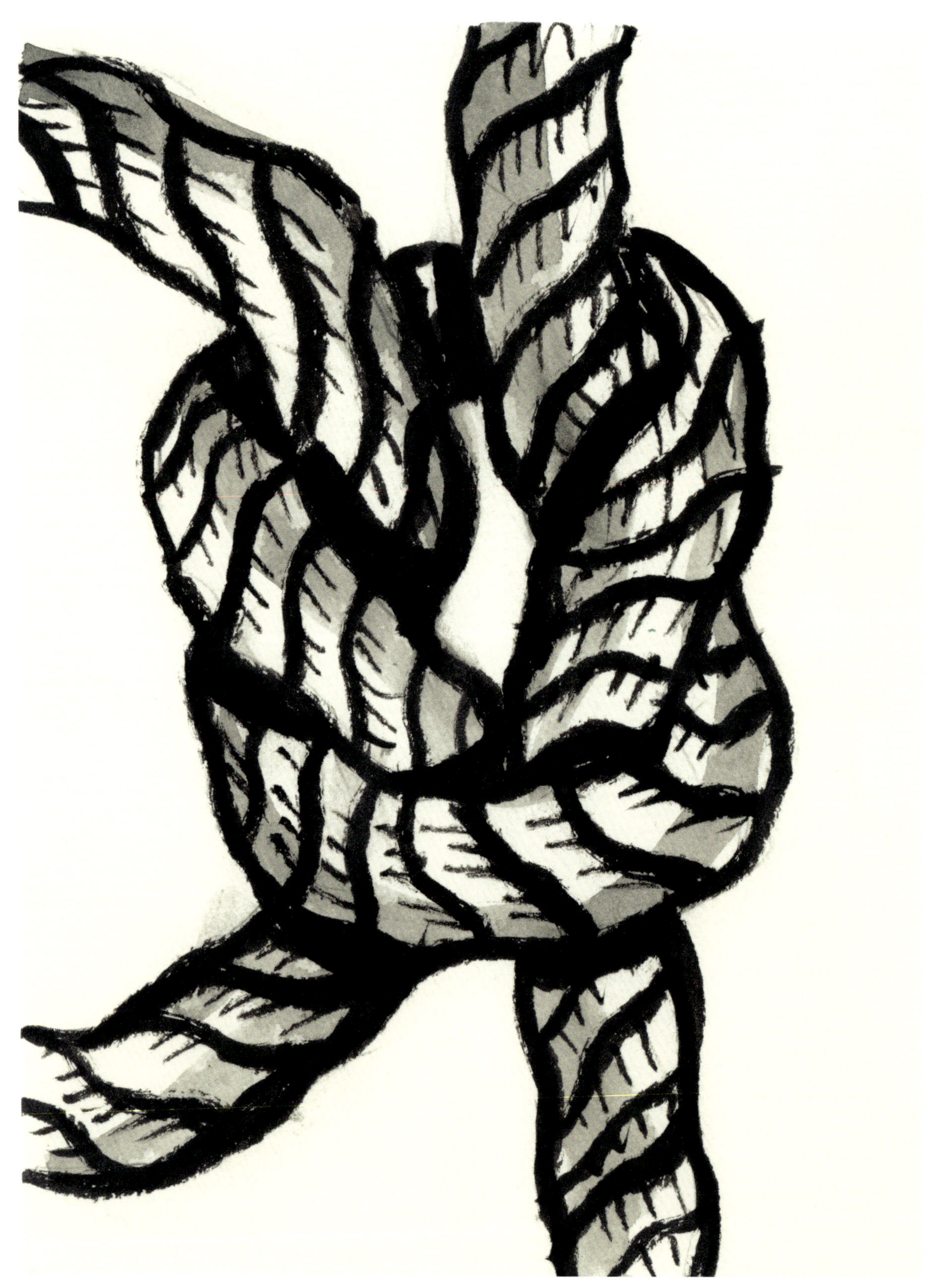

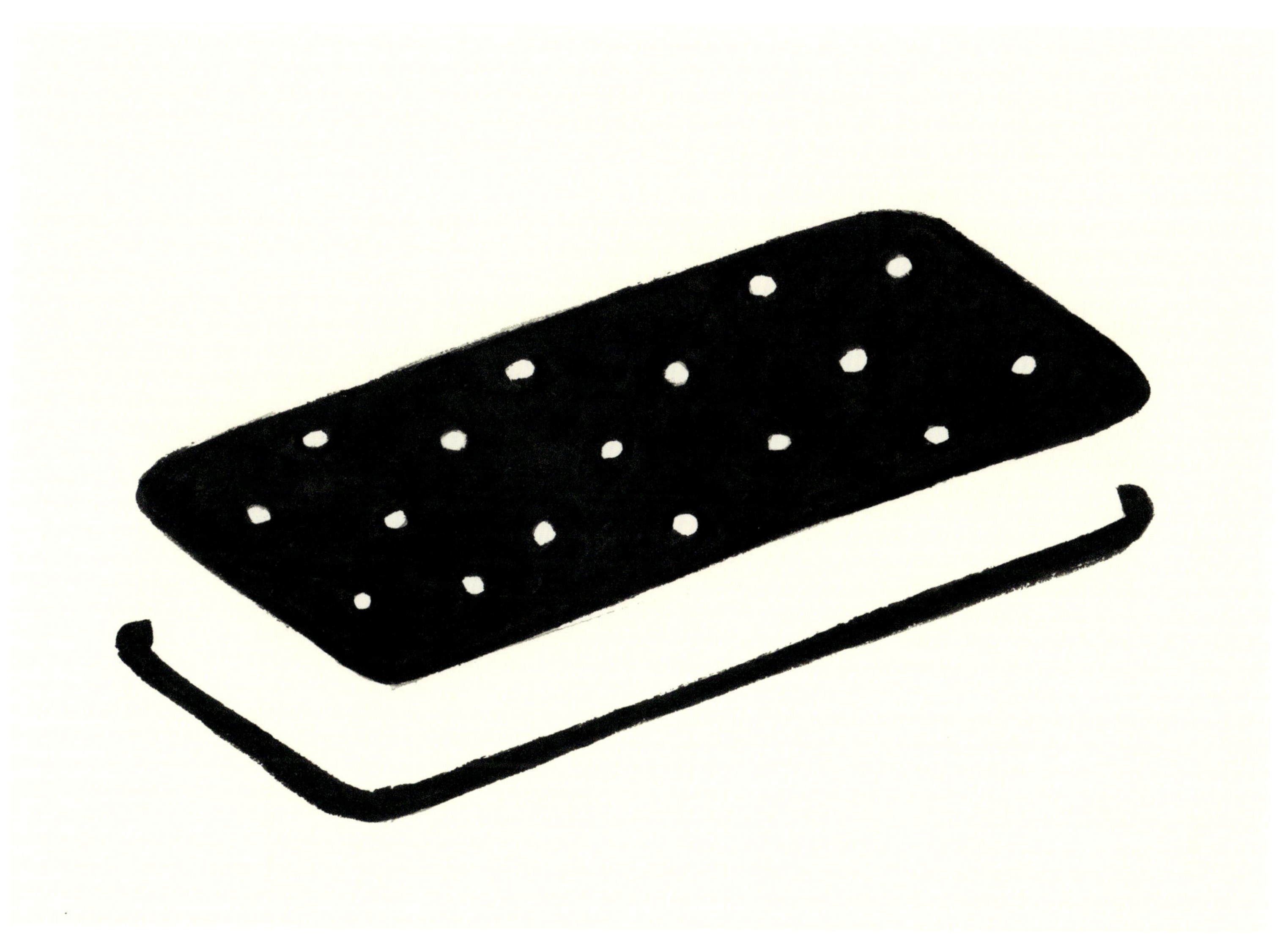

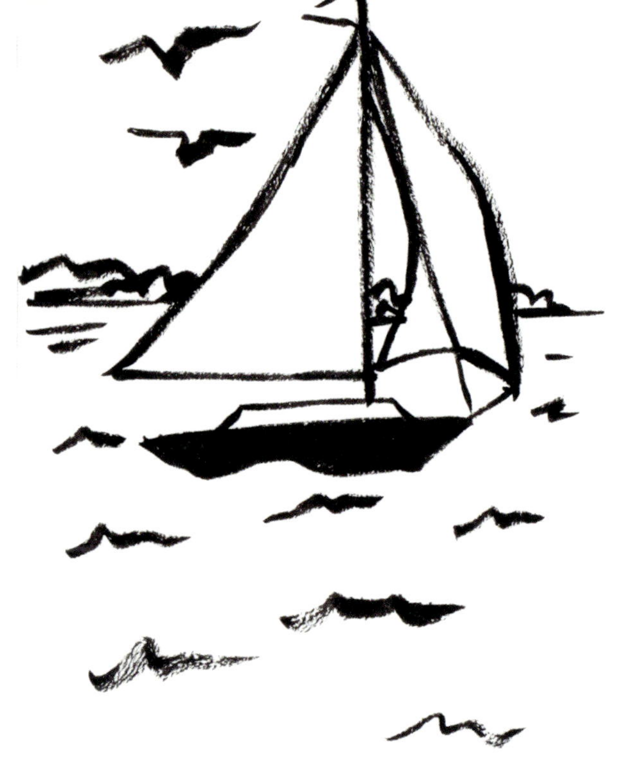

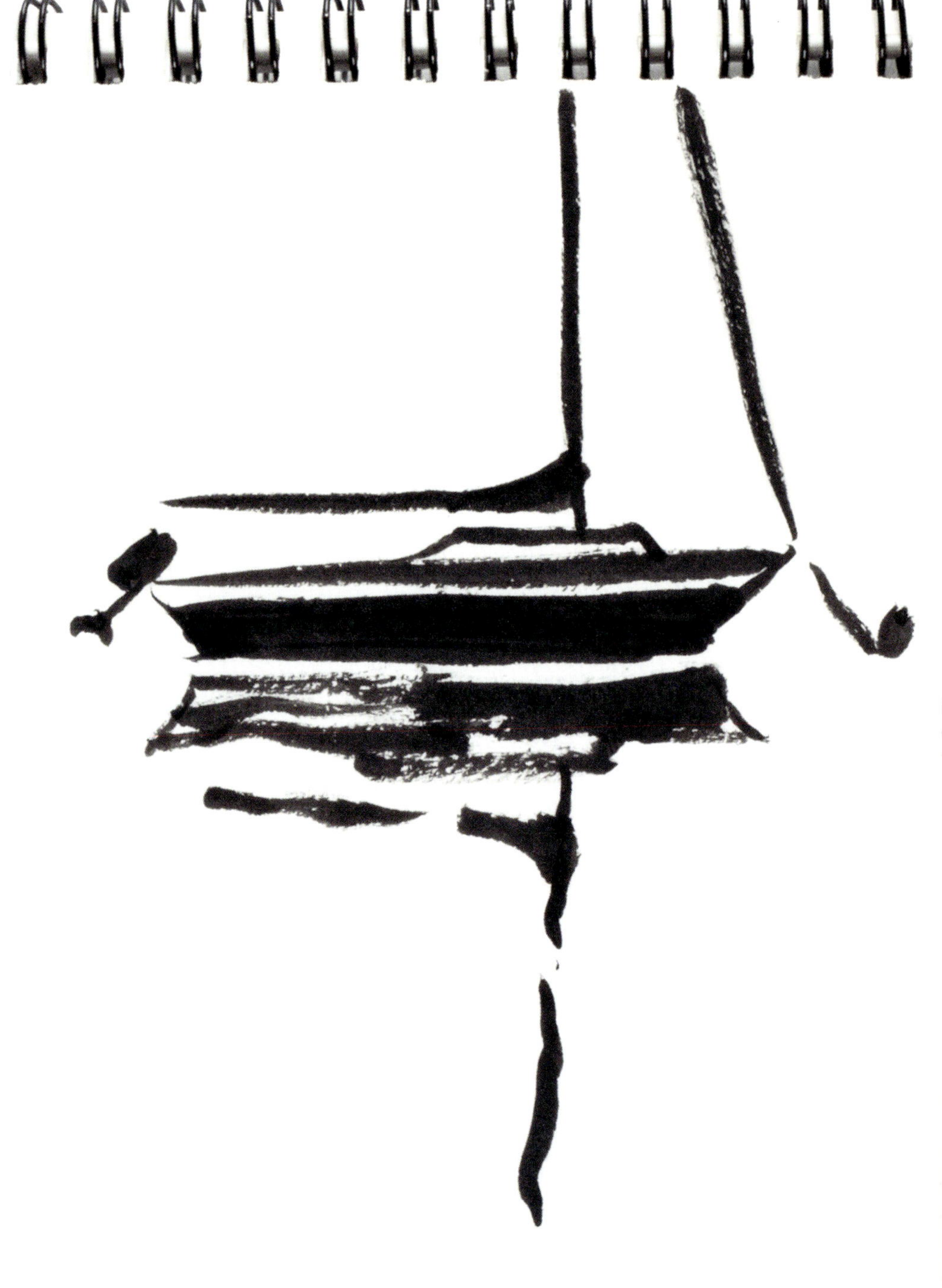

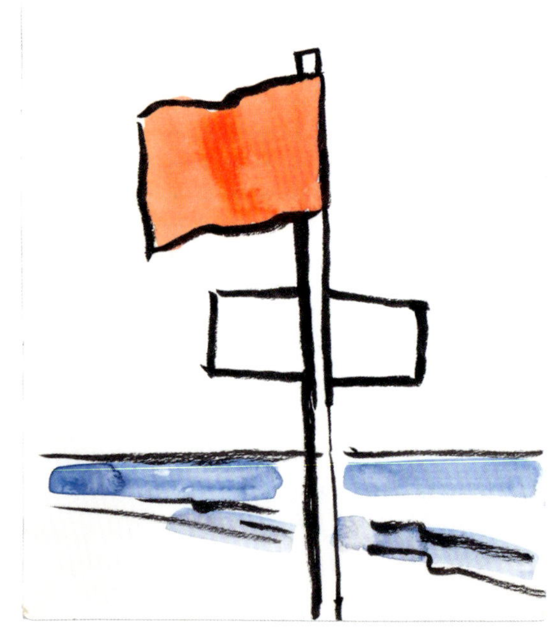

light Blue
green Blue
Red
WOODSHOLE
NANTUCKET
Grey
Tom 08

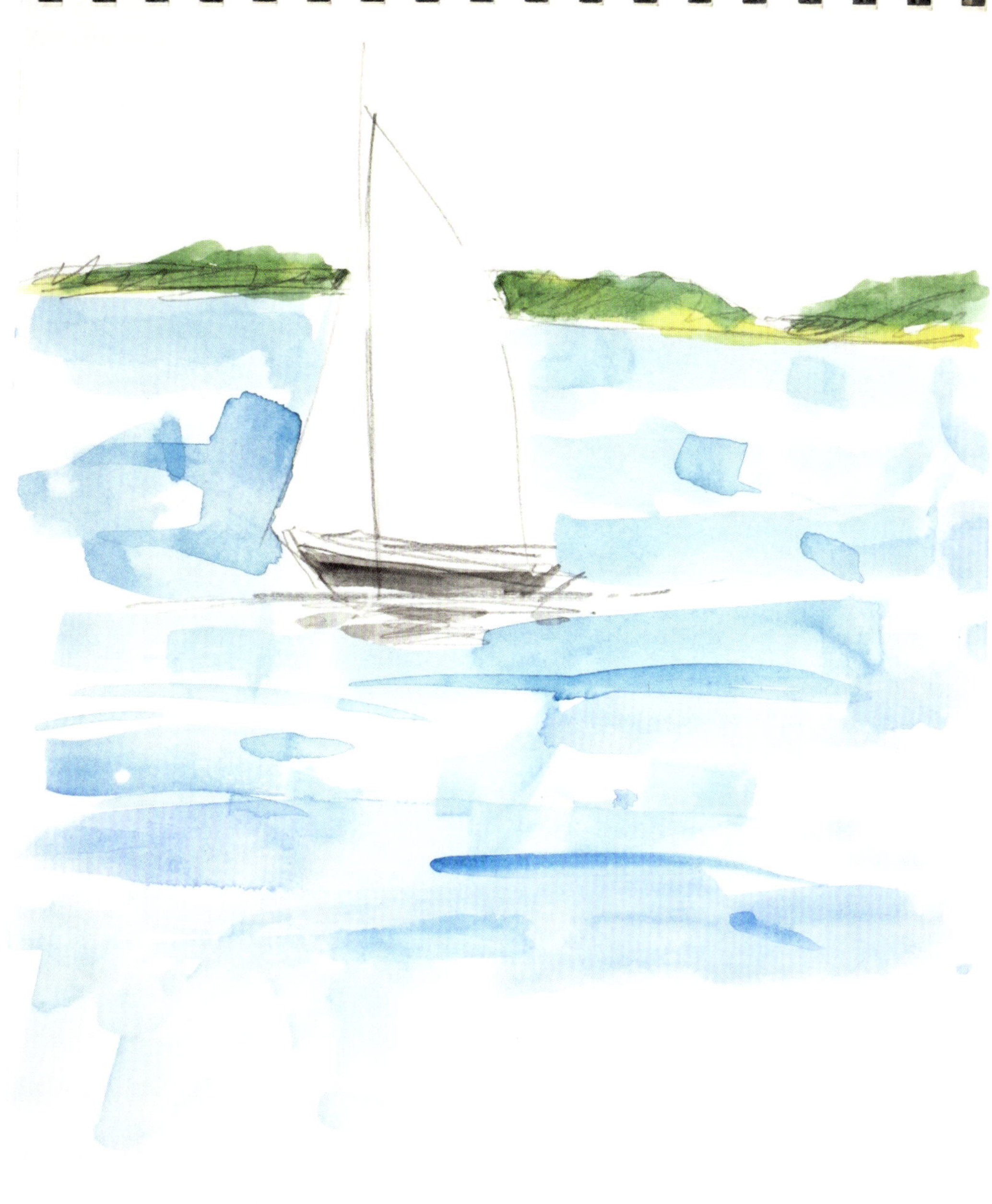

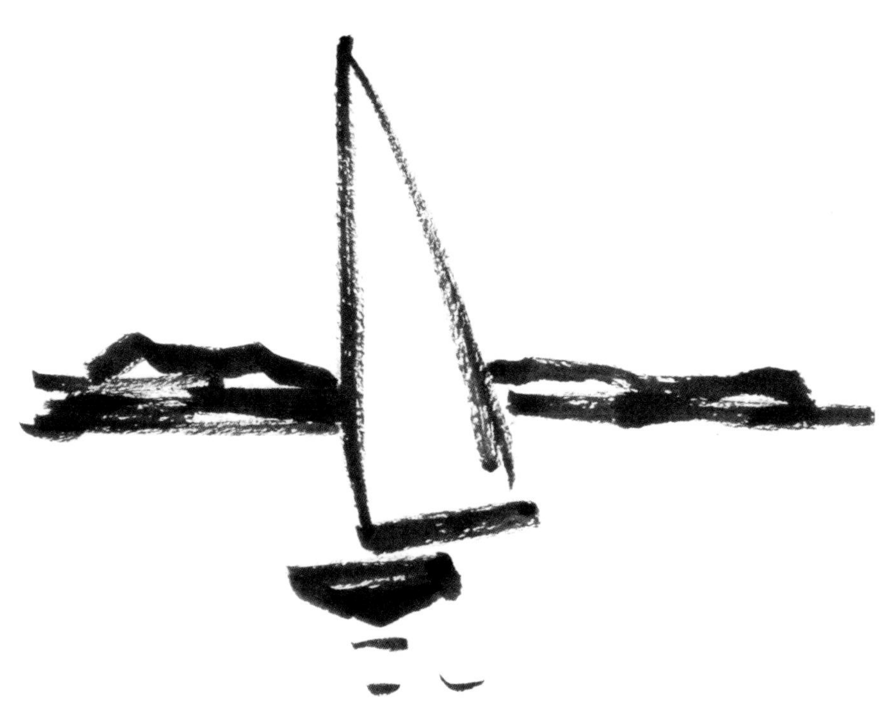

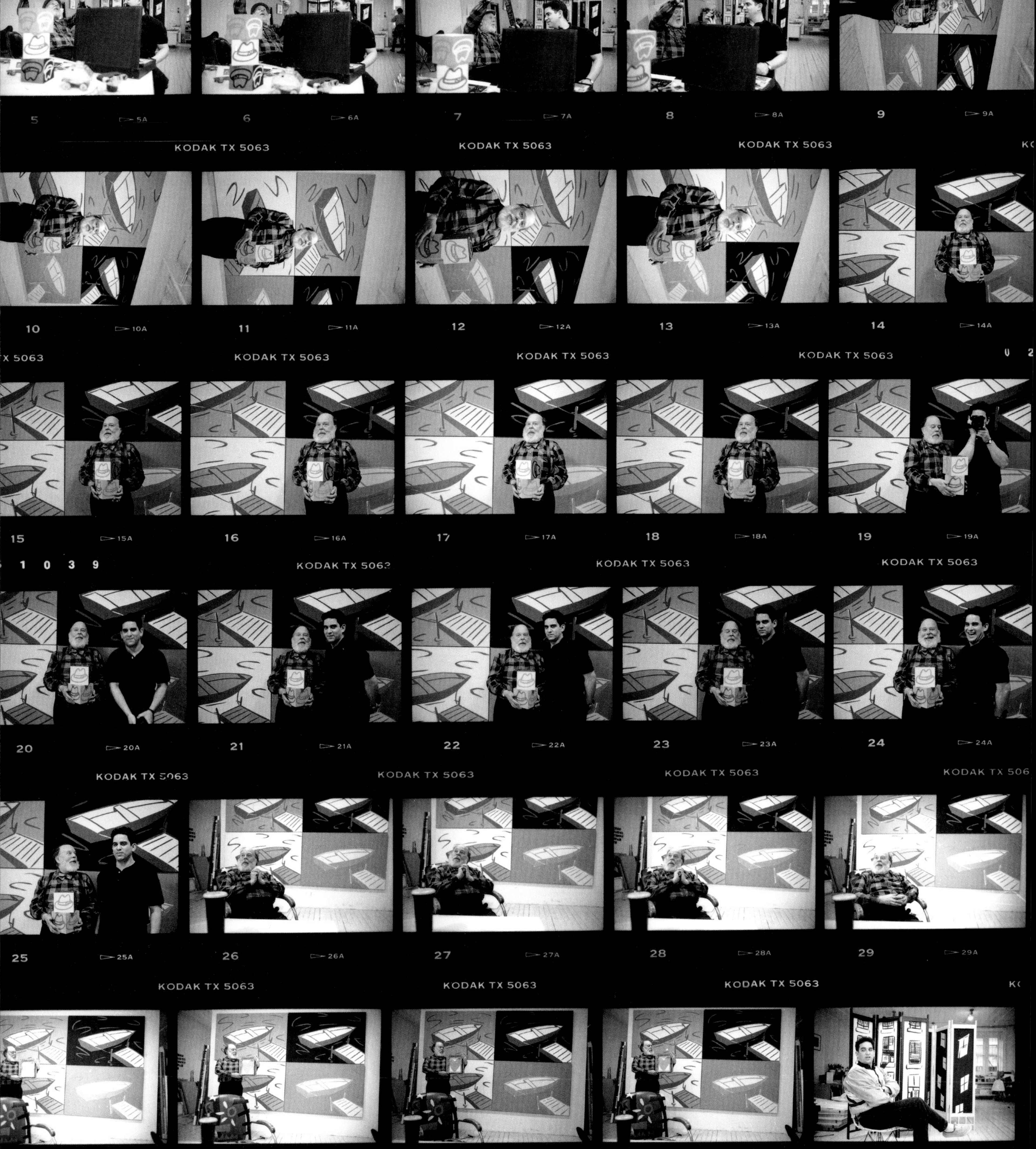

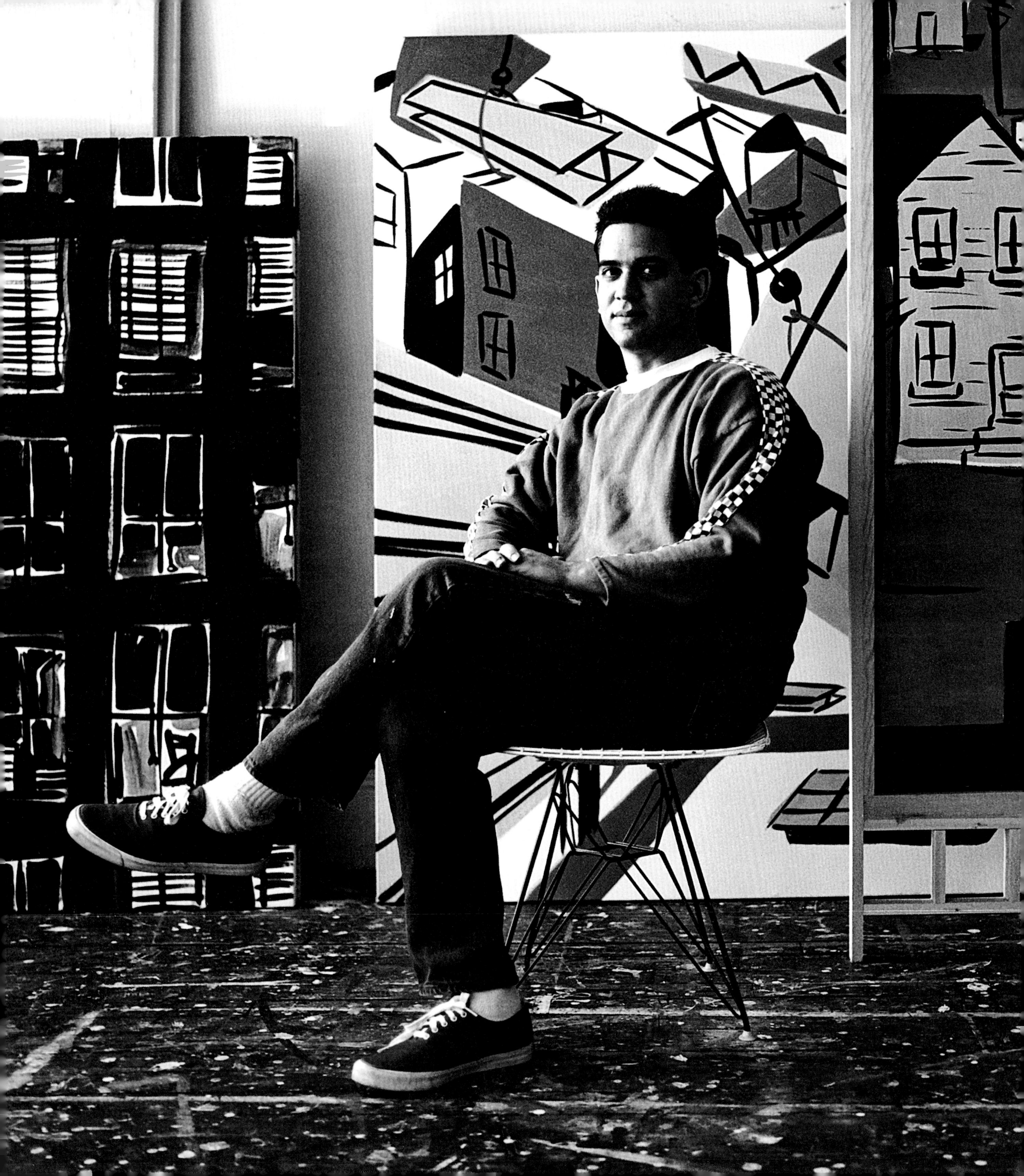

UNMISTAKABLY HIS

An interview, conducted in 2017, with five
of Slaughter's contemporaries.

HJ: How did you meet Tom?

JPR: I first saw Tom's work at George Mulders's house—it was one of those classic city paintings, just two colors, much more raw, more like Franz Kline than some of Tom's other work. So I was really quite taken. George was sort of making this shift, in publishing prints from, let's just say from Keith [Haring] and Andy [Warhol] to this younger group of artists that Henry Geldzahler was championing a little bit. And Tom was really the first project that George was doing with that.

And then when we met, in 1987, it was pretty much a hit right away. I think we met at the loft on Broadway the first time, and we talked about the prints and all that stuff. And I was still working for Rupert [Jasen Smith] so we actually started working together, kind of with Durham Press but not at Durham Press—at Rupert's in New York. So our first experiences were these really late nights after work, working at Rupert's studio, just Tom and me. It was always just really a lot of fun; for one, it was my own new thing, and for another, I was working with this new artist and we were just these two young people having a lot of fun making new work. It was a lot of excitement, working late into the night, until two or three in the morning on these prints.

All I can say is that it was sort of this immediate connection and relationship—we were immediately just up to no good. I knew I wanted to publish under my own business and we were even already conjuring up a project as we were finishing the work with George. Tom was really one of two people who were the first people to print with Durham Press, both of whom started in New York and by the time we got to Pennsylvania, there was already this relationship going.

SH: I can't really remember the first time we met, because it's one of those relationships that just always was. I think it was through a West Coast dealer, Robert Barman, who was putting together the American Pop Culture Now show in Japan. So, we knew each other's work. We all had overlapping bonds before we even met. That's one of those neat things—in art there's nowhere to hide. Once you see a painting, you know the guy, so you tend to know each other from the work before you know the people. I knew right off the bat that Tom and I were going to be tight. I can't separate his work from the spectacular personality. I couldn't see the guy without cracking up. I mean, he had more deadpan wisecracks than anyone.

Interviewers:
Hannah Jocelyn - **HJ**
Nell Jocelyn - **NJ**
Jimmy Mezei - **JM**

Interviewees:
Jean-Paul Russell, Owner of Durham Press - **JPR**
Stephen Hannock, Painter - **SH**
Robert Harms, Abstract painter - **RH**
Scott Kilgour, Artist - **SK**
Ray Charles White, Photo-based artist - **RCW**

We were all under the radar of the vast commercial success that the neo-Expressionists were enjoying. Julian [Schnabel] was breaking plates and Jean-Michel [Basquiat] had this brilliant, natural sense of graphic design but we weren't swept up in that. But things were happening—I took over the pop shop space from Keith [Haring], and Scott [Kilgour] got kicked out of yet another space, so we shared the spot, and Tom had Crosby street. I think we were, ironically, more of a group than the Expressionists who were really in competition. We were just making stuff and hanging out.

The mystery to a lot of us was why Tom, who was armed better than any of us to be just a juggernaut through the culture, was so restrained when it came to his own stuff. When he met Henry, Henry could just tell he had heart. That is perfectly descriptive of Tom as a painter in this culture. Calvin [Churchman] gave Henry a painting of Tom's. Just a little boat. And the painting went from the dining room, and then through the house, and finally to the bedroom so that Henry could see it all the time, and he realized, Holy shit.

RH: It stuck with him. Henry would pick something up, bring it home, and see what it felt like after a while. And that's what happened with Tom's painting. He liked it more and more as he had it. And then he wanted to meet him. Tom told me that story of getting a call and Henry saying, "I think it's about time I come to your studio."

SH: He started writing to Tom and championing him. When Henry came to your place, you knew it was just a privilege for him. He was so honored to come by and see art being made, he got a kick out of it, he respected it. But for us, having Henry come to your studio, you just knew you were on the right track.

RCW: None of us would be here without Henry. He affected all our lives. We all ended up in SoHo because of Henry.

SK: Because of Henry, we got an opening into New York that was extremely unusual.

RCW: A real insider's view.

RH: And it grabbed people's attention because once people saw you with him, they would wonder who you were.

RCW: Reflected status.

RH: And it was nice to have him come to your studio and talk to you about the world. You don't meet too many fucking people that can talk about art like that—I haven't.

SK: I had met Henry in 1982, and a few years later, I think '87 or '88, Henry brought Tom to my studio—I had a place in Hell's Kitchen, on 54th street. So my first experience with Tom is when Henry was doing the runs. The two of them connected instantly so Henry was taking him places, studios, galleries, everything.

RCW: I met Tom late '86, also a studio visit with Henry. We came to the loft with Peter Morton, who started the Hard Rock Cafes, and with Ann Biderman who was with Roger Vadim at the time. We had lived in the same area and we shared a lot. I had been working for Andy [Warhol] and *Interview* magazine and living in a crazy, crazy five-thousand-square-foot loft. Peter was wearing a very slick Armani suit, and they were going around the different studios to see what they should buy, who they should collect, and Henry was obviously advising them.

The loft thing was one thing Tom and I shared. The issue of loft living, and Soho living. We really had a connection over living that way in New York in the early eighties—such a specific way of life.

HJ: Yes, Tom and Marthe [Jocelyn] had just recently moved into the loft. He was coming back from Seattle.

RH: He was prospecting! Looking cute. With his cowboy hat and his truck.

NJ: In Truth or Consequences, New Mexico.

RCW: But so, Henry had this power to bring people together. And Tom also had that in him. This ability to kind of put people together, and to recognize things in people. He wasn't afraid to introduce people and share people. Henry and Tom were both so inclusive in a way, and so they probably shared that as a kinship.

And I think it's one thing to be a nice person and an interesting person and a genuine and authentic person—and certainly both Henry and Tom appreciate that—but it's quite another to have some ability, an eye, something that you can do. And I think Henry saw that in people, and he certainly saw that in Tom. I think he saw a genuine authentic person who was also an unbelievably talented artist.

RH: And he wouldn't waste any time. He really liked the work. Moving Tom's painting around the house—that was real. It's not just a story.

RCW: He'd take paintings he liked in a little bag on the Jitney! He connected to the work.

SK: We were all a part of Henry's aesthetic. We were connected in a little way, by some kind of Henry eye.

RCW: When I think about what that was, what he saw in our work and Tom's work—it was an authenticity of the person, and that translated into an organic ability.

RH: And a sort of a sensuality to it, too.

RCW: Stripped down.

RH: I met Tom in '89 I think. A couple years after he met Henry. I had met Henry on the Jitney going into the city. He was by then living in Southampton, so he started coming to my studio and then one by one he wanted me to meet these guys because they all knew each other by then for a couple of years. I think I met Tom first at Scott's studio in Hell's Kitchen. He just showed up, and I didn't know

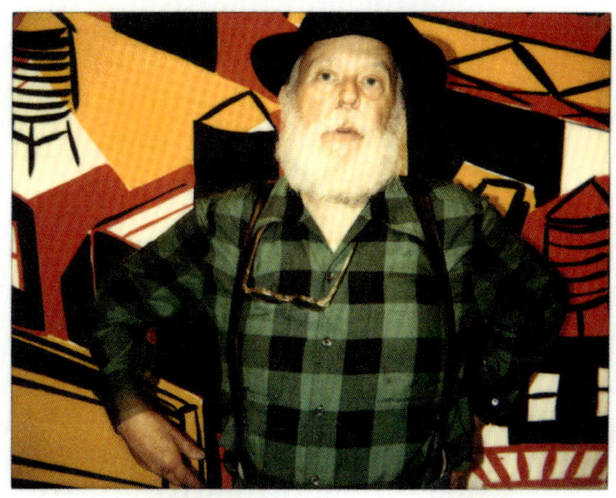

Henry Geldzahler

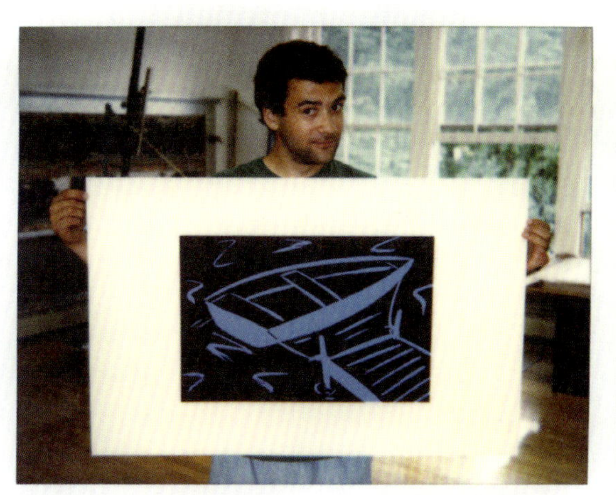

Jean-Paul Russell

anybody except for Henry so I was a little nervous and then Tom comes bounding in. He's got this big voice and I'm like, "Who the fuck is this guy?" And then what I remember about Tom—we were leaving the studio and we went downstairs and Tom was across the street by then and he bellows across the street, "Henry meeting you is like getting the *Good Housekeeping* seal of approval!" Being so cheeky! And, I mean, I was intimidated by Henry then and I'm thinking, This guy is kind of cool. And he had those big brown eyes and he was shouting across the street and I thought, He's fun. So I liked him right away.

And it was like, in two, three years from there, Tom was on a rocket ride that was just, whoa! It was crazy. Then the first set of prints was a big success. A water tower, hat, construction. And then it went straight into another set of prints and it just kept on going. That's when it all took off.

RCW: I remember they did four shows, maybe five. And they set up an exhibition in the Netherlands. Ruth Seigel, on 57th street, she had work from floor to ceiling. And then we did a show in Boca, the four of us, with this woman called Dorothy Blau. She was a wonderful woman from a society family. She sold the most Warhol portraits of any dealer, and she was really kind of renowned and knowing. She had a gallery in an industrial strip-mall kind of place that had been reconfigured and we agreed to do this show.

She had another gallery in Bal Harbour and we went down there a few years later and did a July 4th show. And I remember it was so great. We stayed at my friend's house in Miami Beach with beautiful nineteen-twenties Spanish art decor, gorgeous house right on the beach and Tom was suddenly something else. He was not Mr. New York. And Miami then was not what it is now—it was very casual and a little haphazard. And Tom jumped right in the water. And I remember seeing Tom in the sun with the water and the palm trees and he just seemed really relaxed, really comfortable. And it was just a really nice moment, thinking back.

SK: But the thing is about Tom—he didn't like to leave SoHo. He knew every street.

RCW: Such a New York guy, such a SoHo guy. He hated cabs.

RH: Yeah, but you see that in his work. It's so much here. I can't walk down a block in SoHo; everywhere I look I see him. The water towers. The work depicts the things that were really here, and this neighborhood. Even though Henry talked about his work like it's imagined, and heightened, always a brilliant sunny day, I still think it's really rooted in the actual place. And once he had the place in Long Island, he did the same out there.

JM: It's also a snapshot of the time he was painting.

RCW: When I look at the images of the water towers and the buildings from SoHo in that era, I never figured it out in my mind, was that an actual, real depiction or his interpretation?

RH: I think it's both—there is a real specificity to where it is, and then it's seen sort of through his lens. I mean, he would sketch all the time. Constantly. How many sketchbooks do you have?

NJ: Hundreds and hundreds.

RH: He always had a sketchbook.

RCW: He was a good photographer, too. He had the observation. He had the eye, and the sensibility.

RH: He always did it. When you got a letter from him, you'd get the place, where he was, on the envelope. He'd write the note, and on the envelope would be a watercolor from wherever he was, Santa Monica, the hotel stationery, in Martha's Vineyard with Mike [Ridgway]. So maybe he traveled better than we thought.

HJ: Who was Tom to you?

SH: Tom, for me, was the personification of where the rubber meets the road. I think that's a quote from Frank Stella, and what that means is he always used to tell us that there's no such thing as a good idea for a painting or a bad idea for a painting—they are just good paintings or bad paintings, so don't talk about it, just do them. And *then* you discuss them. And that is so brilliant if you are making art around here [SoHo] because you go over a block west to Fanelli's and you have a beer at the bar, and there's always painters there—not as many as there were back in the day, but they're still lingering around here—and you have a beer and you hear a couple of cool things, ideas for paintings and stuff like that. You go back five years later and some of these guys are still talking about the same painting. And that type of behavior is just so far removed from the way Tom worked—it's not even funny. He was just like, BANG. He put the canvas down and he just, BANG. I would get so envious of the way he would just put down that canvas, flag down the tap, and just get that brush wet and go in and paint. So rich, and the depth, and that mood! His work was—without question—the most real, and primary. Those colors. The prince of primary colors.

RCW: I always thought of Tom as an older brother. We talked a lot, we shared a lot—a curiosity and appreciation of life and people. He taught me a lot of funny lessons; he always had these great sayings. One of them was "Pay the twenty bucks." I love that phrase—I think it was a family saying, maybe from his dad. It's sort of like, sometimes there's a cost. You might not like it but swallow your pride, get on with it, and move forward with your life. I think that's an important lesson—to remember now and always to just keep moving forward and not let those things get in your way. So I always think of Tom in those situations.

And he was so charming—instantly reading you, and able to put you at ease and make you feel better about yourself. He loved meeting people, putting them together and seeing things come together. You know—there are certain people in New York that you meet—and you don't meet very many of them—who are charming in the

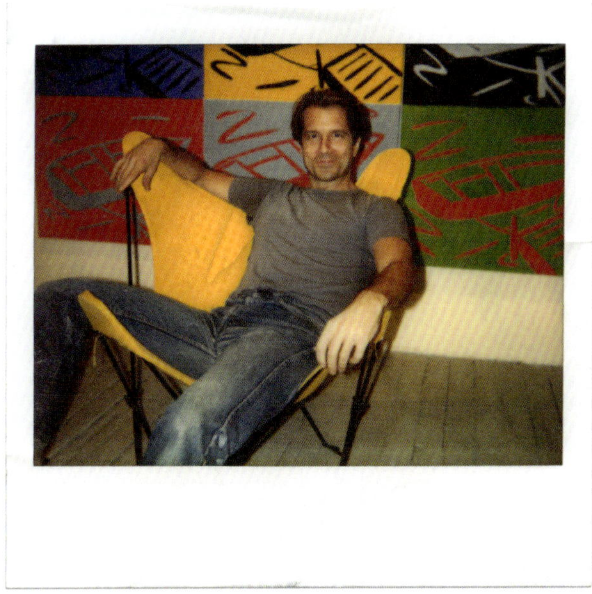

Stephen Hannock

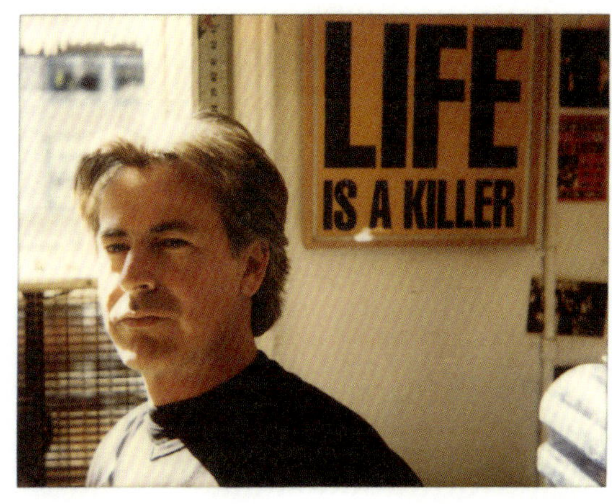

Robert Harms

sweetest way. He was one of these guys that if you were unsure or not feeling good, or you had some uncertainty, he always had that ability to strip it down and make you feel able to handle the dilemma you were in.

RH: One thing I think about a lot is that he did have this sort of great sarcastic sense of humor. But also he could be really supportive, you know? With my work, and in the studio. . . I think of the last few times he visited. They were great. He was genuinely interested in the work—he could see it, he could talk about it—without the humor, without trying to be funny or jokey. He just had a real, genuine love of art. He just really loved painting. Painting and friendship—and that was wonderful.

He would come up—I had this little window in my house before you got to the door—and this was Tom, he'd come up without telling me he was coming and BANG! on that fucking window. I'd practically jump out of the house. He just, like, appeared, and he was there whether you liked it or not. But then, you know, he was a great friend and just genuinely really helpful. Over years and years, we're talking like twenty-five years.

HJ: Did you ever watch him paint?

RH: I saw him create—new cut-outs and paintings up there in the studio. He'd be working—I remember the different tables—that always fascinated me. He had a table here for this, a table here for that. And all these tools—he had scissors and knives and jars of paint. The whole studio had its own personality. I remember him squinting when he was painting, looking at it. He'd always step back and do that. I remember once he came over, he got out of his car, he had his little sketchbook and next thing I know he's standing in the middle of Little Fresh Pond Road drawing the fucking road! I thought "Boy, he's really getting down to work." Like all of a sudden. He wasn't scared; he didn't have a lot of hesitation.

RCW: I remember watching him paint. There was an eleganance and quickness to his brush stroke when you watched him paint. His energy was quicker on the surface—brash but then equally sensitive—kind of like his work. There was an incredible sweetness about him. Henry [Geldzahler] used to say that "kindness is the greatest virtue" and Tom personified that. It's reflected in his ability to draw quickly and more than accurately. He cut through—he was out there—bold, quick, concise. And by more than accurately I mean when you see the depictions of SoHo it comes across as this idea about literal translation. What is it in our minds that we remember? And I think about his work in terms of that quick deftness of his hand, his touch. You could see him just painting. It was very assertive. It was bang on, and right. He had that ability—his paintings were more than real. They brought so much more than that.

SK: It is more than what's there. I remember him saying, "This is two toothbrushes. It's a painting about a relationship."

SH: When you see a painting of Tom's, you see the process. You're thinking, There has to be more to it, he's got to be projecting images, because how can each painting be so goddamn perfect? But it's simple. He just put stuff down. There was no finicky, "Oh let's try this juxtaposed here, or move this here. . . ." No. It was just . . . done. No fuss, no muss.

More than any of us, in our little group, more than any artist that I can remember, he was a part of the culture we feel connected to. Nobody had ideas as profound as Tom's were. And he just put them to paper, or canvas, or whatever medium, and that was the nature of that. It was a real inspiration for me. I think every artist has insecurity, a feeling that it could always be better, but the way Tom painted was the way he was—so direct. It resonates, affects today's audience—everybody is desperate for a fundamental simplicity. And Tom's stuff just provides it.
Some of the paintings he would do, of just a dock and a boat—those really, really rocked me. Because it's an impossible subject matter to do without being David Hockney, or too Hamptons-y, but Tom just put a boat on water and it was that simple.

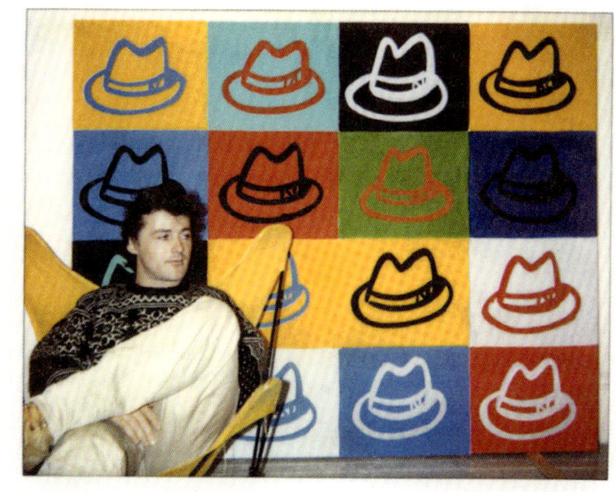

Scott Kilgour

HJ: How do you see Tom's later work, as compared to the work he was making as he was first starting to find success?

JPR: In a weird way, when I initially saw that a shift was happening, if it happened at all, was when he started making children's books, and a little bit more what you might call "commercial art." Maybe at first I thought it was a bad thing, but in the end, when I think about it, with the bigger picture, it was all the same. It was always what he wanted to do: just to make really great pictures, in the way that he made them. And it didn't really matter, at the end of the day—it didn't matter whether he was an artist who just made paintings versus one who branched out more, and did more with design, because it was always still him.

The early work definitely showed a kind of a direction, but he could have been just as happy designing wallpaper, or designing anything, or painting—as long as he was making pictures. It always had vitality. The simple method was always there. Very few people are able to put images out in the world with so little, you know, action, and make it so complete. Like, you don't have to make a boat any more complicated than he would make it. You could, if you wanted to, shade it all in and do all that nonsense, but he always just maintained this remarkable way of representing something that gave you the exact sense that that's how the thing should be—or how he wanted it to be.

RCW: In my mind, there was always this delineation between people who did commercial, graphic work and those who did fine art. And that was always a bit of a thing, particularly if you were in the commercial, editorial world and you wanted your work to be taken more seriously or critically—your personal work. But the interesting thing about Tom, and this is true of a lot of interesting artists, was that there was no delineation, no "is it this or is it that." He always seemed to do a little bit of both and very successfully.

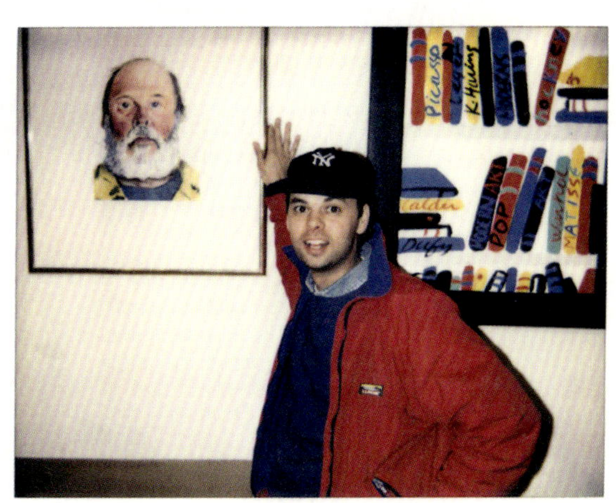

Ray Charles White

RH: To me, when I think about his work, it's just unmistakably his. The images are iconic. And it's not just from doing the same image over and over—I think that's part of it—but I think the thing was that he had such a sure hand. It was like his personality, too. He didn't hesitate. It just came out. He was so assured. And no matter which discipline it was, a more commercial one, or a more fine arts one, I think that came through.

SK: When you see the etchings, and the nude series, the tree series—he was going in a whole new direction. Around 2001. Refined in a way. Subtle. A more mature Tom coming into play.

RH: In a way, it's more lyrical.

SK: I love those trees. They get better with time.

RCW: That's the other thing, by the way, it's going to last. The earlier work, the later work, it's all the same energy and strength. He had a great understanding of process and I think he understood, like Hockney does, this idea of, Don't fight the process. Make the work so it takes advantage of the parameters of the process. Tom had a mind like that. He could see it clearly. He really understood that.

SK: The one that really blew me away, *October* in 2001. And *Two Trees*. So here, this work has the same energy as the early stuff, even though it was a new direction and a new process.

RH: It's still his hand.

RCW: He always kept that curiosity about him, that interest, that sense of wanting to learn and experience.

SK: I remember Henry saying that when an artist goes back to black and white, it's like they're trying to get back to some kind of origin.

RH: Like, what's there under the color. The bones of it.

RCW: It became looser and lighter and more of the moment. More almost spontaneous, when we think about it . . . to the sort of far more formal, static dynamic that was in the earlier work. He got more open, also sweeter.

RH: Right, I mean, you think of those big construction paintings—which were the first ones that I saw Henry was collecting, I mean, it took up the whole fucking stairway. And these from the early aughts are these little intimate, beautiful pieces.

RCW: It's interesting, that idea, if we think about later works, the sweet pictorial scenes, from Stratford or Noyac. The early pieces are so bold, and brash, and strong, and you wonder if the later ones offer a sense of a sort of letting go of ego. He had accomplished a lot! And so he was letting go a little, maybe.

RH: Realizing for it to be meaningful it didn't have to be twelve foot by twelve foot. He was in touch with why he wanted to do it. Even when he would talk about wanting to make a jaunty sailboat, something inside him knew it was really what he wanted to do. So it was more secure.

JM: He liked that you could take the watercolors anywhere.

SK: What type of work was he doing the most in the last two years?

NJ: His last show was the hotel stationery work at a gallery in East Hampton.

JM: He was doing a lot of work on paper, a lot of cut-outs, a lot of brush pen and watercolor on paper. When we were getting ready for one of the last group shows, *The 80s: Past and Present,* at the Bleecker St. Arts Club, we were looking at the big paintings again and he was actually getting excited about them.

RH: This is what I mean, who knows what would have happened for the next twenty years. He could have done anything.

RCW: But the thing is, when you make an image, a beautiful image, and you die, too early, the image stays.

RH: It still has the power.

HJ: What was his role in the artistic or cultural environment of New York City?

JPR: I just think he really represented well where he lived and what happened there. He had impact.

SH: This was a time when the closest thing to punk art that was happening was graffiti, and so much graffiti—all done with the aerosol spray, from the street. And it had a good story—it was seen as dangerous and rugged and stuff—but the truth is that a lot of it wasn't very good. Tom's work was so much smarter than the work that was coming out. He was smart like Keith Haring. The high graphics, so brilliant, that just weren't translated into finished paintings anywhere but in Tom's stuff. In Tom's work, every mark was a finished painting—whether he used one color, two, eight. And it was as whimsical as Matisse, his lines moved in that way. Effortless but so strong. Bold. Johnny Rotten was just about to retire, and so that's why I called Tom "Johnny Matisse." It was a perfect combination of street and fine art. He's still listed that way in my phone.

RH: I think he was definitely a part of a generation of artists in a time in New York that started in the early eighties with Basquiat and Haring . . . and all those artists. That's what you were seeing if you moved down here. And he was hanging out with Henry and that's who Henry was talking about and I think he was definitely part of that milieu. Where you showed or didn't show—it was an atmosphere he was in, this neighborhood.

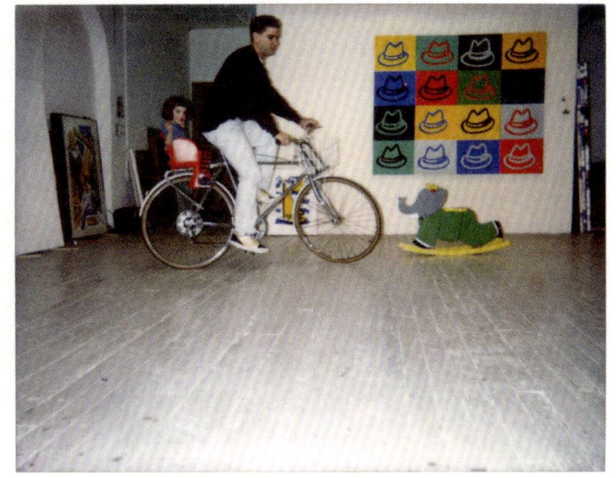

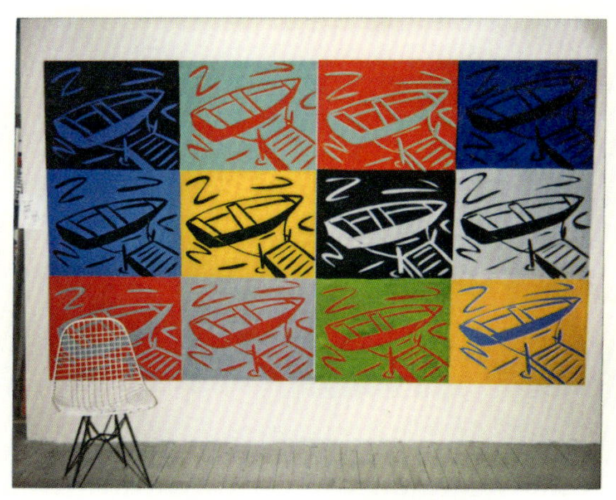

RCW: That scene was happening. And what was interesting about that scene, in SoHo, was that there were many different strata of people who were contributing on many levels, and it was all part of the same group. And even in the earlier days when he wasn't as well known, he was still contributing, still a known personality within that world, very much so. And that grew of course.

RH: That was what was going on. It was in the air. I mean, if you were an artist, and you were paying attention, you're living right in the middle of it.

RCW: Thirty years ago the art world was a closer community, a more tightly knit community and I think there was a real importance put on the quality of the work. A kind of stewardship of the work. There was a level of interest and seriousness about it. And there was a camaraderie, like a group. That was the art world we came up in.

HJ: What piece first comes to mind when you think of Tom's work?

RCW: In my head, I always think of the quintessential Tom painting—

RH: You can't think of Tom without thinking of those things! The water tower, the hat—

RCW: Yes! And the cityscape.

RH: Those fucking cranes with the I-beams. I see them all day long! And then the boat.

RCW: And the interesting thing is that, whether it's a small cityscape or moderately sized—it still has strength. It still has that immediacy, that's like, Wow! The impact.

SK: It's definitely got to be the water tower. That's his first statement. And the interesting thing about it is that his work is still going to have impact. It's still going to find an audience. It's still so contemporary. It withstands the test of time.

RCW: Good art probably always does, right?

SK: It's powerful.

RH: That's the hope, right?

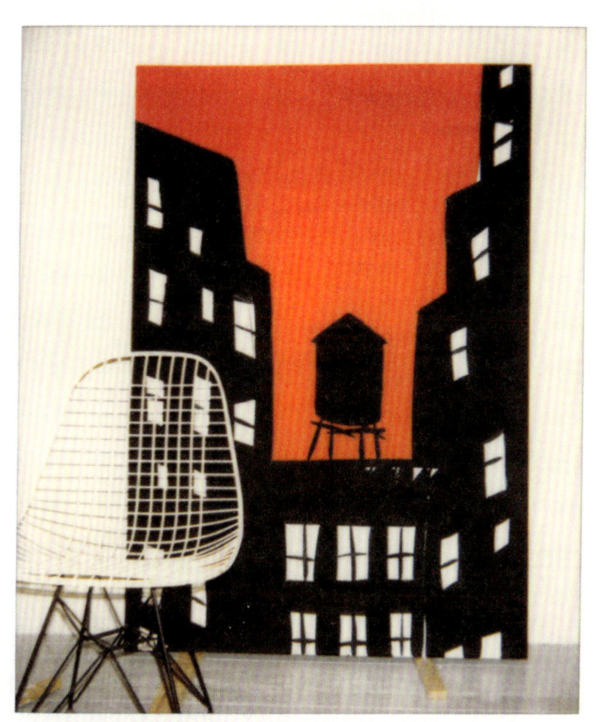

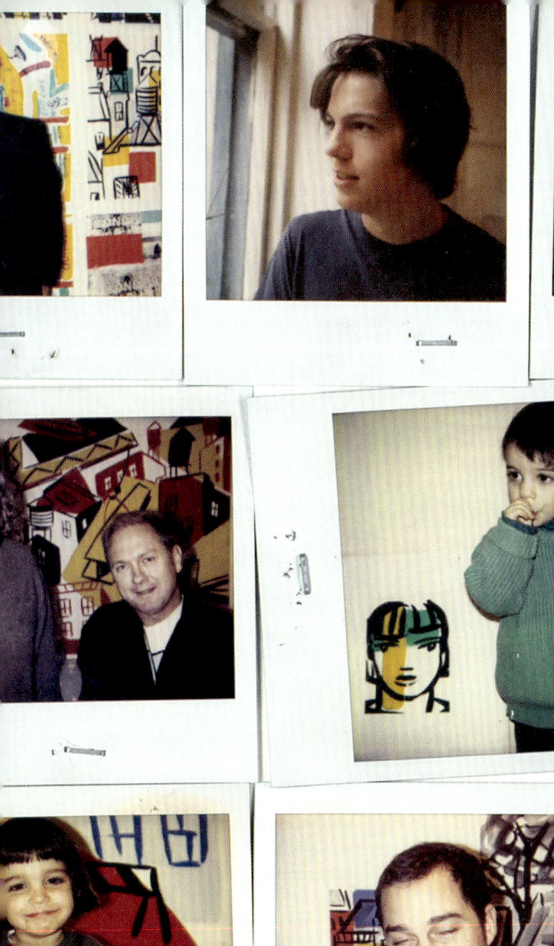
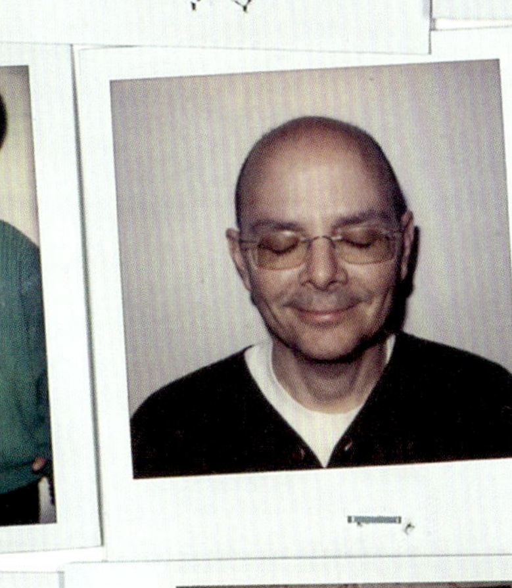
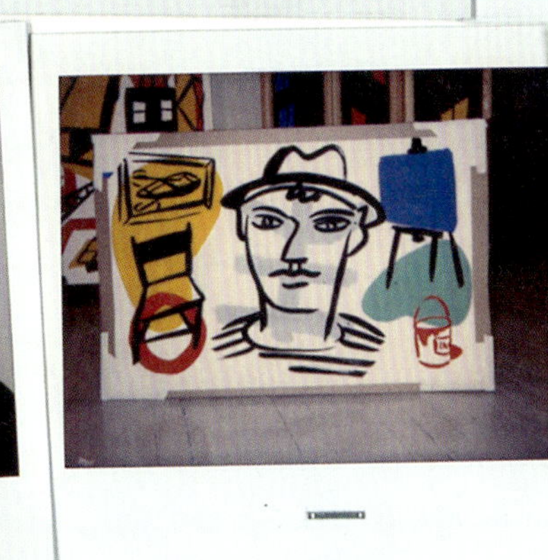
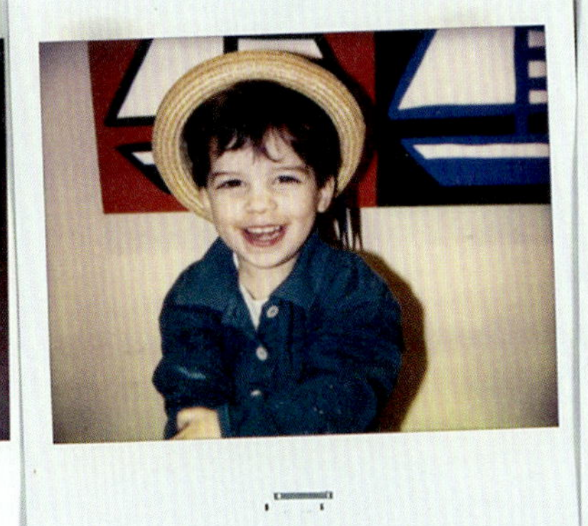
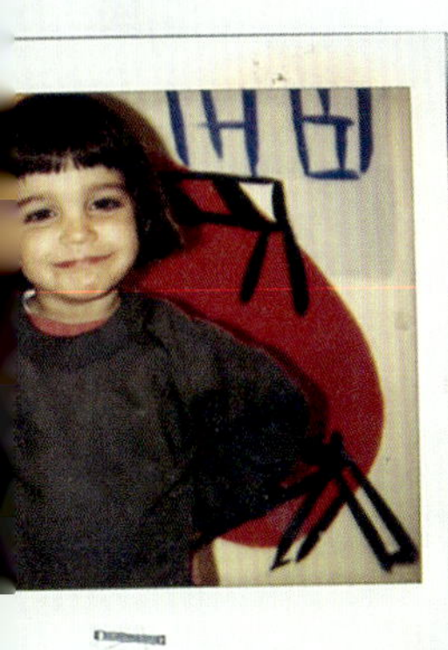
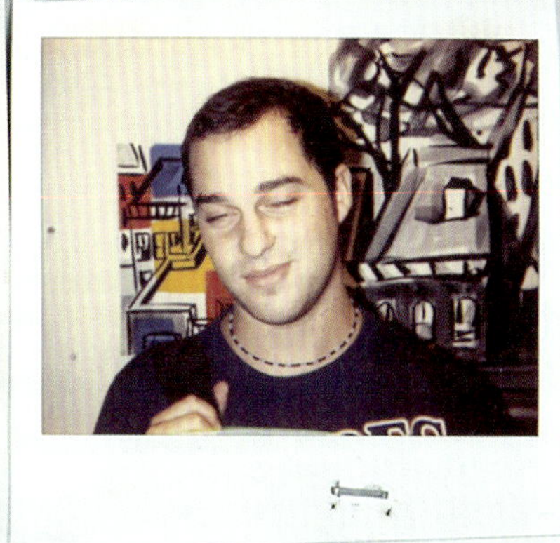
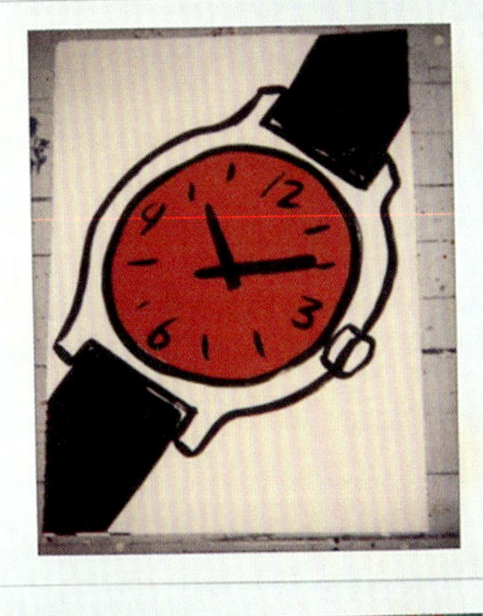
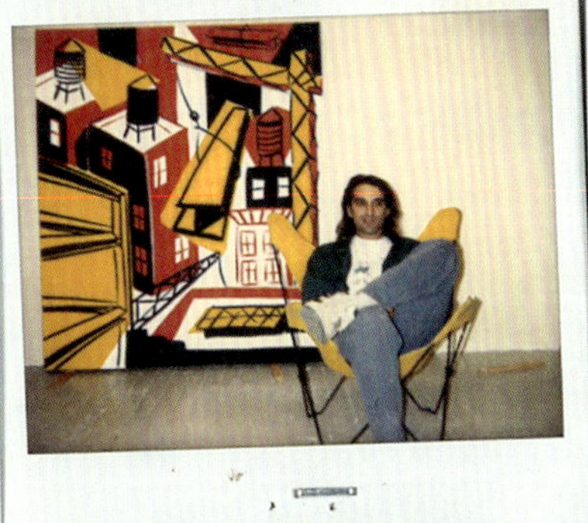
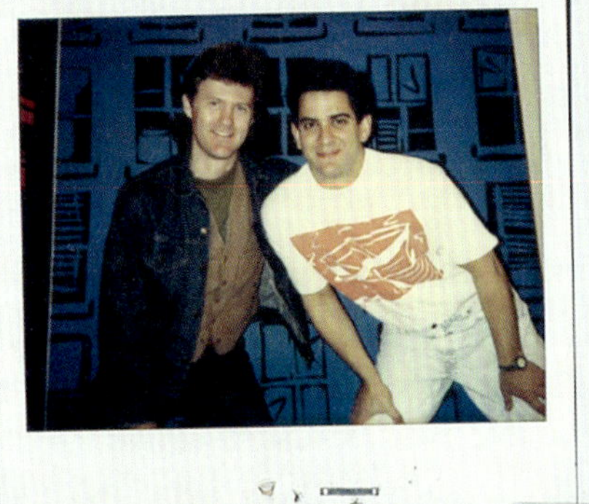
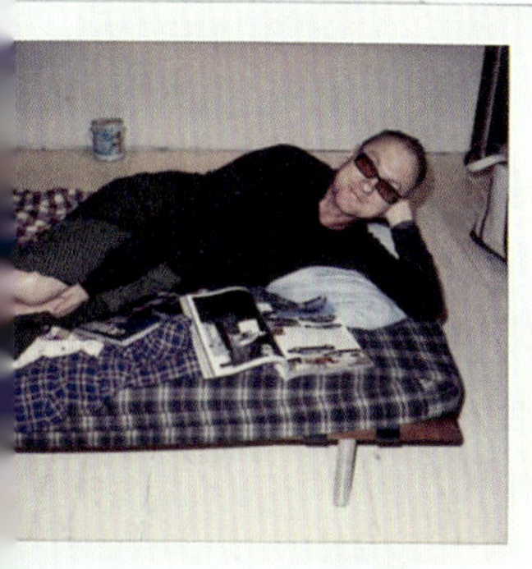
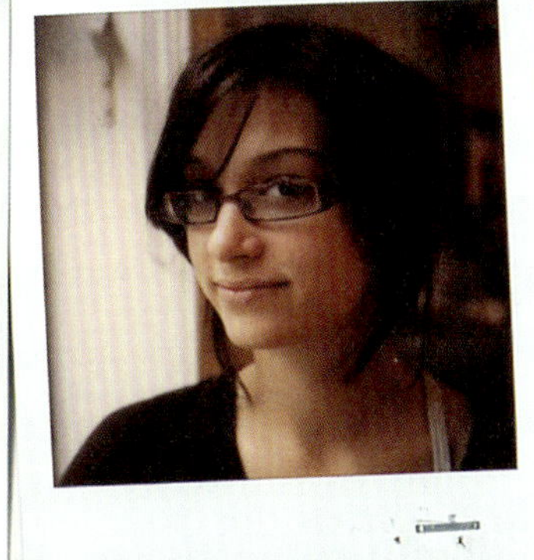
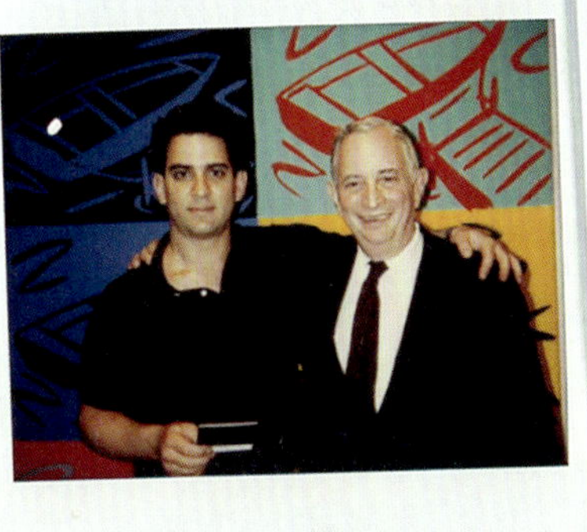
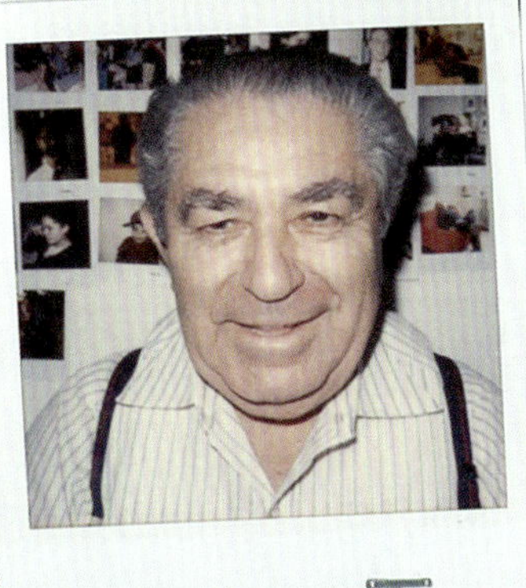
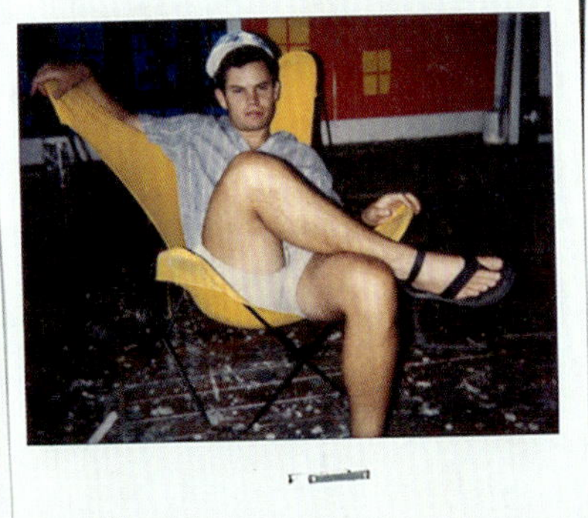
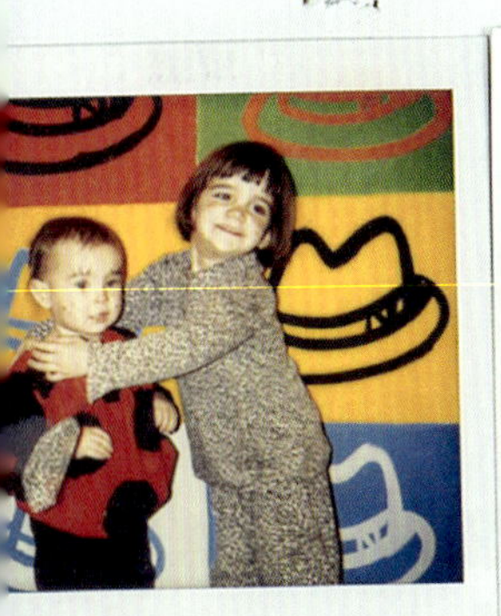
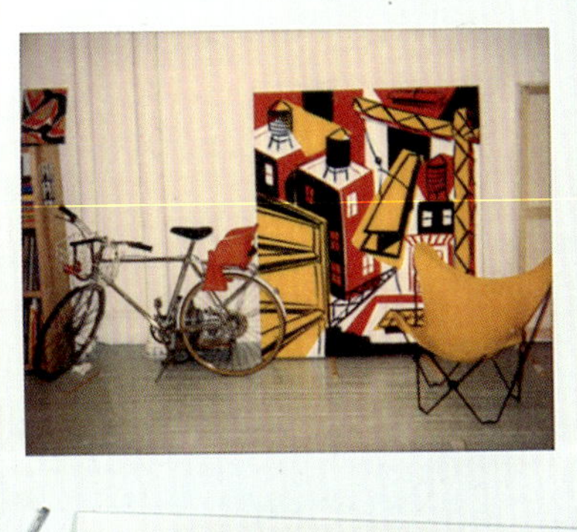
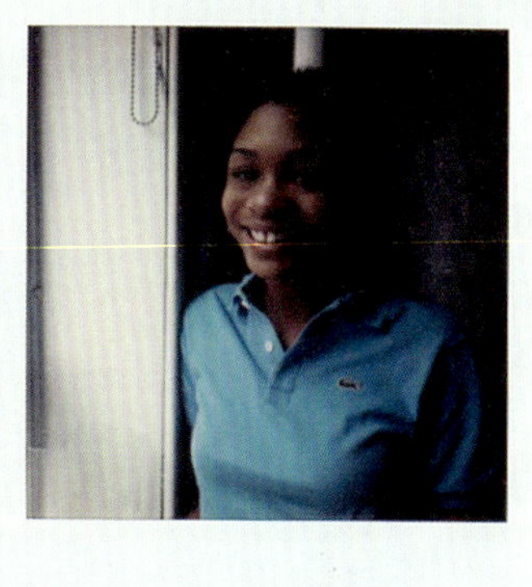
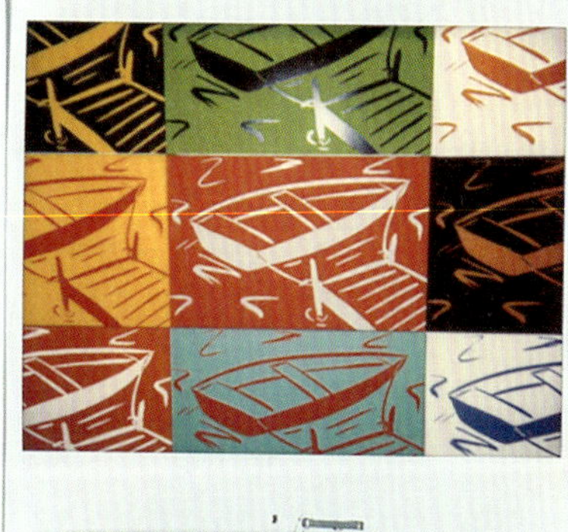
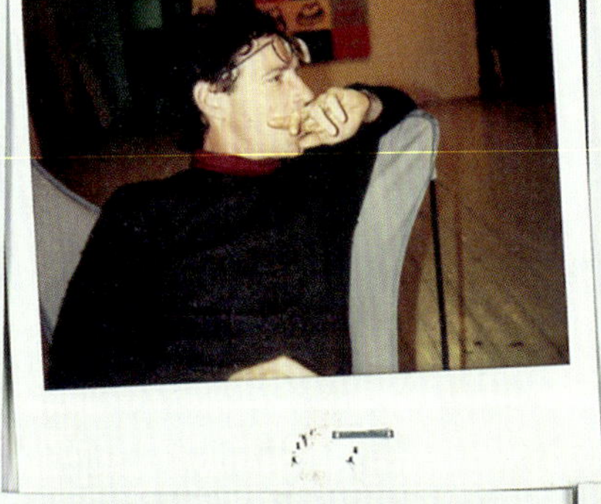
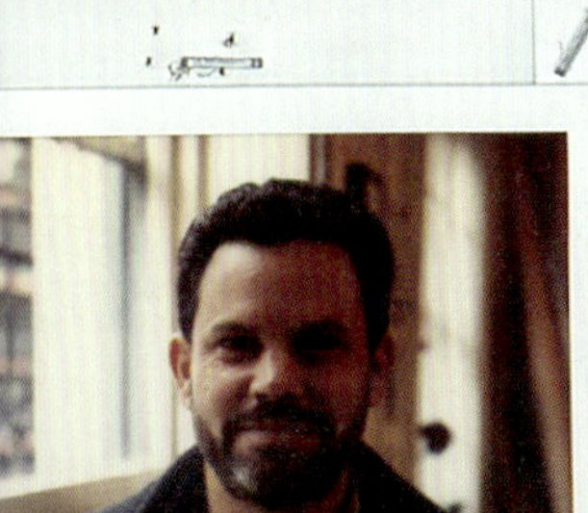
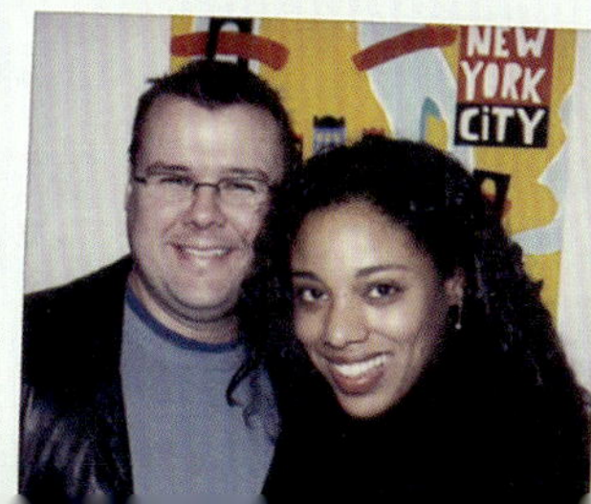
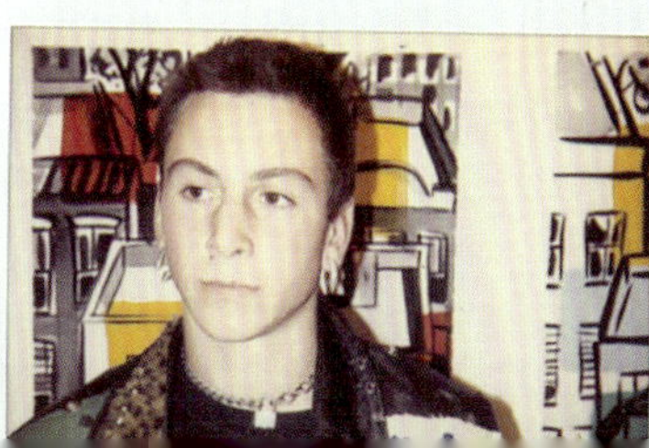
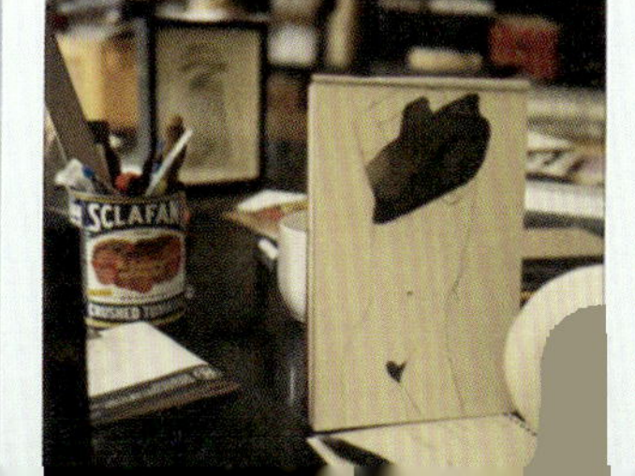
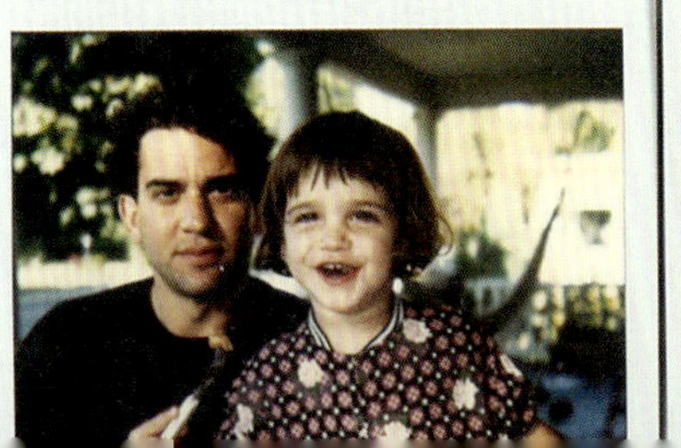

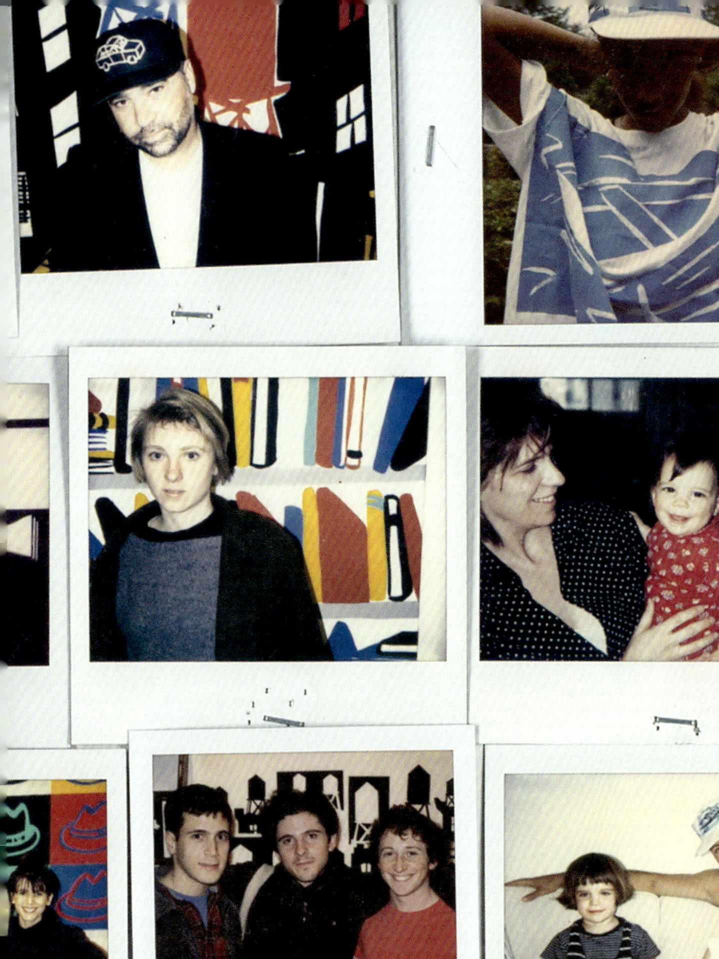
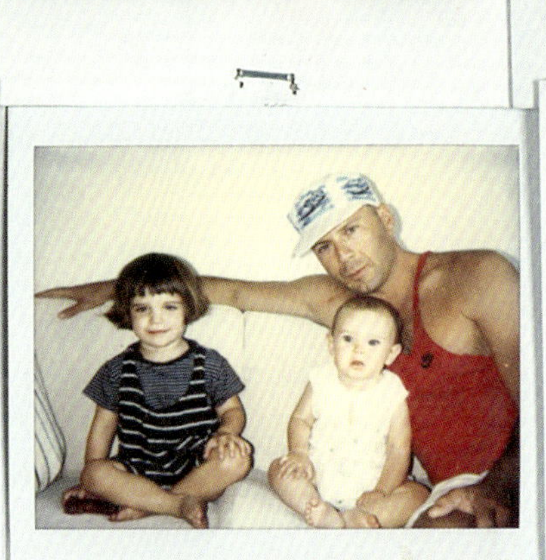
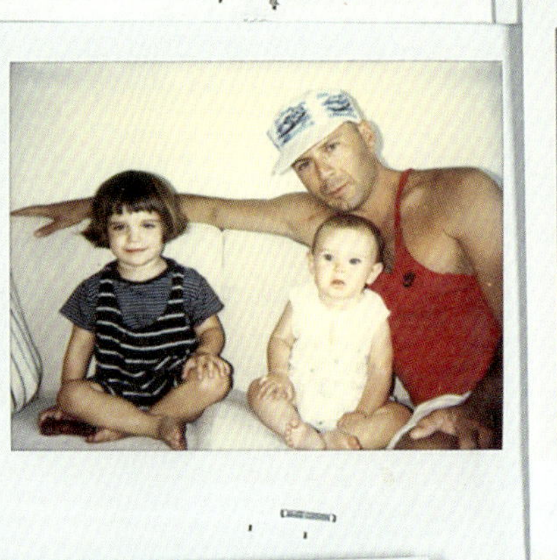
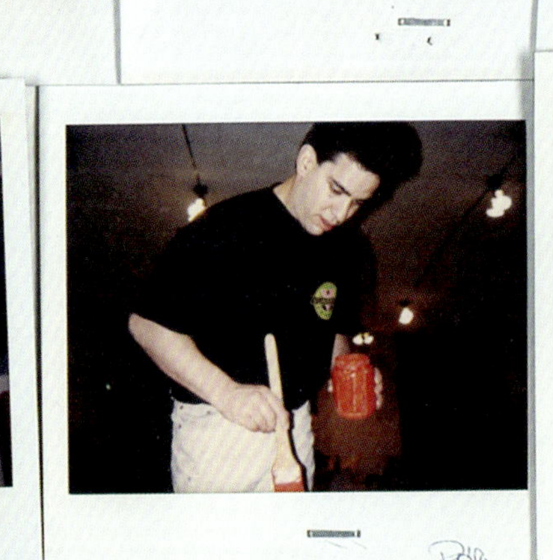
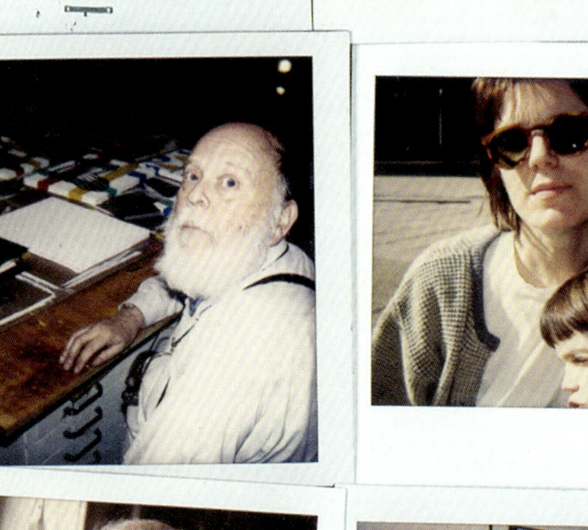
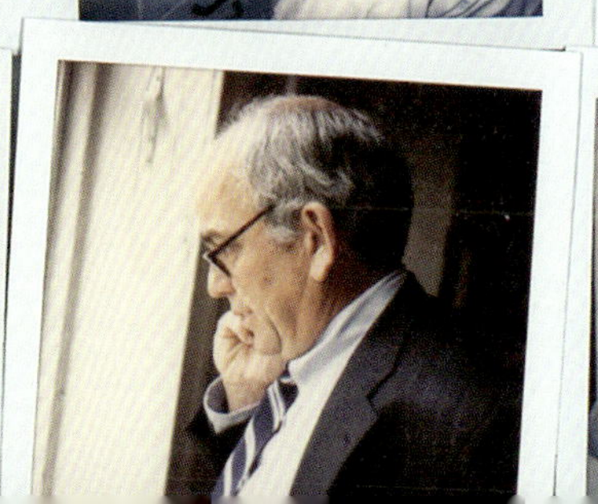
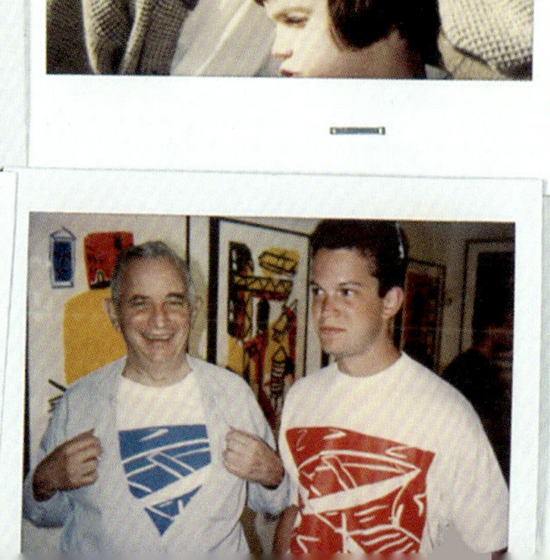
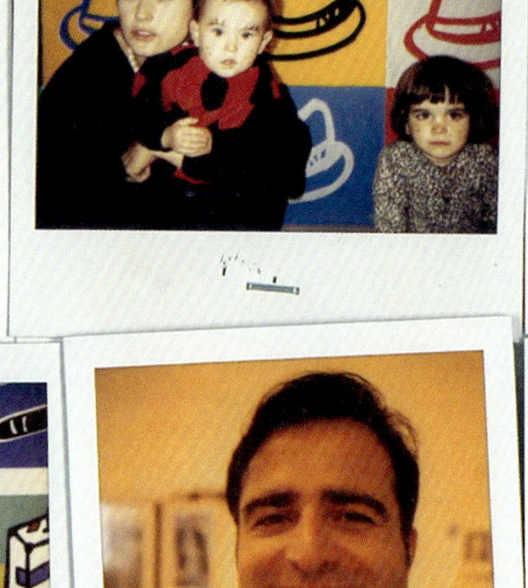
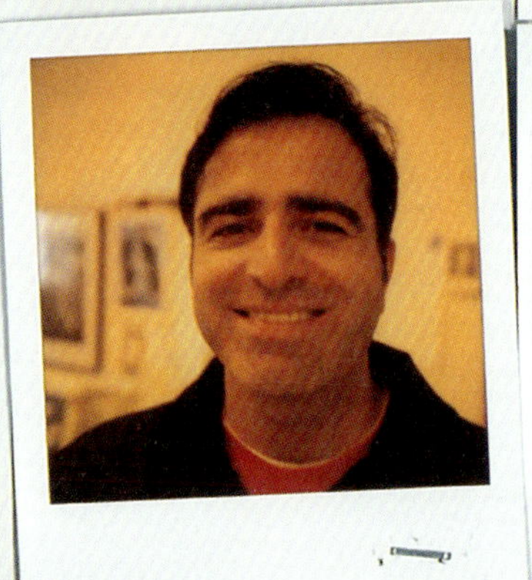
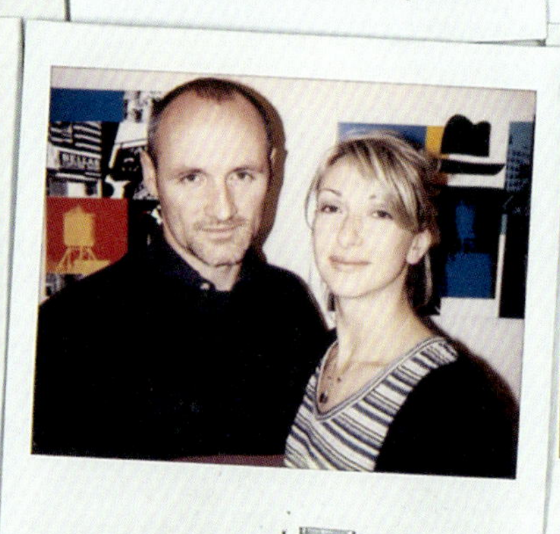
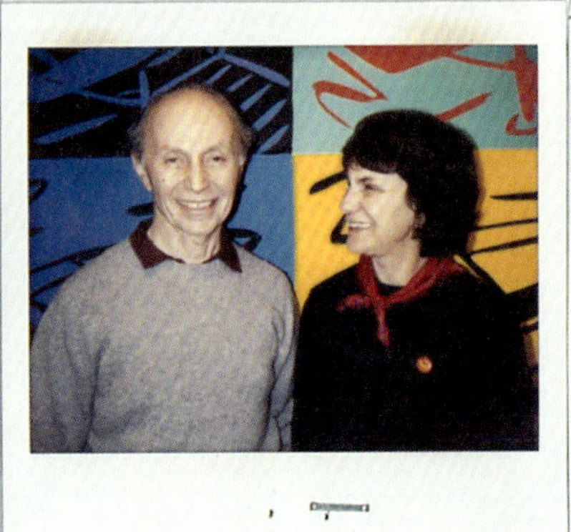
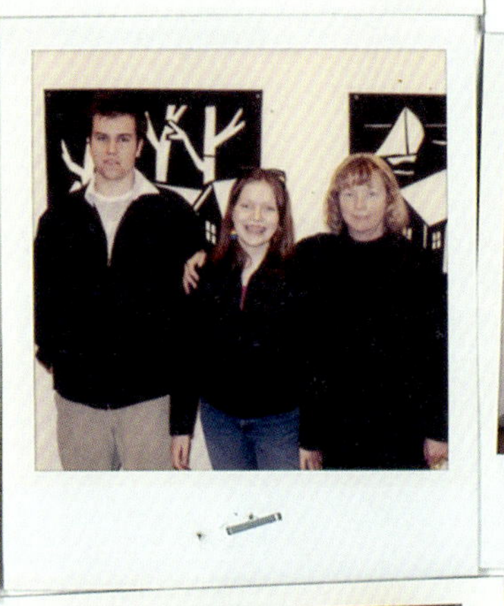
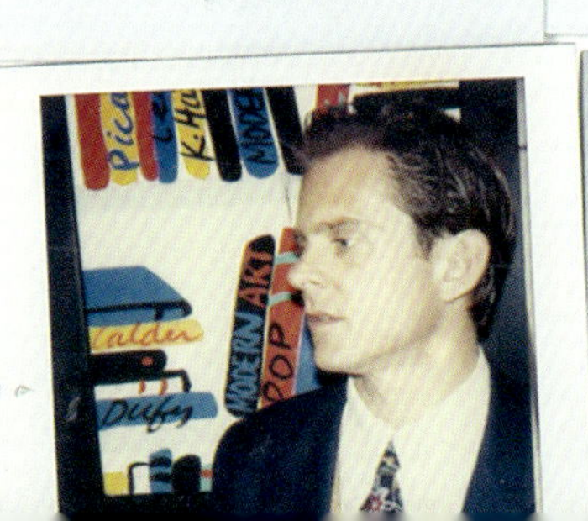
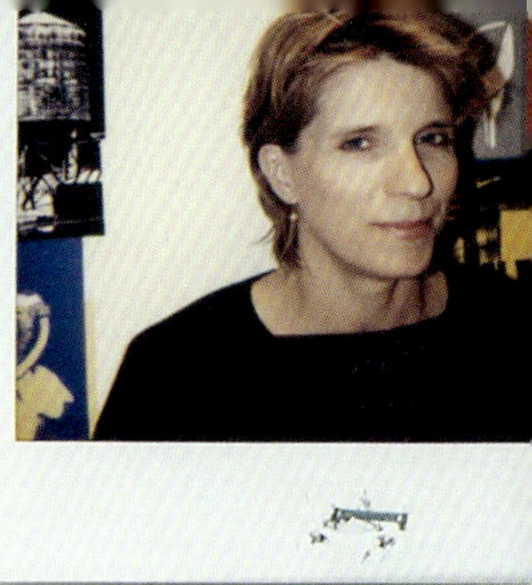
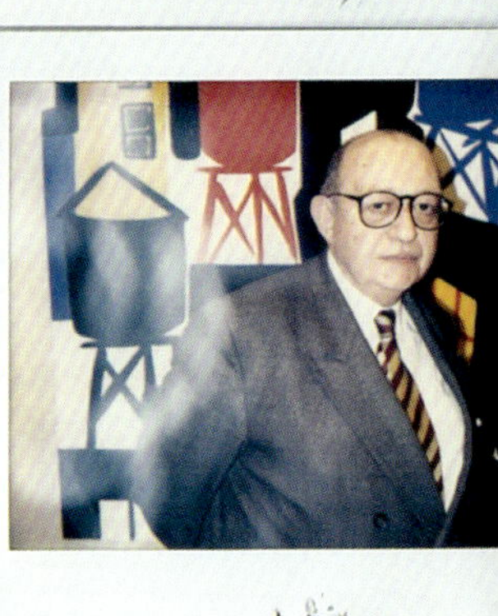
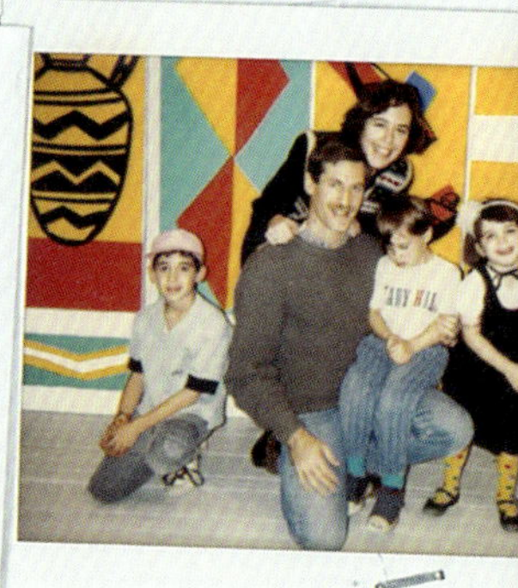
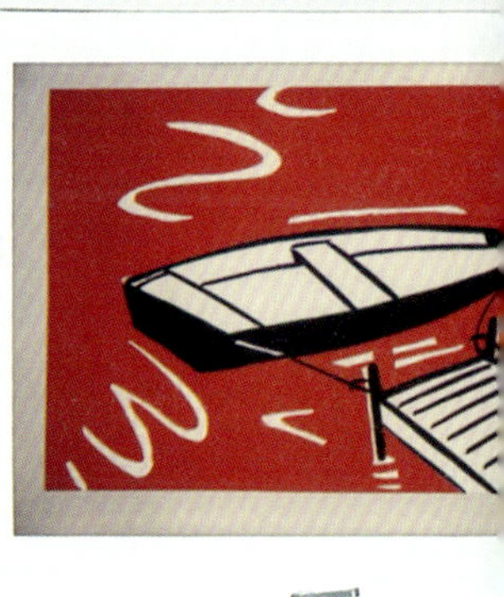
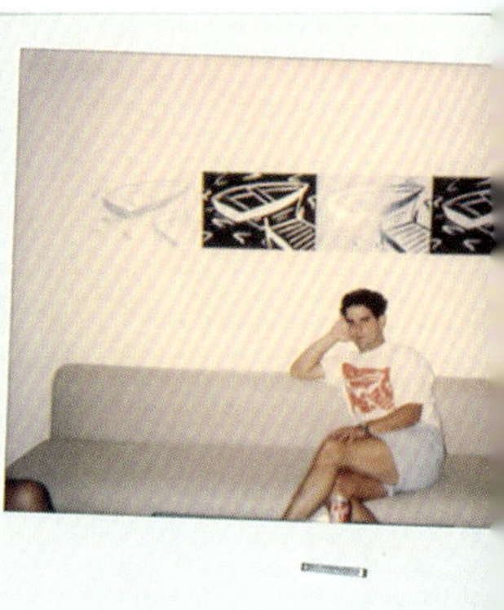
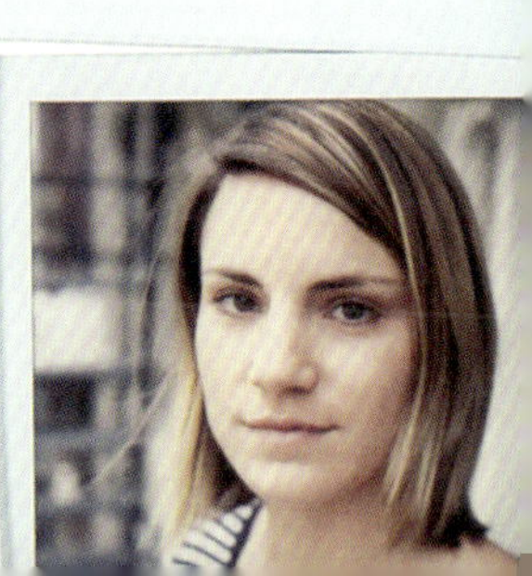
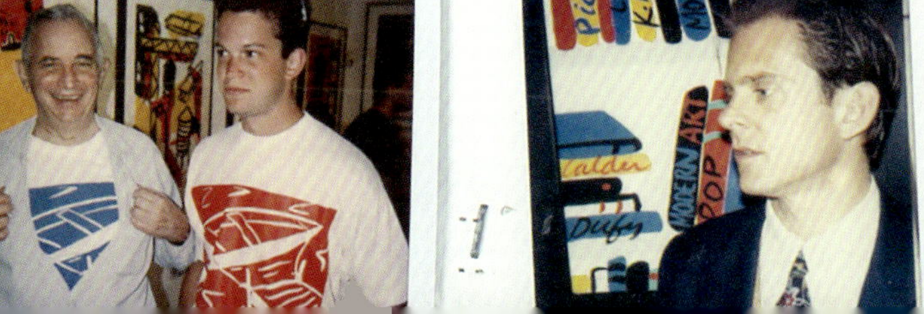
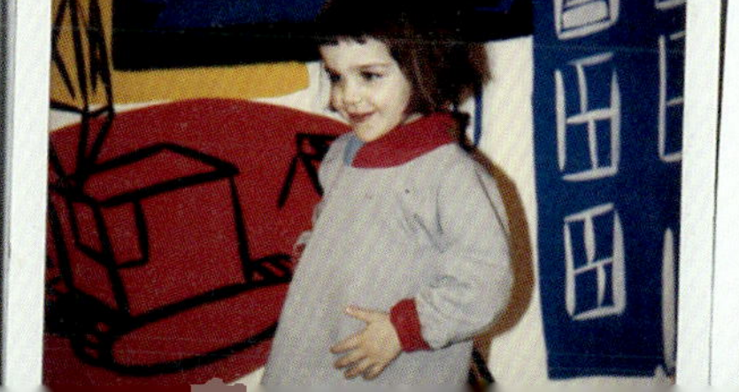

LIST OF PLATES

To the best of our knowledge at the time of this printing, unless otherwise noted the photographs and Polaroids that appear in this book were taken by Tom Slaughter.

HALF TITLE

Pp. 2–3: Tom in his studio, ca. 1991, by Ray Charles White.

CONTENTS

P. 6: Tom in his studio, ca. 1990.

FOREWORD

P. 8: Tom's street corner in SoHo, ca. 1992.

P. 9: Glenn Lowry in the studio, ca. 2001.

P. 10: *Art History*, 1991. Acrylic on canvas.

INTRODUCING TOM SLAUGHTER

P. 12: Tom and Hannah in the loft, ca.1988, by Marthe Jocelyn.

P. 13: Top: Hannah Jocelyn in the studio, ca. 1991;
bottom: Nell Jocelyn in the studio, ca. 1993.

P. 14: Top: *Untitled (Rowboat)*, ca. 1990. Flashe paint on paper;
bottom: *Untitled (Hats)*, 1990. Flashe paint on canvas.

P. 16: *Untitled (Dock)*, ca. 2010. Flashe paint on cut paper,
8.5 x 11 in. (21 x 28 cm).

THE NEGATIVE SPACE

P. 18: Tom, ca. 1977, by Michael Zeigler.

P. 19: David Marshall Grant in the studio, ca. 1987.

P. 20: *Untitled (Houses)*, ca. 2005. Flashe paint on cut paper.

Pp. 22-23: The Polaroid wall in Tom's studio, 2018,
by Nell Jocelyn.

1980–1990

P. 25: *Untitled (Train)*, 1987. Flashe paint on paper,
4 x 11 in. (10 x 28 cm).

Pp. 26-27: Various works, ca. 1985–1990. Flashe paint on paper.

P. 28: *Untitled (Georgian Bay)*, ca. 1985. Flashe paint on paper.

P. 29: *Untitled (Cactus)*, ca. 1981. Flashe paint on paper.

P. 30: *Tim*, 1983. Flashe paint on paper, 22 x 29 in.
(55.8 x 73.7 cm).

P. 31: *Untitled (Crane with I-beam)*, 1989. Flashe paint on paper.

P. 32: *Untitled (Self-Portrait)*, ca. 1986. Flashe paint on paper.

P. 33: Folding screen in loft, 1986. Acrylic on wood, 3 panels,
74 x 50 x 2 in. (188 x 127 x 5 cm).

P. 34: *Untitled (Cottage)*, ca. 1990. Flashe paint on paper,
60 x 30 in. (152.4 x 76.2 cm).

P. 35: *Untitled (Bench)*, ca. 1991. Flashe paint on paper, 6 x 9 in.
(15.2 x 22.9 cm).

P. 36: *Untitled (Jesse)*, ca. 1985. Flashe paint on paper.

P. 37: *Untitled (Paris Chairs)*, ca. 1990. Acrylic on paper, 12 x 9 in. (30.5 x 22.9 cm).

P. 38: *Untitled (Suitcase)*, ca. 1990. Flashe paint on paper, 5 x 7 in. (12.7 x 17.8 cm).

P. 39: *Untitled (Self-Portrait with Boat)*, ca. 1990. Flashe paint on paper.

P. 40: *Untitled (Blue Vase)*, 1990. Flashe paint on paper, 30 x 15 in. (76.2 x 38.1 cm).

P. 41: Top: *Untitled (Portrait)*, 1989; bottom: *Untitled (Vase Sculpture with Bums)*, ca. 1989.

P. 42: Top: Vases hanging on the wall in the loft, ca. 1989; bottom: *Untitled (Vase Sculpture)*, ca. 1989.

P. 43: Left: *Untitled (Red Vase)*, 1989. Flashe paint on paper, 30 x 15 in. (76.2 x 38.1 cm); right: *Untitled (Yellow Vase)*, 1989. Flashe paint on paper, 30 x 15 in. (76.2 x 38.1 cm).

Pp. 44–45: The loft wall, featuring *Red Yellow Black Construction*, ca. 1989. Flashe paint on canvas.

P. 46: *Self-Portrait*, ca. 1987. Flashe paint on paper.

P. 47: *Untitled (Red Sky)*, ca. 1989. Flashe paint on canvas.

P. 48: *Untitled (Black and White Window)*, ca. 1989. Flashe paint on paper.

P. 49: *Untitled (Yellow Windows)*, 1989. Flashe paint on canvas, 72 x 60 (182.9 x 152.4 cm).

P. 50: *Blue Building*, ca. 1988. Flashe paint on canvas, 72 x 60 in. (182.9 x 152.4 cm).

P. 51: *Construction City*, ca. 1989. Flashe paint on canvas, 54 x 68 in. (137.1 x 172.7 cm).

P. 52: *Untitled (Red Windows)*, ca. 1990. Flashe paint on paper.

P. 53: *Untitled (Blinds)*, ca. 1990. Flashe paint on paper.

P. 55: *Untitled (Night City)*, 1989. Flashe paint on canvas, 72 x 60 in. (182.9 x 152.4 cm).

P. 56: *Untitled (Water Tower)*, ca. 1990. Flashe paint on canvas, 72 x 60 in. (182.9 x 152.4 cm).

P. 57: *Untitled (Yellow Windows)*, ca. 1990. Flashe paint on canvas, 72 x 60 (182.9 x 152.4 cm).

P. 58: Tom signing *Hats*, 1989.

P. 59: Contact sheet of Jean-Paul Russell and Tom at Durham Press, 1989.

Pp. 60-61: Durham Press Print Series (edition, 75 numbered and signed copies, plus 15 artist proofs). From left to right: *New York View*, 1989. 44 x 30 in. (111.8 x 76.2 cm); *Construction Work*, 1989. 44 x 30 in. (111.8 x 76.2 cm); *Hats*, 1989. 44 x 30 in. (111.8 x 76.2 cm); *Boats*, 1989. 44 x 30 in. (111.8 x 76.2 cm).

P. 62: *Untitled (Blue Windows)*, 1989. Silkscreen on paper.

P. 63: *Untitled (Primary Windows)*, ca. 1987. Silkscreen on paper.

P. 64: Folding screen in loft, ca. 1991. Acrylic on wood, 3 panels, 74 x 50 x 2 in. (188 x 127 x 5 cm).

P. 65: *Untitled (Blue Windows)*, 1989. Flashe paint on canvas.

P. 66: *Untitled (Yellow Shutter)*, ca. 1987. Flashe paint on paper.

P. 67: *Blue Chrysler*, 1991. Gouache on paper, 30 x 22 in. (76.2 x 55.9 cm).

THE OBJECT MAKER

P. 68: Tom in the studio, ca. 1989.

P. 69: Various small works on canvas, ca. 1990.

P. 70: *Untitled (Binoculars)*, ca. 1990. Flashe paint on paper.

Pp. 72–73: The studio, ca. 1995, by Jeremy Pollard.

1990–1998

P. 75: *Untitled (New York Windows)*, 1989. Flashe paint on canvas.

P. 76: *Untitled (Books)*, 1991. Flashe paint on canvas, 20 x 30 in. (50.8 x 76.2 cm).

P. 77: *Untitled (Self-Portrait)*, 1991. Flashe paint on paper.

Pp. 78–79: Disassembled folding screen in the studio, ca. 1991. Canvas-wrapped wood panels, 74 x 50 x 2 in. (188 x 127 cm).

Pp. 80–81: Assorted art works in the studio, ca. 1990–1996.

Pp. 82–83: *Untitled (Rooftop Diptych)*, ca. 1992. Flashe paint on canvas, 72 x 60 in. (182.9 x 152.4 cm).

P. 84: *Untitled (City Boy)*, ca. 1990. Flashe paint on paper.

P. 85: *Night Music*, 1995. Flashe paint on canvas, 60 x 48 in. (152.4 x 121.9 cm).

P. 86: *Untitled (Red Window)*, ca. 1991. Flashe paint on paper.

P. 87: *Untitled (Books)*, ca. 1992. Flashe paint on paper.

Pp. 88–89: Tom printing at Durham Press, ca. 1992.

P. 90: *Book Prints*, 1991. Silkscreen on paper, 31 x 33 in. (78.7 x 83.2 cm), edition of 72.

P: 91: Selected *Recession Prints*, 1991–1996. Each 13 x 17 in. (33 x 43.2 cm).

P. 92: Tom's studio, 1991, featuring *Pee-Boy* and *Fish*.

P. 93: *Pickup Trucks*, 1990. Silkscreen on canvas.

P. 94: *Untitled (Hannah)*, ca. 1993. Flashe paint on paper.

P. 95: *Color of Night II*, 1996. Silkscreen on paper, 44¼ x 30½ in. (112.4 x 76.2 cm), edition of 50.

P. 97: *Untitled (Red Windows)*, ca. 1994. Flashe paint on canvas, 72 x 60 in. (182.9 x 152.4 cm).

P. 98: *Untitled (Four Boats)*, 1991. Flashe paint on paper.

P. 99: *Untitled (After Matisse)*, 1993. Flashe paint on paper.

P. 101: *Two Boats*, 1991. Flashe paint on paper, 60 x 30 in.
(152.4 x 76.2 cm).

P. 102: Top: *Untitled (Glasses)*, ca. 1997. Flashe paint on paper;
bottom: *Three Books*, ca. 1992. Flashe paint on canvas.

P. 103: *Untitled (Two Fish)*, ca. 1992. Flashe paint on canvas.

P. 104: *Chair*, ca. 1992. Flashe paint on paper.

P. 105: *Untitled (Hats)*, ca. 1995. Silkscreens on twelve panels.

Pp. 106–107: Paints in Tom's Stratford studio, ca. 1995.

EXCERPT FROM JON ROBIN BAITZ

P. 108: *Untitled (City Triptych)*. Flashe paint on canvas.

1990–1998 CONTINUED

P. 110: *Untitled (Four Windows)*, ca. 1992. Flashe paint on
canvas, 14 x 10 in. (35.6 x 25.4 cm).

P. 111: *Untitled (City Signs)*, 1995. Flashe paint on canvas,
40 x 30 in. (101.6 x 76.2 cm).

P. 112: *Untitled (Study)*, ca. 1995. Flashe paint on paper,
60 x 30 in. (152.4 x 76.2 cm).

P. 113: Various small pieces, ca. 1992–1998. Flashe paint on paper.

P. 114: Various small pieces, ca. 1992–1998. Flashe paint on paper.

P. 115: *Untitled (Stratford)*, 1995. Flashe paint on paper.

P. 116: *Untitled (Fruit Bowl)*, 1995. Flashe paint on paper.

P. 117: *Untitled (Boats)*, ca. 1993. Flashe paint on canvas.

P. 118: Top: *Untitled (Umbrella)*, 1995. Flashe paint on paper,
7 x 9 in. (17.8 x 22.9 cm); bottom: *Untitled (Pen and Pencil)*,
ca. 1995. Flashe paint on paper, 7 x 9 in. (17.8 x 22.9 cm).

P. 119: *Untitled (Boats)*, ca. 1992. Flashe paint on paper,
44 x 30 in. (111.8 x 76.2 cm).

P. 120: *Untitled (Shirt and Tie)*, 1998. Flashe paint on paper,
9 x 7 in. (22.9 x 17.8 cm).

P. 121: *Untitled (Red Bikini)*, ca. 1997. Flashe paint on paper,
7 x 5 in. (17.8 x 12.7 cm).

Pp. 122–123: *Ultramarine*, 1998. Portfolio of 6 woodblock prints,
each 20 x 15 in. (50.8 x 15 cm), edition of 38.

Pp. 124–125: Various nudes, ca. 1997. Flashe paint on paper,
each 12 x 9 in. (30.5 x 22.9 cm).

P. 127: *Untitled (Nude)*, ca. 1997. Flashe paint on paper, 12 x 9 in.
(30.5 x 22.9 cm).

EVERY SUMMER

P. 128: Tom's attic studio in Stratford, Ontario, ca. 1997.

P.129: Marthe Jocelyn, ca. 1986.

P. 130: Maquette of *One Some Many*, ca. 2003. Flashe paint
cut-outs on paper.

P. 131: Abecedarian book, work in progress, ca. 1988.

Pp. 132–133: Various works, ca. 2002-2010. Flashe paint on paper,
cut out, and collaged.

Pp. 134–135: Tom Slaughter's children's books and paper cuts,
2018, by Nell Jocelyn.

COMMENT FROM JIM KEMPNER

P. 136: Tom in the loft, ca. 1986.

1998–2006

P. 139: *Untitled (Seaside)*, ca. 1999. Flashe paint on cut paper.

P. 140: Left: *Untitled (New York Times)*, ca.1998. Flashe paint
on paper; right: *Untitled (Press Hat)*, ca. 1995. Flashe paint
on cut paper, 7 x 9 in. (17.8 x 22.9).

P. 141: *Untitled (Water Towers)*, ca. 1999.
Flashe paint on cut paper, 12 x 9 in. (30.5 x 22.9 cm).

P. 142: *Untitled (Rooftops)*, ca. 2001. Flashe paint on paper,
60 x 30 in. (152.4 x 76.2 cm).

P. 143: *One Way*, ca. 1999. Silkscreen on paper.

Pp. 144–145: Various silkscreens, ca. 2001.

P. 146: *Home Cooking* from *The Old Neighborhood* series, 2001.
Silkscreen on paper, 23 x 18 in. (58.4 x 45.7 cm), edition of 65.

P. 147: *Export & Domestic* from *The Old Neighborhood* series,
2001. Silkscreen on paper, 23 x 18 in. (58.4 x 45.7 cm),
edition of 65.

P. 148: *Honeymoon* from *The Old Neighborhood* series, 2001.
Silkscreen on paper, 23 x 18 in. (58.4 x 45.7 cm), edition of 65.

P. 149: *American Pie* from *The Old Neighborhood* series, 2001.
Silkscreen on paper, 23 x 18 in. (58.4 x 45.7 cm), edition of 65.

Pp. 150–151: *Arts and Letters* series, 2000. Etching, each 11 x 15 in.
(27.9 x 38.1 cm), edition of 35.

P. 152: *Sparse Woods*, 2000. Sugarlift with aquatint, 12 x 18 in.
(30.5 x 45.7 cm), edition of 30.

P. 153: *Durham Road & Dogwood Lane*, 2000.
Sugarlift with aquatint, 12 x 24 in. (30.5 x 61 cm), edition of 20.

P. 154: *Two Trees II*, 2000. Sugarlift with aquatint,
7 x 5 in. (17.8 x 12.7 cm), edition of 60.

P. 155: *October*, 2000. Sugarlift with aquatint, 12 x 9 in.
(30.5 x 22.9 cm), edition of 40.

Pp. 156-157: From left to right: *Nude I*, 2005. Hardground with
drypoint, 22 x 15 in. (55.9 x 38.1 cm), edition of 29;
Nude II, 2005. Hardground with drypoint, 22 x 15 in.
(55.9 x 38.1 cm), edition of 29; *Nude III*, 2005. Hardground with
drypoint, 22 x 15 in. (55.9 x 38.1 cm), edition of 29; *Nude IV*,
2005. Hardground with drypoint, 22 x 15 in. (55.9 x 38.1 cm),
edition of 29.

P. 158: *Untitled (Girl in White I)*, ca. 2005. Flashe paint on
cut paper, 7 x 5 in. (17.8 x 12.7 cm).

P. 159: *Untitled (Girl in White II)*, ca. 2005. Flashe paint on
cut paper, 7 x 5 in. (17.8 x 12.7 cm).

P. 160: *Untitled (Country)*, ca. 2005. Flashe paint on cut paper.

P. 161: *Untitled (White Bikini)*, ca. 2005. Flashe paint on
cut paper, 12 x 9 in. (30.5 x 22.9 cm).

P. 162: Various works, ca. 2000–2006. Flashe paint on cut paper.

P. 163: *Untitled (Espadrilles)*, 2006. Flashe paint on cut paper,
9 x 12 in. (22.9 x 30.5 cm).

P. 164: *Untitled (Yellow Map)*, ca. 2007. Flashe paint
and cut-paper collage.

P. 165: *NYC Map*, 2009. Flashe paint and cut-paper collage,
30 x 22 in. (76.2 x 55.9 cm).

P. 166: *Gingham Shirt and Tie (Red)*, 2012. Flashe paint
and cut-paper collage, 16 x 12 in. (40.6 x 30.5 cm).

P. 167: *Gingham Shirt and Tie (Light Blue)*, 2012. Flashe paint
and cut-paper collage, 16 x 12 in. (40.6 x 30.5 cm).

P. 168: Studio wall, featuring *Untitled (Telephone Pole)*, ca. 2005.
Flashe paint on cut paper. Photograph by José Picayo.

P. 169: *Dockside*, 2004. Watercolor on paper, 5 x 7 in
(12.7 x 17.8 cm).

P. 170: *Untitled (Stratford Porch)*, ca. 2001.
Watercolor in notebook.

P. 171: *Untitled (Robert's Truck)*, ca. 2005.
Watercolor on notebook paper, 8 x 6 in. (20.3 x 15.2 cm).

COMMENT FROM ANDY FABO

P. 172: Studio still life, 2014, by Nell Jocelyn.

OBJECTS

P. 175: *Anchor Paper Weight*, 2010. Powder-coated, water-jet-
cut steel in hand-screened canvas envelope, 4 x 6 in.
(10.2 x 15.2 cm), edition of 100 red, plus 5 AP, and 100 blue,
plus 5 AP. Published by Dale Nigel Goble.

P. 176: *Untitled (Fish Toy)*, ca. 1989. Mixed media (flashe paint
on wood, hardware).

P. 177: *New York Window (Red)*, ca. 1990. Acrylic on wood,
   3 panels, 74 x 50 x 2 in. (188 x 127 x 5.1 cm).
P. 178: Silkscreen model buildings with water towers, ca. 1993.
P. 179: Watches, designed and produced ca. 1992.
P. 180: Top: Flashe-painted wooden toys created by Tom,
   ca. 1989, left to right: *Black Dog with Wheels* and *Giraffe*;
   bottom: Painted hat boxes, ca. 1993. Flashe paint
   on cardboard.
P. 181: Wooden toys created by Tom, ca. 1989. Top, left to right:
   Red Truck with Ladder and *Zebra with Red Wheels*;
   bottom, left to right: *Tiger with Red Wheels* and *Elephant with
   Red Wheels*. Mixed media (flashe paint on wood, hardware).
P. 182: Top, left to right: D. Hussey in Slaughter hat and T-shirt and
   painted Adirondack chair; bottom: *Hatboxes*, 1992.
   Screenprint on wood.
P. 183 *Untitled (Water Towers and Fire Escapes)*, ca. 1999.
   Silkscreen on wood, 3 panels, 74 x 50 x 2 in. (188 x 127 x 5 cm).
Pp. 184–185: *Pigeon,* 2009. Powder-coated, water-jet-cut steel,
   9 x 7 in. (22.9 x 17.8 cm), edition of 8, plus 2 AP. Published by
   Dale Nigel Goble and Gordon Johnson. Photograph
   by Jamie Slaughter.

LOOK, AND REALLY SEE
P. 186: Tom painting glasses with flashe paint, ca. 1995,
   by Jeremy Pollard.
P. 187: Anne Pasternak, ca. 2010.
P. 188: Wallpaper designed by Tom Slaughter and produced
   by Cavern Home, 2010.
Pp. 190–191: Studio still lifes, 2014, by Nell Jocelyn.

2006–2014
P. 193: *Untitled (Undress)*, ca. 2010. Brush pen and watercolor
   in notebook, 6¼ x 4 in. (15.9 x 10.2 cm).
Pp. 194–195: Various watercolor notebook pages, ca. 2006–2011.
P. 196: *Untitled (Toothbrushes)*, 2005. Flashe paint on cut paper,
   7 x 5 in. (17.8 x 12.7 cm).
P. 197: *Flip Flops*, ca. 2007. Flashe paint on cut paper.
P. 198: *Montauk*, 2012. Silkscreen on paper, 16 x 20 in.
   (40.6 x 50.8 cm).
P. 199: *Yes We Can*, 2008. Silkscreen on paper, 20 x 32½ in.
   (50.8 x 82.5 cm).
Pp. 200–201: Various valentines, ca. 2009–2011. Flashe paint on
   paper (and on cut paper), each approx. 9 x 6 in.
   (22.9 x 15.2 cm).

Pp. 202–203: Various seagulls, ca. 2011. Brush pen, watercolor,
and pencil paper, each approx. 8 x 6 in. (20.3 x 15.2 cm).
P. 204: *Menemsha*, ca. 2007. Watercolor in notebook.
P. 205: *Summer*, 2005. Flashe paint on cut paper, 14 x 11 in.
(35.6 x 27.9 cm).
P. 206: *Untitled (Houses)*, ca. 2010. Watercolor on paper.
P. 207: *Untitled (Boat Berth)*, ca. 2009. Watercolor in notebook.
P. 208: *La Réserve de Beaulieu*, 2003. Watercolor on hotel
stationery, 11¼ x 8 in. (28.6 x 20.3 cm).
P. 209: *Room Service La Réserve*, 2003. Watercolor in notebook.
P. 210: *Untitled (St. Barthes I)*, 2005. Watercolor in notebook,
8 x 6 in. (20.3 x 15.2 cm).
P. 211: *Untitled (St. Barthes II)*, 2005. Watercolor in notebook,
8 x 6 in. (20.3 x 15.2 cm).
Pp. 212–213: Various envelopes, ca. 2005–2012.
Watercolor on stationery.
P. 214: Various works in notebooks, ca. 2009.
Brush pen and watercolor on paper.
P. 215: *Untitled (Elmer's Glue)*, ca. 2008. Pen on paper,
7 x 5 in. (17.9 x 12.7 cm).
Pp. 216–217: *After Hopper*, 2007. Various works, from top left:
scratch paper, pen on paper, watercolor on paper, watercolor
on paper, watercolor on envelope.
Pp. 218–219: Various works, ca. 2010. Brush pen and watercolor in
notebook, 8 x 6 in. (20.3 x 15.2 cm) and 6 x 4 in.
(15.2 x 10.2 cm).
Pp. 220–221: Various works on stationery and in notebook,
ca. 2012. Pencil, brush pen, and watercolor on paper.
P. 222: *The Shore Club (Girl in Red)*, 2012. Watercolor, brush pen,
pencil on stationery, 8 x 11 in. (21.6 x 27.9 cm).
P. 223: *Four Seasons Vancouver (Girl Curled on Chair)*, 2012.
Watercolor, brush pen, and pencil on stationery,
7½ x 10¼ in. (19 x 26 cm).
Pp. 224–225: Various notebook spreads, ca. 2005.
Watercolor and pencil.
P. 226: Various notebook pages, ca. 2008. Brush pen and
watercolor on paper.
P. 227: *Untitled (LL Bean Tote)*, 2008. Watercolor on paper,
5 x 7 in. (12.7 x 17.9 cm).
P. 228: *Starfish Cottage*, ca. 2011. Watercolor on notebook paper,
8 x 6 in. (20.3 x 15.2 cm).
P. 229: *Grant's House*, ca. 2006. Watercolor on notebook paper,
8 x 6 in. (20.3 x 15.2 cm).
P. 230: *Other Desert Cities*, 2011. Flashe paint on paper.

P. 231: Various portraits, ca. 2013. Brush pen in notebooks.
Pp. 232–233: *Untitled (Motorboat and Tow)*, 2012.
Brush pen in notebook.
P. 234: *Square Knot*, ca. 2012. Brush pen on paper.
P. 235: *Ice Cream Sandwich*, ca. 2011. Brush pen on paper.
Pp. 236–237: Various notebook pages, ca. 2008–2013.
Brush pen and watercolor.
P. 239: *Untitled (Circle Beach)*, 2013. Brush pen in notebook.
P. 241: Contact sheet of Tom and Henry Geldzahler in the studio,
ca. 1990, by Ray Charles White.

UNMISTAKABLY HIS

P. 242: Tom in the loft, ca. 1989.
P. 245: Top: Henry Geldzahler in the studio, ca. 1989;
bottom: Jean-Paul Russell at Durham Press, ca. 1993.
P. 247: Top: Stephen Hannock in the studio, ca. 1995;
bottom: Robert Harms in the studio, featuring a
John Giorno print, ca. 2007.
P. 249: Top: Scott Kilgour in the studio, ca. 1991;
bottom: Ray Charles White in the studio, ca. 1992.
P. 251: Top: Hannah and Tom in the studio, ca. 1989;
bottom: *Rowboats*, with chair, ca. 1992.
P. 253: *Untitled (One Water Tower)*, with chair, ca. 1993.
Pp. 254–255: Polaroid wall in Tom's studio, 2018, by Nell Jocelyn.

CHRONOLOGY

P. 262: *The Artist at Fifty*, 2005, by Colm Feore.

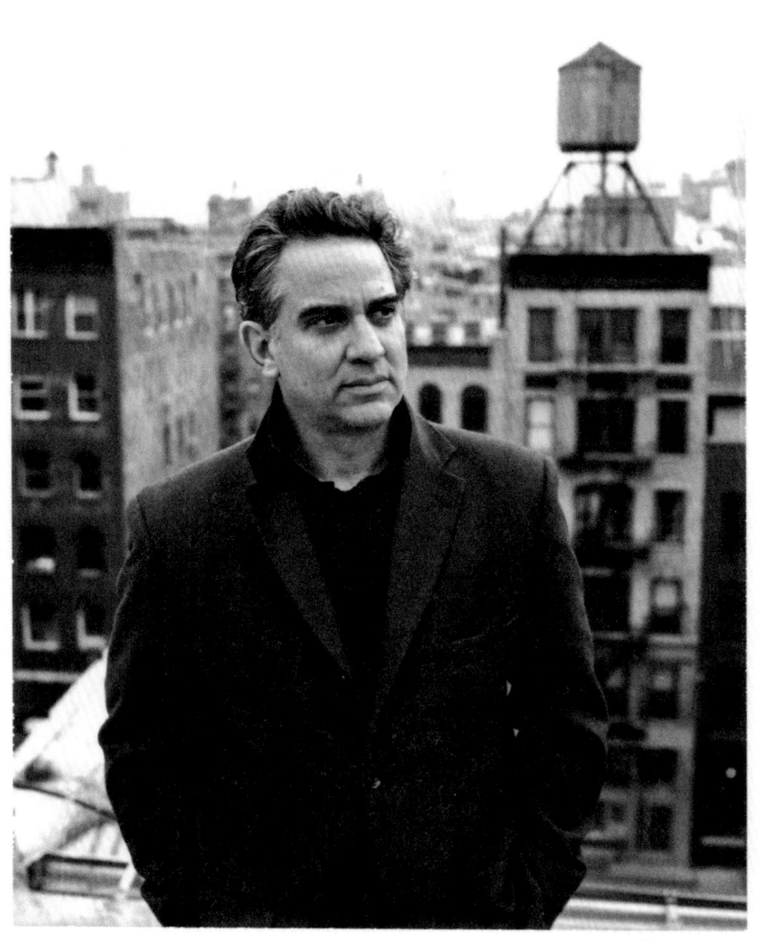

1955: Thomas Robert Slaughter is born March 29 at Lenox Hill Hospital in New York City to Robert Redell Slaughter and Virginia Berman Slaughter, and older brother Bill Slaughter; brothers John, Chuck, and Jamie follow in the nineteen sixties.

1962: The family moves to Westport, Connecticut.

1965: John Slaughter passes away.

1973: Tom graduates from Staples High School, Westport, Connecticut.

1973–1977: Attends Connecticut College, majoring in art history.

1977–1980: Prospects for tin in New Mexico, where, in 1978, he buys an acre of land in Truth or Consequences; works construction in Seattle.

1981: Returns to New York and moves with Marthe Jocelyn into the SoHo loft, where he will live for the rest of his life.

1983: First group shows, *Selections 21* at the Drawing Center on Wooster St., curated by George Negroponte; *Crime Show* at ABC No Rio Gallery, New York, NY; and *Chromaliving* at Chromazone Gallery, Toronto, Ontario.

1985: Marries Marthe Jocelyn, on April 26, at City Hall.

1987: Tom and Marthe's first daughter, Hannah, is born in April.

From 1987 until 2005, the family spends summers in Stratford, Ontario.

1988: Meets Henry Geldzahler; rents a separate studio space on the floor above the loft.

1989: First solo show (Mark Humphrey Gallery, Southampton, NY); first international show (Galerie Berbert, Rotterdam, Netherlands).

From 1989 until his death in 2014, Tom's work appears in over sixty solo and group exhibitions in New York, California, Florida, Pennsylvania, Massachusetts, Germany, the Netherlands, France, Japan, and Canada.

1990: Second daughter, Nell, is born in June; publishes first prints, *Watch* and *Cityscape*, with Durham Press, beginning a collaboration with Jean-Paul Russell with whom he will continue to make prints for twenty-five years.

1991: Robert Slaughter passes away.

1992: Joins the board of the Horace W. Goldsmith Foundation.

2002–2003: Lives in Stratford, Ontario for a year.

2003: Publishes first children's book, *123* (Tundra).

From 2003 through 2013, Tom will illustrate ten children's books.

2005: Becomes art director of New Victory Theater; separates from Marthe Jocelyn.

2006: Joins the board of The Public Theater.

2008: Joins the board of MoMA PS1.

2010: First summer at new home in Noyac, Long Island.

2012–2013: Diagnosed with multiple myeloma; undergoes a stem-cell transplant and recovers.

2014: Last solo show, *Hotel Stationery*, at Grey Gallery, East Hampton, New York; and last group show, *The 80s: Past and Present*, at Bleecker St. Arts Club, New York City.

Following a battle with brain cancer, Tom passes away in October, at age fifty-nine.

SELECTED PUBLICATIONS

CHILDREN'S BOOKS

Ziefert, Harriet. *What Is Part This, Part That?* New Jersey:
    Blue Apple Books, 2013.

Shea, Susan A. *Do You Know Which Ones Will Grow?*
    New Jersey: Blue Apple Books, 2011. 2012 Notable American
    Library Association Book of the Year.

Slaughter, Tom. *Boat Works*. New Jersey: Blue Apple Books, 2012.

Jocelyn, Marthe. *Which Way?* Toronto: Tundra Books, 2010.

——. *Same Same*. Toronto: Tundra Books, 2009.

——. *EATS*. Toronto: Tundra Books, 2007. The Toronto Public
    Library First & Best Top Picks award.

——. *ABC x 3*. Toronto: Tundra Books, 2005.

——. *Over Under*. Toronto: Tundra Books, 2005.

——. *One Some Many*. Toronto: Tundra Books, 2004.

Slaughter, Tom. *123*. Toronto: Tundra Books, 2003.

ARTISTS' BOOKS

Slaughter, Tom. *Trees of Bucks County*. Durham, PA:
    Durham Press, 2001.

Baitz, Jon Robin. *Whatever We Lose*. Durham, PA:
    Durham Press, 1998.

Mayer, Marc. *Tom Boat*. Toronto: Obscure Knight, 1987.

PRINT SERIES

2013 *Ice Cream Sandwich*, Exhibition A, New York, NY

2012 *Peconic Bay, New York Valentine*, and *Route 27*, 20 x 200,
    New York, NY

2005 *Nudes I–IV*, Durham Press, Durham, PA

2001 *Old Neighborhood*, Durham Press, Durham, PA

2001 *Tree Series*, Durham Press, Durham, PA

2000 *Arts & Letters*, Durham Press, Durham, PA

2000 *Prince & Broadway*, Durham Press, Durham, PA

1997 *Fanelli's*, Durham Press, Durham, PA

1996 *Ice Tea* and *Cappuccino*, Galerie Kunst Parterre, Germany

1996 *Recession Prints IV*, Durham Press, Durham, PA

1996 *I-Beam Large*, Durham Press, Durham, PA

1996 *Color of Night*, Durham Press, Durham, PA

1994 *Recession Prints III*, Durham Press, Durham, PA

1994 *Sneaker*, Durham Press, Durham, PA

1993 *Summer*, Durham Press, Durham, PA

1992 *Tom Slaughter & John Giorno: Whatever Window Is Your
    Pleasure*, George Mulder, Amsterdam and New York

1992 *Hatboxes*, Durham Press, Durham, PA

1991 *Recession Prints I and II*, Durham Press, Durham, PA

1990 *Cityscape*, Durham Press, Durham, PA

1990 *Watch*, Durham Press, Durham, PA

1989 *Tom Slaughter: New York View, Construction Work, Hats
    and Boats*, George Mulder, Amsterdam and New York

CATALOGUES

Made in the USA. Rotterdam: The Caldic Collection, 1993.

Tom Slaughter: Views of New York. Amsterdam and New York: George Mulder Fine Arts, 1992.

Tom Slaughter & John Giorno: Whatever Window Is Your Pleasure. Amsterdam and New York: George Mulder Fine Arts, 1992.

Tom Slaughter: New York View, Construction Work, Hats and Boats. Amsterdam and New York: George Mulder Fine Arts, 1989.

BOOKS AND MAGAZINES

Baitz, Jon Robin. "Tom Slaughter." *BOMB* magazine 84 (July, 2003) https://bombmagazine.org/articles/tom-slaughter/ (accessed August 27, 2018).

Franzen, Jonathan. "First City: Why America Should Have More New Yorks." *The New Yorker* (February 19, 1996): 85.

Geldzahler, Henry. *Making It New: Essays, Interviews, and Talks*. New York: Mariner Books, 1996, cover.

———. "The Familiar Turned Phenomenal." *Graphis* (September–October, 1991): 74.

Gerber, Robert. "Where Henry Hangs His Hat." *House & Garden* (July, 1992): 64–69.

Jocelyn, Tim. "Artists' Furniture and Functional Art in New York," *Impulse 12*, no. 1 (1985).

Lane, Anthony. "The Power of One." *The New Yorker* (April 28, 1997): 228.

———. "Byte Verse." *The New Yorker* (February 20, 1995): 103.

Perry-Zucker, Aaron, and Spike Lee. *Design for Obama*. Taschen (New York, 2009): 8.

"Reviews." *ARTNews* (March, 1992): 130.

Slaughter, Tom. " 'Ultramarine' and 'Room Service.' " *Art on Paper*, *Special: Prints 3*, no. 2 (Nov/Dec, 1998): 55.

Solomon, Andrew. "Florida Fun House." *House & Garden* (May, 1992): 102–103.

Szabo, Julia. "Regarding Henry." *New York Magazine* (January, 1995): 42–47.

Van Veelen, Ijsbrand. "An Outsider Inside the Art World." *Haage Post* (Amsterdam, Netherlands) (July, 1989): 49–52.

Wert, Hal Elliot. *HOPE: A Collection of Obama Posters and Prints*. Zenith Press (London, 2009): 20.

SELECTED SOLO EXHIBITIONS

2014

Hotel Stationery, Glenn Horowitz Bookseller / Grey Area,
  East Hampton, NY

2012

Summer Pop Up, Jim Kempner Fine Art, New York, NY

2008

Contemporary Watercolors, Harrison Gallery, Williamstown, MA

2006

Tom Slaughter, Harrison Gallery, Williamstown, MA

2005

Hanging, Galarie Benden & Klimczak, Viersen, Germany

2002

Ahlum Gallery, Easton, PA

Comerford & Hennessy, Bridgehampton, NY

Fine Art & Artists Gallery, Washington, DC

2001

Lufthansa Corporation, Frankfurt, Germany

2000

Views of New York, Galerie Benden & Klimczak, Viersen, Germany

Summer Group Exhibition, David Beitzel Gallery, New York, NY

1999

David Beitzel Gallery, Project Room, New York, NY

Fine Art & Artists Gallery, Washington, DC

1998

Wallpainting and More, Galerie Benden & Klimczak,
  Viersen, Germany

Senior & Shopmaker Gallery, New York, NY

1997

Jaffe Baker Blau Gallery, Bay Harbor, FL

Dorothy Blau Gallery, Scottsdale, AZ

1996

Marcia Rafelman Fine Art, Toronto, Canada

Selected Prints by Durham Press, 1987–1996, West Bank Cafe,
  New York, NY

1995

Molinar Gallery, Scottsdale, AZ

Jaffe Baker Blau Gallery, Boca Raton, FL

Roger Smith Gallery, New York, NY

Miliani Gallery, Marseilles, France

1994

Gallery Organic, Osaka, Japan

Jaffe Baker Blau Gallery, Boca Raton, FL

1993

Recent Paintings, Earl McGrath Gallery, Los Angeles, CA

Equinox Gallery, Vancouver, Canada

Hanqu Department Store, Tokyo, Japan

1992

Basque Exhibition, Fukuoka, Japan

Galerie Kunst Parterre, Viersen, Germany

Independent Editions, London, England

Molinar Gallery, Scottsdale, AZ

George Mulder Foundation, Amsterdam, Netherlands

1991

Ruth Siegel Gallery, New York, NY

Hokin Gallery, Bay Harbor Islands, FL

New Work, Robert Berman Gallery, Santa Monica, CA

Equinox Gallery, Vancouver, Canada

1990

Hokin Gallery, Bay Harbor Islands, FL

B-1 Gallery, Santa Monica, CA

Equinox Gallery, Vancouver, Canada

Phillip Samules Fine Art, St. Louis, MO

Casa Sin Nombre, Sante Fe, NM

1989

Galerie Bébert, Rotterdam, Netherlands

Hokin Gallery, Bay Harbor Islands, FL

Mark Humphrey Gallery, Southampton, NY

SELECTED GROUP EXHIBITIONS

2017

Highlights from the Collection 2017, Galerie Klaus Benden, Cologne, Germany

The Nude in Print, Childs Gallery, Boston, MA

2014

The 80s: Past and Present, Bleecker St. Arts Club, New York, NY

Summer in the City, Galerie Klaus Benden, Cologne, Germany

2013

Remembering Henry, Harrison Gallery, Williamstown, MA

2008

Coney Island Maybe, The Puffin Room, New York

Manifest Hope, Manifest Hope Gallery, Denver, Colorado, and Washington, DC

2004

Friends from New York, The Harrison Gallery, Williamstown, MA

2002

25th Anniversary Exhibition, Drawing Center, New York, NY

Pop Art Show, Equinox Gallery, Vancouver, BC

2001

The Book as Object, Senior & Shopmaker Gallery, New York, NY

Fine Art & Artist Gallery, New York, NY

2000

The Print Center, Philadelphia, PA

Pop, Michael Haber Gallery, New York, NY

1999

New Prints, Cindy Bordeau Fine Art, Chicago, IL

Summer Group Exhibition, David Beitzel Gallery, New York, NY

Wooster Projects, New York, NY

1998

Marcel Sitcoske Gallery, San Francisco, CA

1997

Loft Pioneer Show, The Puffin Room, New York, NY

1995

Jaffe Baker Blau Gallery, Boca Raton, FL

Roger Smith Gallery, New York, NY

Miliani Gallery, Marseilles, France

Store Next Door, Whitney Museum, New York, NY

1994

Red Windows, Barneys New York, New York, NY

Centro Colombo Americano, Medellin, Colombia

1993

Roy G Biv Gallery, Columbus, OH

1992

New Editions, Equinox Gallery, Vancouver, Canada

1990

The Power of Childhood, Wessel O'Connor, New York, NY

Whatever Window Is Your Pleasure, George Mulder, New York, NY, with John Giorno

1989

Home Work, Garnet Press Gallery, Toronto, Canada

1987

Cobalt Blue, Attack Gallery, Los Angeles, CA

1986

Architects and Designers Building, New York, NY

1985

East Village Funktional, Rosa Esman Gallery, New York, NY

Gallery Artists, Rosa Esman Gallery, New York, NY

The Red Studio, New York, NY

1984

Artful Objects, Meredith Contemporary Art, Baltimore, MD

1983

Selections 21, The Drawing Center, New York, NY

Crime Show, ABC No Rio Gallery, New York, NY

Chromaliving, Chromazone Gallery, Toronto, Canada

SELECTED PUBLIC & PRIVATE COLLECTIONS

Caldic Collection, Rotterdam, Netherlands
Cooper-Hewitt, Smithsonian Design Museum, New York, NY
Museum of Modern Art, New York, NY
Whitney Museum, New York, NY

Gordon and Peggy Davis, New York, NY
Asher Edelman, New York, NY
Colm Feore, Stratford, Ontario
Jonathan and Janet Geldzahler, New York, NY
Ashton Hawkins and Johnnie Moore, New York, NY
Dorothy Lichtenstein, New York, NY
Joe Mantello, New York, NY
Keith Miller, New York, NY
Paige Powell, New York, NY
John Reinhold, New York, NY

PHOTOGRAPHY CREDITS

Ray Charles White: 2–3, 241

Marthe Jocelyn: 12

Michael Zeigler: 18

Nell Jocelyn: 22–23, 134–135, 172,
175,176–177, 183, 190–191, 254–255

Jeremy Pollard: 72–73, 186

José Picayo: 168

Jamie Slaughter: 184–185

Colm Feore: 262

ACKNOWLEDGMENTS

Thank you to the contributors: Glenn Lowry, David Marshall Grant, George Negroponte, Marthe Jocelyn, Jon Robin Baitz, Andy Fabo, Anne Pasternak, Jim Kempner, Stephen Hannock, Ray Charles White, Scott Kilgour, Robert Harms, Jean-Paul Russell, Ann Marshall, Colm Feore, José Picayo, Jeremy Pollard, Michael Zeigler.

Thank you to the Tom Slaughter collectors who shared with us the pieces they love so that we could compile this book, especially Keith Miller and Gordon Davis. For all your help, thank you to David Haskell, Kristine Eng, Elyse Leyenberger, Nicole Giusti, Harry Cepka, Peter Stroumos, Deeno. Graphic Imaging and Fortress Holdings.

Thank you to Josh Smith, Richie and Marcy Glanz, Mike Ridgway, Steve Olsen, Louis Black, Jef Kaplan, Jon Berne. To the Mezei family, Todd Bishop, Matko Tomicic, Lucy Hogg, Sarah Bielicky. To the Slaughter brothers and their families.

Thank you to all the collaborators and to The Artist Book Foundation.

This publication is released on the occasion of a mural
installation at the Massachusetts Museum of Contemporary
Art (Mass MoCA) in North Adams, MA, and an exhibition
at The Artist Book Foundation's gallery on the
campus of Mass MoCA to commemorate what would have
been Tom Slaughter's sixty-fourth birthday, with a
book launch at MoMA PS1 in Long Island City, NY, on
May 2, 2019.

First Edition

© 2019 The Artist Book Foundation
Tom Slaughter by Hannah and Nell Jocelyn, foreword
by Glenn Lowry, essays by David Marshall Grant,
George Negroponte, Marthe Jocelyn, Jim Kempner,
Andy Fabo, and Anne Pasternak

All rights reserved under International and Pan-American
Copyright Convention. Except for legitimate excerpts
customary in review or scholarly publications, no part
of this publication may be reproduced or transmitted
in any form or by any means, electronic or mechanical,
including photocopying, recording, or information
storage or retrieval systems, without permission in
writing from the publisher.

Published in the United States by
The Artist Book Foundation
1327 MASS MoCA Way, North Adams, MA 01247

Distributed in the United States, its territories and
possessions, and Canada by ACC Distribution
www.accdistribution.com/us

Distributed outside North America by ACC Distribution
www.accdistribution.com/uk

Publisher and Executive Director: L. Pell van Breen
Art and Production Director: David Skolkin
Design: Jimmy Mezei
Editor: Deborah Thompson
Proofreader: Nicole Barone

Manufactured in Canada

ISBN 978-0-9962007-8-3

Library of Congress Cataloging-in-Publication Data

Names: Grant, David Marshall. | Negroponte, George, 1953-
  | Jocelyn, Marthe. | Pasternak, Anne, 1964- |
  Lowry, Glenn D., writer of foreword.
Title: Tom Slaughter / essays and contributions by
  David Marshall Grant, George Negroponte, Marthe Jocelyn,
  and Anne Pasternak ; foreword by Glenn Lowry.
Description: First edition. |

North Adams : The Artist Book Foundation, 2019. |
  Includes bibliographical references.
Identifiers: LCCN 2018045416 | ISBN 9780996200783
Subjects: LCSH: Slaughter, Tom,
  1955-2014--Criticism and interpretation.
Classification: LCC N6537.S5665 T66 2019 | DDC 709.2--dc23
LC record available at https://lccn.loc.gov/2018045416